URBAN
SOCIETY
FIFTH EDITION

NOEL P. GIST
PROFESSOR OF SOCIOLOGY
UNIVERSITY OF MISSOURI

And

SYLVIA FLEIS FAVA
ASSOCIATE PROFESSOR OF SOCIOLOGY
BROOKLYN COLLEGE OF THE CITY
UNIVERSITY OF NEW YORK

THOMAS Y. CROWELL COMPANY
New York   Established 1834

Designed by Anne Churchman

Preface

Some three decades ago, when the first edition of *Urban Society* was published, barely half of the American population was living in cities, and suburbanism was still in an early stage of expansion. Big cities there were, here and elsewhere, but the age of metropolitan regionalism, in which almost two-thirds of the American population live in metropolitan complexes, had not fully emerged.

Subsequent editions of the book have recorded many of the epoch-making developments associated with the urbanization of society. So pervasive have been the changes accompanying the upsurge of urbanism that countless numbers of people, in many parts of the world, have experienced a virtual revolution in their modes of life, work, and thought. Many societies have already developed a social order dominated by the values and behavior characteristic of the city. To describe and interpret such changes have been especially the responsibility of the urban sociologist.

This edition of *Urban Society* gives explicit recognition to the nature and importance of urbanism as a world phenomenon—appropriately, the authors believe, since many of today's issues stem from the changes associated with the process of urbanization in various countries. The main focus of attention is necessarily on urbanism in the United States, partly because more relevant data is available for the United States than for most other countries. But the selection of materials is such as to emphasize that the urbanization of America is merely a part of a worldwide trend, which of course varies considerably from one country to another.

The central emphasis in this Fifth Edition is on social change as it is manifest in various aspects of urbanization. The dynamic character of the city and the impact of the urban trend on nonurban communities or societies makes such a focus logical. But the organizational and structural aspects of urban communities are also given extensive treatment.

Those familiar with this work in its earlier editions will note many changes. About three-fourths of the present volume, which is somewhat longer than its predecessor, consists of entirely new or completely rewritten material. The treatment has been brought up to date by the use throughout of 1960 census data for the United States and the latest available statistics for other countries.

To increase in scope the historical and cross-cultural discussion of urbanism, Part One, The Growth of Cities, has been expanded from four to five chapters. Chapter One, which is entirely new, includes description of preurban settlement patterns and ancient cities. It also delineates three significant factors in urban development, which succeeding chapters then apply to the later development of cities. Chapter Five, "Classes and Types of Cities," has been almost wholly rewritten and presents another framework for urban analysis. Part One makes clear the importance of metropolitan development as a characteristic form of modern urban growth, and the phenomenon is further explored in the later sections on ecology, social organization, social-psychological aspects, and redevelopment policies.

Part Two, Urban Ecology, has been thoroughly revised to focus on recent theory in human ecology and on the far-reaching effects upon public policy stemming from the movement of population and business enterprises into suburban and fringe areas.

In Part Three, The Organization of Urban Life, the opening chapter, "Urbanization: Process and Impact," has been completely rewritten to stress the importance of exploring the world's very rapid urban transformation. And to the section's revised chapters on systems of status and occupation, the family, and formal and informal associations has been added a new chapter on leisure, reflecting the increased prominence of this aspect of urban life in an age of growing affluence.

Other emerging aspects of urban life are treated in Part Four, Social Psychological Aspects of Urban Life, in two new chapters: "Adjustment of Migrants to Cities," and "The Image of the City." The two chapters making up Part Five incorporate much new information on urban housing and planning in the United States and abroad.

Readers acquainted with the earlier forms of this work will note a change in authorship in this edition. The late Dr. L. A. Halbert has been succeeded as co-author by Dr. Sylvia F. Fava of Brooklyn College. Although the present authors have maintained a continuing interchange of ideas and criticisms, Dr. Fava was primarily responsible for the chapters on the growth and ecology of cities, and for the treatment of social-psychological aspects, while Dr. Gist assumed the major responsibility for the discussions of the organizational characteristics of city life and for the chapters on housing and planning.

Works of this kind depend heavily on the researches and theories of many persons, and to them the authors wish to express their appreciation and acknowledge their indebtedness. Those whose published works have been drawn upon are given credit in the form of footnotes or other references. All interpretations of these or other data are, of course, the sole responsibility of the authors.

Noel P. Gist
Sylvia F. Fava

March, 1964

Contents

PART THREE

The Organization of Urban Life

PART FOUR

The Social Psychology of Urban Life

Tables, Figures, and Illustrations

TABLES

FIGURES

ILLUSTRATIONS

The Growth of Cities

PART ONE

The Origin and
Development of Cities

What are cities? This question is unavoidably involved with the question of when cities began, for we cannot define cities without implying when and where urban traits first existed.

The most impressive fact about the origin of cities is that they appeared so recently in the history of mankind. This is true despite the fact that the first cities appeared about five or six thousand years ago (that is, 3000–4000 B.C.).[1] Although this span encompasses all of written history, for record-keeping emerged only with cities, it is very short when compared either with the half-million years the human species has been on earth or with the 40,000 years that physically modern man, *Homo sapiens,* has existed. Put another way, the 6,000 years of man's urban existence represent only slightly more than one per cent of his total existence on earth and only about 10 per cent of his existence as physically modern man. Furthermore, cities remained a rarity and were the place of residence of only a tiny fraction of the human population until the last cen-

[1] Because of the absence of written records, the scarcity of archeological remains, problems of classifying the surviving artifacts, and conceptual problems (that is, what constitutes agriculture, village life, and the like), there is great confusion and uncertainty over the dating of all events before historic times. Wide variations exist for all the dates employed here. For example, many authorities would assign a date of 700,000 to a million years for the appearance of the human species on earth. Authorities also differ on the dates for the beginning of the Neolithic in various parts of the world, the first emergence of cities, of metal working, and so on. All of the dates employed in this chapter should, therefore, be regarded as tentative and subject to revision, pending further investigation and classification. In general we have followed the dating suggested in Robert Braidwood and Gordon Willey (eds.), *Courses Toward Urban Life* (1962); S. Piggott (ed.), *The Dawn of Civilization* (1961); and S. Washburn (ed.), *The Social Life of Early Man* (1961).

tury or so. Even today only about 20 per cent of the world's population lives in cities.

CAUSES AND OVERVIEW OF PREURBAN SETTLEMENT

Three major factors have been recognized as shaping the development of cities.[2] (1) Environment, that is, the degree to which a given climate, topography, and set of natural resources can support a species with the physical requirements of man. The environment changed significantly in the recent geologic past and is, of course, constantly changing to some extent. (2) Technology, that is, the degree to which man's tools and inventions can make use of the resources of a given habitat. Urban settlement requires a high technological competence to produce enough food and other necessities for dense populations living permanently in a fixed place. (3) Social organization, that is, the extent to which man's cultural institutions and attitudes are consonant with a given community pattern. The study of human communities is part of the social sciences for precisely this reason.

It cannot be overemphasized that *all three factors—environment, technology, social organization—are necessary for urban development; no single factor is sufficient.* In the preurban phase of man's existence, technology and environment loom large because man's skill at coping with nature was so limited.

THE OLD STONE AGE (PALEOLITHIC)

Man has spent most of his history on earth as a nomad, a wanderer without any settled habitation. This lack of permanent settlement was related to an extremely unproductive level of technology. Men had only crude unpolished stone tools and subsisted by hunting wild animals and gathering edible plants. And because the yield from this method of exploiting the environment was low and erratic, the quest for food was the full-time occupation of the entire group, which was also compelled to follow the food supply as the seasons changed or a given area's growth of animals and plants was exhausted. A more precise name for this technological level is the Old Stone Age or Paleolithic (from *paleo,* old; *lith,* stone). From man's beginnings 500,000 years ago until about 9000 B.C., all human groups lived at this technological level, with only small improvements in tools and skills occurring over long intervals. There are a few groups today, such as the Australian Aborigines, who still live at a Paleolithic level.

Important environmental forces were also at work between 500,000

[2] Cf. Gideon Sjoberg, *The Preindustrial City* (1960), p. 27ff.

and 9000 B.C. During this period, which geologists call the Pleistocene, glaciers several times covered, receded, and then covered again what is now Canada, the northern United States, northern Europe, and northern Asia. During most of the Pleistocene, man was further handicapped in coping with his environment, for he had not attained his fully modern physical and mental characteristics; physically modern man emerged about 40,000 B.C. The Pleistocene came to an end about 9000 B.C. when the glaciers retreated. Great changes in climate, wild life, and rainfall were ushered in on most of the world's surface and necessitated re-adjustment of man's way of living. We must, however, guard against invoking environmental determinism in explaining the origin of cities, because the climatic and other changes of 9000 B.C. had occurred several times before but had never been responded to technologically and socially as they now were.[3] The environmental changes brought about by the melting of the glaciers were not uniform. In northern areas, such as northern Europe, these changes marked the extinction of herds of woolly mammoth, hairy rhinoceros, giant bear, and other big game; instead, forests grew on what had been tundra, and small game flourished. Some parts of the world were inundated by the release of waters from the melting glaciers. Other areas, formerly blooming, became semi-arid as the rainbelts shifted. Some areas were relatively unaffected.

MIDDLE STONE AGE (MESOLITHIC)

Most human groups responded to their changed environment by a more intensive system of food gathering and by other technological improvements that enabled them to exploit more fully the food resources. In other words, they decided to stay put and adjust to the new conditions instead of trying to hold on to their old way of life by migrating. This new technological level is called the Middle Stone Age, or Mesolithic (*meso,* middle; *lith,* stone). The Mesolithic achievements of man included the domestication of the dog, which was a considerable help in hunting; the invention of axes and adzes for felling trees and working wood; the invention of fishing nets and boats with paddles; and improvements in techniques for making a greater variety of specialized tools from stone, bone antler, and wood. The length of time that particular human groups remained at a Mesolithic level varied widely, although the period was always extremely short compared to the preceding Paleolithic. The settlements of a few contemporary Mesolithic societies, the Eskimo, for example, are characteristically small and impermanent.

[3] Braidwood and Willey, *op. cit.,* p. 342.

NEW STONE AGE (NEOLITHIC)

The Mesolithic was essentially a transitional phase between the crude hunting-gathering technology of the Paleolithic and the farming villages of the last stone-age economy, the Neolithic (*neo*, new; *lith*, stone), or New Stone Age. Although it is difficult for us today to imagine a world without agriculture and animal husbandry, it must be emphasized that they are inventions. Their importance is so great that the period of their emergence has sometimes been called "The Neolithic Revolution." [4] In addition to the domestication of plants and animals, other hallmarks of the Neolithic are the grinding of stone tools to give them a sharper edge, weaving, pottery, and similar inventions.

The more intensive hunting-gathering-fishing and greater technological skill of the Mesolithic had acquainted men thoroughly with the ways of the plants and animals in their environment. In a few areas of the world the close observation of native flora and fauna was followed by food production. The best current evidence indicates that the first area where crops were tilled and animals domesticated was the hills flanking the so-called Fertile Crescent, a roughly semicircular area in southwestern Asia lying astride present-day Iran, Iraq, Turkey, Syria, Israel, and Jordan. Its hills were the natural habitat of the wild species of grains and animals which were the ancestors of later domesticated species.

Excavations at Jarmo in the Fertile Crescent show that it was inhabited as an agricultural village for several hundred years around 6500 B.C.[5] Jarmo was a permanent, year-round settlement with about two dozen several-roomed, rectangular, mud-walled houses that showed signs of frequent repair and rebuilding, so that the excavations showed about a dozen distinct levels of occupancy. The people grew domesticated barley and wheat; domesticated goats, dogs, and possibly sheep were also kept. Evidences of other Neolithic inventions were also found at the site —tools and stone objects of fine workmanship based on new stone-working techniques, weaving, and pottery. The pottery objects were found only in the upper, hence later, levels of the excavations.

Other aspects of life in Jarmo are indicated in the finding of large numbers of clay figurines used as religious cult objects. The people of Jarmo may also have done some trading for they had tools of obsidian, a volcanic glass with a cutting edge much sharper and harder than stone, whose nearest source was 200 miles away. There were many other Neolithic villages in the Fertile Crescent, particularly by 5000 B.C., but Jarmo

---

[4] See, for example, Chapter 5 in V. Gordon Childe, *Man Makes Himself* (1951).

[5] This description is based on Braidwood and Howe, "Southwestern Asia beyond the Land of the Mediterranean Littoral," in Braidwood and Willey, *op. cit.*, pp. 132–46; and R. Braidwood, "The Agricultural Revolution," *Scientific American*, 203 (September, 1960), 130–52.

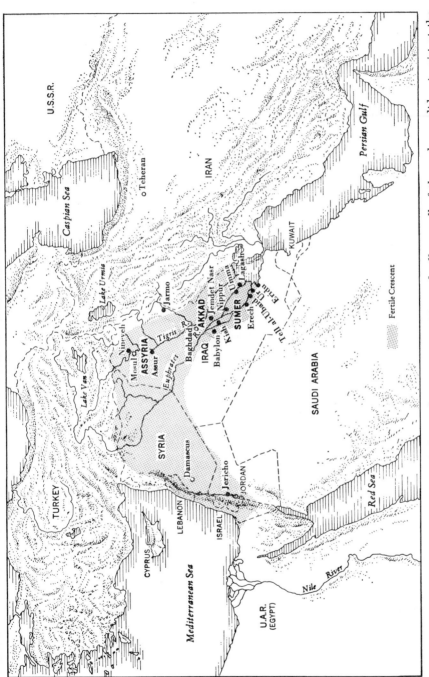

Figure 1. The Fertile Crescent. Black dots indicate ancient cities and villages; all of those shown did not exist at the same time. The modern Tigris and Euphrates rivers flow along different routes than the ancient courses shown. Open dots indicate present-day cities. National boundaries shown are also modern. SOURCE: Adapted with permission from Robert Braidwood, "Agricultural Revolution," *Scientific American*, September, 1960. Copyright © 1960 by Scientific American, Inc.

and Jericho,[6] which lies at the opposite end of the Crescent from Jarmo, were among the very earliest of these farming villages.

These earliest villages, unable to produce all of the food they needed, still depended to a considerable extent on hunting and gathering. The transition from the intensive hunting-gathering economies of the Meso-lithic to the Neolithic was a gradual one, and there is sometimes confu-sion over the labelling of the two periods. A fully Neolithic technology included major reliance for food on domesticated crops and/or animals and only minor reliance, if any, on hunting-fishing-gathering; the making of stone tools by grinding and polishing instead of the earlier techniques of flaking and chipping; weaving as in clothing, basketry, rugs, or mats; and pottery. The importance of the Neolithic villages cannot be exag-gerated, for they represent the first settlements of man that were intended to be permanent. From this point on, changes accumulated so swiftly that the next few thousand years would transform man's way of life more than had the previous half-million.

Some indication of the importance of Neolithic technological advances is shown by comparing the size of Neolithic settlements with earlier ones. Estimates are that the technological level of the Paleolithic supported human populations of about one-half to one human being per square mile, while Neolithic technology supported densities of 30 or more per square mile.[7] For example, it is probable that one square mile was needed to support each individual of the peoples with an advanced Paleolithic technology who produced the well-known cave paintings of the Spanish peninsula.[8] In contrast it has been calculated that approximately 150 people lived at Jarmo at a density of 27 people per square mile.[9]

The Neolithic Revolution occurred independently at least twice and perhaps three or four times, as a result of a similar constellation of en-vironmental, technological, and cultural factors. There is general agree-ment, however, that the "revolution" occurred earliest in the Fertile Cres-cent. Agriculture and animal husbandry also appeared very early in the valley of the Nile in Egypt—by 5000 B.C.; in the valley of the Indus River in India by 3500 B.C.; and in the Yellow River basin in China by 2500 B.C. On the basis of chronology and other evidence it is possible to de-duce that farm-village development in these areas was derived from that in the Fertile Crescent, but the archeological record is meager and the data inconclusive.

However, the independent origin of methods of food production in the

[6] Kathleen Kenyon, "Jericho and Its Setting in Near Eastern History," *Antiquity*, 30 (December, 1956), 184–95. See Braidwood's critique (June 1957 issue) of her con-clusions about Jericho for an illustration of the theoretical and practical difficulties in classifying and dating early sites.

[7] V. Gordon Childe, "The Urban Revolution," *Town Planning Review*, 21 (April, 1950), 4–5.

[8] Luis Pericot, "The Social Life of Spanish Paleolithic Hunters as Shown by Levan-tine Art," in Washburn, *op. cit.*, p. 210.

[9] Braidwood, "The Agricultural Revolution," *op. cit.*, p. 143.

New World is generally accepted. The core area in which agriculture developed was Central Mexico about 3000 B.C., and from there it diffused to Central, North, and South America.[10] From the two original nodes in the Fertile Crescent and in Middle America (and possibly other original areas of cultivation in Egypt, India, and China) the Neolithic skills of farming and animal husbandry spread eventually to all parts of the world. A few groups, such as the native societies of New Guinea, remain even today at a Neolithic level.

THE CITY AND CIVILIZATION

Neolithic technology set the stage for the emergence of cities by making it possible, through a stable food supply, for man to remain permanently settled on a given site. But Neolithic villages were just collections of farmers; they were not cities. Much more than technology was needed to build cities. How much more is indicated by the fact that although the first farming-villages appeared in the Fertile Crescent between 7000 and 6000 B.C., and became widespread in the area by 5000 B.C., the first cities did not appear in the region until approximately 3500 B.C., in that section of the Fertile Crescent variously called southern Mesopotamia, Sumer, Babylonia, and now, southern Iraq. This area was not in the hilly uplands where the domestication of plants and animals had begun, but in the more level portion of the Crescent lying between the Tigris and Euphrates rivers, which flooded and thus fertilized much of the lowlands every year. Some of the early cities were Eridu, Kish, Ur, Ubaid, Erech (Uruk, Warka), Jemdet Nasr, Nippur, Lagash, Umma, and, somewhat later, Babylon, Ashur, and Nineveh.

Although it is true that a maturing technology, like environment, played an indispensable part in the origin of cities, it was not the key ingredient necessary for their formation, as is indicated by the fact that many societies based on Neolithic skills endured for thousands of years, some of them resisting urban development when this new way of life was brought to them. A few exist even today. All early cities arose in regions of benign climate and good growing conditions—as in the river valleys of the semitropics—in which Neolithic technology was adequate to enable farmers to produce more than they themselves could consume. The crucial additional element, however, was a social organization that could effectively distribute this surplus so that some individuals would not have to engage in food production, but would be free to perform other tasks and to live apart from the farms.

[10] G. Willey, "Mesoamerica," in Braidwood and Willey, *op. cit.*, p. 86; and G. Bushnell, "The Crimson-Tipped Flower: The Birth and Growth of New World Civilization," in Piggott, *op. cit.*, p. 360ff.

SOCIAL ORGANIZATION OF URBAN SOCIETY

Because cities are linked with a particular kind of social organization, commonly called "civilization," they cannot be adequately described or explained by geography, engineering, or architecture, but require analysis by the social sciences. As the term "civilization" is used here it is not a value term implying that civilization is better than other types of social organization; rather, it refers to a complex social system which involves its participants in a different set of interactions than do noncivilized societies.

Civilization precedes cities. Logically, changes in social structure precede the creation of cities, which are, in turn, one result of these social changes.[11] Thus, it would be possible for civilization to exist without cities. There is some indication, as will be discussed below, that the Maya may have approached this. Some experts also believe that Egyptian civilization existed for 2,000 years before cities appeared in it. The emergence of cities in turn brings about other social changes. In practice, therefore, cities are both the result of a civilized society and the cause of further civilizing changes. This dual relationship of cities and social structure is a major analytical problem for urban sociology and underlies the discussion in Parts III and IV of this book. It need not detain us now from examining the occurrence of particular social patterns with urban life.

The major contrast between civilized and primitive societies lies in the nature of the bonds unifying the society. Although their technologies differed, hunting-gathering groups and Neolithic farm-villages were alike in being small, even though the latter were, of course, larger than the former. Both were self-contained, for virtually all the group needed was obtained within its own confines. They were homogeneous, for even though the Neolithic allowed permanent settlement, both of these technological levels required every individual to devote full attention to obtaining food; thus, the major distinctions were those of age and sex, since all individuals had the same occupation and attendant property and wealth. In all Stone Age societies kinship was very important and the family, performing economic, educational, leadership, and other functions, was the major social unit. Finally, religion and art reinforced the values of this small world, as in the cave-paintings to magically insure success in the hunt, or in the "fertility goddesses" of much of the Neolithic Near East.

The individuals constituting such societies shared the same experiences and expectations, and were thus primarily knit together by similar senti-

[11] Robert Adams, "The Origin of Cities," *Scientific American*, 203 (September, 1960), 154; and Rushton Coulborn, *The Origin of Civilized Societies* (1959), pp. 18–20.

ments and points of view. Redfield has described this kind of social bond as resting on " . . . the binding together of men through implicit convictions as to what is right, through explicit ideas, or through similarities of conscience." He contrasts it with the social bonds resting on impersonal, specialized relations which

result from mutual usefulness, from deliberate coercion, or from the mere utilization of the same means. In [this] . . . order men are bound by things, or are themselves things. They are organized by necessity or expediency. Think, if you will, of the orderly way in which automobiles move in response to the traffic light or the policeman's whistle, or think of the flow of goods, services, and money among the people who together produce, distribute, and consume some commodity such as rubber.[12]

Precivilized societies are those in which the first-noted order, that based on personal, total involvement, is the main way in which the activities of men are coordinated. In civilizations the order based on indirect associations and the interdependence resulting from a specialized society assumes much greater importance. This does not mean it replaces the other type of social coordination. It simply means that a new dimension has been added to social control.

CHILDE'S DEFINITION OF THE CITY

V. Gordon Childe's ten criteria defining cities show the dependence of the city on such a complex differentiated social structure.[13] (1) Full-time specialists, such as draftsmen, transport workers, officials, and priests, are found in cities. These specialists exchanged their services for food produced by the farmers, but, it is important to note, it was not a direct exchange but one mediated by other agencies. In the ancient cities of southern Mesopotamia, for example, the priests were fed, housed, and clothed by the temple administration which in turn obtained these items from the tithes collected from farmers.[14] Although cities had emerged, only a small portion of the population lived in cities or engaged in specialized urban tasks. Farm technology still produced only a small surplus, and hence it was impossible for more than a tiny minority to be relieved of growing their own subsistence. Estimates are that only about five per cent of the labor force of ancient Sumer was employed in spe-

[12] Robert Redfield, *The Primitive World and Its Transformations* (1953), p. 21. Redfield's formulation has many similarities to Durkheim's contrast between mechanical and organic solidarity, to Cooley's distinction between primary and secondary groups, and to such typologies as *Gemeinschaft-Gesellschaft.*

[13] Childe, "The Urban Revolution," *op. cit.,* pp. 3–17.

[14] Sumerian examples derived from M. Mallowan, "The Birth of Written History— Civilized Life Begins: Mesopotamia and Iran," in Piggott, *op. cit.,* pp. 65–96; and Braidwood and Willey, *op. cit.*

cialized occupations and, at a somewhat later period in Sumerian development, less than 20 per cent were so employed.[15]

Several of Childe's other urban traits also relate to a more complex differentiation of labor. (2) Larger, denser populations are found in cities than in Neolithic villages, because urbanites do not need space to produce their own food. Sumerian cities are judged to have included between 7,000 and 20,000 people, although Uruk extended over 1,100 acres and contained possibly 50,000 people.[16] (3) Great art was produced by full-time specialists in that field, while others invented (4) writing and numerical notation, which were vital in keeping the records and accounts so prominent in the many indirect transactions now necessary. Sumerian writing, a cuneiform script incised on clay tablets, was used mainly for documentary purposes, such as temple accounts, inventories, receipts, and records of land transferral. (5) The exact and predictive sciences, such as arithmetic, geometry, and astronomy, were invented by the literate segment of society and served to help plan major projects. The Sumerians used time calculations based on astronomy to determine the appropriate time for irrigating their fields, and their temples could not have been constructed without advanced mathematics.

The foregoing urban criteria have been interpreted as dealing with the importance of full-time specialists, supported ultimately by the ability of farmers to produce a food surplus, as an index of complex social structure. The remainder of Childe's criteria may be interpreted as dealing with ways in which the surplus produce was collected and used, other than for support of the specialists. (6) Tribute or taxes were paid by farmers to a religious or secular administration, thus allowing for the concentration of the surplus product. Without centralized authority, the tiny surplus of individual producers would not have added up to effective working capital. In Sumerian society, the temple authorities were important in performing this function. (7) The formation of the state underscores the previous point, for it means that society was organized on the basis of residence instead of, or on top of, a basis of kinship. Taxes were a function of the allegiance and duties the individual owed to the state. Sumerian cities originated as city-states, were welded about 2400 B.C. into a short-lived empire under Sargon of Akkad, and later suffered much warfare and shifts of political hegemony to the Babylonians and finally to the Assyrians. (8) Monumental public buildings symbolizing the society's surplus product were built in cities. Sumerian cities were focussed on the *Ziggurat* or raised platform and temple, which towered above the flat plains. (9) "Foreign" trade was also made possible by the surplus product and was important for even the earliest cities, indicating the widespread net of interdependence beyond merely local boundaries. Stone and wood were scarce on the Sumerian flood plain and were regu-

---

[15] Adams, *op. cit.*, p. 168.
[16] *Ibid.*, p. 166; and Childe, "The Urban Revolution," *op. cit.*, p. 9.

larly traded for. (10) A class-structured society emerged from the unequal distribution of more plentiful property and from specialized activities. The elite contributed important functions to the society—usually religious, political, or military—but nevertheless the gap between their life and that of the peasant-farmer was very wide. The magnificent jewelry, household objects, musical instruments, and other items found in the royal tombs at Ur, an important Sumerian city mentioned in the Bible, testify not only to the high aesthetic and technical level of the culture but to the luxuries enjoyed by the privileged.[17]

All or almost all of the ten traits described are found in all early cities, and in present-day cities as well: full-time specialists, large dense populations, great art, writing and numerical notation, exact and predictive sciences, levies that concentrate the surplus food production, the state, monumental public architecture, long-distance trade, and a class-structured society. Sumerian cities displayed all of these traits, some only in incipient form, by about 3500 b.c. and reached the height of their development between 3000 and 2500 b.c. The general layout of Sumerian cities is indicated by several well-excavated sites.

Radiating out from the massive public buildings . . . toward the outer gates, were streets, unpaved and dusty, but straight and wide enough for the passage of solid-wheeled carts or chariots. Along the streets lay the residences of the well-to-do citizenry, usually arranged around spacious courts and sometimes provided with latrines draining into sewage conduits below the streets. The houses of the city's poorer inhabitants were located behind or between the large multiroomed dwellings. They were approached by tortuous, narrow alleys, were more haphazard in plan, were less well built and very much smaller. Mercantile activities were probably concentrated along the quays of the adjoining river or at the city gates. The marketplace or bazaar devoted to private commerce had not yet appeared.

Around every important urban center rose the massive fortifications that guarded the city against nomadic raids and the usually more formidable campaigns of neighboring rulers. Outside the walls clustered sheepfolds and irrigated tracts, interspersed with subsidiary villages and ultimately disappearing into the desert. And in the desert dwelt only the nomad, an object of mixed fear and scorn to the sophisticated court poet. By the latter part of the Early Dynastic period [c.2400 b.c.] several of the important capitals of lower Mesopotamia included more than 250 acres within their fortifications.[18]

ANCIENT EGYPTIAN CITIES

Childe himself noted that the ten common factors in early cities were quite abstract and that the actual civilizations were "as different as the

---

[17] For a description of the city by its chief excavator, see Sir Leonard Woolley, *Ur of the Chaldees* (1929).

[18] Adams, *op. cit.*, p. 10. Reprinted with permission. Copyright © 1960 by Scientific American, Inc. All rights reserved.

plans of their temples, the signs of their scripts and their artistic conventions." [19] Egyptian cities were not generally as large or densely settled
as Sumerian, but they suffered from fewer conquests and reconquests
and rested on a civilization remarkable for surviving several thousand
years with relatively few changes.[20] Egyptian society revolved around the
concept of the god-king, or pharaoh, whose capitals were such cities as
Memphis and Thebes. Most of the full-time specialists were attached to
the god-king or his temple-court where they produced masterpieces of
sculpture, painting, and architecture. Most notable are the Sphinx and
great pyramids, the largest of which, built in 2600 B.C., rises 480 feet
above the desert. The god-king was also the head of an elaborate centralized civil service. This bureaucracy had at its service clerks, or scribes,
trained in hieroglyphic writing; paper (papyrus) and ink, which the
Egyptians invented; and the world's first calendar, also an Egyptian invention and similar to the 365-day one we use today. The bureaucracy conducted an annual census, collected taxes, and maintained a system of
courts. The Egyptians were skilled in the medical sciences and produced
treatises on anatomy, surgery, and pharmacy. For most people, "the
splendor that was Egypt" is symbolized by the riches uncovered with
the only unplundered royal tomb ever found, that of a minor pharaoh
Tut-ankh-Amon, who died in 1344 B.C. at age 18.

CITIES OF ANCIENT INDIA

The remains of another of the early civilizations, that of the Indus
River valley, in what is now West Pakistan, are not as plentiful as those
of Egypt, partly because, in the 1850's, a British engineer accidentally
discovered one of the cities and used the bricks of the buildings as ballast
for a railway line he was building! Nevertheless, we know that the major
cities of the Indus civilization, Mohenjo-daro and Harappa, met Childe's
urban criteria. The two cities were 350 miles apart on the Indus River and
appear to have been the twin capitals of a huge empire covering a territory 950 by 700 by 550 miles.[21] Each of the cities covered at least a square
mile and probably contained a population of 20,000. The civilization they
headed is characterized as having been highly controlled and planned,
and very stable for a period of a thousand years. For example, a standard system of weights and measures existed and was applied to bricks,
pottery, and other items which were uniform over the whole territory
of the empire. Mohenjo-daro and Harappa themselves are built on identical plans. On the western edge of the city a citadel, about 1,200 feet by

[19] Childe, "The Urban Revolution," *op. cit.*, p. 16.
[20] Description based on L. Barnett, "The Epic of Man," *Life* (Part I, October 1, 1956; Part II, November 26, 1956).
[21] Description based on S. Piggott, *Prehistoric India* (1950).

600 feet, was located, built atop a raised mud-brick platform roughly 30 feet high. The complex included ceremonial and public buildings such as a public bath, a large pillared hall, a large building suggesting study activity, and another building, probably a temple. In each city, streets, ships, and the homes of the main population lay below the citadel and were laid out in a grid pattern of blocks of approximately equal size. It is likely that different sections of the city were set aside for particular groups—workers, artisans, merchants, and the ruling group. Large public granaries and flour-mills were found on the outskirts of the cities, indicating centralized control of food production. There is evidence that the Indus society traded with Sumerian cities and possibly other areas. The script of the Indus River valley civilization has not yet been deciphered, but the civilization is also enigmatic on other grounds. There are no clear indications of who its founders were or when or from where they came; its ending is also obscure although it appears to have been violently conquered about 1500 B.C.

EARLY CITIES IN THE WESTERN HEMISPHERE

The first civilization produced in the New World, that of the Maya, is a paradoxical one.[22] The Maya had an agriculture based on maize and other plants, but domesticated few if any animals; nor did they invent the plough, which meant they had to rely entirely on human labor to clear and plant the tropical rain-forests of the Yucatan peninsula where their civilization reached its height. The Maya developed a form of hieroglyphic writing and an elaborate and very accurate calendar. They were also accomplished astronomers and mathematicians, even employing the concept of zero, but they never invented the wheel or discovered the use of metals. It is likely that the Maya invented agriculture and other Neolithic skills such as weaving and pottery independently of the Old World about 3000 B.C. By 1500 B.C. they were established in farm-villages.

Mayan religion was based on nature worship, and by 1000 B.C. their characteristic raised mounds surmounted by temples which, along with related ceremonial buildings were the major features of Mayan cities, began to appear. Cities grew up between 300 B.C. and A.D. 300. There is some debate as to whether these were true cities, for the main permanent inhabitants were probably the priests and their attendants. The rest of the population lived on farms and villages and collected at the temples for frequent rituals. Each religious center had a ruler or priest(s) who maintained contacts with other independent rulers. Mayan civilization

---

[22] Description based on Willey, *op. cit.* in Braidwood and Willey, *op. cit.*; Bushnell, *op. cit.*, in Piggott, *The Dawn of Civilization, op. cit.*; and Alfonso Caso, "New World Culture History: Middle America," in Alfred Kroeber (ed.), *Anthropology Today* (1953), pp. 226–38.

was, therefore, not an empire but a loose widely-scattered federation of equals sharing a common culture. At its height, between A.D. 300 and 900, this federation included a vast territory encompassing central Mexico, the Yucatan peninsula, and Guatemala. The Maya still flourished on the Yucatan peninsula at the time of the Spanish conquest, but they had already lost their position of prominence. In sum, we may say that at its zenith Mayan civilization and cities met all of Childe's urban criteria except that of large densely settled populations.

A derivative civilization was later formed in the valley of Mexico by the Aztecs, whose religion was based on human sacrifice.[23] The Aztecs built true cities, and their capital, Tenochtitlan, with a population of 100,000, much impressed the Spanish under Cortez who conquered the Aztecs and their ruler, Montezuma II, in 1519. Tenochtitlan was on the site of modern Mexico City.

The only other indigenous New World civilization was that of the Inca in the Central Andes, in what is now Peru and Bolivia.[24] The Inca, too, fail to meet one of Childe's criteria. Although they developed a system of numerical notation in the *quipu*, a knotted string, they never developed a system of writing. This lack probably also accounts for their failure to develop very far in such sciences as calendrics, astronomy, or mathematics. Although agricultural practices were diffused to the Central Andes after 2500 B.C. from the north, ultimately from the Maya, the South American civilization was very different from the Mayan. After 750 B.C., agricultural practices, weaving, pottery, and village life were well established along the Peruvian coast.

Collier notes that five of Childe's urban traits existed among the Inca by the beginning of our Christian era: monumental architecture, great works of art, capital in the form of food surplus, full-time craft specialists, and long-distance trade. All of the additional criteria, with the exception of writing, developed by about A.D. 900. The Inca cities clustered around stone temple pyramids covered with beaten gold in honor of the sun god and were planned on a rectangular grid pattern enclosed by defensive stone walls. The Inca conquered the independent local kingdoms between A.D. 1100 and 1400 and formed the only true empire in the New World. The tremendous area, five times the size of Europe, was linked together administratively by a centralized governmental bureaucracy under a god-king and by a stupendous 10,000-mile system of highways.[25] Even before the Inca unification, some cities, such as Chanchan, the Chimu capital, reached 50,000 in population. The Inca capital was located at Cuzco. The modern city of the same name stands on the site and has many buildings constructed with stones from ruined Inca buildings. Inca

[23] Description based on Bushnell, *op. cit.* in Piggott, *The Dawn of Civilization, op. cit.*

[24] Description based on D. Collier, "The Central Andes," in Braidwood and Willey, *op. cit.*, pp. 165–76.

[25] Victor Von Hagen, *Highway of the Sun* (1955), p. 295.

wealth, power, and "welfare statism" were reflected in their elaborate public works such as bridges, canals, and terrace systems, as well as in their large-scale social and economic planning such as resettlement projects, "valley authorities," and city planning. In contrast to the Maya, the Inca had discovered metal-working at an early date. By 1000 B.C. they used gold, silver, and soon thereafter copper, and by A.D. 1000 were working in bronze. The Inca were conquered by the Spanish led by Pizarro in 1532.

The brief compass of this chapter does not permit description of other early civilizations and their cities. The list would include China and Crete, both of which attained a civilized level sometime after 3000 B.C. It is important to note that although the various Old World civilizations and cities described here—Mesopotamian, Egyptian, and Indian—flourished several thousand years before Christ, even crude Neolithic skills were not found in Europe until after 4000 B.C., and civilization and cities were not formed there until much later.

THE ROLE OF RELIGIOUS AND POLITICAL ORGANIZATION

Although we have described the origin of early cities in conjunction with civilization, that is, with a complex social order, a final question remains. Can we point to any forces which set the process of complexity in motion? Religious and political organization have often been pointed to in this regard. In fact, many of Childe's criteria hinge on the more underlying assumption of a strong central authority which directs the formation, concentration, and distribution of the surplus product. Religious or political allegiance provide such a focus.

Several of the early civilizations combined sacred and secular authority. The Egyptians and the Inca had god-kings, while the Indus civilization was probably a theocracy. Although the local units of the Maya civilization enjoyed autonomy, political and religious authority were closely linked within local units, and the very core of the civilization was a common religion embodied in the ceremonial city centers. Mesopotamian civilization, too, rested more on religious than political unity, although it is noteworthy that political authority grew in importance in Mesopotamian history.

Some authorities have assigned the major position to religious organization, arguing that each of the early civilizations was associated with a new religion which gave

the settlers in great river valleys the courage to clear the land, to keep it cleared, and to bring the water to it. . . . [Religion also] serve[d] to encourage settlers in a rain forest to undertake the far greater task of clearing the land in a tropical rain forest, where, however, the water came direct. . . .[26]

[26] Coulborn, *op. cit.*, pp. 176–77.

However, as we have guarded against attributing the origin of cities exclusively to environment or technology, so here we must guard against invoking cultural determinism, that is, viewing religious, political, or other features of social organization as the sole determinants of civilization and, ultimately, cities. No amount of religious exaltation or of political control could have originally concentrated and administered a surplus product if environmental and technological conditions had not made such a surplus possible. Nevertheless, the creation of cities was not an inevitable consequence of a society's possession of such surpluses alone; rather, it was through the interaction of social, technological, and environmental factors that cities were formed. But the catalytic function of political and religious organization, the seemingly more "abstract" aspects of social structure, exemplifies the role of new, complex forms of society in making efficient use of surpluses.

SELECTED BIBLIOGRAPHY

BOOKS

Braidwood, Robert, and G. Willey (eds.), *Courses Toward Urban Life.* Viking Fund Publications in Anthropology, #32, 1962. Distributed by the Aldine Publishing Company, Chicago.

Childe, V. Gordon, *Man Makes Himself.* New York: The New American Library, 1951.

―――, *What Happened in History.* New York: Penguin Books, 1946.

Clough, Shepard B., *The Rise and Fall of Civilization: An Inquiry into the Relationship between Economic Development and Civilization.* New York: Columbia University Press, 1961.

Cottrell, Leonard, *Lost Cities.* New York: Holt, Rinehart and Winston, 1957.

Coulborn, Rushton, *The Origin of Civilized Societies.* Princeton: Princeton University Press, 1959.

Frankfort, Henri, *The Birth of Civilization in the Near East.* Bloomington: Indiana University Press, 1951.

Kraeling, Karl, and Robert Adams (eds.), *City Invincible: A Symposium on Urbanization and Cultural Development in the Ancient Near East.* Chicago: University of Chicago Press, 1960.

Piggott, S. (ed.), *The Dawn of Civilization: The First World Survey of Human Cultures in Early Times.* London: Thames and Hudson, 1961.

Redfield, Robert, *The Primitive World and Its Transformations.* Ithaca: Cornell University Press, 1953.

Singer, Charles, E. J. Holmyard, and A. R. Hall, *A History of Technology.* Vol. 1, *From Early Times to Fall of Ancient Empires.* New York and London: Oxford University Press, 1954.

Sjoberg, Gideon, *The Preindustrial City,* chs. 2 and 3. Glencoe, Ill.: The Free Press, 1960.

Steward, Julian, "Development of Complex Societies: Culture Causality and Law: A Trial Formulation of the Development of Early Civilization," in

Steward (ed.), *The Theory of Culture Change.* Urbana, Ill.: University of Illinois Press, 1955.

ARTICLES

Adams, Robert M., "The Origin of Cities," *Scientific American* (September, 1960), 153–72.

Braidwood, Robert, "The Agricultural Revolution," *Scientific American,* (September, 1960), 130–52.

Childe, V. Gordon, "The Urban Revolution," *Town Planning Review,* 21 (April, 1950), 3–17.

Coe, Michael D., "Social Typology and the Tropical Forest Civilizations," *Comparative Studies in Society and History,* 1 (November, 1961), 65–85.

Freeman, Linton C., and Robert Winch, "Societal Complexity: An Empirical Test of a Typology of Societies," *American Journal of Sociology,* LXII (March, 1957), 461–66.

Conditions of City Growth
in Historic Times

TWO

The interplay of the same factors that promoted the growth of ancient cities continued in historic times, that is, the period of roughly 5,000 years for which we have some written records. The city has waxed and waned as have its environmental, technological, and social bases. In this chapter we shall consider the interplay of these factors as they have been affected by the Industrial Revolution, describing first city growth before the Revolution, then discussing growth since the Revolution.

CITY GROWTH BEFORE THE INDUSTRIAL REVOLUTION

Environmental and Technological Factors

In the limited time span of recorded history, environmental factors do not loom large as having affected urban growth, partly because environment changes slowly, and partly because technology rendered many environments more suitable to urban life. Therefore, environmental and technological factors will be discussed jointly for the period before the Industrial Revolution.

Technology made steady although slow advances before the Industrial Revolution, the processes of metal-working becoming especially important. Copper was the first useful metal man discovered, and by approximately 3000 B.C. bronze, an alloy of copper and tin, was in use. Tools such as axes, ploughs, and hoes made of bronze were much more efficient and durable than those of stone, wood, or bone. Invention of techniques of iron-working about 1000 B.C. brought even more efficient tools into being and still further enhanced man's ability to obtain sustenance from the environment. These dates refer to the discovery of the processes, not to the period during which their use was widespread or common.

Significant advances in building materials and skills in wood-working, spinning and weaving, pottery, irrigation and water supply, methods of transportation, weights and measures, the decorative arts, and many other areas, continued to accumulate before the Industrial Revolution.[1]

Cities expanded in the wake of this technological development, but environmental factors were more important in city growth before the Industrial Revolution than they have been since then. Technology was still very limited so that natural conditions provided more of an obstacle to the establishment of cities. A survey of preindustrial cities noted that cities were not established early in areas whose location or terrain posed problems of accessibility, cultivation, or transport.[2] Although we may think of the cities of mainland Greece as very old, they were not established until fairly late in historic time when improvements in sailing ships and agricultural techniques made the area more accessible and the mountain slopes more productive. The city of Lhasa in the Himalayan fastnesses of Tibet was not established until the early years of the Christian era.

The relative inefficiency of preindustrial technology and consequent hampering of urban expansion are also indicated in the small percentage of population living in cities and in the small size of preindustrial communities. In countries where cities existed, usually no more than 10 per cent, and perhaps less than 5 per cent, of the population were able to live in the urban settlements. In the preindustrial period cities of 100,000 or more were very rare, although under certain social as well as economic conditions some surpassed even this size. Rome in the second century A.D., Constantinople as the later political successor to Rome, Baghdad before A.D. 1000, the cities of Sung China between A.D. 1100 and 1300, and Edo (Tokyo), Kyoto, and Osaka in seventeenth- and eighteenth-century Japan all had populations well above 100,000, and in some cases, possibly even a million. However, most preindustrial cities, including many important ones, had populations of five to ten thousand.[3]

---

[1] These advances are well described in C. Singer, E. J. Holmyard, A. R. Hall, and T. I. Williams (eds.), *A History of Technology* (1956–57), especially vols. II and III. Another valuable study, though of a shorter time period and with a more deterministic view of the effects of technology on social organization, is Lynn White, Jr., *Medieval Technology and Social Change* (1962).

[2] These statements are based on Gideon Sjoberg, *The Preindustrial City* (1960), pp. 82–85.

[3] *Ibid.*

Preindustrial versus industrial cities. Above: Carcassonne, France, a well-preserved example of the walled cities that dotted medieval Europe. Modern Carcassonne lies in the background. Below: A general view of Sofara, in Mali, a newly independent African nation. Timbuctoo, a renowned preindustrial city, is also located in Mali. Facing page: Note the striking contrasts of Carcassonne and Sofara with the modern industrial city of Houston. (Courtesy French Government Tourist Office, United Nations, and Cities Service Company [photograph by Anthony Linck].)

SOCIAL FACTORS

Cities have continued to be associated with complex societies. The Western civilizations of historic times indicate the continued special importance of political and other aspects of social organization.

Cities in Ancient Greece and the Roman Empire. Some of the cities of ancient Greece developed as self-governing communities—city-states with political independence. Among these were Athens, Sparta, Corinth, and Miletus. Athens not only was the largest of these cities but it also developed one of the most brilliant civilizations of the ancient world. During the fifth century B.C. the city probably had as many as 150,000 inhabitants.

The largest ancient city in the Western world was Rome, capital of an empire extending over Europe, the British Isles, Asia Minor, and North Africa. At its peak Rome had a population variously estimated at from 250,000 to 1,000,000 inhabitants. Certainly it was the largest European city until the rise of Constantinople and London. The decline of the Roman Empire saw the eclipse of Rome as a great administrative capital. Rome had been the hub of a vast network (52,000 miles) of well-maintained, well-policed roads which facilitated the free movement of goods

and people throughout the empire. As the empire slowly disintegrated under invasions and internal troubles, surplus production could no longer be drawn from a wide territory nor, concomitantly, could specialists and others be maintained apart from the soil. It is difficult to assign a specific date to the "fall" of the Roman Empire, but the last Roman emperor in the West was deposed in A.D. 476. By the fourteenth century A.D., Rome was little more than a straggling town.

Revealingly, the only other very large European city until the rise of modern industrial cites was also the capital of an empire. Constantinople (modern Istanbul) was the capital of the Roman Empire of the East from A.D. 330–1453, and thereafter was the capital of the Ottoman Empire until that empire fell in the twentieth century.

Cities of Medieval and Post-Medieval Europe. After the Roman Empire went into eclipse there was a long period of cultural and economic stagnation when cities ceased to flourish over large parts of Europe. This was the so-called Dark Ages. From the fifth to the tenth centuries cities generally declined, trade languished, and intellectual life was at a low ebb. The glories of the cities of ancient Rome and Greece faded into the past.

Feudalism was the characteristic political structure of the European Middle Ages. The orientation was toward the soil and local self-sufficiency. The many petty kingdoms and the constant warfare between them further inhibited contacts and trade over long distances. These conditions prevented concentration of effective surpluses and the support of a specialized division of labor. Significantly, the Roman Catholic Church, the one most nearly universal institution in Europe at this time, and the one resting on a literate specialized clergy, was also an important means of preserving the heritage of Western civilization.

The ruralism of the Middle Ages was gradually transformed under the impact of increasing trade and expanding intellectual horizons. Much long-distance trade was generated by the movement of thousands of Crusaders back and forth across Europe from 1096 to 1291. Their need for food, clothing, shelter and transportation had to be met at numerous places en route. The Crusaders also brought back new objects, new wants, and new ideas.

Beginning with the eleventh century, cities among the Mediterranean felt the effects of renewed commercial activities. Florence, Genoa, Venice, Pisa, and other cities of the Italian peninsula were among the first to enjoy the benefits of a commercial renaissance. Along the northwest coast of Europe and in the Baltic area, city growth increased under the stimulation of trade. In central Europe the growth was slower, but there was growth nevertheless.

A merchant class grew in power and ultimately gained ascendancy over the feudal nobility. The merchants represented a way of life based on craft and service specialization, on the concentration of surplus production, and on living apart from the farms. Thus, they laid the foundation for the large-scale reappearance of cities in Europe.

Sjoberg's Study of Preindustrial Social Structure. The preceding section has indicated something of the religious, political, and other social aspects of preindustrial cities in Western civilization. It appears that certain features of social organization are common to all preindustrial cities, thus emphasizing that cities depend on an adequate social base, as well as on technological and environmental factors. This does not mean that all preindustrial cities have identical social structures, but rather that their diversity is a series of variations on the same theme.

Sjoberg's pioneering study of preindustrial cities, old and relatively new, Western and non-Western in culture, concluded that these cities are characterized by particular systems of social stratification, family and kinship, political organization, religion, education, and communication.[4]

Manual and economic activity is given a low value in preindustrial cities, and hence there is little social encouragement for expanding productive activities. Commercial or manual activities are "beyond the pale" for the elite, who control the much more highly regarded political and religious realms. Political and religious systems are typically static and dedicated to preserving tradition. Political behavior is hierarchical and highly influenced by family and status. Religious considerations, which include many magical practices and beliefs, permeate all phases of life.

In short, the preindustrial social order tends to be rigid, tradition-bound, and oriented away from economic productivity. However, many preindustrial cities of today are undergoing modernization and exhibit some attributes usually thought to be characteristic of industrial cities, such as local newspapers, radio stations, and modern schools and universities.

CITY GROWTH AFTER THE INDUSTRIAL REVOLUTION

By far the greatest urban growth, associated with a complex series of events called the Industrial Revolution, has occurred in the past 200 years. For the first time in history, man was capable of utilizing sources of energy besides domestic animals or his own muscle; steam power was the earliest source developed, but later electricity, oil, natural gas, and atomic power were made available. For the first time, too, man had machines, rather than just tools, to assist him in the performance of work. The social order also underwent far-reaching changes under the impact of the Industrial Revolution, but it would be an oversimplification to say

[4] *Ibid.*, pp. 323–38. Sjoberg's description of the preindustrial city is a "constructed type." Apart from providing a basis for historical description, this construct also provides a basis for analyzing contemporary preindustrial cities. A more detailed discussion of Sjoberg's study of the social characteristics of preindustrial cities is found in Chapter 5, "Classes and Types of Cities."

Port cities. Location on major bodies of water has often been an important environmental factor favoring the growth of large cities at these sites. The picture above is a panoramic view of Istanbul (formerly Constantinople), Turkey. The bridge crosses famous Golden Horn harbor and connects Galata and Stamboul, parts of the metropolis separated by the body of water. The aerial view on the facing page is of the piers lining the Hudson and East rivers along lower Manhattan as the island juts into New York harbor. (Courtesy Pan American Airways and Trans World Airlines, Inc.)

that social structure was altered *because* of the technological advances. Rather, social and technological factors interacted reciprocally, and several important alterations in social structure and values *preceded* commercial and industrial innovations.

ENVIRONMENTAL FACTORS

The importance of environmental factors as determinants of city growth is reduced still further under the impact of industrial technology. Thus, a huge aggregation like Los Angeles can grow up in an area of limited rainfall because water can be brought to it from rivers hundreds of miles away. Air-conditioning, airplanes, automobiles, and trucks have rendered a wider variety of areas comfortable for permanent habitation or made them accessible to a hinterland which could provide the neces-

sary food and other supplies. Temporary settlements have even been made near the South Pole.

Nevertheless, environment cannot be entirely discarded as a force affecting the establishment and growth of cities in industrial times. All the great industrial-urban nations have had plentiful natural resources, especially arable land, timber, water, coal, iron, oil, or natural gas, although it is also true that many areas have these resources, but have not necessarily become heavily urbanized as a result.

Industries dependent on mild climate have become increasingly important in the American economy, and have been an important factor promoting rapid urban growth in California and Florida.[5] The aircraft industry has a special need for mild climate the year round so that planes can be assembled, tested, and delivered without interruption. In 1958 the aircraft industry employed a total of 839,000 people compared with 593,000 employees in motor vehicle manufacturing and 519,000 employees in steel mills and blast furnaces. California's equable climate has attracted so large a share of aircraft employment that it has been an important reason for the state's leading the nation in urban growth. Florida's sunshine has attracted many people to retirement or recreation communities which in turn have attracted business and industry directed to serving leisure needs.

[5] Victor Fuchs, *Changes in the Location of Manufacturing in the United States since 1929* (1962), pp. 24–28.

It has been pointed out that about 80 per cent of the world's large cities (population of 100,000 or more) are in the temperate zone, although there appears to be no inherent reason why societies in tropical regions should not become heavily urbanized.[6] It may simply be that since the Industrial Revolution on which heavy urbanization depended was developed by temperate zone populations, it tended to spread more readily to areas of similar climate.[7] This leaves aside the question of whether the Industrial Revolution could have *originated* in any but the temperate zone; there can be no conclusive answer to this question.

TECHNOLOGICAL FACTORS

The significance of the Industrial Revolution was that it immensely broadened the economic capacity of society. With the application of new and revolutionary forms of technology to manufacturing, transportation, and warfare, the basis was laid for the growth of cities larger than the world had ever seen before. Steam power harnessed to the factory machine made possible the production of far more commodities than could be fabricated in a handicraft technology. With the increase in factory output and the intensification of commercial activities to dispose of fabricated commodities, more and more workers were needed to tend the machines or perform the various tasks related to trade. As the cities of Europe and America became increasingly industrialized, they drew to them vast numbers of country and village folk. The die was thus cast for a new type of community in the Western world—the mass-production city. Manchester, Birmingham, and Pittsburgh were to become symbols of the pervasive economic changes based on the new technology.

The Factory System. As long as industry was in the handicraft stage there was no reason why concentration of population for industrial purposes alone should take place on a very large scale. Certainly the advantages of concentration were outweighed by disadvantages: transportation facilities were not adequate for the distribution of fabricated commodities; sufficient food and shelter for a concentrated population could not be provided; the labor supply was inadequate, for workers were characterized more by their immobility than mobility. Even during the period when factories were operated by water-driven machinery the geographical location of cities usually forbade any great expansion of industries. Only when the steam-driven engine came into universal use did workers concentrate in large numbers in industrial centers.

As the Industrial Revolution in Europe and America gained headway,

[6] Kingsley Davis and Hilda Hertz, "The World Distribution of Urbanization," *Bulletin of the International Statistical Institute,* Vol. 33, Pt. IV (December, 1951), pp. 234–35.
[7] *Ibid.*

Work moves from home to factory. The change in the manufacture of cigars is typical of the mechanization of the Industrial Revolution. Above: Hand-filling of cigars at the turn of the century. Below: The same operation performed at a Richmond, Virginia, cigar factory in 1960. (Courtesy American Machine and Foundry Company.)

new labor-saving devices appeared, and these in turn were instrumental in transferring all kinds of home industries to the factory and thereby accentuating the concentration of population in the industrial centers.

Even before the modern era of steam-propelled machinery, industrialism was making itself felt in some European countries. Adna Weber distinguishes four principal stages in the evolution of industry: first, the household or family system; second, the guild or handicraft system; third, the domestic, or cottage system; and fourth, the factory system or centralized industry.[8] While the second and third stages were conducive to a limited concentration of population in towns and cities, it was only in the fourth stage that the huge agglomerations of people in industrial centers took place.

The modern industrial town or city is, therefore, partly a product of steam and, more recently, electrical power. By its very nature steam is economical when applied to large manufacturing units concentrated within a small area. Consequently, the power-driven machine drew manufacturing out of the home and placed it in a centralized location.

As the factory system expanded to meet the needs and demands of a growing population more workers were required to tend the machines and dispose of the finished products. To the factories in towns and cities, then, flocked rural people, attracted not only by the novelty of city life but also by the possibilities of greater economic rewards. Here they crowded into stuffy and unsanitary quarters near the industrial plants.

City growth in England represents very well the relationship between manufacturing and urbanization. The technological revolution as applied to industry got under way in England earlier than in any other country, and at a time when the world's natural resources were virtually untouched. Vast amounts of raw materials were brought to the British Isles to feed the maws of the machinery, whose insatiable appetites were forever increasing. To the factories and mills came people in search of work, settling in towns and cities close to the places of employment. Thus such cities as Birmingham, Leeds, Manchester, and Sheffield became vast concentrations of factories surrounded by the homes of the people who manned the machines.

Mechanization of Agriculture. While steam and electricity were being utilized to turn the wheels of factories in the great industrial centers, mechanical energy and scientific knowledge were applied to agriculture to increase the output of farm and ranch. But, while the revolution in industry and the expansion of commerce demanded more workers, the revolution in agriculture made it possible for fewer people to supply the basic needs of an expanding population. The result was a gradual divorcement of men from the soil.

In 1750 the great majority of the labor force—about 85 to 90 per cent —in what was to become the United States was engaged in agriculture.

[8] Adna F. Weber, *The Growth of Cities in the Nineteenth Century* (1899), p. 185.

These percentages steadily declined to 80 per cent by 1805 and 70 per cent by 1830.[9] In 1870 over half (50.3 per cent) of the United States labor force was employed in agriculture, while in 1960 only 8.3 per cent of the employed men were engaged in agricultural occupations—farmers and farm managers, farm foremen, and laborers.[10] In 1960 this small group produced not only enough food to maintain the United States as one of the best-fed nations, but great quantities of food and raw materials were shipped abroad, and staggering surpluses piled up in storage bins. This has come about not only through mechanization but also through application of scientific knowledge to increase soil fertility, improve plant and animal strains, and reduce wastage in various ways.

SOCIAL FACTORS

Urban development in Western civilization advanced not only in response to industrialization but as a consequence of a transformation of the social structure. Major debates still rage in the social sciences about the precise role of technological and nontechnological factors in social change. Although we cannot pinpoint the relative contribution of each set of factors, there is no doubt that social organization of a certain type was a precondition for the emergence of urban-industrial communities in Europe and North America. An important question is whether a similar type of social structure is necessary for cities to develop successfully in the little-urbanized parts of the world.

City growth in Europe was stimulated by the demise of feudal systems of government and by the emergence of new political ideals and forms. Nationhood gained currency, first in monarchical and later in democratic forms. Large areas were unified under the impetus of nationalism with a resultant expansion of areas covered by common coinage, long transportation systems, absence of frequent customs and toll collection, and the like.

Whereas Europe in the later Middle Ages had witnessed the multiplication of cities, the post-Medieval period was characterized by agglomerations of population at the seats of political and ecclesiastical power. According to Mumford, the modern state began to take form during the fourteenth century.[11] Its hallmarks, permanent and centrally-located bureaucracies, courts of justice, and archives and records, epitomized the principles of uniformity and centralization. Under their impetus the dispersed feudal estates were consolidated; power and popula-

[9] The accuracy and sources of these figures are discussed in Sidney Aronson, *Status and Kinship in the Higher Civil Service* (1964), ch. 3.

[10] Frederick J. Dewhurst and Associates, *America's Needs and Resources* (1955), p. 732; and *United States Census of Population, 1960: U. S. Summary, General Social and Economic Characteristics*, PC (1) IC, p. 1–216.

[11] Lewis Mumford, *The City in History* (1961), pp. 351–56.

tion were no longer scattered. Cities with royal courts typically embodied central economic as well as political power, for the nobility were a major group of consumers and also the source of capital for economic enter-prises. "After the sixteenth century, accordingly . . . about a dozen towns quickly reached a size not attained in the Middle Ages even by a bare handful: in a little while London had 250,000 inhabitants, Naples, 240,000, Milan over 200,000, Palermo and Rome, 100,000, Lisbon, port of a great monarchy, over 100,000; similarly, Seville, Antwerp, and Amsterdam; while Paris in 1594 had 180,000." [12]

Religious as well as political factors helped lay the foundation for modern Western societies. In the Renaissance a major shift in social val-ues turned men's eyes to the things of this world. The Renaissance marked the freeing of man's intellect from the medieval outlook. The conse-quences of the Renaissance were profound not only for the arts and liter-ature, but for all fields of human endeavor. A spirit of inquiry affected the growth of the sciences. The humanist point of view spurred the un-derstanding and well-being of man. All of these values went into build-ing a civilization more complex and more far-flung than any which had preceded it.

Max Weber has pointed out how certain features of the Protestant Reformation were conducive to the expansion of technology and produc-tion.[13] Weber noted that the puritan aspects of Protestantism fostered economic rationality. High value is placed on an active, rather than a contemplative life, unremitting labor is moral virtue and duty, and the more productive the labor is the more it signifies that the individual per-forming it had found favor in the eyes of God. Hence success, profit, and wealth were not necessarily evils. They were vices only if they led to idleness and dissipation.

Such an outlook was a powerful motivation to work; it also placed a high moral value on the material consequences of one's work. It was a set of beliefs consonant with the technological innovations of industrial capitalism. Weber did not hold that he had proved a causal relationship between Protestantism and the rise of modern industrial society. How-ever, it has been noted that although the ideology of the "Protestant Ethic" originated with small religious sects in the sixteenth century, it spread throughout Western civilization among all religious groups and coincided with the productive expansion of the Industrial Revolution.

SOCIAL FACTORS IN URBANIZATION IN THE UNDERDEVELOPED AREAS

There is no better proof of the importance of the social factors under-lying urbanization than an examination of the economically underde-

---

[12] *Ibid.*, p. 355.
[13] Max Weber, *The Protestant Ethic and the Spirit of Capitalism,* tr. Talcott Parsons (1958). This work was originally published in the early 1900's.

veloped areas. The obstacles to stable urban development in these areas are not only technological but social.

Most of the present-day cities in these areas originated as trading and administrative centers for the industrialized nations of Europe. Hence, cities in the underdeveloped areas did not evolve gradually in conjunction with a social structure suited to urban-industrial living. The problem for these areas is not simply to industrialize rapidly so that their cities will rest on a sound internal economic base. Even more fundamental is the re-education of the people toward the values and practices related to industrial efficiency and productivity.

A recent analysis by Philip Hauser details some of the obstacles which the native cultures of underdeveloped areas place in the way of economic development.[14] His observations were based on South and Southeast Asia, but the general point of the role of social factors holds for other underdeveloped regions. Hauser describes five main elements hindering economic development.

First, he notes that the traditional value systems emphasize spiritual rather than material values and in other ways conflict with material aspirations. Second, these societies are highly stratified into an elite and a lower class, the middle class being very small or nonexistent. The effective utilization of human resources is inhibited by the fact that opportunities for training and advancement are distributed among the elite, often on the basis of criteria other than merit. Third, there is great deference to age, which further inhibits effective utilization of manpower. Age and seniority take precedence over training and competence.

The fourth social factor which Hauser describes as hindering economic development is the prescientific mentality. Views of the universe as controlled by astrological, numerological, magical, animistic, and other nonrational forces often interfere with economic incentives. Fifth, and finally, Hauser points to the atomistic or "loose" social ties in some underdeveloped societies which result in their inability to move in a concerted way toward common objectives. The individual is so immersed in self, family, or local concerns that he does not develop the broad perspective and wider sense of responsibility which are important in maintaining industrial discipline and coordination.

It is revealing to note the many parallels between Hauser's analysis and Sjoberg's description of the social structure of preindustrial cities. Another recent study also points up the importance of social factors in urbanization. Lerner's survey of 54 countries contrasts present-day "traditional" with "modern" societies in terms of social organization. "Modern" societies are characterized not only by urbanization but other traits which proved to be statistically related to urbanization—degree of literacy in the population, availability and use of impersonal media of com-

[14] Philip Hauser, "Cultural and Personal Obstacles to Economic Development in the Less Developed Areas," *Human Organization*, 18 (Summer, 1959), 78–84.

munication (radio, television, movies, inexpensive newspapers and magazines), and degree to which the population participated in the political
process (formation of public opinion on important issues, voting, and
so on).[15]

Hauser believes that we may oversimplify the relationship between
social values and economic development if we assume that social organization in non-Western countries must follow the Western pattern in
order to progress economically.[16] Although we cannot predict the future
course of social change in the underdeveloped countries, it is clear that
their present values and customs hinder technological advance, thereby
also hindering stable urban development.

GROWTH OF LARGE CITIES

Cities have grown as industrialization progressed, but it was not until
the twentieth century that urbanism featured the growth of gigantic
cities that cast their shadow over the whole of society, both urban and rural.
In reviewing the growth of large cities, Davis estimates that in 1800 only
1.7 per cent of the world's population was living in cities of over 100,000,
but that this figure had increased to 13 per cent by 1950. In 1800 around
16 million people lived in cities of over 100,000; by 1950 the figure had
increased to about 314 million, more than 20 times the earlier figure.[17]

Precise data on the number and population of all the great cities of
the world are not obtainable, but it is known that in 1960 there were
upwards of 1,400 cities of 100,000 or more inhabitants and over 60 in
the million class.[18] In 1800 there were probably about 20 cities of over
100,000 inhabitants, but none had as many as a million.[19]

Table 1 shows how important urbanism in general and large cities
in particular have become in many parts of the world. Contrasting the
highly urbanized group with the less urban group suggests that the
highly urbanized countries tend to be the highly industrialized ones.
There are, however, important exceptions. Argentina, Chile, and Venezuela, for example, have about as large a proportion of their population
in cities over 100,000 as the United States but are not heavily industrialized. Many of the world's largest cities—Calcutta, Mexico City, Teheran,
Cairo, for example—have relatively little industry.

[15] Daniel Lerner and Lucille Plevsner, *The Passing of Traditional Society* (1958).

[16] Hauser, *op. cit.*, p. 81.

[17] Kingsley Davis, "The Origin and Growth of Urbanization in the World," *American
Journal of Sociology*, 60 (March, 1955), 433–34.

[18] *Demographic Yearbook* (United Nations, 1960), p. 32 and Table 7. The actual
number of cities in these categories may be higher than shown here since not all
figures are based on 1960 data and some are estimates. Furthermore, since the enumerations were made, a number of cities have probably moved into the 100,000 category
or the million class.

[19] Eric E. Lampard, "The History of Cities in the Economically Advanced Areas,"
Economic Development and Cultural Change, 3 (January, 1955), 82.

TABLE 1

Ten Highly Urbanized and Ten Little-Urbanized Countries

	PER CENT URBAN	PER CENT IN CITIES OVER 100,000
HIGH		
England and Wales (1951, 1958) *	81	51
Australia (1954, 1959)	79	57
Israel (1958, 1959)	76	34
West Germany (1950, 1959)	71	31
United States (1960)	70	28 **
Denmark (1955, 1958)	69	34
Argentina (1947, 1958)	63	40
Chile (1952)	60	30
Japan (1955, 1959)	56	41
Venezuela (1950, 1959)	54	32
LOW		
Yugoslavia (1953)	19	8
India (1951, 1960)	18	9
Ceylon (1956, 1958)	18	5
China, mainland (1956, 1953)	14	8
Cambodia (1958, 1959)	13	9
Haiti (1950, 1958)	12	4
Thailand (1960, 1947)	12	10
Sudan (1956)	8	2
Tanganyika (1957)	4	2
Nepal (1954)	3	1

* If the two types of urban data were not collected in the same year, the first date in parentheses refers to the "per cent urban" column, the second to "per cent in cities over 100,000."

** Refers only to people living within the political limits of the city, thus excluding many suburbanites.

SOURCE: Based on data from *Demographic Yearbook* (United Nations, 1960), Tables 8 and 9, except for the United States data which is from *U. S. Census of Population: 1960.*

On the whole, urbanization and industrialization are closely related as shown in the world survey reported in Table 2. There is a high correlation between the proportion of the population living in cities of over 100,000 and the degree of industrialization (measured by nonagricultural occupations of the labor force in a country).

Large cities are by no means limited to the industrialized areas of the world, however. Many, if not most, of the countries in the underdeveloped areas have at least one city of 100,000 or more in size. China and India each have over 100 cities in that category; some of these cities range into the million class.[20] Nowadays only sparsely settled and isolated areas such as North Borneo have no cities over 100,000 in size.

TABLE 2

Degree of Urbanization in World's Countries and Territories
Classified by Degree of Agriculturalism

PER CENT OF GAINFULLY OCCUPIED MALES IN NONAGRICULTURAL OCCUPATIONS	NUMBER OF COUNTRIES	PER CENT OF POPULATION IN CITIES OF 100,000 PLUS
80–100	11	32.3
70–79	11	23.6
60–69	7	23.2
50–59	7	21.9
40–49	16	17.7
30–39	17	8.9
Less than 30	86	6.3

SOURCE: Adapted from K. Davis and Hilda H. Golden, "Urbanization and the Development of Preindustrial Areas," *Economic Development and Cultural Change*, 3 (October, 1954), Table 1, p. 8. Reprinted by permission.

Many cities in the underdeveloped areas originated from the commercial impact of the industrializing nations. To feed the ever-enlarging industrial machines located in great cities, nations began to look beyond their own boundaries for new sources of raw materials. New political and economic concepts in the form of colonialism and imperialism were devised in order to exploit more effectively the natural and human resources of far-flung lands. As each country proceeded to exploit the resources of its empire, new cities were founded or old ones expanded as trading centers through which could be channeled raw materials destined for the factories at home. Some of these cities also became administrative capitals from which indigenous peoples could be governed by their colonial overlords.

Many of the cities were essentially creations of imperialism. Saigon in French Indo-China, Jakarta in the Dutch Indies, Singapore in British Malaya, Rangoon in Burma, and Hong Kong in China grew to large size as colonial bridgeheads. The three greatest cities of India—Calcutta, Bombay, and Madras—were developed by the British as major seaports and administrative capitals. Rangoon, Saigon, and Singapore did not exist as cities before 1800; likewise Jakarta and Manila, while somewhat older, grew to metropolitan magnitude in the nineteenth century as

[20] *Demographic Yearbook, op. cit.*, Tables 7 and 8.

foreign enclaves or gateway cities.[21] Leopoldville and Elisabethville in the former Belgian Congo and many other African cities had a similar origin in the twentieth century. Much of the Latin American urban population is concentrated into a small number of large cities which were originally established as headquarters for the Spanish colonial system.[22]

The prevalence of large cities in countries with little industrialization presents a situation in which urban agglomerations have developed without an adequate technological base. The separation of urban from economic development, which colonialism was instrumental in bringing about, is the root of many contemporary urban problems in Asia, Africa, and Latin America. Some of these problems are discussed in Chapters 4, 12, and 20.

SELECTED BIBLIOGRAPHY

BOOKS

Hauser, Philip M., *Population Perspectives.* New Brunswick, N.J.: Rutgers University Press, 1960.

Hoselitz, Bert, *Sociological Aspects of Economic Growth.* Glencoe, Ill.: The Free Press, 1960.

Hoyt, Homer, *World Urbanization.* Washington, D. C.: Urban Land Institute, Technical Bulletin #43, 1962.

Lerner, Daniel, and Lucille Plevsner, *The Passing of Traditional Society.* Glencoe, Ill.: The Free Press, 1958.

Mumford, Lewis, *The City in History.* New York: Harcourt, Brace and World, 1961.

Pirenne, Henri, *Medieval Cities.* Translated by Frank Halsey. Garden City, N.Y.: Doubleday Anchor Books, 1956.

Singer, Charles, E. J. Holmyard, A. R. Hall, and T. I. Williams (eds.), *A History of Technology.* Vols. 2-5. New York: Oxford University Press, 1957–58.

Sjoberg, Gideon, *The Preindustrial City,* chs. 5–11. Glencoe, Ill.: The Free Press, 1960.

Weber, Adna, *The Growth of Cities in the Nineteenth Century.* Ithaca, N.Y.: Cornell University Press, 1963. Originally published in 1899.

Weber, Max, *The Protestant Ethic and the Spirit of Capitalism.* Translated by Talcott Parsons. New York: Scribner, 1958.

ARTICLES

Davis, Kingsley, "The Origin and Growth of Urbanization in the World," *American Journal of Sociology,* LX (March, 1955), 429–37.

————, and Hilda H. Golden, "Urbanization and the Development of Pre-

[21] Norton S. Ginsburg, "The Great City in Southeast Asia," *American Journal of Sociology,* 60 (March, 1955), 455–62; and R. Murphey, "New Capitals of Asia," *Economic Development and Cultural Change,* 5 (April, 1957), 216–43.

[22] Harley L. Browning, "Recent Trends in Latin American Urbanization," *Annals of the American Academy of Political and Social Science,* 316 (March, 1958), 114–16.

industrial Areas," *Economic Development and Cultural Change*, III (October, 1954), 6–26.

Golden, Hilda H., "Literacy and Social Change in Underdeveloped Countries," *Rural Sociology*, XX (March, 1955), 1–7.

Kahl, Joseph, "Some Social Concomitants of Industrialization and Urbanization," *Human Organization*, XVIII (Summer, 1959), 53–74.

Young, Frank, and Miriam Young, "The Sequence and Direction of Community Growth: A Cross-Cultural Generalization," *Rural Sociology*, XXVII (December, 1962), 374–86.

The Urbanization
of the United States

THREE

It is no accident that America has become a land of many and great cities. All three of the factors promoting urban growth are present to a high degree in the United States—favorable environmental setting, highly developed technology, and a social organization whose small family system and emphasis on the Protestant Ethic are suited to urban-industrial life. The United States also had the major advantage of coming into being in a land where urban development was unhampered by earlier city forms. The North American Indians did not have cities and were, in any case, ruthlessly pushed from the territory they occupied.

A subcontinent blessed with a superabundance of natural wealth, favorably located for international trade, and inhabited by an energetic people with a flair for technology, the United States has possessed all the necessary ingredients for a civilization that is thoroughly urban. No other country in the world, save perhaps Russia, rests on such a firm foundation of natural resources—iron, oil, coal, forests, fertile soil, vegetation, waterways, wildlife, and favorable climate. When the American people set their hand to the exploitation of the country's natural wealth, the result was an expansion of agriculture, industry, transportation, and trade, together with the universal concomitant of such expansion—the growth of cities.

URBAN CONCEPTS IN THE UNITED STATES CENSUS

Since data on urban developments reflect the definitions and system of classification used in the present or the past, it is important to consider the concepts that have been employed by the United States Bureau of the Census for purposes of definition and classification. Only when these concepts are understood can one comprehend adequately the growth of cities in this country.

It is important to realize that the census counts of rural and urban population serve many purposes. Businessmen use them to determine where new stores, factories, and other facilities might best be located. Politicians are interested in the rural-urban distribution of population for indications of shifts in the base of voting power. Various levels of government—local, state, and federal—use census figures on community growth in deciding on the construction of parks, hospitals, schools, roads, and in formulating public policies such as tax rates, price supports for farm products, federal guarantees for home mortgages, and welfare programs. The federal government is required by the Constitution to take a census every ten years in order to reapportion the seats in the House of Representatives. Heavily urban states typically have larger populations and therefore more Representatives than heavily rural states. The 1960 census returns resulted in the allotment of eight more Representatives to California and lesser numbers to other states, while states of declining population, such as Arkansas were assigned fewer Representatives.

The census is a major research tool for social scientists. Sociologists are particularly interested in using the rural-urban classification as a basis for distinguishing between groups that are different from one another in attitudes, tastes, or behavior. Rural-urban comparisons are often significant in fertility rates, attitudes, family behavior, religious and recreational activities, organizational participation, and other aspects of social life. Also, rural and urban communities usually have different kinds of social problems.

Put another way, the accuracy of a definition of rural and urban is not innate or fixed, but depends on the usefulness of the resulting categories. If businessmen, politicians, government, and researchers find that rural-urban classifications do not help in analyzing or predicting community events, then the definition is not valid no matter how precise it may be.

Typically, rural-urban definitions achieve their utility by a very simple method. The definition consists only of some easily measurable items such as size, density, or legal community status. These simple items are assumed to be associated, in ways that may or may not be fully understood, with more complex items such as socioeconomic behavior. Therefore, by employing the definition based on the simple items one has an index to the more complex items. Lack of validity (hence utility) in the definition results when changes occur in the association between the simple and the complex items. Then the definition cannot serve as a valid (useful) index.

This is precisely what happened in the United States in the three or

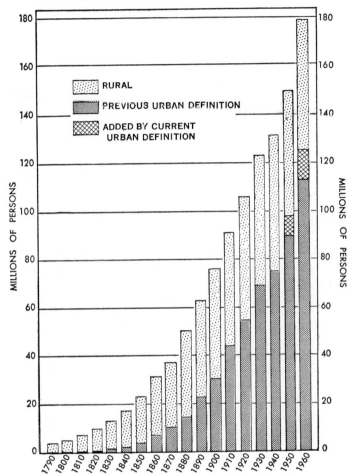

Figure 2. Urban and rural population: 1790–1960. The gradual growth of urban population in the United States transformed a predominantly rural population into a predominantly urban one. In making historical comparisons, one must keep in mind the new urban definition used in the 1950 and 1960 census statistics. SOURCE: *U. S. Census of Population, 1960. Number of Inhabitants, United States Summary.* Final Report PC(1)–1A.

four decades preceding 1950. One of the major changes was that rapid transportation and communication, especially the automobile and telephone, enabled many people to live an urban existence without living in places that were large, densely settled, or legally incorporated as cities. Accordingly, the 1950 and 1960 censuses are based on a new urban definition that tries to reflect the changed conditions.

A NEW DEFINITION OF URBAN

For some time census officials and others were in agreement that the official definition of "urban" as an incorporated place of 2,500 or over was unrealistic. In 1950 the definition was changed to include unincorporated settlements, if they had predominantly "urban" characteristics, as well as a number of incorporated and unincorporated places having populations of less than 2,500. These changes were retained in the 1960 census. The 1960 definition of urban is substantially the same as the 1950 definition.[1]

The 1960 census definition specifies that the urban population will be composed of all persons living in the following types of settlements:

(a) Places of 2,500 inhabitants or more incorporated as cities, boroughs, and villages, and towns (except in New England, New York, and Wisconsin, where "towns" are simply minor civil divisions of counties);

(b) the densely settled urban fringe, including both incorporated and unincorporated areas around cities of 50,000 or more (see Urbanized Areas section below);

(c) unincorporated places of 2,500 inhabitants or more;

(d) towns in New England and townships in New Jersey and Pennsylvania which contain no incorporated municipalities as subdivisions and have either 25,000 inhabitants or more or a population of 2,500 to 25,000 and a density of 1,500 persons or more per square mile; and

(e) counties in states other than the New England states, New Jersey, and Pennsylvania that have no incorporated municipalities within their boundaries and have a density of 1,500 persons per square mile.[2]

This change had the effect of increasing the urban population in 1950 and 1960 over the figure which would have been obtained by the old definition. The rural population was correspondingly reduced.

The new urban-rural definition makes a greater difference in the highly urbanized states than in most of the states that are predominantly rural. This is because of the shift of large numbers of persons to the suburbs and other outlying areas of cities. A great many of these people would have been classified as rural under the old definition. By the same token, the large rural increases of highly urbanized states as shown by the data

[1] The major difference between the 1950 and 1960 definitions is the designation of "urban towns" in New England and "urban townships" in New Jersey and Pennsylvania. This made little difference in the classification of people as urban because most people living in these places were classified as urban anyway by virtue of residence in an Urbanized Area or in an unincorporated urban place.

[2] U. S. *Census of Population: 1960. Number of Inhabitants, United States Summary.* Final Report PC(1)–1A (1961).

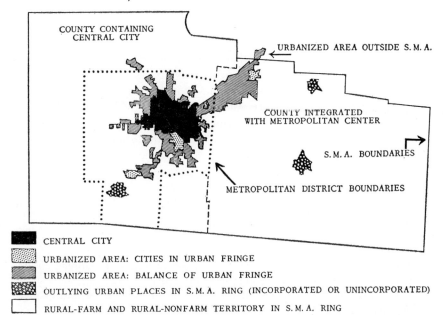

COUNTY CONTAINING CENTRAL CITY

URBANIZED AREA OUTSIDE S. M. A.

COUNTY INTEGRATED WITH METROPOLITAN CENTER

S. M. A. BOUNDARIES

METROPOLITAN DISTRICT BOUNDARIES

■ CENTRAL CITY

▨ URBANIZED AREA: CITIES IN URBAN FRINGE

▨ URBANIZED AREA: BALANCE OF URBAN FRINGE

▨ OUTLYING URBAN PLACES IN S.M.A. RING (INCORPORATED OR UNINCORPORATED)

☐ RURAL-FARM AND RURAL-NONFARM TERRITORY IN S. M. A. RING

Figure 3. Schematic diagram showing relative size and arrangement of a Standard Metropolitan Area. The diagram applies to 1950 census definitions. The Standard Metropolitan Statistical Areas of the 1960 census are comparable to the 1950 Standard Metropolitan Areas. SOURCE: Donald J. Bogue, *Population Growth in Standard Metropolitan Areas* (1953).

reflect the heavy suburban movement in these areas. Among the predominantly rural states, changes in population under the old definition reflect fairly accurately the trends because the suburban population in these states is comparatively small.

The efforts of the Bureau of the Census to make the definition of urban population a valid (useful) reflection of community patterns went much further than the new criteria already described. Two new categories for population enumeration were employed in the 1950 and 1960 censuses: Urbanized Areas, and Standard Metropolitan Areas. In 1960 the term Standard Metropolitan Area was changed to Standard Metropolitan Statistical Area.

The Urbanized Area concept is designed to delineate the limits of the physical city, as opposed to the legal city limits. All population in Urbanized Areas is classified as urban. The Standard Metropolitan Statistical Area concept is designed to delineate the limits of regular daily influence of large cities beyond physically urban territory. The "metropolitan" community, by definition is larger than the "urban" community and may include some population classified as rural.

URBANIZED AREAS

It was generally recognized that many unincorporated places on the edge of a city were quite as urban as the city itself, although prior to 1950 the census excluded these areas in its enumeration of city residents. The Urbanized Areas category was therefore designed to include in the urban population those persons living under distinctly urban conditions on the fringe of the larger cities. By definition, an "urbanized area consists of one or more cities of 50,000 or more and all the nearby closely settled suburban territory, or urban fringe." In striving for some degree of accuracy the Bureau of the Census is rather specific concerning the types of settlements on a city's fringe that are included as a part of an Urbanized Area. The 1960 specifications are:

1. Incorporated places with 2,500 inhabitants or more.
2. Incorporated places with fewer than 2,500 inhabitants containing an area with a concentration of 100 dwelling units or more.
3. Towns in the New England states, townships in New Jersey and Pennsylvania, and counties elsewhere which are classified as urban.
4. Unincorporated territory with a population density of 1,000 inhabitants or more per square mile.
5. Unincorporated territory with a population density of less than 1,000 inhabitants per square mile provided inclusion of the territory meets certain requirements for smoothing the fringe boundaries.
6. Territory devoted to commercial, industrial, transportational, recreational, and other purposes functionally related to the central city.[3]

Obviously, the new category of Urbanized Area had the effect of increasing the population of the larger cities over what would have been the figure if the old definition of urban had been employed. In addition to the foregoing specifications, outlying noncontiguous areas, incorporated or unincorporated, were included in Urbanized Areas if they met certain residential requirements. The new classification was represented by 157 Urbanized Areas in 1950 and 213 in 1960. In 1960, 95.8 million people, almost one-half the total population of the United States, were living in Urbanized Areas.

STANDARD METROPOLITAN STATISTICAL AREAS

Earlier enumerations of the Bureau of the Census included the "metropolitan district" in recognition of the growth of great communities con-

---

[3] *Ibid.* The 1960 specifications for Urbanized Areas and their fringes are similar to those introduced in 1950. Minor changes include reformulation of the density criterion and the use of enumeration districts in the unincorporated parts of the fringe, so that results would be as up-to-date as possible in these usually newly-built-up areas.

sisting of central cities and adjacent settlements. This category was first used in 1910 and applied to 25 metropolitan districts and 19 "other districts containing cities of 100,000 to 200,000 and their adjacent territory."

The emergence of the metropolis as the dominant community form in the United States provides the most striking example of the way in which definitions must be developed to meet the reality of community life. The exodus of population from the crowded central cities to the mushrooming single-family subdivisions far beyond the city's legal limits, the miles of expressways and thruways constructed to meet the growing traffic of cars and trucks, the building of factories and shopping centers in outlying areas, all heralded a new era on the American urban scene. The postwar period saw a "metropolitan explosion," and by the 1950 census the need to develop a comprehensive definition to deal with the metropolitan complex had become pressing.

In 1950 the Bureau of the Census, together with other interested federal agencies, officially adopted the Standard Metropolitan Area to replace the metropolitan district. In 1960 the term was altered to Standard Metropolitan Statistical Area; however, the criteria remained substantially the same as in 1950. Like the 1950 Standard Metropolitan Area classification, the Standard Metropolitan Statistical Area gives recognition to the growth of large multinucleated communities characterized by a central city and surrounding settlements.

Each Standard Metropolitan Statistical Area has as a nucleus a county containing a large central city of at least 50,000 inhabitants. Contiguous counties are added to the metropolitan area if they meet certain specifications in the definition. One type of specification is concerned with the character of the contiguous county as a place of work or as a home for a concentration of nonagricultural workers, and with the density of population. These are intended to measure the metropolitan nature of the contiguous county. The other type of specification is concerned with the degree to which the contiguous county as a unit is integrated into the social and economic structure of the county containing the central city.

For a contiguous [4] county to be included in a metropolitan area, the following specifications must be met, according to the 1960 census:

1. The county must have:
    a. 10,000 nonagricultural workers residing or working there, or
    b. at least 10 per cent as many nonagricultural workers residing or working there as reside or work in the county containing the largest city in the metropolitan area, or

[4] A "contiguous" county either adjoins the county containing the largest city in the area or adjoins an intermediate county integrated with the central county. There is no limit to the number of tiers of outlying metropolitan counties so long as all other criteria are met.

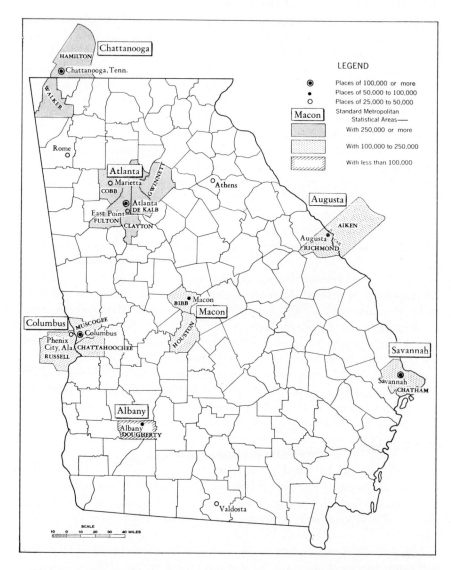

Figure 4. Standard Metropolitan Statistical Areas of Georgia (1960) delineated by the census. Georgia's largest SMSA, Atlanta, includes five counties and three major cities—the central city of Atlanta and the smaller cities of East Point and Marietta. Georgia's smallest SMSA, Albany, consists of only one county and its central city, Albany. Three of Georgia's SMSA's cross state lines, indicating how metropolitan development crosses political boundaries. SOURCE: *U. S. Census of Population, 1960. General Population Characteristics, Georgia.* Final Report PC(1)–12B.

    c. at least half of its population residing in contiguous minor civil divisions with a population density of 150 or more per square mile.

2. Nonagricultural workers must constitute at least 75 per cent of the total employed labor force of the county.

3. There must be evidence of social and economic integration of the county with the county containing the central city as indicated by such criteria as the following:

    a. 15 per cent of more of the workers residing in the contiguous county work in the county containing the largest city in the metropolitan area, or

    b. 25 per cent or more of the persons working in the contiguous county reside in the county containing the largest city in the metropolitan area, or

    c. if criteria 3a and 3b are not conclusive, then related types of information may be used: average telephone calls per subscriber per month from the contiguous county to the county containing the central city; newspaper circulation reports; analysis of charge accounts in retail stores of central cities to determine the extent of their use by residents of the contiguous county; delivery service practices of retail stores in central cities; and official traffic counts,[5]

On the basis of this detailed set of specifications, 212 Standard Metropolitan Statistical Areas were designated in 1960, each consisting of one or more contiguous counties.[6] The total metropolitan population was 112 million in 1960, as compared with 168 SMA's and a metropolitan population of 89 million in 1950. There is no limit to the number of counties that census metropolitan areas may include, provided the counties meet the criteria specified. A metropolitan area may also include counties in more than one state. In 1960, however, the two largest metropolitan areas in the United States, New York and Chicago, were designated as Standard Metropolitan Consolidated Areas. Four Standard Metropolitan Statistical Areas, and two additional counties that do not meet the formal integration criteria but do have strong interrelationships of other kinds, were included in the New York-Northeastern New Jersey Standard Metropolitan Consolidated Area. The Chicago-Northwestern Indiana Standard Metropolitan Consolidated Area includes two Standard Metropolitan Statistical Areas.[7]

[5] *U. S. Census of Population: 1960, op. cit.*

[6] "Town" rather than "county" is the basic geographic unit in New England. Since New England towns are roughly equivalent in territory and function to counties in the rest of the United States, the Bureau of the Census uses towns in defining New England's metropolitan areas.

[7] Comparison of the 1960 Standard Metropolitan Consolidated Areas with 1950 Standard Metropolitan Area data for New York and Chicago can be made as follows: the 1960 New York-Northeastern Standard Metropolitan Consolidated Area consists of 17 counties and is identical with the 1950 New York-Northeastern New Jersey Standard Metropolitan Area; the 1960 Chicago-Northwestern Indiana Standard Metropolitan Consolidated Area is larger by two counties than the 1950 Chicago Standard Metropolitan Area. In effect, the 1960 census divided the very large 1950 Standard

The data compiled by the Bureau of the Census on the basis of the metropolitan classification developed in the 1950 and 1960 censuses have been widely used, much more so than data compiled under the Urbanized Area classification. This is probably so because the metropolitan classification is based on county units for which many other types of information are available. The metropolitan definitions of 1950 and 1960 appear to be serving well the statistical and comparative needs they were designed to fill.

Reactions to the metropolitan classification system, however, are not always objective. "There is, unfortunately, a tendency for local areas to view the establishment of [a metropolitan area] as a sort of gold star awarded by the federal government."[8] One city staged a public parade when its classification as a metropolitan area was officially announced. Some communities press unwarranted claims for metropolitan status because they believe that national advertising is placed only in central city newspapers of such areas or that new industries are more likely to locate in metropolitan areas. On the other hand, some local areas object to metropolitan status, especially if it means their community will be counted as a secondary city in the metropolitan area and not have its name included in the metropolitan area title.

TRENDS IN URBAN GROWTH

Before considering recent patterns of urban growth, it will be profitable to review historic trends in the urbanization of America. In 1790, the year of the first census, no American city had over 50,000 people, and it was not until 1820 that any city had as many as 100,000 inhabitants. The quarter-million mark was reached for the first time in 1840, and the million mark in 1880. The same trend may be pointed up in somewhat different terms. In 1790, the year of the first census, only one in 20 inhabitants was classified as urban; in 1960, seven out of ten persons were so classified. Nineteen hundred and twenty is an important date in the onward march of urbanism, for it marks the first time in the history of the United States that half its population was classified as urban.

First in the order of development in the United States, naturally, were the cities of the eastern seaboard established in the Colonial period. As industry developed and domestic and international trade expanded,

---

Metropolitan Areas of New York and Chicago into several Standard Metropolitan Statistical Areas and then provided the Standard Metropolitan Consolidated Area concept so there would be an over-all unit for New York and Chicago comparable to their 1950 Standard Metropolitan Areas. The problem of finding an appropriate unit for the very large metropolitan complexes may foreshadow future definitional difficulties as such areas become more numerous. The discussion of Megalopolis in Chapter 4 is relevant.

[8] Henry S. Shryock, Jr., "The Natural History of Standard Metropolitan Areas," *American Journal of Sociology,* LXIII (September, 1958), 170.

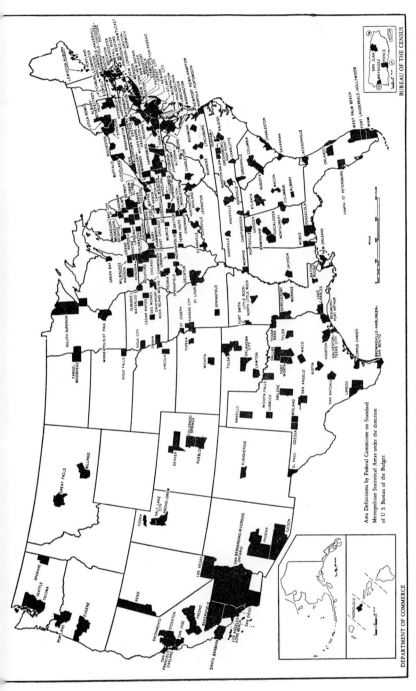

Figure 5. Standard Metropolitan Statistical Areas of the United States and Puerto Rico, 1960. In 1960, two-thirds of the total United States population lived in the 212 SMSA's delineated by the United States Census. SOURCE: *U. S. Census of Population, 1960. Number of Inhabitants, United States Summary.* Final Report PC(1)–1A.

49

these continued to grow, many to great magnitude—New York, Boston, Philadelphia, Baltimore. The conquest of a continent meant the acquisition of raw materials for the industrial machines and the rapid increase in finished products for home consumption or shipment abroad. More manpower was needed—men to till the soil, to mine the iron, to cut the trees, to process the raw materials, to haul them to the factories, to sell the manufactured goods, and to serve and entertain those who were so engaged. Under such a powerful stimulus, combined with a heavy stream of immigration from overseas, population grew rapidly; and with technology increasing the efficiency of primary and secondary production, a larger and larger proportion of the American people found employment in the industries, stores, and offices of the growing cities.

As our agricultural and industrial frontier moved westward, so did population. On the plains and waterways of the Middle West cities grew to impressive size—Cleveland, Detroit, Chicago, St. Louis, Cincinnati, Kansas City, the Twin Cities of Minneapolis and St. Paul, the scores of smaller centers. The growing population alone provided an expanding market for goods and services, and the market places were the cities, large and small. Even before the twentieth century had dawned, the line of conquest had pushed into the Southwest and the Far West, stimulating the growth of settlements in areas that not long before had been considered America's geographic frontier. These grew into the newer cities— Houston, Fort Worth, Dallas, Los Angeles, San Francisco, Seattle, Portland, Salt Lake City, and Denver.

TABLE 3

Per cent of Population Urban, United States, 1790–1960

1960 (new def.)	69.9	1880	28.2
1960 (old def.)	63.0	1870	25.7
1950 (new def.)	64.0	1860	19.8
1950 (old def.)	59.0	1850	15.3
1940	56.5	1840	10.8
1930	56.2	1830	8.8
1920	51.2	1820	7.2
1910	45.7	1810	7.3
1900	39.7	1800	6.1
1890	35.1	1790	5.1

CITY GROWTH BY STATES

By 1850 the major patterns of urban settlement were fairly well established in the northeastern states, whereas in the remaining sections urbanization did not really get under way until considerably later. In Indiana, for example, it was not until 1840 that any settlement was large enough to be classified as a city. At the turn of the century, only eight states, of which six were in the Northeast, had a majority of their population in cities. During the first three decades of the present century thirteen states moved into this category.

Between 1930 and 1940 there was a slump in the urban trend, and no additional state increased its proportion of city residents beyond the 50 per cent mark. But during the 1940's and 1950's, a period of wartime and postwar activity, the rate of urbanization was sharply accelerated. By 1960, 39 of the 50 states had more than half of their population living in cities. The eleven states still predominantly rural are Alaska, Arkansas, Idaho, Kentucky, Mississippi, North Carolina, South Carolina, North Dakota, South Dakota, Vermont, and West Virginia.

Even in preponderantly rural states the population has become increasingly urbanized. In 1900, less than 10 per cent of the population was urban in six states—Idaho, North Dakota, Oklahoma, Mississippi, Arkansas, and North Carolina. Sixty years later none of these states had less than one-third of its population living in cities, and approximately 60 per cent of Oklahoma's people was classed as urban. Even the most rural of the 50 states, North Dakota, had 35 per cent of its population residing in urban communities in 1960.

Just as the states vary greatly as to the proportions of urban residents, so do they differ widely in rate of increase of the urban population. Using the new definition of urban, all 50 states showed increases of urban population between 1950 and 1960. For the United States as a whole the urban population increased by 29 per cent. Generally speaking, states with a high percentage of urban population had a low rate of increase, and vice versa, although there were exceptions like California. Five states, all in the Northeast, had an urban increase, by the current definition, of less than 10 per cent between 1950 and 1960. On the other hand, seven states, all except Florida west of the Mississippi River, had an urban increase of 50 per cent or over.

The most significant urban gain is probably that of California, which added the largest *number* of urban residents—five million—during the 1950–60 decade. This vast increase of urbanites, most of them migrants from other states, swelled California's total population so that by the winter of 1962–63 Californians were able to stage a series of parades and celebrations in honor of their state's surpassing New York as the most populous state. A national television network celebrated the event by presenting a special program entitled "California—The Most."

In contrast to the general and marked urban expansion from 1950 to 1960, the 1960 census revealed that the rural population of the United States declined about one per cent, a particularly significant decline since it marks the first time since census-taking was begun in 1790 that the rural population actually decreased. Although, previously, rural population had always increased at a lower rate than the urban population,

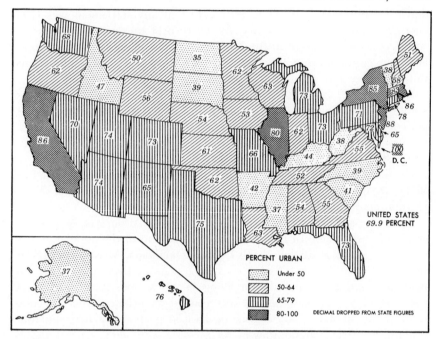

Figure 6. Per cent of population urban, by states, 1960. This map shows clearly the high level of urbanization in the Northeast and West. SOURCE: *U. S. Census of Population, 1960. Number of Inhabitants, United States Summary.* Final Report PC(1)–1A.

nevertheless, it had increased. But now, with continued agricultural advances in rational farming and mechanization, an ever-decreasing labor force is required. For example, in 1940 the average farm worker produced enough to support 13 people; by 1960 he produced enough to support 28 people.[9]

The largest losses in rural population occurred in the more heavily rural states. Oklahoma registered the largest decrease, losing 21 per cent of its rural population in the 1950–60 decade; Arkansas lost 20 per cent and Texas almost 17 per cent. All of the states in the West North Central area lost rural population—Minnesota, Iowa, Missouri, North Dakota, South Dakota, Nebraska, and Kansas. In all, 28 states lost rural population.

REGIONAL DIFFERENCES IN URBANIZATION

Since the northeastern section was the center of early industrial and commercial developments, that area was highly urbanized as early as the

[9] U. S. Department of Agriculture, *Report of the Secretary of Agriculture* (1961), p. 2.

turn of the century. This lead has been maintained. With the shift of population and industry to the South and West, however, other sections of the country are following the Northeast. There is a possibility that the Northeast has reached, or possibly passed, the peak of urbanization because of the exodus of industry from that area.

Although the Northeast still leads so far as degree of urbanization is concerned, the South and West are setting the pace in rate of urban growth. Florida, Texas, Arizona, Nevada, New Mexico, and California have experienced an especially rapid urban expansion. The West is already almost as urbanized as the Northeast region, and at its present rate of urbanization will soon outdistance the northeastern states in the proportion of persons living in cities. With the exception of Texas and Florida, the South still lags behind other sections. The percentage of the population classified as urban in the four regions of the United States in 1960 was Northeast, 80; West, 78; North Central, 69; South, 59.

ELEMENTS OF URBAN GROWTH IN THE SOUTH AND WEST

The rapid growth of cities in the South and West appears to bear both cause and effect relationships to significant changes that have occurred, or are occurring, in the country. Perhaps the most important change has been industrialization of these sections. Until fairly recently the economy of southern and western cities was dominated by trade. But as early as the 1920's there was a sharp increase in manufacturing activities. During the war the location of numerous military bases and defense industries in the South and West had the effect of drawing population to cities in those areas. Postwar years witnessed a continuation of the same trend. Close proximity to a supply of labor, sources of raw materials, and an enlarging body of consumers appear to be the principal reasons for industrial developments in these sections.

Although prospects of industrial employment were one of the principal lures of cities in these regions, some areas like Arizona, Florida, and California widely publicized their climatic assets. No doubt part of urban growth in the South and West has been due to the attractiveness of certain cities as popular playgrounds, health resorts, or places of permanent retirement. During the 1950–60 decade Fort Lauderdale's population increased by 130 per cent and that of Albuquerque by 108 per cent. Houston's spectacular growth in the last few decades reflects her commercial expansion as the main seaport and financial capital of Texas. In 1960 Houston became, for the first time, one of the ten most populous cities in the United States.

NEW ENGLAND AND INDUSTRIAL CHANGE

New England presents the opposite side of the picture. Many cities in this area lost population in recent years, and even greater numbers had only minor increases. Industrial dispersal from New England, especially the shift of textile and leather manufacturing to southern or midwestern locations, has exerted a considerable population drain on the cities. During the war and postwar period New England had little share in the defense industry, one of the important contributors to recent urban growth.

ANNEXATION A FACTOR IN CITY GROWTH

As urban populations have overflowed the political boundaries to settle in suburban districts, municipal governing bodies have looked with favor upon extension of city boundary lines, although their point of view is not always shared by those who live outside the city. A considerable number of persons are added to particular communities each year by annexation of adjacent territory.

In order to permit the analysis of the relative importance of population growth within old boundaries and of population added by annexation, separate counts of the population in annexed areas were made for the first time in the 1960 census. The results indicate that 103 cities of 25,000 population or over annexed territory between 1950 and 1960 which contained 10,000 or more inhabitants. The largest number, 332,000, were in territory annexed by Phoenix, Arizona.

The importance of taking annexations by central cities into account as a factor in analyzing urban growth has its major illustration in the Standard Metropolitan Statistical Areas. Without allowing for changes due to central city annexation, there would be a false impression of the relative rates of growth in the two component parts of the SMSA's, the central cities and the area outside the central cities. According to the 1960 census the population in metropolitan areas outside central cities increased by 49 per cent, a much more rapid rate than the population gain of 11 per cent made by the central cities. Correction for population changes due to annexation shows that these figures seriously understate the growth differentials. The corrected percentage of increase for the metropolitan central cities is only 1.5 per cent, while that for the metropolitan area outside central cities rises to 62 per cent. In other words, most population increase in metropolitan central cities was due to annexation, and since the territory annexed came from areas beyond the central cities the effect was to understate the rapid growth in the metropolitan area outside the central cities.

PROSPECTS FOR THE FUTURE

This chapter has indicated how the rapid growth of urban population and the new conditions of urban life outmoded the definition of urbanism based on the political city. The compact city of the nineteenth century has been superseded by the metropolis.

The large-scale redistribution of the United States population into metropolitan areas, and especially into the suburban sections of such areas, explains many of the seeming paradoxes of the 1960 census. Although the population of the United States was at an all-time high in 1960, more than half the counties of the United States had smaller populations than at the time of the 1950 census. Although the population was more highly urban than ever, many cities lost population in the 1950–60 decade. "On closer inspection these apparent contradictions in the quantitative results yield clear insight into some of the qualitative changes now taking place in the life of the country." [10]

The redistribution of the United States population, as more and more people move to suburban and outlying areas of the metropolis, is at the root of many problems in contemporary American life: deterioration of the city cores, increased racial segregation in many cities, financial and governmental problems, to mention just a few that will be discussed in detail later.[11] Yet it has also brought a higher standard of living and more spacious surroundings to millions of families. The social and economic consequences of metropolitan expansion are controversial, but whether one approves or disapproves, the fact is that the metropolis is here to stay.

SELECTED BIBLIOGRAPHY

Books

Bogue, Donald, *The Population of the United States.* Glencoe, Ill.: The Free Press, 1959.

———, *Population Growth in Standard Metropolitan Areas, 1900–1950.* Washington, D.C.: Government Printing Office, 1953.

Bridenbaugh, Carl, *Cities in the Wilderness: The First Century of Urban Life in America, 1625–1742.* New York: Ronald Press, 1938.

———, *Cities in Revolt: Urban Life in America, 1743–1776.* New York, Knopf, 1955.

Duncan, Otis D., and Albert Reiss, *Social Characteristics of Urban and Rural Communities, 1950.* New York: Wiley, 1956.

Gulick, Luther, *The Metropolitan Problem and American Ideas.* New York: Knopf, 1962.

[10] Philip Hauser, "The Census of 1960," *Scientific American* (July, 1961), 40.
[11] See Chapters 7–10.

Hawley, Amos, *The Changing Shape of Metropolitan America.* Glencoe, Ill.: The Free Press, 1956.

McKelvey, Blake, *The Urbanization of America, 1860–1915.* New Brunswick, N.J.: Rutgers University Press, 1963.

Schlesinger, Arthur M., *The Rise of the City, 1878–1898.* New York: Macmillan, 1933.

Vance, Rupert, and Nicholas Demerath (eds.), *The Urban South.* Chapel Hill: University of North Carolina Press, 1954.

Wade, Richard, *The Urban Frontier: The Rise of Western Cities, 1790–1830.* Cambridge, Mass.: Harvard University Press, 1959.

ARTICLES

Glick, Paul, "The 1960 Census as a Source for Social Research," *American Sociological Review,* 27 (August, 1962), 581–85.

Hauser, Philip, "The Census of 1960," and "More from the Census of 1960," *Scientific American* (July, 1961 and October, 1962).

Lampard, Eric, "American Historians and the Study of Urbanization," *American Historical Review,* LXVII (October, 1961), 49–61.

Schnore, Leo, "Municipal Annexations and the Growth of Metropolitan Suburbs," *American Journal of Sociology,* LXVII (January, 1962), 406–17.

Shryock, Henry, "Some Results of the 1960 Census of the United States," *Rural Sociology,* 27 (December, 1962), 460–72.

———, "The Natural History of Standard Metropolitan Areas," *American Journal of Sociology,* LXIII (September, 1957), 163–70.

Contemporary
World Urbanization

FOUR

Although cities have spread throughout the world and are found in every major area, except for the Arctic and Antarctic regions, nevertheless, their distribution is uneven. The fact that urbanism is more marked in some regions of the world than others is not accidental. Contemporary world urbanization falls into three distinct levels, the examination of which reveals more fully the roles environment, technology, and social organization play in promoting urban growth. Cross-cultural comparisons provide a means for discovering what is unique in the Western pattern of of urbanization as well as revealing the universal patterns.

A discussion of world urbanization inevitably involves comparing the levels of urbanization among countries or regions, but several factors make accurate comparisons difficult. International urban data are scarce, but even when available they usually have not been gathered by the same methods—some are based on censuses of varying degrees of accuracy while others are merely estimates. In many countries the most recent statistics are out of date, being ten, twenty, or even thirty years old.

By far the most important factor affecting international urban comparisons is the widely varying definition of "urban" from one country to another. Three major types of definition of the term are used by various nations.[1]

1. The most common definition is to classify localities as urban on the basis of size. The lower limit accepted as urban varies greatly. In Den-

[1] The following discussion is based on *Demographic Yearbook* (United Nations, 1960), p. 34 and Table 9.

mark urban status is granted to places with as few as 250 inhabitants, while in Korea the number is 40,000. Fortunately, most nations' definitions of urban size do not vary quite so extremely.

2. Another type of definition is based on legal and governmental criteria. Localities are defined as urban if they are the administrative center of minor civil divisions, the remainder of the territory being classified as rural. Thus, in Northern Ireland and Bulgaria urban means places with certain administrative functions, regardless of size.

3. The final type of urban definition is a composite. Definitions based on governmental or legal status are combined with one (or more) additional criterion. In other words, minor civil divisions are classified as urban only if they meet another requirement, which may be type of local government, number of inhabitants, or per cent of population engaged in agriculture. In Israel, for example, urban means localities which are predominantly nonagricultural, while in Malta urban is defined as built-up areas devoid of agricultural land.

Many of the difficulties posed by varying definitions of "urban" may be avoided by using as the standard of urbanization the proportion of a country's population living in cities of 100,000 or more. Although this standard also presents problems of definition, it shows much less variation among nations than do other definitions of urbanization.[2] For one, because the inherent nature of urban agglomerations of 100,000 or more inhabitants makes it impossible to overlook them, all countries that have localities of this size have some statistics available about them. In addition, there is a high correlation between the proportion of a country's population living in large cities and other measures of urbanization, as the data in Tables 1 and 2 indicate (pages 35 and 36). Thus, the following discussion of world urbanization is based on the proportion of a nation's population living in cities of 100,000 or more.

THREE MAJOR LEVELS OF URBANIZATION

Applying the yardstick of proportion of the population living in cities of 100,000 or more suggests three levels of urbanization among the countries of the world. The three levels are not scattered randomly over the world but correspond roughly to its major areal and regional divisions, as shown in the upper map of Figure 7 (page 63).

1. The most heavily urbanized areas, those with over 20 per cent of their populations living in cities of 100,000 or over, exhibit greater cultural and economic variety than one might expect. Highly urban countries may be subdivided into three groups—the "established urban-industrial," the "newly industrial," and the "overurbanized." The established urban-industrial group consists essentially of the countries in

---

[2] See, for example, *ibid.*, pp. 33, 369.

which industrialization originated, which became thoroughly industrial at an early date, and which also developed new social forms in the family, government, religion, and education. Urban-industrial development proceeded in these countries throughout the nineteenth century, usually reaching high levels by the end of the century. This subgroup includes England and the countries of northwestern Europe as well as the countries heavily colonized from these areas—the United States, Australia, New Zealand, and Canada. These countries also tend to have the highest levels of urbanization of all. Many established urban-industrial countries, such as England and Wales, West Germany, and The Netherlands, have a third or more of their populations living in cities of 100,000 or over.

The next subgroup, the newly industrial, represents those countries in which industrialization began only in the twentieth century, but has already become a significant force. The traditions and social organization of modern Western civilization are also less evident in these countries. The countries in this category form a belt across southern and eastern Europe—Spain, Italy, Hungary, Poland—and include the USSR. The only non-Western country in this category is Japan, which has recently shown remarkable industrial gains as well as change in its social structure. The proportion of Japan's population in large cities (100,000 plus) rose spectacularly from 12 per cent in 1920 to 41 per cent in 1959, while the proportion of its labor force employed in agriculture dropped, equally spectacularly, from 44 per cent to 29 per cent in the same time period.[3]

The USSR also illustrates recent, rapid urbanization. The proportion of its population in cities over 100,000 rose from 6.5 per cent in 1926 to 14.9 per cent in 1939; even with the upheaval of World War II, the urban population grew to 19.2 per cent in 1955 and increased rapidly thereafter, reaching 23.5 per cent in 1959.

The final subcategory of highly urbanized countries contains many found throughout the underdeveloped regions; they are the overurbanized countries. Venezuela, Argentina, and Uruguay, three South American countries included in this group, are very highly urbanized—well over 30 per cent of their populations are in cities of 100,000 or over—but they are not heavily industrialized. Their high level of urbanization is a result of high birth rates in urban as well as rural areas, an early pattern of substantial immigration from abroad, and a system of large cities established under Spanish rule. Venezuela, however, is now experiencing rapid economic growth.[4]

In most of the other countries in the overurbanized subgroup—Mexico,

[3] Irene Taeuber, "Urbanization and Population Change in the Development of Modern Japan," *Economic Development and Cultural Change,* 9 (October, 1960), pt. 2, p. 15; and *Demographic Yearbook, op. cit.,* Table 8.

[4] Harley L. Browning, "Recent Trends in Latin American Urbanization," *Annals of the American Academy of Political and Social Science,* 316 (March, 1958), 111–20. Browning also discusses, from a somewhat different point of view, whether these countries are "overurbanized."

Costa Rica, Cuba, Jamaica, Colombia, Egypt, Syria, Lebanon, and Korea
—the level of urbanization (between 20 and 30 per cent of their populations in cities of 100,000 or more) is somewhat less than in Venezuela,
Argentina, and Uruguay. Nevertheless, it is considerably higher than is
warranted by their economic and social development and is indicative of
the heritage of colonial administrative centers to which migrants from
overpopulated rural areas are now flooding.

The degree of a country's overurbanization can be measured by comparing industrial employment with the level of urbanization.[5] For example, Egypt had 22 per cent of its population in cities of at least 100,000 in
size in 1958, while over half the labor force (56 per cent) was still employed in agriculture.[6] In contrast, the United States has 28 per cent of
its population in cities of 100,000 or over and just 8 per cent of its labor
force in agriculture. On the other side of the coin, Egypt had only about
6 per cent of its labor force in urban middle class occupations—merchants, clerks, professionals—while urban Western countries have one-
third to two-fifths of the labor force in such occupations.[7] Overpopulation,
ever-smaller land holdings per farmer, and the exactions of absentee
landlords have brought extreme poverty to Egypt's rural areas. The villagers flock to cities where it is more difficult for the government to ignore
them. In the cities many can find employment only in marginal service
occupations which are financially unrewarding and also add little to
building an industrial economy. In short, economic organization in the
cities does not afford employment for all in-migrants, a familiar pattern
in highly urban, little-industrialized countries.

2. The second level of urbanization—between 10 and 20 per cent of
the population in cities of 100,000 or more—is associated with low levels
of industrialization. Countries in the underdeveloped areas begin to be
numerous in this category and countries in the Western industrialized
areas to be infrequent.

Middle and South America figure importantly at this level of urbanization, with Guatemala, Nicaragua, Ecuador, Peru, Brazil, Bolivia, and
Paraguay falling into the category. The Near East is also important, contributing Turkey, Iraq, and Iran. The rim of South and Southeast Asia
includes several countries barely within this level of urbanization—Thailand, Malaysia, Vietnam, Indonesia, and the Philippines. Africa north of
the Sahara is another important component, since Algeria, Tunisia, Libya,
and probably Morocco, have reached this level of urbanization. It is noteworthy that in Asia and Africa this middle level of urbanization is found

[5] Kingsley Davis, and Hilda H. Golden, "Urbanization and the Development of Preindustrial Areas," *Economic Development and Cultural Change,* 3 (October, 1954),
16ff.; and Bert Hoselitz, "Urbanization and Economic Growth in Asia," *Economic
Development and Cultural Change,* 6 (October, 1957), 42–54.

[6] Morroe Berger, *The Arab World Today* (1962), p. 203; *Demographic Yearbook,
op. cit.,* Table 8.

[7] Berger, *op. cit.,* pp. 274–75.

at the edges of these continents where crossroads trade tends to flourish.

This middle level of urbanization is poorly represented in industrialized regions. There are no countries at this level in North America and only a scattering in Europe, mainly in the south and east—Romania, Bulgaria, Greece, Czechoslovakia, East Germany, Portugal, Norway, and Finland.

3. Despite the penetration of cities to all parts of the world, there are still major regions where low levels of urbanization—less than 10 per cent of the population living in cities of 100,000 or more—prevail. In modern times the least urbanized nations are those with the least industrialization and the least similarity to Western culture. Asia (except Japan) and Africa, only slightly industrialized, are most heavily represented in the lowest level of urbanization. An index to their relative economic development is found by comparing their annual per capita incomes with those of the industrialized areas: Asia $50, Africa $75, Europe (exclusive of the USSR) $380, USSR $310, North America $1,100.[8]

There are no countries in North and South America at this lowest level of urbanization except small countries such as El Salvador and the Guianas. In Europe there are only two countries—Albania and Yugoslavia.

Almost all of Africa and Asia are included in the lowest level of urbanization—less than 10 per cent of the population lives in cities of 100,000 or more. All of the vast territories of native Africa, including such independent nations—old and new—as Liberia, Ethiopia, Ghana, Nigeria, and the Republic of the Congo, are little urbanized as yet. Nor are the many sizable countries whose very names are unfamiliar to many Americans—Mauritania, Mali, Niger (not the same as Nigeria), Chad, the Malagasy Republic, Upper Volta, and still many others. Except for the eastern and western edges of Asia, the rest of that continent is only lightly urbanized. The two giants, India and Communist China, each have only about 8 per cent of their populations living in cities of 100,000 or more. Burma, Cambodia, Ceylon, Laos, Nepal, Pakistan, and Saudi Arabia have well below 10 per cent of their populations in large cities.

URBANIZATION IN THE UNDERDEVELOPED AREAS

Although the foregoing analysis of the distribution of urbanization throughout the world has demonstrated that high urbanization is associated with the technically advanced nations and with Western culture, it would be wrong to assume that the underdeveloped non-Western countries are unimportant in understanding contemporary urbanism. Figure 7 (lower map), which graphically illustrates the significance of the little-urbanized areas to world urbanization, is drawn to scale in terms of the proportion which the *total* population of each major world area made

[8] P. Hauser, *Population Perspectives* (1960), Table 1.

to the total population of the world in 1960. Thus, although Canada and Communist China each occupy roughly the same amount of geographic territory, Canada is reduced to small size on this map because its total population of 18 million is only a small part of the world total of three billion, while Communist China is expanded in size because its 700 million population is about a quarter of the world total. The three levels of urbanization described previously are shown on the upper map. It is readily apparent that the most highly urbanized areas—North America and Europe—are not those with the largest total populations.

Some of the least urbanized areas of the world have very large populations, so that even a small proportion of such populations living in cities is considerable. This is one important reason why analyses of urbanism cannot be restricted to the highly urbanized regions. For example, in terms of absolute numbers there are about as many people living in large cities in Communist China as in the United States. Although China has fewer than 10 per cent of its population living in cities of 100,000 or more, and the United States has almost 30 per cent of its population in such cities, the total number in large Chinese cities is approximately 48 million, while in the United States it is about 50 million. Latin America, Africa, and the rest of Asia also have large populations, which means that their low levels of urbanization nevertheless yield large numbers of city dwellers.

Sheer numbers are not the only reason why city dwellers in the little-urbanized, but populous, nations are important. Cities in these areas are also growing faster than cities in the more urbanized countries of the world. In general, the *rate* of urbanization tends to slow down in countries having a high proportion of population in cities. If the rate of urbanization is taken as the increase or decrease in the proportion of people residing in urban localities, then the period of rapid increase for many highly urban countries lies in the past.

Urban growth rates reached their peak in the highly urban-industrial nations during the late nineteenth century. In contrast, such rates began to accelerate in the twentieth century in the slightly urbanized areas and have not yet reached their peak. India's rate of urban growth, an excellent example of this process, has not begun to slow down as have those of the United States and England and Wales. India and the other underdeveloped countries of Asia appear to be in only the initial phase of urban expansion. Japan is the only Asian country in which urban population has already reached a high level and where urban growth rates may, therefore, be expected to level off.

Davis believes that city growth in Africa is proceeding more rapidly than anywhere else in the world.[9] Certainly the growth of individual cities there is impressive. Elisabethville, for example, was founded in 1910; in 1959 it had well over 180,000 inhabitants. Leopoldville was a

[9] Davis and Golden, *op. cit.*, pp. 20–21.

urbation in England is that centering on Manchester, the city sometimes cited as the place where the Industrial Revolution "began." The Manchester conurbation is near that of Liverpool and there are signs that they may eventually merge into a huge city-region.[19]

Belgium and the Netherlands have large metropolitan complexes. As industry expanded rapidly there after World War II, the demand for workers often outstripped the nearby housing supply. Workers most commonly commute by motorized bicycle or by railroad.[20] In western Holland, Amsterdam, the Hague, Rotterdam, Utrecht, Leiden, and many smaller cities are located within a short distance from each other. If it were not for national planning restrictions, which maintain greenbelts, many of the cities would actually merge.

The Ruhr Valley in West Germany, the center of a major iron and steel industry, is closely built-up and contains three very large cities— Essen, Dortmund, and Dusseldorf, as well as a score of smaller cities. Essen and Dortmund, together with Duisburg, form an almost unbroken urban belt along the principal canal leading to the Rhine, and have a combined metropolitan population of about 5.5 million.

Metropolitan areas have also developed in nonindustrialized countries and are growing very rapidly there. However, the high general rate of population increase in these countries is not the only factor governing urban growth. In some little-industrialized countries a single metropolitan area overshadows all other urban communities. All the major urban functions tend to concentrate in this one metropolis—government, banking, institutions of higher education, headquarters for business and industry, tourist accommodations, "bright lights" entertainment, artistic and cultural life, and so on. Often the pattern is a holdover from the country's period as a colony, when the occupying power established a single administrative center for all of its operations.

Once established, such centers usually "snowball" and attract the overwhelming share of growth. Montevideo, Uruguay, contains roughly a third of that country's population and is seventeen times as large as the second ranking city.[21] This pattern, which is characteristic of Latin American countries, also holds for the Middle East. In Iraq, Baghdad has a population of a half-million, while Mosul, the second largest city, has only about 100,000; Egypt's two major centers, Cairo and Alexandria, have 3.3 million and 1.5 million inhabitants respectively, while the third largest city, Port Said, has only 300,000.[22]

The existence of metropolitan areas in the underdeveloped and slightly urbanized regions of the world prevents us from making oversimplified generalizations about the causes of metropolitan growth. Statistical anal-

[19] T. W. Freeman, *The Conurbations of Great Britain* (1959), p. 3ff.

[20] Robert E. Dickinson, "The Geography of Commuting: The Netherlands and Belgium," *Geographical Review,* XLVII (October, 1957), 521–38.

[21] Browning, *op. cit.,* p. 115.   [22] Berger, *op. cit.,* p. 196.

ysis of the relationship between urban-industrial and metropolitan development also shows that although highly urban-industrial nations have
the most metropolitan development, the association between level of
metropolitan development and level of industrialization and urbanization is not invariable.[23]

One must be particularly cautious about generalizing on the basis of
developments in the United States. Automobile and truck transport were
important in United States metropolitan growth, but vast metropolitan
areas have grown up in India and Japan where such vehicles are rare.
The spread of purchasing power which enabled more and more people
to buy their own homes in outlying areas—and the cars to reach them—
were characteristic of metropolitan expansion in this country. But in
other parts of the world poverty may be just as compelling in stimulating
metropolitan expansion, as people erect squatters' hovels on public or
empty land on the outskirts of the metropolis.

In the United States, metropolitan development was preceded by gradual urbanization, but in some regions, Africa being a notable example,
metropolises spring up with few intervening stages and exist in the midst
of "a sea of rurality." Finally, the American metropolis shows a predominance of service occupations among its labor force; so do the metropolises
of emerging countries, but the resemblance ends there. The services performed by the United States metropolitan labor force are mainly administrative, technical, and professional, and require a high degree of education and skill, while the services performed by some other metropolitan
labor forces are primarily "busy-work," simply enabling an illiterate and
unskilled population to eke out a living. A description of Middle Eastern
cities notes:

Shops and offices have several messengers for different kinds of errands.
Apartment and office buildings have several kinds of doormen, messengers,
cleaners, some of whom are not actually employed but simply are around for
whatever task comes up and for whatever they can earn. In the streets there
are men who help drivers find and squeeze into parking places, and there are
others who help the helpers. In many barber and beauty shops there is so refined a division of labor that the operator commands a small crew of aides.[24]

The world will doubtless be metropolitan in the future, but it may be
metropolitan in a different way and for different reasons than the metropolises of the United States.

[23] Thomas Wilkinson, "Urban Structure and Industrialization," *American Sociological Review*, 25 (June, 1960), 356–63.

[24] Berger, *op. cit.*, p. 99.

METROPOLITAN AMERICA

One of the most important recent developments in the United States has been the growth of numerous metropolitan communities, to the extent that today the majority of Americans live in census-defined metropolitan areas. Thus, it is more accurate to speak of metropolitan, rather than urban, America.

The metropolitan community is an extensive geographic unit whose social and economic activities form a more or less integrated system centering around a large city. Metropolitan development differs from previous urban development in that the community is much larger in area and in population, and the linkages among the specialized territorial components are more complex. No segment of a metropolitan community is self-sufficient in its day-to-day activities. For this reason there is constant and intense movement among the various parts of the metropolis. The travel of commuters from "dormitory suburbs" to "downtown"; "local" deliveries of mail, newspapers, and department store merchandise over a wide area; the trucking of produce from near-by farms and of manufactured goods from outlying factories—all testify to the interdependence among the various segments of the metropolitan community.

Metropolitan growth

In 1960 almost two-thirds (63 per cent) of the population of the United States lived in the Standard Metropolitan Statistical Areas delineated by the census.[25] Using the boundaries of the SMSA's as defined in 1960, we find that 58 per cent of the United States population lived in these areas in 1950 and 49 per cent in 1940. Clearly, in recent decades metropolitan areas have come to be the characteristic dwelling place for Americans.

Metropolitan development in the United States is essentially a twentieth-century phenomenon. Table 5 indicates that the metropolitan areas have grown faster than the rest of the United States in every decade since the turn of the century, except for the depression years 1930–40. In 1960, for example, the metropolitan area population increased by 26.4 per cent over that of 1950, while that of the United States as a whole increased by only 18.5 per cent, and that of population in nonmetropolitan areas by only 7.0 per cent. Streams of migrants have been leaving rural farm areas, villages, and small towns, and flocking to the supercities so that most of the population growth is taking place in metropolitan areas.

---

[25] See Chapter 3 for a description of the census definition of SMSA.

Los Angeles, symbol of modern growth. View of a section of Los Angeles shows the low building density and system of superhighways which have led to urban sprawl in modern American cities. (Courtesy Los Angeles Chamber of Commerce [photo by Modernage].)

THE DECLINE OF THE CENTRAL CITY

The metropolis as a whole has gained enormously in population, but this growth is not distributed evenly within the metropolitan area. The central cities of metropolitan areas have grown relatively little and in some cases have actually lost population. Some of the many reasons include the sheer unavailability of space for further building, the obsoles-

TABLE 5

Percentage Increase in Population in the United States, in Metropolitan Areas and in Area Outside of Metropolitan Areas, 1900–60

	1950–60	1940–50	1930–40	1920–30	1910–20	1900–10
Total U. S. Population	18.5	14.5	7.2	16.1	14.9	21.0
All metropolitan areas						
reported	26.4	22.0	8.1	28.3	26.9	34.6
Central cities	1.5 *	13.9	5.1	22.3	25.2	33.6
Suburban areas	61.7 *	35.6	15.1	44.0	32.0	38.2
Area outside metro-						
politan areas	7.1	6.1	6.5	7.9	9.6	16.4

* These figures are corrected for population changes due to annexation of territory between 1950 and 1960; see the section on annexation in Chapter 3.
SOURCES: W. S. Thompson, "The Growth of Metropolitan Districts in the United States: 1900–1940," U. S. Government Printing Office (1947); *U. S. Census of Population: 1950. Number of Inhabitants,* Vol. I, PA; *U. S. Census of Population: 1960. Number of Inhabitants, United States Summary.* Final Report PC(1)–1A (1961), p. XXV and Table Q. The student should keep in mind that the criteria defining metropolitan districts from 1900 to 1940 differ somewhat from those used in defining metropolitan areas in 1950 and 1960. See Chapter 3 for a description of the differences.

cence of housing and industrial plants in core areas, deliberate programs of urban renewal and redevelopment aimed at reducing population density, and the availability of rapid, cheap methods of communication and transportation. Table 5 shows that the suburban ring of the metropolitan area has consistently grown at a much higher rate than the central cities. Furthermore, the discrepancy is increasing: the contrast between central city and suburban percentages of increase was 33.6 and 38.2 in the 1900–10 decade, but by 1960 the contrast in percentages was 1.5 and 61.7. The proliferation of housing subdivisions and factories in outlying areas is everyday evidence of this trend.

More than one-quarter of the central cities of Standard Metropolitan Statistical Areas actually lost population in the 1950–60 decade, the 1960 census being the first to show population declines in a considerable number of large cities. These losses do not usually reflect economic decline but rather the decentralization of population and institutions within the metropolitan area. In most cases population decline in the central city was accompanied by population growth in the rest of the Standard Metropolitan Statistical Area. Losses were particularly marked in the larger cities and those in the north central and northeastern regions. Of the five cities in the million class (New York, Chicago, Los Angeles, Philadelphia, and Detroit), all except Los Angeles lost population in the 1950–60 decade, whereas all five had gained during the previous decade.[26] In

[26] One reason why the Los Angeles central city area did not show a decline in

contrast to central city declines, all five of these metropolitan areas showed considerable population growth in the rest of the metropolitan area, as shown in Table 6.

TABLE 6

Percentages of Population Change in the Central City and the Territory Outside the Central City in the Largest Standard Metropolitan Statistical Areas in the United States, 1950–60

	IN CENTRAL CITY	OUTSIDE CENTRAL CITY
New York *	−1.4	75.0
Chicago *	−1.9	71.5
Los Angeles	27.1	82.6
Philadelphia	−3.3	46.3
Detroit	−9.7	79.3

* Figures are for Standard Metropolitan Statistical Areas, not for Standard Metropolitan Consolidated Areas.
SOURCE: *Changing Metropolitan Markets 1950–60: Population Trends in Standard Metropolitan Statistical Areas,* Office of Marketing Services, U. S. Department of Commerce (1961).

MEGALOPOLIS

The large-scale movement of population into the outer rings of metropolitan areas may be ushering in a new phase of metropolitan development. In regions where there are many Standard Metropolitan Statistical Areas, as the outer ring of one metropolitan area expands it often overlaps with the outer ring of another metropolitan area. The result is a continuous band of urban and suburban development, sometimes stretching for hundreds of miles. This phenomenon has been called variously "strip city," "city region," "super-metropolis," and "megalopolis."

The largest and most intensively studied megalopolis is that of the northeastern seaboard.[27] The main axis of the northeastern megalopolis extends about 600 miles from southern New Hampshire to northern Virginia and extends inland 30 to 100 miles from the Atlantic shore to the Appalachian foothills. The total area, over 53,000 square miles, had a population of about 37 million in 1960, approximately one-fifth of the total population of the United States. This megalopolis encompasses all of Massachusetts, Rhode Island, Connecticut, New Jersey, Delaware, and

population is that the city includes within its political boundaries an extensive area which in other cities may be classified as suburban.

[27] Jean Gottmann, *Megalopolis: The Urbanized Northeastern Seaboard of the United States* (1961). Gottmann, a French geographer, directed an extensive research of this area in the 1950's.

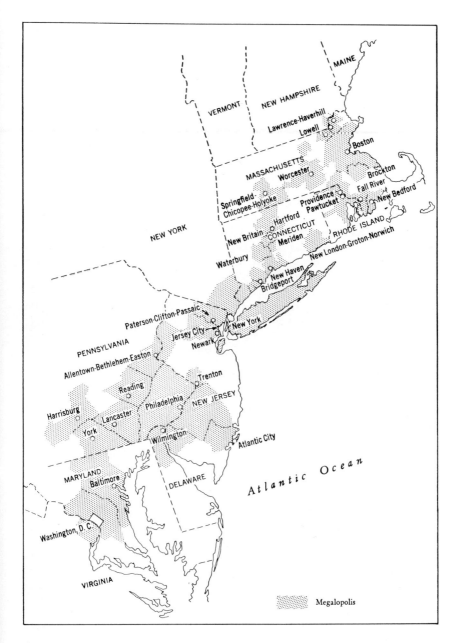

Figure 8. Eastern Megalopolis consists of 34 SMSA's and extends from the southeastern tip of New Hampshire to Washington, D. C. All SMSA's except Jersey City gained in population. Of the 45 central cities they contain, however, 28 lost population: Washington, D. C., and three counties of the New York SMSA are shown as white areas; other central cities that lost population appear as white dots. SOURCE: Adapted from Philip Hauser, "The Census of 1960," *Scientific American*, 205 (July, 1961), p. 42. Reprinted with permission. Copyright © 1960 by Scientific American, Inc. All rights reserved.

the District of Columbia, most of Maryland, large chunks of New York State and Pennsylvania, and slices of New Hampshire and Virginia.[28]

Gottmann describes megalopolis and its meaning for future urban life as follows:

As one follows the main highways between Boston and Washington, D. C., one hardly loses sight of built-up areas, tightly woven residential communities, or powerful concentrations of manufacturing plants. Flying this same route one discovers, on the other hand, that behind the ribbons of densely occupied land along the principal arteries of traffic, and in between the clusters of suburbs around the old urban centers, there still remain large areas covered with woods and brush alternating with some carefully cultivated patches of farmland. These green spaces, however, when inspected at closer range, appear stuffed with a loose but immense scattering of buildings, some of them residential but some of industrial character. That is, many of these sections that look rural actually function largely as suburbs in the orbit of some city's downtown. Even the farms, which occupy the larger tilled patches, are seldom worked by people whose only occupation and income are properly agricultural. And yet these farm areas produce large quantities of farm goods!

Thus the old distinctions between rural and urban do not apply here any more. . . . In this area, then, we must abandon the idea of the city as a tightly settled and organized unit in which people, activities, and riches are crowded into a very small area clearly separated from its nonurban surroundings. Every city in this region spreads out far and wide around its original nucleus; it grows amidst an irregularly colloidal mixture of rural and suburban landscapes; it melts on broad fronts with other mixtures, of somewhat similar though different texture, belonging to the suburban neighborhoods of other cities. . . . This region serves thus as a laboratory in which we may study the new evolution reshaping both the meaning of our traditional vocabulary and the whole material structure of our way of life.

. . . So great are the consequences of the general evolution heralded by the present rise and complexity of Megalopolis that an analysis of this region's problems often gives one the feeling of looking at the dawn of a new stage in human civilization. . . . Indeed, the area may be considered the cradle of a new order in the organization of inhabited space. . . .

Separation between place of work and place of residence creates within the area the system of daily "tidal" movements involved in commuting. Over these are superimposed other currents, some seasonal and some irregularly recurrent. These reflect relations between different parts of Megalopolis that stem from more complicated needs than the simple journey from home to work. These other needs grow more complicated and more general as average family income rises and both goods and activities that were once considered dispensable come to be regarded as necessary by large number of Megalopolitans. . . .

New *patterns of intense living* that have become normal in Megalopolis affect not only land use. They also exert a strong influence on the economic and social foundations of society. . . . The density of activities and of movement of all kinds is certainly the most extraordinary feature of Megalopolis, more characteristic even than the density of population and of skyscrapers. It has become a

[28] *Ibid.,* pp. 25–26.

means of maintaining economic growth and stabilizing society; but how far can it go without destroying itself? . . . The self-defeating effect of dense concentrations may be observed also in other fields than transportation. . . .

It is easier to accept responsibility for solutions than to provide them. The many millions of people who find themselves *neighbors in Megalopolis,* even though they live in different states and hundreds of miles from one another, are barely becoming aware of the imperatives of such a "neighborhood." . . . Responsible public opinion is becoming conscious of the problems involved, and the struggle to find solutions has started. It is especially difficult because no one problem can be tackled without affecting others. Transportation, land use, water supply, cultural activities, use and development of resources, government and politics—all are interrelated. . . .

Megalopolis stands indeed at the threshold of a new way of life, and upon solution of its problems will rest civilization's ability to survive.[29]

SELECTED BIBLIOGRAPHY

BOOKS

Berger, Morroe, *The Arab World Today.* Garden City, N.Y.: Doubleday, 1962.

Gibbs, Jack P. (ed.), *Urban Research Methods.* Princeton, N.J.: Van Nostrand, 1961.

Gottmann, Jean, *Megalopolis.* New York: The Twentieth Century Fund, 1961.

Hauser, Philip (ed.), *Urbanization in Latin America.* Unesco Tensions and Society Series, 1961.

——, *Urbanization in Asia and the Far East.* Unesco Tensions and Society Series, 1958.

Hoyt, Homer, *World Urbanization,* Technical Bulletin #43, Washington, D. C.: Urban Land Institute, 1962.

International African Institute (London), *Social Implications of Industrialization and Urbanization in Africa South of the Sahara.* Unesco Tensions and Society Series, 1956.

International Urban Research, *The World's Metropolitan Areas.* Berkeley and Los Angeles: University of California Press, 1959.

Schnore, Leo, "Urban Form: The Case of the Metropolitan Community," in Werner Z. Hirsch (ed.), *Urban Life and Form.* New York: Holt, Rinehart and Winston, 1963.

Sjoberg, Gideon, "Comparative Urban Sociology," in Robert K. Merton, Leonard Broom, and Leonard S. Cottrell, Jr. (eds.), *Sociology Today.* New York: Basic Books, 1959.

Turner, Roy (ed.), *India's Urban Future.* Berkeley and Los Angeles: University of California Press, 1962.

ARTICLES

Bascom, William, "Some Aspects of Yoruba Urbanism," *American Anthropologist,* 64 (August, 1962), 699–709.

[29] *Ibid.,* pp. 5–16 *passim.* Reprinted by permission.

Gibbs, Jack and Kingsley Davis, "Conventional vs. Metropolitan Data in the International Study of Urbanization," *American Sociological Review*, 23 (October, 1958), 504–14.

———, and Leo Schnore, "Metropolitan Growth: An International Study," *American Journal of Sociology*, LXVI (September, 1960), 160–70.

Friedmann, John, "Cities in Social Transformation," *Comparative Studies in Society and History*, 1 (November, 1961), 86–103.

Little, Kenneth, (ed.), "Urbanism in West Africa, a Symposium," *The Sociological Review* (England), 7, N.S. (July, 1959), 5–126.

Morse, Richard, "Latin American Cities: Aspects of Function and Structure," *Comparative Studies in Society and History*, 4 (July, 1962), 473–93.

Schnore, Leo, "Metropolitan Development in the United Kingdom," *Economic Geography*, 38 (July, 1962), 215–33.

———, "Metropolitan Growth and Decentralization," *American Journal of Sociology*, LXIII (September, 1957), 171–80.

Taeuber, Irene, "Urbanization and Population Change in the Development of Modern Japan," *Economic Development and Cultural Change*, 9 (October, 1960), pt. 2, 1–28.

Wilkinson, T. O., "Urban Structure and Industrialization," *American Sociological Review*, 25 (June, 1960), 356–63.

Classes and Types of Cities

Most scientific analyses involve the construction of some kind of classificatory scheme wherein the things that are studied are classified and arranged in some kind of a logical order. A study of cities is no exception. Indeed, the very concept of "city" implies a classification which distinguishes certain kinds of communities from others. Any broad classification may be further classified according to particular characteristics exhibited by some cities to a greater degree than by others. The specific characteristics selected would depend on the purpose of the classifier. Explicitly or implicitly, any classification of cities involves the notion of a "type." This does not mean that all cities of a given type are identical, nor does it mean that differences between types of cities are absolute. The differences are more likely to be relative. To classify cities (or any other phenomena) is not to "explain" them; it is only the first step in the direction of explanation and interpretation.

Any conceptual device for the classification and analysis of cities must be applicable to communities and even societies in a continuing state of transition. Throughout the world, cities and entire social systems, are undergoing profound changes. The same is true of towns and villages. The isolated folk communities which Redfield and others studied so meticulously are changing under the impact of an expanding urban culture. And the cities themselves, whether preindustrial or "modern," are likewise undergoing changes. Consequently, any conceptualization of the city, whether a typological device or some other, must be related to the empirical realities of situations if it has value for analytical purposes. A continuing re-examination and possibly revision of the typological constructs must be made if they are to have value as analytical tools.

FUNCTIONAL TYPES OF CITIES

A typology of cities based on dominant functions is commonly employed. Seldom if ever in modern society does a "pure" type exist, for the reason that any particular function tends to stimulate the development of other functions. As cities grow in size there is a tendency toward internal differentiation of functions, which logically leads to functional interdependence and reinforcement. The modern metropolis is multifunctional and the trend is apparently toward greater diversification even though a particular function may be dominant. Cities that manufacture goods, for example, also distribute them, and the institutions of such cities also perform numerous other functions.

A classification of cities based on dominant functions depends on how "dominant" is defined and interpreted—whether in general terms or by means of some specific quantitative criterion. For economic functions several criteria may be used, but a yardstick commonly employed is occupational, that is, the proportion of workers engaged in particular activities. In a functional classification worked out by Kneedler, for example, a city was "typed" as manufacturing if 50 per cent or more of the gainful workers were employed in industry and if employment in retail trade was less than 30 per cent of the total labor force. Similar yardsticks were used to classify cities as retail, wholesale, government, recreational, or educational.[1]

For the purposes of this volume a generalized description of city functions, rather than specific quantitative criteria, will be employed as a basis of classification. Thus the cities to be assigned to particular types will be selected primarily on the basis of their respective reputations, and hence no claim for precision is made. Here the emphasis is on "dominant" functions, as that term may be defined in general terms. In some instances, no doubt, a particular city may have two or more kinds of functions or activities which are more or less equal in importance. At any rate, the following functional types will be illustrative.

1. Manufacturing or production centers
2. Centers of trade and commerce
3. Political or administrative centers
4. Cultural or educational centers
5. Health or recreation centers
6. Military cities

[1] Grace M. Kneedler, "Functional Types of Cities," *Public Management,* 27 (1945), 197–203. A similar system was employed by Chauncey D. Harris, "A Functional Classification of Cities in the United States," *Geographical Review,* 33 (1943), 86–99.

PRODUCTION CENTERS

Production in cities is of two types: primary production, based on ex-
tractive industries, and secondary production, based on the fabrication
of raw materials into finished commodities. Sometimes a city combines
primary with secondary production, but ordinarily these two specialized
activities are located in different cities. Centers devoted to primary production rarely reach great numerical magnitude; the number of inhabitants is limited in the main to those engaged directly in extraction of natural resources and a few others necessary to supply the needs of the primary workers. Mining, fishing, lumber, and oil towns are examples of
communities whose dominant activity is extraction. Routes of transportation connect them with other, larger cities, where the extracted products may be disposed of directly to distributors for immediate consumption or to industrialists for manufacturing.

Manufacturing centers, like the primary production centers, acquire
individualities of their own, although the fact that most of them engage
in commercial and trading activities tends to make for uniformity and
similarity. The reputations they acquire and traditions they build up are
determined by the principal product manufactured. The type of industry
leaves its imprint upon the city. Thus Detroit is famous for its automobiles; Grand Rapids for its furniture; Akron for its rubber; Pittsburgh,
Gary, Youngstown, Chattanooga, and Birmingham for their steel; Elgin
and Waterbury for their watches and clocks; Tampa for its cigars; Lawrence and Fall River for their textiles.

Looking at other countries one finds numerous cities with reputations
based largely on specialized manufacturing. Thus Dresden is noted for
ceramics, Lyons for silks, Kimberly for diamonds, Ahmedabad for
cotton goods, and Manchester for textiles. To be sure, these cities manufacture other things; in some instances they have rather diversified manufacturing activities. Sometimes a city is pre-eminent in a specialized form
of industrial activity although the particular industry may employ only
a small proportion of the local force. Amsterdam is one of the world's
leading diamond-cutting centers, but that alone hardly affords it a reputation as a manufacturing center.

COMMERCIAL CITIES

All cities are centers of commerce, but not all cities are dominated by
commercial activities. Some serve as a distributing center for commodities consumed in the immediate locality or region. Others are interme-
diaries for national or international trade and are known as *entrepots*. In-

stead of functioning as a distributing center for the local area, the entrepot becomes a distributing point for commodities destined for areas far
removed as well as for the immediate locality.

If a city is a distributing center for products destined for foreign countries it is a world entrepot. New York, London, Rotterdam, Bombay, São
Paulo, San Francisco, Naples, and Hamburg are examples of world entrepots. In earlier centuries single cities from time to time dominated
world entrepot trade; thus commercial supremacy was held in turn by
Venice, Bruges, Antwerp, Amsterdam, and London. Today there are
many national and international entrepots; and because finance and
commerce are so interdependent, great commercial cities are invariably
centers of finance.

Some of the great commercial cities control and direct the distribution
of certain commodities although the products themselves are never actually transported to the distributing center. The movement and final
distribution of wheat grown on the plains of the Dakotas may be determined at Chicago, although the wheat itself is never sent farther east
than the Mississippi. Cotton grown in the South may be shipped from
Norfolk to Liverpool at the direction of London distributors; from
Liverpool it may go to Manchester for fabrication, thence to Sweden as
a finished product. The business of purchasing the raw materials, con-
trolling their movement, financing the manufacturing, and finally dis-
posing of the finished products in a foreign land may fall, either directly
or indirectly, to the lot of London financiers. Similarly, New York
financial and mercantile interests may direct the growing of fruit on a
Central American plantation, although the fruit is shipped directly across
the Atlantic or Pacific to foreign ports for consumption.

POLITICAL CAPITALS

Before the Industrial Revolution virtually all the great cities of the
world were national capitals. Indeed it was not a coincidence than many
political and administrative centers were commercial cities with an expanding trade. During the last century or so great commercial capitals
have developed apart from political capitals. But the early impetus that
many centers of government received made it possible for these to maintain their supremacy or in some instances outdistance their competitors.

In most of the world the leading or the largest city is the political
capital. Among these, in Europe, are London, Paris, Brussels, and Berlin;
in Latin America, such political capitals as Mexico City, Havana, and
Lima; in Asia, the capital cities of Bangkok, Saigon, and Rangoon; and
in the Middle East such centers as Teheran, Baghdad and Cairo. Only in a
few countries is the national capital a lesser city than the commercial

capital; such capital cities, for example, are Washington, New Delhi, and Ottawa.

Taking the world as a whole, there are literally dozens of provincial or state capitals—seats of government for major political subdivisions of a country. Sometimes these are large cities, but if so their size is probably due more to economic than strictly political factors. In the United States many state capitals are commercially small—Topeka, Lincoln, or Olympia—but there are also large state capitals, such as Columbus, Atlanta, or Indianapolis.

CULTURAL OR EDUCATIONAL CENTERS

Cultural centers and resort towns are numerous. For many cities of the Old World the cathedral has played an all-important role. Indeed the cathedral and the market square have constituted the nuclei around which have grown large metropolitan centers. Even today, in cities like Rheims and Amiens, the cathedral occupies a central position. The many cathedral towns of England and the Continent are witnesses to the influence of religion in the origin and social organization of urban communities. Rome is a political center, but it is perhaps more widely celebrated as the religious capital of the Roman Catholic faith. Mecca became the holy city for the Mohammedans, and Jerusalem the destination of thousands of pilgrims representing several world religions. Mecca and Jerusalem are symbols of religious faiths just as Rome symbolizes the Catholic Church. In this country there are notable examples of cities and towns that developed as religious centers.

Cities are frequently identified with outstanding cultural and educational institutions. Not a few college and university towns owe their existence almost entirely to institutions of higher learning that bring each year thousands of students to their doors. Such university towns as Columbia, the seat of the University of Missouri, and Ann Arbor, where the University of Michigan is located, are examples. European cities sometimes owe their name and fame to educational institutions in their midst. Oxford is identified with the famous university, and Heidelberg, a German town, is known more for its university and famed scholars than for any other characteristic. The name of Oberammergau, a German town, is associated with the religious drama that it sponsors every decade.

Some cities have religious, others literary, artistic, or historic backgrounds that make them notable. The prestige that historic leaders or famous institutions lend to certain localities gives them a peculiar attraction for many people. Throngs of persons each year journey to Mecca, Jerusalem, Lourdes, and other cities to express their veneration for great historic personalities or for individuals representing important religious institutions. Benares in India is a city that is peculiarly holy, and for this reason it has become a shrine, as Lourdes is for the afflicted and crippled. In a similar way certain cities are cultural shrines. To Stratford-on-Avon, the birthplace of Shakespeare, flock great numbers of tourists to pay homage to the renowned English bard. A town of little commercial importance, its streets are bustling with activity during the tourist season in the summer months. Athens, Rome, and other historic cities that were in their day centers of brilliant civilizations, attract students and tourists from all parts of the world.

Resort cities

Such places as Atlantic City, Palm Beach, San Sebastian, Monte Carlo, and Nice are largely concerned with providing recreation and housing for multitudes of tourists and for others seeking respite from rigors of climate or the confinements of a metropolis. Such cities are commercialized playgrounds—cities of smart hotels, of bathing beaches, or of mountain scenery. They attract a cosmopolitan population, but only for a day, or at most a "season." The resort city is comparatively new, mainly a development of the nineteenth or twentieth century. Hot Springs, Aix-les-Bains, and Saratoga Springs are known far and wide as health resorts.

Military cities

In earlier historical periods military defense was one of the major functions of cities. Some of these cities were essentially military garrisons that existed behind ramparts. With the rise of the political state and in part the result of technological changes in weaponry that made the walled city vulnerable to military attack, the function of defense was transferred to the state. In the era of modern warfare, however, cities have grown up having military defense, not just for themselves but for the entire societies, as a major function. Such cities as Oak Ridge, Cape Kennedy, and Los Alamos are centers of scientific research and experimentation, primarily for military purposes. Some military establishments are so vast that they resemble an urban community having numerous functions subsidiary to the principal function. Cities like San Pedro or Southampton are distinctive as military bases, and a few like Gibraltar take on the character of a fortress.

Occupational classification of cities

Any classification of modern cities must take cognizance of the occupational structure. This is particularly true because the occupational

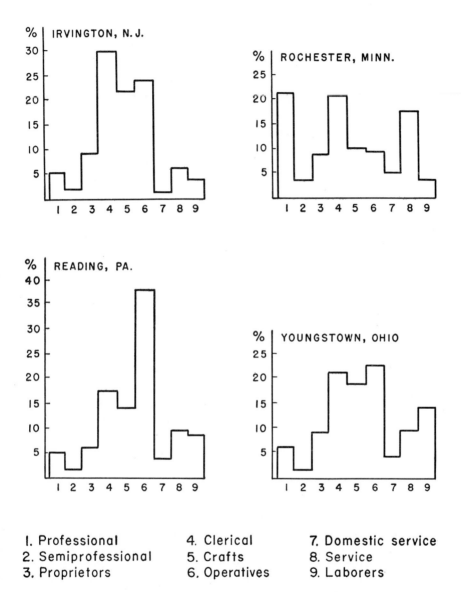

1. Professional	4. Clerical	7. Domestic service
2. Semiprofessional	5. Crafts	8. Service
3. Proprietors	6. Operatives	9. Laborers

Figure 9. Occupational profiles of four cities. Many cities can be typed according to distribution of occupations. SOURCE: Adapted from P. B. Gillen, *The Distribution of Occupations as a City Yardstick* (1951), by permission of King's Crown Press, New York, Publisher.

system underlies many of the functional characteristics just described. Occupation, next to size, is perhaps the most common criterion used in the classification of urban communities, but there are various classificatory schemes based on the distribution of occupations. Alexanderson, for example, presents a system of classification of American cities in which jobs are classified by the proportion which function to supply the needs for goods and services *within* a given city compared with the proportion related to supplying the needs of *other* cities or rural areas.[2]

A somewhat different method was used by Gillen for classifying cities occupationally.[3] A scoring system was worked out based upon the percentage distribution of workers in nine occupational categories—professional, semiprofessional, clerical, skilled workers, and so on. Cities with a large proportion of the population in occupational categories representing high income and educational levels, for instance, had a high rating on the scoring system. By this means it was possible to classify the cities on the basis of their occupational scores.

OTHER TYPOLOGIES OF COMMUNITIES

The ideal type

The concept of an "ideal type" has been applied to communities as it has to other social phenomena. This conceptual device is a constructed proposition which designates the hypothetical characteristics of a "pure" or "ideal" type. As used in this sense the term "pure" or "ideal" has nothing to do with subjective evaluations of the phenomena being studied. The concept merely hypothesizes certain qualities or characteristics of the phenomenon in question, in this instance the community. Actually, no single city or town would conform absolutely to the ideal type that is postulated, but the concept has the value of providing a focus for the study of community life. A problem for the social scientist is to examine empirically the attributes of particular communities from the standpoint of the type that has been hypothesized. This procedure clearly implies a comparative analysis, since communities may be compared on the basis of their actual as well as hypothesized attributes.

In the following discussion, some ideal types of communities will be considered. For the purposes of this book, only the most abbreviated and elementary analysis is possible.

Folk, Feudal, and Metropolitan Community Types. Redfield, the anthropologist, has provided a typology of a folk society or community which is by implication the polar opposite of an urban community.[4] The

---

[2] G. Alexanderson, *The Industrial Structure of American Cities* (1956).
[3] Paul B. Gillen, *The Distribution of Occupations as a City Yardstick* (1951).
[4] Robert Redfield, "The Folk Society," *American Journal of Sociology*, 52 (January,

folk community (or society) as it is viewed by Redfield is "small, isolated, nonliterate, and homogeneous, with a strong sense of group solidarity. . . . Behavior is traditional, spontaneous, uncritical, and personal; there is no legislation or habit of experiment and reflection for
intellectual ends. . . . The sacred prevails over the secular; the economy
is one of status rather than of the market." This, clearly, is stated as an
ideal type; it may not conform precisely to any particular community.

A criticism of the folk-urban concept of community has been made by
Lewis, who restudied the Mexican town of Tepoztlan some years after
Redfield had conducted research in the same community and formulated
his well-known typology. It is Lewis' criticism that the folk-urban concept "focuses attention primarily on the city as a source of change, to the
exclusion or neglect of other factors of an internal or external nature,"
and that "culture change may not be a matter of a folk-urban progression, but rather an increasing or decreasing heterogeneity of culture elements" in the society at large, and that the incorporation of these elements do not necessarily make the community more "urban." [5]

Sjoberg finds the concept of "folk" community acceptable provided
it is not applied to relatively complex communities. He would reserve
the concept of "feudal" community for those units that include a relatively
large peasant population and a small elite. Such communities, as he views
them, are more heterogeneous, more stratified, and more occupationally
differentiated than the folk communities. There is a small corps of literate
persons in the community, a government apparatus, and a priestly class.
The folk community as the term is applied by Redfield may be more
appropriate for tribal communities than for communities that are made
up of peasants "who have a fairly complex form of social organization
and who have fairly frequent contacts with the outside world." [6]

A similar distinction is noted by Foster,[7] whose concept of "peasant"
community is similar to that of Sjoberg's feudal community. The typical
tribal community, according to Foster, is self-sufficient both economically
and culturally. It produces its own food and artifacts, maintains its own
indigenous social system, and exists in a state of cultural isolation—or
has until recent times. The peasant community, on the other hand,
"represents the rural expression of large, class-structured, economically
complex, preindustrial civilizations, in which trade and commerce and
craft specializations are well developed, in which money is commonly
used, and in which market disposition is the goal for a part of the pro-

---

1947), 293–308. Redfield initially developed this idea in his *Tepoztlan: A Mexican
Village* (1930). Subsequently, he modified this theory somewhat in his *The Little
Community* (1955).
    [5] Oscar Lewis, "Tepoztlan Restudied," *Rural Sociology*, 18 (June, 1953), 130–31.
    [6] Gideon Sjoberg, "Folk and 'Feudal' Societies," *American Journal of Sociology*,
58 (November, 1952), 231–40.
    [7] George M. Foster, *Traditional Cultures: The Impact of Technological Change*
(1962), pp. 46–49.

ducer's effort."[8] The peasant (or feudal) community is not a new type; it has existed for thousands of years, and exists in large numbers today, mainly in the underdeveloped areas of the world. Vestiges of such communities remain even in the industrial societies of the West. Although the peasant community represents a distinct way of life, its contacts with the city, however tenuous they may be, have served as channels for the diffusion of urban culture into the smaller community. This aspect will be considered more fully in a later chapter.

While it is certainly true that the concepts of both "urban" and "folk" (or similar terms) are so broad that they are invariably vague, it is the view of this book that they do provide a perspective and that even with these limitations are valuable conceptual tools. In any case, a community typology should be considered a "first step" in community analysis.

By implication, at least, the metropolis would be at the polar extreme of the folk or tribal community. The essential character of the metropolis has been stated by Wirth in a famous essay, "Urbanism as a Way of Life."[9] Among these distinguishing characteristics of the metropolis, aside from large size and relative density of population, are heterogeneity of people and cultures; anonymous, transitory, and impersonal relationships; occupational specialization; secularization of thought; and the predominance of segmental and secondary contracts. This conception of the metropolis is, manifestly, an ideal construct. Although any particular metropolis would deviate, in greater or lesser degree, from the "ideal," the very preponderance of these "typical" characteristics differentiates it quite distinctly from the folk or peasant community.

Paradoxical as it may seem, the city as a type of community may be less important in the modern world than in earlier periods, despite the fact that most societies are becoming increasingly urbanized in a cultural and social-psychological sense. The justification for such a proposition stems from the fact that communities—rural and urban alike—are enmeshed in the institutional network of the larger society and are no longer detached or semi-isolated units related to the outside world only by tenuous connections.

Furthermore, the growth of clusters of communities to form gigantic "urban regions" has been an important development in the twentieth century. In an earlier chapter we considered the growth and development of megalopolis, an emergent "type" of "community."[10]

---

[8] *Ibid.*, pp. 47–48.

[9] Louis Wirth, "Urbanism as a Way of Life," *American Journal of Sociology*, 44 (July, 1938), 1–15.

[10] See especially Chapter 4, pp. 75–77, for an extensive quote from Jean Gottmann, *Megalopolis* (1961), for a description of the vast metropolitan complex that extends from New England as far south as Washington, D.C.

THE CONCEPT OF A CONTINUUM

The various community typologies have suggested a somewhat different approach in which the concept of a continuum is postulated. In the very nature of the typological approach particular communities deviate from the ideal type. Some conform fairly closely to the hypothetical ideal; in others the similarities are less apparent. For particular traits the designated communities may be placed in positions on a continuum representing a range and frequency of traits selected for comparative purposes. Thus, communities may be compared as to the frequency with which any particular trait may exist in different communities.

The concept of a continuum has been employed in comparing rural with urban communities in a particular country or region. Loomis and Beegle, for example, have constructed a continuum by means of which communities may be placed on a scale according to such values as social solidarity, sacredness, and the like.[11] Other yardsticks have been used for comparative purposes for such characteristics as mortality and fertility rates, the percentages of the population in designated occupational categories, rates of crime, delinquency, and divorce, incomes, and so on. Queen and Carpenter have used such an approach in an attempt to construct a quantitative index of urbanism.[12]

Like the folk-urban and other typologies, the rural-urban continuum has definite limitations. Although it does provide a perspective for viewing rural and urban communities, and has been the basis for the accumulation of a considerable body of factual data on cities and towns, it has not been especially fruitful as a conceptual device for theoretical analysis. As one writer has expressed it, the continuum is "real but relatively unimportant, for the reason that it throws little light on the actual nature of social organization and relationships." [13] Nor does it reveal much about the changes that are continually occurring in urban societies or about the processes that are involved in these changes. It can, however, supplement the typological constructs such as those we have discussed in this chapter.

"MODERN" AND "PREINDUSTRIAL" CITIES

A typology of cities that involves many variables—social, economic, political—has been developed by Sjoberg.[14] In his analysis both of histori-

[11] Charles P. Loomis and J. Allen Beegle, *Rural Social Systems* (1950), pp. 811–14.
[12] Stuart A. Queen, and David B. Carpenter, *The American City* (1953), ch. 3.
[13] Richard Dewey, "The Rural-Urban Continuum: Real but Relatively Unimportant," *American Journal of Sociology*, 56 (July, 1960), 60–66.
[14] Gideon Sjoberg, *The Preindustrial City* (1960). See the discussion of Sjoberg's typology in a historical context in Chapter 2 of this text.

cal and contemporary cities, he observed numerous differences that distinguish "modern" cities from "preindustrial" communities. As he defines them, preindustrial cities not only existed in earlier periods of history, but they may also be found in certain regions of the world today, notably in parts of Asia, Africa, and the Middle East. Many cities exhibit characteristics both of the modern and the preindustrial types, indicating that urban centers are undergoing a transition toward modernization. Some of the characteristic differences which Sjoberg and others have observed are considered below:

1. In the industrial or modern city the nuclear family, loosely organized, is predominant. The extended or joint family system, with members of a larger kinship group commonly residing in a single household, is characteristic of preindustrial cities.

2. The class system in industrial cities tends to be flexible, social mobility occurs frequently, and the characteristic feature of the system is a large middle class, whose members are not readily distinguishable from those on higher or lower levels. The social structure of the preindustrial city is relatively rigid, social mobility between strata is slow or infrequent, and a small elite class, easily recognizable, is sharply separated from the masses.

3. A symbol of the industrial type of city is the complex machine whose application has helped to accelerate social change and create a society oriented toward mass production and distribution of goods and services. In preindustrial cities most of the manual work is performed by man or beast; technology consists mainly of simple tools which may be used by craftsmen for limited production of finished articles.

4. In modern industrial cities economic units tend to be large, and prices, weights and measures, marketing procedures, and the quality of products are usually standardized. The characteristic economic establishment in the preindustrial city is the small retail shop or cottage industry. Neither measures nor products are extensively standardized.

5. In modern cities, at least in democratic societies, governmental functionaries are commonly selected on the basis of expertness, experience, competence, or voter appeal, and community issues are often settled by mass expression or public sentiment. The political system of preindustrial cities is usually dominated by a "ruling clique" representing a small elite class, and positions in government are usually filled on the basis of tradition or personal influence, with little effective expression of public opinion on community problems or issues.

"Developed" and "underdeveloped" countries and
their communities

Following Sjoberg's typology of modern and preindustrial cities, it is possible to compare "types" of cities characteristic of developed and underdeveloped countries. Since, as discussed in earlier chapters, the historical circumstances of urban growth in the developed countries (the United States and those of western Europe, for example) were generally different from prevailing conditions in the underdeveloped countries of Asia, Africa, and the Middle East, cities arising under such divergent conditions have exhibited rather different characteristics. In some respects cities in the underdeveloped regions today are similar to those of America and Europe a century or two ago.

Density of population is usually lower in the industrial cities than in cities of underdeveloped countries. In the latter there is usually a preponderance of males, due mainly to selective migration, while in the former there is likely to be a preponderance of females, or at least a fairly even balance between the sexes. There are also differences in the way people and institutions are distributed spatially. The expanding economies of the developed areas have provided employment in cities for most in-migrants, and also a rising level of living; often the institutional needs for manpower exceed the supply. In the relatively static economies of the underdeveloped areas the cities have been unable to absorb all the migrants into the labor market, with the result that there has commonly been a piling-up of a mass of unemployed or underemployed persons, or persons whose employment adds little to the economic growth of the community. Such differences, and many others, tend to support a typology such as we have suggested above.

SELECTED BIBLIOGRAPHY

BOOKS

Anderson, Nels, *The Urban Community: A World Perspective,* chs. 2 and 3. New York: Henry Holt, 1959.

Bergel, E. E., *Urban Sociology,* chs. 7 and 8. New York: McGraw-Hill, 1955.

Boskoff, Alvin, *The Sociology of Urban Regions,* chs. 2 and 3. New York: Appleton-Century-Crofts, 1962.

Hatt, Paul K., and A. J. Reiss, *Cities and Society,* pp. 22–35, 175–214. Glencoe, Ill.: The Free Press, 1957.

Jonassen, Christen T., "Community Typology," in Marvin B. Sussman (ed.), *Community Structure and Analysis.* New York: Thomas Y. Crowell Company, 1959.

Sjoberg, Gideon, *The Preindustrial City.* Glencoe, Ill.: The Free Press, 1960.

Weber, Max, *The City.* Translated by Dan Martindale and Gertrud Neuwirth. Glencoe, Ill.: The Free Press, 1958.

ARTICLES

Dewey, Richard, "The Rural-Urban Continuum: Real but Relatively Unimportant," *American Journal of Sociology,* 66 (July, 1960), 60–66.

Hillery, George, Jr., "The Folk Village: A Comparative Analysis," *Rural Sociology,* 26 (December, 1961), 337–52.

Hoselitz, Bert F., "Cities in Advanced and Underdeveloped Countries," *Confluence*, 4 (October, 1955), 321–34.

Gottmann, Jean, "Megalopolis: Urbanization of the Northeastern Seaboard," *Economic Geography*, 33 (July, 1956), 189–200.

Lewis, Oscar, "Tepoztlan Revisited," *Rural Sociology*, 18 (June, 1953), 121–36.

Miner, Horace, "The Folk-Urban Continuum," *American Sociological Review*, 17 (October, 1952), 529–36.

Redfield, Robert, "The Folk Society," *American Journal of Sociology*, 52 (January, 1947), 293–98.

———, and Milton B. Singer, "The Cultural Role of Cities," *Economic Development and Cultural Change*, 3 (October, 1954), 53–73.

Stewart, C. T., "The Urban-Rural Dichotomy," *American Journal of Sociology*, 64 (September, 1958), 52–58.

Urban Ecology

PART TWO

The Ecological Approach

The city may be many things—a legal entity, a "state of mind," a census definition—but ultimately we must take cognizance of the fact that the city is a physical entity, possessing buildings, streets, and people which exist—or have existed—in time and space. It is a common observation that the land area of a city is put to a variety of uses. There are districts serving primarily commercial uses and others manufacturing and transportation. There are areas wholly residential, and sections that are used for leisure time activities and for the official functions of the community. These areas are not always distinct and clearly defined in terms of use or occupancy; frequently they overlap and interpenetrate in such a fashion as to give the impression that they have multiple uses, as indeed they may have.

THE NATURE OF HUMAN ECOLOGY

The high visibility both of the city and of the diversity within it makes it hardly surprising that one of the earliest and most widely-used approaches to understanding the city has been in terms of the interplay between physical and social conditions. It is implicit in human ecology that although the city (and the human groups inhabiting it) is not merely a physical thing it does have a physical component. The science of human ecology alerts us to this component and deals with it systematically.

As a physical entity, the city and its various parts compete for space with other types of communities and land uses, find some localities more congenial for their development than others, and have characteristic ways of adjusting to the world around them. This point of view may be applied in two ways: (1) to the city as a whole, in which case it leads to under-

standing the chronology, distribution, location, and types of cities; and
(2) to the component parts of cities that strike the eye so forcefully—
apartment house areas, retail shopping areas, hotel districts, racial, religious, or ethnic ghettos, prestige address sections, and so on. In this
case, ecology leads to an understanding of the internal structure of the
city, the functions performed by the various districts, and the changes
in population type or land use within subareas of the city. Chapter 11 will
deal with the first type, the application of human ecology to the city as
a whole.[1] This chapter, as well as Chapters 7–10, will be concerned with
the second type of application, the description and analysis of areas
within the city.

THE ECOLOGICAL SYSTEM

While human ecology is concerned with the interrelationships among
men in their spatial setting, urban ecology is specifically concerned with
these interrelationships as they manifest themselves in the city. Urban
ecology includes the study of such external expressions of ecological interrelationships as the distribution of cities or their internal structure
and composition. Because urban ecology devotes much attention to the
description of these external manifestations, the fact that its main concern is the system producing these external patterns, not with the patterns
themselves, is sometimes obscured.

Much of the sociological literature on ecology is concerned with the
distribution in space of people and institutions. But spatial distribution
is only a starting point in ecological analysis. Human ecology goes farther
than merely determining where designated groups are located or where
particular functions of these groups are performed. It is also concerned
with interactive relationships between individuals and groups and the
way these relationships influence, or are influenced by, particular spatial
patterns and processes. It is concerned with cultural, racial, economic,
and other differences insofar as preferences and prejudices associated
with these differences serve to bring people socially or spatially together
or keep them apart. It is concerned with social organization insofar as the
organization of human activities influences, or is influenced by, the spatial
distribution of people or of institutions. Above all, it is concerned with
the dynamics of the social order insofar as change in the structure and
functions of institutions, or changes in patterns of human relationships,
bring about ecological changes, and vice versa.

It should be kept in mind that human ecology as a science does not
deal with individuals as individuals; rather it is concerned with groups

[1] It should also be noted that in the discussion of the prehistory and history of cities
in Chapters 1 and 2, ecological elements are included, although they are not labelled
as such.

of individuals having some common characteristic such as age, sex, income, education, race, marital status, and the like. Nor does human ecology deal with individual business firms or industries but with types such as financial institutions, light manufacturing, service enterprises, and so on. The concern of human ecology with categories of people or institutions arises from its attempt to describe the system of interrelationships underlying the visible city. Single individuals or commercial enterprises are not self-sufficient but dependent on others who in turn are dependent on them. Accruing from this interdependency is a complex interplay of forces. Furthermore, the properties of the interrelated whole are different than the properties of the component parts. For these reasons, human ecology is always concerned with collectivities.

ELEMENTS OF THE ECOLOGICAL SYSTEM

The ecological system has been described as having four elements: population, environment, technology, and organization.[2] A fifth element, social-psychological factors, is added in this discussion.

Population. Human ecology always deals with a specific concrete population of human beings. Population groups have characteristics which affect their adjustment. Thus a population has a rate of increase or decrease which helps determine the degree of competition for space. For example, it was easier to find houses and apartments in the 1930's when the urban marriage and birth rates were low and few people migrated to cities than in the post-World War II period when marriage and birth rates and immigration were at high levels. Populations can also be described in terms of their density or other aspects of their distribution.

Movement, another characteristic of populations relevant to urban ecology, may be of various types: permanent or transitory, within the city or between cities, or between city and countryside. For example, such phenomena as migration and immigration, commuting, moving from one address to another, the summer exodus from the city, the "rush hour," and holiday and weekend travel have definite regularity and meaning. The daily ebb-and-flow movement in the city, resulting from the separation of work place and place of residence which is a significant aspect of modern urbanization, offers an interesting example. In this respect one may contrast the American farmer with the city dweller. For most farmers the place of work is the place of residence; the two are almost inseparable. Yet even in agriculture there is some tendency toward divorcement of place of work from place of residence. Many farmers live in a

---

[2] Otis Dudley Duncan, "Human Ecology and Population Studies," in P. Hauser and Duncan (eds.), *The Study of Population* (1959), pp. 681–84. This presentation is broadly based on Duncan's analysis, except that he does not include the fifth element.

village or city, commuting daily by car or truck to and from their farms.

The daily urban ebb and flow of workers is characterized by main currents, countercurrents, and crosscurrents of movements; some, perhaps the majority, move centripetally to the center of the city during morning hours, some move in a centrifugal direction to outlying work places, others move laterally across the city. Some movements are short, possibly a few minutes' walk; others are long, often as far as forty or fifty miles in the larger metropolitan areas.

Environment.   Populations exist in a given natural environment, which is broadly defined here to include location, climate, natural resources, flora and fauna, topography, natural disasters, and geologic change. The population must cope with this environment to exist, and environments differ in the resources they offer for survival. Environment sets limits to the size and density of the population, but the process of adjustment is continuous and reciprocal because man in turn modifies the environment via his technology and culture. The transformed environment may then support populations at entirely different levels, as a comparison of present-day Manhattan or Chicago with those same areas when occupied by the Indian readily shows.

In the city, man's modification of the natural environment reaches a high level. Most native plants and animals are destroyed and new ones introduced intentionally (the English sparrow) or unintentionally (the brown rat). Waters are polluted by sewage and industrial wastes and the air by smoke and smog. The terrain is altered by roads, railroads, swamp drainage, the construction of reservoirs and canals, the development of golf courses and beaches, and by bombing and other war damage.[3]

Despite man's increased ability to cope with the natural environment, it is still a factor to be reckoned with in analyzing cities, as the following discussion of two aspects of the natural environment—terrain and rivers —indicates.

If all cities were located on level plains, completely removed from waterways, hills, and mountains, their ecological patterning would be mainly the result of man-made factors unhampered by topographic characteristics. But few cities are located on sites devoid of surface irregularities. Indeed, an irregular terrain has often been selected for initial settlement because of advantages offered for defense or transportation, as in the case of many early European and American settlements that later grew into urban centers. It is the viewpoint of this book that topographic conditions are not so much direct causes of particular ecological configurations as they are limiting factors to which some kind of ecological adjustment can be made.

Cities located on waterways, especially rivers, make a rather typical ecological adjustment to this physical fact. Probably most cities on rivers were initially located on one side of the bank; but as they grew in size

[3] Lee Dice, *Man's Nature and Nature's Man* (1955), pp. 77–78.

and became more specialized in their functions, they tended to spill over the river to the opposite bank. Population and institutions on one side of the river are commonly quite different from those on the other. One side, especially if it is on low ground and considered less desirable for residential purposes, may be devoted mainly to heavy manufacturing. East St. Louis, North Kansas City, and Camden, N.J., are examples of highly industrialized developments on opposite sides of major rivers in the United States. On the right bank of the Rhine, at Cologne, is a similar development. Budapest is likewise a city divided by a river: Buda on the hill side of the Danube, Pest on the flat plains on the opposite side of the stream.[4] Buda is an old town with winding streets; the hill is the historical nucleus of the city. Pest is modern in lay-out and contains most of the commercial and industrial establishments and residences of the workers. Cities on irregular terrain show the effect of topographic irregularities in the pattern of growth. Wedged between Lake Superior and a high escarpment is Duluth, whose expansion can occur in only two directions, along the waterfront. The result is a city stretching for twenty or more miles along the lake but extending scarcely a half-mile back from the shore line. The extreme density of population in Bombay is partly due to the fact that the city is located on an island and cannot expand territorially beyond the water's edge.

Technology. The adjustment of a population to its environment is obviously conditioned by the available technology. This is implied in what has been said about the modification of the natural environment by man. The carrying power of a given environment varies according to the means man has developed to make use of it. The city as we know it—the industrial city—depends on a complex specialized technology which makes it possible for a considerable proportion of the population to live apart from direct concern with agriculture.

The internal spatial patterns of cities are also, to a very considerable extent, the creation of technology, especially the technology of factory and transportation. As technological changes have taken place, the ecology of the city has correspondingly undergone changes. Wherever cities are characterized by small-scale manufacturing and distributive enterprises, the place of work and place of residence are unseparated for many families. This pattern prevailed in early European and American cities, and is still widespread in cities of economically underdeveloped countries such as those of the Orient. Dual functions are carried out in the same building. A retail merchant may operate his business on the first floor and house his family in the rear of the building or on the second floor; or a craftsman may carry out his operations in the rear of a structure which also houses his family. Sometimes the same structure is used for three purposes: residence, manufacturing, and merchandising. Increased mechanization which required factories altered these locational patterns.

[4] Robert F. Dickinson, *The West European City* (1951), p. 209.

In the early days of the Industrial Revolution, factories were located in the inner zones of cities; or, perhaps more accurately, cities tended to develop around the factories, with workers residing close to the place of employment. The result was high residential density, families stacked on families in crowded tenements occupied by workers and their dependents. But as transportation technology changed, as speed and size of vehicles increased, workers tended to break the ties that bound them to the vicinity of a factory site.

With the growth of large-scale industrial and commercial organizations in many countries of the world, the detachment of the work place from the place of residence became more and more a distinguishing feature of city life. On the basis of the 1960 census, of the 47 million wage earners in American cities, only 2.9 per cent worked at home.[5] Not only has detachment occurred; actual distance from place of residence to place of work has increased—and is still increasing. Long-distance commuters in smaller cities as well as in metropolitan areas shuttle back and forth between their place of work and their suburban or rural residence beyond the city. Almost 14 per cent of the urban workers in the United States reported that they worked in a county different from the one they lived in.

Obviously technological developments have greatly affected the ecology of cities not only with reference to the distribution of business and industry but also with reference to the distribution of the people. As technological changes continue, there can be no doubt that other ecological changes will occur.

Organization. A crucial element in the ecological complex is organization. For human beings organization is always *social* because they cannot exist on a sustaining basis apart from other human beings. As interdependent creatures, it is necessary that they organize, that is, make their activities regular and systematic when they are living in the same group, whether that group be as small as the family or as large as the metropolis or the nation. Without some form of organization, chaos would result, as sometimes happens in times of disaster, revolution, rapid social change, or other instances where the social order is temporarily disrupted.

Urban ecology is, of course, concerned with those aspects of social organization which impinge upon the community level. Foremost among these is the division of labor, for the network of occupational interdependence is very extensive and we are often unaware of many of its ramifications. Thus, the feasibility of staggered working hours to reduce rush hour congestion hinges on whether studies can uncover what kinds of business can operate for part of the day without the services of other types of enterprise. There is no point in having type "A" firm begin work

[5] *U. S. Census of Population 1960. General Social and Economic Characteristics, United States Summary.* Final Report PC(1)–1C, Tables 93 and 94.

at 8:30 A.M. while type "B" firms begin at 9:00 A.M., if the former cannot function without the latter.

The ramifications of interdependence are often brought to light during a prolonged strike. Typographers would seem far removed from retailing, the theatre and entertainment, fashion, café society, charity balls, and real estate and employment agencies. Yet, the lengthy strike by the typographers union against the leading New York City newspapers in 1962–63 ultimately had serious effects on all of these groups, who were without their customary advertising and publicity.

Since much organization of human activities in the city is embodied in economic organization, it is inevitable that human ecology devotes much of its attention to cost and to the locational factors affecting cost—time and distance. Economic exchange, since it does not require personal contact or acquaintance, is well-suited to the large populations of the city. Economic organization, however, is only part of social organization; social organization also involves such concepts as status, position, and role. Thus, we cannot understand the occupational division of labor in Western society, for example, without recognizing the status of women or youth or the position of Negroes and immigrants within society.

The physical pattern of the city mirrors some of the organizing principles of social structure. Is the skyline dominated by the cathedral, the fortress, or the office skyscraper? Do groups occupy separate residential areas on the basis of race, religion, ethnic affiliation, wealth, caste occupation, social class, or other criteria? Is movement within the city unimpeded or is it restricted by such governmental controls as curfews, passes, ghettos, police, and check-points? To what extent is commercial or residential location a matter of laissez-faire, and to what extent is it directed by the government through zoning laws, building restrictions, subsidized housing, rights of eminent domain, and so on?

The Social-Psychological Element. A fifth element, social-psychological aspects of human ecology, should be added to the four ecological elements posited by Duncan. If man is anything at all, he is a creature of wits and sentiments. He is a purposive animal, capable of making choices of his own volition, capable of certain action patterns in accordance with the sentiments and values he has acquired. Commonly he is a person of prejudice, and his likes and dislikes of other individuals and groups influence the character of his associational life and frequently affect his position in the ecological structure of the community.

Preferences, values, attitudes, and beliefs must be common to a significant number of individuals who act or are willing to act on them, in order to qualify as social-psychological elements in human ecology; purely idiosyncratic individual tastes are unimportant.

Several examples, of which the pattern of Negro residential segregation in American cities is noteworthy, illustrate the social-psychological element in human ecology. Spatial segregation of Negroes in slums is, of course, related to their limited economic means, but their low economic position is in turn related to many social-psychological factors such as attitudes, prejudice, motives, public opinion, rumor, gossip, and propaganda.

Firey's study in central Boston indicated that two social-psychological aspects were at work in land use there, in addition to the expected economic competition. (1)" . . . Space . . . also [has] an additional property, *viz.*, that of being at times a symbol for certain cultural values that have become associated with a certain spatial area." (2) " . . . Locational activities are not only economizing agents but may also bear sentiments which can significantly influence the locational process." [6] Sentiment and symbolism may supersede other considerations and result in noneconomic, "nonrational" use of land. Thus, Beacon Hill, with its historical, literary, and "old-family" associations, has remained a fashionable residential area, despite the fact that its central location would bring much higher financial return if it were put to commercial use. The Boston Common, several colonial burying-grounds, and historic churches and meeting houses stand in the heart of Boston. The retention of these landmarks is expensive, but public opinion runs high against demolishing the edifices in which major events of the Revolution took place.

Firey points out that sentimental and symbolic attachment to spatial location is not restricted to historic or upper class areas. The foreign-born Italian immigrants tend to remain in the North End of Boston even when their means permit them to move elsewhere, for the North End provides the traditional Italian community life not available in other sections of Boston.

A recent study of zoning in Austin, Texas, also demonstrates the role of values and volition in human ecology.[7] Analysis of the proceedings of the Austin City Planning Commission and the Commission's Zoning Committee, 1956–60, and interviews with the participants revealed that the central problem in urban zoning is resolution of the conflict among competing values and beliefs about effective land use. Willhelm describes three major sets of opposing values: economic versus protective values; collective versus individual values; present-time versus future-time values.

INTERRELATIONSHIPS OF THE ECOLOGICAL ELEMENTS

Environment, population, technology, organization, and social-psychological elements all mutually modify one another, an interaction that can be seen clearly if the elements are expressed schematically. The case of

[6] Walter Firey, "Sentiment and Symbolism as Ecological Variables," *American Sociological Review*, 10 (April, 1945), 141.
[7] Sidney Willhelm, *Urban Zoning and Land-Use Theory* (1962). The title of this volume belies its general relevance for the study of human ecology.

suburban expansion of United States cities after World War II may serve as an example. The symbols, E, P, T, O, and SP, respectively, stand for environment, population, technology, organization, and social-psychological elements.

Few residential buildings were constructed in American cities during the Depression of the 1930's and World War II, and many of the earlier industrial and residential structures were built in a period of rapid growth and industrialization with minimum restriction and planning. Thus, by the mid-1940's the central areas of most American cities were characterized by polluted air and beaches, and by little open space for parks or recreation or for further industrial or residential expansion (O, SP, T → E). During this same period most immigrant groups had been assimilated into the middle class; increased mechanization drew more people to cities, the proportion of the labor force in unskilled jobs was reduced, the amount of leisure time available increased, and values about early marriage and child-bearing changed. All of this resulted in a rapidly expanding, prosperous, middle class, urban population with many young children (O, SP, T, → P). The change in the size and composition of the urban population pressed on the already crowded city cores which were undesirable in terms of middle class amenities for children, thereby complicating the adjustment of urban middle class living (P → E, O, SP). Ownership of cars and homes (especially since mass-production techniques had been applied to housing) was widely possible for the middle class and made possible an explosion of residential suburbs which replaced farms or relatively open land on the outskirts of American cities. (O ⟷ T → E).

The new communities, based, as we have noted, on a series of adaptations and new interrelationships among the five ecological elements, set still further changes in motion. Social scientists have been particularly interested in the organizational and social-psychological changes resulting from these new communities (E, P, T, O_1, SP_1 → O_2, SP_2). These include the drive for a metropolitan form of government, the concern among politicians with the shift of many voters to areas outside the city limits, the research studies and debates about the quality of religious and family life in homogeneous suburbs, discussion of the values exemplified by suburbia, and proposals to control urban sprawl by zoning and better planning.

This schematic analysis indicates that the ecological community is in a constant cycle of adaptation and re-adaptation.

THE SOCIAL COMPONENT IN HUMAN ECOLOGY

Although all human ecologists have recognized the importance of social factors, various schools of thought differ sharply in the relative position

Weekly shopping in contrasting ecological systems. Above: A town market in Mali, an African nation, attracts Dogon tribesmen from remote areas every five days. Below: The Garden State Shopping Plaza in Paramus, New Jersey. Differences in size of population, geographical environment, technology, values, and social and economic organization underlie the striking contrast. (Courtesy United Nations and Cities Service Company [photograph by J. Alex Langley].)

they assign to social factors within the ecological framework. One recent survey of human ecology has classified these schools of thought as the "classical," "neo-orthodox," and "sociocultural." [8]

The so-called "classical" position, exemplified by Park and Burgess, included an emphasis on cultural elements as separate from and, to a large extent, dependent on, the noncultural ecological elements. The classical ecologists used many concepts such as competition, natural area, biotic community, and symbiosis which derived from plant and animal ecology and from Social Darwinism.

Beginning in the late 1930's, the classical position was criticized and modified. Generally speaking the more recent schools of thought have assigned social factors a more central position in human ecology. The so-called "neo-orthodox" approach has done this either by retaining the emphasis on the noncultural elements but indicating they can only be understood in terms of culture (Quinn) or by concentrating on those cultural elements reflected in the economic aspects of community structure (Hawley). The "sociocultural" position is the only view of human ecology to assign cultural factors a major causative influence. Walter Firey, an important exponent of this point of view, notes in his study of Boston that sentiment and symbolism often resulted in inefficient uneconomic uses of land, and further, notes that other types of ecological approach do not account for such land uses.

Although this presentation is oversimplified, it does serve to suggest the variety of ways in which the social factor may be conceptualized in human ecology. All of these approaches have produced research results and, except for the strict classical position, are currently being used. The analysis of the ecological complex presented in terms of environment, population, technology, organization, and social-psychological elements would probably be called a sociocultural approach.

ECOLOGICAL PROCESSES

CENTRALIZATION

Ecological literature makes use of a few basic concepts. These will be introduced in this section and considered more thoroughly in later chapters. One of these concepts is *centralization*. Centralization may be defined as the tendency for people to gather at some pivotal point in a city in order to satisfy their interests, fulfill their needs, or carry out desig-

[8] George A. Theodorson, "Introductions" to Parts I and II in Theodorson, (ed.), *Studies in Human Ecology* (1961). Rather similar distinctions are made in Willhelm, *op. cit.*, chs. 2 and 3. Willhelm uses the terms, "traditional materialism," "neoclassical materialism," and "cultural" to describe the three major types of emphasis on social factors in human ecology. The following discussion is based on Theodorson and Willhelm.

nated social or economic functions. In common usage the term implies the tendency to gather at a *central* pivotal point. Such a place is the *central business district.* The term centralization is also applied to institutional functions: thus we refer to centralization of administrative controls or to centralization of certain economic operations such as particular types of retailing.

DECENTRALIZATION

A second concept is *decentralization.* Interpreted literally, decentralization is the tendency to move away from, rather than toward, a central point. But centralization and decentralization may occur simultaneously. This is true because the concepts actually refer to somewhat different phenomena. An individual may carry out highly centralized functions in the central business district, but at the same time make a series of residential changes, all away from the center of the city. This centrifugal shift of location we refer to as residential decentralization.

Decentralization may also have reference to the shift of institutions from the center of the city toward the periphery. Decentralization often results in the development of subcenters in the outer areas of the city. Decentralization of residential population and decentralization of institutions are closely related developments. Both kinds of decentralization are important in recent metropolitan growth.

The growth of population or institutions on the periphery of a city may not be due entirely to decentralization as we have used the term— movement from a central area in a community. This is because people and institutions may move to an outlying area from some other locality. A family moving from Topeka to a suburb of Los Angeles would hardly be an example of decentralization in the strict meaning of the term. Similarly, a new industry springing up in a London suburb would not represent industrial decentralization.

SEGREGATION

There is a widespread tendency for persons to select as intimate associates other individuals with whom they share similar interests, values, and perhaps social positions. These associational preferences commonly reflect differences in occupation, religion, race, nationality, education, and so on. When they are manifest in spatial relationships as the tendency of individuals to reside near others with similar characteristics the phenomenon is known as *segregation.* Urban districts that are populated largely or entirely by members of the same race, religion, or nationality would be examples of ecological segregation. As the term is employed in this book, segregation may be voluntary or involuntary. Segregated districts are often referred to as *natural areas*. They are "natural" because they are seldom the results of a preconceived plan.

When individuals or groups abandon a residential area and move into another district, the phenomenon is known as ecological *invasion*. Invasion is of particular interest to sociologists if people moving into an area are different from the occupying residents in race, religion, nationality, economic status, or some other important attribute. If the occupants of the invaded areas are completely displaced, the result is *succession*. Residential invasions may also occur when people move into a vacant area or an area used for business or industrial purposes. Similarly, institutional invasions occur when business, industrial, or other kinds of establishments move into an area which has heretofore been put to a different use.

ECOLOGICAL PATTERNS OF URBAN GROWTH

Are there uniformities in the ecological patterning of cities and if so what is the nature of such patterns? If such uniformities exist, can they be presented in forms of principles or generalizations? A number of urban ecologists have attempted to go beyond mere description to the formulation of a set of theories or hypotheses concerning the ecological pattern of the city. In their efforts to formulate systematic principles they are aware of the fact that scientific theories are generalizations which may not fit all the details of each individual city. Theoretical constructs concerning ecological structure postulate a kind of ideal type which may not actually exist in all details but which may be only an approximation of the patterning of particular areas or cities. If the theoretical construct departs too far from what actually exists, its validity is open to question, or at least has limited applicability. On the other hand, a theory of urban ecology may have validity without having universal application; if it is designed to apply only to cities of a certain country or region, or to cities of a particular type, then it may be valid, provided it is accurately descriptive of the spatial configurations that actually exist.

Three theories of urban ecology have been particularly interesting to sociologists. The first is the "concentric zone theory" of urban growth, formulated many years ago by E. W. Burgess. The second is the "sector theory" of city growth, developed more recently by Homer Hoyt. The third is Harris and Ullman's "multiple nuclei theory." Each theory is, in a sense, an ideal construct, a set of generalizations. Burgess is particularly explicit in noting that his concentric zone theory has no reference to any particular city but that it is an abstraction representing a kind of generalized ecological profile of cities, presumably American communities. Each of the theories is concerned with ecological change and with the spatial patterns that have emerged from these changes. Each was developed on the basis of knowledge concerning the ecology and growth of American cities. Whether their authors ever intended them to apply to cities in other countries is not clear, but whatever validity they possess is higher for American communities than for cities outside the United States. As we shall observe later in this volume, certain cities in Latin America and the Orient differ quite markedly from American cities in their ecological configurations.

BURGESS' CONCENTRIC ZONE THEORY

Burgess has suggested that the modern city assumes a pattern of concentric zones, each with certain distinguishing characteristics.[9] These zones, according to Burgess, are idealized concepts; no city conforms absolutely to his scheme. Physical barriers such as rivers, lakes, hills, and gulches tend to distort the zonal pattern of a community. Lines of transportation, such as railroads and automobile highways, divide the zones into smaller sections.

a. The Central Business District.   The first or inner zone, according to the Burgess theory, comprises the central business district. This is where skyscrapers, department stores, cheap variety emporia, hotels, restaurants, theatres, and motion-picture houses are concentrated to meet the needs of downtown shoppers or transients. The inner zone is essentially an area of retail trade, light manufacturing, and commercialized recreation. In Chicago it is called the "Loop," in New York the "Midtown" and "Downtown" areas, and in Pittsburgh the "Golden Triangle." In American cities, at least, the central business district occupies a relatively small proportion of the entire area of the community.

b. The Zone of Transition.   The zone surrounding the central business district has been designated by Burgess as the "area of transition," because it is in the immediate path of business and industrial expansion and has an ephemeral character. Unlike the business district, which is a nonresidential area for the most part, the zone of transition tends to be heavily populated by the lower income classes, by Old World immigrants and rural migrants, by unconventional folk, and by social outcasts such as criminals and prostitutes. Typically, the zone of transition also contains some high-cost luxury housing—the "Gold Coast."

c. The Zone of Workingmen's Homes.   The third zone in Burgess' scheme is designated the "area of workingmen's homes." Superior to the

[9] E. W. Burgess, "The Growth of the City," in R. E. Park and E. W. Burgess, *The City* (1925), p. 51.

area of transition in physical appearance, but falling short of the residential districts of the middle classes, it is populated largely by workers whose economic status enables them to have many of the comforts and even some of the luxuries the city has to offer.

d. *The Zone of Middle Class Dwellers.* Beyond the zone occupied by the working classes is a broad area populated mainly by professional people, owners of small businesses, the managerial group, clerical forces, and the like. There are hotels and apartment houses, and detached residences with spacious yards and gardens.

e. *The Commuters' Zone.* On the outer pheriphery of the city is the commuters' zone. Beyond the political boundaries of the city are satellite towns and suburbs, existing in a mutually dependent relationship to the metropolis. These towns and hamlets, dubbed by some writers "bedroom" towns, may house many of the city's workers by night but are largely vacated during the day.

Burgess gives empirical support to his hypothesis by presenting sociological data, mainly from Chicago, which in their distributive patterns take the form of a series of gradients. He shows that, in passing from the center or Loop of Chicago to the periphery, delinquency rates, sex ratios, and percentages of foreign-born persons tend to decrease, while home ownership is inclined to increase.[10] In certain instances the gradients are uniformly continuous. These gradients are also observed by Shaw and McKay [11] in their ecological studies of delinquency and by Faris and Dunham [12] in a study of the ecology of insanity in Chicago.

HOYT'S SECTOR THEORY OF URBAN GROWTH

On the basis of data provided by real-property inventories of 142 American cities, Hoyt has formulated the sector theory of urban development.[13] Briefly, the theory holds that high-rent areas tend to be located on the outer fringes of one or more sectors or quadrants of the city, and that in some sectors the low-rent districts assume the shape of a cut of pie, extending from the center to the city's periphery. As cities grow in population the high-rent areas move outward along one sector; districts thus abandoned by the upper-income groups become obsolete and frequently deteriorate as people of lower economic status move in. Instead of forming a concentric zone around the periphery of the city, Hoyt insists, the high-rent areas are ordinarily located on the outer edge of one or more

[10] "The Determination of Gradients in the Growth of a City," *Publications of the American Sociological Society*, 21 (1927), 178–84.

[11] Clifford Shaw, and Henry McKay, *Juvenile Delinquency and Urban Areas* (1942).

[12] R. E. L. Faris, and H. Warren Dunham, *Mental Disorders in Urban Areas* (1939).

[13] Homer Hoyt, *The Structure and Growth of Residential Neighborhoods in American Cities* (1939), ch. 6. See also his article, "The Structure of American Cities in the Post-War Era," *American Journal of Sociology*, 48 (January, 1943), 475–92.

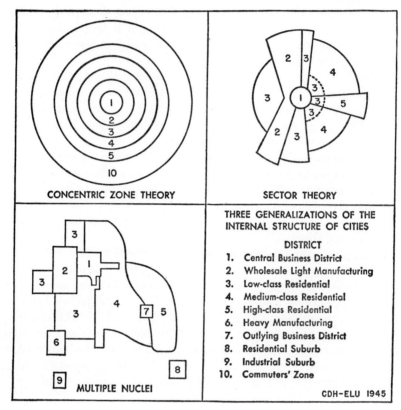

Figure 10. Schematic illustration of three theories of city growth. SOURCE: C. D. Harris and E. L. Ullman, *Annals*, November, 1945.

sectors. Furthermore, industrial areas develop along river valleys, water courses, and railroad lines instead of forming a concentric zone around the central business district. In recent decades there has been a tendency for factories to locate on outerbelt lines near the edge of the city. Hoyt likens the pattern of the American city to an "octopus" with tentacles extending in various directions along transportation lines.

Hoyt observes that the high-rent residential areas tend to be located along established transportation routes, usually on high ground and away from the "flats." In some cities these districts are situated on attractive waterfronts not used for industrial purposes. Chicago, for example, has a high-rent area stretching along the lake front from the Loop to the northern city limits; beyond the city's northern boundaries is a string of upper-class suburbs which follows the lake shore for thirty or forty miles and is connected with Chicago by rapid transit lines. A similar pattern of development may be noted in Madison, Wisconsin, a much smaller city, where the two areas of maximum rentals are along the shore of

Lake Mendota, beyond the city's boundaries near the eastern and western extremities of the metropolitan district.

HARRIS AND ULLMAN'S MULTIPLE-NUCLEI THEORY

Harris and Ullman's theory differs from both the Burgess and Hoyt theories in that it postulates not one center for the city, but several.[14] Each of the centers tends to specialize in a particular kind of activity— retailing, wholesaling, finance, government, recreation, education, and the like. Several centers may have existed from the beginning of the city, or have developed later in a division from one center. London is an example of the first type, where the financial and governmental centers were separate from the inception of the town. Chicago illustrates the second type, for while heavy industry was originally concentrated in the downtown area, it later tended to concentrate in an area of its own in the extreme southeast of the city.

Multiple centers develop for the following reasons: (1) certain activities require specialized facilities and concentrate where these facilities occur. Thus heavy industry requires large acreage and long-distance connections, in contrast to retailing which requires much less space and easy local accessibility. (2) Similar activities benefit from location close to one another. For example, the clustering of retail establishments concentrates potential customers. (3) Certain dissimilar activities may be disadvantageous to one another. Industry which requires large space and may have "nuisance" features is incompatible both with retailing which depends on heavy pedestrian and street traffic and with high-class residential development. (4) For some urban activities a downtown location is too expensive and would not be the most advantageous site in any case.

The major urban activities often form subnuclei on the following pattern. The central business district contains the major retail shopping area but, especially in large cities, financial and governmental districts may form separate concentrations within it. "Automobile row" may also be a separate part of the central business district. Wholesaling, light manufacturing, heavy industry, high class and low class residences—each tends to occupy separate nuclei apart from the central business district. Multiple nuclei may assume many patterns, only one of which is shown in Figure 10.

LIMITATIONS OF THE THEORIES

A general criticism of the concentric-zone theory is offered by Alihan, who declares that a zone can have significance only if its boundaries mark

[14] C. D. Harris, and Edward L. Ullman, "The Nature of Cities," *The Annals*, 241 (November, 1945), 7–17.

a distinction between gradients.[15] If, as the name implies, gradients are continuous, zonal lines can be drawn arbitrarily at any radius from the center. In other words, it would be as logical to have twenty zones as five. Apparently, however, the Burgess theory, according to Alihan, implies a certain homogeneity of phenomena within a particular concentric zone, and the same idea appears to be implicit in the sector theory.

After examining land utilization maps for a number of cities, Davie found that the Burgess hypothesis had little value so far as those cities were concerned. He says:

> The hypothesis of the concentric-zone pattern . . . clearly does not apply to New Haven. Nor does it appear to apply to the sixteen self-contained cities in which Bartholomew made detailed field surveys of land utilization. Nor does it apply to Greater Cleveland, where Green by analyzing social data by census tracts mapped the "cultural areas" of Cleveland and the four largest adjacent cities. Low economic areas, characterized by smaller incomes, fewer radios and telephones, fewer home owners, fewer one-family dwellings, more two- and multi-family dwellings, more murders, houses of prostitution, juvenile delinquents, dependent families, unemployed, illiterates, and higher birth and infant mortality rates in proportion to population—low economic areas, while in general near the center of the city, are by no means confined there but are found in every zone. They are generally adjacent to industrial and railroad property.[16]

Davie's main criticism of the Burgess theory is that it fails to take account of the factor of industrial and railroad utilization. Industrial activities, he notes, may be found in any zone, and this he insists is as true of Chicago as of other cities. An examination of twenty zoning maps of cities of varying types and sizes located in this country and Canada disclosed: "(1) a central business district, irregular in size but more square or rectangular than circular, (2) commercial land use extending out along the radial streets and concentrating at certain strategic points to form subcenters, (3) industry located near the means of transportation by water or rail, wherever in the city this may be—and it may be anywhere, (4) low-grade housing near the industrial and transportation areas, and (5) second- and first-class housing anywhere else. These seem to be the general principles governing the distribution of utilities. There is no universal pattern, not even of an 'ideal' type." [17]

In a penetrating critique, based upon a study of land use in Boston, Firey found both the concentric-zone and sector theories inadequate for that city.[18] The distribution of particular population groups in Boston shows much greater variability than either the Burgess or Hoyt schemes

---

[15] Milla Alihan, *Social Ecology* (1938), p. 225.

[16] Maurice R. Davie, "The Pattern of Urban Growth," in G. P. Murdock (ed.), *Studies in the Science of Society* (1937), p. 159.

[17] *Ibid.*   [18] Walter Firey, *Land Use in Central Boston* (1947), pp. 41–86.

permit. He points out, for example, that Beacon Hill and the West End, situated in what would be the "zone of transition," are populated by sharply contrasting people. One part of Beacon Hill is a fashionable residential district; adjacent to it, within the same concentric zone, is a low-income area populated in the main by lower-class immigrants and their descendants. These two contiguous areas have for the past century and a half been sharply set off from one another in terms of class status, population characteristics, housing, and reputation. Furthermore, Firey observed, the two adjacent areas do not represent a "gradation" in accordance with the Burgess and Hoyt theories, but are in certain respects "polar opposites."

Firey also demonstrates that the distribution of income classes, based upon rentals, does not conform to the concentric-zone hypothesis. In the inner zone are both the highest and lowest rental areas. Similarly, the outermost zone includes low-rent and high-rent areas. "Not a single concentric zone reveals any homogeneity in its rental classes." [19] Firey found that the "sector" lying southwest of Boston was characterized both by upper-class and lower-class residents and could not therefore be considered homogeneous. The working-class towns in the metropolitan district do not conform to the sector theory, with the exception of the North Shore, but are distributed at random.

There is reason to believe that each theory fits certain types of cities more accurately than it does other types. Gilmore is of the opinion that the concentric zone hypothesis is more suited to commercial cities, where "most of the low income families may live in second-hand houses, originally built by the upper classes, and the older houses are likely to be closer to the central business section than the new." [20] This is due to the fact that the older houses were constructed when working-class people traveled mainly by walking—before the automobile age; hence they tended to be as close as possible to the business district. In manufacturing cities, according to Gilmore, the supply of second-hand houses may be insufficient to house the workers; hence a residential sector built especially for laborers.

An important recent study demonstrates that both the Hoyt and Burgess descriptions have some validity, but for different aspects of urban life.[21] This conclusion was drawn from a study of residential areas in four United States cities ranging in population between 200,000 and 500,000—Akron, Dayton, Indianapolis, and Syracuse. It was found that areas characterized by many apartment buildings, families with few young children, and families in which the wife works were most frequent near the city center and gradually declined in relative frequency toward

[19] *Ibid.*, p. 77.
[20] Harlan W. Gilmore, *Transportation and the Growth of Cities* (1953), p. 145.
[21] Theodore Anderson and Janice Egeland, "Spatial Aspects of Social Area Analysis," *American Sociological Review*, 26 (June, 1961), 392–98.

Ecological patterns. Above: The semicircular canal system is the dominant feature of Amsterdam. Facing page: Chicago, showing the grid system of streets and the massive downtown buildings typical of United States cities. Amsterdam was an important city even in medieval times, while Chicago is a nineteenth-century city, one factor explaining the differences in handling location on flat terrain near a large body of water. (Courtesy Netherlands Information Service and Cities Service Company [photograph by Anthony Linck].)

the periphery. In other words, these traits were distributed in a concentric zonal fashion. On the other hand, characteristics associated with the prestige of residential areas, as measured by the education and occupations of the inhabitants, were distributed in sector fashion, although the position of the sector varied from one city to another. In each of the four cities there was a segment of territory that extended from the center to the periphery and was inhabited with a higher proportion of people with at least a high school education and with nonmanual jobs than the rest of the city.

The multiple nuclei theory of Harris and Ullman has not been as thoroughly studied as the Burgess and Hoyt theories. It is, perhaps, the most flexible of the three. None of the three theories, however, appears to be complete and universal in its application. Each represents a particular perspective, a way of looking at the city at a particular time and place. Outside the United States, urban patterns often exhibit significant

differences.[22] However, even in a given country, ecological patterns may change as social values, income distribution, and technology change.

HUMAN ECOLOGY AND METROPOLITAN DEVELOPMENT

An illustration of emerging ecological relationships in the United States is provided by post-World War II metropolitan development. Although the ecological patterns of the metropolis have not been fully investigated, preliminary analysis suggests they are more related to the multiple nuclei than to the concentric zonal or sector patterns.[23]

The sheer extension of territory and population, which is one aspect of metropolitan development, has made it almost impossible to concentrate activities in a single center. More importantly, physical centralization of activities is no longer necessary as new means of transportation and communication—automobile, bus, truck, airplane, telephone—make distance less of an obstacle to contact and coordination. Decentralization in such diverse fields as entertainment, housing, manufacturing, and retailing is evident in the growth of motels, outdoor movies, "campus" factories, residential suburbs, and outlying shopping centers. The major

[22] See the section on foreign cities in Chapter 9.
[23] Sylvia F. Fava, "Some Implications of Metropolitan Development for Urban Ecology," paper presented at the annual meeting of the Eastern Sociological Society, April 8–9, 1961, New York City.

activity to remain centralized in the urban core is administration and office work, which merely underscores the point that various activities no longer have to be located at the center in order to be effectively coordinated. Even offices, as in the case of insurance firms, have shown some tendency to decentralize.

A new factor in residential location is the relative gain in income among blue collar as opposed to white collar workers. Many blue collar families now own their own homes in the suburbs.

The increased role of planning and the conscious control of urban location have also contributed to the rise of subcenters in the metropolis. Government and private enterprise have created civic centers, cultural centers, and industrial parks which, typically, replace districts of more varied land use. Land use is also increasingly controlled by zoning laws, urban renewal and slum clearance developments, large-scale highway programs, master plans, subsidized housing, and various laws and financial arrangements designed to encourage specific kinds of building or occupance or discourage others. The impact of these laws has not been assessed, but it seems likely they are often disruptive to any preexisting zonal or sector pattern.

SELECTED BIBLIOGRAPHY

BOOKS

Alihan, Milla, *Social Ecology: A Critical Analysis*. New York: Columbia University Press, 1938.

Carson, Rachel, *Silent Spring*. Boston: Houghton Mifflin, 1962.

Dice, Lee, *Man's Nature and Nature's Man: The Ecology of Human Communities*. Ann Arbor, Mich.: University of Michigan Press, 1955.

Duncan, Otis Dudley, "Human Ecology and Population Studies," in P. Hauser and O. D. Duncan (eds.), *The Study of Population*. Chicago: University of Chicago Press, 1959.

Hawley, Amos, *Human Ecology*. New York: Ronald Press, 1950.

Hoyt, Homer, *The Structure and Growth of Residential Neighborhoods in American Cities*. Washington, D. C.: Federal Housing Administration, 1939.

Park, Robert, *Human Communities: The City and Human Ecology*. Glencoe, Ill.: The Free Press, 1952.

Quinn, James, *Human Ecology*. New York: Prentice-Hall, 1950.

Theodorson, George (ed.), *Studies in Human Ecology*. Parts I and II. Evanston, Ill.: Row, Peterson, 1961.

Willhelm, Sidney, *Urban Zoning and Land-Use Theory*. New York: The Free Press of Glencoe, 1962.

ARTICLES

Duncan, Otis Dudley, and Leo Schnore, "Cultural, Behavioral and Ecological Perspectives in the Study of Social Organization," *American Journal of Sociology,* LXV (September, 1959), 132–46.

Firey, Walter, "Sentiment and Symbolism as Ecological Variables," *American Sociological Review,* 10 (April, 1945), 140–48.

Form, William, "The Place of Social Structure in the Determination of Land Use: Some Implications for a Theory of Urban Ecology," *Social Forces,* 32 (May, 1954), 317–23.

Rodwin, Lloyd, "The Theory of Residential Growth and Structure: Evaluation of Prevailing Theories," *Appraisal Journal,* 18 (July, 1950), 295–317.

Schmid, Calvin, E. H. McCannell, and M. D. Van Arsdol, "The Ecology of the American City," *American Sociological Review,* 23 (August, 1958), 393–401.

Wirth, Louis, "Human Ecology," *American Journal of Sociology,* 50 (March, 1945), 483–88.

Ecological Segregation

Ecological segregation stems from the fact that city people, like others, differ from one another. They are also interdependent. In the competition both for status and for desirable spatial location in the city these differences and interdependences enter into determining what space people consider desirable and into their ability to obtain it. The result is ecological segregation—the clustering together in the same residential area of people with similar characteristics.

THE NATURE OF SEGREGATION

From the ecological point of view, the most important differences and interdependencies are those that affect large numbers of people, for these will have the greatest impact on the spatial structure of the city. Therefore, the differences and interdependencies embodied in the socio-economic structure will have the greatest relevance to understanding ecological segregation. Differences of social class, religion, ethnic origin, and race are among the major characteristics toward which social attitudes, beliefs, and customs are directed. It is no accident that our major types of residential area follow these lines—Gold Coast and exclusive suburb, Black Belt and Chinatown, Little Italy and Swedetown, and so on. The division of labor reflects the most important interdependencies; the network of reciprocity is long and often indirect and unnoticed in all of its ramifications.

The division of labor and social differences often reinforce one another. A given racial or ethnic or class group is associated, sometimes by preference and sometimes by social pressure, with a particular occupation— Negro laborers, Chinese laundrymen, low-caste leather workers, Italian

118

fruit-sellers, white Ivy League executives of corporations or banks, Jewish small businessmen or professionals. Occupying these positions has, in turn, repercussions for income, power, and social standing, as well as other factors differentiating groups from one another.

VOLUNTARY AND INVOLUNTARY SEGREGATION

Some of the differences and interdependencies between themselves and others are quite clear to people and provide a basis for action, while others are not. Hence, some aspects of ecological segregation are matters of choice or planning, while others are unplanned or involuntary. Voluntary segregation occurs when the individual, on his own initiative, seeks to live with others of his own kind and apart from those who are different in some fundamental (to him) respect. Motives may vary from one individual, group, or area to another. Certain individuals may elect to live with others of similar characteristics because of the prestige such residence accords them; some may choose to live in a segregated area because such residence may afford them a sense of security or otherwise provide emotional satisfactions not attainable elsewhere; others may select such a residential location because they know or imagine that they are not welcome in areas occupied by persons who are different. These reasons are not mutually exclusive; any or all of them may apply to a particular individual.

This is the psychologically positive aspect of segregation. It emphasizes preference and not prejudice. If, however, those identified with a particular group regard with hostility or fear another group whose members are different in certain respects, it is unlikely they will choose the same residential neighborhoods unless forced to do so by economic or other circumstance. The tensions involved in living among people whom one dislikes or considers inferior, or the anxieties provoked by the awareness that one is not wanted in a particular neighborhood or district, are sufficient to provide the basis for much residential separation reflecting human differences.

It may happen, however, that an individual has neither preferences nor prejudices with respect to race, religion, nationality, or other attributes, but he may, for some reason, gravitate to a neighborhood occupied by others who *do* cherish strong preference or prejudices. Thus, whatever may be his motivations and values, he is a contributing party to the principle of ecological segregation.

Involuntary segregation may occur in two ways. An individual or family may be required by law or custom, or both, to reside in a designated area, or may be prevented from living in an area occupied by others who are different in certain respects.

Involuntary segregation also occurs through the operation of impersonal economic forces. Individuals or families tend to seek their own economic level; ordinarily they live in areas where they can *afford* to live, not necessarily where they would like to live. Obviously a family with a two-thousand-dollar-a-year income cannot live on the Gold Coast or Park Avenue whatever might be their aspirations. They are forced by sheer economic circumstances to confine their choice to areas occupied by people of middle or low incomes.

These two forms of involuntary segregation are likewise not mutually exclusive. An individual or family may be forced by custom, law, *and* economic circumstances to live in, or apart from, a particular district. Economic pressure sometimes becomes a technique for enforcing segregation. An individual or family forced by economic circumstances to reside in a particular area might have selected the area anyway, irrespective of economic considerations.

LIMITED SEGREGATION

The process of segregation does not necessarily result in the formation of areas inhabited solidly by persons of a certain race or culture. More often than not there is a mixture, particularly on the fringes. Recent studies of 12 of the largest cities in the United States showed that from 22 to 78 per cent of the white population lived in census tracts that were classified as "mixed"; that is, from one to 49 per cent of the population was nonwhite.[1] It is probably true that some of these areas were "mixed" because they were in the process of changing to predominantly Negro occupancy.

One of the Seattle districts, designated by Hatt as a "polyethnic" area, showed a considerable variety of ethnic types living side by side: Gentile whites, Jews, Chinese, Japanese, Filipinos, and Negroes.[2] The mixed block with no single type occupying more than half the dwelling units was the most frequent pattern. Blocks with a preponderance of a single type were not necessarily contiguous, indicating that whole blocks, or even groups of blocks, were skipped by the population in the course of residential changes.

Similarly, a study of an Italian area in Boston showed that only 42 per cent of the population were first- or second-generation Italians, 10 per cent were first-generation Jewish immigrants, 9 per cent were of Polish background, 8 per cent of "other Slavic" background, 5 per cent were of Irish ancestry, and the remaining quarter was distributed among a variety of ethnic groups.[3]

---

[1] Davis McEntire, *Residence and Race* (1960), Table 6.

[2] Paul Hatt, "Spatial Patterns in a Polyethnic Area," *American Sociological Review,* 10 (June, 1945), 352–56.

[3] Herbert Gans, *The Urban Villagers* (1962), pp. 8–10.

SEGREGATION AND SOCIAL RELATIONS

The segregation of population, whether voluntary or involuntary, may affect the entire fabric of relationships between people in a community. People who do not associate intimately with each other because they differ in certain fundamental respects tend to live apart from those who are different. Obviously this segregation does not always occur, but there is a tendency in that direction.

Similarly, social isolationism is reinforced by spatial isolationism; the more people are spatially segregated, the less likely are they to come into intimate contact with each other. At least the possibilities of close relationships on the basis of social equality are greatly reduced. Instead, contacts tend to be formalized, confined principally to the market place or the work situation. People who work together on the job, or who have contacts of a strictly economic character, may live in entirely different social and ecological worlds.

An example is provided by Mack in an ecological analysis of an industrial port located on Lake Erie.[4] During the rapid industrial expansion of the city in the late nineteenth century there was a heavy influx of Swedes and Finns, who became collectively categorized as "the Swedes." Their residential locality, called "Swedetown," was situated near the docks and railroad repair yards. Around the turn of the century a heavy influx of Italians occurred. Since the Italians also found employment at the docks and yards, they initiated an invasion of "Swedetown," which ended in complete succession, although the original name was still retained in common usage. The "Swedes," considering the Italians their social inferiors, moved into another area which came to be known as "the Harbor." These two areas, as Mack points out, are not only ecologically separate but are also distinct sociological communities, membership in which is determined by the ethnic label. If one is a Swede (or Finn), he cannot become a member of the Italian community, and vice versa.

To the Swedes, any residence east of the dock-line tracks is looked down on as being "Dago" or "Wop." The Italians, on the other hand, define residences on the west side of the same dividing line as being undesirable, since they are not "in the community" but among the "dumb-Swedes," a popular compound on the Italian side of the line.[5]

Now this pattern of social and ecological segregation is carried over into work relationships in the same city. Both Italians and Swedes are

[4] Raymond W. Mack, "Ecological Patterns in an Industrial Shop," *Social Forces,* 32 (May, 1954), 351–56.
[5] *Ibid.,* p. 352.

employed in the railroad car repair shop. By agreement with management, only Italians are assigned to light repair work and only Swedes to heavy repair work in which railroad cars may be completely dismantled and rebuilt. The "lights" and "heavies" work on different sides of the yard. They are two distinct groups, with different tests of admittance, different roles, and different norms of relations among the members. They are kept apart not so much by ethnic differences as such as by prevailing prejudices and stereotypes. The Italians regard the Swedes as "dull, stupid, stolid work-horses"; the Swedes consider the Italians as "flighty, erratic workers" and look upon themselves as "real men," steady and capable.

The social distance between these two groups is especially interesting because they have much in common in terms of minority ethnic status, blue collar occupation, and economic position. An even greater social distance may exist between other residentially segregated groups.

RESIDENTIAL SEGREGATION AND GOVERNMENT

Governmental actions affect residential segregation in several ways. Sometimes these actions are deliberately designed to do so. They illustrate the role of conscious directed planning in the ecological process. The efforts are not always successful, thus serving as reminders that ecological segregation is also the result of complex interrelationships, many of which are imperfectly understood. For example, while government in the United States, at all levels, has acted to ban residential segregation by race, such segregation appears to be increasing because a larger proportion of the Negro population is concentrated in very large cities and because the low social and economic position of Negroes limits their range of residential choice. This means that the role of government must be understood in a larger context.

In 1948, the United States Supreme Court unanimously ruled that judicial enforcement of racially restrictive covenants was unconstitutional. Hence, while restrictive real estate covenants based on exclusion of racial, religious, or ethnic groups are still widely used, they are not legally binding. Since that time there has been a spreading movement by state and local governments to enact legislation which prohibits racial and religious discrimination in various parts of the housing market. In the early stages, the trend was to ban discrimination in housing that received government aid, such as public housing or housing covered by federal government mortgages. In recent years, however, the trend has been to extend the prohibitions to the general housing market, that is, to homes that are privately financed. By mid-1963, 18 states and 55 cities had adopted legislation banning discrimination in housing. Of these, 11 states and 7 cities (including New York, Philadelphia, Pittsburgh, and Toledo) had barred discrimination in private housing.[6]

The legal unenforceability of discriminatory restrictive covenants and the increasing number of state and municipal laws banning housing discrimination in various forms have led to the development of new devices for housing discrimination. Chief among them is the "private club" or corporation to which an individual must be admitted before he can purchase property in a given area.[7]

Sometimes governmental action with respect to housing segregation is unintended. Subsidized housing in the form of "projects" for low income groups or tax-abated developments for middle income groups were designed to provide more and better housing. But the imposition of income and other restrictions may increase residential segregation along these lines. The percentage of public housing occupied by Negroes in New York City rose from 28 per cent in 1951 to 39 per cent in 1957. This increase is at least partly the result of income restrictions, for, in 1957, Negroes occupied 23 per cent of the city-aided housing units with family income limits of $4,000, but less than 7 per cent of those with income limits of $6,900. Similarly, Puerto Ricans occupied 24 per cent of the units with the lower income limits and less than one per cent of the units with the higher income limits.[8] Urban renewal programs, often involving wholesale demolition of neighborhoods, may disperse voluntarily segregated groups. For example, the West End in Boston, a low income Italian area, was razed in the urban redevelopment program and replaced by luxury apartment buildings.[9] Extensive government activity in the housing field is relatively recent and its precise impact is still not known.

In the United States, government policies are directed at reducing housing segregation based on arbitrary racial and religious restrictions, but in some countries, policies may be directed at keeping certain groups residentially separate. In cities of South Africa the African and colored peoples, as well as those of Asian background, are required by law to reside in designated sections of the city. Laws are passed and enforced by the white population and are a part of a general policy of segregation called *Apartheid*.[10] About half of the urban Africans live in "controlled" districts. Wherever the law operates to the disadvantage of white resi-

---

[6] *State Statutes and Local Ordinances and Resolutions Prohibiting Discrimination in Housing and Urban Renewal Operations.* Washington, D. C.: Office of the Administrator, Housing and Home Finance Agency, revised December, 1961; and *Trends in Housing,* bimonthly publication of the National Committee against Discrimination in Housing, New York City.

[7] N. C. Belth (ed.), *Barriers: Patterns of Discrimination against Jews* (Anti-Defamation League of B'nai Brith, 1958), especially the selections by Arnold Forster and Sol Rabkin.

[8] Oscar Handlin, *The Newcomers* (1959), Appendix, p. 146.

[9] Gans, *op. cit.,* p. 281ff.

[10] Leo Marquard, *Peoples and Policies of South Africa* (1951), pp. 48–49.

dents, there is a tendency to overlook its enforcement, as evidenced by the presence, in the city of Johannesburg, of at least 50,000 African domestic servants living in white quarters. Durban, on the east coast of South Africa, grew in a few decades from 60,000 to over a half-million, and in the process penetration and encirclement of European areas by the native population and by Asian groups occurred.[11] In order to achieve thorough racial segregation, plans were drawn in 1952 for the displacement of 55,000 Indians and 80,000 Africans. The plans are slowly being implemented, although with some modification, and the difficulties encountered—cost, political pressure, humanitarian considerations, industrial inefficiency, and sheer physical effort—indicate the problems of compulsory segregation.

NATURAL AREAS

Ecological clusters resulting from the tendency of individuals to reside in areas occupied by people of similar racial, cultural, or economic status have been termed *natural areas*. The term "natural" suggests that such ecological configurations are the outcome of unregulated competition and conflict rather than the products of deliberate design. Unfortunately, the term carries the implication that segregation is strictly unplanned. A segregated area may be, in part or in whole, a product of design. For example, a modern trend in the housing field is the development of whole communities, often complete with shopping and recreation facilities and schools. Stuyvesant Town and Peter Cooper Village in New York City are downtown apartment examples, while the Levittowns on Long Island and in Pennsylvania are suburban examples. As noted earlier, various government activities, such as antidiscrimination legislation, housing subsidies, zoning, and urban renewal, also affect residential segregation.

The size, shape, and location of so-called natural areas may be influenced by physical conditions. But geographic factors appear to *limit* rather than *determine* the formation of such areas or other ecological phenomena. A body of water or a precipitous cliff, for example, may define the boundaries or limit the size of a natural area, or even prevent the segregation of people, but such geographic conditions could hardly bring a natural area into existence. Ecological segregation and the formation of natural areas are, rather, essentially *social* in character. If in a particular city high-income people cluster together in elevated districts and the poor reside in the valleys, the determinants for such distributive patterns lie in the values of the people themselves. Geographic factors involved in segregation must therefore be interpreted within the context of the value systems of a particular community or society.

[11] Leo Kuper, *et al.*, *Durban: A Study in Racial Ecology* (1958).

MAJOR TYPES OF SEGREGATED AREAS
IN CITIES OF THE UNITED STATES

The principal types of segregated areas in American cities reflect the major differences customarily recognized and acted on in American society—race, ethnic affiliation, and occupation—and underscore the fundamental point that ecological segregation is not random or the result of merely personal preferences and individual motivation, but also reflects the position of groups in a network of interdependence, some of whose ramifications may be obscure to the participating individuals. It is for this reason that human ecology always involves social organization as well as social psychology.

Racial and occupational segregation will be covered in this section and ethnic segregation in the next chapter.

SEGREGATION OF NEGROES IN AMERICAN CITIES

As a minority group, Negroes in the United States occupy the lowest social and economic position. Residentially, they are also the most highly segregated group in American cities, for both voluntary and involuntary reasons. Their segregation is complicated by the high visibility of skin color and by the false impression that Negroes are somehow innately inferior to other races. Although many people oppose racial segregation, the weight of the social structure and the predominance of prejudiced values still tend to support it. Negroes still encounter much difficulty in acquiring or renting property in areas not previously entered by nonwhites, and they also have difficulty in finding banks to accept their mortgages. Public opinion is passively or actively opposed to their entry in many neighborhoods, and various methods, sometimes subtle, sometimes violent, are used to discourage them.

In a study of 12 large United States cities in 1950, the proportion of the Negro population living in census tracts that were predominantly Negro (at least half of the population nonwhite) ranged from a low of 26 per cent in San Francisco to a high of 81 per cent in Chicago. Most frequently, 65 per cent or more of the colored population lived in such segregated tracts: Detroit, 74 per cent; St. Louis, 76 per cent; Atlanta, 70 per cent; Birmingham, 75 per cent; New York City, 68 per cent.[12]

More precise statistical measures, applied on a block, rather than census tract, basis, also revealed high levels of Negro segregation from 1940 to

[12] McEntire, *op. cit.*, Table 6.

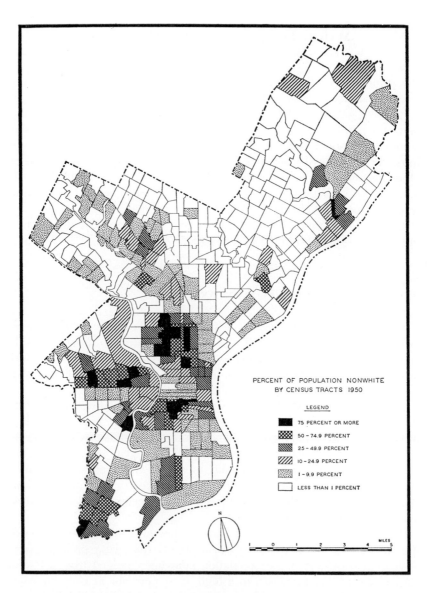

PERCENT OF POPULATION NONWHITE
BY CENSUS TRACTS 1950

LEGEND

■ 75 PERCENT OR MORE

▨ 50 - 74.9 PERCENT

▨ 25 - 49.9 PERCENT

▨ 10 - 24.9 PERCENT

▨ 1 - 9.9 PERCENT

□ LESS THAN 1 PERCENT

Figure 11. This map of the city of Philadelphia, showing nine distinct areas of nonwhite concentration of population, reflects clearly the typical northern pattern of one major segregated area and several minor ones. SOURCE: Davis McEntire, *Residence and Race* (Berkeley: University of California Press, 1960). Reprinted by permission.

Metropolitan segregation—the contrast between the heavily Negro core cities and "lilywhite" suburbs—is perhaps the most significant aspect of current racial segregation. Estimates are that by 1975 nonwhites will constitute 21 to 28 per cent of the population in the central cities of large metropolitan areas, and by the mid-1980's will constitute one-quarter to one-half the population in at least 10 of the largest central cities.[22] One observer has commented, "The city can be saved only if it faces up to the fact that 'the urban problem' is in large measure a Negro problem."[23]

AMERICAN CHINATOWNS

During the latter part of the nineteenth century, according to Lee, many Chinese settled in American cities, mainly on the West Coast and in the Rocky Mountain area.[24] Since women were relatively scarce in these cities, some of the Chinese men performed "women's work," that is, cooking, washing, and domestic service. Others were employed as laborers in lumbering, railroad construction, and mining. The majority were located in smaller cities. As technological and economic changes reduced their occupational security, they tended to migrate to metropolitan centers in which there was a demand for their services. The result has been that Chinatowns in small cities have either declined in population or disappeared altogether. More and more the Chinese are being concentrated in great metropolises like Chicago, New York, and San Francisco. In 1960, 96 per cent of the Chinese in the United States were classified as urban.[25]

The present-day Chinatown illustrates the principles of interdependence in the ecological community. According to Lee, Chinatown provides services which are demanded or needed, and in turn benefits by the economy of the metropolis. The Chinese hand laundry, in competition with steam laundries, can exist only in a large city where there are enough people who want their clothing laundered by hand. Similarly, Chinese restaurants serving exotic foods under novel conditions can compete with standard restaurants and lunch counters only when there is sufficient demand for this kind of special service. Such a demand exists only in the large city, especially in the city where there are many tourists and other transients unable to secure these services at home. Thus, the modern Chinatown has become something of a tourist attraction, featuring special foods, services, and works of Oriental craftsmanship. But it is more than a mere tourist

[22] Morton Grodzins, "Metropolitan Segregation," *Scientific American,* 197 (October, 1957); and McEntire, *op. cit.,* pp. 21–24.

[23] Charles E. Silberman, "The City and the Negro," *Fortune,* LXV (March, 1962), p. 89; see also James Conant's *Slums and Suburbs: A Commentary on Schools in Metropolitan Areas* (1961).

[24] Rose Hum Lee, "The Decline of Chinatowns in the United States," *American Journal of Sociology,* 54 (March, 1949), 422–32.

[25] *Statistical Abstract of the United States, 1962,* p. 29.

mecca. In a real sense it is a community, a miniature society having a distinctive organization and style of living.

The nature of the interdependence between Chinese groups and the rest of the urban community may be changing. At least this is suggested by the tendency of the Chinese, since 1940, to move from Chinatowns to more dispersed locations in the city. It may be that, like other immigrant groups, as they become assimilated into American society they also becomes less concentrated residentially. Another reason is that the large Chinatowns, for all their exotic character, are slums, and many Chinese desire better housing. In 1940, 70 per cent of San Francisco's Chinese lived in Chinatown, but by 1950 only 40 per cent were living there.[26] Similarly, New York's Chinatown contained half of New York's Chinese in 1940 but not quite a third in 1950. However, an opposing trend should also be noted. The possibility exists that the influx of refugees from Hong Kong, admitted under a presidential order in May, 1962, may temporarily offset the exodus from American Chinatowns.

RESIDENTIAL SEPARATION OF OCCUPATIONAL GROUPS

The social and economic differences between occupational groups are reflected in the tendency for people in the same broad occupational group to cluster together residentially. A study of the 22-county New York metropolitan region employed an index of residential specialization to measure the degree to which an occupational group's residential distribution differed from the overall distribution of residences.[27] The metropolitan region was also divided into four rings differing in distance and accessibility to Manhattan, which was the first "ring." The index of residential specialization was applied to determine whether a given occupational group's homes were over- or underrepresented in any of the rings or were the same as that of homes in general.

It was found that the homes of those in upper white collar occupations (professionals and managers) were overrepresented in the third ring, the suburban commuting zone, about 20 to 30 miles from Manhattan. To some extent, the upper white collar groups were also overrepresented in the high rent areas of Manhattan. The lower white collar groups (clerks and sales personnel) were concentrated in the second ring, the New York city boroughs and one New Jersey county that borders Manhattan. This area is served by subway and elevated train and has many apartment and attached single-family houses. The blue collar workers were overrepresented in the fourth or outer ring, a diverse area beyond the regular commuting distance, composed of industrial satellite communities, spacious

---

[26] McEntire, *op. cit.*, p. 45.

[27] Edgar M. Hoover and Raymond Vernon, *Anatomy of a Metropolis* (1959), pp. 154–76.

Figure 13. Ecological segregation based on occupation. It is clear from this chart, based on Wichita, Kansas, data, that professionals and laborers tend to be ecologically separated in the city. SOURCE: Donald O. Cowgill, *A Pictorial Analysis of Wichita.*

exurbs, and resorts. Within the fourth ring, subgroups of blue collar workers were further segregated residentially—craftsmen and foremen preferred suburban-like communities while semiskilled workers and laborers tended to live in industrial sections. Finally, the service workers (domestics, barbers, elevator operators, and the like) were heavily concentrated in the first ring, Manhattan itself. Obviously, people of every occupation lived in almost every type of area, but these were the main features of residential specialization.

The study noted that the differences in residential location of the various occupational groups were related to, but by no means completely explained by, differences in their incomes and by their choice of homes close to the areas in which they worked. A value element was also involved: In the New York area, for example, rather than use their high incomes to live in Manhattan, where a large proportion of their members work, upper white collar groups evidently prefer low density areas of private homes and are willing to accept a long commuting trip to attain them.

A study of the Chicago metropolitan area also examined the tendency of the various occupational groups to live apart from one another.[28] Various measures of segregation were applied to the residential distribution of eight occupational groups over the census tracts and 104 zone-sector parts of metropolitan Chicago. One of the major findings was that the top and bottom occupational groups are the most residentially segregated from the rest of the labor force and from one another. Segregation indexes are highest for the professionals and for laborers, and gradually decline toward the center of the occupational hierarchy. "This finding suggests that residential segregation is greater for those occupational groups with clearly defined status than for those groups whose status is ambiguous." [29]

Like the New York metropolitan study, the Chicago study also found that while differences in income among the occupational groups accounted for some of the variation in residential distribution, it did not account for all. The most interesting case is that of the clerical workers who were found to have generally lower income levels than the craftsmen and foremen group. Nevertheless, the clerical workers tended to live among other white collar groups rather than among blue collar groups. Social prestige and community of interest were evidently more determinative of residence than income. The study also shed some light on even more underlying factors in the ecological process. Dissimilarity in residential distribution was more highly associated with the occupational status of one's father than with one's own present socioeconomic status. Further investigation is needed, but this finding suggests that one's taste in housing and resi-

[28] Otis Dudley Duncan and Beverly Duncan, "Residential Distribution and Occupational Stratification," *American Journal of Sociology*, LX (March, 1955), 493–503.
    [29] *Ibid.,* p. 497.

dential areas is formed relatively early and exerts an influence apart from one's present educational attainments and economic position.

SEGREGATION AND THE BURGESS ZONAL PATTERN

The New York and the Chicago studies provide a test of the Burgess zonal pattern; both tend to confirm it. The New York metropolitan region study was not directed at examining Burgess' theory but, nevertheless, shows rings 1, 2, and 3 (the limits of the urban territory encompassed by Burgess' five zones) inhabited by progressively higher occupational levels. The Chicago study included examination of the degree to which the residences of various occupational groups were concentrated toward the core of the city and found that the concentration was in accord with Burgess' zonal pattern; that is, the higher the occupational level the greater the tendency to locate away from the center.[30] However, the Duncans also found evidence that sector distributions modified the zonal tendencies.

Racial segregation also approximates the concentric zonal pattern. This is particularly clear in noting the tendency for Negroes to be increasingly segregated in the central city and whites to locate on the outskirts of the city or in the suburbs beyond the corporate city limits.

SEGREGATION IN OTHER COUNTRIES

BRAZIL

In Bahia, Brazil, according to Pierson, residential segregation exists as a carry-over from early days in which the Europeans settled on the elevated ridges and the Africans, either slaves or propertyless freedmen, were assigned to the valleys.[31] This pattern persists to a considerable degree, with the whites and the lighter "mixed-bloods" occupying the more attractive and more healthful ridges of the city, and the blacks and darker mixed-bloods being located in the low-lying areas and in the less accessible sections on the outskirts of the city. What appears to be strictly racial segregation, in the opinion of Pierson, is also segregation by economic and educational status, since color and economic class in this city tend to coincide. But the situation is fluid, and as darker residents, blacks or mestizos, move up the economic and educational scale they are not denied admittance to predominantly white areas, as often occurs in the United States. Areas settled mainly by mestizos are somewhat intermediate between the European sections and those occupied by blacks. There is,

---

[30] *Ibid.*, pp. 499–500.   [31] Donald Pierson, *Negroes in Brazil* (1942), pp. 20–25.

indeed, considerable overlapping as blacks or mestizos become economically able to move into areas occupied by whites.

In one respect the Bahia pattern of segregation differs sharply from the
form which racial segregation usually assumes in cities of the United
States. In Bahia, the outskirts of the city as well as the valleys are populated mainly by blacks and darker mixed-bloods who are also low in the
economic scale. In fact, says Pierson, Bahia somewhat resembles a "medieval city surrounded by African villages." [32] In the United States, Negroes and other racial minorities have tended to be centrally located in
the so-called area of transition.

India

Segregation in Indian cities reflects differences in caste and occupation as well as in religion and economic status. Among the Hindus there
is a strong tendency for members of the same caste to seek their own
communal level in residential locations. One may find areas occupied
mainly or exclusively by Brahmins, the highest caste; areas occupied solely
by scheduled or "untouchable" castes; or areas occupied by other castes
holding intermediate positions in the social hierarchy. Segregation on
the basis of caste automatically means segregation on the basis of religion
to the extent that Hindus are segregated from other religious groups. In
the Muslim group there is an equally strong tendency toward residential
segregation. Most of the larger Indian cities have fairly large Muslim
populations which reside, for the most part, in distinct Muslim districts.
Christians also manifest the same tendency.

But economic segregation tends to cut across caste and religious lines;
hence, a tendency for wealthy or well-to-do families to live in fashionable
high income districts occupied by representatives of numerous castes or
religions. Thus a wealthy Brahmin may live alongside a wealthy Parsee
or Christian or Muslim; and because of similar occupational, political,
intellectual, or social interests they may have more in common with each
other than with certain members of their own religious or caste group.
Segregation in Indian cities is essentially voluntary; certainly it is not
legally compulsory, although the dictates of custom are strong, prejudices
do exist, and there is undoubtedly some discrimination. An untouchable
moving into an area occupied by orthodox Brahmins would not be welcome, and possibly attempts would be made to keep him out or evict him
after he moved in. But since most untouchables are impoverished, economic as well as social factors determine where they can reside.

[32] *Ibid.*, p. 20.

ENGLAND

In Oxford, the residential distribution of occupational classes is the reverse of that found in most American cities. The highest ranking occupational groups are concentrated near the center of Oxford, and the occupational rank of the dominant residential group declines with distance from the city center. We cannot assume that the same distribution necessarily obtains in other English cities. Oxford was almost exclusively a university town until 1914, which may be an important factor in the central location of high-ranking occupational groups; more recently the municipal housing "estates" were built on the outskirts of the city, which may explain the outlying location of low-ranking occupational groups.[33]

In London, where thousands of Negroes from the West Indies and Africa have settled since the war, there are "no Harlems."[34] Only two streets are occupied almost entirely by a colored population, and even in areas where Negroes are heavily concentrated most of the population is white. The lack of residential segregation may be due to the relatively small numbers of Negroes in London, but, more importantly, it may merely reflect the lack of a crystallized position for Negroes in the British social structure. The permanent residency of Negroes is so recent in Great Britain that there are no laws banning racial restriction in housing, employment, or other activities, for in the past there had been so few nonwhites to discriminate against. It is unlikely that the British will enact discriminatory legislation in housing, places of public accommodation, and the like, but it will be revealing to study residential trends as the position of Negroes crystallizes in British society. Legal steps have already been taken to restrict the in-flow of migrants to Britain.

AFRICA

In South Africa, segregation of whites from other races is not solely a matter of choice; it is also a matter of law. There are, however, many types of voluntary segregation within the racial restrictions, one of the most important being between "Red"[35] and "School" natives. The "Red" group emphasize and practice traditional African forms of dress, religion, entertainment, and social customs, while the "School" group emphasize and practice European forms. Both groups consist of poor peasants who segregate from one another, both in the countryside and in cities. A re-

[33] Peter Collison and John Mogey, "Residence and Social Class in Oxford," *American Journal of Sociology*, LXIV (May, 1959), 599–605.

[34] Ruth Glass, *Newcomers: The West Indians in London* (1960), p. 40ff.

[35] This term has no political connotations; it probably arises from the "Red" custom of smearing the face with red ochre on festive occasions.

Famous districts in cities. Every large city has distinctive subareas, called "natural areas" by the early human ecologists, but some have achieved international fame. Above: A street in the Casbah of Algiers. Facing page: Fisherman's Wharf in San Francisco. (Courtesy Trans World Airlines, Inc.)

cent survey of East London, a South African city of over 100,000, showed that the Bantu had segregated themselves residentially along the "Red"– "School" division.[36] Most native districts in East London were either predominantly "Red" (two-thirds or more of the inhabitants "Red") or predominantly "School."

In most of the rest of Africa, racial segregation also occurs, but on a voluntary basis, influenced by other factors such as tribal affiliation, religion, and economic status. Investigation of Freetown, Sierra Leone, a former British colony and protectorate in West Africa, disclosed five major areas in the city, the vast majority of whose population are natives.[37] The high-status, good-quality residential district was occupied largely by Creoles (Christian, Europeanized descendants of nonlocal tribes; some Creoles have racially mixed ancestry). Two areas were inhabited largely by local tribal populations (most of whom are recent Muslim converts from paganism), one old, settled, and stable, the other unstable and with many newcomers. There are also two areas of mixed Creole-tribal occu-

[36] Philip Mayer, *Townsmen or Tribesmen* (1961), ch. 2, Appendix II, and end map.
[37] Michael Banton, *West African City* (1957), chs. 5 and 6.

pancy, one of which appears to be of higher economic status. In addition, there are also areas where the small European, Indian, and Lebanese populations concentrate separately from one another and the Africans.

The rapid changes in the political and social structure of African society will undoubtedly bring many changes in the segregative patterns of the cities. As more African countries become self-governed and as a greater variety of occupations are entered by natives, segregation based on race is likely to be overlaid by economic and other criteria. In several independent African states there are, for example, Europeans who, as civil servants or private employees, are the inferiors of the African elite in terms of power, prestige, and economic standing.[38]

THE JEWISH GHETTO

Among the notable examples of segregation in the Western world is the Jewish ghetto in predominantly non-Jewish cities. In most of the cities of continental Europe during the Middle Ages, and in some of them until the nineteenth century, Jews were required by law and custom to live in segregated districts. Forced back upon their own cultural resources, Jews within these ghettos developed a strong sense of spiritual kinship.

[38] See, for example, Hugh Smythe and Mabel Smythe, *The New Nigerian Elite* (1960).

In Warsaw, Frankfurt, Vienna, Prague, Moscow, and many other cities of Europe, the ghettos were unspeakably crowded, some existing behind walls to isolate the Jews from the remainder of the population. Dickinson believes that the walled ghetto originated in the western Mediterranean area during the Byzantine period and spread from there to Europe, especially eastern European cities.[39]

In the course of time, legal barriers supporting the ghettos were removed in most cities, but the ghetto as a well-established type of community life tended to survive, partly because of discrimination against the Jews, partly because of the attitudes that had developed among the Jews during their period of enforced segregation. Even in cities where segregation has never been legally enforceable, such as Paris, London, Chicago, and New York, many Jews have selected residential districts populated mainly by persons having similar cultural and religious interests. Wirth's analysis of two ghettos, those of Frankfurt and Chicago, is probably the best in sociological literature.[40]

MEASUREMENT OF SEGREGATION

A methodological problem confronting urban ecology is the objective measurement of segregation. Accordingly, a number of persons have addressed themselves to the problem of constructing a scale or index that will measure empirically the degree of segregation in any area. Such a measuring device, however intricate, is based on certain simple principles. If, for example, members of a particular group are distributed at random throughout a city, there is no segregation so far as the members of this group are concerned. Thus, if 10 per cent of the population of a given city are Negroes, and if 10 per cent of the residents in each section of that city are also Negroes, there is no segregation in the ecological meaning of the term, whatever might be the nature of their social relationships. But if they constituted 5 per cent of the residents of some areas, 50 per cent of other districts, and 100 per cent of still others, there is evidence of segregation.

Specific indexes

We shall summarize in nontechnical terms some of the attempts to develop a segregation index. The Jahn-Schmid-Schrag team, whose efforts were among the earliest, developed several indexes of segregation, using census tract units as the basis of their evaluations.[41]

[39] Robert E. Dickinson, *The West European City* (1951), p. 515.

[40] Louis Wirth, *The Ghetto* (1928); see also Amitai Etzioni, "The Ghetto: A Reevaluation," *Social Forces*, 37 (March, 1959), 255–62.

[41] J. Jahn, C. F. Schmid, and C. Schrag, "The Measurement of Ecological Segregation," *American Sociological Review*, 12 (June, 1947), 293–303.

The Cowgills have criticized this procedure on the grounds that a census tract is too large an area to provide the basis for a sensitive index.[42] They point out that a particular group might be represented in a census tract in the same proportion as in the population of the city as a whole, but that within the census tract there could be segregation.

Recently, the Cowgills have refined their index, which originally utilized block statistics in computing separate indexes for the various cities and suburban communities of the metropolis. The new index is still based on block statistics, but is now computed for an area approximating, but not identical to, the Standard Metropolitan Area.[43] The Cowgills made the change because they believe that segregation is a matter of the distribution of nonwhites in the total community, so that measuring separately any part of the community gives an incomplete picture. Under the separate indexes, many suburban cities had low segregation scores which gave false impressions of residential integration. "Thus, the important thing is not whether the few nonwhites living in Oak Park, Illinois, are segregated within Oak Park (this is what the separate index measures); the important thing is whether there is a tendency for nonwhites to avoid Oak Park entirely and to live in other parts of the large community, Chicago."

The Duncans have subjected segregation indexes, including the Jahn-Schmid-Schrag and Cowgill indexes, to searching criticism, describing a number of their mathematical inadequacies.[44] They suggest that the basic difficulty with such indexes may be that residential segregation is a multidimensional phenomenon which cannot be measured by a single index. They have developed a series of indexes to measure the various aspects of segregation, the most widely used being the index of dissimilarity.

The index of dissimilarity is a measure of the extent to which two distributions are nonoverlapping, that is, dissimilar. It is defined as one-half the sum of the absolute values of the differences between the respective distributions, taken area by area. In the hypothetical example below, the index is one-half of 40 per cent, or 20.[45] This means that 20 per cent of Group A would have to move to a different area in order to make their distribution identical to that of group B. The index may range from zero, meaning the distributions of the populations are identical, to 1.00 (or 100

[42] Donald O. Cowgill and Mary S. Cowgill, "An Index of Segregation Based on Block Statistics," *American Sociological Review*, 16 (December, 1951), 825–31.

[43] Donald Cowgill, "Segregation Scores for Metropolitan Areas," *American Sociological Review*, 27 (June, 1962), 400–412.

[44] Otis D. Duncan and Beverly Duncan, "A Methodological Analysis of Segregation Indexes," *American Sociological Review*, 20 (April, 1955), 210–17; and Duncan and Duncan, "Measuring Segregation," *American Sociological Review*, 28 (February, 1963), 33.

[45] Otis D. Duncan and Beverly Duncan, "Residential Distribution and Occupational Stratification," *American Journal of Sociology*, LX (March, 1955), 494. Reprinted by permission of the University of Chicago Press. Copyright 1955 by the University of Chicago.

AREA	A	B	DIFF.
1	10%	15%	5%
2	20	15	5
3	40	25	15
4	30	45	15
	100%	100%	40%

per cent), meaning the distributions are completely dissimilar, totally segregated. Indexes of dissimilarity may be computed for other than areal or racial distributions.[46]

RESULTS OF DIFFERENT INDEXES

As the techniques for measuring segregation become more sophisticated and presumably more descriptive of the true state of affairs, they reveal an increasingly higher level of segregation. Thus, the results of the Cowgill indexes are generally higher than the results of the Jahn-Schmid-Schrag index for the same cities. It should be remembered that the Cowgill index is based on census blocks while the other index is based on census tracts, and that the two indexes are arrived at by different formula. The results support Cowgill's contention that the Jahn-Schmid-Schrag index is not sufficiently sensitive to measure much of the actual segregation that exists and that it is therefore somewhat misleading.

Comparison of the two Cowgill indexes shows that the index for metropolitan areas is usually higher than the separate indexes for the component parts of the metropolitan area. The 78 component cities had separate indexes ranging from .000 to .972, but when these cities were combined into their 21 metropolitan areas the indexes ranged only from .662 to .929. The Duncan index appears to give results at least as high, and probably higher than the Cowgill metropolitan index. Taeuber's study, previously discussed (p. 127), used the Duncan index in measuring nonwhite residential segregation and found very high levels of segregation. The more refined the measure of segregation the more segregated American cities are disclosed to be.

SHEVKY-WILLIAMS-BELL METHOD

A trail-blazing methodological study in Los Angeles County by Shevky and Williams was designed to further the scientific development of an

---

[46] *Ibid.;* and Otis D. Duncan and Beverly Duncan, *The Negro Population of Chicago,* (1957), p. 57.

urban typology by combining the methods of ecology with other sociological procedures.[47] A later study by Shevky and Bell applied the approach to San Francisco Bay region data for 1940 and 1950 and elaborated many of the concepts and procedures.[48] The particular problem to which the studies addressed themselves was to develop a procedure for delineating "social areas," going beyond the methods commonly used in delineating "ecological areas." Such areas could, if carefully delineated, be used effectively as a basis for comparative studies, either of areas within a particular city or between different cities.

Three indexes were employed by Shevky, Williams, and Bell: (1) "social rank," representing measures of occupation and education; (2) "urbanization," representing measures of fertility, gainfully employed women, and single-dwelling or multiple-dwelling residence; and (3) "segregation," representing measures of ecological segregation of ethnic or racial groups. The census tracts of Los Angeles and San Francisco were then typed according to their characteristics as related to these three basic indexes.

We are concerned here particularly with the measures of segregation. Shevky, Williams, and Bell constructed several segregation indexes, only one of which will be described here.[49] This index showed the number of times the concentration (segregation) of a group was greater than the group's proportional representation in the total area. If members of a group were evenly distributed in all census tracts, the index, theoretically, would be 1. But if members were concentrated in certain tracts and not found in others, the index would be above 1.

A group was considered highly segregated if the index obtained was 3 or over; that is, if its average concentration was 3 or more times what it would be if distribution over the whole area were strictly at random. In the Los Angeles area five groups had index figures of 3 or over. These five groups were also found to be closely associated with one another; that is, Mexicans and Orientals were found in predominantly Negro tracts, Mexicans and Italians were found in Oriental tracts, and so on. Because of these interassociational characteristics another index was calculated for the five groups taken together.

The Shevky-Williams-Bell social area indexes have been widely tested and a number of studies have found them an accurate analysis of the major areal dimensions of American cities.[50] However, the social area ap-

[47] Eshref Shevky and Marilyn Williams, *The Social Areas of Los Angeles* (1949).

[48] Eshref Shevky and Wendell Bell, *Social Area Analysis* (1955).

[49] They were not always called indexes of segregation; one, for example, was called the index of social isolation.

[50] See the summary in Wendell Bell, "Social Areas: Typology of Urban Neighborhoods," in Marvin Sussman (ed.), *Community Structure and Analysis* (1959), pp. 61–92.

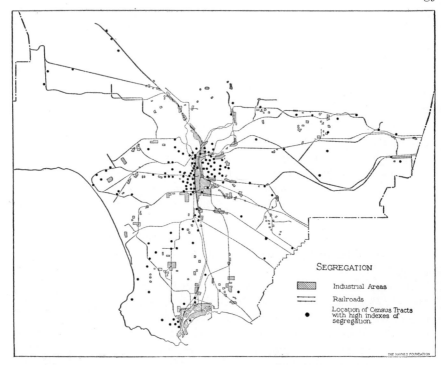

Figure 14. Ecological segregation in Los Angeles. Dots show location of census tracts having high indexes of segregation. Shaded portions are industrial areas, and lines are railroads. Note that tracts with high indexes tend to be located near industrial districts. SOURCE: Eshref Shevky and Marilyn Williams, *The Social Areas of Los Angeles* (Berkeley: University of California Press, 1949). Reprinted by permission.

proach has been criticized on both theoretical [51] and empirical grounds [52] and its status is still ambiguous.

OTHER APPROACHES NECESSARY

However valuable an empirical instrument may be for studying segregation quantitatively, it actually does not provide much insight into the social and psychological aspects of the phenomenon as an ongoing process. Segregated areas are ordinarily not static; the people who live in them are usually becoming *more* or *less* segregated. To understand the phe-

[51] Amos Hawley and Otis Dudley Duncan, "Social Area Analysis: A Critical Appraisal," *Land Economics,* 33 (November, 1957), 337–44.
[52] Maurice D. Van Arsdol, Jr., Santo Camilleri, and Calvin Schmid, "An Investigation of the Utility of Urban Typology," *Pacific Sociological Review,* 4 (Spring, 1961), 26–32.

nomenon of segregation, and particularly why segregation in any area may be increasing or decreasing, or even why it has occurred at all, we need to know a great deal about the status system of a society and about the values and behavior of people who are on different economic and social levels or who represent different cultural backgrounds. We can deal with people in the mass, as census data, and secure some understanding of the problem; but segregation is also an individual matter insofar as it is the person, not the mass, that is motivated (or not motivated) to reside in a particular area. Personalized data secured from individuals should illuminate the problem, but not much empirical evidence of this type is available.

SELECTED BIBLIOGRAPHY

BOOKS

Brush, John, "The Morphology of Indian Cities," in Roy Turner (ed.), *India's Urban Future*. Berkeley and Los Angeles: University of California Press, 1962.

Gans, Herbert, *The Urban Villagers*. New York: The Free Press of Glencoe, 1962.

Handlin, Oscar, *The Newcomers: Negroes and Puerto Ricans in a Changing Metropolis*. Cambridge, Mass.: Harvard University Press, 1959.

Kramer, Judith, and Seymour Levantman, *Children of the Gilded Ghetto*. New Haven: Yale University Press, 1961.

Kuper, Leo, *et al.*, *Durban: A Study in Racial Ecology*. New York: Columbia University Press, 1958.

Lieberson, Stanley, *Ethnic Patterns in American Cities*. New York: The Free Press of Glencoe, 1963.

McEntire, Davis, *Residence and Race*. Berkeley and Los Angeles: University of California Press, 1960.

Miner, Horace, *The Primitive City of Timbuctoo*. Princeton, N.J.: Princeton University Press, 1953.

Sjoberg, Gideon, *The Preindustrial City*, ch. 4. Glencoe, Ill.: The Free Press, 1960.

Theodorson, George (ed.), *Studies in Human Ecology*. Part III. Evanston, Ill.: Row, Peterson, 1961.

ARTICLES

Bascom, William, "Some Aspects of Yoruba Urbanism," *American Anthropologist*, 64 (August, 1962), 699–709.

Coughlin, Richard, "The Chinese in Bangkok: A Commercial-Oriented Minority," *American Sociological Review*, 20 (June, 1955), 311–16.

Duncan, Otis D., and Beverly Duncan, "Residential Distribution and Occupational Stratification," *American Journal of Sociology*, LX (March, 1955), 493–503.

Etzioni, Amitai, "The Ghetto: A Re-evaluation," *Social Forces,* 37 (March, 1959), 255–62.

Gist, Noel P., "The Ecology of Bangalore: An East-West Comparison," *Social Forces,* 35 (May, 1957), 356–65.

Grodzins, Morton, "Metropolitan Segregation," *Scientific American,* 197 (October, 1957), 33–41.

McElrath, Dennis, "The Social Areas of Rome," *American Sociological Review,* 27 (June, 1962), 376–90.

Sharp, Harry, and Leo Schnore, "The Changing Color Composition of Metropolitan Areas," *Land Economics,* 38 (May, 1962), 175–82.

Yuan, D. Y., "Voluntary Segregation: A Study of New York's Chinatown," *Phylon,* 24 (Third Quarter, 1963), 255–65.

Ecological Change,
Invasion, and Succession

EIGHT

The distinctive segregated subareas of a city are never permanent. In fact, the Burgess, Hoyt, Harris-Ullman, and other descriptions of city patterns are predicated on change.

Any of the five ecological elements described earlier may produce changes in the natural areas of the city. (1) *Environmental* conditions, such as flood or fire, may force rebuilding and relocation.[1] Such changes, at least on a large scale, occur relatively infrequently, but their impact, nevertheless, is immediate and far-reaching. (2) *Population* may change in numbers or composition. After World War II the general increase in the birth rate and the migration of large numbers of Negroes to cities had profound effects on both the character and availability of particular kinds of areas within the city. (3) *Technological* changes, particularly the automobile and the bus, alter the time-distance-cost factor with respect to many sections of the city. Housing advances render earlier home styles obsolete. (4) The *organization* of the community changes as a higher (or lower) general standard of living prevails. (5) *Social-psychological* values and attitudes may shift, as when ethnic groups improve their social standing or are assimilated. Or a new emphasis on leisure, the home, and "togetherness" may provide an added reason for suburban residence. The examples given do not exhaust the kinds of changes that may be initiated by these five elements.

Neighborhood changes stemming from each of these ecological ele-

[1] For an interesting example, see Robert W. Janes, "A Study of a Natural Experiment in Community Action," in Marvin Sussman (ed.), *Community Structure and Analysis* (1959), pp. 157-72.

147

ments will be apparent in the discussion in this chapter. The discussion will center first on the way in which certain groups become less segregated from one another as they remain longer in the city. Second, we shall deal with invasion-succession—the changes that occur in natural areas as they are "invaded" by new groups.

RESIDENTIAL DESEGREGATION

In this section we shall examine the tendency toward residential desegregation in the city. For a variety of reasons, groups that once tended to live together may begin to disperse residentially and become scattered in localities occupied by people having different characteristics. Ecological desegregation is a countertendency to the segregative processes, thus preventing the formation of permanently frozen homogeneous islands within the city. The operation of both segregative and desegregative processes leads to the constant forming and reforming of such islands—natural areas based on ethnic, religious, occupational, or other traits.

Decentralization of ethnic groups

The centrifugal shift of racial and ethnic groups in Chicago is revealed in a study by Cressey.[2] By computing the median distance from the city's center of nine groups in 1898 and again in 1930, Cressey compared the extent of centrifugal movement of these people, taking the groups as a whole. For all nine groups there had been a centrifugal shift, but the ethnics from northwest Europe—Swedes, Irish, and Germans—had moved farthest out, whereas the Negroes and Italians still remained fairly close to the center of the city. However, in 1898 the Swedes, Irish, and Germans were already three or more miles from the central point of the city; hence, the distance moved over the 32-year period was actually not much greater than the distance moved by some of the other groups. Since the ethnics from eastern and southern Europe arrived considerably later than those from northwestern Europe, and since they tended to settle first in central locations, it is not surprising that they were less widely diffused in 1930. Using a similar technique, Ford followed up the Cressey study, bringing the data to 1940.[3] There was a continuation, he found, of the scattering that Cressey had earlier observed—a movement toward the periphery of the city or even beyond it.

[2] Paul F. Cressey, "Population Succession in Chicago, 1898–1930," *American Journal of Sociology*, 44 (July, 1938), 59–68.
[3] Richard G. Ford, "Population Succession in Chicago," *American Journal of Sociology*, 56 (September, 1950), 156–60.

A still more recent study than Ford's, by Duncan and Lieberson, shows that the decentralization of ethnic groups in Chicago has continued.[4] This trend has been particularly obvious among those foreign-born groups most centralized in the earlier years—the "new" immigrant groups from southern and eastern Europe (Poland, Czeckoslovakia, Austria, the USSR, Lithuania, and Italy). In 1950 these groups were much more decentralized than in 1930, although they were still not as decentralized as the "old" immigrant groups (England and Wales, Ireland, Sweden, and Germany). The outward movement of immigrant groups is a general phenomenon in American society. A study of nine large cities in addition to Chicago— Boston, Buffalo, Cincinnati, Cleveland, Columbus, Philadelphia, Pittsburgh, St. Louis, and Syracuse—compared the degree of centralization of immigrant groups in 1930 and 1950.[5] In all these cities the groups had become less centralized over the 20-year period. The tendency for immigrant groups from the southern and eastern European countries to remain somewhat more centralized than those from northern and western Europe was also generally found.

Studies of immigrant groups in American cities indicate that many ethnic communities established in the nineteenth century have tended to disintegrate, whereas communities established by later migrations are still fairly distinct. But time alone is not the only factor. Earlier immigrants —Scandinavians, Germans, English, Irish, Dutch, Danes—actually set the cultural standards. Protestants for the most part, with strong addictions to cleanliness, godliness, and hard work, they arrived at a propitious time, just as the industrial and commercial expansion was getting in full sway. Most of them prospered.

After the turn of the century, many immigrants came from southern and eastern Europe—Poland, Italy, Greece, Bulgaria, Rumania, Czechoslovakia, Russia, Hungary. Predominantly Catholic or Greek Orthodox, they represented cultures often at considerable variance from the ones that had become firmly established. Arriving fairly late on the American scene, after most free agricultural land had been acquired by earlier immigrants, and after the industrial expansion was well under way, they crowded into the larger cities, establishing segregated cultural or ethnic islands in the midst of a polyethnic community. They were not only poor and ignorant, for the most part, but they arrived too late to become established on the ground floor of the great American boom. Hence they were at an economic as well as a cultural and psychological disadvantage.

If Italians or Poles are more segregated in American cities than, say, Germans or Swedes, the explanation is at least partly in terms of these historical and cultural differences.

---

[4] Otis Dudley Duncan and Stanley Lieberson, "Ethnic Segregation and Assimilation," *American Journal of Sociology*, 64 (January, 1959), 368–69.

[5] Stanley Lieberson, *Ethnic Patterns in American Cities* (1963), pp. 101–8.

DECENTRALIZATION, DESEGREGATION, AND ETHNIC ASSIMILATION

Decentralization of ethnic groups is of interest largely because of its relationship to their desegregation and assimilation into American society. The classic hypothesis is that as the immigrant groups move outward from the central areas of first settlement they also become less segregated from the native white population. The underlying dynamic of the relationship is assumed to be that they have become assimilated, that is, more like the native white population in terms of socioeconomic status, culture, and values. In other words, as the social distance between ethnic and native white populations has declined so, too, has the physical distance between them.

Decentralization is not necessarily associated with desegregation—a group may move out from the city center without becoming less segregated—but in the case of the immigrant groups, decentralization and desegregation generally go hand in hand. Table 8, listing the average indexes of residential segregation for 10 large American cities, shows that residential segregation between ethnic and native white groups decreased during the same period that the previously discussed studies by Cressey, Ford, and Duncan and Lieberson showed decentralization of ethnic groups. As with decentralization, the decreases in desegregation were more marked for the "new" immigrant groups, although these groups were still considerably more segregated than the "old" ones. The indexes in the table may be interpreted as percentages, as the following example indicates: In 1930 an average of 40.4 per cent of the total immigrant population in Boston would have had to move to another census tract in order to achieve the same residential distribution as native whites; in 1950, only 37.5 per cent would have had to move to another census tract.

Having established the linkage between ethnic decentralization and residential desegregation, we shall also find that decentralization is linked with assimilation. All the ecological models of the American city indicate that the residential zones or sectors gradually increase in socioeconomic status with distance from the city core. If these models are even roughly accurate, then movement toward the city periphery is an indication of assimilation in the sense of successful achievement according to prevailing standards. Lieberson tested the validity of Burgess' zonal model in the 10 cities in which he (Lieberson) also studied the distribution of ethnic groups.[6] He found that among the general population, higher socioeconomic status, as measured by professional occupations, was indeed associated with decentralized residence. When ethnic groups

[6] Lieberson, *op. cit.*, pp. 101–4.

TABLE 8

Average Indexes of Residential Segregation of "Old" and "New"
Ethnic Groups from the Native White Population, 1930–50

City and Groups		(Census Tract Basis) 1930	1950
Boston	Old	26.2	25.4
	New	54.6	49.6
	All	40.4	37.5
Buffalo	Old	30.0	28.4
	New	55.7	48.1
	All	42.8	38.2
Chicago	Old	27.7	27.8
	New	47.1	41.4
	All	39.4	35.9
Cincinnati	Old	28.4	28.7
	New	51.6	49.2
	All	41.0	39.9
Cleveland	Old	28.8	27.0
	New	51.8	45.7
	All	44.9	40.1
Columbus	Old	28.4	24.3
	New	57.2	46.3
	All	46.7	38.3
Philadelphia	Old	29.3	28.4
	New	52.9	48.0
	All	44.3	40.8
Pittsburgh	Old	25.1	24.1
	New	52.7	46.6
	All	42.6	38.4
St. Louis	Old	26.1	27.6
	New	61.9	43.4
	All	48.8	37.6
Syracuse	Old	33.2	27.2
	New	59.2	48.9
	All	47.6	39.3

SOURCE: Stanley Lieberson, *Ethnic Patterns in American Cities* (1963), Table 13.

151

decentralize (in these cities, at least), we may presume that they are likely to have moved up the socioeconomic ladder.

Assimilation is a complex concept, as Lieberson points out, although a useful criterion is the tendency for one group become more like another.[7] He used various measures of the degree to which ethnic groups are like the native white population—ability to speak English, citizenship, educational level, and intermarriage—and found that these factors (plus the independent factor of length of residence in the United States) were related to the degree of residential segregation. Again, the "new" immigrant groups scored more poorly on the measures of assimilation than the "old" groups.

DIFFUSION OF ITALIANS IN NEW HAVEN

In an analysis of the residential diffusion of Italians in New Haven, Myers has shown how ecological position and socioeconomic position are interrelated, how changes in one may be associated with changes in the other.[8] Using a "quota fulfillment index" to indicate changes, Myers calculated the extent of underrepresentation and overrepresentation of Italians in each of six ecological areas and in each of six occupational groups, and also showed the changes that had occurred for six census decades. A quota fulfillment index of 100 signifies that the proportion of Italians in a given area or occupational group is what would be expected if they were uniformly distributed. An index above or below 100 signifies that the Italians are overrepresented or underrepresented in the area or occupational class.

For the first three census periods (1890, 1900, and 1920), there were no Italians living in Area I, the fashionable residential district populated mainly by professionals and business executives. The quota fulfillment index was therefore 0. In 1920 the index was 3.39, and by 1940 had risen to 11.36. For Area II, occupied mainly by office workers and small business proprietors, the index had changed from 0 in 1890 to 18.86 in 1940. Obviously the Italians were moving into the "better" residential districts, many of them coming from Area VI, the poorest residential district. In 1890 the index for Area VI was 181.46; it increased to 230.88 in 1920, dropped to 222.74 in 1930, and to 205.96 in 1940. The decline in the index through the years indicates a tendency for the Italians to move from this area. In all the other areas representing higher socioeconomic levels there was a tendency for the index to increase.

Using the same procedure, Myers found that the quota fulfillment for unskilled workers showed a tendency to decline after 1920, whereas indices

[7] *Ibid.*, pp. 7–13.

[8] Jerome K. Myers, "Assimilation to the Ecological and Social Systems of a Community," *American Sociological Review*, 15 (June, 1950), 367–72.

for the higher occupational levels tended to increase. In 1890, for example, the index for professionals was 0, but by 1940 it was 43.90. Although the Italians were still underrepresented among the professionals, there nevertheless had been a pronounced movement into the professional occupations. On the other hand, the index for unskilled laborers in 1910 was 201.02, but by 1940 it had declined to 123.90. In all the occupational levels above that of unskilled workers there had been an increase in the representation of Italian personnel.

Movement up the occupational ladder was therefore associated with ecological diffusion of the New Haven Italians. Upward occupational mobility is often accompanied by residential movement from areas considered socially or physically undesirable. Insofar as upward occupational mobility means higher incomes, those who move to higher occupational levels are in a financial position to pay for better housing. Myers points out, interestingly enough, that some Italians remain in Area VI, even though they have moved up the occupational scale, preferring to remain in the area for sentimental or other reasons. Thus, there is no one-to-one relationship between occupational and ecological mobility, but only a high correlation.

The diffusion of the Italians in New Haven provides an almost classic case of the relationship between physical and social movement. On the basis of a number of ecological studies and of general knowledge of American cities, there has been rather widespread acceptance of the theory that ecological diffusion is associated with the assimilation of ethnic groups and that such diffusion tends to proceed from the center to the periphery of the city. However accurately this theory may apply to the ecological history of certain cultural groups, it does not fit the ecological facts of all.

There are exceptions to the linkage between decentralization, desegregation, and assimilation of ethnic groups. The Dutch in Chicago are an example of a group whose ecological position indicating decentralization is neither a result of movement from the center of the city nor associated with desegregation.[9] In the late nineteenth century, the Dutch settled heavily in an area about 12 miles from the center of Chicago where they were close to their jobs as farmers or railroad construction workers. Their high decentralization index is the result of the city's growing out to encapsulate their neighborhoods.

NEGROES AND RESIDENTIAL DESEGREGATION

As pointed out in the preceding chapter, Negroes have tended to become more rather than less residentially segregated in American cities. Yet within this segregative pattern there is the same general relationship

[9] Duncan and Lieberson, *op. cit.*, p. 369.

between physical and social distance as among the white population. Negroes vary greatly as to socioeconomic status, education, family patterns, and value systems. In Chicago there is a tendency for Negroes of higher status to live apart from those of lower status. With numerous exceptions, Negro areas near the center of the city are the lowest in terms of socioeconomic status of the inhabitants and the highest in terms of density and housing congestion.[10] On the whole, the centrally located areas are more heavily populated by Negroes, and had been so for a longer time, than the less centrally located Negro areas. There are too many exceptions to state it as a hard and fast generalization applying to all American cities, but these facts suggest that as the Negro community expands, the higher-ranking Negroes move to less centralized areas. This would conform to the characteristic pattern of the white community (and of the Burgess hypothesis of urban growth), namely, the association of decentralization of residence with improved social position.

THE "GILDED GHETTO"

Jews in the United States have never been officially confined to ghettos as was formerly the case in many European countries, but, nevertheless, they have often formed distinct residential clusters in American cities. Voluntary segregation on the basis of religious and kinship ties is obviously important, but there is also an involuntary element in their segregation. Discrimination against Jews in housing, employment, and social contacts was, and is, still practiced to some extent. The Jews in the United States are highly urbanized. In 1950 one-quarter of the over-all United States population lived in the 12 largest metropolitan areas, but almost three-quarters of the Jewish population lived in these areas.[11]

A study in "North City," a midwestern metropolis, showed changes in the location and function of Jewish residential areas from one generation to another.[12] The first generation consisted of Jews who came to North City in the 1860's from Germany, Austria, and Hungary; in the 1900's they were joined by Jews from eastern Europe. Most of the first generation settled in an area called the North Side. In 1910 over 80 per cent of all Jews in the city lived there. The second generation, that is, the native-born children of the immigrants, were less likely to live on the North Side. Many, particularly the financially successful descendants of the early German immigrants, moved to better neighborhoods on the South Side. The authors call these areas "gilded ghettos" because, although such areas were a far cry from the crowded slums of the North Side, Jews resi-

[10] Otis Dudley Duncan and Beverly Duncan, *The Negro Population of Chicago: A Study of Residential Succession* (1957), pp. 252–63.

[11] Fred Massarik, "The Jewish Community," in Marvin Sussman (ed.), *op. cit.*, pp. 240–41.

[12] Judith Kramer and Seymour Leventman, *Children of the Gilded Ghetto* (1961).

dent in them still carried on their social life almost exclusively within their own group. Thus, the second generation had become assimilated in terms of standard of living but not in terms of social relationships. The third generation, native-born grandchildren of the original immigrants, definitely tended to settle away from the North Side. Indeed, by 1957 only 38 per cent of the Jewish population still lived there. The third generation, for the most part "young marrieds" and in white collar occupations, have moved to the southside suburbs, where they have many non-Jewish neighbors and friends. Jews of the third generation have not rejected the heritage of their forefathers; but they appear more interested in living in high status communities than the ghettos—gilded or not—of the first and second generation.

This study and others showing the physical dispersion and upward mobility of ethnic groups raise the basic question of how assimilated the ethnic groups in American society are likely to become. There has been a noticeable decline in prejudice and discrimination against ethnic groups, in large part due to the recognition of the contribution these groups have made to American life. For the members of many ethnic groups there is no longer any significant stigma attached to their ethnic origin. Therefore, for these groups, interest in and practice of the tradition of immigrant ancestral groups need not be rejected on account of connotations of social inferiority. But, can skills in and meaningful knowledge of ethnic customs be acquired without living in neighborhoods populated largely by others with the same ethnic interest? Can the telephone, the automobile, formal ethnic organizations, and other devices overcome the relative absence of physical concentration? We do not yet know the answers to these questions, but they are important in determining the future shape of ethnic residential segregation in United States cities.

THE NATURE OF INVASION-SUCCESSION

When population moves into an area for residential purposes, the phenomenon is termed ecological *invasion*. If the original occupants are completely displaced by the invaders, the term *succession* is commonly applied to describe what has occurred.

Ecological invasion and segregation are closely associated phenomena; indeed, they are often merely different aspects of the same general process. An area undergoing an ecological invasion may at the same time be undergoing the processes of segregation, dispersal, and diffusion. As the invaders increase in numbers, they may, if they are homogeneous in respect to certain attributes, become a segregated group. If they displace residents who already occupy the area, the displacement may mean the gradual movement of the group into another area or the scattering of its members. Invasion, however, may merely represent movement into an unoccupied area; in this instance there is no displacement of residents, but the land may be put to a different use. Fringe areas of growing cities in the United States are constantly undergoing invasions of this type. Invasions into residentially unoccupied areas may or may not result in racial or ethnic segregation, but often such invaded areas manifest a certain degree of economic segregation in the sense that the settlers are fairly homogeneous as to income.

Ecological invasion may be viewed as a kind of barometer reflecting both the dynamics of a social order and the direction of certain social changes. In a society having little social or spatial mobility, invasion would probably not figure importantly in community life. It appears to be most characteristic of societies having an expanding economy, strong personal and institutional competitiveness, and widespread preoccupation of individuals with pecuniary and status objectives.

Although ecological invasion probably occurs in one form or another in cities of every country, it is especially manifest in the dynamic American metropolis. If, however, the American economy loses some of its dynamic qualities, if city growth slows down or stops altogether, vertical social mobility will become increasingly difficult, and social values will undergo certain changes. Ecological invasions then will probably become less important as a phase of urban life.

There is some evidence that patterns of ecological invasion vary greatly in character and volume from one society or city to another. Observations of ecological change in certain cities of Latin America indicate that invasions are of a decidedly different character from what they are in a large American city. Some cities of the Orient are also different from American cities in this respect. Although many of these centers have been growing rapidly in population, this growth has usually not been paralleled by a centrifugal expansion of the central business district. Nor has there been a pronounced decentralization of population resulting in successive invasions.

Voluntary and involuntary invasion

As in the case of segregation, ecological invasions may be voluntary or involuntary. Probably most of them are voluntary. But there are numerous instances in which residential areas are themselves invaded by business or industry and the occupants forced to move; or instances in which families victimized by adversity are forced to shift to neighborhoods which they would hardly choose under more auspicious circumstances. If their incomes are low, or if they are subject to racial or cultural discrimination, their choice of a new residential location may be narrowly limited. Often their move is merely from one deteriorated district to another, with no advantages, real or imagined, to be gained. Highway construction and urban renewal are other causes of involuntary residential relocation.

Voluntary residential invasions are usually a matter of infiltration by individuals or families motivated by a desire for more pleasant surroundings, occupational advantages, social prestige, or any number of things that rank high on their scale of interests. Ethnic or racial invasions are no exception. Except in cases of forced evacuation, residential movement —which is both movement *away from* an area and *into* a different area— is highly individualized behavior. While the movement may superficially assume the appearance of collective action, actually it is nothing more than shifts of individuals or families each motivated by its own particular reasons. The appearance of collective action arises from the fact that the movements may be similar in direction and destination, and the people moving may be similarly motivated.

Invasion should be considered in relative terms. Just as "one swallow does not a summer make," neither does the movement of one individual or family into an area ordinarily constitute an invasion of much sociological significance for the area unless the presence of the invading individual or family meets with resistance, creates a problem for the residents, or alters the existing pattern of neighborhood relationships.

In common usage the concept of invasion is applied to the movement of a considerable number of individuals or families into a particular area. The specific number is unimportant; what *is* important sociologically is the character of the invaders, the relationships between the invaders and the residents, and the effect on physical properties and social institutions. The movement of a half-dozen Negroes into a white area of an American city may be of greater sociological significance than the movement of a hundred Polish-Americans into an Italian-American district. In the final analysis the sociological significance of ecological invasions into residential areas already occupied reflects the prevailing values both of the occupants and of the invaders.

INSTITUTIONAL INVASION

The character of land use may also result from institutional change. In an expanding, dynamic city there are frequent changes in the economy of an area as commercial, industrial, or other types of institutions invade a particular district, or as such buildings are removed to make way for an invasion of residents.

Institutional invasion may occur independently of population movement, it may precede or follow an invasion of population, or the two types of invasion may occur more or less concurrently. An invasion of an area by industry may be followed by a residential invasion of industrial workers who want to live close to the place of employment. An institutional invasion may also be the signal for an exodus of the residents of an invaded area because property values may be adversely affected or because the area becomes less suited to residential purposes.

The exodus of population from a residential area or the change in character of an area's population as a result of invasion may affect institutional functions. Sometimes churches are forced to move because members have left the area and the invaders are of a different religious persuasion. Church buildings often remain, but church organization may be shifted in the direction of relocated members. The invaders, on the other hand, may take over the church property and put it to a somewhat different use.

It has been generally observed that in growing American cities the area immediately surrounding a central business district is in a state of transition as land use is changed from residential to commercial or industrial purposes. It is that fact which prompted Burgess to refer to this area as a "zone of transition." If business or industrial establishments press farther out, claiming space used for residential or other purposes, land values tend to rise out of proportion to the incomes derived from residential occupancy. Since the land is held primarily for prospective increases in value when it is put to institutional use, existing residential properties are commonly allowed to deteriorate. The last ounce of profit is squeezed out of speculative holdings as tenants are crowded into dilapidated rookeries before demolition squads take over. It is this fact as much as any other that accounts for the central slum in most American cities.

Sometimes institutional invasion involves the movement of one type of establishment into an area occupied by another type. An expanding business district may result in the movement of commercial enterprises into areas already occupied by, say, light industry. Or commercial and industrial establishments may move into unoccupied areas, possibly replacing agricultural operations. The growth of various types of enterprises along main highways near cities is an example. Sometimes such commercial establishments become the nucleus for subsequent suburban or satellite settlements arising from the decentralization of population.

Central business districts of some American cities are no longer expanding, and the time will probably come when such districts in many cities will cease to grow. Extensive invasions by business or industry of adjoining areas will then cease. Land values that have been inflated in anticipation of business or industrial invasion will probably decline, and the blight that is already so conspicuous may continue to spread unless concerted efforts are made toward reconstruction of the area. This day seems to be hastened by the growth of outlying shopping centers and by the decentralization of residential population in metropolitan areas.

INVASION AND SOCIAL MOBILITY

There is considerable evidence that invasions in American cities are commonly associated with vertical social mobility, either upward or downward. Movement of an individual or family into a particular area is often a means to higher social or economic position or an indication that higher status has already been achieved. Individuals or families moving to a higher social position commonly expect to display the symbols appropriate to that position—a larger house, a more expensive car, a suitable residential location. The kind of neighborhood a family lives in is a fairly accurate criterion of its class status; to improve that status the family may seek a "nicer" area than the one already occupied. We have already noted how the desegregation of ethnic groups in American cities is associated with the socioeconomic advancement of the immigrants.

This relation between ecological and social mobility in America appears to obtain when the social system is functioning normally and the avenues for social ascendancy are open. In times of economic distress, as in economic depressions, the channels for upward mobility tend to be closed, or at least greatly narrowed, so far as the masses are concerned. It is in these periods of depression that the direction of ecological mobility tends to change considerably. As individuals move down the economic scale, as a result of loss of job or reduction in income, they may be forced to move into less espensive areas, regardless of their social aspirations. The march to attractive suburbs slows down, construction of new homes declines, and there is an invasion of the slums or blighted areas by families victimized by misfortune. Others, more fortunate but nevertheless troubled by insecurity, may lay aside their plans to move to a neighborhood symbolic of the status they would like.

FACTORS INITIATING RESIDENTIAL INVASIONS

Cressey mentions 10 conditions which he believes may be associated with the invasion process: "(1) desire for increased social prestige, (2) pressure of wife and children, (3) increased economic resources, (4) desire for better living conditions, (5) activity of real estate agents, (6) desire for home ownership, (7) pressure of vacant homes, (8) changes in transportation facilities, (9) desire to be near one's place of employment or place where employment is sought, and (10) movement of industrial areas." [13] Gibbard offers a somewhat more satisfactory analysis of the factors that tend to initiate invasions. They are: "(1) change in the size

[13] Paul F. Cressey, *The Succession of Cultural Groups in the City of Chicago.* Unpublished doctoral dissertation, University of Chicago (1930).

of the population aggregate in the community, (2) change in the racial
or ethnic composition of the population, (3) development of a status hierarchy within the minority group, (4) commercial or industrial changes
that affect the relative economic status of different groups in the community, (5) residential displacements in other areas, (6) taking over of
residential property for business or recreational use, (7) obsolescence of
neighborhoods, (8) establishment of large factories, and the consequent
creation of employment, in suburban areas." [14]

NEW ORLEANS: A CASE STUDY

In an analysis of the ecological history of New Orleans, Gilmore described the various invasions that have occurred during the nineteenth
and twentieth century, relating these invasions to the topography of the
city as well as to the segregation of ethnic and racial groups.[15] The earliest
settlers were French, who came to be known as Creoles. Together with
Spanish settlers later on they developed a distinctive cultural life. Many
of them prospered, their influence being based primarily on the plantation
labor of slaves or the cheap labor of free Negroes. Upper class families in
New Orleans had a retinue of Negro servants.

With expansion of the city's economy an influx of migrants occurred.
The first of these were Americans whose money-making interests led them
into business and industry. The area of first settlement was near the
French quarter, in the central part of the city. Large numbers of Irish
immigrants were also attracted.

As the wealth of the Americans mounted and their numbers increased,
they moved farther west on land adjacent to the Mississippi River, where
they developed a pretentious residential district. The area they abandoned was filled up by Irish immigrants and came to be known as the
Irish Channel. The centrifugal movement of the Americans meant an
invasion of the Negro residential fringe and their truck gardening zone.

With the growth of the Creole population in the central area and the
deterioration of their residential properties, many Creole families also
moved outward, not in the direction of the Americans, whom they disliked, but northward along one of the ridges. There they developed an
attractive residential district.

In the early days the Negroes lived on the premises of their masters
or clustered in a horseshoe-shaped fringe around the Creole or American
residential areas. When street cars later came into use, it was no longer

[14] Harold Gibbard, *Residental Succession: A Study in Human Ecology.* Unpublished
doctoral dissertation, University of Michigan (1938).
[15] H. W. Gilmore, "The Old New Orleans and the New," *American Sociological
Review,* 9 (August, 1944), 385–94. This is one of the best ecological analyses of an
American city because it brings into focus the historical, geographic, ethnic, economic, and technological factors involved.

necessary for the Negroes to live in the immediate vicinity of the place of work. Since the outer Negro fringe was invaded by the whites, displaced Negroes turned toward the center of the city, moving into deteriorated areas or into the swamp zone between the districts occupied by whites.

Gilmore makes it clear that the topography of New Orleans, particularly the river and swamp areas, imposed limitations on the direction of invasions. But cultural differences and tensions between ethnic groups, especially between the Creoles and Americans, fostered segregation and operated to direct population movements toward different sections of the city.

A more recent study showed that topography and ethnic relations continue as the most important determinants of change in the ecology of New Orleans.[16] Because New Orleans is a growing, prosperous city, not only have the prices of the limited suitable land risen substantially, but the drive for new land by dredging and filling the swamps and by building crossings over the Mississippi River and Lake Pontchartrain is being pressed. The Negro population has expanded more rapidly than the population in general, but in the context of scarce high-priced land, the gap between the Negro need for housing and the supply appears to be widening. Also, all the new housing, public and private, built for Negroes is designed for all-Negro occupancy. This is contrary to the earlier residential pattern of New Orleans, which did not emphasize racial segregation in housing. New Orleans is still relatively unsegregated in terms of residence, but changes may be anticipated. An important change has taken place among the white population which may also effect the ecological pattern of New Orleans, including racial segregation. The white population, a much larger proportion of whom live in apartment houses than is general in American cities, has "discovered" the virtues of single family home ownership. Consequently, many are moving to more outlying areas where property values are beyond the income level of Negroes. Finally, with the increased use of the automobile after World War II there has been a decline in the *bistro* culture among both Negro and white lower and middle class groups. The *bistro* culture emphasizes the local community, for group activity centers on small local bars and restaurants where socializing with friends and kin takes place.

INVASIONS IN BOSTON

Changes in land use and type of occupants of Boston's Back Bay, once occupied almost exclusively by the city's elite, are illustrative of ecological transformations occurring in many American cities.[17] Although

---

[16] Forrest LaViolette, "The Negro in New Orleans," in Nathan Glazer and Davis McEntire (eds.), *Studies in Housing and Minority Groups* (1960), pp. 110–34.
[17] Walter Firey, *Land Use in Central Boston* (1947), ch. 7.

rigid deed restrictions designed to preserve the prestigious character of the district afforded some protection, changes in land use and character of occupants have nevertheless occurred, and these in turn have affected the cultural tone of the area. Nineteenth-century Back Bay featured brownstone front houses extending continously along tree-lined streets, the homes of Boston's pedigreed blue-bloods. It was an area of sumptuous living.

As invasions or changed land use in the twentieth century threatened the prestige of the area, Back Bay elite began their exodus, many of them going to such fashionable suburbs as Newton, Milton, or Weston. Some of the brownstone mansions were demolished to make way for apartment buildings, or were transformed into kitchenette apartments or respectable middle-class rooming houses to accommodate students, young professionals, and white collar workers. High rentals prevented an influx of low-income families. Although business houses encroached upon the area, there has been selective invasion, limited mainly to establishments featuring luxury items for women. The area has become increasingly the metropolitan focus of medical practice; about 700 physicians, one-fourth of the practicing doctors in Boston, were residents of this district in 1942.

Beacon Hill, another of Boston's areas of fashionable occupance, has undergone a somewhat different ecological history.[18] During the latter part of the nineteenth century, Beacon Hill families migrated from the area, possibly because of a threatened invasion of people without prestige. Some of the homes with halos were converted into rooming-houses, several apartment houses were constructed, and such business establishments as tailor shops, stores, and clubs began moving into the district. But for many of the established families, particularly those with impressive pedigrees as well as the *nouveaux riches* in search of pedigrees, such incursions into sacred territory were resented. The Beacon Hill Association, backed by influential families, was formed to carry on resistance against such invasions as would imperil the symbolic reputation of the Hill. Its activities met with considerable success; there was a revival of upper class interest in the area and a restoration of the district as a symbol of prestige. Firey interprets this as a refutation of ecological theories that view economic functions as the determinants of spatial phenomena. The preservation of the character of the area had cultural determinants running counter to the interests of those who might have made money by changing the residential amenities of Beacon Hill.

REPEATED INVASIONS IN A SINGLE AREA

An urban area may witness a series of invasions within a relatively short time. The near west side of Chicago, for example, has been popu-

[18] *Ibid.*, ch. 3.

lated by a succession of racial and cultural groups, one following on the heels of another.[19] The district was first settled by Czechs, but when the Jews began to crowd into the area after the Chicago fire of 1877 the original occupants, accustomed to spacious surroundings, forsook the region for more desirable quarters. With the egress of the Czechs went also the Irish, who had occupied a portion of the district. But the Jewish residents had hardly become firmly intrenched when the Italians came. Between 1910 and 1918 more than half the Jewish population, their security and status threatened by the influx of a people with a different cultural background and a somewhat lower standard of living, moved to other parts of the city. The coming of Negroes proved an added stimulus to the Jewish exodus. A considerable portion of the zone that was once in the heart of the ghetto had become a "black belt," and with this change has gone all but a mere remnant of the culture of an alien people who had selected this site as their abode. Here, for example, a large structure, once used as a synagogue, was transformed into a Negro Protestant church—a symbol of the far-reaching changes that have taken place.

The area has continued to deteriorate and plans are now afoot for wholesale demolition, including the famed Hull House, which is located there.[20] If the renewal plans are carried out, the history of the area will recapitulate the successive downgrading of many centrally located neighborhoods and their "final" redevelopment under government auspices.

RESISTANCE TO INVASIONS

The rate of displacement depends on a number of interrelated factors—economic, geographic, cultural, psychological. Each situation has unique features. An impending invasion of a white area by Negroes may signal a wholesale exodus from the district, resulting in rapid displacement of white families by Negro families; or it may mean a last-ditch fight by whatever available devices to prevent the Negroes from moving in. The reaction to an invasion by Negroes in New York may be quite different from the reaction to such an invasion in Atlanta, San Antonio, or Johannesburg. Or the reaction in 1900 may have been different from the reaction in 1964, even in the same city.

The degree of resistance to invasion seems to be related to the following factors: (1) The socioeconomic status of the invading group. Groups regarded as equal or superior are rarely resisted. (2) The stand taken by leadership groups including the clergy, real estate men, citizen's associations, and the government. (3) Ability to secure equivalent housing elsewhere. If the housing market is tight, resistance is likely to stiffen.

[19] Maurice H. Krout, "A Community in Flux," *Social Forces*, 5 (December, 1926), 278–82.

[20] Symposium, "The Future of Hull House," *Social Service Review*, 36 (June, 1962), 123–28.

(4) The meaning of housing to the individuals, particularly if it is primarily a status symbol. (5) Length of residence in the area. Highly transient areas tend to have few individuals with an economic or sentimental stake in the community. (6) The stage of the family cycle. Families with young children are most apt to be concerned with the impact of the newcomers on educational or recreational facilities.

PROPERTY VALUES AND INVASION

Resistance to residential invasion has often been defended on the grounds that otherwise property values would decline. This viewpoint has been particularly strong with regard to the movement of Negroes into white neighborhoods. Until recently, even the policy of the federal government agencies dealing with housing held that racial separation in housing protected property values. Despite widespread contention on this matter there was little evidence to substantiate or refute it, until Laurenti made a careful study which provides some information to enable us to assess the relationship between property values and segregation.[21] Laurenti obtained the sales prices for homes sold from 1943 to 1955 in 20 neighborhoods in San Francisco, Oakland, and Philadelphia that had formerly been all white but had undergone some degree of nonwhite entry, ranging from less than two to over 29 per cent. Home sale prices in each neighborhood were compared with a "control" area—a similar neighborhood in the same city except that it had remained all white during the 1943–55 period. Almost 10,000 individual home sales were involved in the study. It should be noted that while the neighborhoods represented a variety of home price categories, most were in the middle-price range, and all the neighborhoods were in single-family residential areas occupied by owner-occupants and were located outside the heart of the city.

The study did not support the idea that nonwhite occupancy necessarily lowered property values.

The major statistical finding of the present study is that during the time period and for the cases studied the entry of nonwhites into previously all-white neighborhoods was much more often associated with price improvement or stability than with price weakening. A corollary and possibly more important finding is that no single or uniform pattern of nonwhite influence on property prices could be detected.[22]

Specifically, the study found that in 44 per cent of the comparisons, prices in the test areas entered by nonwhites ended relatively higher than prices in the control areas, by margins ranging from over 5 to 26 per cent; in 15 per cent of the comparisons, test area prices were relatively lower than control area prices by margins of 5 to 9 per cent; and in 41

[21] Luigi Laurenti, *Property Values and Race* (1960).   [22] *Ibid.,* p. 47.

per cent of the comparisons, test area prices stayed within 5 per cent of control area prices, indicating no significant differences in price behavior in the test and control areas. Price changes were not predictably related to the price class of the neighborhood or to the percentage of Negroes who moved into the neighborhood.

Laurenti's findings suggest that home prices in the kinds of neighborhoods studied are not necessarily adversely affected by Negro entry. We might add that "panic" selling, if it occurs, may indeed lower home sale prices temporarily. This appears to be an instance of the "self-fulfilling prophecy." If white owners expect property values to fall when non-whites move into the area, then many owners may put their homes on the market at once, thereby creating oversupply and bringing about the price decline they fear.[23] There is debate over the facts of what happens in these instances of the self-fulfilling prophecy, particularly whether the process and the resulting behavior are irrational.[24] Certainly both Laurenti's results and the theory of the "self-fulfilling prophecy" make it clear that the relationship between property values and race should not be dismissed in stereotyped terms but merits further consideration.

STAGES OF INVASION-SUCCESSION

Several efforts have been made to identify different stages in the invasion-succession cycle in American cities. Burgess notes four, including the initial movement into the area, reaction on the part of the occupants, general influx of newcomers, and the climax or period of complete displacement.[25] On the other hand, Gibbard concluded from his study of Detroit that the invasion cycle was characterized by five stages,[26] while the Duncans' study of Negro population distribution in Chicago disclosed four stages.[27] These theoretical schemes are essentially alike: the differences are probably due to the fact that the invasion may vary in differing communities or population groups. In the following discussion we shall follow essentially the four-stage theory by Burgess.

The initial stage

The initial stage is characterized by the movement of a small number of individuals or families into an area. Frequently, though not always,

[23] Robert K. Merton, "The Self-Fulfilling Prophecy," in his *Social Theory and Social Structure* (1957), pp. 421–36.

[24] Eleanor Wolf, "The Invasion-Succession Sequence as a Self-Fulfilling Prophecy," *Journal of Social Issues,* 13 (1957), pp. 7–20.

[25] E. W. Burgess, "Residential Succession in American Cities," *Annals,* 140 (November, 1928), 112.

[26] *Op. cit.*   [27] *Op. cit.,* ch. 6.

this movement passes unnoticed by the original occupants. If cultural and racial differences between the old residents and the newcomers are not great, a considerable penetration may take place before the occupants are aware of it, or at least before there is a marked reaction. Sometimes the first newcomers take special precautions to conceal their racial or cultural identity, thereby postponing the time when a reaction will set in. Most invasions start slowly, gaining momentum as time passes. In Detroit, Gibbard noted that at least two or three years elapsed before a Negro invasion reached significant proportions, and in one district it took about 10 years.[28]

The rate of invasion-succession varies widely. In Chicago, the Duncans reported, one census tract that changed from 0.2 per cent to 98.4 per cent nonwhite occupance between 1940 and 1950, while another tract changed from 0.3 per cent to only 12.4 per cent over the same decade.[29]

In the case of Negro invasions in Detroit there seems to be a tendency for the first newcomers to represent a higher social and economic status than the majority of their group.[30] Their presence gives the locality a certain prestige, and therefore tends to attract other Negroes who may be on a slightly lower level but who nevertheless aspire to associate with the more successful members of the race. As the movement continues, the social and economic status of the incoming group tends to be lowered. This suggests that as an area continues through the process of racial succession, we might expect a decline in the socioeconomic status of the inhabitants and in housing standards. This expectation is theoretically valid, but neglects the fact that racial succession occurs in the context of general social and business conditions. The over-all socioeconomic position of American Negroes has been rising, and since the end of the 1930's there has also been general prosperity and a high level of employment. These factors have combined to minimize the downgrading associated with racial succession. For example, the Duncans' study in Chicago showed that census tracts that had experienced racial succession from white to Negro between 1940 and 1950 nevertheless showed increases in the educational level of their population.[31] Although Chicago Negroes still ranked below whites in educational attainment in 1950, the advances in both groups had evidently been great enough for Negroes to outrank the whites' attainment of only 10 years earlier.

THE REACTION

Once the original occupants are aware of the invasion, a reaction may set in. Its intensity may be influenced by a number of conditions, includ-

---

[28] *Op. cit.*, p. 178.   [29] *Op. cit.*, p. 121.   [30] Gibbard, *op. cit.*, p. 181.
[31] *Op. cit.*, p. 241.

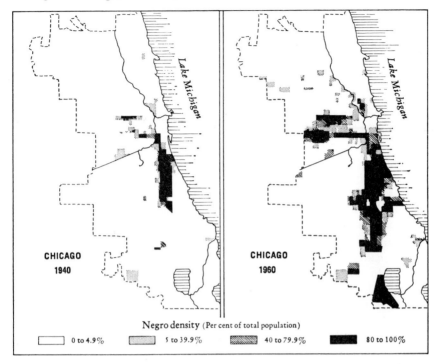

Negro density (Per cent of total population)

0 to 4.9%	5 to 39.9%	40 to 79.9%	80 to 100%

Figure 15. The changes in distribution of Negro population in Chicago in 1940 and 1960 resulted largely from invasion-succession. The total Negro population of Chicago increased from 277,700 in 1940 (8 per cent of the city's population) to 813,000 in 1960 (23 per cent of the city's population). The Chicago suburbs, not shown on these maps, have a much smaller Negro population, both numerically and proportionally. SOURCE: Charles E. Silberman, "The City and the Negro," *Fortune*, March, 1962. Courtesy of *Fortune* magazine.

ing the prevailing attitudes toward the invaders, cultural or racial characteristics of the newcomers, the degree of community or neighborhood solidarity among the older residents, and the extent to which the occupants are socially rooted by virtue of home ownership, acceptance of community traditions, or interest in community welfare. Almost always a Negro invasion is resented from the outset by white occupants, though the intensity of resentment will vary among cultural and economic groups. An invasion of Jews, Poles, Italians, Greeks, Russians, and other cultural groups is often opposed, but if the first newcomers occupy an economic position comparable to that of the residents, little attention may be paid to them. Indeed, they may be accepted. This seems to indicate that the invaders may be opposed not so much as individuals but as members of a class that has been assigned an inferior status.

This is particularly clear with Negro invasions. Single Negro families often are accepted without incident into a white neighborhood on a long term basis.[32] But when larger numbers of Negroes move in, the implication that the area is losing status causes whites to leave, more or less rapidly. This may be one of the factors underlying the "tipping" process, that is, the phenomenon of whites moving out of a neighborhood once the proportion of nonwhites exceeds a given point (the "tip point"). The tip point varies from one city and one neighborhood to another.[33] It is also revealing to note that several studies show that status considerations often override favorable attitudes toward Negroes in the decision of white families to leave racially changing neighborhoods.[34] It appears that analyzing reactions to Negro invasion is not merely a matter of understanding personal prejudice.

The role of status considerations in the reaction to Negro residents is illustrated in the case study of Levittown, Pennsylvania.[35] Construction of this large suburban development began in 1951, and, by 1957, 15,500 families, about 60,000 people, lived there when William Myers, a 34-year-old veteran, college-educated and employed as a refrigeration engineer, purchased a four-year-old house and moved in with his wife and three young children. The Myers were the first Negroes to live in Levittown. Pro- and anti-Myers factions quickly developed.

Myers' opponents were almost wholly recruited from the ranks of the relatively uneducated urban proletariat in the process of uncertain transit to the suburban middle class. . . . A high degree of ethnocentrism is a common phenomenon in the sub-college stratum, and as might be anticipated a goodly number of Levittowners had chosen to live in this community precisely because it offered an escape from "mixed" neighborhoods and those facing imminent desegregation. Moreover, these initial biases among industrial workers were frequently reinforced by status anxieties arising from their equivocal position in the class structure. A skilled or semi-skilled laborer employed by the United States Steel Company, Kaiser Metal Products, or other local enterprises might well sense the disparity between his relative economic affluence and his modest occupational prestige. One method of resolving this ambiguity consists of borrowing prestige from his community which if it is to serve this purpose satisfactorily must then represent a pure distillate of middle-class life styles. The working class addiction to the coy middle-class symbolism so prevalent in Levittown, its "Sweetbriar Lanes" and "cook-outs," its "patios" and enthusiastic agronomy, is to an appreciable extent a simultaneous exercise in self-persuasion and ritualistic affirmation whose purpose it is to demonstrate that life patterns in the community, and not the job, constitute the only valid basis for class

[32] Arnold Rose, Frank Atelsek, and Lawrence McDonald, "Neighborhood Reactions to Isolated Negro Residents: An Alternative to Invasion and Succession," *American Sociological Review* 18 (October, 1953), 497–507.

[33] Morton Grodzins, *The Metropolitan Area as a Racial Problem* (1958), pp. 6–7.

[34] Wolf, *op. cit.*, p. 16; and J. Fishman, "Some Social and Psychological Determinants of Intergroup Relations in Changing Neighborhoods," *Social Forces*, 40 (October, 1961), p. 50.

[35] Marvin Bressler, "The Myers' Case: An Instance of Successful Racial Invasion," *Social Problems*, 8 (Fall, 1960), 126–42.

assignment. The appearance of a visible threat to the social status of the community in the persons of a Negro family could be expected to produce considerable apprehension among the inhabitants of a poorly defined no man's land on the margins between two classes.

. . . . .

If Myers' fiercest antagonists exhibited an intense preoccupation with the social reputation of the local community his most vigorous defenders represented the cosmopolitan orientation. . . . College educated and career oriented, the cosmopolitan had not moved to Levittown in order to improve his social status. He had come for idiosyncratic reasons, out of economic compulsion, or because repeated references to a "planned" community had led him to indulge in the soon dispelled vague fantasy that he was being introduced to a sort of contemporary New Harmony. But whatever his motivations he was often embarrassed by his "Levittown address." Members of his occupational reference groups in Philadelphia sometimes behaved as if they regarded his tenure in Levittown as evidence of some unsuspected eccentricity and wondered when he intended to join his fellows in the more elegant western suburbs.

Moreover, the occupations of a significant proportion of the cosmopolitans inclined them to reject parochialism. Physicians, clergy, educators, and social workers, for example, are routinely accustomed to think and act according to universalistic norms. As recent graduates of American institutions of higher learning the majority of the cosmopolitans had been "broadened" in race relations courses and workshops. They had heard that decent men must forswear prejudice, that contact produces amity, that the UN was man's best hope, and one or two had even entertained foreign students.

Myers was to find his chief allies among these cosmopolitans, persons who refused to define the situation primarily and exclusively in terms of its impact on the tight little island of suburbia. The whole complex of the personal and ideological influences which had shaped their lives had rendered them peculiarly sensitive to the value system and the symbolic vocabulary of the liberal intellectual with whom they identified.

The ideal-typical social constructs distinguishing Myers' adversaries from his supporters should not obscure the fact that numerous Levittowners did not behave as expected and that by far the greater number remained watchfully inert during the entire period of the crisis.[36]

Harrassment of the Myers continued for several months until a court injunction forbade interference with their or any other Negroes' rights of residence. It had also been clear all along that the governor and the state police would not tolerate violence or intimidation. In succeeding years several Negro families moved into Levittown without incident.

Various methods may be employed to block an invasion, once it has started, or to avoid the possibility of an invasion. A common device is the neighborhood association, commonly called "protective associations," "civic associations," or "improvement associations." Their one important

---

[36] *Ibid.*, pp. 133, 137. Reprinted by permission.

purpose is apt to be the exclusion of individuals representing unwanted racial, cultural, or economic groups. As members of the neighborhood association, property owners enter into an agreement, called a covenant, not to rent or sell to individuals who by specific designation are undesirable.[37] Such associations have proved to be more effective in areas having a high percentage of home ownership and considerable rapport among the residents than in areas having a high population turnover. Such organizations, in fact, may not exist in a highly mobile community.

Real estate companies also enter into agreements to protect certain areas against unwanted elements, but since such agencies do not ordinarily handle all the sales and rentals in a given district, they have been less effective than other forms of protection. A third method of protecting an area, at least in slowing down an invasion, is the erection of economic barriers by increasing property values.

Not infrequently, invasions have been met with physical force or mob violence. So far as we are aware, however, mob resistance has been directed only against Negroes; opposition to whites has tended to take nonviolent forms. Attempts have been made to drive out Negroes by blasting their homes, planting "pineapples" under their front porches, shooting through their doors or windows, threatening the newcomers with personal violence, and otherwise making life miserable for them.

The Myers were never subjected to physical violence, but a picture window in their home was broken, crowds up to 600 gathered around their house, noise and lights were directed at them during the night, and their sympathizers also were subjected to threatening letters and phone calls, cross-burnings on their lawns, defacement of their homes by KKK insignia, and the planting of a bomb at one home.

In recent years there has been a noticeable movement to achieve stable racially integrated neighborhoods by stemming the white exodus from areas invaded by Negroes. Neighborhood associations may form to prevent panic selling by white residents and to promote racial harmony. Signs saying "Not for Sale—We Believe in Democracy" may be posted. Public and private agencies may assist such groups with professional guidance and support.

In some cities and states the combatting of racial and religious discrimination in housing is a matter of public policy which official agencies may be charged to implement directly. For example, the City of New York's Commission on Human Rights, established in 1955, administers the municipal laws prohibiting discrimination in housing and is also empowered to take action in areas where intergroup tensions may develop, out of housing or other causes. In a pioneer case, the Commission sent a trained worker to help the residents of a racially changing area prevent

---

[37] See Chapter 7 for a discussion of the legal status of such covenants.

panic selling and "ghettoization."[38] Since then there have been many such cases.

One of the best-known attempts, apparently successful, to halt the invasion-succession cycle is that of the Hyde Park-Kenwood area adjacent to the University of Chicago.[39] In this community the efforts at racial integration extended over many years, involved large-scale citizen participation, included physical replanning and rebuilding of the neighborhood, and benefited by the special conditions of proximity to the university. The general effectiveness of neighborhood groups and public agencies in achieving residential integration under more usual conditions is not yet clear. At the present time, once the "tipping point" is passed, neighborhoods most frequently proceed to further stages of racial succession. The ultimate goal is to make race less dominating as a factor in residential location. Some observers believe that as a temporary measure it may be desirable to place a quota on the proportion of Negroes in a neighborhood in order to maintain racial balance.

THE GENERAL INFLUX

In the third stage of the invasion process a general influx takes place and is often accompanied, or possibly preceded, by the abandonment of the area by the original inhabitants. It is hardly correct, however, to say that the occupants are crowded out; they usually go of their own volition, choosing to live in a different district rather than have as neighbors persons whom they dislike or consider inferior. Sometimes the dispersion is motivated not by threatened invasions but by the desire to escape from an area that is already becoming less attractive. Deterioration of buildings or streets, or the development of industry in adjacent districts, may cause the region to decline in prestige as a residential section and therefore hasten the departure of the inhabitants. Their exodus creates a sort of social vacuum, and hard-pressed groups may immediately move into the vacated structures which may be superior to those they have left. Thus the usual sequence of invasion and dispersion may be reversed, with dispersion preceding rather than following the influx into the area.

THE CLIMAX

The final stage or climax occurs when complete displacement of the original population has occurred. But the process involves more than

[38] Peter Kihss, "Queens Homeowners Seek to Keep Racial Balance," *The New York Times*, November 22, 1958, p. 1.
[39] Julia Abrahamson, *A Neighborhood Finds Itself* (1959); and Peter Rossi and Robert Dentler, *The Politics of Urban Renewal: The Chicago Findings* (1961).

mere displacement of people; it involves also the social reorganization of the area. The receding group takes its culture patterns, leaving behind, perhaps, certain physical properties; the newcomers must perforce modify their institutional structures to meet the needs of people living under a new set of conditions. Frequently these changes involve modifications of the family system, alteration of religious practices, and new forms of recreation and earning a living.

INVASION SUCCESSION AND BLIGHT

Completion of the invasion-succession cycle should not lead us to assume that "climax" areas are necessarily completely different than they were before their invasion. Residential invasion-succession has two distinctly different aspects—the character of the population and the character of the neighborhood—which must be considered in analyzing the ultimate changes in an area. It is possible, and indeed frequent, for the population to change while the nature of the neighborhood, that is, its ecological function, remains the same. There are many areas in large cities where indices of disorganization such as infant mortality rates, delinquency rates, public assistance, and so on, have remained high for decades while successive groups of varying religion or nationality have inhabited the area. It would seem that as each group advanced economically, educationally, and otherwise, it left that area and was succeeded by a group having the same general socioeconomic status the preceding group had when it first settled in the area. We have long been familiar with this aspect of invasion-succession among immigrant groups. Apparently it also prevails in racial successions; at least this is suggested by the Duncans' study of racial succession in Chicago. At the various stages of the invasion-succession cycle, census tracts occupied by Negroes tend to keep the same relative position in terms of housing characteristics and socioeconomic indicators compared with other census tracts, as when the areas were occupied by whites. In sum, middle class Negroes tend to invade middle class white neighborhoods and lower class Negroes, lower class white neighborhoods, so that the character of the neighborhood remains roughly the same, although the race of the occupants changes.

The relative stability of the ecological position of some neighborhoods as they undergo population succession stems in part from the preexistent physical facilities of the areas—type of housing, convenience to transportation, and the like—which continue to exert a selective pull on the population.

In the displacement of one population by another that constitutes the process of residential succession, the incoming population does not distribute itself at random among the various areas in which succession occurs. Rather the succession process is a selective one, in that the incoming population tends to be differentiated according to residential areas, in many respects, in much the same way as the population being displaced.[40]

The foregoing sections have been concerned with the dynamics by which population characteristics may change but an area may retain the same ecological function. But what of the situation where the area's ecological function changes; or where changes from one type of residential land use to another occur,[41] as when apartment houses come to predominate over single-family homes in an area, or residential structures become obsolete ("walk-ups" compared with elevator buildings), or sparsely settled areas become fully built up with homes? When one type of residential use is succeeded by another, the area usually becomes less desirable as a place to live. In ecological terms it has taken a lower position in the hierarchy of residential areas. A change in residential land use does not inevitably mean downgrading, but in actuality cases of neighborhood deterioration far outweigh cases of improvement.

There are some instances of the later residential land use being on a higher level than the preceding one. Georgetown in Washington, D.C., was an abject slum in the 1920's, but gradually private individuals restored the crumbling homes, many of them mansions from pre-Civil War times, to their former splendor. Georgetown is now an expensive and very attractive neighborhood in which many high government officials and business and professional leaders live. It was from Georgetown that the late President Kennedy, then a Senator, moved to the White House.

As a result of governmentally supported urban renewal programs, some slum areas have been replaced by new residential or commerical construction. In many of these cases the original population has been displaced and relocated.

Regardless of whether a neighborhood's attractiveness relative to other neighborhoods increases or decreases, the change in ecological position inevitably brings a change in the character of the population drawn to the neighborhood. As the row houses of the 1920's become obsolete, they attract a different group. As high-rise apartments in an area come to outnumber single-family homes, the kinds of people interested in living there change, too.

The foregoing discussion has focussed on two aspects of residential invasion-succession—population characteristics and ecological rank of the area. That these phenomena occur separately is shown by the fact that new racial, religious, or nationality groups may "take over" an area while the area retains the same rank *vis-à-vis* other parts of the city. In cases where the ecological rank of an area has changed, then we observed that

[40] Duncan and Duncan, *op. cit.*, p. 277.
[41] An area may change from residential to nonresidential land use (housing succeeded by industry). See the discussion, pp. 157–58.

the resident population inevitably shifts, for the basis of attraction to the area, or repulsion from it, has also changed. Since the new ecological rank is usually lower, the incoming population is typically on a lower socio-economic level.

THE NEIGHBORHOOD CYCLE

Having established that population characteristics and residential land use are separate elements in invasion-succession, we may now indicate how they sometimes interact. One study, based on data from the New York metropolitan region, described the typical sequence of residential land use and population change as follows.[42] (1) Vacant land is developed with houses in the popular style of the period—whether Victorian gothic, brownstones, row houses, terrace apartments, or split-level single-family homes. Often the predominant home style in an area enables us to date the period when the neighborhood first grew. At this stage the neighborhood attracts middle and high income groups, and families with children. (2) The second stage marks the continued growth of residential building in the area, usually with apartment houses, because land values have increased and the continued growth of the city has given the area a more central location. Population density increases and single individuals and childless couples are more frequent residents. (3) At the third stage there may be signs of downgrading in residential land use— the conversion of apartments into smaller units, the appearance of "Rooms to Let" signs on private homes, and the resulting increases in population density. It is at this point that lower income families or ethnic or racial minorities begin to "invade" an already declining area. The minority groups are usually in the child-bearing ages and this adds to the congestion and overtaxing of neighborhood facilities. Blight, which had been underway before these groups moved in, is accentuated. (4) The fourth stage involves the "maturing" of the area as a low income minority group place of settlement. Often the population density ultimately declines as the children marry and leave. The area may then be ripe for invasion by another low income group. Negroes and Puerto Ricans are moving into many such areas in New York City. (5) If the area is close to the city center, it may be residentially upgraded again. Luxury apartments are likely to result from private development and low or middle income housing if there is governmental assistance. It is important to stress that this sequence is not inevitable; a neighborhood may remain at any stage almost indefinitely. Equally important is that if change occurs it is likely to be in the direction of neighborhood deterioration. Few urban neighborhoods ever attain the "renewal" of Stage 5. In New York City, where public and

---

[42] Raymond Vernon, *Metropolis 1985* (1960), pp. 135–42; and Edgar Hoover and Raymond Vernon, *Anatomy of a Metropolis* (1959), pp. 190-207.

private efforts at rebuilding have been massive, less than one per cent of the dwellings were replaced per year in the span from 1946 to 1957.[43] Urban blight is a spreading problem whose solution requires, among other approaches, an understanding of the invasion-succession cycle.

ZONES, SECTORS, AND ECOLOGICAL CHANGE

Although there are exceptions, the processes of residential desegregation and of invasion-sucession generally confirm the Burgess hypothesis of urban growth. The modifications of Burgess' zonal hypothesis introduced by Hoyt's sector theory and the Harris-Ullman multiple nuclei proposal also seem valid. In examining the desegregation of ethnic groups, we found that the most segregated areas were toward the center of the city. Ethnic desegregation was associated with decentralization and higher social position, thus supporting Burgess' contention that the city is composed of concentric progressively "better" zones. The invasion-succession sequence is related to the process of desegregation and also fits in with the Burgess hypothesis. Invasion-succession typically occurs in a "ripple" fashion, as the more affluent groups move further and further out to modern areas as the city expands, and the neighborhoods they leave behind are settled by progressively lower ranking groups. However, the Burgess, Hoyt, and Harris-Ullman models are not necessarily applicable to cities in other countries having different historical, economic, and cultural elements.[44]

SELECTED BIBLIOGRAPHY

BOOKS

Duncan, Otis Dudley, and Beverly Duncan, *The Negro Population of Chicago: A Study of Residential Succession.* Chicago: University of Chicago Press, 1957.

Dobriner, William, *Class in Suburbia,* ch. 4. Englewood Cliffs, N.J.: Prentice-Hall, 1963.

Firey, Walter, *Land Use in Central Boston.* Cambridge, Mass.: Harvard University Press, 1947.

Glazer, Nathan, and Davis McEntire (eds.), *Studies in Housing and Minority Groups.* Berkeley and Los Angeles: University of California Press, 1960.

————, and D. Moynihan, *Beyond the Melting Pot: The Negroes, Puerto Ricans, Jews, Italians, and Irish of New York City.* Cambridge, Mass.: Harvard University Press, 1963.

Hoover, Edgar, and Raymond Vernon, *Anatomy of a Metropolis,* ch. 8. Cambridge, Mass.: Harvard University Press, 1959.

[43] Vernon, *op. cit.,* p. 142.   [44] See Chapter 7, pp. 135–39.

Laurenti, Luigi, *Property Values and Race*. Berkeley and Los Angeles: University of California Press, 1960.

Lieberson, Stanley, *Ethnic Patterns in American Cities*. New York: The Free Press of Glencoe, 1963.

Marris, Peter, *Family and Social Change in an African City: A Study of Rehousing in Lagos*. Evanston, Ill.: Northwestern University Press, 1962.

Rossi, Peter, *Why Families Move*. Glencoe, Ill.: The Free Press, 1955.

————, and R. Dentler, *The Politics of Urban Renewal: The Chicago Findings*. Glencoe, Ill.: The Free Press, 1961.

ARTICLES

Bressler, Marvin, "The Myers' Case: An Instance of Successful Racial Invasion," *Social Problems*, 8 (Fall, 1960), 126–42.

Caplow, Theodore, "The Social Ecology of Guatemala City," *Social Forces*, 28 (December, 1949), 113–33.

Dotson, Floyd, and Lillian Dotson, "Ecological Trends in Guadalajara, Mexico," *Social Forces*, 32 (May, 1954), 367–74.

Gilmore, H., "The Old New Orleans and the New," *American Sociological Review*, 9 (August, 1944), 385–94.

Lieberson, Stanley, "Suburbs and Ethnic Residential Patterns," *American Journal of Sociology*, LXVII (May, 1962), 673–82.

Richey, Elinor, "Kenwood Foils the Block-Busters," *Harper's*, 227 (August, 1963), 42–47.

Taeuber, Karl, and Alma Taeuber, "The Negro as an Immigrant Group: Recent Trends in Racial and Ethnic Segregation in Chicago," *American Journal of Sociology*, LXIX (January, 1964), 374–82.

Wolf, Eleanor, "The Invasion-Succession Sequence as a Self-Fulfilling Prophecy," *Journal of Social Issues*, 13 (1957), 7–20.

Urban and Suburban

Residential Areas

—

NINE

Among the many kinds of residential areas in the city, slums and suburbs have received the lion's share of attention. Slums often arouse humanitarian concern as well as the desire to protect society from the physical and social blight they may contain. Suburbs, although relatively recent arrivals in the American landscape, are now so pervasive that it is impossible to describe American cities without including them. In many ways, slums and suburbs contrast sharply, thereby providing insight into various urban ways of life. For these reasons, slums, suburbs, and an emerging residential type, the rural-urban fringe, will be examined in this chapter. The patterns found in the United States are not universal, however. In the concluding section of the chapter a cross-cultural comparison is made with cities in other countries of the world, especially Latin America, Asia, and Europe.

THE URBAN RESIDENTIAL SLUM

The term "slum" has many connotations. Because it means different things to different people, the term itself has limited value for sociological and ecological analysis. Nevertheless, it has wide currency, sociological and otherwise. One way of viewing the slum is that it is an area characterized by deteriorated houses densely occupied by impoverished people whose way of life and standard of conduct are often at variance with those of people on higher socioeconomic levels. Such a definition should be considered relative because of the many exceptions to it.

177

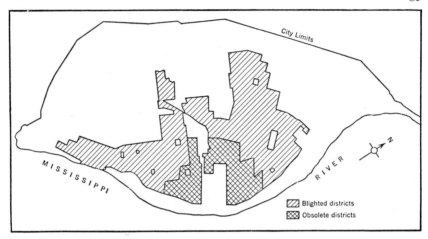

Figure 16. Slums are spreading in many cities. St. Louis is an example. The obsolete district shown on this map surrounds the central business district. Some measures have been taken toward slum clearance and redevelopment. SOURCE: *St. Louis after World War II,* courtesy St. Louis Planning Commission.

THE NATURE OF THE SLUM

The residential slum in an American city springs from a combination of factors and circumstances. In expanding cities, competition for favorable sites by business, industry, and residence sets in motion a continuous process of change in land-use patterns. In some sections, notably those adjacent to the business district, or on the periphery of the settlement, this change may be quite rapid, especially in a growing city. This is why Burgess called the central slum an area of transition. Its transitional and unstable character is undoubtedly due in part to the lack of effective land-use planning in the past. Since residential land was to be put to a different use some time in the future, buildings were allowed to deteriorate as property owners squeezed the maximum rental revenues from them.

The physical deterioration itself makes the area relatively unappealing as a residential area, at least to most persons. But one thing is in its favor: comparatively cheap rents. For this reason it is populated by people who ordinarily cannot afford to live elsewhere. Poverty and physical deterioration thus go hand in hand. The slum area has been a port of entry for millions of impoverished and dispossessed migrants: Old World immigrants, Negroes from the South, uprooted village and farm folk, Mexican laborers from across the border, Puerto Ricans from the slums of San Juan.

The convenience of the area to downtown, coupled with its low rents, also attracts students, artists, "bohemians," and some intellectuals. Criminals and social deviants of various types are attracted by the opportunity for anonymity provided by density of population and by the lack of organized resistance to their residence. These various groups may live in separate sections of the slums or be intermingled to some extent.

Whether a slum is interpreted in terms of the sector or concentric zone theory or some other proposition, its general location in most American cities is fairly obvious. Ordinarily it is situated around or near the central business district, near heavy industries, or on major transportation routes such as rivers or waterways. Many cities have small-scale slums lying just beyond the municipal boundaries in one or two sectors of the community.

THE SLUM AND SOCIAL DISORGANIZATION

The residential slum has commonly been interpreted as an area of social disorganization. Yet what often passes as disorganization may be only a different form of social organization, possibly organization of an unconventional type. As Whyte points out, human behavior in the slum may be as highly organized and social controls quite as effective as in a fashionable suburb, except that the slum residents may not always conform to middle class standards of propriety and respectability.[1] The tightly organized groups of delinquents and criminals, the alliance between crime and politics, and between business and crime, the systems maintained by racketeers and other denizens of the underworld, are forms of social organization.

Although there may be a greater tolerance of nonmarital sexual relationships and illegitimacy in slum areas than elsewhere, this does not mean that anarchy prevails. Sexual relations are organized around definite values and conducted according to accepted custom. Kinsey also found that although people of lower socioeconomic status, most of whom we may assume to be slum residents, deviated from middle class sexual standards, they did adhere to their own standards. Many of them were, in fact, shocked by accepted middle class sexual behavior.[2]

The whole question of the relationship between slums and social disorganization has become more important as urban renewal and slum clearance have gained momentum. A study of turn-of-the-century housing reform points out that Americans have long had a simple faith that social betterment would inevitably result from the improvement of housing conditions.[3] To the contrary, an increasing number of professional and civic studies show that poor housing is not necessarily associated with social pathology—and even when it is, improving the housing will not

[1] W. F. Whyte, "Social Organization in the Slum," *American Sociological Review*, 8 (February, 1943), 34–39. Cf. Whyte, *Street-Corner Society* (1955); and Whyte, "A Slum Sex Code," *American Journal of Sociology*, 49 (July, 1943), 24–31.

[2] Jerome Himelhoch and Sylvia F. Fava (eds.), *Sexual Behavior in American Society: An Appraisal of the First Two Kinsey Reports* (1955), sec. IV.

[3] Roy Lubove, *The Progressives and the Slums: Tenement House Reform in New York City, 1890–1917* (1963), pp. 245–56.

guarantee improvement of the social pathology. The relationship between housing and social life is much more complex than that.[4]

As the wrecker's ball approaches ever more city slums, it becomes more urgent than ever to ask, "What is being destroyed"? Jane Jacobs' controversial book, *The Death and Life of Great American Cities* (1961), contends that the mixed land use, density of population, and old buildings on small blocks, which usually lead to labeling an area as a slum, may not create slums in a social sense. She discusses Greenwich Village in New York City, among other cases, and urges re-examination of the haphazard destruction of so-called slums. After conducting a participant-observation study of the West End, an Italian neighborhood in Boston, prior to its replacement by luxury apartment buildings, Gans, a sociologist and city planner, concluded that the West End was a low-rent area with a cohesive, stable social structure, albeit not organized around middle class standards of success.[5] He urges that a distinction be made between *low-rent* and *slum* districts. Although both have deteriorated housing, only in the slums is the deterioration associated with harmful effects on the individual or the larger society.[6]

Ironically, social disorganization came to many former West Enders as a result of being forced to leave. The higher rents in other parts of the city strained limited budgets and separation from kin and friendship groups weakened the bases around which social life was organized. Half a world away, in Nigeria on the West Coast of Africa, a slum clearance project in Lagos, the capital city, had similar results and provoked similiar criticism of redevelopment policies.[7]

All of this should not blind us to the fact that there are areas of physical, social, and moral degradation which deserve to be called slums in any sense of the word and should be eliminated. We are calling attention here only to the uncritical assumption that physical and social blight necessarily go hand in hand.

SLUMS AS PROBLEM AREAS

Changing land-use patterns, high residential mobility, excessive density, physical blight, race discrimination, and poverty in the midst of plenty all contribute to the creation of problem areas. Such areas in time develop a social character that distinguishes them from other areas. If they attract impoverished people, they may also attract social misfits and pariahs. Their social climate may be such as to encourage and foster unconven-

---

[4] Irving Rosow, "The Social Effects of the Physical Environment," *Journal of the American Institute of Planners*, 27 (May, 1961), 127–33.

[5] Herbert Gans, *The Urban Villagers* (1962).   [6] *Ibid.*, p. 308ff.

[7] Peter Marris, *Family and Social Change in an African City: A Study of Rehousing in Lagos* (1962).

tional behavior, or at least to tolerate it. Evidence points to a higher-than-average incidence of crime and delinquency, sex deviations, and forms of personal disorganization such as insanity and suicide.

A comprehensive report on the ecology of delinquency and crime in 21 American and Canadian cities shows the highest incidence of such behavior in the inner zones of cities, usually in slum areas.[8] These ecological configurations are based on the place of residence of delinquents and criminals. Allowing for errors in reporting, or for the fact that slum residents are more subject to police control and arrest than people in other sections of the same city, there is nevertheless reason to believe that certain forms of crime and delinquency abound in the slum. Although reliable data on sex deviations are difficult to obtain, there is evidence that organized prostitution and perversion are practiced more extensively in the slums than elsewhere in the city.

Studies of insanity in a number of American cities, based upon the residence of persons committed to psychopathic hospitals, show quite consistently that the highest rates are centered in the inner zones, in the so-called areas of disorganization or transition—the slums. In a well-known study conducted in Chicago, Faris and Dunham found this pattern to be characteristic of the various insanities, with the exception of manic-depressive psychoses.[9] This ecological patterning of insanity conforms fairly closely to the patterning of suicide and desertion.

There is also evidence that the death rate is considerably higher in the inner sections of cities than in areas removed from the central business district. This also applies to various diseases—especially tuberculosis, venereal diseases, and nutritional disease—and accidents. The chances of being murdered are considerably greater in the inner districts than elsewhere.

It would appear that the forces and conditions that produce any of these so-called pathologies are similarly related to others. A study of the 352 health areas into which New York City is divided showed high rates of social problems were concentrated in particular areas.[10] Juvenile delinquency rates, welfare payments, infant mortality, venereal disease, psychiatric clinic cases, and overcrowding in dwelling units were the indices of social problems. Ten areas, all of them slums toward the center of the city, had high rates on all six indices. In a similar vein, a complex statistical investigation of 20 American cities with populations between 200,000 and 500,000 showed that groups with low income, low education, and unskilled occupations were highly concentrated in particular areas of the city.[11]

[8] Clifford R. Shaw and Henry D. McKay, *Juvenile Delinquency and Urban Areas* (1942).

[9] R. E. L. Faris and H. Warren Dunham, *Mental Disorders in Urban Areas* (1939).

[10] "Interaction of 'J.D.' and Other Social Problems," *Youth Board News* (New York City Youth Board), 2 (May, 1959), 3–4.

[11] Calvin Schmid, E. H. MacCannell, and M. D. Van Arsdol, "The Ecology of the American City," *American Sociological Review*, 23 (August, 1958), 392–401.

SLUMS AND RACE

In the past the slums have been only a temporary abode for many of their residents. Immigrants, students, artists, and those temporarily "down-on-their-luck" usually moved on when their economic position improved. Today, however, there is danger that many slum residents, and their descendants, may become permanently trapped in the slums, primarily because so many slum residents are nonwhite. Significantly, almost all of the 10 high-problem areas in the New York City study were nonwhite ghettos. The large-scale movement of the white population to suburban areas and the replacement of immigration from abroad by internal migration from the rural south have dramatically increased the proportion of Negroes in cities.[12] To a far greater extent than for the white immigrant groups which preceded them as ghetto residents, the nonwhite minorities have found discrimination focussed primarily on the unchanging genetic characteristics of skin color rather than on the relatively flexible cultural characteristics of distinctive dress, speech patterns, or customs of individual or group behavior.

Racial discrimination acts doubly to isolate Negroes in slums. Discrimination in education and employment places them in an economic position where few can afford any but low-rent housing. The 1960 census indicated the median income of white males was $5,137 while that of nonwhite males was only $3,075. The ecological study of 20 major American cities showed that residentially Negroes were clearly concentrated in areas of low socioeconomic status.[13] Sometimes the slum does not even provide inexpensive housing for Negroes. Because landlords realize Negroes have "nowhere else to go," apartments may be subdivided and each room rented to a family on a weekly basis, resulting in high rental costs. Or "furnished" apartments may be the basis for high rents for inferior facilities. Race discrimination also operates to restrict the residential mobility even of those Negroes who have the means and desire to move from the slums.

A broad range of programs is underway throughout the nation to break the vicious cycle of Negro ghettoization. Several cities are "bussing" Negro children to schools in white neighborhoods to achieve school integration despite residential segregation. Others have instituted specially enriched curricula for schools in Negro neighborhoods. Sit-ins, protest marches, civil rights legislation, and lawsuits are challenging the denial of equal opportunity to Negroes in housing, employment, political affairs, and places of public accomodation. On their outcome hinges whether the majority of urban Negroes will be forced to live in slums.

---

[12] See Chapters 7 and 8 for details of Negro urban migration and segregation.
[13] Schmid, MacCannell, and Van Arsdol, *op. cit.*, p. 400.

THE SUBURBS

DEFINITIONS OF SUBURBS

Suburbs are much-discussed but ill-defined. One reason for the variety of definitions is that the census provides no criteria for suburban status. In the voluminous literature on suburbs there are, however, two general approaches to the problem of definition. The first relies on objective, relatively easily measurable characteristics, such as demographic characteristics of the population or the type of land use. The second emphasizes the social organization and values of suburbanites. The two approaches are not mutually exclusive, but the distinction is a useful one. The following are examples of the first type of definition.

A. An inclusive definition which has the virtues of simplicity and comparability defines as suburban all the territory within the census Standard Metropolitan Statistical Area but outside the central cities. On this basis, almost 40 million Americans were suburbanites in 1950 and almost 55 million in 1960.

B. A more refined definition of suburbs is based on the census delineation of Urbanized Areas. The suburban population may be defined as that within the Urbanized Area but outside the central cities. On this basis about 21 million Americans were suburbanites in 1950 and almost 38 million in 1960.

Whichever of these or similar definitions is used, clearly suburbs are an important and growing aspect of the American landscape.[14]

When defined in terms of social organization, "suburbanism as a way of life" has been said to include neighboring,[15] emphasis on family values,[16] status-seeking, and conforming behavior.[17] Obviously such items are less precisely measurable, although techniques do exist. Later in this chapter we shall discuss the evidence for a suburban way of life.

One need not choose between defining suburbs in objective geographic terms or as a distinctive type of social organization. Both are necessary to the study of suburbs. The real difficulty lies in relating the two types of definition. Do the demographic and locational characteristics of suburbs produce the social characteristics; or do certain social traits produce suburban settlement patterns; or is there some combination of these types

[14] Several varieties of suburban definitions based on Metropolitan Area and Urbanized Area concepts are developed in Otis Dudley Duncan and Albert Reiss, *Social Characteristics of Urban and Rural Communities, 1950* (1956), chs. 11 and 14. See Chapter 3 of this text for explanations of Metropolitan Area and Urbanized Area.

[15] Sylvia F. Fava, "Suburbanism as a Way of Life," *American Sociological Review*, 21 (February, 1956), 34–37.

[16] Wendell Bell, "Social Choice, Life Styles and Suburban Residence," in W. Dobriner (ed.), *The Suburban Community* (1958).

[17] William H. Whyte, Jr., *The Organization Man* (1956), Pt. VII.

of causation? These are basic ecological questions in suburban dress, the full answers to which are not yet available on the basis of current research. It is the point of view of this book that both types of causation operate in the ecological process generally, and will be found to do so in the suburban situation, too.

STAGES OF SUBURBAN GROWTH

Viewing decentralization as a long-time trend, a social historian, Frederick Lewis Allen, has identified five stages of suburban development in the United States.[18] These periods, by no means clearly distinct but tending to overlap, are especially applicable to great metropolitan areas.

The first stage, the horse-and-buggy period, began in the latter years of the nineteenth century and lasted until about the close of World War I. Many well-to-do people all along had maintained country homes which they occupied part of the year, but late in the century some of them adopted the practice of year-round living in their rural or semirural homes, commuting to work by train or trolley. As the advantages of outlying residence gained wider appeal, numerous persons moved to the rim, settling in clusters within walking distance of railroad or interurban stations. Families financially able to afford a stable and coachman could locate a little farther from the station.

The second period, according to Allen, covered approximately the 1920's. A period of revolution in transportation, the number of automobiles increased from 9 million in 1920 to around 26 million in 1930. Open cars were replaced by all-weather closed cars, and road-building was undertaken on an unprecedented scale. Railroad and interurban lines carried increasing numbers of persons, but the number transported by private cars grew by leaps and bounds. Undeveloped tracts on the outskirts of cities were criss-crossed with streets as suburban developments were carried out to accommodate the thousands of families bent on moving to the country.

The third period covered the depression years of the 1930's and World War II. When the Great Depression which started in 1929 began to stifle the nation's economy, the headlong flight to the suburbs was stopped. Real estate developments that had been blithely undertaken on a shoestring collapsed, partly because families that had purchased property on an equally slender shoestring were unable to keep up their payments, partly because uncommitted families would not risk their savings in suburban property. As the country regained its economic health in the late 1930's, there was a resumption of suburban developments but on a modest scale. Much of it was what Allen calls "filling in the chinks" around the

[18] Frederick Lewis Allen, "The Big Change in Suburbia," Part I, *Harper's Magazine*, 208 (June, 1954), 21–28.

edge of cities, between cities and nearby suburbs, or along radial thoroughfares. Heavy government expenditures in peripheral areas for parkways, bridges, cloverleaf intersections, and express highways laid the stage for another flight to the suburbs. But building and transportation restrictions imposed by the war prevented it from occurring. During the whole of this period, from 1930 to 1945, population growth in the suburbs was about the same as for the country as a whole.

The postwar period, in Allen's view, represents the fourth and fifth stages. The fourth stage featured the mass-produced suburb built for war veterans and other young families with limited means. Unlike many suburban developments, which occurred mainly by slow accretion as new houses were gradually added one by one, the mass-produced suburbs around the great cities were constructed as large-scale engineering enterprises. Levittown near New York, Drexelbrook in the Philadelphia area, Park Forest outside Chicago, Parkmerced near San Francisco, and Lakewood outside Los Angeles are examples of entire communities being constructed on the assembly-line principle.

These suburbs were built for the young people of an intensely domestic generation, who want to have babies, and take their parental duties seriously; who cannot afford servants and would not know what to do with them if they had them; who enjoy sharing the work in and about the house; who fully subscribe to the do-it-yourself credo of a generation of household tinkerers; and who subscribe equally fully to the current cult of informality, getting into slacks or shorts as soon as they reach the suburb and continuing to wear them until they leave for town.[19]

By no means all of suburban growth during the postwar period took the form of large-scale enterprises. Wealthy or well-to-do families, as well as many families of limited incomes, built private homes according to individual tastes and interests. Nevertheless, even in the vicinity of small and medium-sized cities much of suburban growth was of the development type, but on a small scale.

Park Forest, about thirty miles south of Chicago, is an example of a postwar suburb built on the principle of mass production. Built on an open-country site of about 2,400 acres, Park Forest was designed as a commuter's suburb of about 30,000 residents. All of the planning and development was done by a private corporation; so far as the accommodations and facilities were concerned, the community was ready-made.

Allen's fifth period is what he calls the "discovery of the suburbs by business." This trend is discussed in Chapter 10 dealing with decentralization of business and industry. Although there has been considerable movement of business to the suburbs in past decades, the postwar period witnessed an unprecedented shift of business activities from the center to the periphery.

[19] *Ibid.*, pp. 25–28.

Superhighways in the American metropolis symbolize the suburban trend. Such highways carry a heavy daily load of passenger traffic moving between outlying areas and the central zones of the city. The Garden State Parkway is shown as it passes near Perth Amboy, New Jersey. (Courtesy Cities Service Company [photograph by Anthony Linck].)

PORTRAIT OF SUBURBIA

ECONOMIC AND DEMOGRAPHIC CHARACTERISTICS

The suburban population differs in many significant ways from that of the central city. Including as suburban the Urbanized Area population outside of central cities, Duncan and Reiss found that child-rearing and high socioeconomic status were associated with suburban residence.[20] Thus, suburbs had a higher fertility ratio than central cities, an "excess" of population between 0–13 years and a "deficit" of those over 45; a larger proportion married; and a more evenly balanced sex ratio than the central cities. The median income was higher in suburbs, and the suburban population aged 25 and over completed a median of 11.3 years of school compared with 10.3 for central city residents. Suburbs also have higher proportions of their workers employed in professional and managerial occupations and in the higher blue collar ranks of craftsmen and foremen. Finally, native whites are proportionately more numerous in suburbs than in central cities.

Duncan and Reiss note that not all of these contrasts are exclusively suburban-central city contrasts. Although small cities outside the orbit of Urbanized Areas show the same pattern of marital and fertility characteristics and high proportions of native whites as suburbs, they do not have the high socioeconomic characteristics of suburbs. Duncan and Reiss conclude that the particular constellation of characteristics found in suburbs is a consequence of the fact that suburbs are specialized areas within a larger economic city, although many are politically independent. On the whole, Duncan and Reiss' data, which covered suburbs on a nationwide basis for 1950, confirm the impression that suburbs are disproportionately occupied by white middle and high status population in the child-rearing phase of the family-cycle.

The growth of suburbs has been accompanied by a persistence of central-city suburban differences, although the gap is narrowing in some respects. At least this is suggested in a recent analysis of changes from 1950 to 1956.[21] The family-cycle characteristics of suburbs are borne out by the increasing concentration there of large families (three or more children) and young family heads (under 45 years). High income groups ($7,500 or more per year) and more expensive housing (rent over $100 or value over $10,000) are also increasingly concentrated in suburbs. However, with respect to educational attainment and occupation, city-suburban differences are not as marked as they had been. Apparently suburbs are no longer so exclusively a residential center for middle class families.

SUBURBAN SOCIAL ORGANIZATION

Suburban social structure has been described in topics ranging from family values, religion, education, formal and informal participation, to politics, leisure, and general "philosophy of life." Unfortunately, the use-

---

[20] Duncan and Reiss, *op. cit.*, ch. 11.

[21] Bernard Lazerwitz, "Metropolitan Residential Belts, 1950 and 1956," *American Sociological Review*, 25 (April, 1960), 245–52.

fulness of many such studies is diminished because no comparative norms for urban or rural areas are presented. The question of suburban social organization has also brought forth a flood of opinions, critiques, and value-judgments. Dobriner makes the apt distinction between "commentators" and "scientists." The commentators are uniformly opposed to suburbs, regarding them as "homogenized" communities where "social and personal differences are submerged beneath a great wet blanket of conformity." [22]

Social Consequences of Suburban Location and Population Characteristics. Several observers have noted that the objective characteristics of suburbs have fairly predictable social consequences. Thus, Fava has pointed out that the relatively small size, low density, and greater homogeneity of population in suburbs are conditions favorable to informal neighborhood contacts.[23] Her later study in the New York metropolitan area confirmed that higher levels of neighboring were indeed more characteristic of suburbs than of central city areas.[24]

Martin has pointed out that in addition to relatively low community size and density of population, such characteristics of suburbs as outlying location and commuting to work in the central city may be important in determining the type and frequency of social interaction.[25] Thus, a daily trip to a work-place separated from home by long distance, social differences, and, perhaps, political jurisdiction, may produce a division of suburbanites' participation and interests. Daily commuting prolongs the absence of men from their place of residence and may therefore also result in more important roles for women in suburban activities. Both Fava and Martin stress that migration to suburbs has been selective of white, native-born, middle class couples who are rearing families. The resulting homogeneity may produce a high degree of community involvement. These hypotheses require further testing, but are suggestive of the possible social consequences of objective suburban characteristics. Obviously, if the external characteristics of suburbs change in time—if, for example, suburbs become larger, more densely populated, and more heterogeneous in population composition, and if more suburbanites have nearby jobs than commute to the central city—then any related social consequences would also change.

Values and Suburban Social Organization. Suburban and urban social organization may differ, not only as a consequence of socially relevant external characteristics of population and location, but also as a consequence of differences in values, standards, beliefs and preferences. There is some evidence that the dominant values of suburbanites emphasize

---

[22] William Dobriner, *Class in Suburbia* (1963), p. 5.   [23] Fava, *op. cit.*

[24] Sylvia F. Fava, "Contrasts in Neighboring: New York City and a Suburban County," in William Dobriner (ed.), *The Suburban Community* (1958). See Chapter 17, pp. 408–9, for a summary of the study.

[25] Walter Martin, "The Structuring of Social Relationships Engendered by Suburban Residence," *American Sociological Review*, 21 (August, 1956), 446–53.

TABLE 9

Percentage Distribution of First Choices in Each of the Life Styles, by Suburban or City Residence and Neighborhood Economic Status

	City		*Suburban*	
LIFE STYLE	JACKSON BLVD. (LOW ECON.)	NEAR NORTH SIDE (HIGH ECON.)	BELLWOOD (LOW ECON.)	KENILWORTH (HIGH ECON.)
Familism	55%	45%	75%	61%
Career	18	27	17	17
Consumership	27	28	8	22
	100%	100%	100%	100%

SOURCE: Wendell Bell, "Social Choice, Life Styles and Suburban Residence," in W. Dobriner (ed.), *The Suburban Community* (New York: Putnam's, 1958), p. 241.

familism, the local group, and direct participation to a greater extent than do the values of urban residents.

A study in several suburbs in metropolitan Chicago disclosed a greater emphasis on familistic values, defined as the orientation of life goals and activities around the home and children, than on alternative value systems centered on career aspirations or enjoyable consumption.[26] The three values and related life styles—familism, career, and consumership—are to some degree antithetical, often forcing the individual to make a choice. For example, devotion of time and money to the family may interfere with upward occupational mobility and with achieving as high a standard of living as possible. Familism was measured by asking the suburbanites why they had moved from the city. Eighty-three per cent gave responses classified as familistic—"more healthy for children," "nicer children for playmates," "better schools," "home ownership provides greater security for children than living in an apartment." Only 10 per cent gave responses involving upward social mobility, and only 43 per cent gave responses classified as consumership. Since many suburbanites gave more than one type of reason, the percentages total more than 100.

In another phase of the study, suburban and urban residents were forced to make a choice between familistic, career, and consumership responses on a questionnaire. Table 9 shows that, although familism obtained more first choices than either career or consumership in each of the suburban and urban communities, the predominance of familistic responses was greater in the suburban communities. The table also shows that familism varies by economic status as well as by city or suburban location, but that suburbs have a higher proportion of familistic choices than economically equivalent urban areas. Thus, suburban Kenilworth

[26] Bell, *op. cit.*

Planned suburban developments present a wide variety of ecological configurations. In the United States most of these developments are by private enterprise, but in Europe they are often carried out by municipalities or cooperatives. Above: A cooperative housing project in an Oslo suburb. Below: A suburban development in the vicinity of St. Louis, Missouri. (Courtesy Norwegian Information Service and Missouri Resources Division [photograph by Massie].)

residents gave familistic responses 61 per cent of their first choices, compared with 45 per cent of the residents of the urban Near North Side.

Whyte's well-known study of Park Forest indicated that suburban social organization exemplifies a broad shift in American values from the frugality, hard work, and individualism of the Protestant Ethic to the "fun morality," "belongingness," and "togetherness," of the Social Ethic.[27] Whyte proposed that the shift in values, together with widespread bureaucratization, upward mobility, and physical transiency, led people to a search for "new roots." In his study of Park Forest, Illinois, a large post-World War II housing development near Chicago, he found much frantic socializing in the community, a high degree of dependence on the group, and education, leisure, religion and consumption patterns centered around conformity. Wood, on the other hand, has argued that the local participation so evident in suburbs, especially in government, is representative of a renaissance of traditional democratic values rather than the emergence of a new set of values.[28] A major difficulty with such studies is determining what features, if any, of the values described are unique to suburbs.

A NEW LOOK AT SUBURBIA

A new trend has emerged in the literature on suburbs, stressing the diversity of suburban populations and the variety of suburban life styles. Obviously this limits generalizations that can be made about "the suburbs." This does not mean that suburbs do not have distinctive characteristics but simply that greater care is exercised in describing them. The reasons for the reappraisal lie both in changes taking place in suburbs as they come within the financial means of a broader range of socioeconomic groups, and in increasingly sophisticated research and theoretical tools which emphasize the importance of social class in urban and suburban social organization. Some of the differences that were thought to exist between cities and suburbs are perhaps not quite so pronounced as had originally been thought.

Heterogeneity of Suburban Economic and Social Characteristics. As noted earlier in this chapter, suburbs generally are characterized by higher income and occupational and educational status than urban areas. These contrasts persist, but some changes are under way, particularly with regard to occupational composition. Changes in population characteristics of metropolitan residential belts from 1950–56 disclosed that "the high income families living in the suburban belt are being joined by an increasing number of families of skilled and semiskilled workers (who live in low and moderate cost subdivisions.)"[29] An interesting conse-

[27] Whyte, *op. cit.* See Chapter 2, p. 32, of this text for a description of the Protestant Ethic.
[28] Robert C. Wood, *Suburbia—Its People and Their Politics* (1958).
[29] Lazerwitz, *op. cit.*, p. 252.

quence is that some suburbs have moved through an invasion-succession cycle from white collar to blue collar occupancy.[30] Such a process is apparently underway in Levittown, Long Island, where 62 per cent of the male residents were in white collar jobs in 1950–51, but in 1961 only 50 per cent were so classified.[31] During the same period the proportion of blue collar residents rose from 38 to 45 per cent.

One recent study suggests that urban-suburban contrasts in socioeconomic characteristics may be a function of the maturation of the metropolitan area.[32] In older metropolitan areas, deterioration and obsolescence at the core tend to be marked; hence, higher status families are likely to move to outlying suburban areas, resulting in high socioeconomic characteristics for the suburban areas. In newer metropolitan areas, central city deterioration is not as marked; hence many high status families remain in the central city. Schnore found that 1960 census data confirmed this view, for in older metropolitan areas suburbs generally outrank the central cities in income, education, and occupation whereas in newer metropolitan areas the reverse occurs—central cities outrank the suburban areas in socioeconomic status. Schnore notes that there is no guarantee that high status groups in the newer metropolitan areas will repeat the history of the older metropolises by shifting to suburban residence.[33]

Social Class and Suburban Diversity. It is becoming increasingly clear that residential location is only one of the many factors influencing suburban social organization and behavior. Suburbanites come from many backgrounds, and, as indicated above, the heterogeneity of suburban population is increasing rather than decreasing. Groups and individuals retain many of their former activities and allegiances in the suburbs. For example, urban Democrats appear to continue to vote for that party after they move to suburbs, rather than joining the Republican majority found in many suburbs.[34] Church attendance among Protestants and Catholics is as frequent among suburban as among urban residents, contrary to the belief that religious participation is more frequent among suburbanites.[35] Patterns of ethnic segregation also persist in suburbs. A study of 10 large metropolitan areas disclosed "that first- and second-generation groups have patterns of segregation from each other and from native-white population that are frequently similar to those of their central-city members." [36]

[30] See Chapter 7, pp. 132–35, for description of occupational segregation and Chapter 8, p. 155ff., for discussion of invasion-succession.

[31] Dobriner, *Class in Suburbia, op. cit.*, p. 98.

[32] Leo F. Schnore, "The Socio-Economic Status of Cities and Suburbs," *American Sociological Review*, 28 (February, 1963), 76–85.

[33] See also the discussion of emerging aspects of metropolitan ecological structure in Chapter 6, pp. 115–16.

[34] Bernard Lazerwitz, "Suburban Voting Trends, 1948–1959," *Social Forces*, 39 (October, 1960), 29–36.

[35] Bernard Lazerwitz, "National Data on Participation Rates among Residential Belts in the United States," *American Sociological Review*, 27 (October, 1962), 691–96.

[36] Stanley Lieberson, "Suburbs and Ethnic Residential Patterns," *American Journal of Sociology*, LXVII (May, 1962), 773–81.

Although ethnic and religious affiliation provide variations in the suburban (and urban) way of life, the chief variation is provided by social class. On the basis of a field study of 100 working-class families living in a suburb of the San Francisco Bay area, Berger pointed out that "there is no reason to believe that what is characteristic of organization men or of the 'new' middle classes is also characteristic of the mass-produced suburbs." [37] Most of the men of the families he studied were employed in blue collar jobs in a nearby Ford plant. He found that the families lived for the most part as they had before they moved to the suburb, rarely participating in formal associations or engaging in mutual visiting with suburban neighbors. They continued to vote for Democratic party candidates and their church participation remained low. Berger also found "little evidence of pronounced striving, status anxiety, or orientations to the future." [38] Life in this working-class suburb contrasted markedly with that of middle class groups in Park Forest or Crestwood Heights.[39]

More recently, Dobriner has compared life styles of the working-class and middle class groups within Levittown, Long Island.[40] The middle class values are privacy, initiative, and upward mobility; the working-class places less emphasis on privacy or appearances and is more concerned with living for the moment than planning for the future. In leisure time pursuits the middle class emphasizes reading more than television, while the reverse is true of the working-class. Middle class Levittowners are less concerned with maintaining traditional sex roles in home and child-rearing than are working-class Levittowners. The middle class group appears to do more entertaining and visiting with business associates and non-Levittown friends and less entertaining of relatives than does the working class group. Dobriner notes that these differences in outlook and activities have led to friction within local neighborhoods in Levittown.

Dobriner's general evaluation of urban-suburban differences in life style relative to social class differences bears repeating, for it is indicative of the direction of much current research on suburban social organization.

Life in the suburbs . . . may be expected to differ from life in the city in terms of social relationships and life styles arising out of transportation characteristics; extent and degree of informal relationships at the neighborhood level; degree of home-centered activity, such as gardening, do-it-yourselfing, and the like; and ease of child-rearing, particularly in the early years. As to political conversion, religious reawakenings, status climbing, attitudes toward education, basic family structure, and so forth, there is no indication that the suburban situation in any way significantly modifies basic class patterns. I hesitate to summarize these four suburban characteristics in whole or singly into a total way-of-life which sharply distinguishes suburbs from cities. The

[37] Bennett Berger, *Working-Class Suburb* (1960), p. 91.   [38] *Ibid.*, p. 92.
[39] See Chapter 24, pp. 559–60, for a description of life in Crestwood Heights.
[40] Dobriner, *Class in Suburbia, op. cit.*, pp. 106–8.

urban and suburban upper-middle class share many more significant characteristics between them than either shares with the working class.[41]

SUMMARY

The chief points about suburbs may be briefly noted as follows:

1. As suburban living has become characteristic of more and more Americans, a greater variety of suburbs and suburban life styles has developed than the simple, middle class, child-rearing suburb.

2. There are still many urban-suburban differences, but they co-exist with ethnic, religious, and, especially, social class differences within urban and suburban communities.

3. Further changes may be underway in suburbia as metropolitan areas grow older, potentially initiating a new phase of invasion-succession.

THE RURAL-URBAN FRINGE

Until fairly recently most decentralized families remained within easy access of the city's public facilities—city water, gas, electricity, bus routes, railroads. Freedom from the noise and congestion of the city was desirable, but not to be purchased at too dear a price, certainly not at the price of sacrificing modern conveniences associated with the comforts of living. Therefore the suburban movement, by and large, tended to be limited mainly to those outlying areas that were served by extensions of city services. But in recent decades, residential expansion has encompassed still further territory, the so-called rural-urban fringe.

THE NATURE OF THE FRINGE

The new centrifugal movement in the United States has by no means replaced the familiar suburban trend but has, instead, been an extension of the traditional march to the suburbs. In a very real sense it is a march *beyond* the suburbs. A detailed analysis of growth rates for various sections of the metropolitan area indicated that the more outlying portions of the ring are growing at a faster rate than the inner portions.[42] The ring was defined as the metropolitan territory outside the central city and was subdivided into urban and rural portions. In this study the "urban ring" is roughly equivalent to the suburbs and the "rural ring" to the rural-

---

[41] *Ibid.*, pp. 58–59.
[42] Leo F. Schnore, "Metropolitan Growth and Decentralization," *American Journal of Sociology,* 63 (September, 1957), 171–80.

urban fringe. Since the 1930–40 decade the rural ring has been growing much faster than the urban. In the 1940–50 decade the urban ring increased its population by 26 per cent while the rural ring increased by about 45 per cent. Within the rural ring, growth rates were computed separately for incorporated and unincorporated areas; the unincorporated areas grew more rapidly than the incorporated areas. These are precisely the areas most likely to fall into the rural-urban fringe category. In the 1950–60 decade the census shows that the total ring grew by almost 49 per cent. Detailed breakdowns for the suburban and fringe portions of the ring are not yet available but will undoubtedly show a continuation of heavy fringe growth.

CONTRIBUTING FACTORS

What, then, has facilitated such a trend? For one thing, automobiles are faster and more comfortable than ever before, and all-weather highways radiate outward in all directions from most cities. But these improvements in transportation, while important, are not the only changes that have encouraged the movement to the country. Rural electrification has made it possible for the open-country dweller to have electric power, heat, and light. The electric pump and the septic tank have made rural residents independent of city water and sewage systems. Fuel oil for space heating and bottled gas for cooking afford them independence from coal dealers and city gas mains. Television and radio provide the same satisfactions (or dissatisfactions) that are afforded city residents, and there may be little difference in the quality of their telephone or telegraph services. Hence the inconveniences or even hardships once associated with rural life are not necessarily present in the rural-urban fringe.

Yet technology alone cannot explain the trend; there are economic, social, and psychological factors as well. Some families undoubtedly move because it is fashionable to have a country estate or an acreage, others because they wish to supplement their incomes by part-time farming. Still others move for health reasons or because they wish their children to have the advantages of open-country life. No doubt many forsake the city because of adverse housing conditions, or because they wish to escape the tax collector or a disagreeable landlord. Among some the "back to nature" idea has become a consuming interest which can be realized only by abandoning the city.

In Europe, decentralization of population has occurred in urban areas, but the movement of city-occupied families into rural or semirural areas beyond the immediate suburbs has not happened to any extent. There are several reasons.[43] One is that only well-to-do people can afford automo-

---

[43] Personal correspondence from Professor E. W. Hofstee, Agricultural University, Wageningen, Netherlands.

biles. Commuters must therefore depend on buses or railroads. This means that commuters must locate near a bus stop or railway station. They tend to live, therefore, in compact settlements within easy walking distance of transportation routes. Secondly, agricultural land is too expensive for most urban residents. Thirdly, in several European countries, notably England and the Netherlands, a strict system of land-use planning for agriculture, industry, parks, and residential purposes limits choice of locations. Because land is scarce in most of these countries, strict regulations are imposed on the amount of space that individual families may have. Fourth, there seems less longing for the wide open spaces in Europe than in America or Canada. European peoples have long been accustomed to living in settled communities; even farmers are usually villagers by residence. Hence their desire for fresh air and sunlight and space is perhaps satisfied in garden-city suburbs rather than in open-country residence. Finally, part-time farming is simply not an important aspect of the European way of life. Agricultural operations of city people seldom extend beyond cultivation of a flower or vegetable garden.

DEFINITION OF THE FRINGE

Analysis of life in the rural-urban fringe has been handicapped by poor definition of just what areas should properly be included in this category. Often the problem is that one researcher's fringe is another's suburb. A recent analysis attempts to distinguish these two types of residential areas by the following criteria: (1) location; (2) land characteristics; (3) growth and density; (4) occupation; and (5) governmental structure.[44] On the basis of these criteria, the fringe was defined as "location beyond the limits of the legal city, in the 'agricultural hinterland,' exhibiting characteristics of mixed land use, with no consistent pattern of farm and nonfarm dwellings. The residents are involved in rural and urban occupations. The area is unincorporated, relatively lax zoning regulations exist, and few, if any, municipal services are provided. The area shows potentialities for population growth and increasing density ratios. Present density ratios are intermediate between urban and rural."

In contrast the suburbs are defined as "location beyond the limits of the legal city (possibly contiguous), with a consistent nonfarm residential pattern of land use. The residents are primarily employed in urban occupations, mostly in the central city. The area may either be incorporated or unincorporated, depending upon the type of suburb under investigation. However, some municipal services are provided even in the unincorporated suburbs; this is a responsibility assumed by real estate in-

[44] Richard A. Kurtz and Joanne B. Eicher, "Fringe and Suburb: A Confusion of Concepts," *Social Forces*, 37 (October, 1958), 32–37.

terests. Population growth may be taking place on the periphery, and density ratios are intermediate between urban and fringe." [45]

The underlying characteristic of the rural-urban fringe is well expressed in its designation—it is neither urban nor rural. Hence the fringe exhibits an amazing variety of people and land uses, both of which are not neatly separated into clusters but intermingled without much rhyme or reason. One study found that the fringe differed from suburbs precisely in that homogeneous communities on various levels of income, occupation, and so on, were characteristic of suburbs but not of the fringe.[46]

In the wide rural-urban zone that surrounds American cities, the population varies greatly as to occupation, economic status, and social interests. There is no neat formula that describes what the fringe or its people are like. In this zone one may find, often side by side, junk yards, trailer camps, roadhouses, hot dog stands, golf courses, truck gardens, tourist courts, oil depots, commercial farms, factories, cemeteries, airports, middle class homes, fashionable estates, and residential slums, not to mention vacant spaces that are too expensive for agricultural use and undesirable for residential occupancy.

Some of the residents are strictly agricultural by occupation; some are part-time farmers for whom the urban job is a major source of income; others are rural by residence only—persons whose interests, values, occupation, and style of life are those of the city or the metropolis. There are wealthy business or professional people whose spacious estates are exhibits of conspicuous consumption; middle class folk whose land holdings range from small plots to large farms operated by tenants or members of the family; working class families who perform the dual role of part-time farmer and urban worker. Within the zone are residential community developments of varying size, density, and character; areas in which families are sparsely and unevenly distributed in the open country; areas in which residence and business establishments are strung in monotonous rows along the main radial thoroughfares. Many families have moved from the nearby city or its suburbs to the rural-urban fringe; others have moved from distant points—from farms, villages, and cities. Culturally and psychologically, some are more urban than rural, others are more rural than urban.

A number of studies of the rural-urban fringe have been made in the United States, and the Bureau of the Census had taken into account fringe developments in its enumeration of population. However useful these studies may be, the varied definitions of the rural-urban fringe impair their value in the formulation of generalizations concerning the phenomenon for the country as a whole. Nevertheless, the researches that

[45] Comparison of this definition with those noted earlier in this chapter indicates that it has elements of both the objective and the social-organization approaches to community definitions.

[46] Leslie Kish, "Differentiation in Metropolitan Areas," *American Sociological Review,* 19 (August, 1954), 388–98.

have been undertaken, as well as the enumerative work of the U. S. Bureau of the Census, bring the phenomenon into focus and throw considerable light on its character. Some of the studies raise as many questions as they answer, but that is usually true of any scientific inquiry.

THE CHICAGO FRINGE

On the basis of published and unpublished 1950 census data, Duncan and Reiss made a thorough study of the rural-urban fringe of Chicago, Illinois.[47] The chief feature of their study was that the fringe population was divided into three groups: urban (residents of that portion of the urbanized area within the metropolitan district, but outside of incorporated places of 2,500 or more); rural-farm (farm residents within the metropolitan district but outside urban territory); rural-nonfarm (all other residents of the rural territory of the metropolitan district). By this definition the fringe occupied a belt up to 25 miles from the center of Chicago. The area included might have been larger under other definitions and would, in any case, be larger today as transportation and other factors have improved.

The social, economic, and demographic characteristics of these fringe groups were compared with the city and suburban populations of Chicago and also with the satellite population living beyond the rural-urban fringe. One important finding was that on most characteristics the urban and rural-nonfarm residents of the fringe are quite similar and resemble the city and suburban populations rather than the rural-farm population of the fringe. Such findings strongly suggest that the rural-nonfarm population in the vicinity of large cities consists primarily of urban-oriented residents.

The rural-farm component of the fringe illustrates the mixed influences of the fringe. Although it differs from the urban and rural-nonfarm components of the fringe, it also differs from the rural-farm population beyond the fringe. For example, the fertility ratio of the fringe rural-farm population is lower than that of the rural-farm populations that are a greater distance from the metropolis. The rural-farm population of the fringe seems to be "less urban" than the rural-nonfarm and urban components of the fringe but "more urban" than other rural-farm populations.

THE COLUMBIA FRINGE

The characteristics of the rural-urban fringe around Columbia, Missouri, a city of less than 50,000 population in 1960, may be compared with those for the Chicago metropolis. The Columbia study selected only

[47] Duncan and Reiss, *op. cit.,* ch. 12.

open-country families which had one or more members employed in the city and in which residential location was at least one-half mile from the city's corporate limits.[48] Excluded were families in the immediate suburban zone and in villages or towns within the area. The 460 families selected for interviewing represented, by conservative estimate, at least three-fourths of the families having direct occupational ties in the city. Some of them lived as far as 15 or 20 miles from the place of employment; others were within a few minutes' driving distance of work.

Slightly less than half of the families (49 per cent) had moved from Columbia; the remainder had migrated from other localities—30 per cent from farms in Missouri, 11 per cent from cities, and about 5 per cent from villages. Only 5 per cent had migrated from out of state.

When the decentralized families, that is, those which had moved from Columbia to the fringe, were compared with the nondecentralized families that had migrated from other places, some striking differences were apparent. Two-fifths of the decentralized families, but only one-fifth of the nondecentralized families, lived within three miles of the city. Beyond the five-mile point the proportions were reversed.

Decentralized families maintained closer associational ties with the city than was the case of the nondecentralized families. These differences were demonstrated empirically by means of indices developed to gauge the extent of membership and participation in organized groups, participation in unorganized or informal recreation, visiting relationships, and sharing in joint undertakings with neighbors or friends. Especially impressive were the differences between the decentralized and nondecentralized families in the membership-participation index for organized groups. Whereas the decentralized families had a higher membership-participation index for city groups, the nondecentralized families had a slightly higher index for groups located in the open country. Furthermore, decentralized families had a much higher index of membership-participation in city groups than the nondecentralized families had in rural groups. There may be several possible reasons for this difference. Decentralized families, in general, were younger and better educated that the others, and more representative of business, white collar, or professional occupations. No doubt many of the decentralized families continued to participate in city groups which they had joined before moving to the open country. Since there are actually more possibilities for formal-group membership in the city than in rural areas, "joiners" may be expected to utilize the city's resources in this respect.

The Columbia research examined attitudes of the population toward fringe residence. In the Columbia study, 90 per cent of the husbands and 88 per cent of the wives among the decentralized families, compared

[48] Noel P. Gist, "Ecological Decentralization and Rural-Urban Relationships," *Rural Sociology,* 17 (December, 1952), 328–35; and Gist, "Developing Patterns of Urban Decentralization," *Social Forces,* 30 (March, 1952), 257–67.

with 93 per cent of the husbands and wives in the nondecentralized group, were either reasonably satisfied or highly satisfied with this living arrangement. Since the men, by virtue of their occupational connections in the city, are perhaps less isolated or inconvenienced than the women, it is not surprising that the men were somewhat better adjusted to this arrangement. A study of the rural-urban fringe of Eugene-Springfield, Oregon, revealed similar attitudes.[49]

THE FRINGE—ASSET OR LIABILITY

THE PROBLEM OF ORGANIZED CONTROL

In most fringe areas there is no over-all planning for systematic land use; this appears to be true, at least, of unincorporated and sparsely settled areas in the outer reaches of the zone, and in some localities it is characteristic of the entire belt, from the city limits outward. Such lack of planning and orderly regulation of land use betokens the varied character of the occupants and the conflicts of their interests.

A considerable portion of the outlying population lives in unincorporated settlements that have no local government but are subject only to formal controls imposed by the county or state. Some of these settlements are strung along radial highways. Because of the distinctive ecological patterning of such settlements, often a mixture of residences and business establishments catering to the traveling public, neither local community sentiment nor community organization can develop to any marked extent. In many areas there are no effective agencies for dealing with such problems as crime, sanitation, or transportation. Students of government have frequently proposed an over-all agency that would have jurisdiction over an entire metropolitan area, including the city and its outlying fringe districts. Vested interests and community rivalries have made this proposal difficult if not impossible to put into effective operation.

Divergent values and conflicting interests of fringe occupants often stand in the way of effective community organization. The issue of extending municipal services to adjacent fringe areas has been a subject of heated debate among residents. Families engaged in part-time or full-time agricultural activities may oppose extension of utilities, or the development of other communal enterprises, on the ground that higher tax levies would make it impossible for them to stay in business, or merely that, after all, such things are unnecessary luxuries. On the other hand, residents with urban backgrounds, especially those on the higher income levels, may support such developments because modern utilities are important aspects of their preferred mode of living.

[49] Walter T. Martin, *The Rural-Urban Fringe: A Study of Adjustment to Residence Location* (1953).

Whether the social and economic advantages of fringe residence outweigh the additional economic costs is a matter which would have to be determined on the basis of specific families, taking into consideration a number of factors, including distance from the city, kinds of transportation, differences in property taxes, and expenditures for certain forms of conveniences and services. But even then no accurate assessment can be made because there are noneconomic values as well as economic considerations. Stated simply, large numbers of persons are willing to pay handsomely in time, money, inconvenience, and energy for the satisfactions of living in a rural-urban fringe.

SOCIAL RELATIONSHIPS AND FRINGE RESIDENCE

There is some reason to believe that conditions imposed by fringe residence affect family relationships and roles.[50] Since the majority of employed male adults work in the central city or adjacent suburbs and are therefore away from home most of the day, usually leaving early and returning late, the responsibility of managing the home and rearing the children falls on the mother. The family tends therefore to become what Mowrer has called the matricentric or mother-centered group. While this situation also prevails in the city, it appears to be accentuated in the fringe.

Conditions of residence in the rural or semirural fringe, plus the fact that such residence is often a considerable distance from the centers of social activity in the city, may make it easier for parents to exercise effective supervision over the activities of young children. Mere distance to the urban centers of social activity—movies, sports events, the playgrounds, the organized groups of one sort or another—undoubtedly forces many children and parents back on their own resources, whatever they may be. If the fringe family is engaged in part-time agriculture, as many are, whether gardening, livestock-raising, or even extensive cultivation, there is usually work that needs to be done, or enterprises that can be undertaken on a family basis. No doubt one of the reasons for the comparative solidarity of the farm family has been the functional interrelatedness of roles played by parents and children.

But if the conditions of living in the rural-urban zone, at least in the more remote parts of it, make it necessary and possible for families to exert effective control over the behavior of young children, the same conditions may introduce difficult problems of control over them when they reach the adolescent age. Often there are no high schools in the immediate vicinity, which fact makes it necessary for the teenagers to be transported to a school in the central city or in one of the suburbs. If

[50] See especially the discussion by E. G. Jaco and I. Belknap, "Is a New Family Form Emerging in the Urban Fringe?" *American Sociological Review*, 18 (October, 1953), 550–57.

school buses are available, this may entail no inconvenience or hardship; but if transportation is provided by the family, some obvious difficulties may be encountered. What is probably more important is the tendency for high school students to make social commitments that pull them away from their respective families and neighborhoods. Such commitments commonly involve participation in social activities in evenings and after-school hours—extracurricular activities or activities that are strictly social. The transportation problem may create tensions between members of the family, or impose upon the parents the role of chauffeur for their pleasure-bent children.

Most of the studies point to the paucity of voluntary associations in the rural-urban fringe, and some of the associations that serve this zone have little or no appeal to persons whose social interests are mainly in the city. Here again one should be cautious about making easy generalizations, for the interests and tastes of urbanized persons who live in the fringe are by no means uniform. Some families have identified themselves with the rural community, participating actively in local organizations and maintaining a close relationship with farm families. Others, however, are *in* the rural-urban zone, but hardly *of* it. Their relationships outside the home are almost entirely with city people. Neighbors, to them, are merely nigh-dwellers.

EFFECTS ON THE CENTRAL CITY

The centrifugal movement is not without its serious impact on the economy of the central cities. As the march to the suburbs or the open country continues, the city's financial structure undergoes increasing strains because of the loss of revenue through migration of the taxpayers. There is, at the same time, another side of the picture. Probably all cities, large and small, are dependent in considerable measure on the support of families that reside beyond the municipal boundaries, whether in the immediate suburbs or in the rural or semirural fringe. Without them organized city life could hardly function, at least as at present. As numerous studies have shown, the occupational structure is maintained both by persons who live "inside" and those who live "outside." But there are many other city groups and associations that depend upon the outsiders for leadership, financial support, and ordinary services associated with active participation. The extent to which residents of the rural-urban fringe participate in associational activities centered in the city is evidence of the reciprocal relationships that exist between the city and its adjacent hinterland. They are mutually dependent, and never the twain can be severed short of serious damage to both.

It should be apparent that many pertinent questions concerning the rural-urban fringe are unanswered in anything like precise terms, although some of the systematic studies that have been completed do throw some light on the phenomenon. One may, therefore, appropriately pose certain questions that can only be answered by means of further systematic investigation. Some of these might be stated as follows:

Do the fringe areas surrounding manufacturing or mining cities differ in land use, population characteristics, and forms of social relationships from cities that are predominantly commercial in character?

Does the size of the central city have any bearing on the social, economic, and other characteristics of the fringe?

What differences, if any, exist between the fringe areas surrounding American cities and those within the orbit of cities in other countries—the cities of western Europe, for example?

Is there developing in fringe areas a mode of life that is neither distinctively urban nor rural, but a blending of the two; and if so, what are its principal characteristics?

RESIDENTIAL PATTERNS IN OTHER COUNTRIES

As we have noted earlier, the growth of cities appears to be universal in modern times, although the pattern and nature of such growth vary from one city or society to another. Thus, while it is probable that the populations of all of the world's large cities spill over their outer boundaries, the location and characteristics of their slums and suburbs offer many contrasts with one another as well as with those of the United States.

City growth is not necessarily synonymous with suburbanization in the sense of adjacent settlements which are socially integrated with the city. In French cities, according to Caplow, the outward dispersion of population does not necessarily create American-style suburbs: many suburbs around the cities of France are of ancient origin and are not populated by families moving away from the central city.[51] In Latin America and India the rising urban population has not necessarily resulted in the growth of dependent suburban communities. A number of peripheral villages around Bangalore, India, for example, are suburban in a geographical sense, but they are apparently very old and not the result of an expanding metropolitan population. Rather, the expanding metropolis caught up with them, so to speak. Such villages are characteristically found on the outskirts and interstices of even the largest Indian cities. They have few, if any, urban physical amenities, and maintain traditional social forms. They are near the city, but not "of" it in the social sense.[52]

[51] Theodore Caplow, "Urban Structure in France," *American Sociological Review,* 17 (October, 1952), 546.
[52] Richard A. Ellefsen, "City-Hinterland Relationships in India," in Roy Turner (ed.), *India's Urban Future* (1961), pp. 94–117.

If suburban communities of the type familiar in the United States have not developed extensively in many areas, there are undoubtedly economic and technological factors involved. But possibly just as important are the cultural values of the people. For many, suburbanism as a way of life may have little or no appeal. Dotson's view is that even when upper income Mexican families establish residence on the urban fringe, it is not necessarily because suburban life is idealized as in the United States.[53] Caplow notes that in French cities residential density does not necessarily decrease toward the periphery, which suggests, though does not prove, that French city people prefer urban residence with high density to suburban residence with lower density.[54]

In much of Europe, high prestige is traditionally associated with residence toward the center of the city, a reversal of the situation in the United States. Rome [55] and Budapest [56] are among the cities showing this pattern, which had its origin in the central location of the king, court, and religious hierarchy.

In some cultures, kinship and family ties inhibit suburban "overspill" from crowded cities. Among the Yoruba, a major tribe of Nigeria, city homes and plots are owned and inherited by the extended family, rather than by individuals. Such property is a symbol of family and social unity and has a significance far beyond its physical facilities, which may be meager. Attempts in central Lagos, Nigeria, to raze some of these homes and relocate their residents in suburban developments are meeting with only limited success because the new Western-style homes are not on the "ancestral sites" nor do they provide for the close family life on which Yoruba society is based.[57]

RESIDENTIAL PATTERNS IN LATIN AMERICAN CITIES

Traditionally, upper class families tended to locate on or near the central plaza, the underprivileged were situated on the periphery, and between the inner and outer zones were families of moderate status and means. But as the population of cities increased and business or industrial districts expanded, this residential pattern underwent considerable change. Dotson observes that upper class families in Guadalajara have often been forced to move from the plaza area because of commercial or industrial expansion. They have tended to move westward, forming

[53] Floyd Dotson and Lillian Ota Dotson, "Ecological Trends in the City of Guadalajara. Mexico," *Social Forces*, 32 (May, 1954), 373.

[54] Caplow, *op. cit.*

[55] Dennis C. McElrath, "The Social Areas of Rome," *American Sociological Review*, 27 (June, 1962), 389–90.

[56] Erdmann D. Beynon, "Budapest: An Ecological Study," *Geographical Review*, 33 (April, 1943), 256–75.

[57] Marris, *op. cit.*

a sector reaching from the center to the edge of the city. But unlike American cities, there has been no mass development of middle class and upper class suburbs. Middle class workers prefer to live as close as conveniently possible to their work and to shopping or recreation centers because of difficulties in transportation. Consequently, numerous apartments and small row houses are being constructed in the inner zones of the city. Guadalajara is surrounded by a belt of low-grade housing occupied by low-income families.[58] Whatever may be the preferred locations of these residents, rents in the inner zones are too high for them, even if houses were available. Consequently they build their own sun-baked adobes on vacant land at the edge of the city. As the city grows in size these people are pushed farther out, except those few who have increased their incomes sufficiently to afford rentals in higher-priced areas. Public housing in the inner zones of the city has been primarily for middle class occupants rather than those at the bottom.

Much the same residential pattern was observed by Caplow in Guatemala City.[59] Although there has been considerable movement of upper class families toward the periphery, they are still heavily concentrated in the center. Low-income families form an outer belt around the city— only one area of extremely low-grade housing is within two miles of the commercial center.

The Dotsons recently surveyed the ecological patterns of the 11 largest Mexican cities and 20 smaller ones.[60] Architectural features of homes were used as a guide to socioeconomic status on a five-point scale, ranging from "modern-international style" to "adobe huts." On the basis of observation, the areas of the cities were then classified and maps constructed. The Dotsons concluded that there is a recurring ecological pattern in Mexican cities. There are three concentric zones: the interior zone contains the homes of white collar workers (Class III in the five-part housing scale); the next zone is that of the better manual workers' homes (Class IV); and then the lowest class of homes, V, encircle the city. The highest classes of homes, I and II, are not numerous, but the new ones tend to be located in enclaves in the outer areas of the city. The pattern of generally declining quality of homes toward the outskirts of the city contrasts markedly with Burgess' description of the content of the concentric zones of American cities. However, the Dotsons believe the movement of the middle class to the periphery of Mexican cities will accelerate as this class grows. With the deterioration of the inner section, the lower income groups are likely to move to the central area.

---

[58] Dotson and Dotson, *op. cit.*, pp. 372–74.

[59] Theodore Caplow, "The Social Ecology of Guatemala City," *Social Forces*, 28 (December, 1949), 113–33.

[60] Floyd Dotson and Lillian Ota Dotson, "La Estructura Ecologica de las Ciudades Mexicanas." *Revista Mexicana de Sociologia*, 19 (January–April, 1957), 39–66.

In Mexico City the classical ecological configuration has already been altered by population shifts.[61] Wealthy or well-to-do families have tended to push westward toward the periphery of the city, forming a sector with the highest grade residences near the city's boundaries. At the same time, a horseshoe of high land-value slums has developed around the expanding central business district. Thus the slums are tending to become more centrally located, whereas high-grade residential areas are becoming more decentralized. Yet these changes have not gone as far as in American cities. There is still a marked tendency for low land-value slums to encircle the city. In 1960 this ring of slums was broken only twice by sections of first-class residence, both of them toward the southwest. The outlying slums persisted despite very heavy growth in these areas; the area adjacent to the political boundaries of Mexico City grew eight times as fast as the city from 1950 to 1960.

THE RESIDENTIAL PATTERN OF BANGALORE, INDIA

The residential district of highest prestige in Bangalore is High Ground, a slightly elevated district in the northwestern part of the city, about a mile or so inside the municipal limits and about the same distance north of the major business area. Most of the homes in this district are spacious and comparatively expensive, obviously maintained by the elite. There are several upper middle class residential districts, but all are well within the city limits. Wealthy or well-to-do families, unlike their counterparts in the United States, have shown little inclination to establish suburbs beyond the city's boundaries. Much of the new public housing constructed for low and middle income families is on the outskirts of the city.

The areas of highest residential congestion are near the two municipal markets; here population density sometimes exceeds 100,000 persons per square mile. But these areas by no means represent the poorest housing; the slums are farther out, some of them peripherally situated. At least a half dozen mud-hut slum areas can be identified, but their location has little reference either to a business district, industrial developments, or transportation routes. These areas appear to have been occupied originally by migrants who were too poor to afford a rented house and who therefore built their own shacks on unoccupied land on or near the outskirts. As the city expanded some of these areas were surrounded; hence they are presently well within the city limits, but by no means centrally located.

The ecology of Bangalore's slums apparently resembles that of Calcutta. Ghosh observes that in Calcutta, India's largest city, "most of the

---

[61] Norman S. Hayner, "Mexico City: Its Growth and Configuration," *American Journal of Sociology*, 50 (January, 1945), 294–304; and Hayner, *Mexico in Transition: A Study of Town and Metropolis, 1941–1961* (forthcoming).

slums are located in the eastern and southern parts of the city, although some of the worst still exist in the very heart of northern Calcutta as well." [62]

SELECTED BIBLIOGRAPHY

BOOKS

Berger, Bennett, *Working-Class Suburb*. Berkeley and Los Angeles: University of California Press, 1960.

Berger, Morroe, *The Arab World Today*. Garden City, N.Y.: Doubleday, 1962.

Dobriner, William, *Class in Suburbia*. Englewood Cliffs, N.J.: Prentice-Hall, 1963.

Fava, Sylvia F., "Contrasts in Neighboring: New York City and a Suburban Community," in W. Dobriner (ed.), *The Suburban Community*. New York: Putnam's, 1958.

Gans, Herbert, "Effects of the Move from City to Suburb," in Leonard Duhl (ed.), *The Urban Condition*. New York: Basic Books, 1963.

Gans, Herbert, *The Urban Villagers*. New York: The Free Press of Glencoe, 1962.

Lewis, Oscar, *The Children of Sanchez: Autobiography of a Mexican Family*. New York: Random House, 1961.

Miner, Horace, *The Primitive City of Timbuctoo*. Princeton, N.J.: Princeton University Press, 1953.

Whyte, William F., *Street Corner Society*. Revised edition. Chicago: University of Chicago Press, 1955.

Willmott, Peter, *The Evolution of a Community*. London: Routledge & Kegan Paul, 1963.

Wissen, G. A., *American Cities in Perspective: With Special Reference to the Development of Their Fringe Areas*. Assen, Netherlands: Van Gorcum, 1962.

Wood, Robert, *Suburbia—Its People and Their Politics*. Boston: Houghton Mifflin, 1958.

ARTICLES

Fava, Sylvia F., "Suburbanism as a Way of Life," *American Sociological Review*, 21 (February, 1956), 34–37.

Gist, Noel P., "Ecological Decentralization and Rural-Urban Relationships," *Rural Sociology*, 17 (December, 1952), 328–35.

Greer, Scott, "The Social Structure and Political Process of Suburbia: An Empirical Test," *Rural Sociology*, 27 (December, 1962), 438–59.

Kurtz, Richard, and Joanne Eicher, "Fringe and Suburb: A Confusion of Concepts," *Social Forces*, 37 (October, 1958), 32–37.

[62] S. Ghosh, "The Urban Pattern of Calcutta," *Economic Geography*, 26 (January, 1950), 257; Noel P. Gist, "The Ecology of Bangalore, India: An East-West Comparison," *Social Forces*, 35 (May, 1957), 356–65.

Lazerwitz, Bernard, "Metropolitan Residential Belts, 1950 and 1956," *American Sociological Review*, 25 (April, 1960), 245–52.

Martin, Walter, "The Structuring of Social Relationships Engendered by Suburban Residence," *American Sociological Review*, 21 (August, 1956), 446–53.

Schnore, Leo, "The Socio-Economic Status of Cities and Suburbs," *American Sociological Review*, 28 (February, 1963), 76–85.

Ecology of Urban Institutions

This chapter will be concerned with the ecological patterns of urban organizations and institutions, changes that are occurring in these spatial configurations, and various factors associated with the formation of particular ecological structures. It will deal primarily with the ecology of business and industry, but will also consider certain ecological aspects of noneconomic institutions.

In examining the ecology of urban institutions, we will find there are basically two different kinds of ecological networks represented in American cities. One, an older system found in the compact cities of the nineteenth and early twentieth centuries, is the "urban" network. The other, the newer ecological system, which is found in the sprawling communities that came to the fore with the technical advances and social changes of the twentieth century, may be called the "metropolitan" network. The metropolitan kind of interdependence is becoming ever more important, although most of the urbanized sections of the United States show aspects of both the old and the new systems. No city has a wholly urban or metropolitan structure, but newer and rapidly growing cities—Los Angeles, for example—usually show greater decentralization than the cities that had their major growth in the "horse and buggy" era. Some of the major differences between the two networks, summarized below, should serve as guideposts to help in understanding the changes occurring in the distribution of business, industry, and other institutions.

1. The urban network is simpler. It is based on transportation by foot or by mass "fixed-track" transportation (trolleys, els, subways, and railroads) and on limited facilities for rapid communication. The metropolitan network is more complex, partly because the development of "rubber-wheeled" transportation (car, truck, and bus) and of instantaneous communication (telegraph and telephone) opens a wide range of locational choices. Metropolitan networks are a

The journey to work. Modes of mass transportation have an important bearing on the social, political, and ecological development of cities. In most cities of the world the daily journey to work is mainly by public conveyance, bicycle, or walking. Only in the United States and Canada is the automobile a vehicle of mass transportation. Above: Automobiles occupy ten traffic lanes on the Saw Mill River Parkway, Westchester County, New York, in a mass journey to work. Facing page: The bicycle work parade in Amsterdam, Holland. (Courtesy Cities Service Company [photograph by Anthony Linck] and Netherlands Information Service.)

characteristic of highly industrialized societies. The affluence of the population, reflected in greater spending power and more leisure time, is also an important determinant in the ecology of business and industry.

2. The "downtown" area, the central business district, in an urban network tends to serve as the site for most of the major activities of the city, except residence. In a metropolitan network the function of the central business district is to integrate activities, many of which are located in other parts of the metropolitan area.

3. It follows that the physical pattern of business and industrial location in an urban network tends to be centralized. A metropolitan network is associated

with a more decentralized distribution of business and industry. The various businesses, industries, and other city institutions are affected to different degrees by metropolitan trends. In general, heavy industry and relatively standardized retailing tend to decentralize most rapidly.

TRANSPORTATION AND ECOLOGICAL CHANGE

So long as transportation was confined mainly to the horse and buggy or to walking, Western cities were compact and distances from one point to another were comparatively short. This compactness of residential occupance, resulting in high density, is still characteristic of cities in technologically underdeveloped countries because mass transportation is mainly by primitive vehicles or by walking.

MASS TRANSPORTATION SYSTEMS

Beginning in the nineteenth century, mass transportation systems, first the steam railway and later the electric street car and interurban train,

progressively altered the ecological structure of the Western city. Workers could live farther from their place of employment or their center of supplies than in the old days, without necessarily spending more time in travel. To escape the congestion of central areas they moved farther out, utilizing street cars and railways to reach their destinations when traveling to other points. These systems of mass transportation were further developed to include the elevated and subway sytems; at the same time steam and electric trains grew longer and traveled faster. Industries began to move out too, since they were no longer dependent on a labor force housed in the immediate vicinity of the factory.

Automotive transportation

With the widespread use of the automobile, passenger bus, and motor truck in the early part of the twentieth century, a new force was unleashed which still further transformed the ecological structure of the city. Whereas the passenger bus merely augmented the existing mass transportation system with a vehicle somewhat more flexible than trains or street cars, the private automobile increased flexibility of transportation still more by reducing dependency on fixed routes and travel schedules. Furthermore, the automobile could go beyond terminal points of bus or street car lines or reach points between the regular routes. As it came to be adopted as a vehicle of mass transportation in the United States and Canada, city people pushed farther and farther out, extending the area of urban occupance and filling in the open spaces between peripheral settlements. Thus the distance of travel within the urban community gradually lengthened.

Private automobile transportation quickly became the major means of daily travel in American cities. By 1960, almost two-thirds of the urban workers in the United States regularly used automobiles in going to work.[1] The next most frequent means of transportation, buses and streetcars, was used by less than 11 per cent of the workers. By 1960, the New York metropolitan area was the only one in which more than half (about 55 per cent) of the workers regularly used public transportation in traveling to work. It is hardly surprising, therefore, that throughout the United States there has been a rash of bankruptcies, curtailed service, and economy measures among commuter railroads, subways, and other means of public transportation.

Because comparatively few city dwellers in many countries can afford private automobiles, long-distance travel within a metropolitan district in these areas is confined largely to fixed systems of railway, street car, and bus. For this reason outlying settlements tend to cluster around the

[1] *U. S. Census of Population: 1960. General Social and Economic Characteristics, U. S. Summary.* Final Report PC(1)–IC, Table 94.

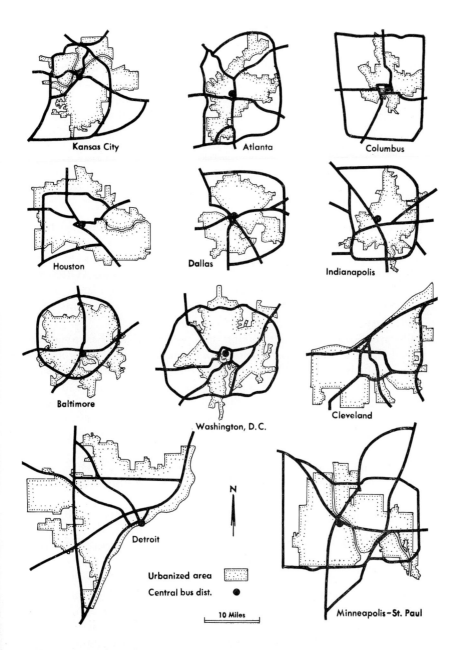

Kansas City

Atlanta

Columbus

Houston

Dallas

Indianapolis

Baltimore

Washington, D.C.

Cleveland

Detroit

N

Urbanized area

Central bus dist.

10 Miles

Minneapolis–St. Paul

Figure 17. The urban freeway systems in these 11 cities, not all of which are as yet completed, are typical of circumferential routes being built in American cities to handle movement generated by the decentralization of many activities. The earlier radial pattern of arteries leading to the city-center is also evident. SOURCE: Adapted from Edgar Horwood and Ronald Boyce, *Studies of the Central Business District and Urban Freeway Development* (Seattle: University of Washington Press, 1959).

stations where passengers are picked up and discharged. For shorter distances within the city the bicycle has been adopted as an important mode of transportation. After World War II, the advent of the motorized bicycle extended the range and reduced the time of commuting. In The Netherlands and Belgium, for example, the bicycle and the railroad are the principal means of traveling to and from work over metropolitan distances. Both of these countries have sizable commuter groups.[2]

TRANSPORTATION AND ECOLOGICAL PATTERNS

As long as mass transportation in cities was limited mainly to trains and street cars having fixed routes, population tended to cluster fairly close to these lines. This was especially true of peripheral zones, where built-up areas developed near radial transportation routes. Within the limits of topographic conditions, the city thus tended to assume a star-shaped pattern, the points of the star being outlying settlements along the outer reaches of urban transportation lines.

Widespread use of the automobile and passenger bus has somewhat modified this star-shaped pattern of expansion. Because the automobile and passenger bus can reach any point in the city if streets or roads are passable, areas between points, off fixed routes, have been filled in by settlers. There is, nevertheless, still a tendency in large metropolitan areas for settlements to stay fairly close to main transportation thoroughfares, whether automobile trafficways or fixed routes. The star-shaped configuration has not been entirely changed.

As American cities grew into sprawling metropolises in which many activities were no longer located in the city core, the linear transportation routes of most subways, els, intracity railroads, and streets leading to the city center were no longer adequate to accommodate the ever-increasing traffic circulating entirely within the metropolitan periphery. As a consequence, there has come into prominence, particularly since World War II, the circumferential highway which links the outlying shopping centers, industries, and communities of the metropolitan area. Not only does the system accommodate visiting, shopping, and entertainment traffic; with the decentralization of business and industry, the proportion of suburbanites who also work in the suburbs is increasing steadily and substantially. According to the 1960 census, almost 58 per cent of the workers living in the suburban rings of metropolitan areas also work in the ring. This is particularly true in the larger metropolitan areas.[3]

[2] Robert E. Dickinson, "The Geography of Commuting: The Netherlands and Belgium," *Geographic Review*, XLVII (October, 1957), 521–38.

[3] *U. S. Census of Population: 1960. Place of Work and Means of Transportation to Work, 1960.* Supplementary Report PC(S1)–41, January 30, 1963.

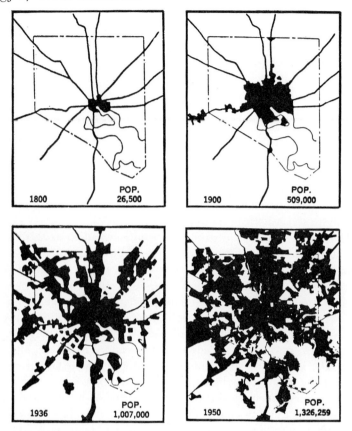

Figure 18. Baltimore's expansion over a century and a half. Decentralization of population is clearly indicated. Note the transition from a compact "walkable" city to a star-shaped pattern, and then the blurring of the star pattern as the automobile age comes into its own.

Decentralization of business, industry, and residence does not necessarily mean shorter work trips, for the employing and residential suburbs may be quite distant from one another, possibly even at the opposite ends of a large metropolitan area. Recreation, education, and shopping may also be far from suburban homes.

SPATIAL PATTERNS OF BUSINESS

Typically, a Western city has a primary or dominant nucleus in which are concentrated economic, political, and social functions of the community or region. This is the central business district. Cities beyond a certain size commonly develop subordinate nuclei which represent a clustering of establishments whose functions are often different from those

of centralized institutions. Ordinarily the larger the city, the more numerous the subordinate nuclei. This has become particularly true in recent decades as cities expand into huge metropolitan aggregations of
territory and population.

The ecological center of the city, the central business district, is the
focus of many functions that affect the entire community or region.[4] The
varied and interdependent functions carried out in the central business
district tie all parts of the community together and integrate the city
with its hinterland. Those considered in the following paragraphs apply
especially to the American metropolis.

a. The central business district has been referred to as the headquarters area of the city. It is the place where decisions are made—decisions
that may affect an entire community or even a region or nation. It is the
power center of the community, for it is here that men of power make
decisions, issue orders, and formulate policies. These men, centrally located, may exercise control over actual economic operations covering a
wide area. Here are the captains of industry, industrial magnates, merchant princes, publishers of newspapers, leaders of labor, high-placed
bureaucrats, executives in positions of authority who find it expedient
to be near the center of political and economic power.

b. The central business district is the center of finance and financial
transactions for the city or region. It is usually here that financial credit
for economic operations may be extended or withheld. Here are broker-
age houses, investment banks, and stock or commodity exchanges run by
specialized personnel who handle transactions in stocks or bonds, or who
manipulate the buying and selling of commodities which neither they
nor their clients actually ever see. Here also are offices manned by personnel whose financial transactions are concerned with risks; by accountants and consulting economists whose skills or advice is of value to the
financiers; by attorneys whose legal talents are purchased by corporations engaged in varieties of transactions or operations; by bookkeepers
and stenographers and private secretaries who perform their endless
paper work as a necessary part of the system.

c. The central business district is a center of transmitted intelligence.
The media of communication converge here where they are used most
intensively. Because of the interdependence of functions and the delicate
balance that must be maintained between various parts of the economic

---

[4] See especially Earl S. Johnson, "The Function of the Central Business District in
the Metropolitan Community," in Paul Hatt and Albert Reiss (eds.), *Cities and Society*
(1957), pp. 248–60. A number of Johnson's interpretations are incorporated into this
section.

This scene on the floor of the New York Stock Exchange illustrates the organizational and managerial functions that remain concentrated in downtown urban areas, while the photograph of the suburban factory (p. 226) exemplifies the decentralization of manufacturing. (Courtesy New York Convention and Visitors Bureau.)

system, speedy and accurate communication becomes an integral aspect of the central district. Johnson has pointed out, for example, that financial institutions of the central business district in a large metropolis are highly sensitized to news concerning economic, political, military, or even climatic conditions.[5] Particularly sensitive to news is the stock market in which the volume of transactions and the prices of securities are greatly influenced by information received from the four corners of the globe. In great cities these financial nerve centers are the foci of a complicated network of communications media—telephone, telegraph, radio,

[5] *Ibid.*, p. 483.

and television—over which is transmitted information of significance to the operations of such institutions. News of a drought in Texas, military operations in Cuba, floods in Brazil, international trade agreements, stoppages in industry, and countless other types of events are of significance to institutions in which buying and selling of securities and furnishing financial credit are major functions.

d. The central business district is the predominant center of retail and wholesale activities and of ancillary establishments that serve the needs of workers and shoppers and others who frequent the area. Here are large department stores, specialized retail shops, hotels for transient guests, publishing firms, legitimate theaters, large movie houses, concert halls, civic auditoriums, travel bureaus, downtown churches, and other establishments providing goods or services to the entire city and its tributary region. Close by are the warehouses—banks of merchandise, as Johnson calls them.

An enumeration of some of the organizations and functionaries in Manhattan's central business district summarizes the nature of centralization in a great city.[6] Manhattan south of Central Park contains the main offices of nearly a third of the nation's 500 largest industrial corporations, four of its 10 largest life insurance companies, about 75 per cent of the national health, civic, and welfare organizations, and 70 per cent of the national advertising agencies. Major wholesaling centers for toys, diamonds, textiles, furs, and other products are also concentrated in this area. The financial section around Wall Street includes the nation's two major stock exchanges, large commercial banks, and investment houses. The Manhattan central business district also contains the ladies' garment industry, in which the designing and selling of the most fashionable dresses, suits, and coats, and some of the cutting and sewing, remain centered in a district of about one-eighth of a square mile. Still other activities concentrated in the central business district are export-import firms, publishing houses, the theatre, and television, film, and radio productions. Yet with all this vast complex of institutions and organizations maintained by a daytime army of functionaries, few people reside in Manhattan's central business district. New York City, of course, is by no means a representative city, but the data do indicate the nature and extent of centralization of integrative activities in a single metropolis.

THE CHANGING FUNCTION OF THE CENTRAL BUSINESS DISTRICT

The two major activities conducted in the central business district are retail sales and office operations, the available data indicating that almost two-thirds of the nonresidential space in the central business dis-

---

[6] Regional Plan Association (New York), *Goals for the Region Project*, Background Booklet Number 1, March, 1963.

trict is devoted to retail and office use.[7] Although these functions remain dominant as a city grows to metropolitan status, they undergo a transformation. But since each is affected differently by the expansion of the metropolis, we shall discuss them separately.

Retail Sales. Some types of retailing follow the consumer to the suburbs, especially since the suburban population represents greater purchasing power than the nonwhite and low income families concentrated in the city core. Retail sales have generally lagged in the central business district. A study of 45 large metropolitan areas showed that over-all retail store sales rose 32.3 per cent between 1948 and 1954, but in their downtown central business districts, retail sales increased by only 1.6 per cent.

Many central business districts have shown an actual decline in retail sales. This has been most marked in larger cities, that is, those more likely to be in the advanced stages of metropolitan development.[8] In Los Angeles, downtown retail sales (in standardized dollars) fell by 6.7 per cent between 1948 and 1954; in Philadelphia by 7.2 per cent; and by 11.2 per cent in Detroit.[9] The magnitude of the shift away from downtown shopping is more fully revealed by noting that in the same time period retail sales in the Los Angeles metropolitan area rose by over 50 per cent, in Philadelphia by 30.6 per cent, and in Detroit by 39.4 per cent. New York's was the only central business district in a metropolitan area over a million in size not to show a decline in retail sales.

Some aspects of retail trade and consumer service are resistant to decentralization, expensive items and those dependent on "style" being prime examples of the new retail specialization of the central business district. Such goods and services have a limited clientele, and the stores must be centrally located to draw on the widest market. Thus, jewelry, fur, and furniture shops remain highly concentrated in the central business district, as do expensive or exotic restaurants and art galleries. A recent study of the New York metropolitan region described the new pattern of retail distribution as follows:

. . . The lines of retail activity which are tied closely to neighborhood populations—food stores, for instance, and laundries—are already well scattered throughout the Region and can be expected to keep moving outward as residences shift. At the other extreme, those which demand extensive comparative shopping or which rely on out-of-towners for a considerable portion of their sales will resist the continuing dispersion of populations and will cling much more tenaciously to the central shopping areas. In between these extremes are the department stores and other activities that can satisfy comparative shopping

[7] Edgar Horwood and Ronald Boyce, *Studies of the Central Business District and Urban Freeway Development* (1959), p. 28.
[8] *Ibid.*, pp. 28–44.
[9] Murray Dessel, "Central Business Districts and Their Metropolitan Areas," *Area Trend Series,* United States Department of Commerce, November, 1957.

needs with clusters smaller than those in the central shopping areas. These may create—indeed, already have created—new retail nuclei from time to time at shopping centers spaced through the Region.[10]

This pattern is probably typical for the larger metropolitan areas, and indicates that except for the central labor force and the resident central population the central business district is visited only occasionally and for major shopping needs. In the smaller metropolitan areas and cities, the central business district is visited frequently for almost all shopping needs. One study suggests that the major trend toward decentralization in retailing occurs where the population of the metropolitan area reaches 150,000.[11]

The changes in the distribution of retail outlets may be analyzed in terms of the five ecological elements. Thus far, the discussion suggests that the changes are primarily responses to population, technology, and the resulting new relationships (organization) between the city core and the rest of the metropolis. These are certainly the major determinants in accounting for retail decentralization. A fourth element, environment, does not appear to play a large part, but the fifth element, personal values or preferences, deserves consideration. A survey in Columbus, Ohio, showed that, holding distance constant, the more highly educated, higher income groups, persons having urban or metropolitan backgrounds, and females were most attracted to downtown shopping.[12]

Although metropolitan Columbus grew from 306,000 in 1940 to almost 700,000 in 1960, the area is still not among the largest metropolises. As travel distances and costs mount, the disadvantages of downtown shopping may eventually outweigh the advantages in the value scales of more groups. Outlying shopping centers may also become more diversified and appeal to a wider clientele.

Offices and Administration. Retailing is not the only activity that becomes decentralized as the city expands into a metropolis. Manufacturing, too, increasingly moves to the broad acres of satellite towns or suburbia, as do household and consumer services, following in the wake of the suburban residential boom. What activity, then, remains in the central business district, and is becoming dominant? The answer to this question is provided by the growing importance of office space, for as more and more activities become decentralized in the metropolis, the more pressing becomes the need for their integration.

In the postwar period, there appears to have been a moderate increase in total central office space in cities of over 100,000. Significantly, the larger cities not only have been adding office space at a greater rate than the smaller cities, but they have been adding such space at a greater rate

---

[10] Edgar M. Hoover and Raymond Vernon, *Anatomy of a Metropolis* (1959), p. 122.

[11] Horwood and Boyce, *op. cit.,* p. 44.

[12] C. T. Jonassen, *Downtown versus Suburban Shopping* (1953).

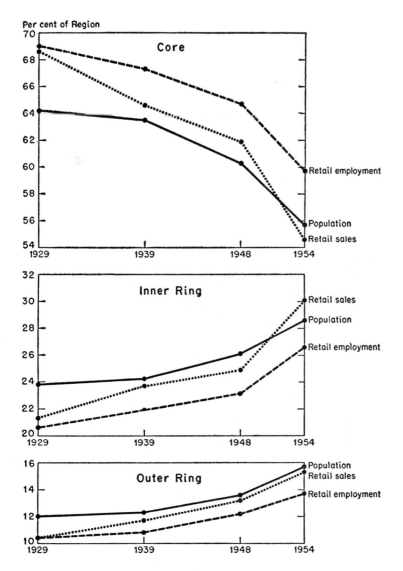

Figure 19. Trends in retail employment, retail sales, and population in main zones of the New York metropolitan region, 1929, 1939, 1948, 1954 (region = 100 per cent). The region is an excellent example of the way in which the distribution of retailing is linked to the redistribution of population. Retail sales and employment in the core area of the region have declined consistently in line with the declines in residential population. On the other hand, the two suburban rings show consistent retail increases as their population increases. SOURCE: Edgar M. Hoover and Raymond Vernon, *Anatomy of a Metropolis* (Cambridge, Mass.: Harvard University Press, 1959).

than they are adding residential population.[13] This trend underscores the integrative function of the central business district, for it is in the larger cities that decentralization of manufacturing, retailing, and other activities has proceeded furthest.

In Manhattan, the core of America's largest metropolitan area, over 56.8 million square feet of rentable office space, in 162 new buildings, were added between 1947 and 1963.[14] The competition for office space in Manhattan is so acute that luxury apartment buildings and smaller office buildings are being razed and replaced by office towers. Park Avenue is undergoing a succession from residential to business use as the "barracks of the rich" are demolished to make way for prestige office buildings.

Offices do locate in suburban areas, of course, but decentralization of offices to such areas is limited and highly selective. At least this is suggested by an investigation in the San Francisco metropolitan area of the location of new offices and the relocation of established ones.[15] From 1948 to 1954, the proportion of top administrative offices concentrated in downtown San Francisco dropped from 61 per cent of all San Francisco metropolitan area top administrative offices to 49 per cent of such offices. However, further analysis disclosed that almost all of the suburban offices relocated or initially established in this period were attached to non-office facilities such as manufacturing plants, warehouses, or transportation terminals. Less than one per cent of the relocation of new offices in the suburbs was of detached headquarters offices. The supremacy of the central business district in attracting new offices and holding existing ones is clear. Total downtown office space in San Francisco grew from 10.2 million square feet in 1946 to 13.2 million in 1956.[16]

THE FUTURE OF THE CENTRAL BUSINESS DISTRICT

The metropolitan economy is not simply a matter of direct negotiation between the producer of raw materials and the manufacturer, nor between the manufacturer and the consumer. The movement of a bushel of apples or a bale of cotton from the farm to its ultimate use as food or clothing involves a long series of facilitating moves by processors and manufacturers, by legal and governmental agencies and inspectors, by advertising promotion, by wholesalers, and by large-scale retailers.

Under the influence of modern transportation systems and methods of communication, the location of these various specialized parts of the

---

[13] Horwood and Boyce, *op. cit.,* pp. 46–57.
[14] "Manhattan Office Building Construction," *New York Times,* January 12, 1964, p. 1R.
[15] Donald L. Foley, *The Suburbanization of Administrative Offices in the San Francisco Bay Area* (1957).
[16] Horwood and Boyce, *op. cit.,* p. 48.

economy is characterized by great selectivity. No longer must the inter-related parts be centralized to be unified. Standardized, routine opera-tions, whether in retailing, manufacturing, or management, desert the central business district for the lower costs, accessibility, and spaciousness of the metropolitan ring. Thus, retailing of everyday, medium-priced shoes becomes decentralized, but outlets for high-style, high-priced, or specialty shoes (ballet, orthopedic, custom-made) remain highly con-centrated in the core. Similarly, large-scale bulk printing of books and magazines is seldom found in the central business district, but "short-order" specialty plants serving newspapers or printing department store handouts remain firmly attached to downtown.

The activities concentrated in the core are those which are predomi-nantly unstandardized and hence require constant communication and revision; those requiring personal contact (judging the "mood" of Wall Street or the qualities of a prospective executive; planning legal, govern-mental, or industrial strategy); and those small-scale producers who benefit from the "external economies" of the many downtown services (cafeterias, window cleaners, tax and accounting experts, and the like) they would not be able to maintain on their own in a suburban setting. Epigrammatically, the emerging function of the central business district is "people, paper work, and parcels." [17]

None of the scattered parts of the metropolitan economy is self-suffi-cient. The integrative function performed by the central business district promises to become even more important as specialization, bureaucrati-zation, and decentralization proceed. The nature of the unifying function of the central business district is revealed by noting the types of offices highly concentrated there: financial and banking institutions; insurance and real estate firms; other business and professional services such as advertising, employment agencies, law offices, and market research firms; and offices of the various branches of government.

The central business district is changing, and for the largest cities its future appears to be bright. Among smaller cities, however, some of the functions of the central business district are being taken over by the dominant city in the geographic center, a process apparently the result of improved communications and transport. In some types of activity, extreme centralization may be possible. For example, a national cor-poration may decide that it is unnecessary to have many scattered semi-autonomous branch offices throughout the country; information can be transmitted by long-distance telephone, and with air travel, face-to-face contacts of executives can be easily arranged. Thus, a single home office in New York, Chicago, or San Francisco may control the company's ac-tivities throughout the country. The extent to which smaller cities have been bypassed is revealed by the pattern of office-building construction in the postwar period. Over 40 per cent of the total number of square

[17] *Ibid.*, p. 15.

feet of office construction has been concentrated in the central business district of New York City.[18] The smaller cities have not generally shared in the office-building boom. On the other hand, it appears that much of the shopping, entertainment, and banking activities of small towns and villages is being transferred to neighboring cities. Thus, both positive and negative influences are evident for the central business districts of many cities. If their districts are to retain their vitality, adjustments to the new conditions will have to be made.

PATTERNING OF SUBCENTERS

Outside the central business district retail developments tend to assume two different ecological patterns. One pattern is the elongated nucleus, the commercial street, in which retail stores line one or both sides of a thoroughfare for varying distances; the other pattern is the circular nucleus, represented by a clustering of retail establishments.[19]

The circular type of subordinate retail nucleus commonly ocurs at the intersection of transportation routes, or in the vicinity of large institutions whose employees are potential customers of local stores. Sometimes the circular nucleus, located at the convergence of transportation routes, expands along the adjacent streets to assume a star-shaped pattern—a combination of the two types of development. The specific configuration of the circular or elongated nucleus may vary greatly in size and character, ranging from the familiar grocery-store–drug-store–filling-station–barber shop pattern to large developments having a wide variety of retail stores and serving customers from a considerable area. Country Club Plaza, some 40 blocks from downtown Kansas City, is an example of a major nuclear development. In Los Angeles in 1959 there were more than a score of so-called "regional" shopping centers which accounted for 38 department store openings between 1945 and 1958.[20]

In 1960 the United States Department of Commerce estimated that in the period following World War II some 2,500 shopping centers were built in the United States.[21] Some of these are inside municipal boundaries; others are in suburban areas.

THE SPATIAL PATTERN OF INDUSTRY

The ecological patterning of industrial establishments is easily distinguishable from the patterns of retail commercial enterprises and office

[18] Committee for Economic Development, *Guiding Metropolitan Growth* (1960), p. 18.

[19] Richard U. Ratcliff, *Urban Land Economics* (1949), pp. 388–89.

[20] Arthur L. Grey, Jr., "Los Angeles: Urban Prototype," *Land Economics*, 35 (August, 1959), 234.

[21] George Sternlieb, "The Future of Retailing in the Downtown Core," *Journal of the American Institute of Planners*, 29 (May, 1963), 109.

activities. Yet industry, too, shows the effects of decentralization brought about by metropolitan growth.

How far has industry decentralized?

Before discussing this question it should be clear that industrial decentralization may assume the form of *diffusion* or *dispersion*. Diffusion has reference to the relocation of factories from the central section of a city to positions farther out, as in the case of a shift to a suburban site. Dispersion refers to a wider redistribution of factories from locations in a particular community to positions elsewhere, either in the same region or in another region. A shift of an industry from, say, Boston to a town in Georgia would be an example of dispersion. That both types of decentralization have occurred in the United States and Europe is generally recognized.

Dispersion of industry in the United States has resulted in greater equality of manufacturing employment among the regions of the nation.[22] Although the Northeast and North Central states still predominate in manufacturing, the South and West have gained manufacturing jobs at a faster rate, thereby increasing their share of manufacturing employment. Reasons for the regional shifts of industry include (1) the phenomenal growth of aircraft manufacturing and air transportation which are more suited to the year-round outdoor climates of the South and West; (2) increasing reliance upon oil and natural gas, rather than coal, for manufacturing plants; (3) the decline in the availability of cheap manpower in the Northeast as immigration was curtailed; and (4) the mechanization of agriculture, which made many farm workers surplus in the South and West.

However, although industrial dispersion has redistributed industry among the regions of the United States, industry is still clustered in or near large cities. In 1929 almost 60 per cent of the manufacturing jobs in the United States were located in 48 large metropolitan areas; by 1954 almost 56 per cent of such jobs were still located there.[23]

Turning to cities and metropolitan areas, we find evidence of decentralization in terms of diffusion. Industry is tending to locate in suburban and fringe areas rather than in the central city. One yardstick is the proportion of manufacturing production workers in metropolitan areas located in the central cities. In the 48 largest metropolitan areas, the central cities' proportion of manufacturing production workers declined from 66.5 per cent in 1929 to 57.5 per cent in 1954.[24] One study carried

---

[22] This discussion is based on Victor Fuchs, *Changes in the Location of Manufacturing in the United States since 1929* (1962).

[23] Raymond Vernon, "Production and Distribution in the Large Metropolis," *Annals*, 314 (November, 1957), 17n.

[24] Raymond Vernon, *The Changing Economic Function of the Central City* (1959), pp. 74–75.

Much manufacturing, especially of standard products, has decentralized to outlying areas, such as this Westinghouse plant in Metuchen, New Jersey, which makes radio and television equipment. The vast amount of space consumed by the factory and its parking areas would be prohibitively expensive in the downtown area. (Courtesy Westinghouse Electric Corporation [photograph by Arthur Swoger].)

these measures back to 1899 for 13 major cities and their metropolitan areas. The data, presented in Table 10 for 10 of these central cities, show that decentralization of industry from the central cities to the outlying parts of the metropolis has been underway at least since the turn of the century.

TABLE 10

Central Cities' Proportion of Manufacturing Production Workers in 10 Metropolitan Areas, 1899–1954

	1899	*1929*	*1954*
Baltimore	91.8	85.5	62.9
Buffalo	74.7	59.8	43.1
Chicago	88.0	73.6	65.2
Detroit	83.6	75.2	53.5
Los Angeles	83.4	66.6	42.3
New York City, Jersey City, Newark	69.9	69.8	63.0
Philadelphia	78.4	65.7	56.0
Pittsburgh	53.1	27.1	22.6
Saint Louis	80.6	69.9	63.9
San Francisco, Oakland	81.2	68.2	50.4

SOURCE: Raymond Vernon, *The Changing Economic Function of the Central City* (New York: Committee for Economic Development, 1959), pp. 74–75.

Because decentralization is frequently measured by different methods, or because techniques are followed that are not altogether valid or accurate, it is difficult to obtain a precise picture of the situation, either in the United States or elsewhere. For example, industrial diffusion may be interpreted as a shift *across* a city's boundaries into peripheral areas, excluding similar shifts in the same direction but *within* a municipality. This procedure manifestly does not furnish a complete picture of industrial diffusion.

LIGHT VERSUS HEAVY INDUSTRY

Industrial production covers many activities in which spatial and other needs are varied. Certain types of industrial enterprise require a great deal of space; other types can operate within narrow spatial limits. Some require great quantities of raw material and fuel; others need small amounts of raw material. Special transportation facilities are necessary for certain types of industry but not for others.

Manufacturing of products of small size and weight is generally classified as light industry. The production of jewelry, time-pieces, drugs,

candy, cosmetics, cigars, wearing apparel, and leather goods are examples. Printing and photoengraving are similar in certain respects. Because
light manufacturing processes can be carried on in a limited space, such
establishments are commonly near the center of the city, at the edge of
the central business district. Sometimes wholesaling and light manufacturing establishments are located in the same general area. But not all
light manufacturing is centrally located.

Manufacturing which requires a great deal of ground space and which
turns out bulky products, or utilizes bulky raw materials, is designated
heavy industry. Industrial establishments producing automobiles, airplanes, petroleum products, farm machinery, flour, sugar, lumber, steel,
cement, meat products, and railroad cars and locomotives are examples.
Until the late nineteenth century heavy industry in Europe and the
United States tended to locate in the central portions of the cities, near
wharves, docks, and railroad sidings, and close to the center of labor
supply. During the twentieth century heavy industry has developed along
railroad lines, river valleys, and ocean or lake fronts, commonly on the
outskirts of the city or even well beyond the city's boundaries.

There is reason to believe that diffusion of industry has proceeded
farther in the large and complex industrial cities than in smaller ones.[25]
It is also probable that changes in locational pattern vary considerably
with kinds of industries. Decentralization of capital and durable goods
has apparently been more pronounced than for plants producing consumer or semidurable goods. This is another way of stating that heavy
industry is more decentralized than light industry.

One measure of the decentralization of heavy industry is that for 48
large metropolitan areas in 1954, the average manufacturing firm in the
central city had 38 employees while the average manufacturing firm in
the ring had 62 employees.[26] Not all large firms are heavy industries, of
course, but generally speaking this tends to be true.

The characteristics of heavy industries suggest reasons for the tendency
to locate on the outskirts. They are (1) comparatively large size, (2)
time or service factor unimportant, (3) large ground area per person
required, (4) nuisance features frequently present (odors, noise, fire
hazards, and the like), (5) specialized buildings required, (6) serious
problem of waste disposal, and (7) large quantities of fuel or water required. Several of these characteristics, such as large acreage, are accentuated by modern assembly-line technology. In contrast, the characteristics of light industry: (1) no specialized type of building ordinarily
required, (2) time or service factor an important element, (3) specialized, unstandardized, or highly skilled work in certain types of industries, (4) small ground area per worker required, (5) obsolete build-

[25] Coleman Woodbury (ed.), *The Future of Cities and Urban Redevelopment*
(1953), p. 287.
[26] Vernon, "Production and Distribution in the Large Metropolis," *op. cit.*, p. 22n.

ings suitable, (6) comparatively small scale operations, (7) close contact with the labor market required, (8) highly seasonal, fluctuating labor force, and (9) importance of fashion or styles.

INDUSTRIAL PARKS

An important aspect of industrial decentralization is the development of industrial parks, which are planned aggregations of manufacturing concerns, usually located on the city's outskirts. Industrial parks are essentially a post-World War II phenomenon. A study of 272 out of an estimated 1,000 industrial districts in the United States and Canada disclosed that 40 per cent of those studied were in metropolitan areas of one million or more, and an additional 31 per cent were in metropolitan areas of 100,000 to one million in size.[27] This suggests that decentralization in industry, as with retailing, is most pronounced in the large metropolitan areas. Industrial parks are not "out in the sticks," however, because accessibility is a primary consideration in the choice of their sites. Most are within 10 miles of the central city, nearly all are adjacent to major highways, and 90 per cent are served by railroads.

The industrial parks studied had been sponsored by real estate developers, railroads, local community groups, government, and some were jointly sponsored by government and private interests; the largest districts were sponsored by port authorities. The planning of industrial parks is another instance of the growing importance of conscious control in the ecological process. The kinds of industry that can be induced to locate in industrial parks are revealing of the underlying factors which the planning maximizes. The most frequent total area of industrial parks is from 100 to 200 acres, and the industries most frequently represented are light manufacturing and assembly plants occupying half- to 5-acre plots and employing less than 50 people. These are probably the small-scale industries that do not require continuous central city contacts, but that are too small to locate alone in an outlying site where access roads, electricity, gas, water, sewer connections, and other ancillary services are not so likely to be readily at hand. Large plants are in a much better economic position to locate alone in an outlying site where all the amenities must be provided by the firm.

REASONS FOR INDUSTRIAL DECENTRALIZATION

Several types of reasons, including changes in technology, population distribution, economics, and social standards, account for the shifting

[27] Robert Boley, *Industrial Districts Restudied: An Analysis of Characteristics,* Urban Land Institute, Technical Bulletin #41, April, 1961.

pattern of industry. The following discussion will focus on the causes of diffusion of industry to the suburbs. Although industrial relocation is partly a response to the changing distribution of population—to some extent industry tends to follow the labor force—this is a more important motive for dispersion to the low-wage regions of the nation than for diffusion to the metropolitan periphery. However, the suburbanization of population has led to industrial diffusion in other ways; some industries, the manufacturers of house paints, for example, find it economically wise to locate their plants near their markets.[28]

Certain technological developments have increased industrial flexibility, allowing for a wider choice of sites. One is the change-over from machinery driven by water or steam to factories operated by electric power. In terms of available power, one site in a metropolitan area is about as favorable as any other. Second, the motor truck for transportation of materials, raw and finished, together with the passenger automobile for transportation of workers, has increased the freedom of industry to operate successfully in locations far from the older terminals in the city's center. The growing reliance of industry and workers on the truck and automobile has often led to moves away from the traffic congestion of the urban core. Outside the central city, industrial firms can afford the large sites required for truck-loading areas and for parking employees' cars. Third, production techniques in modern factories often require horizontal assembly-line methods, thus outmoding many of the multistory factories built in an earlier industrial era. The effects of the new processes on land requirements of industry are phenomenal. A study of plants in the New York metropolitan region showed the following average square footage of plot space per worker: (1) 1,040 square feet for plants built before 1922; (2) 2,000 square feet in plants built from 1922 to 1945; and (3) 4,550 square feet in plants built after 1945.[29] The large amounts of land required for one- and two-story horizontal-line plants are difficult to assemble in the central city and would, in any case, be prohibitively expensive. Land costs for a factory site of 160,000 square feet in Manhattan are roughly 2.5 million dollars while a comparable suburban factory site would be less than a half-million dollars.[30]

Changes in social standards are fairly important in the redistribution of industry and provide an excellent example of nontechnological, noneconomic factors operating in the ecological system. First, public opinion has more strongly supported urban zoning in recent years and has translated its support into zoning laws with "teeth." Industries seeking a centrally located site often find there simply are not suitable sites zoned

---

[28] Vernon, "Production and Distribution in the Large Metropolis," op. cit., pp. 18–20.
[29] Edgar M. Hoover and Raymond Vernon, Anatomy of a Metropolis (1959), p. 31.
[30] Ibid., Appendix C, p. 271.

for industry. Increasingly, other controls have also been imposed on industry, notably legislation specifying the disposal of industrial wastes and pollutants. Such legislation has been passed as the public became more aware of the dangers of air and water pollution in densely populated areas and as general standards of environmental sanitation improved. Because the costs of meeting these standards are often high for industry, it will seek an outlying location where there is sparse population or where less stringent regulations obtain.

Zoning and other regulation of industrial location illustrate not only changes in the "laissez-faire" attitude toward industry but also the role of conscious control and planning. Public attitudes and their legislative implementation are obvious, too, in various programs designed to attract industry to suburban communities. Special tax concessions, zoning provisions, and other inducements may be offered, but, significantly, suburban communities typically offer these advantages exclusively to light industry or administrative and research installations. Each community wants only the industry whose factory resembles a college campus, whose employees are all college educated, and whose manufacturing process smells like a rose.

Other elements in the decentralization of manufacturing are the new attitudes of employers and employees. Industry has come to realize the advertising potential and public relations value of a modern plant in a landscaped setting. In a day when "fringe benefits" are so important, these assets also help to attract and hold employees. The rise of union power plays a part in decentralization, mainly in the *dispersion* of industry to the less "organized" regions of the nation. However, *diffusion* to the outlying areas of the metropolis also occurs because these sections, too, tend to have less labor union strength and hence lower wage standards.

Changes in consumer demand have entered into the decentralization of some industries, notably the garment industry.[31] After World War II a "revolution in clothes" ushered in a widespread trend toward casual, sporty clothing for women. A host of reasons lie behind the revolution: the general trend toward informal, suburban, and outdoors living; more leisure time; increases in the marriage and birth rates (mothers spend less on their clothing than other women of the same age); and the eclipse of clothing by the home as a status symbol. Informal clothing is not highly styled and therefore need not be manufactured in the city's garment center where fashion news and changes concentrate. The relative standardization of casual clothing also makes possible mass production by minimally skilled workers. Without a pressing need for a central city location, the manufacture of casual clothing, which is an increasing por-

[31] This discussion is based on Roy B. Helfgott, "Women's and Children's Apparel," in Max Hall (ed.), *Made in New York: Case Studies in Metropolitan Manufacturing* (1959), pp. 77–134.

tion of the clothing output, is moving toward cheap labor areas. Consequently, garment manufacturing is decentralizing, both through dispersion toward economically depressed regions of the nation and through diffusion toward the outskirts of the metropolis where labor costs are lower.

All of the causes of industrial decentralization—technology, population distribution, economics, social standards—may operate in two ways. Industrial plants may either be *attracted* to outlying districts or be *squeezed* out of the central city. This is the difference between voluntary and involuntary decentralization. An industry may be shifted because the advantage of outlying location is greater than the advantage of an inner site. Sometimes industrial plants are shifted not so much because of present as of future advantages when later expansion is anticipated. Industrial establishments may be forced out because of changing property restrictions or because sufficient land space is unavailable within the city. New industries may locate on the periphery because space in centralized areas is unavailable. Involuntary decentralization may or may not be to the advantage of the particular establishments. Probably in a good many instances the outward movement lags behind the need to move. Some industries are undoubtedly unsuited to their original locations, but there is always a certain inertia because of costs and inconveniences in moving, not to mention actual financial risks. Such an example would be the Chicago stockyards, once in the outskirts of the city but now in the heart of it.

ECOLOGY OF BUSINESS AND INDUSTRY IN OTHER COUNTRIES

The separation of business and industrial areas from residential districts, the prevailing pattern in American cities, is by no means characteristic of cities in other parts of the world. One important reason for the difference is that many of these cities originated in preindustrial times and still retain many preindustrial ecological as well as social features.

THE ECOLOGY OF BUSINESS AND INDUSTRY IN PREINDUSTRIAL CITIES

The ecology of preindustrial cities is primarily affected by the fact that these cities are products of societies which have neither the technology nor the values which maximize economic production.[32] People and goods move by foot, horse carts, wagons, chariots, or similar vehicles. Obligations to religion, kin, and rulers are paramount. Cities serve mainly as politico-administrative-religious centers and as forts. Markets and hand-

[32] This discussion is based on Gideon Sjoberg, *The Preindustrial City* (1960), pp. 80–107. For further description of preindustrial social structure, see Chapter 2, pp. 25 and 33, and Chapter 5, pp. 89–90, in this text.

The central business district in American cities. Kansas City, Missouri, with the central business district indicated by the tall buildings. Compare with the photographs of Houston, New York City, and Chicago (pp. 23, 27, 115) for evidence of the generality of this pattern in American cities. (Courtesy Missouri Resources Division [photograph by Massie].)

crafts represent "business and industry." According to Sjoberg, the technology and values of the preindustrial city give rise to three major ecological contrasts with the industrial city. (1) The central area, usually a plaza or square, is given over to public buildings and religious structures; the main market is located here but is not the dominant feature of the landscape or of the activity at the city center. (2) The city is divided into rather self-sufficient "quarters" which are inhabited by distinct ethnic and class groups. The tradesmen and craftsmen typically work in the houses in which they live. (3) It follows that land use is not highly differentiated in the preindustrial city. Commercial, craft, and residential functions are scattered throughout the city and are often served by the same site.

THE PREINDUSTRIAL CITY TODAY

Many cities in the world, particularly in areas where industrialization has only recently penetrated, show elements of the preindustrial pattern.

In Bangkok, for example, the Chinese, as the largest minority group, are residentially segregated but in a district that also supports varied types of establishments, including retail and wholesale businesses, small shops, banks, factories, theatres, restaurants, and dance halls.[33] Furthermore, in Singapore, Saigon, Manila, Jakarta, Rangoon, and other cities of Southeast Asia, a dominant type of Chinese house is the so-called "shophouse," a structure combining residence and business activity, with shops on the ground floor and living quarters behind and above.[34]

In Africa the division of the traditional African town into fairly autonomous districts inhabited almost wholly by people from a given tribe persists. Within these districts, home, shop, storehouse, and workshop are often combined in one dwelling. Sometimes one room is used as a store, beauty parlor, or office during the day and as a bedroom at night. Work, recreation, and domestic functions also spill out into the adjoining streets. A description of a section of Lagos, Nigeria, is illustrative.

A group of children squat on a porch, while their Arabic teacher takes them through a verse of the Koran; a woman plaits her neighbour's hair; in the late afternoon, men carry their game of draughts or table tennis into the lane; and on a Thursday or a Saturday night, the street may be filled from end to end by a wedding or a funeral party, sipping their beer and whisky under a shelter of matting. In the back yards, carpenters and millers, printers and blacksmiths run their workshops. On the verandahs, tailors bend over their machines. Signboards advertise building contractors, football pool agents, wireless repairers, importers. And in every yard and doorway and verandah, from booths and shops, or hawking up and down the lanes, women are trading—in cottons, velvets, muslin, damasks from Lancashire, Madras, Japan; enamel-ware from Hong Kong; incense from Bombay; dried stockfish from Norway; cigarettes, tinned foods, cola nuts; fruits and vegetables brought by canoe across the lagoon; fried plantains for office workers and bowls of porridge for dockers from the waterside.[35]

In the cities of India, centralization of commerce is clearly less pronounced than in United States cities. The main bazaar or *chowk* is centrally located but is not equivalent to the central business district of the American city. The upper and rear rooms in the *chowk* are generally the homes of the merchants. Also, the commercial function is widely diffused in the city because many other bazaars are located in neighborhoods inhabited by groups of a particular caste, clan, or community origin.[36]

[33] Richard J. Coughlin, "The Chinese in Bangkok: A Commercial-Oriented Minority," *American Sociological Review*, 20 (June, 1955), 315; cf. Coughlin, *Double Identity* (1961).

[34] Norton S. Ginsburg, "The Great City of Southeast Asia," *American Journal of Sociology*, 60 (March, 1955), 459.

[35] Peter Marris, *Family and Social Change in an African City* (1962), p. viii.

[36] John E. Brush, "The Morphology of Indian Cities," in Roy Turner (ed.), *India's Urban Future* (1962); and R. Mukerjee, "Ways of Dwelling in the Communities of India," in G. Theodorson (ed.), *Studies in Human Ecology* (1961).

Preindustrial cities which have been subject to Western influence often develop two commercial centers. A Western-style center with fashionable stores stocked with the latest American and European goods co-exists with the preindustrial center of native stalls and merchandise spread upon carts and the ground. The two "centers," which may or may not be near one another, present a marked physical contrast which reflects the dual nature of the social and economic structure of these societies. Dual commercial centers are a feature of many large cities in India, Southeast Asia, the Middle East, Africa, and Latin America. The retail structure of Manila, in the Philippines, combines many Eastern features with Western influences from Spain and the United States.[37]

DISTRIBUTION OF BUSINESS AND INDUSTRY IN BANGALORE, INDIA

A major retail and wholesale district adjacent to the central municipal market in Bangalore, India, a city of about one and a quarter million population, corresponds only roughly to the central business district in an American metropolis.[38] Central Market represents a major focal point of buying activities for such consumer goods as fruit, vegetables, flowers, baskets, articles of inexpensive clothing, and the like. On streets in the immediate vicinity are shops specializing in such merchandise as silk and cotton goods, silverware, hardware, drugs, jewelry, and hemp products. Shops having the same type of merchandise tend to cluster together, sometimes creating specialized streets.

About a mile north of Central Market is a "big business" street on which are concentrated banking and insurance firms, film distributing companies, a large transportation firm, and numerous business offices. Within a distance of about two blocks are seven major movie theaters. Another center of finance and credit is located a mile or so south of the Central Market in which are concentrated several cooperative institutions and banks. There are several minor commercial districts, each being more or less distinct in terms of types of merchandise or services. Various clusters of stores scattered over the city serve as neighborhood shopping centers.

Wholesale and retail functions in Bangalore are more closely identified than in an American city. There is a major wholesale street, some four or five blocks southeast of Central Market, which handles grains and vegetables. Within the central business district, wholesale and retail businesses are sometimes combined under the same roof. Manufactured products such as silverware or drugs may be sold on the premises. In this

---

[37] See Wallace E. McIntyre, "The Retail Pattern of Manila," *Geographic Review*, XLV (January, 1955), 66–80.

[38] Based on Noel P. Gist, "The Ecology of Bangalore, India: An East-West Comparison," *Social Forces*, 35 (May, 1957), 356–65.

The dominant features of the central areas of the preindustrial city are religious, administrative, or military buildings, around which shopping facilities may cluster, often in the open air or in makeshift stalls. Above: Marketplace in front of the old court house in Wuppertal-Elberfeld, a town in the north Rhine region of West Germany. Facing page: Sunday market near a church in Cuzco, the third largest city in Peru. (Courtesy the German Tourist Information Office and Standard Oil Company, New Jersey.)

general area, especially near the railway station, there are numerous small hotels and roominghouses, but the major hotels are dispersed in various parts of the city. Even municipal or government buildings like the city hall, post office, courts, and telegraph office are some distance from the central business zone.

In American cities the development of business, financial, and industrial chains has enhanced the importance of the central business district as a center of economic control. In Bangalore there are few chain establishments, and none at all comparable in size to those in an American city. Hence outlying business centers, while dependent on wholesale establishments for supplies and on banks for credit, are nevertheless relatively independent of the central business district.

PATTERNS OF BUSINESS IN LATIN AMERICAN CITIES

In an excellent ecological description of a Latin American city, Caplow has shown that the distribution of business and industry by no means follows the North American pattern.[39] The central business district of Guatemala City is much larger in area than a central district in an American metropolis of comparable size. This is because there is less concentration of business enterprises, indicating less competition for a central

[39] Theodore Caplow, "The Social Ecology of Guatemala City," *Social Forces*, 28 (December, 1949), 113–33.

location. Actually, says Caplow, there is no clearly defined central point. The principal retail stores are located at various points in the area, and factories are likewise scattered over the district. Lawyers' offices are distributed at random. Certain types of businesses, however, tend to cluster along particular streets, such as the row of tourist shops opposite a leading hotel, or expensive shops found near the central plaza.

In Guatemala City there is no sharp break between the commercial district and the residential zone; rather, the business area tapers off gradually, and with the exception of "foreign type" suburbs to the south there is no residential area completely without business or industrial establishments. In a random sample of 100 city blocks, representing about half the municipality, Caplow found only 11 that were entirely residential and none that were purely nonresidential. Shops, textile factories, printing plants, churches, government buildings, barber shops, dressmaking establishments, and grocery stores are widely distributed. The outlying or suburban shopping center or industrial district, familiar in the United States, is not a feature of the ecological pattern of Guatemala City.

Many Latin American cities have a central plaza on or near which are located the cathedral, city hall, municipal market, and possibly other government buildings. This plaza design, a feature of earlier city plans, has been observed in Sucre, Bolivia,[40] Guadalajara, Mexico,[41] and Mexico City,[42] and Caplow noted it in Guatemala City. With the growth of commerce and industry and the development of modern forms of transportation, the traditional plaza design has been altered, although some of the original features are still present. Latin American cities are outgrowing their original plans.

DECENTRALIZATION IN OTHER COUNTRIES

Rapid industrial growth in peripheral areas of great cities appears to be a widespread phenomenon, possibly a universal trend. Berlin, for example, has followed this pattern of growth.[43] About 1900, industry began to shift from points within the *Ringbahn*, a concentric railroad encircling the built-up area, to various outlying areas designed for industrial expansion. Although at the time of World War II over two-thirds of Berlin's industry was within the built-up area, large-scale engineering in-

[40] Harry B. Hawthorne and Audrey E. Hawthorne, "The Shape of a City," *Sociology and Social Research*, 33 (November, 1948), 87–91.

[41] Floyd Dotson and Lillian Ota Dotson, "Ecological Trends in the City of Guadalajara, Mexico," *Social Forces*, 32 (May, 1954), 367–74.

[42] Norman S. Hayner, "Mexico City: Its Growth and Configuration," *American Journal of Sociology*, 50 (January, 1945), 295–304.

[43] The discussion of Berlin, Paris, and Vienna is based on Robert E. Dickinson, *The West European City* (1951), pp. 228–50.

dustries had developed in outlying districts, especially along the Spree River and at junctions of belt and radial railway lines.

Until the turn of the nineteenth century, industrial development in Paris took place inside the fortified walls, but after 1900, according to Dickinson, a wide industrial-residential fringe developed outside the city. Factories sprang up along the Seine River valley, on canals that were constructed north of the city for industrial haulage, and along roads and railways. Vienna also experienced the same trend. Although there are many small factories and workshops within Vienna, heavy industrial developments have occurred on the periphery, some in the area southeast of the city designed exclusively for industrial purposes, some along the Wien River valley, and others on the north side near the Danube River.

The industrial pattern in London is much the same as in other European cities. Although industry is still heavily concentrated in the city, large-scale enterprises requiring considerable space have become increasingly decentralized. Since World War II the British government has taken the initiative in industrial planning, emphasizing the necessity of decentralization and offering inducements to industries moving to the countryside. "New towns" near the larger industrial cities of England have been developed since World War II with the idea that industrial establishments and their employees can be attracted to outlying areas because of better working and living conditions. Most of the industrial establishments that have moved into the new towns are small-scale enterprises. A "light" industrial district has also developed in northwest London.

The outlying location of industry in European countries is partly the result of historical, cultural, and political factors which were influential during the preindustrial existence of most of their cities.[44] In many cases, industry has not so much decentralized as it has always tended to be on the city's outskirts. Most European cities date from medieval or even Roman times. Hence, their centers, already built up, often with venerable structures and high-prestige residences, were seldom suitable for the introduction of industrial establishments, particularly those of any size. The walls surrounding many European cities accentuated the crowding and lack of space. When the walls were torn down the space was often used for an industrial "belt" or for wide circling streets ideally suited for access to industrial suburbs. Vienna's aptly named *Ringstrasse* is an excellent example. The lower-income groups tend to live on the periphery in European cities, in contrast to United States cities; this stems from the preindustrial period when the nobility, clergy, and rulers occupied the more prestigious (and more protected) city center. The presence of a suitable labor force encourages industry to locate at the periphery.

---

[44] Some of these factors are discussed in Francis L. Hauser, "Ecological Patterns of European Cities," in T. Lynn Smith and C. A. McMahan (eds.), *The Sociology of Urban Life* (1951), pp. 370–88.

Finally, government planning has been much more important in setting the relative location of industry and residence than in American cities. Paris, Vienna, and Stockholm have a long history of over-all planning.

Nor is peripheral growth of industry confined to cities of the West. In Bangalore, India, for example, the trend is definitely toward peripheral development of heavy industry. On the east side of the city, five or six miles from the city's boundaries, are two large-scale industries, recently established, which manufacture telephones and airplanes; on the northeast, at the edge of the city, is a large tobacco factory; and on the west, within the city limits, a textile mill employing several thousand workers. Just west of the city the municipality has reserved a large area for industrial development. Thus the factor of planning has influenced the location of industry.

On the whole, however, industrial decentralization in India has been limited. The extreme poverty forces most workers to walk to work or use bicycles and thereby inhibits any tendency to locate large-scale industries in uncongested areas on the periphery of cities.[45] Sometimes special work trains are used to transport workers to outlying locations.

Studies of Mexican cities also show little peripheral industrial development.[46] Tlalnepantla, 13 miles north of Mexico City, has emerged as an important industrial suburb, but this is still the exception rather than the rule. Whether the decentralization in Mexican cities will increase is not yet clear. The basic reasons working against it have not been technological but political and cultural, including the low prestige of residence in outlying areas.

ECOLOGY OF CULTURAL AND RECREATIONAL INSTITUTIONS

THE PATTERN OF RELIGIOUS INSTITUTIONS

Churches in American cities are sensitive to the locations of their actual or potential patrons. Hence, there is a tendency for them to follow the main trends of population, keeping fairly close to the residential locations of the majority of their members. In small cities the decentralization of population has not materially increased the distance from the city's center, and for this reason the traditional centralized pattern of the churches has been retained, although even in these localities there is some peripheral movement. It is mainly in the large metropolitan areas that the shifting of churches has occurred on a large scale.

[45] Brush, *op. cit.*, pp. 68–69.
[46] Floyd Dotson and Lillian Ota Dotson, "Urban Centralization and Decentralization in Mexico," *Rural Sociology*, 21 (March, 1956), 41–49.

As Douglass points out, there are three alternatives for a church in a growing city: first, to follow its members to a different part of the city; second, to remain in the same locality and attempt to draw its old constituency from a greater distance; and third, to remain and attempt to attract a new constituency.[47] The majority of churches, however, have followed the path of least resistance and deserted the inner zones of the city. Those that are marooned in the areas of deterioration are frequently missions, gospel halls, and storefront churches that attract the various sects and cults. The larger organizations remaining in the center have greater difficulty in functioning than those that have moved outward. The higher rate of residential turnover in the central areas makes it increasingly difficult for the downtown church to develop an effective organization. Probably every American metropolis, however, has at least one large downtown church which serves a citywide membership as well as visitors from the outside.

The redistribution of population within the metropolis has especially acute consequences for the various Protestant churches. White Protestants are heavily represented among the peoples from northern and western Europe. Having come to the United States earlier and, partly for that reason, now generally occupying high economic and occupational positions, these groups have been in the vanguard of the suburban migration.[48] The exodus of white Protestants from central city areas has probably been underway since about 1870 and has been pronounced since 1920.[49] The Protestants moving into the cities are mainly rural Negroes. Within some Protestant groups there has been a concern that some churches are oriented too exclusively to white, middle class, suburban populations, and are therefore inadequately serving urban, lower class populations, especially Negroes.[50] Whether the concern is justified cannot be answered here, but it is suggestive of some of the issues raised by the relationship between social and spatial mobility. Several studies have been undertaken of the congregations served by urban and suburban Protestant churches of various denominations.[51]

Roman Catholic, Jewish, and other religious institutions have also participated in the suburban movement. Negroes are a negligible proportion of the Jewish population and a minority among Catholics, but the changing composition of the urban population may have affected

[47] H. P. Douglass, *The St. Louis Church Survey* (1924), p. 76.
[48] See Chapter 8 for data on residental segregation of ethnic groups in American cities.
[49] Gibson Winter, *The Suburban Captivity of the Churches* (1961), p. 39ff.
[50] *Ibid.;* and Truman B. Douglass, "The Job the Protestants Shirk," *Harper's Magazine* (November, 1958).
[51] Winter, *op. cit.;* Walter Kloetzli, *The City Church—Death or Renewal* (1961); L. K. Northwood, "Ecological and Attitudinal Factors in Church Desegregation," in M. Sussman, (ed.), *Community Structure and Analysis* (1959), pp. 355–87; and Paul Musselman, *The Church on the Urban Frontier* (1960).

these religions, too. The increasing proportion of Puerto Ricans and Mexi-can-Americans in cities affects mainly Roman Catholic churches.[52]

DISTRIBUTION OF CHURCHES IN DETROIT

A survey of the Detroit area in 1958 provided data on the geographical distribution of religious groups within a very large city and its suburbs.[53] Four major socioreligious groups, accounting for 95 per cent of the popu-lation, were examined: white Protestants, white Catholics, Negro Prot-estants, and Jews. Detroit and its suburbs were divided into "twelve major areas which have emerged as spontaneous and unplanned by-products of the growth of the metropolis." A striking finding of the sur-vey was that in all but two of these areas one or another of the four re-ligious groups constituted an absolute majority among the residents, despite the fact that none of the religious groups constituted a majority of the total Detroit metropolitan population.

Starting at the ecological center of Detroit, the "inner city," and pro-ceeding outward in the same way as the city grew, the survey disclosed the following distribution of religious groups. (1) Negro Protestants pre-dominate in the "inner city" areas. (2) No religious group constitutes a majority in the "middle city" areas, probably because many of these sections are undergoing succession from white Catholic to Negro Protes-tant occupancy. (3) In the "outer city," the area of most recent settle-ment *within* the city boundaries, white Catholics are the major group in the eastern portions, Jews in a central section, and white Protestants in the western portion. (4) White Protestants constitute the majority of the population in all the suburban areas except the southern, where the white Catholics predominate.

The distribution of religious groups is not necessarily a result of volun-tary religious segregation, although this is undoubtedly a factor. Ethnic, racial, and social class factors also play an important part. Other por-tions of the Detroit study show that in terms of occupation and income, Jews and white Protestants generally outrank the white Catholics and Negro Protestants.[54]

CULTURAL AND RECREATIONAL INSTITUTIONS

Cultural and recreational organizations, like retail stores, are usually operated for the direct benefit of consumers except that services rather

---

[52] Oscar J. Lee, "Religion among Ethnic and Racial Minorities," *Annals,* 332 (No-vember, 1960), 120–21.
[53] G. Lenski, *The Religious Factor* (1961), pp. 15–16, 69–74.
[54] *Ibid.,* p. 73 and ch. 3.

than commodities are sold or otherwise distributed. Their locations are therefore determined by the number, interest, purchasing power, amount of leisure time, and location of consumers of the particular services offered. Each type of service has its own distinctive ecological pattern, and doubtless there are great variations in this pattern according to the size of the city, social interests of its inhabitants, and character of its transportation system.

The ecological patterning of motion picture establishments is highly variable. In small cities motion picture houses are highly centralized, except that the outdoor movie, a creation of automotive transportation, is located on the city's fringe or in the open country. The outdoor movie is apparently an American and Canadian phenomenon because in no other country is there mass automotive transportation. Drive-in movies are an aspect of decentralization of recreation following in the wake of a motorized suburban population. Another technological innovation, television, has also contributed to the decline of movie houses. The uses to which vacated movie houses have been put is an interesting example of succession. Some have been demolished to make way for office buildings, but others have been converted to warehouses, bowling alleys, theatres, or television studios.

In the downtown metropolis, movies are shown in palatial establishments accommodating mass audiences drawn from all parts of the city and from the outside. The highly specialized type of movie house presenting exclusively news, documentary, or art films is also usually found in the city's center. In deteriorated areas on the fringe of the business district, areas populated mainly by transients, homeless men, and denizens of the underworld, the honky-tonk movie and burlesque show, commonly combined, is a familiar institution, while neighborhood movie houses and drive-ins usually feature films for the family.

SELECTED BIBLIOGRAPHY

Books

Brush, John, "The Morphology of Indian Cities," in Roy Turner (ed.), *India's Urban Future*. Berkeley and Los Angeles: University of California Press, 1962.

Gillmore, Harlan, *Transportation and the Growth of Cities*. Glencoe, Ill.: The Free Press, 1953.

Horwood, Edgar, and R. Boyce, *Studies of the Central Business District and Urban Freeway Development*. Seattle: University of Washington Press, 1959.

Lenski, G., *The Religious Factor*, ch. 2. Garden City, N.Y.: Doubleday, 1961.

Liepmann, Kate, *The Journey to Work: Its Significance for Industry and Community Life*. New York: Oxford University Press, 1944.

Mayer, Harold, and Clyde Kohn (eds.), *Readings in Urban Geography.* Sections 11–14. Chicago: University of Chicago Press, 1959.

New York Metropolitan Regional Study. Vol. 2: Max Hall (ed.), *Made in New York;* Vol. 4.: Martin Segal, *Wages in the Metropolis;* Vol. 5: Sidney Robbins, *et al., Money Metropolis;* Vol. 6: Benjamin Chinitz, *Freight and the Metropolis.* Cambridge, Mass.: Harvard University Press, 1959–60.

Sjoberg, Gideon, *The Preindustrial City,* ch. 4. Glencoe; Ill.: The Free Press, 1960.

Vernon, Raymond, *The Changing Economic Function of the Central City.* New York: Committee for Economic Development, 1959.

ARTICLES

Ginsburg, Norton, "The Great City in Southeast Asia," *American Journal of Sociology,* LX (March, 1955), 455–63.

Gist, Noel P., "The Ecology of Bangalore: An East-West Comparison," *Social Forces,* 35 (May, 1957), 356–65.

Myers, George, "Patterns of Church Distribution and Movement," *Social Forces,* 40 (May, 1962), 354–63.

Sternlieb, George, "The Future of Retailing in the Downtown Core," *Journal of the American Institute of Planners,* 29 (May, 1963), 102–12.

Vernon, Raymond, "Production and Distribution in the Large Metropolis," *Annals of the American Academy of Political and Social Science,* 314 (November, 1957), 15–30.

The Metropolitan Region
and Urban Dominance

A rural or small-city resident knows, if he stops to reflect, that his community is geared more closely than ever before to the big city, that he has become increasingly dependent on the central metropolis for certain types of services and commodities, and that his thinking and daily habits are influenced by the stream of ideas flowing outward from the city and by his own experiences when he visits the metropolis. He may subscribe to a metropolitan daily; if he wants to consult a medical specialist, attend a theatrical production, go to the circus, visit a public library, buy furniture or a new suit of clothes, or sell something he has produced, he may find that the central city offers greater opportunities or has more adequate facilities than his own community. Even if he chooses to do none of these things, he may be aware that his chances of securing a job or holding the one he has are influenced by institutional changes in the metropolis. Should he be a merchant, physician, hotel proprietor, preacher, or manufacturer, he can hardly escape being affected by his metropolitan competitors.

RISE OF THE METROPOLITAN REGION

In its structural and spatial aspects the metropolitan region consists of the metropolis and its surrounding settlements; *functionally* the region is a complex web of economic, cultural, and political relationships that bind these settlements and the larger metropolis into a unit with a dominant center and subordinate parts.[1] Although topographic or climatic factors certainly affect, or at least limit, regional developments, the metropolitan region as here conceived is essentially a cultural phenomenon. It is the product, to a great extent, of new methods of transportation and communication—the automobile, transport truck, rapid transit public conveyances, newspaper, telegraph, radio, and telephone. By means of these technological facilities the subordinate settlements have become integrated with each other and with larger nuclear centers.

THE METROPOLITAN REGION AND TRANSPORTATION

Metropolitan regionalism in this country has been manifest in two ways: by the development of subordinate communities within the immediate orbit of a metropolis, and by the orientation of these and more distant communities around an urban center to assume a more or less integrated unit.

Although the basic pattern of urban settlement in the United States was laid down during the period of water transportation, it was not until the era of railroad development that something resembling the metropolitan region began to emerge.[2] Railway lines were extended in different directions from the main cities, thus bringing the larger centers into a closer economic relationship and providing a greater degree of integration for the entire national economy. On the railway lines that usually ran from one large city to another were located towns and villages, and these communities were brought more closely within the economic and cultural orbit of the great centers.

Thus the form and character of the metropolitan region began to emerge, manifest mainly by the rise of dominant commercial and industrial centers and the development of tributary settlements in the hinterlands. The reciprocal relationship between the larger centers and the subordinate communities was not uniform for the entire hinterland: many towns and villages not touched by railroad lines were relatively isolated, even though they did not escape entirely the influence of the dominant city. Moreover, the pattern of railway lines resembled not so much a network as a wheel with the spokes radiating outward from the hub in different directions. Therefore, the outlying settlements, while becoming more closely integrated with the dominant community and the emergent regional economy, tended to be isolated from other subordinate communi-

[1] Mumford and Odum criticize the concepts of the metropolitan region as too narrow and arbitrary. That it is a restricted view we readily admit. But we must insist that the relationship between the city and its hinterland is an important aspect of modern urbanism and as such should be presented in a study of urban sociology. See Lewis Mumford, *The Culture of Cities* (1938), p. 367; Howard Odum and Harry E. Moore, *American Regionalism* (1938).

[2] R. D. McKenzie, *The Metropolitan Community* (1933), pp. 139–40.

ties located on different radial transportation routes extending into the hinterland.

The automobile and transport truck speeded up regional development. Automobile highways have been constructed to connect one large center with another, sometimes running parallel to the railroads, and local roads have been developed to fill in the transportation gaps in the axiate railway pattern. Every large American city is now the center of a veritable network of motor-car routes radiating out from the central community, encircling the city, or connecting subordinate settlements that lie within the sphere of influence of the metropolis. Even communities in remoter parts of the hinterland are commonly located on or near motor-car routes that make the metropolitan center accessible. Thus it is clear that the automobile and the hard-surfaced highway have been important factors in the development of an organic regional unity and particularly in the creation of what McKenzie calls the metropolitan community. Towns and villages that were once relatively independent and isolated are in the process of being incorporated into a larger functional unit, and outlying communities and farming areas have been brought more closely within the economic and cultural orbit of the dominating metropolitan center.

The development of air transportation is another factor in metropolitan regionalism. Initially, commercial air routes, like the earliest railroads, tended to be interregional, connecting only large cities. But since World War II, air transportation networks have been extended to include secondary regional cities, many of which have direct air connections with larger cities. To what extent the airlines are used for shopping, business, or pleasure trips to larger cities is not known, but the amount of such travel is considerable. Air transportation also provides faster postal service between the metropolis and outlying cities as well as between regions. So far there has been little development of regular air commuter services for personnel employed in cities. However, first steps in this direction have been taken. "Air shuttles" operating between Washington, D. C., New York City, and Boston leave on a regular schedule, usually every hour; there are no reservations, and fares are collected on board. A similar service operates between Frankfurt and Hamburg, Germany.

LARGE-SCALE ORGANIZATION AND METROPOLITAN DOMINANCE

In certain respects large-scale organization has been as important as transportation and communication in regional developments. The growth of the chain-store principle in merchandising, finance, and certain types of services has extended the influence of the metropolis far into the hinterland. As a result of such developments, the metropolis exercises a coordinating and directing control over economic functions performed in outlying settlements. Branch or chain banks, grocery stores, drug stores, department stores, movie theatres, and apparel shops are all familiar aspects of chain organizations whose hinterland operations are managed from a central metropolis, which in turn may be subordinate to a national headquarters.

Even establishments not parts of an ordinary chain are highly dependent upon a central organization whose policies determine the kinds of merchandise they can carry, prices they can charge, and some of the conditions under which they can operate. Stores carrying "name" brands of merchandise, even though nominally independent, may be little more than links in a great merchandising organization whose metropolitan headquarters formulates many of the policies of local distribution within the region. This principle of large-scale organization has been carried further in the United States than elsewhere, and for this reason metropolitan dominance may assume a somewhat different form in regional growth than in other countries.

SPECIALIZATION AND INTERDEPENDENCE

Metropolitan regions as a whole tend to be heterogeneous rather than homogeneous in their economic and cultural characteristics, and within a region specialization has proceeded apace. To the extent that specialization within a region occurs, to that extent there must be interdependence of the parts one on another. Within regions some communities are highly specialized in commercial or industrial functions.

Agriculture especially tends to become specialized. Immediately surrounding the metropolis is an open-country zone devoted largely to truck gardening, cultivation of flowers and shrubs, or production of small fruits and berries. As one proceeds from this area toward the periphery of the region, agriculture is more diversified, although geographic and climatic conditions may alter this pattern considerably.

In highly industrialized regions in the United States specialization has become pronounced. As McKenzie points out, many industries are operated on an assembly-line basis; the different parts are manufactured in separate establishments scattered throughout the region, then transported to an assembly plant where the finished product is turned out. The automobile industry in the Detroit region is an example of this increasing specialization and interdependence. Automobile parts are manufactured in factories located in Detroit or scattered throughout southern Michigan, Indiana, Ohio, or Illinois. Thus the automobile industry really consists of a large number of industries scattered over a considerable area and closely integrated with each other and with the central assembly plant. This regional coordination of industrial output is made possible by modern methods of communication and transportation. "The transportation channels along which the different units are conveyed to the assem-

blying factory," says McKenzie, "might almost be considered as extensions of that factory's assembly lines, as the intake from the trucks and
railways is about as sensitively adjusted to the time factor in production
as is the speed of the belt lines within the factory itself. Moreover, the
entire process is directed and controlled from central offices, most of
which are located in the city of Detroit." [3]

SPACE, TIME, AND COST

Metropolitan regions are not distinct political units, nor are they isolated socially and economically. For these reasons the periphery of the
region can never be sharply defined: regions not only touch each other,
they also interpenetrate. The outlines of the region may indeed be arbitrarily delineated for purposes of analysis or administration, but there
is always a marginal area that is influenced fairly evenly by two or more
dominant centers and which therefore belongs quite as logically to one as
to another.

The influence of a dominant center tends to diminish with increasing
distance. At least this is true of economic influence. As distance from
the metropolis increases, a point is reached (which actually may be quite
a wide belt) where specific influences of one metropolis may be equalled
by those of another. Since metropolitan centers are constantly competing, the size of a region is subject to change. St. Louis, for example, once
dominated rather completely a vast area in the Mississippi Valley, but
Kansas City, Chicago, and other cities have so extended the territorial
limits of their influence that the St. Louis region has been reduced in size.

The territorial extent of a metropolitan region bears no necessary relationship to the size of its dominant center. The Twin Cities, for example,
represent the nucleus of an area that is much larger than the metropolitan regions of Boston or Philadelphia, although both of the latter cities are
more than twice as large as the Minneapolis–St. Paul combination. The
eastern portion of the country is characterized by a considerable number
of large cities, each of which has tended to carve out a sort of regional
empire. Because of the number of centers, however, and the competition
between them, the areas dominated by each are relatively restricted in
size, although the number of people and institutions within each eastern
region may exceed those of some of the larger regions of the Middle
West and Far West. In general, the eastern metropolitan regions have a
greater density of population and more intense industrial activities than
those west of the Mississippi Valley.

The relation of a metropolitan center to the surrounding region is also
influenced by time and cost of travel, shipment of goods, and transmission
of ideas and information. Time-cost distance is a variable, depending

[3] *Ibid.*, p. 79.

largely upon the nature of the transportation and communication facilities and the costs incurred in their use. In general, distance computed in terms of time is decreasing. Ideas also tend to flow in channels of lowest cost. Although the time element has been reduced through transmission of ideas by telephone, telegraph, radio, television, press, and film, the element of cost still bulks large.

Costs incurred in communication between cities as well as between cities and their surrounding areas are important factors in regional developments. Not only do they have a bearing on relationships between cities but they also limit the degree of interaction between the metropolitan center and outlying settlements.

The remarkable changes in speed of land transportation in recent years have tended somewhat to offset the low costs of inland water transport. Regions once relatively isolated from other areas now find the time-distance factor reduced to a fraction of its original figure. Air transportation will still further reduce the time-distance factor, although cost-distance may be greater than for other means of transportation.

MEASUREMENT OF METROPOLITAN DOMINANCE

THE RANGE OF METROPOLITAN DOMINANCE

Although the complex interdependence of urban society makes it difficult to delineate the geographic boundaries of metropolitan dominance, generally speaking the range of dominance can be measured either narrowly, using direct contact as the measure, or broadly, using indirect contact. These standards enable us to distinguish three areas of metropolitan influence—primary, secondary, and tertiary.[4]

Direct contact, which defines the primary area of dominance, comprises the range of daily movement to and from a center, typified by commuting and shopping. Indirect contact on a daily or almost-daily basis— through the telephone, radio, and newspapers—and some direct contact by the frequent circulation of individuals, identify the secondary area of dominance, which radiates roughly up to 50 miles from the metropolitan center. Both the primary and the secondary areas have been extensively enlarged by modern technology, which enables people to travel more easily and to communicate with one another without actual physical contact.

The influence of the metropolis often extends to vast areas which may even be spatially discontinuous from the metropolitan center. These are the tertiary areas of dominance, where physical contact and communication are on a less-than-daily basis, but the influence of the metropolis is nevertheless clearly felt. The specialized functions of a given metro-

[4] Amos Hawley, *Human Ecology* (1950), pp. 255–57.

politan area may serve a whole region, nation, or may even be worldwide. New York City, for example, is the publishing center for the entire nation. The export area of a metropolis is one measure of its tertiary area.

NEWSPAPER CIRCULATION AND REGIONALISM

One of the most widely used measures of indirect or secondary metropolitan contact is the circulation of metropolitan newspapers. The pattern of newspaper circulation, according to Park's classic study of the Chicago region, tends to take the form of a gradient, the number of subscribers declining fairly regularly in direct ratio to the increase in distance from the metropolis.[5] These gradients, as Park points out, are perhaps a fairly accurate index of the influence of the metropolis; or, stating the matter somewhat differently, of the degree of dependence or independence of the subordinate communities. In the towns around the edge of Chicago the metropolitan dailies are read almost exclusively, or at least in addition to all local papers. Even within a 50-mile radius of the city, the bulk of the daily papers are Chicago journals, although the percentage tends to decline as distance from the metropolis increases.

Another method of studying newspaper circulation in its regional aspects is presented by McKenzie and his collaborators.[6] They selected the Federal Reserve banking centers, main and branch, together with a few additional cities, and then collected data to show the territorial extent of the circulation of a morning newspaper published in each of the cities. The territory assigned to each city included the area in which 50 per cent or more of the morning papers' circulation came from that city. The entire country was then divided into 41 newspaper-circulation areas, each including a dominant metropolis and a "newspaper-reader" hinterland.

Data on newspaper circulation undoubtedly offer significant clues to metropolitan influence. What we need now is more information concerning the functional character of the newspaper and the nature of its influence, if any, by way of spreading metropolitan culture and shaping the attitudes and habits of its hinterland readers. Moreover, we should know if there is any correlation between the regional circulation of newspapers and other factors relating to urban dominance. Does the trade territory of a metropolis, for example, conform to the area of metropolitan newspaper circulation? In general, it does. This reason, among others, prompts "audits" of newspaper circulation, since the results will indicate which stores, entertainment facilities, and services would find it most profitable to advertise in given metropolitan dailies. Not only commercial

[5] R. E. Park, "Urbanization and Newspaper Circulation," *American Journal of Sociology,* 35 (July, 1929), 60–79.
[6] *Op. cit.,* ch. 8.

activities, but the featuring of local sports teams and coverage of local social, religious, and political events, are also affected by knowledge of the
"reach" of metropolitan newspapers.

The linkage of metropolitan dominance with trade areas makes the
measurement of metropolitan boundaries of more than academic interest.
Since market research firms, department stores, banks, and other agencies
are vitally affected by such boundaries, they employ a variety of methods
to measure them, including surveys of the origin and destination of
traffic and the mapping of such information as the delivery areas of department stores, the locations of buyers in the wholesale markets, and the
listening areas of local radio and television stations.

HINTERLAND BOUNDARIES OF NEW YORK CITY AND BOSTON

Green's examination of the areas of dominance of New York City and
Boston indicates the variety of methods that may be used to delimit the
areas of influence.[7] His aim was to find where major orientation to New
York City was replaced by major orientation to Boston. The study
covered such aspects of metropolitan dependence as transportation, communication, recreation, manufacturing, and finance. Among the numerous
measures tested, seven proved most workable in yielding boundaries: (1)
railroad coach ticket purchases; (2) truck freight movement; (3) circulation of major Boston and New York newspapers; (4) long-distance
telephone calls between the two cities; (5) origin of vacationers; (6)
business addresses of directors for major industrial firms in Boston and
New York; (7) New York or Boston banks used in commercial transactions by small-town banks. Taken separately, the various measures did
not produce identical boundaries, since each represented different types
of contact.

When the seven measures were mapped and superimposed, however,
a clear gradation of dominance in the area between the two major centers emerged. Boston's area of dominance was much smaller than that
of New York City, only eastern Massachusetts showing strong attraction
to the former in terms of a majority (usually 90 per cent or more) of the
contacts measured by all seven criteria. On the same basis, the New York
City area included most of Connecticut, portions of Massachusetts, and
the southern fringes of Rhode Island. In addition, the remaining sections
of Connecticut and additional sections of southwestern Massachusetts
and Rhode Island showed a weaker affinity for New York City. Central
Massachusetts and northern Rhode Island were in the outer orbit of Boston's influence.

The problems of measuring metropolitan dominance are illuminated

[7] Howard L. Green, "Hinterland Boundaries of New York City and Boston in
Southern New England," *Economic Geography*, 31 (October, 1955), 283–300.

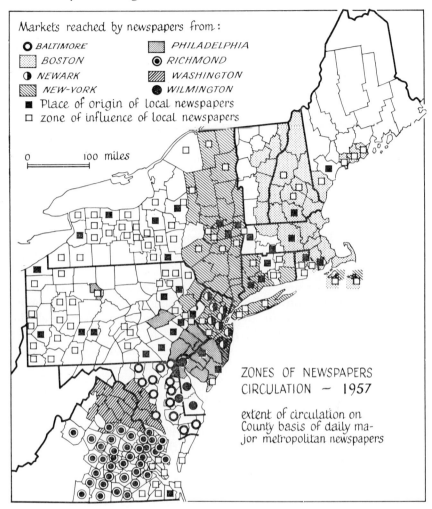

Markets reached by newspapers from:

O BALTIMORE   ▣ PHILADELPHIA

▢ BOSTON   ◉ RICHMOND

◑ NEWARK   ▨ WASHINGTON

▧ NEW-YORK   ● WILMINGTON

■ Place of origin of local newspapers

□ zone of influence of local newspapers

0   100 miles

ZONES OF NEWSPAPERS
CIRCULATION — 1957

extent of circulation on
County basis of daily ma-
jor metropolitan newspapers

Figure 20. SOURCE: Jean Gottmann, *Megalopolis* (New York: Twentieth Century Fund, 1961). Courtesy the Twentieth Century Fund.

by the conclusion of another recent study that New York City and Boston were components of a metropolitan region extending 600 miles from north of Boston to south of Washington, D. C.[8] Gottmann regards this as one region because of its high continuous density of population and the concentration within it of most of the national decision-making activities (government, finance, mass media of communication, institutions of higher learning and research, and so on). The cities, suburbs, farms, parks and decentralized manufacturing plants of this extended region are bound up in such a web of interpenetration and interdependence that

[8] Jean Gottmann, *Megalopolis* (1961). This study is further described in Chapter 4.

the notion of influence radiating from a single center is inapplicable, he says. Although its present structure is nebulous, Gottman views "Megalopolis" as the forerunner of a new kind of metropolitan region whose major characteristics will be polynuclear structure and the inclusion of concentrations of many diverse activities.

METROPOLITAN INFLUENCE IN RURAL AREAS

Various measures of land use and population characteristics indicate the pervasive nature of metropolitan influence as it spreads even to seemingly far-removed farm areas and villages. The so-called "milk shed" is one aspect of metropolitan regionalism. Because milk is a highly perishable commodity, its delivery to city consumers must be done rapidly and with regularity. Owing to improved means of transportation, as well as to improved methods of production and processing, the milk shed around cities has come to encompass an increasingly larger area. Milk trucks range over the hinterland as far as 200 miles from a metropolis, delivering raw milk to the central dairies for processing and local redistribution. Milk delivery trains operate over an even wider area. In general, the larger the city the greater is the milk region. The production and sale of milk within milk marketing areas are regulated by both federal and state agencies, as well as by agreements among the milk producers themselves.

Springdale, a town of about 2,500 in upstate New York illustrates the impact of widening milk supply areas.[9] With the advent of the milk truck, production of butter and cheese and of buckwheat, maple syrup, hay, and sheep was gradually superseded in Springdale by production of fluid milk for daily delivery to urban markets. The mechanized accessories of milk processing outmoded the large farm family, many of whose members migrated elsewhere. Thus, reduced population, mechanization, and increased contact with the outside world transformed the social and economic life of Springdale.

Duncan and Reiss [10] employed a more comprehensive method of testing metropolitan influence on rural areas by classifying all United States counties on a four-part scale from most to least urban: the "most urban" counties contained a metropolis with at least 250,000 inhabitants, while "least urban" counties contained no city as large as 25,000. Examination of the characteristics of the rural farm population in each of the four types of counties revealed that the characteristics varied in a gradient pattern according to the metropolitan or nonmetropolitan nature of the county in which the rural farm population lived. Thus, the fertility rates

[9] Arthur Vidich and Joseph Bensman, *Small Town in Mass Society* (1958), pp. 10–11.
[10] Otis Dudley Duncan and Albert Reiss, *Social Characteristics of Rural and Urban Communities, 1950* (1956), ch. 13.

of the rural farm population increased gradually from the "most urban" to the "least urban" counties, while educational attainment and income gradually decreased. "These results make it clear that blanket characterizations of the rural population tend to be less accurate to the degree that the rural population falls into the area of dominance of urban centers." [11]

Other, less precise measures also indicate the spreading influence of the metropolis in rural areas. Many rural hamlets and crossroads villages are "drying up" as motorized farmers bypass them to shop, bank, and relax in larger, more diverse centers. Most of the surviving small rural towns are firmly under the metropolitan thumb, whether or not they acknowledge it. The many-faceted contacts of rural areas with the metropolis make it clear why there is no longer a sharp distinction between rural and urban ways of life in the United States.

STUDIES OF METROPOLITAN DOMINANCE
IN PRIMARY AND SECONDARY AREAS

As noted earlier, whether we view the extent of the range of metropolitan dominance narrowly or broadly depends upon the measures we use. In this section, we shall consider dominance in the narrow sense, that is, in terms of the influence of the metropolitan center on the primary and secondary zones. Taken together, they represent the way in which a metropolis functions as an integrated community, socially and economically, if not governmentally. Thus, in many ways, analysis of local metropolitan influence constitutes a description of the internal structure of the metropolitan community. In addition, the two-part area is comparable to the Standard Metropolitan Statistical Area as delineated by the U. S. Bureau of the Census. [12]

Suburban Belt and Rural-Urban Fringe

On the basis of a review of several recent studies of metropolitan areas, Dobriner compared the population composition and land use of the primary and secondary areas of dominance with those in the heart of the metropolis itself. [13] Dobriner employs the terms "suburban belt" and "rural-urban fringe," which may be respectively taken as equivalent to the areas of primary and secondary dominance.

1. The central city zone is the heart of the metropolis and contains the major cultural and commercial institutions, including the central business

---

[11] *Ibid.*, p. 168. [12] See Chapter 3 for the definition of an SMSA.
[13] William Dobriner, *Class in Suburbia* (1963), pp. 152–65.

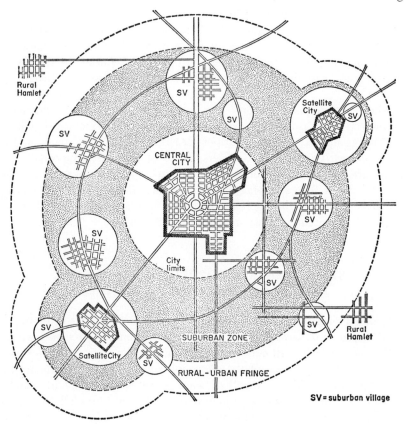

Figure 21. A model metropolitan area showing the relationship between the central city, suburban zone, and rural-urban fringe. SOURCE: William M. Dobriner, *Class in Suburbia.* Copyright © 1963 by Prentice-Hall, Inc., Englewood Cliffs, N. J. Reprinted by permission.

district. Density of population is at a maximum here. Population size is either stable or slowly declining, and its racial and ethnic composition is changing rapidly as more nonwhites move in. The extremes of the social and economic scale live in the central city: the very rich and the very poor; minority groups and the elite of the nation. The central city also tends to contain nonfamily groups: the aged, widowed, and divorced. Consequently, the central city birth rate is low. Women outnumber men.

2. The suburban zone includes residential suburbs of many types and industrial satellite cities. The suburban belt is growing rapidly, as white, middle income families flee the crowded, obsolete core. The birth rate and levels of income and education are generally higher than in the central city. Nonwhite and minority groups are underrepresented.

3. The rural-urban fringe is an area of mixed land use and population

composition because here the urban and suburban commercial, manufacturing, and residential uses are eating unevenly into the countryside.

DIFFERENTIATION AND METROPOLITAN DOMINANCE

An additional element must be added to the preceding zonal analysis
in order to adequately describe primary and secondary metropolitan
influence. The zonal concept implies that zones nearer the metropolis,
and hence more influenced by it, are more specialized—that is, differentiated—in terms of many widely used measures of socioeconomic status
and population composition. The areas closer to the metropolitan center
have little need to duplicate all of the services available in the center.
Outlying areas, however, must provide many more of the services that
their residents require. These areas have less opportunity to specialize.
Differentiation as an aspect of metropolitan dominance was investigated
in a study of suburbs within 12 metropolitan areas.[14] After the suburbs
were classified into concentric zones of distance from the metropolis,
the amount of variation among the suburbs in each zone was computed
statistically. ". . . the 'metropolitan area' investigated here includes
roughly the primary and the secondary communal areas—in order to
contrast the amount of differentiation in the inner primary zones with
that in the outer secondary zones." [15] The suburbs in the inner zones (a
maximum of 15 to 35 miles from the metropolis) were found to be more
differentiated than those of the outer zones (a maximum of 50 miles from
the metropolis). For example, suburbs of the inner zones had either a
low or a high percentage of professional workers as residents; there were
few "mixed" suburbs. In the outer zones, however, suburbs did not vary
greatly in terms of the percentage of professional workers as residents.
Monthly rental value of dwelling units, the proportion of the population
voting Democratic, and the proportion of nonwhite dwelling units also
showed a bimodal distribution among the inner zone suburbs and a uni-
modal distribution among outer zone suburbs. The greater differentiation of inner zone suburbs suggests that, because of greater metropolitan
influence, each suburb serves a special function relative to the metropolitan core—thus, high income suburbs are separate from low income
suburbs, suburbs for professional workers are separate from those for
blue collar workers and for nonwhites. On the other hand, because all
suburbs in the outer zone have roughly the same relation to the metropolitan center, the composition of their populations do not vary much
from one another.

[14] Leslie Kish, "Differentiation in Metropolitan Areas," *American Sociological Review*, 19 (August, 1954), 388–98.
[15] *Ibid.*, p. 390.

STUDIES OF METROPOLITAN DOMINANCE
IN TERTIARY AREAS

Now we turn to consider metropolitan dominance in the area of its furthest influence, the so-called tertiary area of dominance. In some cases the metropolitan "hinterland" is nationwide. We will present two studies, one by Bogue and a second by Duncan, which differ in approach, although both are concerned with tertiary as well as primary and secondary areas of dominance.

BOGUE'S STUDY OF DOMINANCE

In a comprehensive study of metropolitan dominance in the United States, Bogue has clearly shown that economic interdependence actually exists between large cities and their hinterlands.[16] Bogue uses the term "metropolitan community" for those regions which are economically organized around a dominant metropolis and subordinate urban and rural settlements. "Dominance" is defined as the influence which is exerted by a metropolis upon outlying areas. It is Bogue's hypothesis that the economic life of the nation as manifest in commercial and industrial activities tends to be increasingly organized in terms of relationship between a dominant center and subordinate parts.

Method of Study. Bogue's analysis is based on 67 areas centering around major cities of the United States in 1940. On the rough but simplifying assumption that "a metropolis can dominate all the area which lies closer to it than to any other similar city, even if the other metropolis is larger," Bogue delineated the hinterland boundaries at points midway between adjacent metropolises. Through this procedure all of the continental United States fell within one of the metropolitan regions.

Evidence of Dominance. The findings of this extensive study are so numerous and detailed that only a brief summary can be presented in this discussion. Some of the more pertinent results of the study are here designated.

1. Population density tended to decline with increase of distance from the central metropolis. This density was fairly high within the first zone (under 25 miles), but dropped off sharply thereafter. Density of the first zone was about seven times as great as for the entire hinterland (excluding central cities), whereas density in the outer zone (165 miles or over) was only one-third that of the total hinterland. Urban and rural nonfarm residents were much more concentrated near the central cities than were the farm residents. Regions with large central cities (over 500,000) had a higher density at all distances from the center than regions with smaller central cities.

[16] Donald J. Bogue, *The Structure of the Metropolitan Community* (1949).

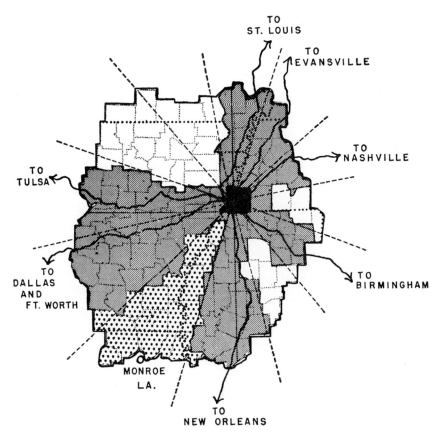

TO
ST. LOUIS

TO
EVANSVILLE

TO
NASHVILLE

TO
TULSA

TO
DALLAS
AND
FT. WORTH

TO
BIRMINGHAM

MONROE
LA.

TO
NEW ORLEANS

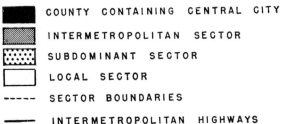

COUNTY CONTAINING CENTRAL CITY

INTERMETROPOLITAN SECTOR

SUBDOMINANT SECTOR

LOCAL SECTOR

----- SECTOR BOUNDARIES

—— INTERMETROPOLITAN HIGHWAYS

Figure 22. Memphis metropolitan region showing intermetropolitan, subdominant, and local sectors. SOURCE: Donald J. Bogue, *The Structure of the Metropolitan Community* (1949).

259

2. Central cities were more specialized in retail trade than were any of the zones in the hinterland. Per capita sales in the central cities ($471) were about 50 per cent higher than in the first two zones and twice as high as sales in the two outer zones. Bogue concludes that residents within a radius of 35 miles were highly dependent upon the central cities for retail goods, but beyond that range the population depended mainly upon retail stores distributed to serve the local population.

3. Wholesale merchandising was concentrated heavily in the metropolis, per capita sales in the central cities being about seven and one-half times the per capita sales in the hinterland portion of the regions. There was some whole-saling within the 25-mile zone, but beyond this wholesale activities were below the average for the hinterland.

4. The dollar value of service activities (mechanical repair services, business and personal services, warehousing, interior decorating, etc.) was about three times as high in the central cities as in the hinterland. Receipts from such services declined steadily with distance from the city.

5. Manufacturing was heavily concentrated within the central city and the 25-mile zone. Value added by manufacturing in the metropolis and within the first zone was almost twice the average for the hinterland and three times that of the outer zone. Per capita value of manufactured products declined regularly with distance from the metropolis.

It is apparent from Bogue's study that the hinterland is economically dependent upon the metropolis and the inner zone. Dependency is especially pronounced for wholesale trade and the various services. Outer zones are dependent upon both the metropolis and inner zones for manufactured products. There is less dependency in the case of retail trade, except for the suburban area. Inability of outlying settlements to provide goods and services necessary to maintain a given standard of living accounts for this economic dependency and for the particular ecological configurations that have developed. Because of such dependency the metropolis is in a position to exercise economic control over various activities in the hinterland. For this reason we are justified in speaking of metropolitan dominance.

There is, of course, a reciprocal relationship; the metropolis is obviously dependent upon the hinterland, and the parts of the hinterland one upon another. It is this interdependence expressed through functional organizations that gives the region its unitary character as a metropolitan community.

Each of the regions was divided into 12 sectors focussing on the central metropolis and extending outward to the assigned regional boundaries—a pie-shaped design in its ideal form, with sectors resembling conventional cuts of pie. These sectors were given a three-fold classification:

a. Intermetropolitan sectors containing major highways connecting neighboring metropolises;

  b. subdominant sectors, the remaining sectors containing a city of 25,000 or more inhabitants and located 10 miles or more from the central city;

  c. local sectors, or all the remaining ones.

SIGNIFICANCE OF BOGUE'S RESEARCH

In interpreting Bogue's findings, it must be remembered that the data apply collectively to 67 metropolitan regions and are not necessarily applicable to any particular region. His study provides an over-all picture, an average of metropolitan regions and the way they are structured economically with reference to functional relationships between metropolitan centers and outlying areas. No doubt there are many variations from this generalized pattern.

One important aspect of Bogue's study is that it approached metropolitan regions as a "closed system"; each of the 67 metropolitan regions he employed was viewed as self-contained. In other words, each hinterland was seen as influenced by a single metropolitan center. An alternative conception, viewing metropolitan regions as an "open system," involves the idea that in many ways the division of labor among metropolises is nationwide. Hence, the hinterland of a given metropolis is also influenced by other metropolitan centers which are geographically separate and distant. Neither the "open" nor the "closed" metropolitan systems can be evaluated in terms of "right" or "wrong"; each emphasizes different aspects of the national organization of metropolitan regions. A study, presented below, by Duncan and his associates, illustrates the "open system" approach.

DUNCAN'S STUDY OF METROPOLITAN REGIONS

Because the analysis of metropolitan regions by Otis Dudley Duncan and his associates is highly complex and technical, only some of their relevant findings can be summarized here.[17] The study's basic premise is that there are various kinds of metropolitan functions, each of which may have a distinct type of regional relationship. Furthermore, the "region" of influence is not necessarily the territory adjacent to the metropolis. In other words, metropolitan influence (dominance) occurs in a variety of ways. Consequently, no one set of regions can adequately describe the pattern of dominance.

Two major methods were employed in the Duncan study. The first concentrated primarily on metropolitan functions and secondarily on regional

[17] Otis Dudley Duncan, W. Richard Scott, Stanley Lieberson, Beverly Duncan, and Hal Winsborough, *Metropolis and Region* (1960).

distribution. Duncan then reversed the telescope as it were by next concentrating primarily on specific metropolitan areas and secondarily reaching conclusions about the functions performed.

First Method. In examining the spheres of influence of various types of metropolitan functions, Duncan found that two major functions, finance-commerce and manufacturing, have different spatial patterns.[18] Data from the Federal Reserve System on the flow of business loans among member banks in 1955 show that an appreciable amount of such borrowing and lending is nonlocal. The geographical extent of financing functions falls into a hierarchy: a few very large metropolises make up a national credit market, while beneath them four other ranks of cities make substantial nonlocal business loans but encompass progressively smaller territories.

Commercial functions, as measured by census data on wholesale sales and receipts from business services (advertising, consumer credit reporting agencies, addressing, and the like), were found to be concentrated in the same cities and in the same hierarchical fashion as bank-lending activities, thus indicating that the metropolitan zone of influence of financial activities coincides with that of commercial activities. It is important to bear in mind that the zones of influence are not necessarily adjacent territory. This is particularly true at the top of the hierarchy.

Duncan also examined the distribution of industrial activities. The measure used to express the economic importance of such activities was value added by manufacture, that is, the market price of goods completed less the cost of materials used. It was found, however, that industry was not concentrated in the same cities as financial-commercial functions, suggesting that manufacturing is less metropolitan in character than financial-commercial activities which serve an integrating function. More importantly, this finding indicates that metropolitan influence stemming from industry has a different spatial pattern than that of banking and trade.

Second Method. Duncan's second method involved construction of "industry profiles" for all Standard Metropolitan Areas above 300,000 population in 1950.[19] The "profile" consists of the degree to which jobs in a given SMA were concentrated in a specific type of employment, relative to other SMA's. "Industry" included all types of employment, not just manufacturing. Evidence was obtained on the location of the major supply areas and major market areas associated with the "profile" industries of each SMA. This provided information on the extent to which a given SMA was associated with a local hinterland in terms of "inputs" of raw material and labor and "outputs" of finished goods and services.

[18] *Ibid.*, ch. 5.
[19] *Ibid.*, chs. 9–11.

Typology of Metropolitan Regions and Functions

Finally, the Duncan study combined the results of the two methods to produce a typology of the 56 United States metropolises over 300,000 in size. This typology classifies the metropolises according to both metropolitan functions and regional relationships. In other words, particular kinds of hinterlands are associated with particular kinds of metropolitan functions.

1. *National Metropolis.* These are the five largest metropolitan areas—New York, Chicago, Los Angeles, Philadelphia, and Detroit. They are pre-eminent in financial-commercial activities, although several have heavy manufacturing concentrations. The national metropolis has a vast local hinterland but exerts strong national and even international influence.

2. *Regional Metropolis.* The areas in this category, including San Francisco, Minneapolis–St. Paul, and Kansas City among others, specialize in finance and trade and in industries whose "inputs" come from contiguous areas. In sum, they are metropolises without the national scope of those in the class above.

3. *Regional Capital, Submetropolitan.* Houston, New Orleans, and Louisville, which are among the areas in this category, are smaller in size than regional metropolises, and their metropolitan functions of finance and trade serve a smaller territory.

4. *Diversified Manufacturing with Metropolitan Functions.* This category includes, among others, Boston, Pittsburgh, and St. Louis. It combines large size and moderate to heavy emphasis on manufacturing with a considerable range of financial and commercial functions. The metropolises show evidence of dominating moderately large contiguous hinterlands, but have strong competition from nearby national centers.

5. *Diversified Manufacturing with Few Metropolitan Functions.* Baltimore, Milwaukee, and Albany–Schenectady–Troy, examples of this class, all have high to very high specialization in manufacturing but little banking, wholesaling, and the like. They do not dominate a large contiguous hinterland.

6. *Specialized Manufacturing Centers.* Textiles in Providence, heavy metals in Youngstown, photographic equipment in Rochester, rubber in Akron, are examples of this type. Wholesaling, trade, and finance are little developed. These metropolises do not dominate a large adjacent hinterland.

7. *Special Cases.* These are metropolises with distinctive and unusual functions: Washington, D. C.; San Diego, San Antonio (major military installations); Miami (tourism); and several others.

The foregoing typology is arranged in a quasi-hierarchy (except for the "Special Cases"), but it is important to note that there is more than one dimension represented. The first three types emphasize the wholesaling, trade, and financial functions of the metropolis; these are associated with large, contiguous, regional, and sometimes national, hinterlands. "However, the hinterlands are overlapping and interpenetrating rather than discrete and clearly demarcated." [20] Types 4–6 emphasize manufacturing, a function that does not appear to be associated with dominance over adjacent territory. This typology conforms to the thesis advanced by Duncan of an "open system" of specialized, overlapping areas of metropolitan dominance.

METROPOLITAN REGIONS OUTSIDE THE UNITED STATES

Metropolitan regions are by no means exclusively American phenomena, although technological developments in transportation and communication have undoubtedly made them distinguishable in certain respects from metropolitan regions in other countries.

GREAT BRITAIN

In Britain there are about 15 large cities which, according to Dickinson, are centers of fairly large regions.[21] Each is the focus of a populous industrial area in which are located a number of minor towns and cities. Each has a large number and variety of industries whose products are marketed mainly in the surrounding area, although some of them have basic industries whose products are marketed on a wider basis. Each is a center of financial and commercial enterprises, the extent and character varying considerably from one city to another. Finally, each city is a shopping center for a considerable area. London, of course, is in many respects a national city whose region is the whole of Great Britain.

The British census officially recognizes six "conurbations," the British term roughly equivalent to metropolitan areas, which contain about 40 per cent of the population of England and Wales.[22] They consist of the built-up areas around London, Manchester, Birmingham, Leeds, Liverpool, and Newcastle. The major conurbations of Scotland are those centered on Glasgow and Edinburgh. Approximately a third of Scotland's population lives in Central Clydeside, the conurbation with Glasgow as its major city.

Metropolitan regions in Britain, as Dickinson points out, tend to be much smaller than those in the United States. Most of the large cities in the United Kingdom are within 50 or 60 miles of each other; hence the regions over which they are dominant are comparatively small in area although in the main densely settled. Because of the proximity of the great cities to one another, there is probably more overlapping of regions

---

[20] *Ibid.,* p. 18.
[21] Robert E. Dickinson, *City, Region, and Regionalism* (1947), pp. 171–77.
[22] T. W. Freeman, *The Conurbations of Great Britain* (1959).

than in the United States, where a central metropolis may almost completely dominate a hinterland for a considerable distance.

GERMANY

Metropolitan regions have developed on the continent in countries where great cities have flourished. In Germany, such cities as Frankfurt-am-Main, Cologne, Munich, Hamburg, Hanover, and Breslau hold sway over commercial, industrial, and cultural regions.[23] Frankfurt, for example, is at the confluence of 10 important railway routes and of a number of automobile highways. Within a radius of 25 miles are several secondary cities whose economic functions are oriented mainly around Frankfurt as the center of dominance. Agricultural activities within the inner zone of the region are mainly concerned with food production for Frankfurt and outlying urban towns and cities. This inner zone is also heavily industrialized along the Main and Rhine rivers.

INDONESIA

City-hinterland relationships in Indonesia illustrate the problems of many developing nations, in which the basic problem is the inadequacy of the internal economic exchange on which a sound relationship between city and hinterland can rest.[24] Indonesian cities are not greatly industrialized and, therefore, have few products to send to the countryside. For their part, the rural villages, under pressure of expanding population and inefficient farming methods, have less and less surplus food to send to the cities. The reciprocal flow of food for manufactured goods is consequently inhibited at both the city and hinterland ends. These deficiencies are alleviated, but the underlying problem untouched, by the importation from abroad of food for city people. In marked contrast to Western cities, where the metropolis is the center of a complex web of national economic interdependence, the cities of Indonesia are political centers rather than national economic centers.

INDIA

A recent study of India demonstrates some differences between metropolitan regions in that nation and those of the United States,[25] differences

[23] Dickinson, *op. cit.*, pp. 186–91, 266–71. Dickinson's data on European regions are taken mainly from the works of German and French social scientists.

[24] Nathan Keyfitz, "The Ecology of Indonesian Cities," *American Journal of Sociology*, LXVI (January, 1961), 348–54.

[25] Richard A. Ellefsen, "City-Hinterland Relationships in India," in Roy Turner (ed.), *India's Urban Future* (1961), pp. 94–114.

that probably apply more broadly between developed and underdeveloped countries. The study examined the nature and extent of the hinterlands of Bombay, Delhi, Madras, Hyderabad, and Baroda, all very large cities of metropolitan stature. Many measures used to delineate the boundaries of metropolitan influence in Western countries are unsuitable in India. For example, rates of metropolitan newspaper circulation as a regional index are of limited value when most of the population is illiterate.

Data from the Indian census were used to measure the degree to which the territory adjacent to the built-up area of the cities exhibited traits which resembled the city rather than the rural villages. Such characteristics as density of population, the proportion of the labor force employed in nonagricultural pursuits, and literacy were shown to decline with distance from the city. This is the usual gradient pattern of metropolitan influence. The pattern of metropolitan hinterlands in India does not extend evenly around the city but radiates along the sectors which are most accessible to the city, thus underscoring the importance of transportation and communication systems in determining the extent of metropolitan influence. Beyond that, the landscape and way of life are typically those of the traditional village.

In India there is a sharp rural-urban contrast, both socially and physically. In the United States and western Europe, metropolitan influence extends further, and differences between city and country are often only matters of degree. Radio, telephone, television, and mass circulation of newspapers and magazines expose Americans, whether in city or country, to the same ideas and standards. Relatively high farm incomes allow American farmers to buy the same goods as city dwellers and widespread transportation systems enable them to come to cities frequently. None of these things pertains to India.

SELECTED BIBLIOGRAPHY

BOOKS

Bogue, Donald, *The Structure of the Metropolitan Community: A Study of Dominance and Subdominance*. Ann Arbor, Mich.: University of Michigan Press, 1949.

Chapin, F. Stuart, Jr., and Shirley Weiss (eds.), *Urban Growth Dynamics in a Regional Cluster of Cities*. New York: Wiley, 1962.

Duncan, Otis D., *et al.*, *Metropolis and Region*. Baltimore: Johns Hopkins Press, 1960.

Ellefsen, Richard, "City-Hinterland Relationships in India," in Roy Turner (ed.), *India's Urban Future*. Berkeley and Los Angeles: University of California Press, 1962.

Gottmann, Jean, *Megalopolis*. New York: Twentieth Century Fund, 1961.

International Urban Research. *The World's Metropolitan Areas.* Berkeley and Los Angeles: University of California Press, 1959.

Mayer, Harold, and Clyde Kohn (eds.), *Readings in Urban Geography.* Chicago: University of Chicago Press, 1959.

McKenzie, R. D., *The Metropolitan Community.* New York: McGraw-Hill, 1933.

Robson, William (ed.), *Great Cities of the World.* New York: Macmillan, 1955.

Schnore, Leo, "Urban Form: The Case of the Metropolitan Community," in Werner Z. Hirsch (ed.), *Urban Life and Form.* New York: Holt, Rinehart and Winston, 1963.

Theodorson, George (ed.), *Studies in Human Ecology.* Part V. Evanston, Ill.: Row, Peterson, 1961.

Vance, Rupert, and Sara Smith, "Metropolitan Dominance and Integration," in Rupert Vance and Nicholas Demerath (eds.), *The Urban South.* Chapel Hill, N.C.: University of North Carolina Press, 1955.

Vernon, Raymond, *Metropolis 1985.* Cambridge, Mass.: Harvard University Press, 1960.

Vidich, Arthur, and Joseph Bensman, *Small Town in Mass Society.* Princeton: Princeton University Press, 1958.

ARTICLES

Dotson, Floyd, and Lillian Ota Dotson, "Urban Centralization and Decentralization in Mexico," *Rural Sociology,* 21 (March, 1956), 41–49.

Gist, Noel P., "Developing Patterns of Urban Decentralization," *Social Forces,* 30 (March, 1952), 257–67.

Keyfitz, Nathan, "The Ecology of Indonesian Cities," *American Journal of Sociology,* LXVI (January, 1961), 348–54.

Kish, Leslie, "Differentiation in Metropolitan Areas," *American Sociological Review,* 19 (August, 1954), 388–98.

Lazerwitz, B., "Metropolitan Residential Belts, 1950 and 1956," *American Sociological Review,* 25 (April, 1960), 245–52.

"Metropolitan Regionalism: Developing Governmental Concepts—A Symposium," *University of Pennsylvania Law Review,* 105 (February, 1957), 439–616.

The Organization
of Urban Life

PART THREE

Urbanization:

Process and Impact

TWELVE

Urbanization as the term is used in this chapter involves the familiar sociological concepts of acculturation, diffusion, assimilation, and even amalgamation—although it involves much more. When nonurban persons acquire the roles, style of life, symbols, forms of organization, and cultural artifacts characteristic of the city, and when they come to share the meanings, values, and perspectives that are characteristically urban, we can say that they are experiencing the process of urbanization. It logically follows that there are degrees of urbanization and ruralization for individuals and groups, though it is difficult to measure such differentials because there is no easy way to determine just what is "urban" and "nonurban" culture. The same person may, and often does, exhibit characteristics which may be defined as both urban and rural.

One may find useful, in developing a theoretical perspective, such ideal-typical constructs as "urbanites" and "ruralites" or "urban society" and "rural (or folk) society." These constructs are probably most applicable to the underdeveloped countries where sharp contrasts exist between the metropolitan elite and the folk or peasant peoples whose contacts with urban culture has been limited or even nonexistent. Probably most people in the United States and western Europe are "urbanized" to a considerable degree, even if they are not actually city dwellers.

The process of urbanization is applicable both to persons who live in cities and those who reside in nonurban areas but have come under the influence of urban culture. In this chapter we will be concerned primarily, though not entirely, with urban influence on nonurban communities and the people who live in them.

Urbanization as we shall use the term implies a cultural and social-psychological process whereby people acquire the material and non-material culture, including behavioral patterns, forms of organization, and ideas that originate in, or are distinctive of, the city.[1] Although the flow of cultural influences is in both directions—both toward and away from the city—there is substantial agreement that the cultural influences exerted by the city on nonurban people are probably more pervasive than the reverse.

Urbanization seen in this light has also resulted in what Toynbee has called the "Westernization" of the world. Europe and the United States got an early start on the road to urbanism and industrialism, and the forces set in motion by these developments have literally penetrated all parts of the globe. Perhaps not a single non-Western society remains unaffected by cultural patterns emanating from the highly urbanized "mass" societies of the West. National as well as municipal boundaries are easily hurdled by the transmigration of cultures.

The preponderant cultural influence of the city on the remainder of a society (or even beyond) stems in part from the fact that cultural innovations undoubtedly occur more frequently in an urban social climate than in a folk or rural milieu. Cities also have been seats of political and economic power, and consequently have exercised a dominance over their respective hinterlands. Not only have they been productive of an "exportable" culture and the means to convey it; they also have the power and motivation to transmit it to other people.

The idea of urbanization may be made more precise and meaningful when interpreted as aspects of diffusion and acculturation. Diffusion refers to the spread of culture either within the same society or in different societies. Urbanization may be manifest either as intrasociety or intersociety diffusion, that is, urban culture may spread to various parts of the same society or it may cross cultural or national boundaries and spread to other societies. It involves both borrowing and lending. On the other side of the diffusion coin is acculturation, the process whereby individuals acquire the material possessions, behavioral patterns, social organization, bodies of knowledge, and meanings of groups whose culture differs in certain respects from their own. Urbanization as seen in this light is a complex process.

The basic processes of urbanization, as we have designated them, apply both to rural and city people, although the specific manifestations of

[1] The term is also used by some to mean the increasing proportion of persons living in cities in a particular country or region. It is well to keep clear the dual meanings attached to the concept of urbanization.

the urbanizing process may vary according to the conditions that exist in each society. Country persons moving to the city, or visiting it, become urbanized to the extent that they acquire characteristically urban ways of behavior and thought, or material objects which, through possession and use, affect their conduct, ideas, and social relationships. Similarly, the farm or village resident may become urbanized as the culture of the city is conveyed to the rural community and there integrated into the ideational and behavioral patterns of the residents. Basically, then, urbanization is both a cultural and a psychosocial process. It involves something more than urban residence (although the term is often used in this sense).

URBANIZATION AS "IMPACT"

Urbanization may also be viewed in terms of its effect or "impact." This, too, is complex, and is manifest in different ways. Once an aspect of urban culture is "borrowed" and incorporated into the system of folkways and thoughtways of another culture or subculture, there may be a kind of "chain reaction" as its effects become cumulative. Inasmuch as a community has a unitary character in which there is a functional interdependence of the various parts, the introduction of cultural elements from the outside may leave an imprint on different aspects of the community. Often the secondary or tertiary effects may be unanticipated. An agricultural implement manufactured in a metropolis and adopted in a rural community may be expected to alter techniques of cultivation and perhaps also raise the standards of living of the user by improving his productivity. But its adoption may alter the social position of the user by affording him an additional measure of prestige; it may modify some of the traditional roles and therefore affect interpersonal relationships; it may undermine some of the folk beliefs concerning agriculture; or engender tensions and feelings of insecurity by creating doubts and uncertainties as to what is right or wrong, good or evil. Like the waves that roll outward in all directions when a stone is cast into a placid pool of water, so does the introduction into a local community of traits from the "outside" tend to pervade various aspects of the receiving culture.

In the following discussion of urbanization and its impact we shall observe how certain reputedly urban characteristics have been diffused, and how this diffusion, and the acculturative process associated with it, becomes a feature of social change. Admittedly the analysis is methodologically imprecise because there are not acceptable criteria for reliably distinguishing between urban and rural cultures, or for that matter between the culture of the larger society in general and that of urban or rural communities. Furthermore, changes in nonurban communities may actually have been self-generated, or they may have been changes of a societal nature, as in the case of upheavals due to revolution or war.

Finally, it is often difficult to measure social change with statistical accuracy, especially when many aspects of change are involved.

MEASURING THE URBAN "IMPACT"

In Chapter 5 on "types" of communities, reference was made to Redfield's folk-urban typology and its value in providing a cultural perspective of community types and the cultures which they represent. Redfield's initial theoretical proposition grew out of his research in a Mexican town, Tepoztlan, which he studied in the 1920's.[2] He was concerned particularly with social change in the town, which he interpreted mainly in terms of urban influence. Certain social trends in Tepoztlan were described in considerable detail and interpreted in terms of his theoretical framework.

Some two decades later another anthropologist, Oscar Lewis, studied the same community but arrived at rather different conclusions concerning the nature of social change.[3] Whereas Redfield reported evidence of increasing family disorganization, secularization, and individualization of behavior of the Tepoztlan residents, Lewis saw little evidence of these changes despite the increased urban influence which brought about certain other changes during these intervening years. Lewis also noted that some of the observed changes may have been generated within the town and were not necessarily the result of diffusion of urban culture.

These two studies are mentioned because they illustrate the difficulties in making valid generalizations concerning phenomena that are exceedingly complex. Some of the lack of agreement between the Redfield and Lewis conclusions may have been due to different kinds of questions asked the residents. In this chapter no pretension will be made to provide a complete picture of the urbanizing process and its effects; indeed, no complete picture is available, either for particular communities or for a society in general. On the basis of what we actually know, it is probable that urbanization is manifest in quite different ways throughout the world, and its impact varies a great deal from one society to another.

URBANIZATION AS PLANNED DIFFUSION

Of special relevance to underdeveloped areas is urbanization through planned cultural diffusion. Recent decades have witnessed various organ-

---

[2] Robert Redfield, *Tepoztlan* (1930).

[3] Oscar Lewis, *Life in a Mexican Village: Tepoztlan Restudied* (1951). See also his article, "Tepoztlan Restudied," in *Rural Sociology*, 18 (June, 1953), 121–36. See Chapter 19, pp. 442–43, for an additional description of the Redfield and Lewis studies.

ized efforts to disseminate Western urban culture to underdeveloped areas. Among the most important of these are the community development programs now being carried on in the rural sections of various countries, often with the assistance of the United Nations or of certain industrialized countries. Through the introduction of modern techniques of agriculture, medicine, and education (mainly Western), it is expected that the level of physical, social, and economic well-being of the villagers will be improved. Many other agencies, private and public, are engaged in the modernization of backward areas: the Peace Corps, Agency for International Development (AID), U. S. Information Service, and the like. The old-time missionary, with the resources of his church behind him, set out to spread Christianity among the "heathen," perhaps including certain medical or economic assistance as a side-line. A more comprehensively planned cultural diffusion may be found in government-sponsored programs, or those sponsored by philanthropic foundations, which include such agents as technical experts, educators, artists, industrialists, editors, and so on.

INTERDEPENDENCE OF CITY AND COUNTRY

URBAN-RURAL INTERACTION

In all societies of the twentieth century there is interaction between city and country, but the forms of this interaction, the frequency and intensity of contacts between urban and rural people, vary a great deal. Certainly distance itself is important. Other things being equal, those residing close to a city may be influenced more than those farther removed. But "other things" are not always equal! The leap-frog principle of diffusion may operate to bypass communities close to a city while affecting those further out.

Communication and transportation facilities are likewise important factors. In highly industrialized countries mass communication and transportation technologies have multiplied and intensified the contacts between urban and rural peoples, even when they are considerably removed from each other in space. Urban mass culture has penetrated even the most isolated communities in these countries, whether communities in the mountain fastnesses of America or western Europe, fishing villages in coastal pockets, or rustic settlements in other remote regions. In the underdeveloped countries, however, there are countless villages that still have limited contacts with cities, and some of them are almost completely isolated both geographically and culturally.

A third important factor is the receptivity of the people themselves to outside culture: whether they are favorably or unfavorably disposed, or indifferent, to cultural innovations. The behavior and attitudes of peo-

Strikingly modern buildings are a symbol of the impact of urbanization and Westernization. Above: A new office building in Baghdad, Iraq. Below: The recently-completed State Library in Accra, Ghana. (Courtesy United Nations.)

ple in this respect are complex, and often unpredictable. There are communities that cling tenaciously to their own indigenous culture, firmly resisting the encroachments of an urbanized mass society. Some of these communities are distinctly religious in their orientation, as in the case of the Amish or Mennonite settlements in America or the sectarian community of Staphorst in The Netherlands. There are many documented cases of resistance to practices and ideas introduced in community development programs in underdeveloped countries.[4] Often these people look with suspicion on the outside world because it represents, to them, a threat to their own values and way of life. But even resistance to outside culture often declines as oncoming generations acquire different values and norms, or as the functional utility of the outside culture is convincingly demonstrated.

VILLAGERS WITHIN CITIES

Some cities, especially those in underdeveloped areas, appear to consist mainly of clusters of residents who are bound together by kinship, tribal, caste, or language ties, and who follow their traditional way of life as much as possible. They are villagers within cities—urban dwellers who are not urbanized. So resistant are they to the processes of urbanization that they identify, not with the city of residence, but with their ancestral communities or groups within these communities. The American or European migrant to cities was generally able to sever his ties with his home community and become identified with his urban place of residence, but Asian and African migrants often retain their traditional loyalties. The remarks of Hoselitz are pertinent in this respect:

> The migrant to the city in underdeveloped countries lives in a strange and foreign place as long as he remains in the city, and this alone increases the psychological stress he experiences. It means, also, that he seeks as associates only persons who come from the same kinship group, village, or province as he himself. . . . He works with men who have the same ethnic and often even the same local origin. He lives in a social structure in which authority and responsibility are distributed according to patterns characteristic of his native culture rather than that of the city and its economic needs.[5]

To some extent this was the picture of American cities during the period of heavy immigration from foreign shores. But in time the immigrants became urbanized, at least to a degree, and their children, reared in an urban environment, were socialized according to city standards. Certainly the process is much slower in underdeveloped countries.

[4] See especially George M. Foster, *Traditional Cultures and the Impact of Technological Change* (1962), chs. 5–7.

[5] Bert F. Hoselitz, "The City, The Factory, and Economic Growth," *American Economic Review*, 45 (May, 1955), 175.

Many people come in contact with urban culture without accepting it except on a superficial level. Certain aspects of the culture are accepted and used and others rejected; and even some of the things that are accepted may be given a different meaning and function. Tumin observed that in a city of Guatamala the Indians live alongside the Ladinos (Europeans) but without taking over much of their culture.[6] They tolerate it but do not incorporate much of it into their own social system. It is cultural contact without extensive acculturation or assimilation. Sometimes there is acculturation without assimilation.

COMMUNITY AND THE LARGER SOCIETY

It has been repeatedly observed in this volume that the community—both rural and urban—is becoming increasingly involved in a vast institutional network representing the larger political, economic, and social order, and that it is unrealistic to view the community as an entity separate and apart from the larger society. Although this trend appears to have gone much farther in technologically advanced countries of the West, it is also apparent in the underdeveloped countries as well. Even in these countries people in all kinds of communities (save indigenous tribal settlements) share in a common core culture, or what Redfield calls the Great Society—a social, economic, or religious system, for example.

Such a social system is societal in scope. A community, while manifesting many distinctive characteristics, which may be unique or shared with other communities, is part of a larger social system and the system part of the community. The development of a social, economic, or political organization that transcends the boundaries of any community and makes community and society interdependent and reciprocal parts of the larger social order has been furthered by modern technology applied to communication and transportation. This trend is readily apparent in the industrialized countries of the West, but it is also evident to a lesser extent in the underdeveloped countries which only recently are becoming "modernized." Communities that have been culturally as well as geographically isolated are being integrated, in varying degrees, into the larger society. One phase of this integration is urbanization. But what appears to be urbanization may indeed be social change on a broader scale, or "Westernization."

Reinforcing the organizational network, in the West particularly, are the communications media which tie a small community into the larger social order. Through the mass media in these countries, rural and urban people alike are subjected to a continuing barrage of words and pictorial impressions that convey and symbolize the mass culture of Western so-

[6] Melvin Tumin, *Caste in a Peasant Society* (1952).

ciety. These media, especially those which purvey advertising, have created new interests, needs, and forms of behavior. They have also substituted vicarious experiences for real ones, and at times have virtually stifled the expression of local ideas and artistic forms.

"Mass culture" in the industrialized societies of the West is almost synonymous with "urban culture," since much of this culture is either the product of an urban milieu or is diffused by urban agencies of communication and transportation. But much of it cannot be identified with a particular city; it is really national or regional, or perhaps even international, in scope. This may be illustrated in various institutional or organizational forms, which have almost blanketed an entire society.

SPRINGDALE

In their study of this small town in New York State, Vidich and Bensman have described the organizational network which connects the villagers with urban mass society.[7] These organizations have provided the mechanism through which outside "mass" culture has been funneled into the local community. Such organizations are national or international in scope. Among them are 4-H Clubs, Future Farmers of America, Boy and Girl Scouts, American Legion, Masonic and Odd Fellow lodges, the National Grange, Parent-Teacher Association, and religious denominations. State and national governments involve Springdale through such agencies as the Social Security Administration, agricultural marketing organizations, university extension, the state recreation commission, and the state department of education. Representatives of these organizations, as leaders or experts, through their personal contacts with the local community, are important carriers of culture from the outside.

PLAINVILLE

Much the same picture is presented by Gallaher in a study of a small town in Missouri.[8] The establishment of federal agencies relating to agriculture was, in Gallaher's opinion, a significant factor in effecting changes through the diffusion of technology and techniques, which have greatly altered the traditional style of work and life. By the same token, connections with private or cooperative organizations have also brought the town into a greater dependency relationship with the larger society. Since Plainville (like many other communities) is confronted with

[7] Arthur J. Vidich and Joseph Bensman, *Small Town in Mass Society* (1958). See Chapter 11, p. 254, for a description of the economic impact of mass society on Springdale.

[8] Art Gallaher, *Plainville Fifteen Years Later* (1961).

problems too complex to be settled by local action alone, the community is forced to accept external authority and assistance through the various organizations which link the town to the wider urban world. Thus, the people of Plainville, through the mass media and through organizational ties with the outside, have been brought into the mainstream of urban America. Gallaher concluded:

And so it goes—the community of Plainville has opened up more to the socio-economic impact and cultural influences of urban American society since 1939–40 than in all its previous history. As urban values steadily penetrate the Plainville subculture, it is little wonder that the people increasingly depend upon external sources of authority for innovations and assistance. They, and similar rural communities, are caught in a complex web of the mass society which now impinges in some form or another upon most institutionalized areas of their behavior.[9]

SPECIFIC ASPECTS OF URBANIZATION

EFFECT ON OCCUPATIONAL ROLES

The growth of cities has had a profound effect on occupational systems, both rural and urban. The application of modern technology has destroyed some occupations while strengthening others or even creating new ones. Rural craftsmen have often been unable to compete with mass production factories. The village smithy was a familiar figure on the American rural scene until well into the twentieth century, when competing factory-made products reduced him to a functionless level. The village miller has likewise been crowded out by the grain processing plants in urban centers. Even artistic craftsmen have turned to machine production to provide cheap consumer goods for the tourist market. Perhaps nowhere has the impact of technology been more impressive than in agriculture, which has been revolutionized by the use of machinery.

The impact of the factory system on craftsmanship appears to be most pronounced in the early stages of urbanization in a particular country. In cities of North Africa, according to LeTourneau, artisans with their age-old techniques have been unable to compete with the flood of factory-made goods produced in America or Europe.[10]

Such concepts as a monetary "wage scale" and "gainful employment," characteristic of industrial societies, are spreading to peasant or folk communities in various countries. These concepts imply a contractual relationship defining duties and responsibilities, as well as specific monetary remuneration for services rendered. They also symbolize the transi-

---

[9] *Ibid.*, p. 247.
[10] Roger LeTourneau, "Social Change in the Muslim Cities of North Africa," *American Journal of Sociology,* 60 (May, 1955), 531–32.

tion of social emphasis from ascription to achievement—from ascribed statuses and roles so characteristic of folk and peasant communities, to achieved statuses and roles characteristically a phenomenon of an urbanized society.

The urban conception of work, with all its specifications and restrictions, has spelled, for many workers, greater freedom of choice and action, as well as greater rewards. This has been particularly important for women in underdeveloped countries because their new roles as wage earners have afforded them more independence, and sometimes more prestige, than commonly exists in a peasant community where work roles are ascribed by custom. Many peasant women migrating to the city engage in *gainful* employment for the first time. But if such work has been an emancipating influence for individuals, it has also taken women from the home and therefore tended to alter their position in the family group.

One of the important distinctions between urban and peasant or rural society lies in the conception and observance of time. In the city, work and life in general are subject to the tyranny of the clock, the wrist watch, or the calendar. City people become acutely conscious of time because virtually every phase of their existence is regulated according to a specific time schedule reduced to hours and minutes. The urbanization of rural migrants to cities involves an accommodation to city time schedules and an assimilation of the meaning of time. As rural communities come under the influence of city culture, particularly through the mass media, time awareness is heightened and behavior patterns altered to meet the demands of the time tyrant. Certainly the clock, a revolutionary invention, has had a profound effect on the course of human society. It has particularly revolutionized the meaning and practice of work.

EFFECT ON CONSUMER BEHAVIOR

The ready availability of factory-made goods in the industrialized countries has brought about profound changes in consumer behavior and interests. There has been increased preoccupation not only with *what* to consume but also with *how* to consume according to acceptable urban standards.

Food culture, for example, has radically changed in rural as well as in urban areas. In the United States, villagers and farmers live out of factory-made tin cans and refrigerators, though not to the same extent as do urbanites. Clothing styles are urban styles, dictated by designers in the great cities, and distributed, often readymade, to rural and urban alike. Residents of Smalltown are not easily recognizable in their attire from those who live in Megalopolis.

EFFECT ON SOCIAL ORGANIZATION

One of the cultural "exports" of cities to nonurban communities has been forms of organization bearing the imprint of urban origin: voluntary associations, for example. As we have noted elsewhere, these organizations form a bridge connecting rural and urban communities with each other and with the larger society. At the same time, they provide social contacts through which the process of urbanization occurs. Some of these associations are national in scope, with "headquarters" located in cities. The number and variety of associations in rural America, as well as in cities, are very great indeed: bridge clubs, book clubs, civic associations, sewing clubs, luncheon clubs, veterans' organizations, religious groups, and so on. The Rotary Club, for example, was organized in Chicago in 1905, but within 30 years about two-fifths of all Rotary clubs were in towns of less than 5,000.[11]

EFFECT ON PERSONALITY

Urbanization as a social process undoubtedly has important ramifications for personality. Although it is an accepted principle of social scientists that personalities are molded by their cultural milieux, there is still limited evidence on the ways personalities of rural or folk peoples differ from urban people, or how personalities are affected by the impact of urban culture. Is there an empirically valid ideal-typical urban personality? Or a similar rural type? The answer to such a question would depend, in part, on the criteria used to ascertain the existence of such types and what they are actually like. Nor do we know, psychologically speaking, what always happens to individuals who are subjected to the influence of an urban or a rural environment. Are rural folk transformed into sophisticated cosmopolites when subjected to urban culture? Not necessarily. But something *may* happen to change their personalities.

There is a good deal of evidence of changes in the attitudes and values of nonurban people who come under the influence of the city. Attitudes toward consumer goods and behavior essentially urban in character, or attitudes toward urban concepts of status and prestige, are illustrations. Then there is the matter of attitudes toward social change in general. It seems to be generally true that the urban impact has the effect of breaking the "cake of custom," which is another way of saying that people under the influence of urban culture tend to be less tightly bound by traditional ways of thought and behavior and more receptive to the new and novel, more willing to experiment, than those who have not experi-

[11] Lewis Atherton, *Main Street on the Middle Border* (1954), pp. 290–93.

enced such influences. But these changes, if they do occur, vary a great deal as between individuals and the specific social situations.

Communities that have felt the urban impact through the importation of various forms of culture from urban sources commonly experience changes in the status system. The diffusion of technology and other material objects, occupational or other techniques, forms of organization, and social values almost invariably bear upon the prestige-ranking system of a community. Gallaher placed considerable importance on these changes in Plainville, noting particularly that imported agricultural machinery and techniques provided an important basis for enhancing the prestige of farmers. "Thus, a farm family derives greater or lesser prestige through ownership of technological equipment which now becomes an end in itself, a symbol of economic achievement. Those who invest heavily in machinery gain, among other things, considerable prestige satisfaction, whereas those who do not are judged as 'backward,' 'behind the times,' and 'tight'." [12] Gallaher is of the opinion that change in the status system of Plainville is a kind of secondary effect derived from possession of agricultural techniques and technology which further economic achievement and therefore symbolize social prestige.

URBANIZATION IN AFRICA

The African family in an urban environment is often shorn of its religious, educational, and economic functions.[13] As in all urban communities, these functions have been taken over by other groups or agencies. But the changes have been so rapid in recent years that serious dislocations have occurred. The lack of a stable community having norms of behavior recognized and supported by general consensus has made itself acutely felt in parent-child relationships. Parental authority is undermined by the influence of gangs, movies, and street life in general. Opportunities for gainful employment have increased the independence and prestige of African women. No longer are they automatically held in a position of subordination. But their new independence has contributed to marital instability, which in turn has been associated with such deviant behavior as illicit sex relations.

New forms of social stratification are emerging in African cities, reflecting occupational and income differentials. Those on the higher levels of

---

[12] Gallaher, *op. cit.*, p. 207.

[13] Unesco, *Social Implications of Industrialization and Urbanization in Africa South of the Sahara* (1956). A summary report of researches conducted in Africa by sociologists, anthropologists, and economists.

Town in Southern Rhodesia. General view of Salisbury, Southern Rhodesia, which has a population of about 170,000, of which 117,000 are Africans. (Courtesy United Nations.)

the emergent social structure are manifesting many characteristics of Western urban dwellers—food habits, dress, etiquette, formal education, recreation, house furnishings, and the like. Diversification of interests has found expression through varied types of voluntary associations, some of which are fashioned after Western models. Breakdowns, stresses, and tensions associated with urbanization have not yet been counterbalanced by new norms of conduct appropriate to city life.

Writing of the new societies in Africa, Hunter observes: "There is a constant coming and going, from town (city) to village and village to town, on labor migration, for education, to visit relations, to trade. Towns in themselves, in any part of Africa, force new ideas upon the visitor." [14]

URBAN IMPACT ON AFRICAN VILLAGE LIFE

In certain respects the urban impact in Africa is felt as keenly in rural tribal communities as in the cities. Migration of males to the cities for

[14] Guy Hunter, *The New Societies of Tropical Africa* (1962), p. 90.

employment may have increased family incomes, but when mainly women and children are left behind, even if only temporarily, the peasant economy is undermined because there may be no one left to cultivate the holdings. Factory-made objects have come to be valued for status symbolism as well as for their utility; hence there is considerable inducement to spend money for luxuries instead of food and other physical necessities. Skills learned in the city by the migrants may have little functional value in the tribal community when the migrants return. Wage earners returning from the city with well-filled pockets and esoteric notions of behavior commonly flout the traditional system of authority and repudiate those responsible for its maintenance.

The increase in village incomes through outside earnings has added an important element to the prestige system in emphasizing status by achievement rather than by tribal or kinship ascription. Marriageable girls accord preferential treatment to men who have returned with glamorous accounts of life in the city; hence individualization of mate selection is encouraged in contrast to the traditional system of selection by families.

These and other influences are affecting family organization, with the resulting increase in broken homes and various forms of individualized deviant behavior. Since family and tribe are integrated into the same social system, the disruptive effects have manifest themselves in what has been called "detribalization." A basic factor in this disruption is the

Country in Southern Rhodesia. Although the native population of Southern Rhodesia covers a wide range of occupations including prosperous businessmen and highly-educated professionals, a large number are still agriculturalists living in tribal areas. (Courtesy United Nations.)

decline in ascribed kinship and tribal authority as urban equalitarian values associated with pecuniary achievement have become widespread. Clearly the villages are going through some kind of transition which may presage the emergence of a different social and economic system.

URBANIZATION IN ASIA

In Asia, as in Africa, the urbanizing process has affected the functions and structure of the family, whether rural or urban. In parts of Asia, though not in all, the "joint" family, or larger kinship group which functions as a unit, has tended to give way in the cities to the nuclear family consisting of parents and children. Occupational differentiation in urban centers has made possible the gainful employment outside the home of married and unmarried women. These role changes have invariably altered the social status of women and affected interpersonal relationships both within and outside the home. The migration to cities of large numbers of males, who leave their families in the native villages, has likewise created problems of deviant behavior since the men are removed, at least temporarily, from the immediate influences of their own families.

Another striking aspect of urbanization in Asia is the alteration of economic behavior, both in rural and urban communities. Consumer habits have been modified and "needs" created in peasant communities as factory-made goods are made available, at prices many can afford. Although cities all along have had a money economy, this system has spread to their rural hinterlands, partially replacing the system of barter, and introducing various kinds of credit and financial facilities. Monetization and its associated attitudes afford precise pecuniary evaluations applied to work and goods, greater freedom of action than has been traditionally the case, and more flexibility of social relationships. Monetization has made possible the extensive diffusion of factory-made goods and therefore new patterns of consumer behavior and new consumer interests. With the growth of cities and the spread of their influence, this aspect of urbanization is bound to become more apparent.

SHAMIRPET, AN INDIAN VILLAGE

In the urbanizing process the diffusion of technology or skills generally occurs fairly rapidly, but changes in social organization or patterns of thought usually take place more slowly. This is brought out by Dube in his study of Shamirpet, an Indian village near the city of Hyderabad.[15] Continuous interaction between the village and city familiarized the villagers with many aspects of the metropolis—and Western culture as

[15] S. C. Dube, *Indian Village* (1955), pp. 212–35.

well. Dube noted that the contacts of the Shamirpet villagers with Hyderabad were varied and numerous. There were frequent visits of the villagers with relatives or friends in the city, or visits of the city residents with their friends or relatives in the village; occasional excursions to the city for shopping or to attend a movie or ceremonial; and a shuttling back and forth of the urban-employed workers between the city of employment and the village they regarded as "home."

In Shamirpet, mill-made clothing and shoes of Western design have partly replaced indigenous attire. Articles having considerable prestige symbolism such as factory-made bangles, sun glasses, fountain pens, watches, and safety razors are in demand. Factories in Hyderabad turn out cheap cigarettes, replacing the hand-made cigarettes produced in the village. Various beverages produced in the city are consumed in quantity. Craftsmen like blacksmiths, carpenters, and tailors are now using factory-made tools and instruments. Modern clinical medicine has become competitive with folk medicine, and many families have cheap patent medicines purchased in Hyderabad or the local dispensary. At the time of the study there was one phonograph in the village, and one crystal radio set, located in the tea shop. In keeping with his exalted position, the headman in the village had acquired an antiquated automobile, the only one in town. Some of the young men played volley ball and cricket, both Western importations, and many patronized the cinema in the city.

Many social and social-psychological changes were also fairly evident in Shamirpet. Dube noted rather widespread dissatisfaction of the younger people with village life; those who had some education tended to idealize city life and have considerable contempt for the rustic ways of village folk. This often created disharmony within family groups and raised serious questions concerning the principles which, by custom, accorded special priorities and privileges to persons on the basis of age and kinship status. Not only had family solidarity declined, in the opinion of Dube, but there had also been a decline in sentimental attachments for the village community. Many caste rules such as prohibitions against inter-dining were relaxed, and new manifestations of political consciousness and interest, including voting behavior, were beginning to appear. "In a small rural community such as Shamirpet, which is situated near a big and modern city and is in everyday contact with it, the prevailing climate of opinion in social, economic, and political matters in the city is bound to influence its general outlook and ways, for apart from their practical value city-ways are gradually coming to be regarded as more 'respectable' and 'progressive.' " [16]

Yet there was also evidence of complete or partial rejection of certain aspects of urban culture. This was manifest in competition between sentiments and loyalties directed toward city culture or the greater social

[16] *Ibid.*, p. 228.

order, and those in support of the regional or local culture with its own customs and values. Many idealize the traditional and familiar, yet tend to follow the lead of the urbanized and powerful elite. The caste and kinship system, though weakened by the impact of urbanism, is still a "going concern," fairly intact so far as structural features are concerned. Independence of action has increased, but parents still select mates for their marriageable children and define their intrafamily relationships in many respects. Secularization has occurred, but most of the people in the village retain their religious ideologies and practice the ancient cere- monies of the Hindu faith. Western conceptions of equalitarianism and achievement are finding acceptance, but adherence to nonequalitarian principles of a rigidly hierarchical social system has not changed very much, and ascribed statuses in all aspects of life are widely observed. It is truly a community in transition.

URBANIZATION OF NAMHALLI, AN INDIAN VILLAGE

Reporting on a study of Namhalli, an Indian village not far from the metropolis of Bangalore, Beals describes in considerable detail the changes associated with modernization or urbanization of the commun- ity from around the turn of the century until the 1950's.[17] During the early part of this period, families began to develop a "need" for machine- made goods. Villagers finding employment in Bangalore, and farmers and artisans marketing their wares in the same city, were reimbursed in cash. Early in the century teachers began receiving *salaries;* by the 1950's one person in six was a salaried government employee, not counting numbers of persons depending on wages or cash profits. This transition to a money economy enabled the visitors to purchase such things as factory-made cloth, iron plows, tile for roofing, bicycles, and the like. Western man- ners and mannerisms were imitated, and European styles of clothing and haircuts for men became the vogue. Village ceremonials were continued, however, but on a reduced scale since urban forms of entertainment, either in Bangalore or Namhalli, are increasingly competitive. These in- clude the movies, radio, horse racing, and recreation in the city's coffee shops. Urban-style courts of justice, introduced in the 1920's, have tended to replace the village *panchayats* in the settlement of disputes. These courts have had far-reaching effects because they have provided new interpretations and definitions of such matters as property rights and interpersonal relations.

Beals points out that Namhalli is only one of many villages which have experienced modernization or urbanization through the influence of Bangalore, as well as influence coming from the larger society. "Buses,

[17] Alan R. Beals, "Interplay among Factors of Change in a Mysore Village," in McKim Marriott (ed.), *Village India* (1955), pp. 78–101.

motor trucks, and railroads carry thousands of villagers to Bangalore every day. Many of them leave with urban gimcracks in their shopping bags and new ideas in their heads." [18]

PERMANENCE AND CHANGE—AN ASSESSMENT

In reviewing the literature on social change in Indian villages, Lambert concludes that the "urban impact" has often been exaggerated, that village social systems have been remarkably stable.[19] Social changes have occurred, of course, but Lambert believes that many of them have been relatively superficial. He cites, for example, the case of the village of Bhadkad, located two miles from a railway line that connects with the metropolis of Bombay. Two studies of Bhadkad were conducted, one in 1913, the other in 1955. Many changes were recorded—changes in food habits, attire, living conditions, work patterns, and so on. But the pattern of caste had not changed appreciably, nor had the customs and ceremonials regulating marriage and family life. The general picture of the village is one of stability, and the changes that have occurred, in Lambert's judgment, "seem not to be linked to urban centers, but to reflect changes in the whole society." [20]

Lambert believes that among the most effective agents of social change are former villagers who have returned from the city to their home community and who bring to the village "not just an urbanized but a Westernized life style." [21] If they have considerable wealth or income—retired pensioners, for example—they are accorded prestige and, through emulation by the villagers, become agents of change. It is also Lambert's opinion that the diffusion into the villages of new functions of cities has resulted in serious rural dislocations.

URBANIZATION OF THE MIDDLE EAST

A penetrating analysis of the urbanizing and Westernizing process is the study by Lerner and Plevsner of social change in the Middle East.[22] The authors here employ the concept of "modernization" in somewhat the same sense that we have used "urbanization." Urbanization, in their terminology, however, refers to the growth of cities and the increasing proportion of population in urban centers.

In the modernizing process, *cities* become the primary variable.[23] This

---

[18] *Ibid.*, p. 78.
[19] Richard D. Lambert, "The Impact of Urban Society upon Village Life," in Roy Turner (ed.), *India's Urban Future* (1962), ch. 6.
[20] *Ibid.*, p. 124.   [21] *Ibid.*, p. 126.
[22] Daniel Lerner and Lucille W. Plevsner, *The Passing of Traditional Society* (1958).
[23] *Ibid.*, pp. 61–65.

is so because urban centers provide the physical and psychosocial conditions that set in motion the need for modernization and the facilities for bringing it about.

The second variable is *literacy*, which the authors consider both an index and an agent. Cities in the modern world invariably require a large literate population in order to function properly.

A third related variable, going hand in hand with literacy, is *media participation*—the use made of the media of communication, or the consumption of its contents.

A fourth variable is *political participation* as indicated by interest in public issues and the expression of this interest in discussion and voting behavior.

These four variables are positively correlated, that is, city growth and the other variables tend to occur together. After a certain proportion of the population residing in cities is reached, however, the further growth of cities becomes less important because the modernizing forces have already been set in motion.

MODERNIZATION OF TRADITIONAL SOCIETIES

Modernization, as the authors see it, then, is the transition toward a Westernized and urbanized society whose characteristic members are literate, consumers of the mass media, capable of imagining themselves in varieties of situations beyond their immediate boundaries, and willing to formulate opinions and make judgments (voting) relative to public issues. Such a society they designate as modernized, and its ideal-typical members are Modern Men. At the other pole of this typology is the society in which the characteristic members are nonliterate, nonparticipants in the mass media, commonly incapable of imaginatively projecting themselves beyond their immediate milieu, and lacking in interest or opinions concerning problems of a community or societal character. Such persons, in this typology, are Traditional Men. In between these two types, and having certain characteristics of both, are the Transitionals. By means of a scaling procedure the authors develop a three-category typology based on quantitative data and used in their analysis of Middle East cultures.

With this conceptual approach the authors explored the modernization (or urbanization) of Middle East countries: Turkey, Lebanon, Egypt, Syria, Jordan, and Iran. Through extensive personal interviews, both in rural and urban communities, they obtained a great deal of data on the nature and process of urbanization (modernization) and of the persons who had (or had not) been influenced by contacts with urban culture. Some of these persons were cosmopolitan in outlook, urbane, intellectually sophisticated, curious about the world around them and the world beyond their own milieu.

But others were Traditional Men without either sophistication or curiosity. "My God! How can you say such a thing?" said a shepherd in Turkey when asked to imagine himself as head of the Turkish government and to state what he would do if he were the head. Such questions when put to the Traditionals were often "baffling, disturbing, and even impious," but when asked of the Moderns they were more likely to be considered interesting and stimulating. The Traditionals characteristically thought public issues beyond their comprehension and actually none of their business; the Moderns commonly had knowledge of the issues and held opinions about them. Table 11 highlights some of the differences that distinguish the three types.

Other distinctive differences were observed by Lerner and Plevsner. The urbanized Moderns are motivated to achieve higher status and to re-evaluate their roles; the Traditionals are more likely to accept the roles and statuses assigned to them. Moderns are more secularized in the sense that their mosque or church attendance tends to decline, while the Traditionals retain their loyalty to religion, family, and village. Moderns join clubs and other voluntary associations, but these groups have

TABLE 11

Percentage Distribution of Turkish Moderns, Transitionals, and Traditionals According to Designated Attributes

	Modern	*Transitional*	*Traditional*
Residents of cities over 50,000	81	61	35
Clerical, professional, and business occupations	85	68	43
Education above elementary level	70	46	8
Literacy	98	71	19
Source of last news received:			
Newspapers	54	46	8
Radio	39	26	10
Word of mouth	6	26	78
Attend movies	88	63	27
Ability to imagine being Turkish President	86	63	35
Know what United Nations is	82	55	10
N =	(105)	(105)	(49)

SOURCE: Daniel Lerner and Lucille W. Plevsner, *The Passing of Traditional Society* (1958); adapted from Tables 1, 2, 4, and 8, pp. 137–44. Reprinted with permission of the publisher. Copyright 1958 by The Free Press, A Corporation.

little influence in the lives of the Traditionals. Familiarity with urban culture, and particularly with the content of the mass media, affords prestige. "When my son comes from the city," said an illiterate Lebanese mother, "he feels like a lord among the neighbors because he reads the newspaper in the city, and he always has many new things to tell the people in the village around." [24]

URBANIZATION OF A CANADIAN VILLAGE

The impact of urban culture on St. Denis, an isolated French-Canadian community, was studied by Miner, who compared the changes that had occurred between 1936–37 and 1949.[25] Although this was not a long period, many changes were nevertheless apparent, both in material and non-material cultural forms. The introduction of farm machinery altered in numbers of ways the traditional mode of life. Store-bought goods such as bakery bread, overstuffed furniture, manufactured soap, and ice cream were introduced into the households during this period, and many houses were supplied with running water and indoor toilets. Homespun clothes were replaced by manufactured attire purchased from a local store or mail-order houses. "Both men and women," says Miner, "want to dress like city people." Judging from the increased circulation of newspapers during the period, the habit of reading had become more widespread. Folk medicine, although still practiced, was being replaced by modern medical techniques introduced by doctors moving into the locality. An immediate effect of the change in medical practice was the decline of infant mortality. The rise of money incomes during the war period made it possible for the people of St. Denis to acquire the symbols of urbanism as manifest in technology, styles, food, and amusements.

SELECTED BIBLIOGRAPHY

BOOKS

Atherton, Lewis, *Main Street on the Middle Border*. Bloomington: University of Indiana Press, 1954.

Foster, George M., *Traditional Cultures and the Impact of Technological Change*. New York: Harper, 1962.

Gallaher, Art, *Plainville Fifteen Years Later*. New York: Columbia University Press, 1961.

Geddes, W. R., *Peasant Life in Communist China: A Restudy of the Village of Kaihsienkung*. Ithaca, N.Y.: Society for Applied Anthropology, 1963.

[24] *Ibid.*, p. 189.

[25] Horace Miner, "A New Epoch in Rural Quebec," *American Journal of Sociology*, 51 (July, 1950), 1–10. Cf. Miner, *St. Denis: A French-Canadian Parish* (1963), which is a reissue of a 1939 study with a postscript covering later developments.

Lerner, Daniel, and Lucille W. Plevsner, *The Passing of Traditional Society.* Glencoe, Ill.: The Free Press, 1958.

Lewis, Oscar, *Life in a Mexican Village: Tepoztlan Restudied.* Urbana: University of Illinois Press, 1951.

Miner, Horace, *St. Denis: A French-Canadian Parish.* Chicago: University of Chicago Press, 1963.

Redfield, Robert, *The Primitive World and Its Transformation,* ch. 2. Ithaca: Cornell University Press, 1953.

Unesco, *Social Implications of Industrialization and Urbanization in Africa South of the Sahara.* International African Institute, London, 1956.

Vidich, Arthur J., and Joseph Bensman, *Small Town in Mass Society.* Princeton: Princeton University Press, 1958.

Whitney, Vincent H., "Urban Impact on a Rural Township," in Marvin B. Sussman (ed.), *Community Structure and Analysis.* New York: Thomas Y. Crowell Company, 1959.

ARTICLES

Beals, Ralph, "Urbanism, Urbanization, and Acculturation," *American Anthropologist,* 53 (January–March, 1951), 1–10.

Bascom, William, "Urbanization among the Yoruba," *American Journal of Sociology,* 60 (March, 1955), 446–50.

Duncan, O. D., "Gradients of Urban Influence on the Rural Population," *Midwest Sociologist,* 18 (Winter, 1956), 27–30.

Hauser, Philip M., "On the Impact of Urbanism on Social Organization, Human Nature, and the Political Order," *Confluence,* 7 (Spring, 1958), 29–34.

Henderson, Julia J., "Urbanization and the World Community," *The Annals,* 314 (November, 1957), 147–55.

Hoselitz, Bert F., "The City, the Factory, and Economic Growth," *American Economic Review,* 45 (May, 1955), 175–87. Reprinted in Paul Hatt and Albert Reiss (eds.), *Cities and Society* (Glencoe, Ill.: The Free Press, 1957), pp. 537–55.

LeTourneau, Roger, "Social Change in the Muslim Cities of North Africa," *American Journal of Sociology,* 60 (May, 1955), 531–32.

McCall, Daniel F., "Dynamics of Urbanization in Africa," *Annals,* 298 (March, 1955), 152–53.

Payne, Raymond, "Leadership and Perceptions of Change in a Village Confronted with Urbanism," *Social Forces,* 41 (March, 1963), 264–69.

Weinryb, B. D., "Impact of Urbanization in Israel," *Middle East Journal,* 11 (Winter, 1957), 23–36.

Urban Status Systems

Systems of social status are universal. Wherever there are differences in the functional roles of individuals, in the power or authority they possess, or in the positions they occupy, a status system emerges because different prestige values are attached to roles, power, and position. Reflecting these prestige values are differential rewards that go to individuals according to the kinds of roles they perform and the way they perform them, the power or authority they posses over others, and the positions which they occupy in the status system.

A status system, then, is a system of social inequality, just as the rewards tend to be unequal. Some kind of status system, or social stratification, is probably inevitable because this is the way various functions essential for the existence of a society or community are carried out, and a system of differential rewards is necessary to motivate individuals to perform these functions. The rewards may be tangible in terms of wealth or property; or intangible in terms of power, privilege, or deference. The rewards are so scaled that individuals or groups performing the important roles from the standpoint of society are rewarded more abundantly than those performing less important roles. The rewards, then, become symbols of prestige as well as devices for getting things done. Whether the distribution of rewards in a society is fair or just, or whether a particular system of rewards is better than another, is not of concern here.

CHARACTERISTICS OF A STATUS SYSTEM

A status system is also an organized system in that roles and relationships are regularized and patterned; they are also defined in terms of right, duties, and responsibilities, with specifications as to the rewards

294

for role performance, the conditions under which roles are carried out, and the nature of the statuses of individuals who perform the roles. In urbanized societies the organization of a status system tends to be more contractual in character than is the case of rural or folk communities. The system generally involves formal associations or institutions in which there is a hierarchical arrangement of status and power, with explicit rules governing role performance, rewards, and interpersonal relationships. The composite of all the elements that make up a status system may be considered a *social structure*.

While certain broad principles concerning the status systems of urban communities may be valid, it is important to remember that individual cities have a degree of uniqueness. Certainly the status system of a city of ten thousand would be different, at least in complexity, from that of a metropolis in the million class. Cities in the industrialized West are probably stratified differently from cities in underdeveloped countries. The industrial cities of Birmingham, Alabama, and Birmingham, England, may be very similar in their structures, but neither probably shows close resemblance to the systems in Atlantic City or the Hague. Bombay has a status system characterized both by caste and social class, which fact would differentiate it from Paris or Atlanta, except that Atlanta has a quasi-caste system based on race. Some of the studies conducted on the status systems of cities in different countries will be considered in this chapter.

ACHIEVEMENT AND ASCRIPTION

In modern urban society, much emphasis is placed on *achievement* of status; in a folk society, status is largely *ascribed*. Achieved status is commonly awarded on the character of role performance, the attainment of a particular position, or the acquisition of certain things which themselves have symbolic significance for the status system. Possibly the most important single source of status in an urbanized society, at least in the West, is the occupational role. But there are other indicators of achieved or ascribed status. Among these are family lineage, race or ethnic background, wealth as income or property, religion, institutional or group affiliations, and such personal attributes as appearance, education, skills, and manners. In a system of social classes individuals or families on different class levels tend to have a "style of life" fairly distinctive of a particular social class. In a caste system the life styles are more clear-cut and distinctive than in a class system.

Status consonance

Adding to the complexity of an urban status system is what Benoit-Smullyan calls "status disequilibrium." [1] Statuses and roles of an urban person may not be consonant with each other. A scion of a wealthy elite family, for instance, may elect to hold a low-status job, live in a slum, and support a radical political party. A Negro university graduate acquires wealth and power through his successful business ventures. An illiterate immigrant develops a lucrative garbage-collection business, capitalizes on his contacts, and gets elected mayor of his city. Where does each of these individuals belong in the status system? Can they be given a categorical status label? To what social class do they belong? These are not easy questions to answer.

In a small peasant community, or even in a rural town in an urbanized society, the status system is less complex, if for no other reason than that a smaller number of persons is involved. In such communities it is fairly easy to "place" individuals in the status hierarchy. This is possible partly because "everybody knows everybody else," partly because the statuses and roles are consonant and easily observed, partly because the definitions and expectations are generally known to all. But even in these communities the status systems are changing under the impact of influences from the "outside."

The values and modes of life and work associated with urbanism have left their imprint on the status systems not only of cities but also of hinterland communities and even entire societies. Particularly in the metropolis, with its heterogeneity of peoples and cultures, the status system is so complex and dynamic that only the broad lines of it may be perceived, and this perhaps unclearly. Indeed, it would be almost impossible, on the basis of facts now available, to perceive the status system of a metropolis in its detailed entirety. One can usually perceive only segments of the system. It is because of this baffling complexity and dynamism of an urban status system that even competent scholars and observers often disagree as to its nature. Much of the empirical research on urban status systems has, for this and other reasons, been concerned with particular facets rather than a system in its entirety.

Weber's three dimensions of social class

Weber viewed social classes in terms of three dimensions, or elements.[2] This three-dimensional approach furnishes a useful conceptual

[1] Emile Benoit-Smullyan, "Status, Status Types, and Status Interrelations," *American Sociological Review*, 9 (April, 1944), 151–61.
[2] H. H. Gerth and C. W. Mills (trans.), *From Max Weber: Essays in Sociology* (1958), ch. 7.

framework and perspective. The first dimension is the economic, that is, the amount and source of income, possession of property, and mode of earning a living. Aggregates of persons who occupy a similar economic position he called a social class, and the organization of their positions and roles the *economic order*. Secondly, he considered the status or prestige dimension as determined by affiliation with various kinds of groups and associations, certain styles of life and behavior, and the display of "honorific" symbols. This dimension he called the *status order*. The third dimension was stated in terms of power or authority exerted over other individuals or groups. Weber referred to this dimension as the *political order*. While there is clearly an interdependence and overlapping of these three dimensions, they are by no means coterminous. Persons who have great power are not necessarily wealthy, or vice versa; but power may be translated into wealth, or wealth into power, and both power and wealth may entitle the individual to deference and other symbols of prestige. Commonly, poor people are without much power and have relatively little prestige.

SOCIAL CHANGE AND STATUS SYSTEMS

Urbanism and industrialism in the modern world have commonly developed together, though cities have often emerged and grown to large size without direct benefits of industrialization. But among the changes accruing from urbanization and industrialization have been alterations of the system of stratification and power. Viewed from the standpoint of the Weberian approach, these things stand out:

1. Urbanism and industrialism, both associated with great changes in science and technology, have profoundly altered the economic basis of stratification. The application of technology to manufacturing has meant the processing of materials which, when distributed, have symbolic value for status as well as utilitarian value for use. Owing to technological and economic changes, many countries, especially those in the West, have experienced an abundance of manufactured materials and a general improvement of income for the masses, both urban and rural. Technological and organizational changes have also altered the worker's actual relation to the productive processes. Through mechanization and now automation he has been relieved of much drudgery, and at the same time his productivity has increased. This has given him (or his children) an opportunity to engage in other occupational pursuits, or time to spend his increased earnings and thereby improve his style of life. Wherever urbanism and industrialism have gone very far there has been a significant growth of the middle classes. At the same time there has been, in these countries, a general decline in size of the unskilled working classes. But in the underdeveloped countries, where urbanism and industrialism are both

in the emergent stage, the middle classes are small while the working and agricultural classes loom large.

2. Associated with the changes accruing to the application of science, technology, and economic organization has been the rise of status groups, which themselves have been made possible by increased incomes and more times for leisure activities. In highly urbanized societies there has been a proliferation of groups or associations which often have a major function of conferring prestige on their members. The number of such groups is legion. These groups, while commonly performing utilitarian functions (sometimes as a mask), become important features of the status system. In the course of time they assume a kind of hierarchical arrangement in terms of the prestige they may confer, so that certain groups become identified with a particular social class. Since the actual existence of such groups and the activities necessary to maintain them depend in considerable measure upon the amount of wealth and leisure time possessed by the individual, the activities themselves have considerable status significance. Certain kinds of leisure-time activities are prestigious, others not. Thus membership in status groups and participation in their activities are symbolically significant for the status system.

The plethora of manufactured goods in highly urbanized societies has served to focus interest on consumption. Not only do consumer goods have symbolic value for status, but the actual behavior involved in their consumption likewise has symbolic significance. In modern urbanized societies there is considerable preoccupation both with *what* and *how* to consume, and under what circumstances. The distinguished American economist, Thorstein Veblen, one of the first theorists to deal systematically with this matter, coined the phrase "conspicuous consumption" to describe the lengths to which the "leisure class" often goes in a frantic effort to gain prestige through wasteful and excessive consumption of both goods and leisure time.[3]

3. The rise of hierarchically structured bureaucracies in modern urban society has had a direct bearing both on the distribution and character of power and on the status system itself. While there are bureaucracies in agrarian as well as urbanized societies, it is in the latter particularly that the great economic governmental and military bureaucracies provide a mechanism for the concentration and exercise of power. Often the men of power are themselves drawn from the upper levels of the status system.

CHANGE IN THE AMERICAN CLASS SYSTEM

Large-scale changes in the major patterns of stratification have been associated with the rise of urbanism in the United States. As Mayer

[3] Thorstein Veblen, *The Theory of the Leisure Class* (1899). Cf. David M. Potter, *People of Plenty* (1954); John Galbraith, *The Affluent Society* (1958); Percival Goodman and Paul Goodman, *Communitas* (1947).

points out, the earlier expansion of the economy as related to industrialism and the growth of cities had the effect of producing a large urban working class.[4] Until well into the twentieth century, this urban proletariat was generally underpaid and overworked. The style of life imposed by adverse conditions reflected their underprivileged position in the economy.

During the past three or four decades, however, a substantial portion of the urban working class has adopted a "middle class" style of life. The basic change making this possible has been the rise of incomes and the shorter work week. So far as incomes are concerned, many manual workers are now in a more favorable position than white collar workers. With higher incomes and more leisure time, opportunities are provided for workers to have and do those things which were possible in the past only for privileged middle or upper class persons. Many have acquired the consumer "needs" of middle classes: modern homes and household equipment, annual vacations and travel, leisure-time activities, and so on. By the 1960's the amount of formal education of skilled workmen approached that of clerical and sales personnel. "As this assimilation of life styles proceeds," in the opinion of Mayer, "the traditional social distinction between white collar and manual occupations, never as sharp in the United States as in Europe, is becoming increasingly blurred. . . . If these trends continue, and there is no reason to assume otherwise at the present time, the class structure of American society will once again become predominantly middle class in the near future."[5]

CHANGE IN THE BRITISH CLASS SYSTEM

One of the world's most urbanized and industrialized countries, Great Britain, has undergone radical changes in its class structure.[6] A century or so ago there was an impressive and influential upper class consisting mainly of wealthy and powerful merchants and industrialists, landed gentry, and titled nobility; (2) a relatively small middle class consisting of shopkeepers, professionals, and clerical workers; and (3) a large body of manual workers employed extensively in manufacturing and shipping, who were underpaid and overworked, and who lived under miserable slum conditions. The middle of the twentieth century presents a very different picture, one contrary to the predictions of Karl Marx and other economic theorists of the nineteenth century. The nobility and landed gentry still exist but with declining significance and influence except for snob appeal; there are still wealthy industrial or business magnates, but their power and influence have been reduced by the socialization of parts

---

[4] Kurt Mayer, "Changes in the Class Structure of the United States," *Transactions of the Third World Congress of Sociology* (1956).

[5] *Ibid.*, pp. 77–78.

[6] G. D. H. Cole, *Studies in Class Structure* (1955).

of the economy and the rise of trade unionism; the middle classes have greatly expanded as white collar occupations have attracted an increasingly large proportion of employed persons; and finally the working classes, while declining in relative numbers, have experienced a great improvement in incomes and working conditions, often making it possible for them to have a standard of living and a style of life comparable to those of the middle classes.

CHANGE IN COMMUNITY STATUS SYSTEMS

Changes in a class system of a mass society have their parallel in changes within a community status system. Viewing American cities in historical perspective one may observe numerous changes that have in turn altered the character of the social structure. The rapid expansion of white collar occupations and professions and the relative decline in numbers of unskilled workers and domestics have been associated with an expanding middle class and the widespread acceptance of a "bourgeois" outlook.

The concentration of certain ethnic or racial groups in large cities has also had an important bearing on the status systems of those communities. This is the case because membership in a particular racial or ethnic group has symbolic significance for the status system. Some groups have high status value, others rank low in the social scheme. The heavy influx into American cities of great numbers of European and Asian immigrants during the nineteenth and early part of the twentieth century added an ethnic dimension to the status system. More recently the great migrations of Negroes and Puerto Ricans to northern cities in this country have further emphasized the racial and ethnic element in stratification.

THE WARNER APPROACH TO STRATIFICATION

Research by Warner and his associates on the status systems of three small American cities has had considerable influence on stratification theory. In terms of the Weberian theory of social stratification, Warner was primarily concerned with the second dimension, namely, status groups and the social order; economic class was not entirely ignored, but the political order, or power system, was given scant attention. The three communities studied were Yankee City,[7] an old Massachusetts seaport with a long history of maritime activities and a population quite varied in ethnic composition; Old City,[8] a Mississippi town with a large Negro

[7] See especially W. L. Warner, and Paul S. Lunt, *The Social Life of a Modern Community* (1941). There are three other volumes in the Yankee City series.
[8] Allison Davis, Burleigh Gardner, and Mary R. Gardner. *Deep South* (1941).

population; and Jonesville,[9] a midwestern town not far from Chicago.

In the Yankee City and Old City studies various methods were used to classify the population according to the existing status system. Individuals were asked to indicate the social positions of themselves and others with whom they were familiar. This information was supplemented by various data relating to education, occupation, group affiliations and activities, and so on. Piecing this information together the investigators located each individual in what was presumed to be his proper place in the status system. In the Jonesville study a somewhat more refined method was used for stratifying the population. Two methods were actually used. One, called "evaluated participation," was based on the belief that the social participation of individuals in formal and informal associations would be known to others, that the prestige of these groups would also be generally known, and that the individual could be fairly accurately placed in the social structure according to his participation and group affiliations. The actual placement was made by panels of local residents. The second method of placement involved a composite "index of status characteristics" based on occupation, source of income, style of house, and type of residential districts. The two methods were considered complementary and together were used in "classifying" the population. Of the three communities studied by Warner we shall discuss only one, Yankee City.

SOCIAL STRUCTURE OF YANKEE CITY

From the Warner method applied to Yankee City there were identified six social classes.[10] The percentage distribution of the population, in terms of class, was as follows: upper upper class, 1.44; lower upper, 1.56; upper middle, 10.22; lower middle, 28.12; upper lower, 32.60; lower lower, 25.22. Much of Warner's analysis of the class system of Yankee City is concerned with the racial and cultural composition of the people on various social levels, their formal and informal associations, behavioral characteristics, and status symbols.

The Social Aristocracy. The upper uppers were, of course, the real elite; below them were the lower uppers, also socially prominent but lacking some of the attributes for full acceptance in the aristocracy. To be eligible for membership in either of these two classes one had to be a long-time resident of New England and a descendant of Old American (Yankee) stock, have proper family connections, own sufficient wealth to maintain acceptable outward appearances, follow a socially approved occupation if gainfully employed, associate intimately with the right

[9] W. L. Warner, *et al., Democracy in Jonesville* (1949). A similar study of the same town is reported by A. B. Hollingshead as *Elmtown's Youth.*
[10] Warner and Lunt, *op. cit.*

people, and exhibit manners appropriate to upper class status. Warner considers manners an important criterion of class.

When affiliated with religious organizations the upper classes selected the Unitarian and Episcopal churches. They participated extensively in social clubs, but were rarely affiliated with fraternal societies, although some belonged to the Masonic lodge. Both men and women participated in organizations devoted to charity. The children attended private schools, where they prepared for college and acquired the forms of etiquette suitable to their class position. There was a tendency for them to purchase their own books, magazines, and newspapers rather than patronize the public library. Many belonged to discussion groups, and their recreational reading frequently was in the fields of biography and history.

The Middle Classes. Whereas *all* the upper classes were Yankees by birth and tradition, 83 per cent of the upper middle class and 67 per cent of the lower middle were so classified. Most of the "ethnics" of these two classes were Irish, but there were also a few Jews, Greeks, French-Canadians, Armenians, and other peoples of recent European extraction. On the upper middle level the great majority were wholesale or retail dealers, but there was also a small percentage of clerks and skilled or semiskilled workers. The lower middle class was heavily weighted with clerical employees and skilled workers.

The pattern of social activities of the upper middle group was similar to that of the superior classes in certain respects; women participated extensively in women's clubs and charitable organizations, but there was limited participation in mixed social clubs. The lower middle class, on the other hand, had limited representation in charity organizations, but participated extensively in fraternal societies and lodge auxiliaries.

The Unitarian Church was favored by the majority of upper middle class folk, with the Baptist, Congregational, and Christian Science churches also drawing heavily from this level; the lower middle classes were attracted mainly to the Congregational and Episcopal churches. Most of the children of the upper middle group attended the public schools rather than preparatory schools, and the great majority of those in high school selected Latin and scientific courses. Lower middle class children also attended the public schools, but less than half were enrolled in the college preparatory courses. The public library received most of its patronage from the upper middle group; about 22 per cent of this group, the highest of any social class, used its facilities.

The Lower Classes. Only about two-fifths of the upper lower class were Yankees, but about half of the Irish, Armenians, Jews, French-Canadians, and Italians, one-third of the Greeks, one-fourth of the Russians, and one-tenth of the Poles were on this social level. At the bottom of the scale were the Negroes, together with the "ethnics" who were not accepted on the higher levels. Members of the upper lower class were employed mainly in shoe factories, retail stores, the building trades, and transportation; a large percentage of the lower lower group were semi-skilled or unskilled workers.

Upper lower persons were associated extensively with fraternal organizations and related auxiliaries, but they did not participate to any great extent in social clubs. This group was mainly Roman Catholic; membership in Protestant churches was low with the exception of the Methodist Church. All of the children attended the public schools, and most of those in high school were taking commercial courses. About 18 per cent made use of the public library. On the lower level, social participation was less than for any other class, little use was made of the public library, and most of the children in high school took the commercial course. The religious affiliations of this group were distributed among the Catholic, Presbyterian, Methodist, Baptist, and Congregational churches.

BLACK METROPOLIS

Employing an approach rather similar to that of Warner, Drake and Cayton conducted a research in the Negro community of Chicago, emphasizing, among other things, the status system and its characteristics. Like the white social structure of any great metropolis, the Negro status system is highly complex and dynamic.[11] Numerous changes have probably occurred in the status system of Chicago's Negro community since the research was conducted in the 1930's, but doubtless the system is essentially the same in its major outlines.

THE UPPER CLASS

Of the Negroes in Chicago, not more than 5 per cent have the qualifications for upper class status. The authors observed that high-status individuals were commonly associated with the professions, mainly law, medicine, journalism, social work, and teaching, and with successful business ventures. In the Negro community, more than in the white group, a college education was a symbol of high prestige and a passport to the upper levels of "society." Only a small proportion of the elite were church-centered; and those who were affiliated with churches were Presbyterian, Congregationalists, or Episcopalians. Fraternal connections were largely with the Masonic lodge or its affiliates. Although the class as a whole was family-centered, much emphasis being placed on a disciplined and orderly family group, social life revolved around highly exclusive bridge clubs, fraternities, and sororities. There was also considerable interest in civic organizations devoted to the uplift of the race, and for many women

[11] St. Clair Drake and Horace R. Cayton, *Black Metropolis* (1945).

such activities were fashionable means of practicing exclusive social rituals. The real uppers of Black Metropolis tended to be conventional in their manners and morals, and conservative in their political and economic philosophy.

Somewhat below the elite were the "shadies." These included the policy kings, gentlemen racketeers, and other members of the *nouveaux riches* whose financial success had not been fully translated into social eminence. Committed to a cult of extravagance and display, of fine clothes, expensive automobiles, and fashionable sports, this group constituted the genuinely leisured class of Chicago's "black belt." For the most part unchurched and uninterested in civic uplift, the shadies and their families were beginning to show interest in culture and upper class rituals as a means of rising to the higher levels.

THE MIDDLE CLASS

About 30 per cent of the people in the Negro district were categorized by Drake and Cayton as middle class. Though this segment included a wide variety of individuals and a considerable range of income, there was a certain amount of unity or consciousness of kind because the group as a whole represented an essentially similar way of life. The characteristic philosophy through which their interests were expressed included respectable living, getting ahead, having a nice home, giving the children an opportunity, and saving something for the proverbial rainy day. These values were especially representative of the upper levels of the middle class group, which was psychologically oriented toward the elite of the community. Belonging to this class, ordinarily, were white collar workers, postal clerks, Pullman-car porters, skilled craftsmen, small businessmen with modest incomes, and even the better-established domestic servants or manual workers.

Recreational activities of this class varied considerably from those of the upper class. Leisure-time interests were channeled largely into age-graded, informal social clubs, of which there were eight or nine hundred. These clubs reinforced the middle class ideals of correct behavior and respectability; at the same time they afforded the members an opportunity for charity work and related civic activities. The most important function of the clubs, however, was to provide outlets for social expression, usually in the form of dances, fashion shows, and elaborate dinners. Older people of the middle class tended to be lodge- and church-centered, but the younger members, while usually retaining church membership, were more inclined to direct their interests to social and civic clubs and labor unions. Church members were usually affiliated with middle class Baptist or Methodist organizations.

THE LOWER CLASS

Two out of every three persons in the Negro district occupied a social position near the broad base of the social pyramid. Unskilled or semi-skilled manual workers for the most part, they were employed in the factories, stockyards, and kitchens of the metropolis, in downtown establishments as cleaners and sweepers, and in work gangs doing the heavy labor of a great city. Many were of recent southern origin.

Because of job uncertainties for the male population, married women found it necessary to seek gainful employment, particularly in times of depression. This assumption of economic responsibility tended to place the woman in a relatively dominant position in the home; at the same time, it lowered the sense of responsibility of the man and weakened his authority. Furthermore, the wandering habits of many lower class men fostered a "love 'em and leave 'em" attitude. Family life, therefore, tended to revolve around the mother, upon whose shoulders often fell the complete responsibility for supporting and rearing the children. Aware of the irresponsible and exploitative habits of many Negro men of this class, lower class women were inclined to be suspicious and hard in their attitudes toward the opposite sex. "I'll live with him until he doesn't act right; then I'll kick him out," was a common reaction. Family tensions characterized by arguing and even fighting were common, and desertion rates were high. This lack of family solidarity was undoubtedly a factor in the high incidence of juvenile delinquency among lower class children.

Even when lower class individuals could afford the costs, their social acceptance by the higher levels was by no means assured. Consequently, much of their recreation took the form of attending cheap movies, playing cards or dancing with friends in informal gatherings, dancing or drinking in public taverns, patronizing policy stations, loitering on street corners, or visiting public parks. The members of this class were uneducated, and there was little interest in cultural or intellectual pursuits.

About half of the lower class adults claimed to be church members, the majority being identified with Baptist, Methodist, or Holiness churches, commonly of the store-front type. However, probably not more than a third of the lower classes were serious about their religious affiliations, and these represented the more stable elements.

SOCIAL STRATIFICATION IN LATIN AMERICA

Generalizations about social stratification in Latin America are indeed hazardous because of the cultural, economic, demographic, and other differences within that vast region. Some of the countries, highly urbanized, are moving rapidly toward an industrial economy; others are just emerging from a feudalistic system. The racial composition varies greatly from one country to another, and the political systems range from dictatorship to democracy. In a few countries most of the people are literate; in most of them there is a high proportion of illiterates.

As in most underdeveloped regions certain broad generalizations can be made, however, with some assurance. In most Latin American countries there is a relatively small middle class—perhaps 20 per cent for the region as a whole, with Uruguay, Argentina, and Costa Rica having a considerably higher proportion, and such countries as Bolivia and Ecuador somewhat less.[12] In a privileged and powerful position is a small elite class, while on the lower levels of the structure are the impoverished and illiterate masses. Under the condition of a feudal or semi-feudal system, the control and ownership of the economic assets is a near monopoly of the elite class; upward social mobility is slow and for vast numbers virtually impossible. Yet with increased urbanization, industrialization, and pressures for economic and educational democracy, there is an expanding middle class, and in such areas as Mexico and Puerto Rico this expansion has been fairly rapid.

Studies of social stratification in two Latin American cities will be reviewed in this chapter.

EL SALVADOR AND SAN JOSE

A study of middle and lower classes in El Salvador and San Jose, the capital cities of El Salvador and Costa Rica, respectively, revealed many differences between the classes in each city and also differences between the two countries.[13] Interviews were conducted in 474 homes selected by sampling procedures from middle and lower class levels. Although both countries belong to a plantation economy, the social system of El Salvador is more rigid than that of Costa Rica, there is a smaller proportion of middle class people, and most of the population are *mestizos* (Indian-European hybrids). At least 40 per cent of the Costa Ricans are white, mainly small landowners and shopkeepers.

In both countries the investigator found marked differences in the "style of life" of middle and lower class people. The middle class was more receptive to social change, more strongly motivated toward mobility, and more positive in outlook, for both the present and the future. Middle class respondents generally were better satisfied with their occu-

---

[12] John P. Gillin, "Some Signposts for Policy," in Council on Foreign Relations, *Social Change in Latin America Today* (1960), p. 25; cf. Ralph L. Beals, "Social Stratification in Latin America," *American Journal of Sociology*, 58 (January, 1953), 327–39.

[13] Robert C. Williamson, "Some Variables of Middle and Lower Class in Two Central American Cities," *Social Forces*, 41 (December, 1962), 195–207.

pational roles and social positions. Marital relationships on this level were more conventional than on the lower social stratum; and individuals tended to be oriented more toward friendship than kinship in their personal relations. Middle class persons were also better educated, more widely educated, more widely traveled, and had higher educational goals for their children.

A larger proportion of lower class persons than those in the middle class tended to view success in life as the result of "luck" rather than hard work. They spent more time listening to the radio, and went to church or confession less frequently. There was relatively little participation by both classes in voluntary associations in El Salvador, but the lower class exceeded the middle class in this respect, which was the reverse of the situation in San Jose. In both cities smaller proportions of the lower classes voted in the last election, but the difference was not very great in each instance.

Certain economic indices point to the wide gap that exists between the middle and lower social classes in both cities. Monthly incomes of the middle class in El Salvador were, on the average, four times higher than for the lower class, and in San Jose they were three times higher. Although the number of children in lower class families was larger than for middle class families, the amount of living space in their homes was much less. Middle class families in El Salvador had, on the average, 4 rooms per family, but there were only 1.5 rooms per family in the lower class. The class difference in room space was somewhat less in San Jose families. This wide disparity of income and living space is probably far greater than would be found in cities in Europe and the United States.

THE UNDERDOGS OF MEXICO CITY

Oscar Lewis has presented a research on what he calls the "culture of poverty," a study of impoverished families in Mexico City and environs.[14] The method followed by Lewis was to record, with meticulous detail, all that he had seen or heard in the course of a single day spent in the homes of each of the families. Although the culture is Mexican, the picture presented of the dynamics of poverty would seem to have a certain resemblance to the submerged classes in other great cities, particularly those in the underdeveloped countries where poverty is brutal and widespread.

A common pattern for the impoverished Mexican families observed by Lewis was the relentless struggle for sheer survival: a never-ending effort to earn enough for basic human needs, with perhaps a little left over at times for "nonessentials." The specter of hunger or exposure or ill-

[14] Oscar Lewis, *Five Families: Mexican Case Studies in the Culture of Poverty* (1959). One of the five families had moved upward into the *nouveau riche* class, and another was located in a small city not far from the capital.

ness was never far away. How to obtain money necessary to provide food, clothing, and shelter was the central problem in life. Economic security was a mirage. The output of energy necessary to keep afloat left little margin for other things.

The picture presented by Lewis is in contrast to the middle class stereotype of the "poor but happy" lower class family. Instead of family life characterized by stable marriages and marital felicity, the marriages were mainly "free unions" whose tenuous bonds were easily and frequently broken. The sexual adventures of husbands and wives, before or after marriage, the prolonged absences of the husbands from their families, or their irresponsible spending of limited earnings, were factors in creating an atmosphere of distrust, tension, and insecurity. In a society in which male dominance is the norm, the absence of the father from the home, or his failure to provide for the family, throws a heavy burden of responsibility on the mother for rearing the children and keeping the group intact. (The *nouveau riche* family was also unstable.) Of the five husbands, two never knew their fathers, and three had poor relations with them; two of the wives had not known their own fathers, and only one had had a satisfactory paternal relationship.

Packed into a single room, the families ate and slept and performed other functions under unspeakably crowded conditions which made harmonious living exceedingly difficult. There was frequent bickering, commonly over family finances. Serious conditions of health existed, but if these were recognized the attributed causes lay outside the realm of science. The adults were either illiterate or had received at the most three or four years of schooling. Generally the parents preferred that their children go to work instead of school, although some of the mothers wanted their sons or daughters to attend a commercial school so that they could obtain a white collar job. All of the families were nominal Catholics, but church attendance was limited mainly to the females, and in general religion appeared to play a relatively limited role in their lives.

These people were not devoid of ambition. But in their aspirations they were realistic concerning the hard facts of life: the levels of aspiration were limited mainly to a job and income that would supply their basic needs, or to enough education to make these things possible. Only one of the fathers, an ingenious and inventive man, was strongly motivated toward financial success, but he lacked the capital and experience necessary to attain his goals.

METROPOLITAN ELITE

With the exception of Black Metropolis and Mexico City, the researches summarized so far have been carried out in small cities. In this section we shall present, in summary form, some of the findings relative to the elite in an American metropolis, Philadelphia.

"PHILADELPHIA GENTLEMEN"

In his study of a metropolitan upper class in Philadelphia, Baltzell treated the subject both historically and sociologically, presenting in rich detail the total "style of life" of those Philadelphians whose inclusion in the *Social Register* attests to their eminent position in the status system.[15] Not only are the "Philadelphia gentlemen" and their families firmly entrenched at the apex of the social structure of this city, but they are generally accepted as qualified members of a national elite representing, in the main, the social aristocracy of other great metropolises. Included in the Philadelphia *Social Register* in 1940 were 5,150 families.

The Philadelphia elite has something of the character of a quasi-caste. Family lineage as well as inherited wealth and an appropriate occupation is an important criterion of membership in this class. Among the more prestigious are the "old families" whose members lay proud claim to descent from illustrious, or at least well-known, ancestors, some of whom played notable roles in American history. Many of the families are extended kinship groups having a strong sense of clan solidarity. Intermarriage between members of these families, as well as with elite families in other metropolitan areas, has added to the castelike character of this class.

Although achieved status does figure very importantly in the social systems of urban society, it may be that achievement is less important on the top echelons than ascription. In the Philadelphia study, Baltzell noted that inclusion in *Who's Who in America*, an honorific recognition of reputed achievement, did not necessarily mean inclusion in the *Social Register*, reserved mainly for properly pedigreed people. Of the 770 persons included in *Who's Who*, only 29 per cent were in the *Social Register*.[16] Clearly, inherited wealth and lineage were of primary importance.

THE STYLE OF LIFE OF PHILADELPHIA GENTLEMEN

Among the associational ties that provide a common basis for class solidarity is membership in exclusive metropolitan clubs, which select their members almost entirely from the elite. Not only does membership in these clubs symbolize the highest level of prestige, but through membership activities the clubs afford a common ground for sharing ideas and experiences that have the effect of isolating the elite from persons on lower social levels. Most of the elite had attended exclusive private schools, and later in college studied at such fashionable universities as Pennsylvania, Harvard, Yale, or Princeton. In the university, as students, they were usually members of exclusive clubs, and as alumni of the uni-

[15] E. Digby Baltzell, *Philadelphia Gentlemen* (1958).   [16] *Ibid.,* p. 33.

versities and clubs they had similar interests and loyalties which found expression in shared associational activities.

Residentially, the elite in Philadelphia are mostly located on what is commonly known as the Main Line, represented by several fashionable suburbs or a section within the city. In the summers they visit, or live in, a few fashionable resorts, where they fraternize with each other and with the elite from other metropolitan areas. By religion, most of them are Episcopalians or Presbyterians. Occupationally, they are mainly business and finance executives, or professionals in the more lucrative and prestigious fields such as medicine, law, or engineering. Mostly they are of Anglo-Saxon derivation; only a few Jews or South Europeans are included, and there are no Negroes.

When Veblen published this *Theory of the Leisure Class* at the turn of the century, he placed considerable emphasis on what he called the "conspicuous consumption" and the "conspicuous waste" of America's elite. This analysis would hardly hold for Philadelphia's elite. Although most of them are in possession of considerable inherited wealth, there is little tendency for them to sensationalize their spending or their leisure-time activities. On the contrary, the ethic of hard work is emphasized and often practiced, and many participate in civic or cultural activities, or accept careers in government service.

SOCIAL MOBILITY AND URBANISM

Social mobility is ordinarily viewed as a change in the social or economic position of an individual or group. This change may be either upward or downward according to the values attached to particular positions or statuses. It may also be horizontal in that movement from one social position to another may occur without any observable change in the prestige of the individual group.

It is fairly clear that urbanized and industrialized societies afford greater prospects for social mobility than agrarian or pre-industrial societies.[17] Highly urbanized societies, or even those moving in this direction, commonly have expanding economies, which means increasing job opportunities and rising incomes. Growing cities, and particularly large cities, have a complex division of labor which involves the creation of new occupations, especially white collar jobs, and a need for personnel to fill these positions. Thus there are opportunities for upward occupational mobility—or prospects for downward mobility. Secondly, urbanized societies are less tradition-bound, in general, than nonurban societies; there is more freedom of action and thought accorded the individual, greater emphasis on achievement than on ascription, and an elaborate system of

[17] See especially Reinhard Bendix and Seymour Lipset, *Social Mobility in Industrial Society* (1960), ch. 8.

rewards to encourage achievement. Aspirations to attain these rewards through achievement mean motivation for upward social mobility. Urbanized societies tend, then, to be "achievement" societies. Such urbanized countries as the United States and those of Western Europe are more favorable to upward social mobility than such traditionalized societies as those of the Middle East, Latin America or parts of Asia.

STATUS VERSUS CLASS MOBILITY

Specific status changes may be readily observed and perhaps easily measured. But it is quite another matter to determine when or what kinds of status changes add up to changes in an individual's class position. This is because the determinants of class position are numerous and varied, making it difficult to delineate class boundaries except in a rather arbitrary manner. The fact that analysts of social systems do not always agree on the number or criteria of classes is in itself evidence of this difficulty. Yet all agree that class mobility within the system does occur.

STUDIES OF SOCIAL MOBILITY

In their studies of Yankee City, Old City, and Jonesville, Warner and his associates observed that class mobility was usually slow and the range of movement narrow, but that it did occur. In fact, Warner believes that upward mobility in a community is necessary if the open-class system is to maintain itself, since the upper classes do not ordinarily produce enough children for replacement, and their places must be taken by those coming up from lower levels. Recent increases in upper class birth rates, however, may reduce the number of high-level vacancies. Conversely, migration of upper class families from a community may have the effect of creating vacancies that may be filled by persons from lower levels or from the outside.

SOCIAL MOBILITY IN YANKEE CITY

Although economic success in Yankee City may pave the way for social ascendancy, according to Warner, wealth alone is no passport to the ranks of the elite. An enterprising Yankee who has accumulated a fortune may, within limits, translate economic success into social success for himself or his family, provided that he has proper family or ethnic affiliations and manifests the appropriate manners and style of living. But if he is a Jew, a Pole, or a Greek he will never qualify for the highest social echelons, whatever the size of his fortune, and if he is a Negro, regardless of wealth,

education, occupation, or manners, he is doomed to a low position in the social structure of the city.

SOCIAL MOBILITY IN OLD CITY

Substantially the same general situation prevails in Old City, except that social distinctions between Negroes and whites are more rigid than in Yankee City. The investigators of Old City utilize the Warner race-caste dichotomy and conceptualize a class system within each race-caste. Social mobility is therefore viewed not as movement from one race-caste to another, but as movement from one social level to another within the same "caste." As in Yankee City, upward mobility was slow. Movement from a subclass to another may be fairly easy, as between lower middle and upper middle, since basic changes in occupation, income, ideology, or manners are not required; but movement from one major class to another becomes difficult, and ascent from lower class to upper class is virtually impossible. Even marriage of a lower class woman to an upper class man hardly guarantees her social acceptance by the elite.

SOCIAL MOBILITY IN POPAYAN AND QUERETARO

In his study of social stratification in two Latin American cities, White-ford presented, in a nonquantitative form, materials on social mobility.[18] As in most nonindustrial communities, upward mobility was slow and difficult for the majority of people. Although there were several avenues for upward mobility, as well as various credentials necessary for social ascendancy, numerous obstacles to movement out of a particular stratum did exist. Whatever may have been the mobility aspirations of individuals in either of the cities, most of them were relatively immobile, at least as far as class mobility was concerned.

A sharp distinction was drawn between those who earned a living by manual labor and those who received incomes in other ways. This barrier was difficult to cross, and for Indians there was the added handicap of race. Indian "blood" and culture, illiteracy, and poverty were interrelated symbols of low class. Certain narrowly restricted channels were open, however, for persons on the lower levels. One was entering a skilled vocation as an apprentice; another was the development of a business sufficient to earn some money and hire helpers; a third was receiving appointments to white collar jobs through political pull. But none of these avenues ordinarily carried the individual very far.

A major criterion for middle class acceptance was education, together with a socially respectable occupation, the wearing of appropriate attire,

---

[18] Andrew H. Whiteford, *Two Cities of Latin America* (1960). The population of Queretaro, Mexico, was about 50,000 and that of Popayan, Columbia, about 33,000.

and the display of manners proper for a middle class station in life. For girls, a common avenue for ascendancy from the lower to higher levels was marriage. Movement into the middle classes was possible but not very frequent, but movement beyond that level was exceedingly difficult. Education, wealth, power, or manners alone or in combination were usually not sufficient for upper class membership unless the individual could establish claim to illustrious ancestry by inheritance or marriage. Hence the avenues for upward mobility beyond the upper middle class were effectively blockaded by the insurmountable barrier of lineage. Those who aspired strongly to these levels often found it expedient to leave the city.

CONSEQUENCES OF SOCIAL MOBILITY

That social mobility has profound implications for almost every facet of the social order can hardly be denied, although the precise consequences for any particular aspect of society are not too well known. Many of the generalizations tend to be in the form of hypotheses subject to further exploration. Some of these may be suggested:

1. Vertical mobility is likely to have disruptive effects on primary interpersonal relationships and on those groups such as family, clique, and neighborhood which are dependent, in the main, on face-to-face relations. This appears to be the case because the mobile person may establish new sets of interpersonal relationships as he moves upward or downward. As new friendships are made and new loyalties develop, the old ties may become less binding. Often vertical social mobility is associated with ecological mobility: those who move "up" may also move "out." Social and ecological mobility taken together is probably one of the factors that create conditions of *anomie* in the city.

2. Vertical social mobility undoubtedly involves considerable stress and strain in the individual. Whether moving upward or downward, the individual experiences new situations, new interpersonal relations, new institutional structures. How to adjust to these is not always clear to the individual. He may be strongly motivated to find acceptance by those whom he meets on a higher or lower level, but may never achieve acceptance, or be haunted with anxieties that he will be rejected. On the other hand, there may be guilt feelings with respect to those who were left behind. In highly competitive societies such as those of Europe or America, status anxieties are common; and those who are striving to achieve upward mobility, or to avoid downward mobility, are doubly beset by these strains. There is reason to believe that the highly mobile person is likely to exhibit syndromes of psychoneuroses, or perhaps even psychoses.

3. The upwardly mobile individual is likely to be successful, in terms of the definitions of his community or society. In the efforts to achieve

these goals we have the psychological conditions favorable to social change (or "progress") and to high productivity as related to the goals. Motivation for social mobility provides the psychological mainsprings for many forms of social change; and it is precisely in the urban social climate that these changes are likely to occur most frequently. It is one of the things that make an urban society a dynamic society.

SELECTED BIBLIOGRAPHY

BOOKS

Baltzell, E. Digby, *Philadelphia Gentlemen*. Glencoe, Ill.: The Free Press, 1958.

Bendix, Reinhard, and Seymour M. Lipset, *Social Mobility in Industrial Society*. Berkeley: University of California Press, 1960.

Drake, St. Clair, and Horace R. Cayton, *Black Metropolis*. New York: Harcourt Brace, 1945.

Hollingshead, A. B., and Fritz Redlich, *Social Class and Mental Illness*. New York: Wiley, 1958.

Kahl, Joseph A., *The American Class Structure*. New York: Holt, Rinehart, and Winston, 1957.

Miller, Herman P., *Rich Man, Poor Man: The Distribution of Income in America*. New York: Thomas Y. Crowell Company, 1964.

Srole, Leo, *et al.*, *Mental Health in the Metropolis*. New York: McGraw-Hill, 1962.

Warner, W. L., and Paul S. Lunt, *The Social Life of a Modern Community*. New Haven: Yale University Press, 1941.

Whiteford, Andrew H., *Two Cities of Latin America*. Beloit, Wisc.: Anthropology Museum, Beloit College, 1960.

ARTICLES

Gist, Noel P., "Caste Differentials in South India," *American Sociological Review*, 19 (April, 1954), 126–37.

Hollingshead, A. B., "Trends in Social Stratification: A Case Study," *American Sociological Review*, 17 (December, 1952), 687–96.

Kahl, Joseph A., "Educational and Occupational Aspirations of 'Common Man' Boys," *Harvard Educational Review*, 23 (Summer, 1953), 317–25.

Kaufman, Harold F., "An Approach to the Study of Urban Stratification," *American Sociological Review*, 17 (August, 1952), 430–37.

Lasswell, Thomas E., "Social Class and Size of Community," *American Journal of Sociology*, 64 (March, 1960), 505–8.

Lipset, Seymour M., "Social Mobility and Urbanization," *Rural Sociology*, 20 (September–December, 1955), 220–28.

Mills, C. Wright, "Middle Classes in Middle-Sized Cities," *American Sociological Review*, 11 (October, 1946), 520–29.

Rosen, Bernard, "The Achievement Syndrome: A Psychocultural Dimension of Stratification," *American Sociological Review*, 21 (April, 1956), 203–11.

Williamson, Robert C., "Some Variables of Middle Class and Lower Class in Two Central American Cities," *Social Forces*, 41 (December, 1962), 195–207.

The Urban World of Work

Urban occupations may be viewed as a *system* in the sense that they represent a complex of more or less interdependent roles and statuses in which a hierarchical principle is manifest in differentials of prestige and power. This hierarchical arrangement of work roles is commonly referred to as an occupational *structure*.

Manifestly the urban occupational system is merely a part of the general occupational structure which includes farm and village work roles as well as those of city people. Many of the characteristics of the urban system are to be found in rural occupations. Certainly changes in any part of the system may be matched by similar changes in other parts. Yet there are differences. Numerous occupations are distinctively urban; some of them are found only in large cities. Steeplejacks and street car conductors are not likely to work on farms or in villages.

THE CHANGING OCCUPATIONAL STRUCTURE

Social changes associated with urbanization in the United States are reflected in the occupational structure. Some occupations have expanded, others have contracted, and new ones have appeared. Technology has had far-reaching repercussions. A rising standard of living, an increase in leisure time for the masses, and the wholesale entrance of women into the labor force have had profound effects on the occupational system.

The occupational changes presented in Table 12 parallel the growth of cities in the United States, and in many respects have been brought about by the rise of urbanism. Some of these changes are spectacular.

The proportion of professional and technical workers, for example, increased by about two and one-half times between 1900 and 1960, while

315

TABLE 12

Percentage Distribution of Persons in Major Occupational Divisions
in the United States, 1900 and 1960

	Direction of *Change*	*1900*	*1960*
Professional and technical	Increase	4.3	10.3
Managers, officials, proprietors	Increase	5.8	10.1
Clerical workers	Increase	3.0	14.4
Sales workers	Increase	4.5	6.4
Craftsmen (skilled workers)	Increase	10.5	12.9
Operatives (semiskilled)	Increase	12.8	17.9
Laborers, except farm and mine	Decrease	12.5	6.2
Private household workers	Decrease	5.4	3.2
Service workers	Increase	3.6	9.2
Farmers and farm managers	Decrease	19.9	4.3
Farm laborers	Decrease	17.7	5.2

SOURCES: *Comparative Occupation Statistics for the United States, 1870–1940* (Bureau of the Census, 1940), p. 187; Bureau of Labor Statistics report, July, 1960. Nineteen hundred and sixty data are not strictly comparable to the 1900 report because of changes in classifications, but the trends are clearly apparent.

the percentage of clerical workers was five times as great in 1960 as at the beginning of the century. But some of the declines were equally pronounced. In 1900, farmers and farm managers accounted for about one-fifth of the labor force, but by 1960 less than one in twenty were so engaged, and a comparable decline occurred among farm and nonfarm laborers. In general, the most pronounced increases were among the white collar workers.

SPECIFIC OCCUPATIONS

Changes in occupational classes conceal changes that occur in specific occupations. Certain specialized workers have more than doubled in a single recent decade, while others have incurred impressive losses. During the decade between 1940 and 1950, for example, the number of industrial engineers increased by 244 per cent, airplane pilots by 217 per cent, radio operators by 160 per cent, office machine operators by 137 per cent, librarians by 54 per cent, and bartenders by 70 per cent.[1] Sharp declines were noted in such occupations as bill collectors (—44 per cent), telegraph messengers (—48 per cent), bus and street car conductors (—33 per cent), paperhangers (—18 per cent), and tailors (—23 per cent).

[1] Data selected from Donald J. Bogue, *The Population of the United States* (1959), pp. 479–82.

Associated with the phenomenal growth of cities in the Western world since World War II have been accelerated activities in such generalized fields as aeronautics, electronics, engineering, nuclear power, scientific training and research, and home construction, all of which have provided a basis for new occupations or the expansion of existing ones—as well as the contraction of others. Similarly, developments in medical care, social welfare, mass communication, mass education, recreation, and consumer interests and behavior have also affected the occupational system. These and other changes reflect the dynamic character of an urbanized society.

WOMEN AT WORK

Women have always worked, but only in urbanized societies have they extensively engaged in gainful employment outside the home. The increasing percentage of persons living in cities is usually paralleled by an increasing proportion of women in the total labor force. At least this is the situation in the United States and western Europe. In communist societies women have been drawn more extensively into the labor force than in noncommunist countries. The influx of women into the labor market during World War II was merely an exaggerated continuation of a trend that has long been under way.

By 1960, over one-third (35 per cent) of the American female population over 14 years of age was gainfully employed; this is an increase from 27 per cent in 1940.[2] One of the striking aspects of this trend is the pronounced increase in the number of married women in gainful employment: from 17 per cent of all married women in 1940 to 32 per cent in 1960.

That this trend is predominantly an urban phenomenon is evidenced by the fact that about four-fifths of female workers in the United States reside in cities, although only about two-thirds of the total population are urban residents. Cities vary considerably in employment opportunities for females. In Washington, D. C., and Charlotte, North Carolina, 45 per cent of the adult females were employed in 1960, but in Youngstown, Ohio, and Wheeling, West Virginia, both centers of heavy industry, the percentages were 30 and 32, respectively. In general, a somewhat larger percentage of women in the central cities than in the suburban fringe is gainfully employed.

AMERICAN MINORITY PEOPLES AND THE OCCUPATIONAL STRUCTURE

Ethnic and racial minorities tend to be concentrated heavily in particular types of occupations. Historically the Jews have been traders, and

[2] *Statistical Abstract of the United States* (1961), p. 213.

in American cities, where the great majority of Jews are located, there has been a tendency for them to continue their occupational traditions. Many Jews have also entered the professions and the manual occupations associated with the manufacture of clothing. Italians and Greeks are oriented toward the preparation and serving of foods; many have also gone into the unskilled or semiskilled manual occupations. Poles have been attracted in great numbers to heavy industries, especially mining, smelting, and manufacturing. The majority of Chinese in American cities have been associated with the restaurant and laundry business. Before World War II the Japanese were heavily concentrated in the vocation of truck-gardening.

Ethnic-group specialization in the United States seems destined to decline, however. An expanding economy and a labor shortage during and after World War II created unprecedented opportunities for employment in all kinds of jobs. Members of ethnic and racial minorities became increasingly acceptable for posts which had not been available to them earlier. Instead of following their fathers' occupational careers, by choice or necessity, they tended to deviate from parental occupations, to ignore work customs, and to strike out into newer and often more promising fields. The assimilation of ethnic groups into the prevailing culture, an increase in their formal education and vocational training, together with rising aspirations toward white collar occupations, had the effect of reducing ethnic specialization.

It appears that many ethnic groups in this country are experiencing a work history similar to that of the Germans and Irish when they began migrating to the United States. At first, the number of occupations available to them, for one reason or another, was limited; hence they tended to concentrate in certain vocations. Eventually they began to enter the occupational structure at all levels; today they are widely diffused. The comparatively late arrivals from southern and eastern Europe and Asia have likewise become somewhat specialized along ethnic lines, but they, too, are becoming more and more dispersed in the occupational hierarchy. The number of names indicative of eastern or southern European family backgrounds to be found in the higher professions is an illustration of this change.

THE CHANGING OCCUPATIONAL STATUS OF AMERICAN NEGROES

The divergent occupational patterns of Negroes and whites are, of course, not due to inherent characteristics of either group but rather to the "job ceiling." This ceiling is imposed at a fairly low level, and regardless of the qualifications of individuals it is extremely difficult to transcend because the white man has reserved most of the choice positions on the higher planes of the occupational pyramid. The result is that urban

Negroes are forced into low-paying jobs. In the higher levels of Negro occupations are some professionals, clerical employees, owners of small business enterprises, and government workers; on the intermediate levels are porters in railway stations, sleeping-car porters, and better-paid servants in restaurants and hotels; at the bottom are unskilled factory and laundry employees, scrubwomen, bootblacks, janitors, elevator operators, household maids, and day laborers. The extensive unionization of Negro workers in cities has been a factor in breaking down the barriers of discrimination.

Legislative and other measures, including mass pressures by the Negroes themselves, have had the effect of opening up many employment opportunities for them, especially in cities of the United States. In some instances, job are available but Negroes cannot qualify because of inadequate educational training or experience. Thus the lag in education due to discrimination or limited opportunity has had the effect of disqualifying Negroes for many jobs that have become available. Table 13 indicates certain changes in Negro employment over a relatively short period.

TABLE 13

**Distribution of Negroes in Major Occupational Classes in 1948
and 1960, Calculated as Ratios**

	Direction of Change	Ratios	
		1948	1960
Professional and technical	Increase	.33	.40
Managers, officials, proprietors	Increase	.20	.21
Clerical workers	Increase	.24	.46
Sales workers	Increase	.17	.22
Craftsmen (skilled workers)	Increase	.36	.43
Operatives (semiskilled)	Increase	1.00	1.14
Laborers, except farm and mine	Increase	2.92	3.07
Private household workers	Decrease	10.40	7.15
Service workers	Decrease	2.30	2.13
Farmers and farm managers	Decrease	1.09	.72
Farm laborers	Increase	2.72	2.82

SOURCE: Calculated from data in *Statistical Abstract of the United States* (1961), p. 216.

These ratios indicate the extent to which Negroes may be underrepresented or overrepresented, proportionally, in the major occupational divisions. If job selection were strictly random, all the ratios should be 1.00. But as the data in the table indicate, the selective process is not random. In 1960, for example, the number of Negroes in the professions was only two-fifths of what it would have been on the basis of chance. At the same time, the number of Negroes employed as household workers was over seven times as large as would be expected on a random basis.

Clearly, the more prestigious and lucrative occupations were under-represented, and the low-paid and relatively low-skilled jobs were greatly overrepresented.

But the table points up another notable fact, namely, the increase in representation of Negroes in the higher occupations, and at the same time a decrease in certain occupations that traditionally have been filled largely by unskilled Negroes and whites. The decline in the ratios for employment in private households, for example, from 10.40 to 7.15 over a 12-year period indicates a major occupational shift from this type of work. Doubtless a considerable part of this decline represents a move into urban unskilled or semiskilled occupations such as factory work. The heavy influx of Negroes into American cities during the past two decades has been accompanied by a general movement upward into the more prestigious occupations, but equality of occupational opportunity is still in the future.

These broad occupational classes tend to conceal even greater differences in the distribution of Negroes. In the professions the Negro group has more than its proportionate share of clergymen, but only about 4 per cent of the accountants, engineers, and chemists. Similarly, Negroes have almost twice their proportionate share of plasterers and cement workers, but only a small fraction of their representation among such occupations as locomotive engineers and toolmakers.

DECLINE OF DOMESTIC SERVICE

Of the occupational changes associated with urbanism in the United States, the decline in numbers of domestic servants is significant. This decline of a servant class suggests both an upward occupational movement by individuals in the course of their work careers and intergenerational mobility in which sons and daughters of servants follow work roles symbolizing a higher level of status. Many servants, or at least their sons and daughters, have entered the ranks of semiskilled or unskilled workers; some of them have even gone into the white collar occupations.

The decades 1940–60 witnessed a sharp diminution in the number of domestics in the United States. That attractive job opportunities provided by industrial expansion during the war years lured countless individuals from domestic service there can be no doubt, but the war decade merely accelerated a trend that had begun much earlier.

The greater prevalence of servants in the South as compared with other sections of the country raises an interesting question: Is the household servant particularly characteristic of a castelike social order which emphasizes rigid status differentials and stigmatizes certain work roles involving physical labor? The prevalence of servants in India, or even in prewar Britain, as well as in the American South, suggests that this may be the case. But if the servant is vanishing, does this betoken increasing flexibility of the social structure as gauged by upward occupational mobility? About all that one can confidently say is that changes associated with increasing urbanization, including industrialization, growth of bureaucratic organization, and, in the United States, an expansion of occupational opportunities in white collar and semiskilled jobs, have tended to pull the household servant out of the home and cast him or her in a different role. One effect of this is to put the housewife back into the kitchen and force her (or her husband) to perform menial tasks.

EMERGENCE OF AN EMPLOYEE SOCIETY

There was a time, in our recent agrarian past, when most workers were "on their own." They were independent proprietors, independent professionals, independent farmers. Even if they were employed by others, as was often the case, they usually worked in small establishments in which the line of authority between employer and employee was direct and the form of communication personal. The employee sold his services in the open market for whatever he could get. The entrepreneur operated his own business; the doctor carried on his own private practice; the lawyer maintained his own law office with a private clientele; the craftsman had his own shop; the farmer was beholden to no one—or so he thought. But the picture has changed. In urbanized America of the midtwentieth century, workers in the labor force have become increasingly wage earners or members of the salariat. There is emerging what Drucker calls "the employee society." [3]

Early in the nineteenth century, when America was predominantly agrarian, probably around four-fifths of the working force were self-employed; by the turn of the twentieth century this proportion had declined to around one-third; and at the middle of the century probably not more than one-fifth were in this category. Thus, as Mills points out, about four-fifths of the occupied members of the labor force were working for the 2 or 3 per cent of the population who owned 40 or 50 per cent of the property of the United States.[4] Drucker feels that equally significant with the emergence of the employee is the appearance of the boss representing the firm, the government, or some other bureaucratic organization. The boss himself is usually an employee who works for other employed bosses. All this, of course, is merely a directional trend associated with

[3] Peter Drucker, "The Employee Society," *American Journal of Sociology*, 58 (January, 1953), 358–63.
[4] C. Wright Mills, *White Collar* (1951), p. 63.

urbanization of modern society. Not all workers by any means are employees. But if such a trend is characteristic of a capitalistic society, such as the American system, it has even greater application in a socialistic or communistic order, in which almost everybody is an employee of the state or one of its political units.

The trend toward an employee society is not confined to the United States. In Australia, a highly urbanized country, the proportion of factory owners declined by half between 1900 and 1948, while the percentage of white collar workers doubled over the same period.[5] The proportion of skilled and semiskilled workers in industry remained about constant over the same period. The expansion of government bureaucracy in Australia has resulted in a corresponding expansion of white collar jobs; presently about one breadwinner in four is employed in a government post. The same trend has also occurred in Britain and the Netherlands.[6]

DIVISION OF LABOR AND PROFESSIONALIZATION

OCCUPATIONAL SPECIALIZATION AND EXPERTNESS

In a society undergoing urbanization and industrialization, the trend is toward increasing emphasis on expertness in work-role performance. An expert, sociologically speaking, is an individual who has gained special competence in the performance of a work role involving particular skills or knowledge. Expertness has developed on two different levels. On one level is the expert whose limited skill or knowledge can be achieved fairly easily: the expert typist or machinist, for example. Even the semiskilled factory operative is an expert whose proficiency is attained with relatively little training. High-level expertness often involves prolonged training or on-the-job experience because of the difficulty in achieving competence to perform certain work roles. Sometimes both training and practical experience are necessary.

The growing importance of expertness in an urbanized society is indicated in the United States by the increasing proportions of persons having highly specialized work roles. Even clerical personnel are usually expert operatives of complex office machinery, performing a highly mechanized work role and nothing else. The office girl who operates a typewriter in a pool of office typists, doing nothing else day after day, probably achieves an expertness that would be difficult of attainment if she performed a dozen tasks around the establishment. But monotony may be the price of such routinized efficiency.

This specialized expertness involves a degree of occupational inter-

[5] S. B. Hammond and O. A. Oeser (eds.), *Social Structure and Personality in a City* (1954), p. 240.
[6] G. D. H. Cole, *Studies in Class Structure* (1955).

dependency which can probably be achieved only through the formal organization of an urbanized society. Reduced to simple terms, occupational specialization means that the specialist ordinarily does only one task and is therefore dependent upon many others to do things for him. To the extent that workers become specialized, to that extent does interdependence exist. People can exist in such a state of interdependence only when there is coordination of work roles.

PROFESSIONALIZATION OF WORK

Occupational expertness associated with urbanization has been accompanied by a trend toward professionalization of work. This trend represents an effort to raise the status of particular work roles and to increase the rewards accruing to those performing such roles. These rewards may be pecuniary or nonpecuniary—or both. Aside from rewards in the form of comparatively high incomes, rewards such as honorific titles, the right to deferential treatment, and status symbols like uniforms or badges may afford prestige to professional workers.

One of the first steps in professionalization of an occupation is the change of name.[7] Thus junk dealers become salvage consultants, embalmers become funeral directors, private secretaries become administrative assistants, traveling salesmen become manufacturer's representatives or sales engineers, laboratory technicians become medical technologists, and so on. Commonly associated with name-changing is the formation of an organization designed to keep out allegedly disqualified or otherwise undesirable persons, or in some instances to keep out competitors, by the imposition of membership tests and standards of competence. Erection of membership barriers is usually accompanied by the adoption of a constitution and a set of by-laws embodying an ethical code to guide the conduct of members. Finally, the group undergoing professionalization often engages in propaganda or political activities to enhance its prestige in the eyes of the public or defend its interests by supporting or opposing particular proposals.

An example of white collar professionalization is the emergence of the professional manager. Many professional managers are trained in university schools of business or public administration for a managerial career in business, industry, government, education, social work, and so on. Curricula for the training of such specialized executives as city managers and hospital administrators are examples of institutional facilities maintained to professionalize certain occupations on the higher managerial levels. Sometimes managers themselves are technical experts who have been selected for managerial roles, as in the case of a corporation lawyer who becomes the executive head of a corporation or a municipal bureau,

[7] Theodore Caplow, *The Sociology of Work* (1954), pp. 139–40.

Automation in factory and office. Industrial development has reached the point where many of the comparatively routine tasks of factory and office workers can now be performed almost entirely by machines. The urban work force will require higher levels of skill and education to meet the demands of automation; unemployment and displacement have occurred for some portions of the labor force. Above: Worker at the controls of an automated bread-making machine. Facing page: Check-processing by 501 computer in a bank. The system can credit or debit an individual checking account in a millionth of a second. (Courtesy American Machine and Foundry Company and Chase Manhattan Bank [photograph by Arthur Lavine].)

or a sanitary engineer or accountant who becomes a city manager or director of public works. Many managers, of course, are still trained in the school of experience, moving upward from lesser positions to increasingly important managerial roles.

AUTOMATION AND THE SCIENTIFIC REVOLUTION

The growth of cities in the West and the Industrial Revolution had the effect of improving human and mechanical efficiency and therefore increasing productivity in almost every sphere of economic endeavor. In the earlier phases of the Revolution there was an expansion of those occu-

pations linked to the manufacturing and to the distribution of the products of factory and mill. As manufacturing came to be located mainly in cities, so also did the distributive processes. In the later phases of the Revolution, the stage was prepared for the expansion of white collar occupations—professionals, clerical workers, sales people, government employees, and so on.

Now at midcentury the urbanized and industrialized countries are entering a new era created by the *scientific* revolution: the era of automation. That its effects will be far-reaching can hardly be denied. Automation will create new jobs, just as it will destroy existing ones. It will involve new knowledge and skills, and will therefore necessitate different training programs. It will make possible a shorter work day or week, and therefore increased leisure time. It will expedite production, and therefore create problems of distribution of goods. It will apply not only to the manufacturing processes, but it will also invade the office, salesroom, and laboratory, where automated machinery may be used for various functions, ranging from complicated mathematical computations to mailing envelopes for mass circulation. Automation is already a reality, though in its first stage. In considering various facets of the problem, Dubin summarized what he considers some of the major consequences of automation will be: [8]

[8] Robert Dubin, *The World of Work* (1958), p. 199.

A. The creation of new specializations will change the skill composition of the total labor force.

B. The needs for much higher skills will have an inevitable impact on formal schooling preparatory to entering industry.

C. Retraining of displaced workers will constitute a major problem for the total economy.

D. A probable shift in the assignment of work by sex may be anticipated.

E. There is a high probability that the areas of more recent economic growth will be favored by automation.

OCCUPATIONAL MOBILITY IN THE CITY

FORMS OF MOBILITY

Movement up or down the occupational structure is perhaps the most important single criterion of social mobility; at least it is objective and lends itself to quantitative measurement. As in social mobility in general, occupational mobility may be *intergenerational,* involving changes in occupational position as between, say, fathers and sons; or it may be *biographical,* with reference to occupational changes occurring during an individual's own work career.

Occupational mobility may also be viewed from the standpoint of changes that occur in the occupational status of particular groups, or changes in an entire stratum of society. Over a period of time the occupational positions of minority groups may change. Certain European or Asian immigrants who came to the United States as peasant or unskilled workers have moved extensively into middle class occupations. There has also been an upgrading of skilled workers *as an aggregate;* their economic position, at least, is fairly comparable to that of sales and clerical workers who make up, by and large, the lower middle classes in Western society.

MOBILITY AND CHANGES IN OCCUPATIONAL STRUCTURE

Changes in the occupational structure may either restrict or expand opportunities for employment. If the status-bearing occupations are expanding, opportunities for upward mobility, from low-status positions, increase correspondingly. A simple illustration may be to the point. Let us take a sample of 100 employable males, 20 of whom are sons of white collar fathers and 80 of manual fathers. Let us further assume that for this sample of sons there are available 20 white collar and 80 manual jobs. If all the 20 sons of white collar fathers entered white collar occupations, there would be no vacancies for the sons of manual fathers. Even if none of the white collar sons entered these occupations, there would be room for only 20 manual sons. If, however, a change occurred

in the occupational structure resulting in an increase of white collar jobs
for 20 to 50, the opportunities for upward mobility would be increased;
and if other factors were favorable, a substantial portion of the sons of
manual fathers could move up to the white collar level. This oversimplified
illustration does indicate what has happened to the occupational system
in numerous countries and the relation of these changes to occupational
mobility.

The concept of occupational mobility implies a related concept: occupational inheritance (or immobility). In every country, even in the most
dynamic open-class societies, many persons continue, by choice, custom,
or necessity, to follow the vocational careers of their parents. This varies
from one society, community, or occupational class to another. In a study
of occupational differentiation in Mysore City, India, Gist found that less
than one-fourth of the male household heads in the professional, managerial, and clerical occupations were following paternal vocations, but
that two-fifths of those in business and three-fifths of the urban manual
workers had inherited the vocations of their fathers.[9] Yet even in a country so committed to tradition as India, it is significant that so large a
proportion of the male workers had deviated from the parental occupations.

STUDIES IN OCCUPATIONAL MOBILITY

OAKLAND

Occupational mobility of 935 working heads of families in Oakland,
California, was studied in 1945–50 by Lipset and Bendix.[10] Because of
the rapid growth of Oakland's population in recent years, occupational
mobility was probably higher for that city than for communities having a
lower growth rate. Generalizations of the investigators may not therefore
be valid for the urban population as a whole, although in certain respects
Oakland furnishes what may be considered a fairly accurate barometer of
occupational mobility in a dynamic Western city.

The 935 Oakland workers had held an average of 4.8 jobs during their
work careers, which averaged 25 years. Shifting from job to job occurred
most frequently in the high-status groups representing professional, semiprofessional, and white collar workers. Most of these shifts, however,
were intra-occupational. Job shifting of manual workers likewise tended
to be mainly within the same occupational class.

Although there was a good deal of interoccupational mobility, shifts

[9] Noel P. Gist, "Occupational Differentiation in South India," *Social Forces*, 33 (December, 1954), 134.

[10] Seymour M. Lipset and Reinhard Bendix, "Social Mobility and Occupational
Work Careers," *American Journal of Sociology*, 57 (January and March, 1952), 366–
74 and 494–504. Cf. Lipset and Bendix, *Social Mobility in Industrial Society* (1960).

were mainly into an adjacent occupational group, and most of them were temporary. The main cleavage was between manual and nonmanual occupations, a gap that was not often permanently bridged. For example, 62 per cent of the nonmanual workers had spent time in manual occupations, whereas 47 per cent of those who worked with their hands had held nonmanual jobs at some time during their work careers. But when viewed in terms of time spent across the major occupational dividing line (manual–nonmanual), these figures become somewhat less impressive. Of the white collar workers in the sample, 20 per cent of their working time had been spent in manual occupations; manual workers, on the other hand, had spent only 11 per cent of their work careers in white collar jobs.

These percentages varied considerably according to occupational class. Professionals, for example, had spent only about 6 per cent of their careers in manual occupations, semiprofessionals 13 per cent, and upper white collar workers had spent 10 per cent; but lower white collar workers had spent 30 per cent, owners of businesses 26 per cent, and salesmen 21 per cent of their careers in manual occupations.

As the investigators indicate, the real test of vertical occupational mobility is the permanence of the shift. The greatest amount of shifting from the manual to the nonmanual job was to self-employment as an owner of a business, but there was also some movement from manual occupations to lower white collar and sales positions. Such shifting did not necessarily mean that the individual was changing his status and income to any considerable degree, if at all. About one-third of the owners of business reported their previous job as a manual occupation, while one-fifth of the lower white collar workers had held manual positions previous to their present job. But most of the professionals, semiprofessionals, and upper white collar workers were recruited from nonmanual occupations. The channel for upward mobility for the lower white collar workers was mainly through a bureaucratic structure.

Although the shift from manual job to self-employment in Oakland was the most important avenue leading from blue collar to white collar occupations, it was full of pitfalls because of serious risks to the small businessman without much capital. This is evidenced by the frequent shifting from, as well as into, the "own business" category; it is further confirmed by census data on the large number of business failures in the country, even in relatively prosperous times. Yet two-thirds of the manual workers and three-fourths of the salesmen "had thought about" going into business for themselves, risk or no risk. Lipset and Bendix conclude: "Self-employment is one of the few positions of higher status attainable to manual workers. That most of these who try it apparently fail does not change the fact that they do try." [11]

Most of the unskilled and domestic workers in the Oakland sample

[11] Lipset and Bendix, "Social Mobility and Occupational Work Careers," *op. cit.,* pp. 502–3.

began their work on the level of domestic and personal service. Of those who started at this point the majority remained at the same level, although some had moved into the class of unskilled labor.

Children of white collar parents were usually employed on the same occupational levels as their fathers, or else had moved to a higher level, whereas children of manual workers tended to hold jobs on the same plane as their parents or had moved downward. Once a worker started on a particular occupational level there was a tendency for him to remain on that level, although some moved upwards or downwards.

INDIANAPOLIS

An analysis by Rogoff of intergenerational mobility in Indianapolis for 1910 and 1940 revealed no significant change in the pattern during the 30-year period.[12] In Table 14 ratios indicate the extent to which employed persons moved from one broad occupational class of origin to another broad class of destination. The three broad occupational classes were white collar, blue collar, and farming. If movement from one broad class to another was strictly random, with no selectivity involved, the ratio would be 1. But if an occupational class drew heavily or lightly from a class of origin, that is, the father's class, the ratio would be higher or lower than 1.

TABLE 14

Ratios Showing Average Interclass Mobility, Indianapolis, 1910 and 1940

Class of Origin	Class of Destination		
	WHITE COLLAR	BLUE COLLAR	FARMING
1910			
White collar	1.47	0.72	0.20
Blue collar	0.69	0.91	0.14
Farming	0.80	1.10	–
1940			
White collar	1.39	0.59	0.21
Blue collar	0.71	.92	.35
Farming	.70	1.29	–

SOURCE: Natalie Rogoff, *Recent Trends in Occupational Mobility* (1953), p. 60.

The ratio of 1.47, for example, indicates that in 1910 white collar occupations drew their personnel from a broad white collar class (origin) almost one and one-half times as frequently as might be expected on the

[12] Natalie Rogoff, *Recent Trends in Occupational Mobility* (1953).

basis of chance selection. On the other hand, the ratio of .69 indicates that white collar occupations attracted workers from blue collar origins only about two-thirds as frequently as might be expected to occur from chance selection. This pattern was much the same in 1940: corresponding ratios were 1.39 and .71. It is apparent that a major barrier exists between head-work and hand-work occupations. To state the matter differently, sons of white collar workers tend to become white collar workers, whereas sons of blue collar workers tend to remain on that level.

OCCUPATIONAL MOBILITY OF BUSINESS LEADERS

A comprehensive study of occupational mobility, by Warner and Abegglen,[13] was designed as a continuation of an earlier research by Taussig and Joslyn.[14] Warner and Abegglen obtained some 8,300 questionnaire responses from business leaders in 1952, while Taussig and Joslyn received comparable information from a similar number of businessmen in 1928. The two studies taken together represent a major longitudinal research on the occupational mobility of two generations of business elite, mainly executives or proprietors of large establishments in American cities.

Both studies gave considerable attention to the social origins of the men who had attained upper class status and prominence in the business world. A significant finding was that a large proportion of the business elite had fathers who were also businessmen; another finding was the small representation in the business elite of men who were born in working class families. But the fact that the working classes *were* represented indicates that upward mobility from that level has occurred.

Several generalizations may be made from the data in Table 15. First, businessmen, both in 1928 and 1952, were recruited heavily from the business and professional classes. Almost three-fourths of the businessmen in 1928 had fathers in business or the professions, while about two-thirds of the 1952 group came from fathers on these levels. Thus the minority came from fathers on the lower socioeconomic levels. Second, occupational inheritance apparently played an important part, as indicated by the fact that about one-third of the 1928 businessmen and one-fourth of the 1952 group had fathers who were major executives or owners of large businesses. Third, the 1952 businessmen were recruited more heavily from the manual occupations than was the 1928 group; at the same time there was a smaller representation from the higher-level occupations of the fathers, with the exception of professionals. Warner and Abegglen consider this evidence of upward occupational mobility.

[13] W. Lloyd Warner and James C. Abegglen, *Occupational Mobility in American Business and Industry* (1955). A nontechnical volume by the same authors is *Big Business Leaders in America* (1955).

[14] F. W. Taussig and C. S. Joslyn, *American Business Leaders* (1932).

TABLE 15

Percentage Distribution of Occupations of Fathers of Business Leaders in 1928 and 1952

Occupation of Father	Business Leaders	
	PERCENTAGE IN 1928	PERCENTAGE IN 1952
Unskilled or semiskilled laborer	2	5
Skilled laborer	9	10
Farmer	12	9
Clerk or salesman	5	8
Minor executive	7	11 *
Owner of small business	20	17
Major executive	17	15
Owner of large business	14	9
Professional man	13	14
Other	1	2
	100	100

* Foremen included in 1952.
SOURCE: W. Lloyd Warner and James C. Abegglen, *Occupational Mobility in American Business and Industry, 1928–1952* (Minneapolis: University of Minnesota Press, 1955), p. 45. Copyright 1955 by the University of Minnesota.

If the fathers of the businessmen in the two samples had been evenly distributed throughout the occupational hierarchy according to the proportional representation of each occupational class in the total labor force, the business leaders would therefore represent proportionally these occupational classes in the labor force. But actually, the fathers were not evenly distributed throughout the occupational hierarchy. The selective recruitment of business leaders in 1928 and 1952 indicated this uneven distribution. This is shown by Warner and Abegglen in Table 16.

Of the business leaders studied by Taussig and Joslyn in 1928, as indicated above, 58 per cent had fathers who were also business executives, although businessmen were represented by only 6 per cent of the adult male population in 1900 (the census date nearest their average birth date). Dividing 58 by 6 gives a ratio of 9.67. Thus the number of businessmen who were sons of businessmen was over nine times as large as would be expected on the basis of random or chance selection (1.00). In the 1952 group of business leaders, 52 per cent had fathers who were also businessmen, although only 11 per cent of the total labor force was so classified in 1920. In this instance the ratio was 4.73, indicating that the number of businessmen drawn from business families was nearly five times as large as it would have been if random selection had prevailed.

TABLE 16

Occupational Mobility Rates and Ratios: 1928 and 1952 Business Leaders'
Fathers Compared with Adult Males of 1900 and 1920

	1928 Leaders			1952 Leaders		
OCCUPATION	THEIR FATHERS	U.S. ADULT MALES, 1900	RATIOS	THEIR FATHERS	U.S. ADULT MALES, 1920	RATIOS
Business exec- utive	58%	6%	9.67	52%	11%	4.73
Professional	13	3	4.33	14	4	3.50
Farmer	12	38	0.32	9	27	0.33
Laborer	11	45	0.24	15	47	0.32
Clerical, sales	5	7	0.71	8	10	0.80
Other	1	1	–	2	1	–
	100%	100%		100%	100%	

SOURCE: W. Lloyd Warner and James C. Abegglen, *Occupational Mobility in American Business and Industry, 1928–1952* (Minneapolis: University of Minnesota Press, 1955), pp. 46–47. Copyright 1955 by the University of Minnesota.

The professional classes were also heavily represented among the business leaders in 1928 (ratio: 4.33) and 1952 (ratio: 3.50). But falling far below a ratio that would represent even chance selection were farmers, manual laborers, clerical workers, and sales people.

There is, however, some evidence from these data that upward mobility from the low-status occupations did occur between the two periods. Warner and Abegglen interpret these changes to mean that the opportunities for upward mobility from the low-status occupations are increasing. For example, the ratio for laborers in the sample increased from .24 in 1928, to .32 in 1952; or the change in ratio of .71 to .80 for white collar workers. That 15 per cent of the 1952 leaders, as compared with 11 per cent of the 1928 businessmen, came from working class families does indicate that the American success myth is sometimes translated into reality. "In the broadest sense," Warner and Abegglen say, "this research indicates that at the levels studied here, American society is not becoming more caste-like; the recruitment of business leaders from the bottom is taking place now and seems to be increasing." [15] But the authors also add that there is not complete freedom of competition. Men born in high places are specially advantaged, and those born on the lower levels are at a disadvantage in the workaday world.

Cities contributed more than their proportionate share of the business leaders in the Warner-Abegglen sample.[16] Approximately three-fourths

[15] *Ibid.,* p. 36.   [16] *Ibid.,* pp. 86–87.

of the 1952 leaders were born in cities, but as of 1900 (the census year closest to the average birth year of the men), only two-fifths of the population were living in urban communities. Furthermore, the large cities furnished a larger proportionate share of the leaders than did the small cities. One-fourth of the men were born in cities of 400,000 or above, although only one person in 11 in the general population lived in cities of that size in 1900. Thus large cities were represented almost two and one-half times more frequently in business leadership than would be expected on the basis of chance selection. Rural communities were represented less than half as frequently as their proportion of the total population would indicate.

OCCUPATIONAL MOBILITY IN BRITAIN

A sophisticated study in Britain by Glass and his associates gives us a picture both of occupational mobility and of occupational inheritance in that country.[17] This research was conducted in a country that not only has a dynamic open-class system but has been overwhelmingly urban for decades. Mobility, as defined in the study, is concerned with movement across the boundaries of categories of occupations, not into or away from specific occupations. Consequently, the picture is an incomplete and imprecise one: mobility related to particular occupations is concealed in the necessary classification of vocations. Operationally, then, occupational mobility and inheritance for this study are interpreted as movement into or out of the different classes of occupations. The persons in the sample were classified into seven occupational categories, hierarchically arranged as follows:

1. Professional and high administrative
2. Managerial and executive
3. Inspectional, supervisory, and other nonmanual (higher grade)
4. Inspectional, supervisory, and other nonmanual (lower grade)
5. Skilled manual and routine grade of nonmanual
6. Semiskilled manual
7. Unskilled manual

Table 17 shows both inheritance and mobility. The italicized figures refer to the percentage of sons in each occupational class whose fathers were also in the same class. For example, 48.5 per cent of the sons in Class 1 (professional and high administrative) had fathers on the same occupational level. Similarly, 50 per cent of the sons in Class 5 (skilled manual and routine grade of nonmanual) were drawn from families on the same level. This may be defined as occupational-class inheritance.

But the figures above and below those in italics indicate upward or

[17] D. V. Glass, *et al.*, *Social Mobility in Britain* (1954).

TABLE 17

Percentage Distribution of 3,497 British Sons by Occupational Status in Relation to Occupational Class of Their Fathers

Fathers' Occupational Class	*Sons' Occupational Class*						
	1	2	3	4	5	6	7
1	48.5%	11.9%	7.9%	1.7%	1.3%	1.0%	0.5%
2	15.5	25.2	10.3	3.9	2.2	1.4	0.7
3	11.7	22.0	19.7	14.4	8.6	3.9	5.0
4	10.7	12.6	17.6	24.0	15.6	10.8	7.5
5	13.6	22.6	35.5	40.5	50.0	43.5	44.6
6	0.0	3.8	5.8	8.7	12.5	24.1	16.7
7	0.0	1.9	7.0	7.0	9.8	15.3	25.0
	100%	100%	100%	100%	100%	100%	100%
	(103)	(159)	(330)	(459)	(1429)	(593)	(424)

SOURCE: D. V. Glass and J. R. Hall, "Social Mobility in Great Britain: A Study of Inter-Generation Changes in Status," Table 2, p. 183, in D. V. Glass, *et al.*, *Social Mobility in Britain* (London: Routledge & Kegan Paul, 1954).

downward occupational-class mobility. For example, slightly over half (51.5 per cent) of the sons in Class 1 were from fathers on lower occupational levels. Presumably this can be interpreted as upward mobility. It may be significant that no sons in Class 1 came from Class 6 or 7 fathers (semiskilled or unskilled). About one-fourth (27.7 per cent) of Class 5 sons, for example, were recruited from fathers on higher levels. This would be downward mobility. On the other hand, 22.3 per cent of Class 5 sons were from fathers in Class 6 or 7, representing upward mobility. Again, one-fourth of the sons in Class 7 (unskilled) were from unskilled fathers; the other three-fourths were recruited from higher levels, but with only 1.2 per cent from the two top ranks.

AUTOTOWN

The American success myth that everybody has a good chance of succeeding provided he works hard and obeys the boss—or marries his daughter—has had much influence on mobility motivations and interests of many people. But the aspirations born of the "American dream" are often unrelated to the harsh realities of the job. In a study of the aspirations of several hundred automotive workers in a midwestern city, Chinoy found that the opportunities for advancement in the industry were severely limited for the vast majority of them.[18] About all that they could

[18] Ely Chinoy, *Automobile Workers and the American Dream* (1955).

hope for was advancement to the rank of foreman or supervisor, but even the number of these positions was small. Many of the workers, disenchanted by the grim realities of the automotive plant, cherished dreams of leaving the industry and acquiring a small business or farm where they could enjoy independence from the relentless grind of factory work. But most of them were unable to accumulate enough savings for this venture, and those that did attempt to translate their dreams into reality were usually unsuccessful because of inadequate capital or experience, or both. So they usually returned to the industry, wiser and poorer, but resigned to this kind of a life career. Two decades earlier, the Lynds found essentially the same situation in Middletown industrial plants.[19] Most of the industrial workers entered the plant near the bottom of the occupational hierarchy; a few rose to the rank of foremen, but the majority remained on the bottom levels as operatives, until they withdrew for another kind of job or retired. Those who moved up the ladder were usually university-trained persons who entered not at the bottom but higher up, and in a channel that could lead to the top.

SELECTED BIBLIOGRAPHY

BOOKS

Bendix, Reinhard, *Work and Authority in Industry.* New York: Wiley, 1956.
Caplow, Theodore, *The Sociology of Work.* Minneapolis: University of Minnesota Press, 1954.
Chinoy, Ely, *Automobile Workers and the American Dream.* Garden City, N.Y.: Doubleday, 1955.
Drucker, Peter F., *The New Society.* New York: Harper, 1950.
Dubin, Robert, *The World of Work.* Englewood Cliffs, N.J.: Prentice-Hall, 1958.
Edwards, G. Franklin, *The Negro Professional Class.* Glencoe, Ill.: The Free Press, 1959.
Frazier, E. Franklin, *Black Bourgeoisie.* Glencoe, Ill.: The Free Press, 1956.
Mills, C. Wright, *White Collar.* New York: Oxford University Press, 1951.
Warner, W. L., and James C. Abegglen, *Occupational Mobility in American Business and Industry.* Minneapolis: University of Minnesota Press, 1955.
Whyte, William H., Jr., *The Organization Man.* New York: Simon and Schuster, 1956.

ARTICLES

Anderson, C. Arnold, and Mary Jean Bowman, "The Vanishing Servant and the Contemporary System of the American South," *American Journal of Sociology,* 59 (November, 1953), 212–80.
Curtis, R. F., "Occupational Mobility and Urban Social Life," *American Journal of Sociology,* 65 (November, 1959), 296–98.

[19] Robert S. Lynd and Helen M. Lynd, *Middletown in Transition* (1937).

Drucker, Peter F., "The Employee Society," *American Journal of Sociology,* 58 (January, 1953), 358–63.

Foote, Nelson, "The Professionalization of Labor in Detroit," *American Journal of Sociology,* 58 (January, 1953), 372–80.

Gist, Noel P., "Occupational Differentiation in South India," *Social Forces,* 33 (December, 1954), 129–38.

Kaplan, S. J., "Up from the Ranks on a Fast Escalator," *American Sociological Review,* 24 (February, 1959), 79–81.

Bureaucratic Organization

and Power

A distinctive characteristic of an urbanized civilization is large-scale organization. Organizational bigness has been particularly manifest in business, industry, government, labor, religion, and education. These trends have occurred not only in industrial societies but also, to a lesser degree, in predominantly agrarian countries undergoing industrialization and urbanization. Although these countries have not produced industrial and commercial giants to the extent that such organizations have grown in highly urbanized societies, many of them have a governmental apparatus of great complexity and magnitude. In all countries the organizations themselves tend to be centered mainly in larger cities.

THE NATURE OF BUREAUCRATIC ORGANIZATION

The most influential theory of bureaucracy was formulated earlier in the century by the German sociologist Max Weber.[1] This theoretical construct of bureaucratic organization was developed as an ideal-type, which was derived by selecting the most distinctive aspects of a number of different large-scale organizations. The Weberian ideal-type of bureaucratic organization can therefore not be matched in detail with any existing organization, but is intended primarily to provide both a way of perceiving such an organization and a bench mark for examining in detail its structural and functional characteristics. The following generalized statements

[1] Hans Gerth and C. W. Mills (trans.), *From Max Weber: Essays in Sociology* (1946). Cf. Weber, *The Theory of Social and Economic Organization*, trans. A. M. Henderson and Talcott Parsons (1947).

concerning the nature of bureaucratic organization are derived in part from the Weberian theory.

In a bureaucratic organization there is a hierarchy of "offices" representing different levels of authoritative power. There is likewise a hierarchy of statuses in which prestige is distributed among the officeholders according to the values assigned to the roles they perform. Any bureaucratic organization is therefore a system in which rights, privileges, obligations, emoluments, prestige, and power are differentially distributed among personnel.

Bureaucratic organization places a premium on occupational specialization, and most bureaucratic personnel are expected to perform more or less specialized technical functions. The man whose sole function is to install spark plugs in motors as they pass slowly before him on an automotive assembly line exemplifies extreme bureaucratic specialization; but in a somewhat different sense the foreman who supervises the spark plug man is also a bureaucratic specialist, as is the office girl whose sole function is typing letters, or the sales manager whose principal concern is distributing a finished product.

Throughout most of a bureaucratic hierarchy, but particularly on the lower levels, the emphasis is upon routinization of tasks in the interest of efficiency. Mechanization of industrial processes has enhanced this trend, especially in manufacturing; more recently the mechanization of office work has resulted in a similar routinization of clerical tasks. Thus the man on an assembly line has his counterpart in the clerical worker whose sole function is to operate a typewriter, an addressograph, or letter-opening machine.

If a bureaucratic organization is to function effectively, there must be responsible performance of roles. Discipline of personnel is therefore necessary and is manifest in emphasis on punctuality, accuracy, and reliability as correlatives of the routinization of work. The time clock has thus become a symbol of bureaucratic punctuality in urban society.

The hierarchical arrangement of status and power characteristic of a bureaucratic organization is commonly systematized and codified, with specifications for the recruitment, training, assignment, promotion, tenure, and retirement of personnel. In the larger bureaucracies there are specified grades or ranks representing different levels of prestige, authority, and income accorded particular roles. A municipal government bureaucracy is an example.

The hierarchy of authority within a bureaucratic organization is likewise systematized into a complex of rules and regulations that define the forms and limits of power an individual has over others—a "pecking order," so to speak. At the peak of the pyramid is the executive, or administrator, or general manager whose authority often encompasses the entire structure; at the bottom are workers who are devoid of any authoritative power, but who nevertheless have certain contractual rights as well as obligations. Between the two extremes most individuals occupy a "pecking position" both of subordination and superordination.

A bureaucracy organized as a behavior system of statuses, roles, and authority is commonly segmentalized into bureaus, departments, agencies, or divisions of one kind or another, depending on the size and functions of a particular organization. These divisional bureaus or departments are themselves aspects of bureaucratic specialization.

Bureaucratic structures may be either public or private. Big business or industry or labor, as private bureaucracies, have their counterparts in big government—public bureaucracy. But bureaucratic structures are by no means independent of or indifferent to other bureaucracies. Bureaucrats in municipal government are commonly men with connections in business or industrial bureaucracies; as government bureaucrats they are in a favorable position to serve certain private bureaucratic organizations. The close tie-in of urban political machines with the bureaucracies of business and industry is well known in urban America.

If the central feature of bureaucracy is formal organization and a hierarchy of authority and status, within this framework there is an informal organization in which relationships between personnel tend to be intimate. Such informal organization, as we have seen, commonly assumes the form of cliques, friendship pairs, and casual visiting relationships among workers having close association on the job. These informal relationships within a bureaucratic structure constitute important channels of communication. Because of their intimate character they tend to soften the harshness of a formal organization that emphasizes impersonal relationships, glorifies efficiency, and isolates personnel on different levels of authority and prestige.

BUREAUCRACY AND EFFICIENCY

There is a widely-held notion that bureaucratic organization is inefficient, almost synonymous with red tape, and that bureaucrats are the overlords responsible for this inefficiency. Actually, bureaucracy may be the most effective form of organization for getting certain things done. Given the conditions of modern mass society, in which specialization and interdependence are basic characteristics, it is doubtful if many institutional functions could be performed as needed except through the mechanism of large-scale organization. The mass production and distribution of, say, automobiles could hardly be accomplished without an industrial bureaucracy to perform these functions; nor could modern government provide all the services and perform all the functions expected of it except through the mechanism of such a complex organization.

This does not mean that a particular bureaucracy is necessarily efficient in carrying out its prescribed functions. Red tape does exist. Stresses and strains do occur between individuals or groups within the organization. Individuals may be incompetent or indifferent. Roles may not be effectively coordinated, or skills effectively used. Activities may be dysfunctional as well as functional. But with all the limitations virtually inherent in bureaucratic organization, such a system is indispensable under modern conditions.

BUREAUCRACY AND POWER

If bureaucracy is indispensable in modern society, it may nevertheless represent such a concentration of potential power that it threatens existing values or even the existing system. It may be either a force for social change or it may harness its forces to resist social change, even change in the public interest. Generally speaking, bureaucracies are strongholds of conservatism, partly because the policymakers of such organizations represent vested interests which they are reluctant to change. Reform movements in almost every city have invariably been opposed by one or more bureaucratic organizations which claim to function in the public interest. "What is good for General Motors is good for the country!"

A bureaucracy may at the same time be both democratic and authoritarian. Its personnel may be selected impersonally, and democratically, on the basis of competence rather than prejudice or pull, but its policies and practices may be authoritarian in nature, formulated and carried out by the managerial elite who sit in the seats of power. Unless restrained by counterforces, bureaucratic power may become tyranny, benevolent or otherwise. With impressive rhetoric, Mills has written of the great bureaucratic strongholds, in American society, of interlocking economic, political, and military power.[2] To him, this interlocking system of power represents a grave threat to the traditional values of the American system.

CHANGES IN STRUCTURE AND FUNCTIONS

The continuous structural-functional changes have witnessed the emergence of new bureaucratic organizations and the expansion or contractions of functions of those already in existence. Out of the competitive-cooperative processes of modern urban society have come coalitions of organizations that challenge or threaten other coalitions. These coalitions sometimes present a formidable combination of power.

Within and between bureaucracies there is an interdependent and interlocking relationship, even among organizations that are competitive. In the modern metropolis, for example, economic organizations are interlaced with the governmental bureaucracy, and both of these exist in a

[2] C. Wright Mills, *The Power Elite* (1956).

state of partial interdependence with complex organizations in other spheres of community life, such as education or welfare. This interdependent relationship may transcend community boundaries and become national in scope. It is through this interlocking system that institutional integration is achieved not only within cities and towns but also in the larger society.

THE PROFESSIONAL MANAGER

The rise of modern bureaucracies has been accompanied by the growth of an influential occupational class: the professional manager. In industrialized and urbanized countries, managers have come to occupy key positions in the institutional structure and community life. Dubin cites estimates to the effect that during the first 50 years of the present century the number of administrative workers for each 100 production workers in industry more than doubled, increasing from 10 to 22; [3] Bendix observed similar trends in Great Britain, Germany, France, and Sweden.[4] The rapid increase in the number of professional "city managers" in American municipalities during the past three or four decades is another indication of this trend.

BUREAUCRATIZATION OF WHITE COLLAR WORKERS AND PROFESSIONALS

The development of great corporate entities, especially in business and government, has proceeded *pari passu* with the expansion of the white collar occupations. Personnel attached to the office force of these bureaucracies carry on endless paper work: issuing, copying, and channeling directives to the proper functionaries; reading and writing letters; sealing and opening envelopes; billing clients; keeping accounts; filing records. Except for the decision-makers on the managerial levels, the tasks become highly routinized.

The growth of bureaucratic organization in government and business has meant larger office forces and consequently the development of intricate status systems within each bureaucratic structure. The office manager, as Mills points out,[5] is clothed with authority and is responsible to his superiors for the proper functioning of lesser personnel. Fairly high in the status system is the private secretary or administrative assistant, whose power is limited but whose closeness to managerial authority affords that office a considerable degree of prestige. Below this level are the office girls—operators of office machinery, stenographers, file clerks, typists,

---

[3] Robert Dubin, *The World of Work* (1958), p. 366.
[4] Reinhard Bendix, *Work and Authority in Industry* (1956), pp. 214–20.
[5] C. Wright Mills, *White Collar* (1951).

White collar workers in a bureaucracy. Clerical workers in large city offices
are commonly skilled operatives of machinery. Tasks are highly standardized
and routinized, and clerks as well as machines are easily replaceable. White
collar clerks thus have much in common with factory operatives. (Courtesy
Remington Rand Office Systems.)

telephone operators, receptionists. They represent, in a real sense, a white
collar proletariat whose rather considerable skill makes them indispensable for the bureaucracy but whose occupational status is fairly low.

The development of an employee society in the United States has resulted in extensive bureaucratization of the older professions. An illustration of this trend is the increasing proportion of salaried professionals, probably most of them bureaucratic employees. As Mills points
out, the proportion of independent or "free" professionals has remained
about constant over the past two generations, about 1 per cent of the
labor force; but the proportion of salaried professionals has increased from
1 to about 6 per cent of all persons at work, and from 4 to 14 per cent
of all middle class persons in the labor force.[6]

Although professionals as a class are highly specialized, they have resisted bureaucratization more effectively than either blue collar workers
or nonprofessional white collar personnel. The very term "free" or "independent" professional attests to this resistance. Probably the legal pro-
fession has shown the least tendency toward bureaucratization of any of
the major professional groups. Yet the metropolitan "law factory" with its

[6] *Ibid.,* p. 63.

junior and senior partners, salaried associates, young apprentice lawyers, office managers, and clerical personnel is evidence of a bureaucratic tendency.[7] Physicians have likewise retained much of their professional independence, but there are many large medical firms with varied specialized personnel, and almost all doctors are integrated into hospital or clinical organizations having an array of functionaries with different levels or kinds of skill. Such professionals as teachers, ministers, and social workers have undergone bureaucratization to a far greater degree than physicians and lawyers. Public school teachers in cities almost invariably function as a part of a large bureaucratic organization with its boards, administrators, supervisors, clerical personnel, and manual workers. This tendency in the social service professions is in general true of engineers, accountants, journalists, even research scientists.

TYPES OF BUREAUCRATIC STRUCTURES

THE MODERN CORPORATION AS A BUREAUCRACY

Growth of large corporate bureaucracies is evidenced by employment trends according to occupational classes. In 1939, 1 per cent of all the 27,000 companies in the United States employed over half of all the workers engaged in business activities. In contrast, the 1,500,000 one-man enterprises accounted for only 6 per cent of the total number of people working in business.[8] Chains of merchandising establishments, financial houses, hotels, newspapers, theaters; giant department stores and supermarkets, often operated on the chain principle; gigantic corporations in the fields of transportation and communication—these bureaucratic structures have become familiar features of the American urban scene. Especially pronounced is the trend toward bureaucratic organization of manufacturing. Small industrialists still exist, performing important functions; but more and more the organization of industry has become bureaucratic and monopolistic. Through mergers, combinations, and interlocking controls, bureaucratic superstructures of almost fantastic magnitude and complexity have arisen. A number of years ago Berle and Means estimated that the 200 largest corporations in the United States, with combined assets of 81 billion dollars, controlled about half of the non-banking corporate wealth of the country; the remaining half was owned by about 300,000 smaller companies.[9] In 1957–58, the 28 largest firms in manufacturing, merchandising, transportation, and utilities had a total of

---

[7] Walter I. Wardwell, "Social Integration, Bureaucratization, and the Professions," *Social Forces*, 33 (May, 1955), 356–59.

[8] See especially Mills, *White Collar, op. cit.*, for a brilliant discussion of these trends.

[9] The classic study of Berle and Means, *The Modern Corporation and Private Property* (1937), records in great detail the bureaucratic developments in the American economy up to the middle 1930's.

three and one-half million employees, and the total assets of nine corporations amounted to 100 billion dollars.[10] General Motors alone has
260,000 employees.

Viewed from the standpoint of internal organization, a business or industrial bureaucracy is a complex of coordinated departments or divisions
each with its hierarchy of personnel. The specific hierarchical pattern, or
the nature of relationships between departments and personnel, varies
with the particular bureaucracy. In industrial bureaucracies there is commonly an organizational dichotomy consisting of a "line" and a "staff"
organization.[11] The line organization, directly responsible for production,
features a hierarchy of personnel ranging from the president, vice-presi-
dents, department heads, foremen, supervisors, and timekeepers to the
workers. In the staff organization, which features specialized or technical
services, the hierarchy runs from the president down through the various
specialists and divisional chiefs such as engineers, cost accountants, sales
managers, research men, personnel managers, private secretaries, clerical
workers, and so on. Save for those on the higher echelons, bureaucratic
personnel function within the confines of a particular department or division.

Merchandising or financial bureaucracies are of course structured differently. In what Mills calls the Great Salesroom [12] (department store) there
are, in addition to the usual top-level executives and boards of control,
buyers, statisticians, market research specialists, personnel managers,
bookkeepers, stenographers, salesgirls (or men), and other functionaries,
including those not directly related to selling. Even local chain establishments such as grocery or drug stores are simply functional units of a
large bureaucracy in which the principle of a hierarchical structure is
carried out. In the large office such as an insurance or investment corporation there is likewise a hierarchy of personnel and departments, with
increasing emphasis upon routinization of clerical work through the use
of mechanical office equipment.

GOVERNMENTAL BUREAUCRACY

Bureaucratic expansion in the American economy has been closely associated with the growth of government bureaucracies. The increase in
the number and character of services provided by government on all
levels has magnified the structural complexity of political organization
to a degree that would have hardly been anticipated a half-century ago.
More than 6,000,000 persons are gainfully employed in government serv-

---

[10] C. Lowell Harris, *The American Economy* (1959), pp. 116–17.
[11] Delbert C. Miller and William H. Form, *Industrial Sociology* (1951), pp. 154–56.
Cf. Wilbert Moore, *Industrial Relations and the Social Order* (1946), ch. 6.
[12] *White Collar*, ch. 8.

ice, most of them being residents of cities and working organizations whose functions are mainly carried out in urban communities. The expansion of various services, some of them hitherto considered the exclusive function of private enterprise, has resulted in the multiplication of agencies, bureaus, departments, and administrative divisions operated by personnel occupying different positions and performing different work roles in the bureaucratic hierarchy.

The complexity of organization apparently tends to increase with the size of the city. In a typical American metropolis the various specialized bureaus or divisions concern themselves with such matters as finance, police protection, public health, traffic control, housing, public works, utilities, education, parks and recreation, the courts, and personnel. Viewing the bureaucracy in its entirety, there is a stratification of authority in which the supreme power of policymaking is vested in a board (sometimes called a commission or council); and in some communities the responsibility for activating and enforcing these policies is delegated to a professional manager. In addition to the employed personnel there are various boards composed partly or entirely of citizens who contribute their time and knowledge.

Supplementing the bureaucratic structure of formal government is the party organization, which in a large city, and even in smaller ones, may be complex. At the base of the organizational pyramid is the precinct worker whose responsibility is to get out the vote in his political division. A little higher up the political pyramid is the ward committeeman, usually a precinct executive who has been promoted because of his diligence and success. His duty is to supervise the precinct workers who operate within his political domain. At the apex of the political pyramid is the boss, the generalissimo of the party. The local party organization is, of course, an integral part of a bureaucracy that is national in scope.

LABOR BUREAUCRACY

One of the newest and most influential bureaucratic structures is the organization of workers. With a membership of about 18,000,000 persons, including about 2,500,000 white collar workers, trade unions in the United States have been mainly a development in large and middle-sized cities. Beginning as a labor movement, trade unions grew rapidly after 1933, becoming increasingly bureaucratized as they gained in size, economic strength, and public acceptance. The organizational transition from social movement to bureaucracy is not yet complete, since at least half of the nation's wage earners and four-fifths of the white collar workers are not identified with a union; but the very existence of some 200 national unions having a formal structure characterized by a hierarchy of power and status is evidence of the bureaucratic trend. Most of these national unions themselves are part of a larger bureaucratic superstructure. The merger in 1955 of the A.F.L. and C.I.O. was a major step toward greater economic and political power through sheer size of labor organization.

Bureaucratization of labor unions in the United States is a matter of degree, varying according to the size and other characteristics of the unions. In a few large national unions, according to Wilensky, bureaucracy is full-blown; in others, bureaucratic features are less developed.[13] But the trend toward bureaucracy is present in all.

In highly bureaucratized unions there is a hierarchy of administrative and supervisory functionaries with specialized roles. Included, also, are such specialized "experts" as accountants, economists, negotiators, trouble-shooters, and so on, in addition to a battery of clerical personnel at the bottom levels of the structure. The division of labor is further exhibited in departments having their own particular functions and specialized personnel. Within the organization there are formalized policies and procedures concerning recruitment, training, promotions, salary and wage scales, tenure, and work roles of the staff and rank-and-file members; externally, there are policies with respect to relations with management and the community at large.

But the foregoing picture is only partially correct, for most unions are not so formally structured. Says Wilensky: "Typically, the division of labor in the national headquarters is still not sharp; the hierarchy of authority not clear-cut. Jobs are loosely defined; jurisdictional areas, even if official, are blurred and shifting. It tries the patience of the participants to figure out the office hierarchy."[14] Contacts with and between officials are often informal, and the influence of the officers is commonly exerted through these informal channels. "Whether they find the process comfortable or not, the experts recognize the importance of the thousands of casual deliverances of opinion in sustained, direct, informal contact with the boss and other line officials."[15]

BUREAUCRATIZATION OF EDUCATION

Urbanization in the modern world has invariably been associated with mass education. Under conditions of city life in a mass society, the educational process cannot be carried out on a mass basis following the simple formula of Mark Hopkins on one end of a log and a student on the other. There must be organization, and large-scale organization at that. To provide educational services appropriate for such a society, an organizational system capable of performing diverse functions has been developed. This

[13] Harold L. Wilensky, *Intellectuals in Labor Unions* (1956), pp. 243–58.
[14] *Ibid.*, p. 249.   [15] *Ibid.*, p. 252.

system is usually part of a government apparatus, although much education is carried on under the auspices of private organizations that may also be bureaucratic in character.

Every American city—and probably most cities in other countries—has a bureaucratic educational organization, its size and complexity depending in the main on the size of the community. This organization provides not only the traditional educational services to all the people but in addition new forms of education unknown to an agrarian society. From kindergarten to college and beyond, these services are offered: regular day schools, night schools, schools for adults, and classes for the mentally and physically handicapped, trade schools and technical schools, special schools for unadjusted children, and schools for adults on higher educational levels.

A veritable army of bureaucratic functionaries, organized hierarchically, is necessary to provide these services. Major policymaking functions are performed by a board whose members are usually elected to office by popular vote of local citizens. Immediate responsibility for carrying out these functions is centered in a hierarchy of professional administrators, who are accorded the necessary authoritative power to keep the system functioning. These include a superintendent, assistant superintendent, principals, and various specialized supervisors of teaching personnel, directors of special curricula, and managers concerned with maintaining the physical equipment. The production workers are the teachers. In addition, there are clerical personnel who do the necessary paper work, and manual workers responsible for the physical operation and maintenance of school facilities. The functions of these personnel must be coordinated within an organizational framework toward the stated objectives of education.

BUREAUCRATIC ORGANIZATION AND SOCIAL WELFARE

Welfare functions have likewise been organized as public and private bureaucracies. Public welfare organization, like public education, is an instrumentality of government and a part of the governmental apparatus; private welfare is privately financed and administered within and by an organization detached from government. Although most private welfare is independently organized, a considerable amount of welfare work is done under the auspices of religious, labor, and fraternal organizations.

The scope and character of activities subsumed under the general category of "welfare" go far beyond what would have been considered appropriate or necessary in a simple agrarian society. There are services for families in need or in trouble, services for the homeless, aged, and physically handicapped, and services concerned with mental and physical illness. Included also are various recreational activities. Obviously such diverse functions can be effectively performed by specialized personnel working within an organizational framework. There are, for example, family case workers, psychiatric social workers, medical social workers, child welfare specialists, visiting teachers, group workers, psychiatrists, probation officers, vocational counsellors, physical therapists, clinical psychologists, and so on. These specialists usually carry on their work in organizations which are themselves integral parts of larger citywide, statewide, or even national or international structures.

In many cities, central agencies have been established whose chief duty is to formulate programs of cooperative endeavor. A central administrative group, generally known as a council of social agencies or welfare council, serves to coordinate the activities of constituent organizations and in some instances exercises certain supervisory functions over their financial affairs. In St. Louis, for example, nearly a hundred organizations constitute a federation of social work agencies. In large cities, agencies doing a specialized type of work usually unite in organizations bearing such names as the Child Welfare Federation or the Association of Day Nurseries. Social service exchanges are maintained in some cities as clearinghouses for information concerning clients served by different agencies. Many of the local organizations or their personnel are identified with national, regional, or state federations such as the American Public Welfare Association, the Child Welfare League of America, National Urban League, or the National Federation of Settlements.

Public welfare bureaucracies in the United States are rather tightly structured, with a complex hierarchy of functionaries in which the chain of administrative command stretches from the local organization to the state or national level in a gigantic social security system. Private welfare bureaucratic organizations tend to be loosely structured, at least so far as interorganizational relationships are concerned, many of them being established on the federated principle.

The organization of health is closely dovetailed with other forms of welfare organization in American cities. Health activities are organized on both a private and a public basis, but public health organization assumes more the character of a bureaucracy than do private medical groups. Thus, there may be municipal bureaus concerned with sanitation, food, drugs, communicable diseases, child hygiene, nursing, and vital statistics. On the policymaking level there is usually a health board or a health officer with authority to direct and coordinate the work of personnel on the staff. Such personnel are themselves commonly affiliated with organizations like the American Public Health Association, National Committee of Health Council Executives, National Organization for Public Health Nursing, and the like.

BUREAUCRATIC TRENDS IN RELIGION

Viewed as a behavioral phenomenon, religion in modern urban society has assumed organizational patterns featuring hierarchies of power and status. In many European countries, organized religion is closely identified with the state, but in the United States religious organizations have had no formal connection with either municipal or national governmental structures. Although the trend is toward large-scale organization, by no means are all organized religious groups bureaucratic in structure. In an American metropolis numerous small sects and cults are completely independent or at best have tenuous connections with related groupings.

In large religious denominations, however, are exemplified organizations in various stages of bureaucratization. Usually the organization extends beyond any single community, assuming the form of a state, regional, national, or even international bureaucracy. One of the most complex bureaucracies is the Roman Catholic Church, a tightly structured international organization with a hierarchy of functionaries ranging from the papal father to the lowly parish priest. In this ecclesiastical hierarchy the flow of authority is from the highest office down through the various ranks of the members. Numbers of Protestant bodies are likewise organized as bureaucracies, but none of them has as elaborate an apparatus for carrying out stated religious functions as the Roman Catholic Church. Most of the Protestant denominations, while evolving toward large-scale organization, are loosely structured on federated principles, with functionaries and members having considerable autonomy in action or belief.[16] A few, such as the Society of Friends, have no formal priesthood. On the other hand, the Salvation Army has a quasi-military structure with centralized authority and with the various ranks of functionaries designated by military titles and insignia.

Coincident with the trend toward bureaucracy has been an expansion of functions far beyond the scope of traditional religious organization. Indeed, the multifunctional character of many religious bodies is facilitated or made possible by the bureaucratic type of structure. In the large American city church, such functions may include, in addition to religious worship, various forms of secular recreational activities, psychiatric services, educational programs, welfare activities, and the like. Churches often maintain day nurseries, children's homes, homes for the aged, publishing firms, hotels for youth, Bible schools, and so on. Manifestly, such diverse functions can be carried out only through the medium of a departmentalized organization and by a staff of specialized personnel. In addition to lay officials and regular pastors or rabbis, there are numerous others, such as nuns, deaconesses, home visitors, nursery matrons, psychiatrists, rec-

[16] Robin Williams, *American Society* (1951), pp. 324–25.

reational directors, Sunday school teachers, and secretaries who perform particular services.

BUREAUCRATIC COORDINATING ORGANIZATIONS

Many bureaucratic organizations in American cities are linked together in a state, regional, national, or international network. One example of such a development is the chain type of organization which has local units in various communities or in different sections of the same city. Some grocery corporations have thousands of local stores whose functions are integrated through a complex organizational structure composed of regional and national offices. These structures are interlaced with other organizations in such fields as finance, manufacturing, and transportation.

Although such chain organizations are competitive with other organizations in the same general area of the economy, presumably they can function most effectively through some kind of associational superstructure. Thus a national association of retail grocers, while composed of competing grocers and grocer organizations, represents a cooperative undertaking to further the interests of affiliated merchants. The United States is overlaid with organizational networks of this type.

These superstructures have numerous functions, but a major purpose is the coordination of activities performed by member organizations. They also serve as propaganda agencies to further the interest of constituent members, frequently maintaining lobbies to influence the course of legislation on a municipal, state, or national level.

Types of Organizations

A survey by the U. S. Department of Commerce revealed the existence of some 4,000 national organizations representing industry, trade, transportation, the professions, labor, agriculture, government, recreation, the military, women, racial and ethnic groups, veterans, fraternalists, and so on.[17] In addition to the national organizations listed, the survey also indicated the existence of upwards of 200,000 local bodies and branch chapters, including 12,000 trade associations, 4,000 chambers of commerce, 70,000 labor unions, 100,000 women's organizations, and 15,000 civic service groups, luncheon clubs, and similar groups of business or professional men and women.

These organizations are thus supported by many thousands of local organizations. In some instances the superstructure assumes a pyramidal arrangement, with local organizations at the base and state or regional associations occupying an intermediary position between the local and

[17] Jay Judkins, *National Associations of the United States* (1949).

national or international levels. Thus, local medical organizations in a particular city support one or more state or regional associations in addition to a national organization. Many cities themselves are members of a statewide league of municipalities, which in turn make up a national league. An endless variety of structural patterns exists, ranging from superstructures with concentrations of power to others that are loosely organized as federations. Most of the organizations have incorporated into their titles words such as association, associated, united, league, union, bureau, institute, society, council, or exchange. The wide range of organized activities represented by these associations may be noted in their very titles: American Dog Feed Institute, National Institute of Diaper Services, Associated Credit Bureaus of America, National Association for the Advancement of Colored People, American Newspapers Publishers' Association, National Congress of Parents and Teachers, National Association of Manufacturers, League of Distilled Spirits Rectifiers, American Society of Lubricating Engineers, Congress of Industrial Organizations, American Association of University Professors, and so on.

Although local organizations may be either urban or rural, predominantly they are urban. State, regional, or national associations are almost invariably located in cities, most of them in large metropolitan centers. In a random sample of 653 national associations selected from Judkins' list, about two-fifths were in metropolitan New York, one-sixth were in Chicago, and one-eighth in Washington. These three cities, together with Philadelphia, Cleveland, Detroit, and Boston, accounted for about three-fourths of the headquarters of national associations in the sample. This associational development has been fairly recent: only about one-tenth were established before 1900, but 45 per cent were organized between 1930 and 1949.

THE POWER STRUCTURE

Social power, by definition, refers to the capacity of an individual or group to command a particular behavior or performance among others. Such power is an inherent element in all social organization, whether rural or urban, primitive or modern. The growth of large-scale bureaucracies as a concomitant of urbanization has made the phenomenon of social power increasingly important.

There are different sources of power, and different ways in which power may be manifest or circumscribed. We are here concerned with authority, or authorized power. Every bureaucracy represents a pyramidal graduation of power by which certain individuals are accorded authority over others. One aspect of power is the decision-making function. The authority to make decisions as well as to carry them out is necessary for the functioning of a bureaucratic organization.

Bureaucratic authority is often slanted both inwardly and outwardly. Within the structure of the system, power means that certain individuals have authority to command a particular form of behavior or service from others, who in turn are obligated to conform to the commands as long as they remain a part of the organization. Such authority may also carry the right to hire and fire. Authority slanted outwardly means that certain individuals who represent a group or organization in its external relations have power to make decisions, exert economic or political pressure, or even use naked force. Thus a corporation or labor executive may not only have authority over others within his organization; he may also be authorized to use certain means to secure the compliance of outsiders.

COMMUNITYWIDE POWER

Supplementing the formal power structures of municipal government and business or industrial bureaucracies is a power system which tends to be somewhat amorphously structured. Many important decisions applying to an entire community are commonly made outside any bureaucratic framework. A decision to float a bond issue, or to have the voters pass judgment on such a proposal, for example, may be made informally by men of prestige and institutional power and transmitted to government bureaucrats for official action. Even though certain decisions affecting an entire community may be made by a small coterie of individuals, often on an informal basis outside the framework of government, community acceptance of such decisions may be decided by a popular vote of the citizens. Free play is thus afforded pressure groups, through propaganda and other devices, to influence community sentiment in support of, or in opposition to, a proposal presented by the decision-makers. No such democratic procedure ordinarily obtains in a business or industrial bureaucracy.

PROBLEMS AND METHODS OF RESEARCH

Most of the research on community power systems has been done fairly recently, although as early as the 1930's the Lynds did their classic studies of Middletown (Muncie, Indiana) in which they analyzed the power system of a medium-sized city.[18] Some two decades later Hunter published his influential study of Regional City (Atlanta, Georgia).[19] Since then, other researches, employing different hypotheses and methods, have been carried on in cities of the United States and Europe. Among the questions that have lent themselves to investigation are:

[18] Robert S. Lynd and Helen M. Lynd, *Middletown in Transition* (1937).
[19] Floyd Hunter, *Community Power Structure* (1953).

a. Is there a single, monolithic, hierarchically structured power system in a community, or are there different power structures, the number and nature depending on the character of the institutional system?

b. Who are the power elite, and how do they exercise power in terms of decision-making and control of institutional functions?

c. To what extent are there interlocking power positions which include authority derived from the economic, political, and social institutions?

d. In what way is a community power structure interlaced with a regional or national power system?

e. What methods and approaches are most effective in the study of community power, and with what results?

How are the roles performed in decision-making and in other manifestations of community power? Is the decision a "one-man show," and the decision-maker a "lone wolf"; or is decision-making a joint undertaking by a few "kingmakers" who operate overtly as teams or covertly in cliques? In the earlier days of political bossism, some of the cities in the United States were ruled autocratically by powerful machine politicians. Tom Pendergast in Kansas City, Edward Vare in Philadelphia, Ed Crump in Memphis, and Big Bill Thompson in Chicago were, each in his own way, undisputed rulers of municipal "empires." But those days have vanished, along with their all-powerful bosses. If the old-style political boss has made his demise, who has replaced him and how does he (or they) operate? In the following discussion, reference will be made to several empirical studies which have attempted to find answers to this difficult question.

Several methods for identifying the power elite of a community have been employed, but three principal ones may be mentioned:

a. The *reputational* method by which a panel identifies the power elite, that is, the leaders and decision-makers in matters pertaining to the community;

b. The *positional* method by which the power elite are identified as the major administrative personnel in the principal organizations of the community;

c. The *functional* approach by which the power elite is identified on the basis of their participation or functions in the decision-making process involving community affairs.

Whatever the strengths or weaknesses of each of these methods (or any variations thereof) may be, the fact remains that the end results tend to differ considerably. The reputational method is highly subjective, depending on the evaluations by a panel of judges who may or may not be qualified to identify the elite. On the other hand, those in high positions in local institutions may not participate in the decision-making processes for the community, but only for their own particular organization. The functional approach may yield valuable information on the exercise of power and the making of decisions only in certain kinds of, but not all, community affairs.

The conflicting findings in the researches reported may reflect in part the differences in community structures, in part the actual methods of study employed. The Lynds and Hunter are not necessarily wrong either in their findings or interpretations of power in Middletown and Regional City. It is highly probable that such power systems do exist, though if different methods of research had been employed in Middletown and Regional City the results might have been different. Continued research should provide a more complete picture of the power systems in a variety of American communities, and similar studies in cities elsewhere would also be revealing. It is through such research that a theory of community power can be developed.

THE STRUCTURE OF POWER IN AMERICAN CITIES

MIDDLETOWN

In *Middletown in Transition* the Lynds described the power system and the way it functioned, using a combination of the positional-functional approach. They identified the power elite as a kinship group (consisting of three brothers and their respective conjugal families) which they refer to anonymously as the X family. Much of the Lynds' analysis is concerned with the "operations" of members of the power elite in the community. Their interpretation is that the X family constituted a highly cohesive power group whose overshadowing influences were felt in many aspects of community life, and that the system as it existed in the 1930's was virtually all-powerful. The Lynds, however, gave scant attention to other facets of the system, particularly to men of power who were not members of the paternalistic X family. What changes have occurred in the system since the study was made three decades ago we do not know. It is possible that the structure as it exists in the 1960's is very different inasmuch as the rise of powerful labor unions has added a new dimension to the power system of many industrial communities. At any rate, the Middletown system as described by the Lynds is (or was) an example of a monolithic power structure in a city dominated by a single type of industry.

The basis of the X family's power lay in the ownership and control of wealth and credit. The family collectively owned a large glass plant, a paper-board factory, and the city's interconnecting railroad. Three members of the family were on the board of directors of a major bank; one of them, the chairman, was on the board of directors of a trust company affiliated with the bank. A son and a son-in-law were also members of the board of directors of the trust company; in addition, a son was director of a building and loan association, and two other sons were directors of a small loan company. Individually or collectively the X family owned the largest department store in the city, two modern dairy farms, a large block of stock in the morning daily newspaper, considerable real estate, and an interest in a brewery in a neighboring city. One member of the family was director of the city's leading furniture store. Members of the foremost law firms were retained to look after the family's diversified interests. One of the lawyers in this firm was also city attorney.

Members of the X family were active in civic and political activities. At the time of the study one member of the family was president of the local school board, and another, a lawyer, was attorney for the Middletown school system. Several X members were on boards of various charitable organizations, and one was serving as park commissioner. A member of the X clan was a Republican National Committeeman, and another was prominent in the local Democratic organization.

Philanthropic contributions were both diverse and generous. The family contributed one and one-half million dollars for a city hospital, and another million dollars to the state toward development of the X Teachers College in Middletown. Money was also supplied for the construction of a gymnasium and arts building. Structures for the Y.M.C.A. and Y.W.C.A. were contributed by the family, and funds were donated for an animal pound, a field house, an athletic field, an armory, a children's recreation center, two summer camps, and a Masonic temple. In addition, the family gave land for an airport, a city golf course, and an American Legion building, and through the X foundation, grants were made to the community chest and various welfare activities. Contributions were also reportedly made to both Republican and Democratic party organizations.

That the X family possessed great power seems evident from the foregoing facts. Precisely how this power was exercised in specific situations is not clearly revealed. Some of the power lay in corporate ownership and control, and the substantial wealth accruing from this ownership and control contributed to the family's unrivalled prestige. This power of ownership was strongly buttressed by control of credit facilities through important connections with financial establishments. By means of credit control especially, the X family was in a position to exert great influence on the economic life of the community.

Charitable and philanthropic contributions plus memberships in various civic and political bodies also gave the family a strong voice in community affairs, although undoubtedly much of the family's influence was informal. The Lynds report, for example, that both personnel and policies of the two "Y" organizations were carefully scrutinized by the X family. That the philosophy and ideas of members of the family entered into decisions made in the fields of education and communication was strongly indicated by the data.

The Lynds are careful to emphasize that the power held by members of the X family was not obtained by connivance of kin, nor was there anything malevolent about it. Individual members of the kinship group were not always in accord in their ideas, and the roles they played were diverse and sometimes uncoordinated. Much of their behavior was undoubtedly motivated by ideals of community service and humanitarian sympathies. But even the community services rendered by various members contributed to the enhancement of their power and prestige, and therefore supplemented the great power held by them through controls over the city's economic life.

REGIONAL CITY

In his study of the power elite in Regional City, Hunter employed the reputational method of identifying the wielders of power.[20] Persons who made the major decisions affecting all or a considerable part of a community were designated the power elite. Closely related to them in the power structure but lower than the major policymaking level were persons whose principal functions were the execution and reinforcement of policy formulated on the higher echelons. Hunter sought, first, to identify the major decision-makers and, second, to describe the actual processes of power formulation and execution.

Identification of specific power leaders was made by citizens familiar with the local community. The list of power leaders in the white community was reduced to 40 persons who figured prominently in the decision-making processes. A similar method was followed by identifying power leaders in the Negro community, which the author refers to as a subcommunity.

Upper-echelon power leaders in the white community were recruited mainly from the business class. Of the 40 power leaders studied, there were 11 executives of commercial enterprises, seven officers of banking and investment houses, five industrialists, four government officials, two labor leaders, six professional persons, and five "leisured" individuals whose leadership derived from membership in social or civic organizations. Five of the professionals were attorneys closely connected with major economic establishments, and one was a dentist. The four government officials included the mayor, city treasurer, and city and country school superintendents. Among the businessmen was the managing editor of a publishing company, but there were no ministers, physicians, or social workers.

The occupational composition of the 24 Negro leaders was quite different. In this group there were 19 professionals, eight businessmen, three banking and insurance executives, two "leisured" persons, one civic

[20] Hunter, *op. cit.*

worker (a retired postal employee), and one politician. Among the professionals were a physician, a lawyer, four educators, six ministers, and seven social workers.

Below the major men of power in the white community was an understructure whose power leadership was represented mainly by professional men and women. This was mainly a level of policy execution rather than policy formulation. In fact, upper-level policymakers depended on the power understructure to put into force the major decisions. For the most part the professionals in the understructure were salaried persons of limited means; in contrast, most of the major men of power possessed considerable wealth and were themselves at the peak of a power pyramid, usually an industrial or business organization, from which position they could direct or influence the behavior of a large number of subordinates. Like leaders in the white understructure, Negro leaders were executors rather than formulators of major policies.

Major decisions were usually made collectively in committees or informally in cliques composed of the power wielders. Rarely were they made in an open forum, though the forum did play an important function in the actual execution of policies. The major policymakers were not usually active in community associations, but rather tended to associate together either in private cliques or in organizations having a highly restricted membership.

Hunter makes it clear that the formulation and execution of power in Regional City is not a conspiracy by malevolent men, except in the case of organized crime. But power systems and institutional structures vary, and what is true of Regional City may not be characteristic of other American cities of comparable size. Indeed, one might expect to find great differences between large and small cities in the United States or elsewhere.

There are two points that stand out in Hunter's analysis. First, there is no single pyramid of power in a city. Rather, there are numbers of pyramidal power structures. The communitywide power structure has its existence only through particular power pyramids, the most important of which are those of the govermental and economic bureaucracies. Second, the power structure of a city is interwoven with power structures on state, national, and international levels. Hunter points out that the major men of power in Regional City often are in policymaking positions on a state or national level, and some of them are prominent in international affairs.

Cibola

A report prepared by Schulze and Blumberg, following a study conducted in Cibola, a small midwestern city, indicated that identifications of the power elite differed sharply according to the methods employed.[21] In addition to the reputational method in which a nominating panel designated the decision-makers, two variations of the positional method were employed: one included the "economic dominants" who were executives of the major industrial and financial establishments in the city; the other designated as "public leaders" those who filled top political or civic positions in the community. These three procedures yielded three rather distinct lists of men of power, with relatively little overlapping. Thus, it appears that the identification of the power elite in a city depends in part on the definitions involved and the methods of research.

After reviewing the role of economic dominants in Cibola for a period exceeding a century, Schulze concluded that an important shift in power had occurred since 1900.[22] Prior to 1900, most of the economic dominants were local residents and executives of locally-owned enterprises. They were not only involved in extensive economic networks in the community, but many of them held civic or political positions. With the growth of giant corporate bureaucracies, the local enterprises tended more and more to become branch establishments, and the erstwhile proprietors became salaried branch managers who were discouraged from participating extensively in local community affairs. Political and civic responsibilities of the city consequently fell almost entirely to local middle class businessmen and professionals, almost none of whom could be considered an economic dominant. Said one general manager, "One sure way to give our firm a black eye would be for me to get myself into things so deeply in town that no matter what I did, I'd end up alienating a lot of people."[23]

New Haven

Using the functional approach, Polsby conducted a study in New Haven, Connecticut, in which he identified community leaders who had been participants in three public issues involving the entire community.[24] These issues centered around urban redevelopment, political nominations, and public education. On the issue of urban redevelopment, 428 persons were actively involved in one way or another; for the political nominations, the number of involved persons was 497; while for public education 131 individuals were identified as participants.

The second step in the research was to conduct lengthy interviews with these participants in order to identify, first, the key decisions that

[21] Robert O. Schulze and Leonard U. Blumberg, "The Determination of Local Power Elites," *American Journal of Sociology*, 58 (November, 1957), 290–96.

[22] Robert O. Schulze, "The Role of Economic Dominants in Community Power Structure," *American Sociological Review*, 23 (February, 1958), 3–9; cf. Schulze, "The Bifurcation of Power in a Satellite City," in Morris Janowitz (ed.), *Community Political Systems* (1961), pp. 19–80.

[23] Schulze, "The Role of Economic Dominants . . . ," *op. cit.*, p. 7.

[24] Nelson W. Polsby, "Three Problems in the Analysis of Community Power," *American Sociological Review*, 24 (December, 1959), 796–803.

had been made in each of the issues, and second, the persons who were involved in these decisions and the roles they played. Polsby found little evidence of a monolithic power structure in the community. There was, indeed, little overlapping of "leadership pools" representing the three issues. The leaders, or decision-makers, were more or less specialized in their interests and activities.

The investigator then attempted to determine how two elites—economic and social—participated in the decisions relative to the issues concerning urban redevelopment, political nominations, and public education.[25] There was some overlapping, but it was not extensive. Of the 239 members of the economic elite, 48 were involved in the urban redevelopment program, but most of them were appointed by the mayor and did nothing more than sit passively on one of the committees. Only six of the economic elite were involved in political nominations, and none at all in the issues centering around public education. Of the 231 members of the social elite, 28 were participants in the urban redevelopment program, two in political nominations, and two in public education. Thus the economic and social elite did participate to a limited extent in the decision-making centering around the three issues, and their participation was probably more extensive than for the depressed groups in the city; but their roles as participants varied a great deal, from relatively passive to highly active and influential. Polsby sees no evidence from the New Haven study to support the idea of a hierarchically structured power system such as Hunter reported in Regional City and the Lynds in Middletown. There is no "crowd" that makes the big decisions for New Haven and transmits these decisions down to individuals in the lower echelons for collective action. It is, rather, a pluralistic system of community power.

Support for a pluralistic interpretation is likewise expressed by Dahl, whose analysis of power in New Haven parallels the findings of Polsby. Dahl traces in great detail the decision-making and strategy-mapping processes in the three "issue areas" considered by Polsby, namely, education, urban redevelopment, and political nominations.[26] For this city, at least, the theories of monolithic power did not apply because they were too simplistic, too indifferent to the role of the politician, too oblivious to the influence of a politically sophisticated leadership elite, and too divorced from public opinion.

EL PASO AND C. JUAREZ

A comparative study by Form and D'Antonio in El Paso, Texas, and C. Juarez, Mexico, was likewise concerned with the problem of whether

---

[25] Economic elite were high officials in major firms or corporations, or persons having an annual income of 250,000 dollars or over. Social elite were members of the "Cotillion Set," a socially exclusive group of ultrahigh prestige.

[26] Robert A. Dahl, *Who Governs?* (1961).

the power elite in those cities represented an integrated, cohesive unity that could, and did, act in concert on matters of community interest.[27] They found a considerable degree of integration and cohesion in both cities, but definitely more in El Paso than in C. Juarez, whose institutional boundaries, especially between business and government, were fairly sharply delineated. In neither city was there evidence of a single, monolithic power system in which decision-making was the monopoly of a coterie of "strong men."

Klapp and Padgett came to similar conclusions based on their study of Tijuana, Mexico, in which the reputational method was used.[28] Of the top 30 influentials identified by a panel of judges, 21 were businessmen. An "important clique" of high-ranking businessmen was observed, and there was evidence of a "loosely-knit and poorly-defined—though identifiable—group of leaders who recently became wealthy, drawn largely from business and the professions." Most of their social life centered around Rotary, Lions, and the country club.

POWER SYSTEMS AND COMMUNITY CHARACTERISTICS

In a comparative study of power systems in six communities, Barth found a relationship between the structure of power and the demographic and institutional base of the community.[29] The structural characteristics of the power systems of the communities studied varied from those which were highly integrated and pyramidal in shape to those having virtually no observable configuration. The rates of growth of the population and the economic structure of the community, in Barth's opinion, are the major determinants of the power structure.

Two of the communities studied, both in the South, had a small and closely-knit group of leaders who collaborated in the decision-making. Among the leaders were men of great wealth. When communitywide issues developed, it was these "influentials" who made the decisions and exerted the necessary leadership to carry them out. The pyramid of power was clear-cut and generally known to the citizens. Both cities were experiencing rapid growth of population; both had great concentrations of wealth.

A second type of power structure Barth describes as a "clique-based truncated pryamid" consisting of as many as 25 persons functioning at about the same level of power. On various issues, two or more cliques

[27] William H. Form and William V. D'Antonio, "Integration and Cleavage among Community Influentials in Two Border Cities," *American Sociological Review*, 24 (December, 1959), 804–14.

[28] Orrin E. Klapp and L. Vincent Padgett, "Power Structure and Decision-Making in a Mexican Border City," *American Journal of Sociology*, 65 (January, 1960), 400–6.

[29] Ernest A. T. Barth, "Community Influence Systems: Structure and Change," *Social Forces*, 40 (October, 1961), 58–63.

of influentials were functioning, more or less autonomously, and sometimes competitively, in the power system. The communities exhibiting this pattern of power, both in the Southeast, were experiencing a rapid growth of population and a diversification of the industrial elements in the community. With rapid economic expansion, new positions of power and influence were created in the institutional structures, and some of the men who filled them helped bridge the power gap when the old leadership group was unable or unwilling to deal effectively with the crucial issues of an expanding community. But there was no single individual, nor clique of individuals, who was dominant; rather the power tended to be somewhat diffuse.

A third type of system observed by Barth could hardly be identified as a power structure at all. What power existed was diffused. There were numerous factions and pressure groups, but no group was in a position to exercise much influence. On community issues action was difficult. The two communities having this kind of power system were characterized by a low rate of population change; one of them actually had no change from 1940 to 1950. In both cities there was a large proportion of absentee ownership of businesses, and both were located near large metropolitan centers.

COMMUNITY POWER IN THE UNITED STATES AND ENGLAND

The composition of the power elite and other leaders in a city may reflect differences in the institutional structure and status system of a community. Using the reputational method, Miller attempted to test this proposition in a study of power and leadership in two cities, one in the United States (Pacific City) and the other in England (English City).[30] Each city had a population of about a half-million. When the results of Miller's study were compared with Hunter's study of Regional City, some rather striking differences appeared. Over half (58 per cent) of the major decision-makers in Regional City were representatives of business, finance, or industry, but only one-third of the key influentials in the other two cities. In Regional City, only 15 per cent were from the combined occupations representing labor, education, government, and regional, but in Pacific City this occupational combination accounted for 48 per cent of the major decision-makers and in English City for 46 per cent. In the latter city, one-fifth of the power elite represented labor alone, higher than for either of the American cities. That this may fairly accurately reflect the position of labor in the power structure of the English City is further indicated by the composition of the city council

---

[30] Delbert C. Miller, "Industry and Community Power Structure: A Comparative Study of an American and an English City," *American Sociological Review*, 23 (February, 1958), 9–15; cf. Miller and Form, *Industry, Labor, and Community* (1960).

in that municipality in 1955: 35 per cent were trade union members, mainly manual workers; 30 per cent represented the business community; and 37 per cent included professionals, housewives, retired persons, and "others."

Miller attributes the difference between Regional City and the other two to the fact that the former is an older community, where the social system has been congenial to the growth of a social aristocracy and where business control tends to be inherited. The composition of the power elites in Pacific City and English City reflects the changing institutions of these communities, the development of new power structures to challenge the older ones, and the rise of a managerial power elite deriving authority from the outside and with limited responsibility for the local community.

POPULAR LEADERSHIP

The preceding discussion has been focused mainly upon the type of leadership that involves the exercise of authority or power. There are, however, community leaders who may occupy no organizational position of authority but who are influential, in varying degrees, in formulating ideas, initiating action programs, directing activities, or in other ways making decisions that effect community life. Some of these may be what Weber has called charismatic leaders—individuals whose personal articulation and role-playing techniques are such as to constitute a popular appeal to persons in various stations of life. The persons who initiate and direct a social reform program in the community, or who assume leadership in opposing such a program, may or may not wield any power that is anchored in the institutional or organizational structure. Leaders of unofficial civic committees, or religious movements, of programs to effect social changes of one kind or another, or to block such changes, may be effective leaders but not wielders of institutional or bureaucratic power. Every community, large and small, has its quota of such leaders. Some may leave a lasting imprint on community life.

All leaders, and particularly the noninstitutionalized ones, deal with public issues which become the focus of public opinion. Such leaders therefore are concerned with the processes of public opinion formation within the community, with the manipulation of public opinion, and often overt behavior, toward certain objectives. Public issues commonly center around community conflict, which may be manifest in various ways within the community.

SELECTED BIBLIOGRAPHY

BOOKS

Dahl, Robert, *Who Governs? Democracy and Power in an American City*. New Haven: Yale University Press, 1961.

Etzioni, Amitai, *Complex Organizations*. New York: Holt, Rinehart and Winston, 1961.

Gouldner, Alvin W., *Patterns of Industrial Bureaucracy*. Glencoe, Ill.: The Free Press, 1954.

Hunter, Floyd, *Community Power Structure*. Chapel Hill: University of North Carolina Press, 1952.

Janowitz, Morris (ed.), *Community Political Systems*. Glencoe, Ill.: The Free Press, 1961.

Lynd, Robert S., and Helen M. Lynd, *Middletown in Transition*. New York: Harcourt, Brace, 1937.

Merton, Robert K. (ed.), *Reader in Bureaucracy*. Glencoe, Ill.: The Free Press, 1952.

ARTICLES

Barth, Ernest A. T., and Baha Abu-Laban, "Power Structure and the Negro Sub-Community," *American Sociological Review*, 24 (February, 1959), 69–76.

Bendix, Reinhard, "Bureaucracy: The Problem and Its Setting," *American Sociological Review*, 12 (October, 1947), 493–507.

McKee, James, "Status and Power in the Industrial Community," *American Journal of Sociology*, 58 (January, 1953), 367–71.

Miller, Delbert, "Industry and Community Power Structure: A Comparative Study of an American and an English City," *American Sociological Review*, 23 (February, 1958), 9–15.

Polsby, Nelson W., "The Sociology of Community Power," *Social Forces*, 37 (March, 1959), 232–36.

Schulze, Robert O., "The Role of Economic Dominants in Community Power Structure," *American Sociological Review*, 23 (February, 1958), 3–9.

Urban Family Life
in Transition

—

SIXTEEN

One of the characteristics of modern urban society is the multiplicity of family patterns to be found within a single community. To speak or write of "the urban family" as a unitary type of grouping is therefore misleading. There are, instead, urban *families,* countless numbers of them, having a range of characteristics that border on the infinite.

In almost any metropolis there are families representing ethnic or religious groups that differ in marriage customs and kinship organization; families organized along authoritarian principles and others organized around equalitarian ideals; families that are loose-structured companionate liaisons between childless couples, and large kinship groups living under a single roof. The conditions under which families live are equally diverse. If these differences in family patterns are to be found within a single metropolis, or even a small city, intercultural differences viewed in world perspective are probably even greater. Family life in Bogota is undoubtedly quite different in certain respects from life in Bangkok or Boston.

By the same token, there are rural and urban differences in family structure and function. Yet it is well to remember that differences between urban and rural families may mean one thing in the United States but something very different in other countries of the world.

URBANIZATION AND THE CHANGING FAMILY SYSTEM

Family systems have been undergoing structural and functional changes the world over. These changes are often in response to changes occurring

364

in the larger social order. As families "adjust" to these broader changes, they invariably undergo modifications in family behavior patterns and in the relationships of family members to each other and to outsiders. It would be hazardous to assume that all of these changes are traceable to the influence of cities, since change may occur in ways that appear to be only remotely related to urbanism, if at all. Nevertheless, the demands of city life have left such a deep imprint on family and kinships systems that changes have occurred in the organization of family life and in the functions of family groups. This "urban impact" may be viewed from two perspectives: (1) changes occurring among families who reside in, or migrate to, cities and (2) changes in nonurban (rural) families who, though not residing in urban communities, nevertheless are affected in one way or another by urban influences. Rural families may therefore be "urbanized" insofar as they acquire behavioral or attitudinal traits that emanate from cities.

RURAL FAMILIES IN THE URBAN MILIEU

Throughout the present century, millions of families, representing a diversity of structural patterns and internal relationships, have settled in cities, large and small. Families settling in an urban community have been forced by circumstances to undergo numerous changes. Many have adapted fairly readily, indicating resourcefulness in coping with various situations and at the same time maintaining harmonious unity of the family or kinship group. Others, weakened by the stresses and strains encountered in urban living, have experienced disruptions often leading to complete collapse of the family organization. The relatively high incidence of divorce and separation of families in cities, especially in American cities, is indicative of widespread disorganization. Family disorganization, in terms of internal group conflicts and other disruptions of family life, is generally more characteristic of urban than of rural society. But disorganization in the city is also more characteristic of certain social classes, racial groups, and ethnic or religious minorities than of others.

Some of the changes in family organization commonly associated with urbanization, especially in the West, may be noted:

1. Changes in the family power structure, which usually means the decline of parental authority over children, and of husbands over wives, with increasing independence and freedom of action on the part of children and wives.

2. Changes in the interpersonal relationships between the sexes, resulting in greater freedom of males and females to associate informally outside the home, to choose their own friends, and to select the persons they wish to marry.

3. Changes in social roles of family members, both within the home and outside it. Behavior tends to be individualized and roles often uncoordinated.

The separation of work roles of family members outside the home usually means a diversification of their interests, with the result that family solidarity may decline.

4. Changes in the proportion of unmarried persons, or of persons who are divorced or separated. Unmarried or separated persons may suffer no appreciable loss of status, at the same time enjoying certain economic advantages as employed workers without the responsibility of supporting dependents.

5. Changes in family structure from the "joint" system toward smaller nuclear families exhibiting a variety of structural and functional patterns. Although joint families do exist in cities, their survival necessitates certain changes in the system.

6. Changes in interpersonal contacts outside the home, with the result that informal friendships, or even formal contacts, tend to supplement, and in some instances replace, intrafamily association.

7. Changes in the ceremonial basis of family life, commonly toward a decline, and in some instances virtual disappearance, of family ceremonies, notably in families on lower class levels.

Some of these trends will be considered at length in subsequent parts of this chapter.

MARITAL STATUS AND SOCIAL CHARACTERISTICS

Numerous changes are occurring in the organization of family life in the United States. These trends are not peculiar to American society but have taken place in certain other countries as well. In Table 18, comparison may be made for a recent period of two decades.

TABLE 18

Percentage Distribution of U. S. Population Over 14, by Marital
Status and Sex, 1940 and 1960

Status	*Male*		*Female*	
	1940	1960	1940	1960
Single	31.8	24.8	24.1	18.4
Married	62.8	70.0	61.0	67.8
Widowed	4.8	3.3	12.9	11.1
Divorced	1.3	1.8	1.7	2.7

SOURCE: *Statistical Abstract of the United States* (1962), p. 37.

Several comparisons from this table may be made, as follows:

1. For both 1940 and 1960, a larger percentage of males than of females was single or married.

2. A much higher percentage of women than of men was widowed.

3. A somewhat higher proportion of women than of men was divorced.

4. Between 1940 and 1960, the proportions of married persons increased sharply. This increase occurred mainly in the 1940's, during and after World War II.

5. Divorce rates showed an increase, a continuation of a trend beginning around the turn of the century.

6. The proportion of widowed men and women tended to decline during this period, but the proportion of widowed women remained high. This reflected in part a higher mortality rate among men, in part a tendency for widowed men to remarry.

7. Corollary to the increase in proportion of married persons has been a decrease in the percentage of single men and women.

Among the countries of the West, the United States ranks at or near the top in the proportion of the population "ever married." This reflects in part the trend toward early marriages. Divorce rates are also higher in the United States than in most countries.

THE SEX RATIO AND ITS SOCIAL IMPLICATIONS

As a general rule, American cities have a slight preponderance of women, although cities with heavy industries may attract more males than females. In cities of preindustrial countries such as those of the Orient and Africa this sex ratio is usualy reversed, there being more urban males than females.

Any tilting of the sex ratio, whether toward males or females, may have far-reaching effects on family life, as indeed it may have on the whole range of social relationships. If the tilting is slight, the effects may be correspondingly slight; if there is a heavy preponderance of males or females, the consequences may be considerable. An idea of how an unbalanced sex ratio affects family life may be obtained by viewing the situation in Africa.

Many cities of Africa are filled with employable men, young and middle-aged, but there are comparatively few native women, children, and aged males.[1] Women and children are commonly left behind to cultivate the farms, although many men are actually accompanied by their families when they migrate to cities for work. In South African cities native workers employed in the heavy industries are especially required to leave their families in the villages and to live in special compounds occupied exclusively by males.

In American cities the sex ratio is only slightly tilted toward females. But this fairly evenly balanced ratio conceals the fact that large numbers

[1] Daniel F. McCall, "Dynamics of Urbanization in Africa," *Annals,* 298 (March, 1955), 151–60.

of unattached men and women live in cities, often under conditions of extreme social isolation. Every metropolis has its Hobohemia populated by homeless and often jobless males who live in barren rooms and eke out a drab existence. These Hobohemias are areas of last resort for the socially uprooted, men who are unable, for one reason or another, to have a normal family life. Higher in the social and economic scale is a veritable army of unattached men and women who reside in rooming houses, bachelor apartments, residential hotels, or "Y" dormitories. Probably most of the younger unattached men and women on the higher social levels eventually marry, but the middle-aged and older persons will likely "go it alone," whether by choice or necessity.

THE CITY AND THE CHANGING FAMILY

CHANGING FAMILY FUNCTIONS

Under conditions imposed by city life, urban families have often been deprived of certain historic functions, or at least prevented from carrying out these functions in the traditional manner. Sometimes these changes are dictated by necessity; often they are chosen from a number of possible courses of action. Whatever the reasons and conditions of their occurrence, they should be viewed as part of a larger panorama of pervasive social change. As new forms of organization have developed or old organizational structures are discarded or modified, functions have been correspondingly added, eliminated, or modified. Often these organizations have performed functions historically carried out by the family group.

Perhaps the most significant development in this respect is the change in certain functions of government—national, state, and local. During the twentieth century especially, the institution of government has expanded its functions to include activities once considered exclusively or mainly of concern to the family group. The role of government in social welfare, housing, medicine, recreation, and education exemplifies this trend.

Economic expansion and differentiation have likewise affected urban family life. Such service establishments as laundries, bakeries, canneries, and cold storage plants, familiar types of enterprises in industrialized America, have taken over functions once performed exclusively in the home if they were performed at all. The whole clothing industry, from textile mill to garment factory, from tannery to shoe-manufacturing plant, has largely displaced the self-service function of the family in attiring its members. The multiplication of hotels, motels, and restaurants attests to the extent urban people, at least in America and Europe, sleep and eat away from home.

Traditionally, the American family as a group was expected to care for children, aged persons, and other members incapable of supporting themselves. In recent decades the economic task of caring for dependent persons has shifted from the family to private and public agencies.

From the cradle to the grave the urban person is served by a vast array of organizations that supplement or replace the self-service functions of the family group. He is entitled to the services of a municipal health clinic or hospital, to an education in the city's schools, to recreation in the city's parks or in its amusement emporia, even to a berth in the city workhouse. An army of specialized or semispecialized functionaries caters to his needs: clinicians, teachers, playground directors, police, turnkeys in the local jail, all at public expense.

The foregoing picture is essentially a picture of urban society in America or industrial Europe. But it does not necessarily fit the facts of city life in the preindustrial cities of the world. Families in technologically underdeveloped countries are less reliant on certain types of outside agencies or organizations. In the Orient, most urban families (or their servants) do their own cooking, washing, sewing, and preserving of foods; they seldom partonize restaurants or hotels; and they are highly self-sufficient in designing their own wearing apparel. They look after most of the needs of their own dependents, whether the young or the old, and a behavior clinic or a home for the aged would be exceptional. Yet even in such cities there has been an expansion of government functions to include various types of social services like housing, medicine, and social welfare.

SOME TRENDS IN AMERICAN FAMILY LIFE

Whether urbanism is associated with any particular trend in family life irrespective of the cultural setting we cannot say, except that family customs and rules of behavior are generally weakened under the impact of city influences. If, however, trends are viewed from the perspective of a particular culture, changes in the family system may be seen in relationship to increasing urbanization. Certain patterns of family change in the United States may be thus designated.

1. Rights and privileges of women have been extended to many spheres of social life. They are accorded the right to invade the occupational world of males, to obtain an education comparable to that of men, to participate in sports, to marry or remain single according to their preferences, to sue and be sued, to take the initiative in courtship, to obtain a decree of divorce, to share equally in the property of the husband, to participate in various undertakings with men other than those of their own families, to emulate males in such things as drinking, smoking, and

wearing apparel. They can even have their cake and eat it too by obtaining alimony if married life is terminated.

2. That supreme egotist, the human male, has had his traditional position of dominance in the household challenged. Like all tyrants, the family autocrat has not always relinquished his authority voluntarily. But this challenge to his authority has been dictated more by external events and conditions than by ideological changes. Inasmuch as the American father or husband spends most of his working hours away from home, responsibility for managing the household has shifted to the mother. And it is this shift of responsibility that has encouraged a shift of authority. This change has been particularly apparent in middle class suburbs. The trend is therefore toward a matricentric family in which authority is being shared on an equalitarian basis by husband and wife.

3. Parental preoccupation with child-rearing is especially characteristic of middle class families. The vast amount of popular and scientific literature on child care both reflects and stimulates this concern about the welfare and happiness of children. In such child-centered families permissiveness of discipline has tended to replace stern punitive measures.

4. Age and sex grading for adults and children has fostered organizational activity outside the home. Participation in voluntary associations has often prevented adults and children from sharing the same experiences.

5. This age and sex grading has also fostered an urban youth culture whose distinct values and roles tend to produce a certain amount of conflict between generations. Such conflict is particularly apparent if parents are identified with a minority racial, ethnic, or religious group and if the children seek to identify with a majority group. The heterogeneous cultures of metropolitan communities are especially conducive to such intergenerational conflict.

6. The urban household is designed for parents and children, sometimes only for husband and wife. There is scant place in it for elders, even if they are wanted. In the small-family system, as contrasted to the kinship group, youth, not old age, is glorified. How to provide for elderly persons is a problem faced in every urbanized society having the nuclear family system.

EMPLOYMENT OF WOMEN

It is one thing to chronicle the trend toward increased employment of urban women, but quite another to assess the effect of such change on family life. Broad generalizations are easy but risky. No doubt family relationships are profoundly affected by such employment, but precisely how to isolate such effects from other influences is not always possible. Furthermore, the effect on family relationships undoubtedly varies greatly from one group to another, depending on particular circumstances and the personalities of individuals involved. With these precautions in mind we present certain trends concerning the significance to family life of gainful employment of women.

1. The average size of families has not been appreciably reduced by the gainful employment of women, especially those in the educated classes. This is evidenced by the fact that birth rates have remained high for the past two decades, a period in which an increasing number of women have entered the labor market. These apparently conflicting trends may be explained partly in terms of changed patterns of female employment: many women are entering the labor market in their thirties and forties, after their children no longer need full-time attention. Thus, increasing urbanism has been accompanied by high birth rates, increasing employment of women, decreasing age at marriage, and a rise in the proportion of females "ever married."

2. Gainful employment of married, widowed, or divorced women has shifted some of the responsibility for child-rearing on other functionaries: the baby sitter, household servant, or day nursery attendant. Other women have thus become mother surrogates for at least part of the day. The recent growth of urban day nurseries for working mothers is an institutional adjustment to the employment of women with children.

3. If both parents are employed, family life tends to be organized around adult rather than children's interests. The drain on a woman's energy in holding a job and at the same time assuming child-rearing and other household responsibilities may result in extreme fatigue, which in turn may foster tensions within the group. Conflict may develop as a result of trying to meet the demands of both occupational and wife-mother roles.

NUCLEAR FAMILY AND KINSHIP GROUP

SOCIAL MOBILITY AND THE FAMILY SYSTEM

There is considerable evidence that vertical mobility, especially when associated with spatial mobility, tends to weaken rather than strengthen family and kinship ties. Upwardly mobile individuals often find it expedient to increase both the spatial and social distance between themselves and their kin. Illustrations are plentiful of the successful person of "humble" parentage who severs his family and kinship ties because his parents or other relatives are social liabilities. The downwardly mobile person may also be alienated from his family, partly by choice, partly because his kin prefer, for status reasons, to sever, or at least minimize, their relationship with him. Skid Row, a familiar theme of novelists, is populated by such persons.

Vertical mobility may also be viewed in its relationships to a particular family system. Upward mobility may be more easily achieved by members of a nuclear than of a joint family. In the nuclear or conjugal family the young adult customarily leaves the parental household and becomes a comparatively "free agent"; and if he (or she) marries, a separate household is established, with obligations primarily to spouse and children, not to parents and other kin. This independence favors the freedom of action often needed for social ascendancy. Hence it is precisely in Western urbanized societies having a nuclear family system, with loose ties to the larger kinship group, that social mobility is maximized.

The joint or extended family system, on the other hand, may provide more security for the individual, though it is less favorable for upward social mobility. Since members of a joint family often live together in a single domicile, they not only identify with the larger unit, but are also obligated to assume certain responsibilities toward all the kin. When they marry the usual procedure is for them to bring their spouse to live in the parental household. Hence their independence and freedom of action are greatly restricted. Their successes, or failures, are also shared by the kinship group. But it is precisely this sharing that acts as a brake on individual mobility. It is not easy for the individual to pull his joint family upward—or downward, for that matter. If the attractive social rewards are for individual success, as in the urbanized societies of the West, and to some extent in large cities elsewhere, the motivations of the individual are likely to be toward success goals for himself, perhaps sharing the rewards with spouse and children, but not with the whole kinship group. This is undoubtedly one of the reasons why the joint family system does not flourish as well in the city's environment as in the traditional village *milieu*.

THE KINSHIP GROUP IN THE CITY

In a critical review of research findings on family systems, Sussman and Burchinal take the position that the urban family can be conceptualized as a "modified extended" system, representing an adaptation of the rural family system to the conditions of urban society.[2] This system consists of nuclear families that are bound together, by affectional ties,

[2] Marvin B. Sussman and Lee Burchinal, "Reappraising Kin Networks in Urban Society," paper presented at a meeting of the American Sociological Association, Washington, D. C., August, 1962.

into a kinship network. These nuclear families comprising the network are functionally related to each other in that they, or at least their members, carry out activities or provide services that are of value to other members of the larger group as well as to their own nuclear unit. Among these activities are the following:

1. Mutual assistance activities, including financial aid, gifts, advice, and so on;
2. Social activities, such as kinship visiting, joint recreational activities, family get-togethers, and so on;
3. Mutual services, such as cooperative shopping, care of children, helping older members of the group, assisting at weddings, and providing various kinds of aid in case of family crises.

That the kinship group assumes many forms in cities is unquestionably the case, whether in America or other parts of the world. Doubtless the strength of such groups is stronger in smaller cities than in larger metropolitan centers, generally speaking. But its typicality is yet to be demonstrated by relevant research. Actually, kinship groups might be placed on a continuum which would be indicative of the degree of "closeness" of the various members—frequency of visiting, of mutual assistance, or of joint activities, and so on. The range would therefore be from closely knit kinship groups to isolated nuclear families having no contacts whatever with their kin. Doubtless there would be considerable variation according to religion, ethnic composition, social class level, and spatial distances separating the groups.

NEW HAVEN AND YANKEE CITY

Dotson found that in New Haven, Connecticut, working-class [3] nuclear families maintained close visiting relations with members of the larger kinship group—brothers, sisters, cousins, and so on—and that much of their leisure time was spent in visiting families related by ties of kinship but living in different sections of the area. In the Warner-Lunt study of Yankee City (Newburyport, Massachusetts) there was considerable evidence that upper class families were especially strong and that close family ties were maintained among the members of the large kinship group. Often elite persons would refer to each other as "cousin" even though they were not blood kin, indicating a strong identification with both class and family.[4]

[3] Floyd Dotson, "Patterns of Voluntary Associations among Working Class Families," *American Sociological Review*, 16 (October, 1951), 690–93.
[4] W. Lloyd Warner and Paul S. Lunt, *The Social Life of a Modern Community* (1941).

RIO DE JANEIRO

In a study of a working-class district in Rio de Janeiro, Pearse noted that while the nuclear family was the characteristic form of organization, the "kin-group" played an important part in the system.[5] Pearse refers to the kin-group as the specific group of relatives with whom the nuclear family interacts more or less regularly, frequently, and intimately. These families did not associate intimately with their neighbors, except perhaps in times of crisis, but their kin relationships were close and influential. "Advice was given, help proffered, and short-term plans made. . . . It [the kin-group] was the first line of defense of the family, and could be relied upon in case of sickness, unemployment, dispossession, accident, etc." [6] It was also the group in which discussion was held concerning the achievements and failures of its various members, and in which evaluations of family problems were made. In a word, the larger kinship circle was an important reference group, supplementing the nuclear family unit.

CRESTWOOD HEIGHTS

In contrast, a study of middle class Canadian families in suburban Crestwood Heights, Toronto, indicated that the larger kinship group in that community was relatively unimportant.[7] Here the geographical separation of the nuclear family members from relatives had its counterpart in social separation. Thus the absence of close kinship bonds tended to free each nuclear family from responsibilities to relatives, but it also deprived these families of whatever stabilizing influence the kinship group might have provided. It also placed on a few individuals, commonly the parents, almost complete responsibility for maintaining a functioning family unit. The kin-group surrogates were close friends, who stood in a relationship similar to that commonly held by relatives—the unrelated "uncle" or "aunt," for example. Also, there was dependence on the services of specialized agencies in the community, especially agencies affording recreation for family members, and also those of an educational and economic character. In these respects Crestwood Heights may be fairly typical of middle class suburban families both in metropolitan Canada and the United States. Apparently, then, the larger kin-group in Western cities is of particular significance for working-class families, groups having strong ethnic ties, and families having upper class status. But in many underdeveloped societies it is relatively more important.

[5] Andrew Pearse, "Some Characteristics of Urbanization in Rio de Janeiro," in Philip Hauser (ed.), *Urbanization in Latin America* (1961); proceedings of a Unesco seminar held in Santiago, Chile, 1959.
[6] *Ibid.*, p. 200.
[7] John R. Seeley, R. Alexander Sim, and E. W. Loosley, *Crestwood Heights* (1956).

In a comparative study of two London suburbs, one a working-class community, the other predominantly middle class, Willmott and Young found that kinship ties in the working-class suburb were, in general, stronger than in the other community.[8] Even in the middle class suburb (Woodford), manual workers had closer ties with relatives than was true of the middle class residents, as indicated by the incidence of visiting with relatives. In a sample of middle class husbands and wives in Woodford, two-thirds had visited with their mothers during the previous week, compared with three-fourths of a similar sample in Bethnal Green, the working-class suburb. In Woodford, 23 per cent of the married persons had visited with their brothers or sisters the previous week, but in Bethnal Green the percentage was 35. The nuclear families in Woodford were relatively independent of their relatives, commonly residing a considerable distance from them, but in Bethnal Green kinship groups often occupied two or more nearby houses, thus making it easy for relatives to "pop in and out" of the homes of their kin.

This frequent "popping in and out," in the judgment of the authors, is a characteristic pattern of kinship behavior on this social level. They note, however, that indirect contacts among relatives may be more frequent among the middle classes than among manual workers. Middle class persons, more than manual workers and their families, are likely to have telephones and are more accustomed to letter-writing. One may therefore deduce, so far as the British data are concerned, that working-class families are more closely identified with the kin group provided they live close enough to permit fairly frequent visiting relationships, but that middle class families living some distance apart are inclined to maintain their kin-group contacts through indirect communication. The authors cite several instances of working-class persons moving away and not communicating thereafter with their relatives.

THE UNITED FAMILY OF PUERTO RICANS IN NEW YORK

The Puerto Rican family in New York is an example of undirected social change that has occurred in the family organization of migrants.[9] Although the basic family unit in New York, as in Puerto Rico, is the nuclear family, there is a larger unit known as the "united family" *(familia unida)* consisting of a number of nuclear families whose members bear a special relationship to their kinsmen such as brothers and sisters,

[8] Peter Willmott and Michael Young, *Family and Class in a London Suburb* (1960), ch. 7; cf. *Family and Kinship in East London* by the same authors (1957).
[9] Elena Padilla, *Up from Puerto Rico* (1958).

uncles and aunts, cousins, and grandparents. Acknowledged members of a united family are relatives who can be relied upon in times of trouble or crises, or on occasions when a helping hand from relatives may be a convenience. There are also special occasions, such as birthdays, weddings, christenings, and celebrations of holidays, when the members get together to express their feelings of affection or respect. In major crises, members of two or more of the related nuclear families may gather and remain in one of the households until the uncertainties have passed. The very existence of these united families implies a strong sense of obligation to kinsmen—though not necessarily to all kinsmen, for there are some who are indifferent to these responsibilities or to united family activities.

But as Padilla points out, the united family is changing as the nuclear families and their members are assimilated into the prevailing culture and integrated into New York metropolitan life. This has been especially true of Puerto Ricans who have been in New York for several years. Their geographic dispersal has often made it difficult for members of the united family to get together. And as social differentiation and status have occurred among the members, as values and interests have been modified, and particularly as the nuclear family unit—parents and children—has become more and more the principal focal point of interest, the united family has declined. Nevertheless, it still functions effectively among the recent migrants who are often in need of the assistance and companionship that only relatives or close friends can give. So long as the heavy stream of migration from Puerto Rico continues, the united family system will probably be supported by the recent arrivals.

THE CITY AND FAMILY LIFE IN SOUTH ASIA

Throughout the rural areas of South Asia, the joint or extended family is predominant. The joint family in its ideal-typical form consists of members of the larger kinship group who reside in a common household, prepare and eat their meals together, hold most of their property in common, and pool their individual incomes. Actually, there are many variations in joint family patterns.

City life does not provide the most favorable environment for the joint family. Consequently, there is a tendency toward the nuclearization of the family unit. There are several reasons for this change. Housing facilities in most cities are usually more suitable for smaller families than for the large kinship groups. Occupational specialization and the separation of place of residence from the work site tend to encourage individualism. Opportunities in the city for occupational mobility and pecuniary achievement help to motivate the worker and his family toward the goal of individual success, for which membership in a joint family may be no advantage.

Actually, the change may be more apparent than real in many instances. In some urban communities members of nuclear families commonly retain their connections with kinsmen and identify with the larger group, even though they live in a small-family unit and hold at least a part of their property and possessions individually. For example, a professor on the faculty of the University of Mysore, India, lives with his wife and child in an apartment in Mysore City, a sizable metropolis. Yet he and his wife retain their village ties, and identify with the larger kinship group, most of whose members live in the "native" village. As a member of the larger group, though living separate from it, he is entitled to certain benefits, such as a share of the grain at harvest time, but he also has certain obligations and responsibilities to the group.

CITYWARD MIGRATION AND FAMILY LIFE

In many ways the impact of urbanism has affected family life both in cities and in villages. Often male villagers, married or unmarried, leave the family circle and migrate individually to urban centers, expecting to gain employment and perhaps later to be joined by their families.[10] For this reason most cities in South Asia have a heavy preponderance of males. Usually these men, if they remain long in the city, make periodic visits to their families in the home village. Village kinship ties normally remain fairly strong. Sooner or later either the men return to live permanently in the village or, if married, bring their families to the city. But not all men residentially situated in the city retain strong identities and loyalties with their immediate families or the larger kinship group. The anonymity of the city, the appeal of the exotic and the romantic, the opportunities for individualized behavior, even deviant behavior, for many has often weakened their sense of family or village loyalty. In this new-found freedom, numbers of men sever their family and village ties altogether.

Nor has the city left unaffected the women who go there to live. As Ross has indicated in her study of the urban Indian family, gainful employment of women has been of particular importance among the factors which have affected family life. Such employment has taken the woman out of the home for long periods of the day, thus reducing the influence she normally exerts in the village family.[11] This has been especially true of working-class families which seriously need the supplemental earnings of the female members.

Although the joint family system is undergoing drastic change in its

[10] Noel P. Gist, "Selective Migration in Urban South India," paper read at World Population Conference, Rome, Italy, 1954. United Nations Document E/CONF. 13/357, p. 9.

[11] Aileen D. Ross, *The Hindu Family in Its Urban Setting* (1961).

adjustment to the demands of metropolitan life in South Asia, the family unit, whether nuclear or joint, remains an effective mechanism for the regulation of the lives of its members. This is well documented in the case of mate selection. As a general rule, with certain exceptions, mates are selected and marriages arranged by the kinship groups of a son or daughter of marriageable age. Among the more emancipated or modernized families, however, the son or daughter may have a voice, or even a veto, in the selection of a spouse.

FAMILY IN COLOMBO

The family and caste system of Colombo, Ceylon, as presented by Ryan,[12] is fairly indicative of "familism" in South Asia. Although the family system has been somewhat altered under conditions of urban living, marriage within the caste is still the prevailing custom, but with numerous deviations from the rule.

Except for a small, westernized bohemian set, specifications of the caste or kinship group in mate selection are usually followed. Youthful sophisticates among the elite often experiment casually with romantic notions concerning marriage, but such fantasies are seldom or never carried to the point of courtship, and public dating would be virtually immoral. Middle and upper classes are in many ways influenced by democratic and secular trends in the metropolis, but in matters of marriage and family life there is little retreat from the traditional forms.

Among the slum-dwelling coolie class, however, there is less adherence to the mandates of custom because family solidarity on this level has been greatly reduced by the conditions of urban living and working. Employment of women outside the home has disrupted normal family life. Marriage customs have been weakened or ignored since many families, through mobility, are separated from the village kinship group and no longer subject to its demands. Without the companionate character of personal relations which often helps to stabilize the Western family group, the low-caste family in Colombo is frequently disorganized, although for the great majority marriage and family rules are generally observed.

AFRICAN FAMILIES AND CITY LIFE

The urbanization of Africa south of the Sahara has had a profound effect on the family life of the indigenous peoples. Because family patterns vary a great deal from one city or country to another in Africa, however, generalizations should be made with caution. Generally speaking, indigenous families of Africans residing in villages are joint or

[12] Bryce Ryan, *Caste in Modern Ceylon* (1953), pp. 308–21.

extended families—kinship groups—and are closely articulated with the tribal system. Under preurban conditions the kinship-tribal system successfully carried out the various functions of family life. Roles were clearly defined and synchronized; authority vested in family heads or tribal chiefs was respected and usually observed; conformity to accepted norms of conduct was expected and enforced.

DISRUPTIVE EFFECTS OF URBAN RESIDENCE

But conditions associated with industrialism and urbanism have brought about many changes in family life, both for families living in the cities and those remaining in the village.[13] African men, and even some African women, often journey in large numbers to industrial centers where they may find employment in the mines and mills and other establishments. Some of the men work under contract for a given period, commonly one year, during which time they are required to live in compounds with other workers. Removed from the village setting, they are no longer subject to the authority imposed by tribal and kinship groups. Deviant behavior in the form of crime and vice often results; and even among those whose behavior remains fairly conventional there tends to be lessened respect for authority and the established norms when they do return to their village homes. Furthermore, with cash in their pockets, their wages for the year are often frittered away on nonessentials in the city's shops, so that their kinsmen, or even their wives and children, are not as well off as before.

Under tribal conditions a man's social and economic status depends on his having a wife, and a woman's security is enhanced through marriage. But in the cities a woman does not necessarily add to prestige, and she may be viewed as a costly luxury. Sexual satisfactions, for men and women, are easily obtained in the city, without the responsibilities of family life. Consequently, illicit sexual behavior in some groups is common, and a considerable proportion of the children are born out of wedlock. Women in the city, in contrast to village life, find gainful employment which enables them to enjoy luxuries and a degree of economic independence beyond the dreams of tribal women. Many of them augment their earnings through prostitution, of which there is a ready market among the males removed from their own kinship group and unable to have a normal family life. Dissolution of marriage is frequent, and deserted or deserting wives and husbands commonly find sexual companionship in temporary unions as well as in prostitution.

[13] Much of the information relating to the urban impact on African families is obtained from the conference held at Abidjan under the auspices of UNESCO and the International African Institute. Reports of the conference were published as *Social Implications of Industrialization and Urbanization in Africa South of the Sahara* (1956).

CHANGES IN THE AFRICAN KINSHIP GROUP

In a survey of research literature concerning family systems in West African cities, Aldous concluded that the extended family is the predominant family organization in these communities and that there is scant reason to believe it will be replaced by the nuclear family in the foreseeable future.[14] The cities included in these studies were Dakar, Senegal; Lagos, Nigeria; and Brazzaville, Leopoldville, and Stanleyville, Congo, all over 100,000 in population. In some instances the kinship group took the form of a voluntary association, Western style, with meetings held regularly, instead of on special occasions. Summarizing these studies, Aldous comments:

> Besides filling recreational, religious, legal, or economic needs of urbanites it [the extended family] substitutes for a non-existent public social welfare system. Kinsmen provide for the elderly and support the sick, the jobless, and the destitute. They give the new arrival from the country shelter and food and help him to get work or an education and to adjust to the bustling city.[15]

Presumably the individual in the West African city is not necessarily isolated or forced to face life alone; rather, he is likely to be involved in a complex network of kinship relations—unless he has voluntarily forsaken his family or kin, or has no relatives in the community.

Owing to the phenomenal growth of West African cities in recent decades due to heavy in-migrations, there has been little time for these peoples to make functional and structural adaptations of family organization to the urban milieu. As we have noted earlier, however, there is already some evidence of weakening of family controls. Whether a nuclear family system will eventually emerge as the city people become more "urbanized" cannot be determined for a number of years, or even decades.

The changing structures and functions of the West African family in Lagos, Nigeria, may be representative of changes occurring in large kinship groups in an urban environment.[16] What might be considered by some as social disorganization may often be a matter of adjustment to the demands and conditions of city life. The traditional family, or kinship group, exists as a loosely-structured unit in a common village abode. But under conditions of urban life this arrangement is not always possible, or even considered by the family members as desirable. Consequently, there is a tendency for nuclear units to break away and establish independent, or semi-independent, households.

---

[14] J. Aldous, "Urbanization, the Extended Family, and Kinship Ties in West Africa," *Social Forces*, 41 (October, 1962), 6–12.

[15] *Ibid.*, p. 11.

[16] Peter Marris, *Family and Social Change in an African City* (1961).

But the kinship ties remain intact, according to Marris; there is still loyalty to the larger group; and the concept of reciprocal assistance to kin, especially to the elders, is a strong force in the lives of the people. Members of the same kinship group, though living separately in nuclear units, meet with considerable regularity, participating in family cere-monies and conducting kinship business. Some of the kinship groups have set up formal organizations by means of which courses of action are planned, decisions jointly made, and responsibilities definitely assigned. Thus "voluntary" associations have tended to develop on the foundations of a kinship group involving a large number of persons bound together by blood ties. Marris points out, however, that the close kinship ties tend to be stronger in the lower class levels than in the higher classes, that families that have prospered have less need for mutual assistance arrangements than those who are economically insecure.[17]

STABILITY AND INSTABILITY IN FAMILY LIFE

Urban families are subject to both disruptive and integrative forces in the community. The separation of work place from residence, pursuit of leisure-time activities away from the family hearth, gainful employment of women outside the home, liberalization of divorce laws and the growth of divorce courts, taking over of traditional family functions by non-family organizations, the decline of family authoritarianism—such are examples of trends that appear to be associated with urbanism. Some of these broader changes have tended to separate family members from one another, as in work or leisure-time activities, and in so doing probably weaken the bonds that tie the family together. Whether these bonds are strong or weak depends in part on the cultural values of the persons in-volved.

But there is another side to the picture: the integrative forces. In the United States the idealization of husband-wife and parent-child compan-ionship has probably enhanced family solidarity. If urban family mem-bers go places and do things separately, they also go places and do things together, often sharing their experiences and interests in a spirit of equal-ity. Such manifestations of family solidarity appear to be more distinctly a middle class than a working-class pattern. The city father who is a stranger to his own children has his counterpart in the parent who par-ticipates with his wife and children in various kinds of joint undertak-ings, both in the home and outside it. The five-day week has at least provided the necessary time for such family activities, and suburban life has afforded a favorable setting.

Then there is the matter of sharing domestic duties. In large families there may be a clear-cut and rigid division of labor, but in families with

[17] *Ibid.,* p. 140.

fewer members the domestic work roles cannot be so effectively differentiated. Futhermore, the virtual disappearance of domestic servants
from middle class homes in the United States has shifted domestic responsibilities to members of the household. Cooking, dishwashing, cleaning, yard care, baby tending, repairing may be viewed as family responsibilities, sometimes undertaken jointly by two or more members. In any
event, household work roles may be performed by any member of the
group, and assignments of individuals to such roles may be only temporary.

The survival of kinship networks and the functional vigor of larger
kinship groups in many of the world's cities would seem to be a counteracting force against fissiparous tendencies that sometimes threaten the
unity or existence of countless urban families. Precisely because the conditions of city life and work represent a marked change from traditional
rural life, at least in most countries, structural and functional adaptations must be made if the family is to survive as a unit. As we have already observed, adaptations *are* being made, in one way or another,
probably with varying degrees of success. The individual counterpart of
these familial adaptations is the adjustment of family members to new
and different family roles and different patterns of interpersonal relationships. Doubtless these changes involve stresses and strains, sometimes
to the point of breakdown of many family units and the demoralization
of their individual members. But it would be premature to conclude
that urbanism has delivered the *coup de grace* to the family as a social
unit. As Key and others have observed, earlier sociological theories that
emphasized disintegration of the family in an urban environment have
not always been supported by recent empirical research, nor is there
convincing evidence that rural-urban differences are as great as they
were once thought to be.[18]

SELECTED BIBLIOGRAPHY

BOOKS

> Bott, Elizabeth, *Family and Social Network*. London: Tavistock Publica
> tions, Ltd., 1957.
> Goode, William J., *World Revolution and Family Patterns*. New York: The
> Free Press of Glencoe, 1963.
> Havighurst, Robert J., *et al.*, *Growing Up in River City*. New York: Wiley,
> 1962.
> Marris, Peter, *Family and Social Change in an African City*. Evanston, Ill.:
> Northwestern University Press, 1962.
> Miller, Daniel R., and Guy E. Swanson, *The Changing American Parent*.
> New York: Wiley, 1958.

[18] William H. Key, "Rural-Urban Differences and the Family," *The Sociological
Quarterly*, 2 (January, 1961), 49–56.

Padilla, Elena, *Up from Puerto Rico,* pp. 101–212. New York: Columbia University Press, 1958.

Ross, Aileen D., *The Hindu Family in Its Urban Setting.* Toronto: University of Toronto Press, 1961.

Seeley, John R., R. Alexander Sim, and E. W. Loosley, *Crestwood Heights,* ch. 7. New York: Basic Books, 1956.

Willmott, Peter, and Michael Young, *Family and Class in a London Suburb.* Glencoe, Ill.: The Free Press, 1960.

ARTICLES

Aldous, J., "Urbanization, the Extended Family, and Kinship Ties in West Africa," *Social Forces,* 41 (October, 1962), 6–12.

Blood, Robert O., and Robert L. Hamblin, "The Effects of the Wife's Employment on the Family Power Structure," *Social Forces,* 36 (May, 1958), 347–52.

Bott, Elizabeth, "Urban Families: The Norms of Conjugal Roles," *Human Relations,* 9 (1956), 325–42.

Key, William H., "Rural-Urban Differences and the Family," *Sociological Quarterly,* 2 (January, 1961), 49–57.

Lee, Rose Hum, "The Established Families of the San Francisco Bay Area," *Midwest Sociologist,* 20 (December, 1957), 19–25.

Masuoka, J., "Urbanization and the Family in Japan," *Sociology and Social Research,* 32 (September–October, 1947), 535–39.

Sjoberg, Gideon, "Familial Organization in the Preindustrial City," *Marriage and Family Living,* 18 (February, 1956), 30–36.

Sussman, Marvin B., "The Help Pattern in the Middle Class Family," *American Sociological Review,* 18 (February, 1953), 22–28.

Voluntary Associations
and Neighborhood Interaction

SEVENTEEN

Social relationships in the city are of many dimensions. In one sphere there are relationships the nature and frequency of which are dictated by traditional rules of family, caste, tribe, or religious body. In another sphere they are determined by political, economic, or juridical institutions.

In a different sphere are the relationships occasioned or determined by voluntary associations. On one level are the relationships of informal associations. On this level there are few explicit rules of conduct. Contacts are commonly intimate, ends in themselves rather than strictly means to an end. There is a wide latitude of permissive behavior.

On another level are the relationships that exist within a formal structural framework. Functions of individuals are more or less explicit. Rules define the conduct of members. Certain individuals are vested with authority. There are specifications as to who shall be included or excluded from membership. Definitions of means and ends may be made in constitutions, by-laws, or other documentary agreements.

Voluntary associations, whether formal or informal, play an important role in the lives of modern men, especially those living and working in an urban environment. In the dynamic cities of the West such associations have flourished without precedent, involving the lives of countless millions. Even among societies in the initial stages of urbanism they are providing mechanisms by means of which many people are making an adjustment to city life. This chapter will focus first on formal voluntary associations and then on informal associations. Participation in such associations varies importantly with such factors as social class.

384

FUNCTIONS OF ASSOCIATIONS

The functions of any particular association may be explicit or implicit, manifest or latent, specific or general. Some associations have a single manifest function; many are multifunctional. Probably the more complex an association becomes the greater the tendency for it to have a diversity of functions, some major ones, others minor.

The number of specific manifest functions performed by groups is legion. Some of the more generalized functions of different associations may be mentioned. (1) Identification with particular associations may confer status or power (or the opposite) on individuals. (2) Some associations provide a mechanism for the socialization of members and their indoctrination with prevailing values and ideologies. (3) As reference groups, they function to marshal public opinion and collective action toward specified goals. (4) They afford a sense of security for the individual, because in conformity there is comfort and in union there is strength, real or fancied. (5) They may offer the pleasures of good fellowship, opportunities for escape from the routine, and surcease from stresses that accompany the competitiveness of modern urban life. (6) They often become ladders for upward social mobility, or escalators for downward movement. (7) In various ways they may bolster the status quo, protect the positions of members through exclusion of outsiders, or foster social change in one form or another. (8) They may have an educational function through the dissemination of information and ideas to the members and others. (9) And they may provide a link that connects the individual with the outer world, thus facilitating his adjustment to the social milieu.

VOLUNTARY ASSOCIATIONS AND URBANIZATION

As societies become more urbanized, in a cultural as well as a demographic sense, traditional forms of organization are often unable to carry out expected functions or to perform other functions necessitated by changing conditions of community life. Presumably urbanization tends to weaken the influence which such institutionalized groups as the family, caste, tribe, or church exercise over their members. Furthermore, the complexities and demands of modern urban life are such that the traditional institutions cannot, by themselves, adequately satisfy all human needs. To meet these needs, however defined by the persons involved, voluntary associations have come into existence. If they did not perform some of these functions they probably would not exist at all.

But their development has not been universally uniform either from one society to another, or even from one community or social class to another in the same society. To understand this diversity of development it would be necessary to examine whole complexes of values, behavior, and social organizations. Mass poverty works against the growth of formal associations; mass affluence favors their development. Mass illiteracy does not provide a favorable social or intellectual climate for their growth; they tend to thrive in an atmosphere created by mass literacy. Where family and caste are the institutionalized hubs around which a social system revolves, as in the case of India, the social and cultural needs of the masses may be effectively met by these traditional mechanisms. Family and caste in India may so encompass the lives of most individuals that only a limited need for voluntary associations is felt.

In France, Rose observed, the Catholic tradition of encompassing the individual within the church, and of encouraging priests rather than laymen to participate in local welfare and improvement activities, tended to deter the formation of associations for civic purposes.[1] It seems probable, also, that authoritarian governments, even in urbanized societies, restrict the numbers of voluntary associations and regulate the functions of those that do exist, in the interest of "national unity."

ASSOCIATIONS IN WESTERN SOCIETY

In the dynamic, democratic societies of the West, urbanization has found expression in the proliferation of vast numbers of voluntary associations, although even here the numbers and character of such organizations have varied considerably. The high incidence of spatial mobility in residential changes of one kind or another, separation of the home from place of work or of recreation, the high incidence of occupational mobility—all these have tended to detach the individual from his traditional moorings and create needs, psychological and otherwise, which existing structures have often been unable to satisfy. Not the least effective in the creation of these needs are the mass media, which touch the lives of people in Westernized societies at many points. Given a competitive social system in which much of the effort of individuals is directed toward the achievement or defense of status, it is not surprising that so many associations function toward these ends.

As Western societies have become increasingly urbanized, there has been a corresponding tendency for urban types of associations to spread beyond the boundaries of cities and become adopted in nonurban communities as well. This diffusion of formal associations, of which there are many instances in American society, has been an important aspect of

[1] Arnold Rose, "Voluntary Associations in France" in Rose (ed.), *Theory and Method in the Social Sciences* (1954), ch. 4.

the "urban impact." Gallaher's study of Plainville provides considerable evidence of the growth of formal associations in a small midwestern village.[2] A study in Denmark, by Anderson and Anderson, was concerned with the changes, over a half-century, of the associational structure in an island community that had been transformed from an isolated fishing town to an urban annex of Copenhagen.[3] During this period the traditional forms of organization declined and were often replaced by new associations around which life tended to be mobilized.

PREVALENCE OF FORMAL ASSOCIATIONS

A number of studies in American and European cities indicate that formal associations are numerous in almost every type and size of community. One of the early studies of associations was done by Warner and his associates in Yankee City, a small New England community. The investigators identified and analyzed 357 associations,[4] which were supported by 6,874 persons, or an average of about two memberships for each member. A similar study in Jonesville, a small town near Chicago, revealed 133 adult organizations and 43 juvenile groups.[5] Axelrod's study of groups in Detroit, based on a sample of 749 persons, revealed that two-thirds (63 per cent) belonged to one or more organizations other than a church, and that 17 per cent were members only of a church.[6]

A survey of voluntary associations in Minnesota in 1957 revealed that the total membership of organizations reporting their size was 2,667,717.[7] Allowing for many unreported memberships, the total membership in the state probably exceeded three million, more than the entire population of Minnesota. Some 294 organizations were large enough to have full-time executive secretaries, and over 400 were statewide in their scope. Most of the larger organizations had headquarters in the Minneapolis–St. Paul metropolitan area. The associations represented a wide range of human activities and interests, including agriculture, science, religion, civic and public affairs, education, health, sports, hobbies, and professional, nationality, veterans' and patriotic groups.

[2] Art Gallaher, *Plainville Fifteen Years Later* (1961).

[3] Robert T. Anderson and Gallatin Anderson, "Voluntary Associations and Urbanization; A Diachronic Analysis," *American Journal of Sociology*, 55 (November, 1959), 263–73.

[4] W. L. Warner and Paul S. Lunt, *The Social Life of a Modern Community* (1941), p. 313.

[5] Marchia Meeker, "The Joiners—Male and Female," in W. L. Warner, *et al.*, *Democracy in Jonesville* (1949), p. 117.

[6] Morris Axelrod, "Urban Structure and Social Participation," *American Sociological Review*, 21 (February, 1956), 13–18.

[7] William C. Rogers, "Voluntary Associations and Urban Community Development." *International Review of Community Development*, No. 7 (1961), pp. 140–41.

The impressive network of formal associations to be found in American cities has helped to create a false stereotype of all urban dwellers as joiners. All the studies indicate that a sizable proportion of the adult urban population is without any formal connections. In a study of social participation of a sample of employed residents of New York City, Komarovsky found that over half (52 per cent) had no organized group affiliations except for church memberships.[8] In Detroit, Axelrod found that 37 per cent of the adults had no formal affiliations.[9] The Lynds estimated that in Middletown the proportion of unaffiliated was 42.[10]

GROUP MEMBERSHIP AND RELATED VARIABLES

Most studies of formal associations have been made in particular localities and have not necessarily been representative of an entire society, both urban and rural. However, two national studies conducted in the United States provide a somewhat more complete picture. One of the studies was conducted in 1954 by the American Institute of Public Opinion (AIPO), and the other in 1955 by the National Opinion Research Center (NORC). For reasons not altogether clear, the results of the two surveys are different in certain respects.[11] For example, the AIPO survey found that 55 per cent of all the persons in the sample belonged to one or more formal associations, whereas NORC found that only 36 per cent were members.[12]

SIZE OF COMMUNITY AND MEMBERSHIP

Both surveys suggested that the proportion of adults having associational memberships was lower in large cities than in smaller centers. In the AIPO study, 47 per cent of the sample of adults in cities over a quarter of a million were members of one or more associations. This percent-

---

[8] Mirra Komarovsky, "The Voluntary Associations of Urban Dwellers," *American Sociological Review,* 11 (December, 1946), 686–98.

[9] Axelrod, *op. cit.,* p. 15.

[10] Robert S. Lynd and Helen M. Lynd, *Middletown* (1929), p. 308.

[11] Murray Hausknecht, *The Joiners* (1962). This is a summary and discussion of the findings of the two surveys. For an analysis of two NORC surveys see Charles R. Wright and Herbert H. Hyman, "Voluntary Association Memberships of American Adults: Evidence from National Sample Surveys," *American Sociological Review,* 23 (June, 1958), 284–94.

[12] These differences may have been due to methods of interviewing. It seems probable that the NORC data on memberships represent an underenumeration.

age increased with decreasing size of cities. In counties with all communities under 10,000, 68 per cent of the residents belonged to associations. The percentages for village and farm residents belonging to associations were 56 and 54, respectively. The NORC findings indicated a similar pattern, though the differences were smaller.[13]

RACE

Comparative data on the incidence of Negro and white memberships in voluntary associations are by no means consistent. Both the AIPO and NORC surveys indicated a larger proportion of whites than of Negroes were members of one or more associations. These percentages were as follows: AIPO—whites 55, Negroes 54; NORC—whites 37, Negroes 27.[14] Since these studies were based on a national sample, they included persons in communities of varying size and social composition.

Other studies, however, reach different conclusions. In his classic study of race relations in the United States, Myrdal concluded that Negroes belong to relatively more associations than whites.[15] He estimated that in 1935 there were some 200 associations among the 7,500 Negroes in Natchez, Mississippi, and about 4,000 organizations maintained by the quarter of a million Negroes in Chicago.[16]

Drake and Cayton also reached similar conclusions based on their study of Negroes in Chicago.[17] Ladinsky identified 46 all-Negro associations among the 2,500 Negroes in Columbia, Missouri, and estimated that 37 per cent of the Negro population were members of one or more associations, with an average number of 1.7 memberships per person.[18] In addition, Negroes were members of 29 liaison associations which were predominantly white.

On the basis of a study of Negro associations in Lincoln, Nebraska, Babchuk and Thompson concluded that Negroes were more disposed than whites to join organizations, though they did not make direct comparisons.[19] Three out of four adults in the sample belonged to one or more associations, exclusive of the church affiliations held by seven out of eight persons in the sample.

These data appear to be consistent with well-known facts concerning

[13] No direct comparisons can be made because the method of classifying cities by size were not the same for the two surveys.

[14] Hausknecht, *op. cit.*, p. 62. The NORC survey included memberships of *all* persons in each family in the sample. Union memberships were also included.

[15] Gunnar Myrdal, *et al.*, *The American Dilemma* (1944), p. 952.

[16] *Ibid.*, pp. 952–55.

[17] St. Clair Drake and Horace R. Cayton, *Black Metropolis* (1945), pp. 526–751.

[18] Jack Ladinsky, *Voluntary Associations and Social Participation of Negroes in a Small City*, unpublished master's thesis, University of Missouri, 1957.

[19] Nicholas Babchuk and Ralph V. Thompson, "The Voluntary Associations of Negroes," *American Sociological Review*, 27 (October, 1962), 647–55.

the restricted position of Negroes in American communities. Since Negroes do not have the same access as whites to many status-lending organizations, or have the same opportunities for achievement that whites enjoy, they tend to create their own social world in the form of associations to which they do have access. The inclination of Negroes to join organizations may, as Babchuk and Thompson observe, also reflect the loose structure of the Negro family, especially on the lower social levels. The implication is that unstable families mean weak kinship ties, which in turn are hardly conducive to visiting and cooperative relationships among members of the same kinship group; hence, the tendency to turn to associations and churches for the personal satisfactions that may be denied them in other situations. Revealingly, many of the associations included in the Lincoln and Columbia studies bore such names as the Birthday Club or the Saturday Nighters Society.

RELIGION

The AIPO and NORC surveys indicated that religious preference or affiliation is an important variable in the associational life of Americans, both showing that Catholics were less inclined than Protestants and Jews to belong to voluntary associations. However, AIPO indicated a higher percentage of Protestants than Jews were members, but NORC showed that Jews were much more disposed to belong to associations than either of the other two groups.

These differences may be explained, at least hypothetically, in terms of other related variables. The fact that Catholics, as a class, rank lower educationally and economically than Protestants and Jews probably accounts in part for the comparatively low percentage of memberships. Restrictions imposed by the Church on the associational life of the members may also tend to limit participation in secular organizations. The Jews, on the other hand, are comparatively well-educated, and most of them are in comfortable financial circumstances. Moreover, they are city dwellers by long tradition.

EDUCATION

Various studies indicate that a positive correlation exists between the amount of formal schooling and the proportion of people holding memberships in formal associations. The AIPO survey revealed, for example, that about three-fourths of the respondents having a college education held memberships in associations, compared with three-fifths of those who had attended only high school, and about two-fifths of those with an elementary education.[20] A similar picture was presented in the NORC

[20] Hausknecht, *op. cit.*, p. 38.

study. Education, of course, is related to income and occupational status, and all of these factors taken together account for some of the leisure time—little or much—the individual has at his disposal. Membership in associations often involves considerable leisure time as well as money. But education also tends to widen the individual's range of interests, which can often be satisfied through participation in formal associations.

CITY AND SUBURB

A study conducted in Flint, Michigan, by Zimmer and Hawley classified the respondents by residential location, either in the central city or in the suburban fringe.[21] In Flint, the percentage of migrant male household heads belonging to associations tended to increase with length of residence in the metropolitan area. This was true of both central city and fringe residents.

One surprising aspect of the Zimmer-Hawley study was the finding that central city residents were more inclined than fringe residents to participate in formal associations. This was true regardless of how the respondents were classified, whether by age, education, occupation, income, or length of residence. An exception was skilled workers. For example, two-fifths of the central city respondents belonged to one or more associations, compared with approximately one-fourth of the fringe residents. One-fifth of the migrants residing in the fringe less than 10 years were members of associations, compared with two-fifths of the migrants living in the central city. Similarly, one-fourth of the migrants who were fringe residents over 10 years were members of associations, while 45 per cent of those residing in central cities for this length of time were participants.

The explanation of these differences between central city and fringe cannot be attributed to demographic or economic differences, as indicated above. Most likely, in the opinion of Zimmer and Hawley, participation in formal associations is an aspect of a more inclusive pattern of participant behavior. They found that the central city residents of Flint exceeded fringe residents in labor union membership, church attendance, election registrations, and in the proportion of persons voting in the last two elections. Labor union members, of course, are primarily manual workers, and these are generally concentrated heavily in central cities.

It would be unwise to generalize from a single study, such as the one conducted in Flint. The character of suburbs and central cities, and the patterns of behavior in them, may vary from one locality to another, depending on the demographic characteristics and social structures of the communities involved.

[21] Basil G. Zimmer and Amos H. Hawley, "The Significance of Membership in Associations," *American Journal of Sociology*, 55 (September, 1959), 196–201.

INCOME AND OCCUPATION

All the available studies point consistently to the tendency for people having high incomes and holding high-status occupations to participate more extensively in formal associations than individuals on lower socio-economic levels. In Detroit, Axelrod found that four-fifths of the respondents with incomes of $7,000 or over belonged to one or more formal groups, compared with two-fifths of those on the bottom levels of $3,000 or less.[22] Middle income persons were about as active in associations as those on the higher levels. The Detroit data also showed that occupational differences are important. For example, three-fifths of the professionals, managers, and proprietors (taken together) belonged to one or more formal associations, compared with two-fifths of the skilled and semiskilled manual workers.

In an earlier study in New York City, Komarovsky found that about three-fifths of the male manual workers, half of the white collar employees, one-third of the businessmen, and a fifth of the professionals were *without* group affiliations.[23] Among the females, almost nine-tenths of the working class women, two-thirds of the white collar women, half of those engaged in business, and one-sixth of the professionals did *not* have group membership.

That income and occupational status are important factors in associational participation is also shown by both AIPO and NORC national surveys.[24] In the AIPO sample, for example, 46 per cent of the respondents with incomes under $2,000 were participants. This increased consistently with larger incomes, and in the high income bracket, $7,000 or over, 69 per cent were members. A similar pattern was revealed when the variables were occupational classes. In the NORC sample, 53 per cent of the respondents classed as professionals, proprietors, managers, and officials were members of one or more associations, compared with 41 per cent of the clerical and sales people, 32 per cent of the skilled workers, and 23 per cent of the semiskilled personnel.

Urban Working-class Associations. Dotson's study of social participation among 50 working class families in New Haven provides further supporting evidence that formal group participation and membership are primarily middle and upper class phenomena.[25] All persons included in the sample were American-born, and all employed adults were in skilled or semiskilled occupations. Three-fifths of the men and four-fifths of the

---

[22] *Op. cit.*, p. 13.   [23] Komarovsky, *op. cit.*, p. 688.
[24] Hausknecht, *op. cit.*, pp. 24–25.
[25] Floyd Dotson, "Patterns of Voluntary Associations among Working Class Families," *American Sociological Review,* 16 (October, 1951), 687–93.

women had no affiliations with formal associations. Even the affiliates of labor unions and fraternal societies were not ordinarily active participants. Associations having the most active participation of members were athletic and church groups.

Similar results were obtained in a study of 480 women in Chicago, Louisville, Trenton, and Tacoma.[26] About three-fourths of the middle class wives were engaged in club work, but only one-fourth of the working class women were so engaged. However, working class wives became more active in voluntary organizations, particularly Parent-Teacher Associations, after they were relieved of full-time responsibilities for child care. Generally speaking, the working class wives tended to join child-centered associations, whereas middle class women were more oriented toward adult-centered organizations such as golf or country clubs, civic organizations, and associations with cultural or artistic interests.

INTEGRATIVE AND DIVISIVE INFLUENCES

Associations may be either integrative or divisive for the community or society. They may bring individuals or groups into more harmonious or cooperative relationships, or they may promote competition or conflict. They may foster the integration or adjustment of the individual, or they may tend to isolate him, and others of his kind, from the rest of the community. Actually, associations may be both integrative and divisive, depending on the perspective from which they are viewed.

There are many associations, characteristically urban, which are integrative in their manifest or latent functions. Occupational or trade associations are, in the main, cooperative organizations in which members of the same occupation combine to further their own interests and objectives, which may or may not parallel the objectives of other groups or the community as a whole. Community teachers' associations or chambers of commerce ostensibly represent both the interests of the members and of the community at large. Federations such as local ministerial alliances, councils of social agencies, or federations of labor unions have the manifest function of integrating certain groups within a given area. Such civic organizations as the League of Women Voters or the Red Cross Board are integrative in the sense that they represent the larger community or society rather than special-interest groups.

Whatever deep social cleavages exist within a community, whether along economic, racial, ethnic, or religious lines, associations tend to develop within these social boundaries, although by no means exclusively so.

[26] Lee Rainwater, *et al., Workingman's Wife: Her Personality, World, and Life Style* (1959).

CANTONVILLE, CANADA

This tendency is well illustrated in Hughes' analysis of the associational structure of Cantonville, a small Canadian city, in which the major cleavage is between the French-Canadians, who are Catholic and French-speaking, and the English-Canadians, who are Protestant and English-speaking.[27] In addition, the French-Canadians are distributed widely in the occupational hierarchy but with a preponderance of shopkeepers and manual workers; English-Canadians are mainly in the managerial and technical occupations.

Some of the Cantonville associations were composed exclusively either of French-Canadians or English-Canadians. On the other hand, several associations cut across ethnic and religious lines, often with membership either preponderantly French or English. Among the associations with mixed membership were golf, baseball, hockey, and tennis clubs, an ambulance corps, and the chamber of commerce. Both the golf club and the chamber of commerce were composed mainly of the successful men in the community, but included some of the minor managers, clerical personnel, and lesser professionals.

NEW HAVEN

Differentiation of associations by racial, ethnic, religious, and prestige cleavages is demonstrated in a study by Minnis of 177 women's organizations in New Haven.[28] These associations, in the view of Minnis, "are not formed according to a simple pattern of functional differentiation and diversity of membership interests, but are born and exist in a complex pattern of interlocking strands of cleavage." [29]

The most rigid distinction was racial, with at least 90 per cent of the New Haven organizations being racially exclusive. Those with racially mixed memberships were mainly in church auxiliaries, veterans' organizations, and associations providing community services supervised by administrative officers.

Three-fourths of the organizations were religiously exclusive, revealing a cleavage between Protestants, Catholics, and Jews. Among these associations, for example, were the Council of Church Women (Protestant), Council of Catholic Women, Council of Jewish Women, Ladies Auxiliary of New Haven Veterans of Foreign Wars, and Sergeant Fish-

[27] Everett C. Hughes, *French-Canada in Transition* (1943), ch. 13.

[28] Mhyra S. Minnis, "Cleavage in Women's Organizations: A Reflection of the Social Structure of a City," *American Sociological Review*, 18 (February, 1953), 47–53.

[29] *Ibid.*, p. 53.

man Auxiliary of Jewish War Veterans. This differentiation by religion had no necessary reference to the functions of the organizations; many of them whose services were of a nonreligious character had religious restrictions on membership.

More than half of the organizations were structured along ethnic lines, representing dominant groups of cultural minorities. Examples of such associations were the Polish Falcons, the Svithiod Lodge (Scandinavian), Daughters of the American Revolution (Old American stock), and Saint Mother Cabrini Society (Italian).

Various combinations of restrictiveness were apparent. Some groups, for example, restricted membership along three lines—race, religion, and ethnic characteristics. An example would be a Catholic group which admitted only Italians of Caucasian ancestry. Others restricted membership along two lines, as in the case of a Negro group admitting only Protestants. Still others drew only one line, say, race or religion. Few groups followed a completely open-door policy with respect to these attributes.

The extent to which the organizational structure is differentiated is well illustrated by the number of junior leagues in the city: Junior League of New Haven (Protestant), Catholic Junior League, Junior Community League (Negro), B'nai B'rith Junior League (Jewish), Swedish Junior League, Italian Junior League, and Polish Junior League. As one might expect, these leagues occupy different positions in the status hierarchy of the city.

VOLUNTARY ASSOCIATIONS IN OTHER COUNTRIES

Sufficient data are not available to permit a detailed comparison of the associational structure of American cities with that of cities in other countries, but on the basis of limited evidence there is some reason to believe that American cities are more organized in this respect than cities elsewhere.

MEXICO

Dotson's study of associational affiliations of 415 adults in Guadalajara, Mexico, a city of about 278,000 revealed that two-fifths of the men and one-third of the women in the sample were members of formal organizations.[30] Only five men and six women in the sample belonged to three or more groups, and only one person held membership in as many as five associations.

[30] Floyd Dotson, "Participation in Voluntary Associations in a Mexican City," *American Sociological Review*, 18 (August, 1953), 380–86.

About four-fifths of the women having associational membership belonged to church-affiliated groups, but only one-sixth of the men were so affiliated. About one-fourth of the men belonged to athletic associations, and an additional fourth to labor unions. Only one in twenty was a member of a professional or learned society.

As in American cities, there was a close relationship between associational membership and economic status. Of those on the lowest economic level (less than 250 pesos [$20] per month) only one-fifth held membership in any voluntary association. Not until a monthly income of 2,000 to 3,000 pesos was reached—roughly a middle class stratum—were more than half of the persons affiliated with such groups.

Relatively few of the associations represented indigenous developments, according to Dotson, but rather were importations, at least in form, from other cultures. Such associations as insurance societies, service clubs, labor unions, country clubs, and professional societies were patterned closely after organizations in the United States and Europe.

CANADA

A vivid account of voluntary associations in Crestwood Heights, an achievement-oriented middle class suburb of Toronto, is provided by Seeley, Sim, and Loosley.[31] In a comparatively new community such as Crestwood Heights, family and reputation are not especially important in the status system since most of the residents are either strangers to each other or have had short acquaintances. Hence they have turned to voluntary associations, partly as a means of enhancing their prestige or strengthening the social positions they have already achieved. The number of associations in the community is sufficiently large and varied to provide social outlets for individuals on different prestige levels. Some of the associations are adult-centered and adult-controlled, some are child-centered and child-controlled, while others are child-centered and adult-controlled.

In Crestwood Heights, where the emphasis is on achieved status rather than lineage, voluntary associations figure prominently as a mechanism for upward social mobility. Speaking of the adult-centered associations the authors say: "The . . . associations operate largely to validate the present social status of the members and to open avenues to higher status in the future. In them it is possible for adults to learn new patterns of behavior under the sponsorship of other adults." [32] By the same token, the child-centered, adult-controlled associations perform the function of conferring status on the child member and preparing him for an appropriate social position in the future.

[31] John R. Seeley, R. Alexander Sim, and Elizabeth W. Loosley, *Crestwood Heights* (1956), ch. 10.
[32] *Ibid.*, p. 300.

A study of voluntary associations in Squirebridge, England, a small commercial city of about 15,000 population, affords a basis for comparison with similar studies of organizations in cities of similar size in the United States.[33] Altogether, the investigator found 135 voluntary associations in the community. Comparisons may be made of the following cities:[34]

	Squirebridge	Boulder	Middletown	Yankee City
Population	15,000	11,985	27,142	17,000
No. associations	135	268	363	357
No. residents per associa- tion	111	45	75	48
Total memberships	14,649	17,324	23,963	12,876
Average membership	109	65	66	36

The foregoing data indicate that the English city was not as highly organized as the three American cities in terms of number of associations. The average number of members for each association, however, was much larger in Squirebridge than in the American cities. No doubt the small membership average for Yankee City groups was due in part to the inclusion of children's organizations in the study.

Many voluntary associations in Squirebridge were dominated by males; in fact, about two-thirds of the memberships were those of men. Such organizations as sports clubs, social clubs, trade and professional associations, charitable organizations, and groups for service or ex-service personnel were composed mainly of men. On the other hand, women predominated in religious, cultural, and educational organizations. Indeed, memberships in churches and church organizations accounted for about two-fifths of all female affiliations.

The tendency for Squirebridge women to dominate the cultural, educational, and religious organizations appears to be true of American urban women as well, although in this country women appear to be more active in charitable and benevolent activities than men.

A study of Derby, England (200,000 population), conducted by Cauter and Downham, revealed that 47 per cent of the adult population (two-thirds of the males and one-third of the females) were members of voluntary associations,[35] not including trade unions and professional organizations. As in American cities, membership rates were highest among the

[33] Thomas Bottomore, "Social Stratification in Voluntary Organizations," ch. 13 in D. V. Glass (ed.), *Social Mobility in Britain* (1954).

[34] In the Squirebridge and Middletown studies, only persons 15 or over were included. The Yankee City study included "subadults" under 20, whereas the Boulder study recorded data only for persons 20 years and over.

[35] T. Cauter and J. S. Downham, *The Communication of Ideas* (1954), pp. 64–66.

well-educated middle classes, and lowest among working-class persons and those with only an elementary education. Only 4 per cent of the working classes belonged to three or more associations, compared with one-fourth of the upper middle class.

FRANCE

Two reports on voluntary associations in France are in only partial agreement. Rose assembled data from three surveys, including a market research in 1951 based on a national sample, and three surveys of small provincial cities in France.[36] The national survey indicated that about 41 per cent of the French adults belong to some kind of formal association. Some 30 per cent were members of an occupational association, 9 per cent of athletic or other recreational organizations, 6 per cent of "cultural" associations, and smaller percentages in political parties, fraternal and social clubs, veterans' organizations, religious associations, and so on. Numerous associations were listed in one of the small-city studies, but the investigators concluded that for this community such organizations were not very important in the lives of the people. Apparently only two or three of the groups provided a strong bond between the members. After interviewing a number of sociologists and other informed persons, Rose concluded that many of the associations are "paper" organizations that do not touch the lives of the members very deeply.

A study undertaken by Gallagher in a French provincial city of 50,000 suggested that voluntary associations were probably more numerous and important than Rose had concluded.[37] In this city there were upward of 300 formal associations, and Gallagher reported that he knew of no person in the three upper classes who did not belong to at least two organizations. Although formal associations may be less numerous than in comparable cities of the United States, the actual numbers, in Gallagher's opinion, are less important than the functions which they perform—and in this respect they also differ from American groups. Generally speaking, they are less important functionally in providing a mechanism for social mobility than associations in the United States. On the other hand, functions related to maintenance, defense, and welfare are important. Groups providing these functions include agricultural organizations, veterans' associations to help needy members, or associations to assist dependent children and widowed mothers. However, because of the major importance both of government and the Catholic Church in providing certain kinds of social services, such groups are probably less vital than in the United States.

[36] Rose, *op. cit.*, pp. 72–77.
[37] Orvoell R. Gallagher, "Voluntary Associations in France," *Social Forces*, 36 (December, 1957), 153–60.

ASSOCIATIONS IN ASIAN CITIES

There is reason to believe that voluntary associations have not flourished in most Asian cities to the extent that they have developed in the West. On the basis of evidence now available it appears that even in Asia there is a wide variation in the number and character of associations existing in any large city. Many of the associations are importations—aspects of the process of Westernization. Among such organizations are Rotary Club, Boy and Girl Scouts, Y.M.C.A. and Y.W.C.A., sports clubs, and so on. Others are indigenous in character.

A survey conducted in the Indian city of Kolhapur, a former state capital of 80,000, revealed only 63 voluntary associations, which included 10 Western-style clubs.[38] Thus there were about 1,200 persons for each association. The investigator concluded that less than 4 per cent of the population of the city had any direct contacts with such organizations. The senior author of this volume observed comparatively few associations in Bangalore, a city of nearly a million. Among the prominent associations were the Western-style social clubs of which there were three in the city. These associations had elaborate facilities for the benefit of a large number of members, many of whom were among the elite of the community. In Indian cities caste, tribe, and kinship are so basic in the fulfillment of many of the needs of the population that voluntary associations have few functions to perform. But as urbanism there, as elsewhere, tends to weaken the traditional institutions, it seems probable that voluntary associations will increase in numbers and importance, filling the gaps in the social systems that are undergoing change.

A sociological study of a middle class district of Tokyo indicated that the residents did not rely very heavily on formal associations.[39] Of a sample of 104 adults in the district, 25 persons reported memberships in 31 associations (excluding those in which membership is conferred automatically by residence). A few leisure-time associations existed, but for the most part the residents found their recreation in informal associations or in attendance at mass sports or theatrical events. Several charitable and civic societies were also in existence, and other organizations promoting particular ideas, but these were supported mainly by women or youth. The investigator concluded that the Japanese are not great joiners, that they are much less inclined to identify with formal associations than the British or Americans.

One exception to the disinclination of most Asians to develop formal associations is the overseas Chinese. A study of the Chinese minority in

[38] N. V. Sovani, *Social Survey of Kolhapur City*, Gokhale Institute of Politics and Economics, Poona (1952).
[39] R. P. Dore, *City Life in Japan* (1958), pp. 245–46, 453, and 220n.

Bangkok, Thailand, indicated that the formal associational structure was highly developed by this ethnic minority consisting of a half-million persons.[40] Apparently most of the adults are members of one or more associations.

The organizations fall into four major categories: (1) surname associations, consisting of persons with the same surname who trace their origin to a single male ancestor or who came from the same region of China; (2) regional or dialect associations, composed of persons speaking the same regional dialect; (3) occupational or business associations, including organizations of businessmen and trade unionists (of this group the most prestigious and influential is the Chinese Chamber of Commerce); (4) benevolent and charitable associations which provide assistance to Chinese individuals or families in distress.

Within the framework of each of these formal associations are informal activities of one kind or another. Since the government of Thailand does not provide very extensively for the welfare of the Chinese, who are considered outsiders, the members of the Chinese community have been forced to depend on their own mutual-aid organizations. Furthermore, these associations provide the mechanism through which authority may be exercised, public opinion molded, social conflicts resolved, economic activity promoted, and the Chinese culture preserved.

ASSOCIATIONS IN AFRICAN CITIES

Numerous observers of urban trends in Africa have commented on the proliferation of voluntary associations in some of the African cities.[41] These associations represent attempts at adjustment to the social conditions of an urban environment. They both symbolize and facilitate a transition from the social system focused on tribe and kinship to a highly differentiated system emphasizing achieved rather than ascribed status. Some of the associations are traditional; some are modifications of traditional organizations; while others are strictly modern, the products of life and work in the city. Some are built around the concept of mutual aid; others emphasize recreation and entertainment; still others are occupational in character. Through the mechanisms of these associations, urban ideas, behavior norms, technical skills, and new forms of social relationships become a part of the experiences and understandings of city people, many of whom have recent village backgrounds. Of this process Little writes:

[40] Richard J. Coughlin, *Double Identity* (1960).
[41] Kenneth Little, "The Role of Voluntary Associations in West African Urbanization," *American Anthropologist*, 59 (August, 1957), 579–96. Cf. Guy Hunter, *The New Societies of Tropical Africa* (1962); Michael Banton, *West African City: A Study of Tribal Life in Freetown* (1957).

Women, and younger people in general, possess a new status in the urban economy, and this is reflected in the various functions which these associations perform as political pressure groups, in serving as a forum for political expression, and in providing both groups with training in modern methods of business. Equally significant is the fact that women's participation in societies with mixed membership involves them in a new kind of social relationship with men. . . . In particular, voluntary associations provide an outlet for the energies and ambitions of the rising class of young men with a tribal background who have been to school.[42]

Such associations, writes Little, assist the newly-arrived migrant in making an adjustment to an urban milieu. For many, they substitute for the extended family, affording an opportunity for social participation and companionship on the basis of common interests. Some associations have a large number of offices, which may enable even the most humble member, if elected to one, to feel that he "belongs."

Such an association also substitutes for the extended family in providing counsel and protection, in terms of legal aid; and by placing him in the company of women members, it also helps to find him a wife. It also substitutes for some of the economic support available at home by supplying him with sickness and funeral benefits, thereby enabling him to continue his most important kinship obligations. Further, it introduces him to a number of economically useful habits and practices, such as punctuality and thrift, and it aids his social reorientation by inculcating new standards of dress, etiquette, and personal hygiene. Above all, by encouraging him to mix with persons outside his own lineage and sometimes tribe, the voluntary association helps him to adjust to the more cosmopolitan ethos of the city.[43]

DISADVANTAGED URBAN MINORITIES AND ASSOCIATIONS

In an earlier section of this chapter the question was posed concerning reasons for the prevalence of voluntary associations among Negroes in the United States. It was suggested that Negroes, being denied privileges and opportunities commonly accorded whites in American society, create numerous associations as a means of satisfying otherwise unmet social needs.

Such a plausible interpretation of Negro associations suggests the hypothesis that ethnic or racial minorities that are the objects of discrimination generally tend to rely extensively on associations of their own creation. The Chinese minority in Bangkok is a case in point. Although the Chinese have prospered and achieved considerable economic power, they are regarded by the Thai people with distrust and even hostility, and are subjected to discrimination in various ways. They cannot, for example, hold public office, or purchase land, or receive benefits of welfare legisla-

---

[42] *Op. cit.,* p. 592. [43] *Ibid.,* p. 593.

tion accorded Thai citizens. Hence they find it expedient to depend on their own mutual-aid and status-conferring associations. A similar situation prevails among the Indians in Durban, South Africa.[44] Restrictive and discriminatory measures imposed by the South African government have forced the Indian minority (and other minorities as well) to develop a *modus vivendi* which can be carried on in part through their own associations. The result is a proliferation of associations in the Indian minority.

INFORMAL GROUPS

Social units having little or no formal structure represent one of the most important types of human groupings in both urban and rural society. Although structural characteristics rather than the nature of social interaction are used here to distinguish formal from informal groups, the differences between the two categories tend to be relative. Organized groups have their elements of informality, just as some informal groups may involve certain formal relationships between members.

STRUCTURAL FEATURES

Some informal groups have only sufficient structure to identify them as a social entity. They have no name, no rules, no formal agreements, no designated purpose; social ties binding the members together are based essentially on mutual attraction of personalities or upon emotional or intellectual satisfactions afforded by intimate association. Old cronies who gravitate fairly regularly to a convenient loafing place in a park; habitués of a tavern or saloon between whom a "we feeling" has evolved into a sense of group-belonging; street-corner hangers-on who drift regularly to the same spot to fraternize with "the boys"; coteries of housewives who regularly hold their midmorning coffees, to the exclusion of other neighbors; small clusters of workers who regularly eat together at lunch time, away from other workers in the same plant or store—these are representative groups characteristic of urban society. Sometimes members of such groups meet together at a designated time and place; sometimes they meet irregularly to suit their fancy or convenience.

Slightly further up the organizational scale are informal groups distinguishable by a name and even by a specified central purpose or activity. Often their names are indicative of their functions or intragroup relationships: the Sewing Susies or Happy Hot Rodders, for example. These groups commonly have some principle for selection of members; leadership-followership patterns emerge; certain canons of conduct are tacitly or explicitly approved.

Informal groups composed of younger persons tend to be sharply age-

[44] Hilda Kuper, *Indian People in Natal* (1960).

and sex-graded, and commonly differentiated also by ethnic, racial, or religious attributes. Among adults, age- and sex-grading is not as rigidly observed, but it is an aspect of social organization nevertheless.

TYPES

Informal groups vary according to their degree of exclusiveness and social solidarity. A clique may be designated as an informal group composed of persons whose friendships are confined entirely or mainly to a single coterie of individuals. Such groupings exhibit a marked degree of social cohesion. They are a distinct social entity, whether or not they have a name. In most informal groups, however, the members have friendships outside the circle or are associated with one or more other such groups. Luncheon cliques may be rigidly exclusive for a lunchtime situation only, but members in their evening or weekend hours of leisure may associate themselves with informal groups having a different membership.

Many individuals, of course, could hardly be considered members of an informal group, yet they may have a wide range of friendships and acquaintanceships. On the other hand, there are undoubtedly persons who not only have no informal group associations but who also have no close friendship ties with anyone.

CLIQUES IN YANKEE CITY

Warner's study of Yankee City revealed the existence of hundreds of informal associations.[45] In fact, some 22,000 clique memberships were recorded. Many persons were members of two or more cliques. Warner was especially interested in the relationship of cliques to the class structure of Yankee City. He found, as one might suspect, that cliques tended to be composed of persons from the same or similar class positions. Warner's contribution was not so much in the discovery and identification of a large number of cliques in the city, but in the analysis of their significance in maintaining the class structure and in providing a means of social mobility. Little attention was paid to the actual dynamics of cliques or to cliqueless individuals.

ELMTOWN'S CLIQUES

In a study of adolescent society in Elmtown (Morris, Illinois), Hollingshead identified 259 cliques.[46] Of these, 106 were composed of boys and girls having intimate associations in the school; 120 were recreational

[45] W. L. Warner and Paul S. Lunt, *The Social Life of a Modern Community* (1941), pp. 350–55.
[46] A. B. Hollingshead, *Elmtown's Youth* (1949), ch. 9.

cliques, centering around recreation outside the school situation; and 33 were institutional cliques which developed in specific nonschool organizations such as Sunday School and Boy Scouts.

As in Yankee City, Elmtown's cliques were class-oriented. Of 1,258 clique members about whom data was secured, three out of five of the clique relationships were between persons in the same prestige class; two out of five were between students in adjacent social classes; but only one in 25 clique relationships cut across two class lines. There were no instances of clique ties crossing three class lines. So far as intimate associations were concerned, students at the upper and lower extremes of the five-class structure were almost completely isolated from each other. Boys and girls from "across the tracks" or "back of the yards" seldom mingled intimately with those living in fashionable sections.

INFORMAL ASSOCIATION IN DETROIT AND NEW HAVEN

In Detroit, Axelrod found a positive, though not a high, correlation between the frequency of informal and formal participation.[47] Contacts with relatives were by far the most frequent, those with coworkers off the job the least frequent. On a six-point status scale there was little difference among the respondents in frequency of contacts with relatives, but frequency of contacts with friends and coworkers tended to increase with status. For example, one-third of the low-status persons interviewed had informal contacts with friends at least a few times a month, compared with three-fifths of those in the highest status category. The same pattern obtained for educational differentials. Eight per cent of the low-educated persons (sixth grade or less) had associations with coworkers at least a few times a month, but this proportion increased to one-fourth on the higher educational levels. Altogether, the frequency of association tended to increase with status as measured by the status scale. One-fourth of the low-status people had 20 or more informal contacts during a two-month period, compared with two-fifths of those on the upper status levels.

Although New Haven working-class families studied by Dotson had comparatively few connections with formal groups, they had many informal associations.[48] The kinship clique was by far the most important type of group in the lives of these people. Leisure-time activities of both husbands and wives in 15 of the 50 families occurred almost completely in association with their own kin, and in another 28 families regular visiting relationships with relatives represented a major feature of their social life. Some of the families had fairly strong neighborhood ties.

[47] *Op. cit.*, p. 119.
[48] "Patterns of Voluntary Associations among Working Class Families," *op. cit.*, pp. 690–93.

PEER GROUPS AMONG BOSTON'S WEST END ITALIANS

In an analysis of the social system of an Italian working-class neighborhood in Boston, Gans concluded that social life outside the place of work tended to revolve around the "peer group," which consisted both of compatible kinsmen and of congenial friends of a similar age, economic level, and cultural interests.[49] These groups were not formally structured, but rather existed as informal collectivities which, in their totality, constituted a network of associations for the district.

The peer groups meet more or less regularly in the kitchens and living rooms of the residents. There are, says Gans, no formal notices of meetings, and no invitations; members drop in for the evening, usually after dinner, and the talk goes on commonly until after midnight. Usually the conversation centers around such topics as weddings and celebrations, recollections of earlier days, local anecdotes, deviant behavior, neighborhood activities, and, for the women, child-rearing and housekeeping. There is little interest in politics or other developments that do not touch their lives more or less directly. Nor is there much interest in formal organizations, with the exception of a few church-related groups, a labor union, and a few informal clubs which meet in halls or vacant rooms leased for this purpose. The West Enders, says Gans, "live within the group; they do not like to be alone." Privacy, so often cherished by the middle classes, has little appeal. From childhood on they have been socialized to belong to a peer group; to be apart from it brings anxieties and discomfort.

INFORMAL NEIGHBORHOOD INTERACTION

Interpersonal communication between persons living in close spatial proximity has doubtless been carried on in almost every conceivable kind of settlement, in urban as well as in folk or rural communities. But the form and content of neighborhood communication are by no means the same in all community situations. Neighborhoods themselves differ in their economic, ecological, demographic, cultural, and physical characteristics; hence patterns of interaction between neighbors may vary greatly, even within the same neighborhood.

Certain stereotyped notions abound concerning the nature of urban neighborhoods and of interaction patterns within them. To state categorically, as did Wirth, that "the contacts of the city may indeed be face to face, but they are nevertheless impersonal, superficial, transitory, and

---

[49] Herbert J. Gans, *The Urban Villagers* (1962), chs. 2 and 4.

segmental" [50] is to ignore the varied forms of social interaction that may actually exist within a neighborhood setting, just as Cooley erred in the other direction by categorically defining the neighborhood as a primary group, ignoring the impersonal contacts that may also exist.[51]

Theoretically, one might arrange the patterns of neighborhood interaction on a continuum. At one end of the continuum would be a neighborhood characterized by extreme personal isolation of the residents. Social contacts would be casual and fleeting. There would be no intimacy, no mutual exchange of favors, no back-and-forth visiting. Such a neighborhood may never actually exist, but possibly the roominghouse district or area of homeless men approaches such an extreme type. Even in such atomized neighborhoods many of the residents doubtless interact on an informal and friendly basis.

FACTORS IN NEIGHBORHOOD INTERACTION

Neighborhood interaction is influenced by varied factors. Individuals who belong to the same associations outside the neighborhood, or have similar vocational, religious, or recreational interests, are likely to have a common basis for personal communication if they reside close together in the same area. Sweetser found in his study of a neighborhood in Bloomington, Indiana, that the factors of sex and age were important.[52] There was a marked tendency for individuals to become intimate only with members of their sex; on the acquaintance level there was no such selectivity. More pronounced than sex selection, however, was the tendency for people of all ages to associate preferentially with their own age group, both on the intimate and the acquaintance level.

INTERACTION IN A ROCHESTER NEIGHBORHOOD

The findings of Sweetser resemble in certain respects the results of a study conducted by Foley in a middle class district of Rochester, New York, a city of about 500,000 inhabitants.[53] Foley justifiably proposes to examine certain widespread generalizations concerning the character of neighborhood communication in light of empirical evidence. Data on neighborhood relationships were secured from 446 persons residing within an area selected for study. Most of the informants had spent most

    [50] Louis Wirth, "Urbanism as a Way of Life," *American Journal of Sociology,* 44 (July, 1938), 15.
    [51] C. H. Cooley, *Social Organization* (1901).
    [52] Frank L. Sweetser, Jr., "A New Emphasis for Neighborhood Research," *American Sociological Review,* 7 (August, 1942), 525–33.
    [53] Donald L. Foley, *Neighbors or Urbanites?* Department of Sociology, University of Rochester (1952), ch. 3 (mimeographed).

of their lives in cities; only about one in ten had grown up in a village or on a farm, 9 per cent were foreign-born, and there were no Negroes in the district.

Foley found that about three-fourths of the residents had at least a "chatting relationship" with other people in the block, but only two-fifths of the informants said this relationship extended to *all* the residents in the block-neighborhood. About the same percentage visited informally in homes of their neighbors. Three out of five expressed their neighborly interests through exchange of favors with others in the area, but only one-sixth engaged in mutual undertakings such as picnics and outings. Thus, one-fourth of the neighbors rarely or never chatted with others. two-fifths did not exchange favors, and three-fifths never visited informally in the homes of others in the district. About two-fifths claimed that none of their best friends lived within five blocks.

So far as this area is concerned it is evident that neighboring, in terms of communication, ranged from the complete absence of social contacts to highly intimate personal relationships. Representative of intimate communication was the woman who said: "Neighbors are in and out all day. I'm in a club with ten women. In the summer we have parties. We entertain neighbor children, have them in for lunch. I like the cosmopolitan character of the neighborhood and the way we get along together." But representative of the other extreme was an elderly woman who said: "We live our own life and don't want anyone to interfere. 'Mind our own business' is my formula for getting on with neighbors."

The conclusions tentatively reached by Foley were: (1) neighboring was less important at the time of the study than in former decades—"people just don't neighbor as they used to"; (2) informal neighboring tended to be restricted to very few families, usually to those residing next door; (3) neighboring was more characteristic of summer than of winter —"we exchange advice about tomato plants"; and (4) neighboring tended to be mainly on an interpersonal rather than an interfamily basis—"we're not so intimate that our husbands get together." [54] Foley's conclusion that neighborly relationships "seldom ran deep" but were in the main superficial, "with an air of reserve permeating most relations," may have some validity, but even a majority of his informants said that one-fourth or more of their best friends lived within five blocks. Foley's measuring instrument tells us very little about the depth of these relationships.

PARK FOREST

In his study of Park Forest, a middle class commuting suburb near Chicago, Whyte observed that much of the neighboring among housewives assumed a definite pattern, the morning kaffee-klatsch.[55] Women

[54] *Ibid.*, pp. 33–36. [55] William H. Whyte, Jr., *The Organization Man* (1956).

participating in these informal sessions lived within a close radius, the exact boundaries of the clique-neighborhoods being determined mainly by the location and proximity of the residences. All of the women were expected to attend the sessions and were viewed rather critically if they declined to participate. As wives of junior executives or young professionals, many strongly oriented toward upward mobility, they tended to talk mainly about the things looming large in their values, namely home management, child care, and their husband's occupational situation, present and future. The men were also neighborly, but their informal contacts tended to be largely an individual matter, mainly backyard visiting or informal social gatherings in the evenings or on weekends. Even though most of the families were fairly mobile, both spatially and socially, the similarities of their situation in Park Forest—similar age, economic position, type of residence, and ecological location—tended to be conducive to informal neighboring.

FACTORS IN NEIGHBORHOOD RELATIONS

Most urban dwellers have intimate contacts on various city levels, some citywide, others locality-centered. The character and extent of local neighborhood contacts are influenced by numerous conditions. A study by Smith, Form, and Stone in a middle-sized city revealed that the higher the economic status of a local area the higher the degree of neighborhood intimacy, and vice versa.[56] They attribute the low degree of neighborhood intimacy in low income areas to the frequent change of residence of families living there. In other words, high residential mobility tends to reduce the probabilities of intimate neighborhood contacts.

However, Fellin and Litwak believe that spatial mobility *per se* is not the crucial determinant of the nature and frequency of neighborhood relations.[57] It is, rather, whether the neighborhood is organizationally structured and psychologically oriented to deal with high mobility. If it is not so structured or oriented, mobility is likely to be disruptive.

NEIGHBORING IN CITY AND SUBURBS

The impressive growth of satellite communities in industrialized countries has raised numerous questions concerning comparative "styles of life" in city and suburb. A few studies, cited earlier, suggest that suburban

[56] Joel Smith, William H. Form, and Gregory P. Stone, "Local Intimacy in a Middle-Sized City," *American Journal of Sociology*, 60 (November 1954), 279.

[57] Phillip Fellin and Eugene Litwak, "Neighborhood Cohesion and Mobility," *American Sociological Review*, 28 (June, 1963), 364–77.

dwellers are less inclined than residents of central cities to join formal associations. Does this situation hold for informal interaction in the form of neighboring? Fava's study of neighboring in the New York metropolitan area indicates that it does not, at least for that locality.[58]

Using the Wallin neighboring scale designed to measure informal contacts and associations with geographic neighbors, Fava obtained data from three samples of residents: one from central Manhattan; a second from Queens, an outer city area; and a third from Nassau County, a suburban area lying beyond the municipal boundaries. Such factors as age, sex, marital status, education, length of residence, nativity, and size of community of childhood residence were held constant by matching subsamples from Manhattan, Queens, and Nassau County.

The results clearly indicated that suburban residents had the highest neighboring scores, those of Manhattan the lowest, while Queens fell about midway between the central city and the suburb. It was found, for example, that married suburbanites were more neighborly than married persons living in Manhattan or Queens, and that single persons in the suburb were more neighborly than single urbanites. "This suggests," Fava observes, "that neighboring gradually increases with distance from the city center." [59]

SELECTED BIBLIOGRAPHY

BOOKS

Babchuk, Nicholas, and Wayne C. Gordon, *The Voluntary Association in the Slum*. Lincoln: University of Nebraska Studies, 1962.

Fava, Sylvia F., "Contrasts in Neighboring: New York City and a Suburban County," in William Dobriner (ed.), *The Suburban Community*. New York: Putnam's, 1958.

Gans, Herbert J., *The Urban Villagers*, chs. 4 and 5. New York: The Free Press of Glencoe, 1962.

Hausknecht, Murray, *The Joiners*. New York: Bedminster Press, 1962.

Hollingshead, A. B., *Elmtown's Youth*. New York: Wiley, 1949.

Minnis, Mhyra S., "Patterns of Women's Organizations" in Marvin B. Sussman (ed.), *Community Structure and Analysis*. New York: Thomas Y. Crowell Company, 1959.

Rose, Arnold, "Voluntary Associations in France," in Rose (ed.), *Theory and Method in the Social Sciences*. Minneapolis: University of Minnesota Press, 1954.

Seeley, John R., R. Alexander Sim, and E. W. Loosley, *Crestwood Heights*, ch. 10. New York: Basic Books, 1956.

Warner, W. L., *et al.*, *Democracy in Jonesville*. New York: Harper, 1949.

[58] Sylvia F. Fava, "Contrasts in Neighboring: New York City and a Suburban County," in William Dobriner (ed.), *The Suburban Community* (1958), pp. 122–30.
[59] *Ibid.*, p. 126.

Whyte, W. F., *Street Corner Society*. Chicago: University of Chicago Press, 1955.

ARTICLES

Axelrod, M., "Urban Structure and Social Participation," *American Sociological Review*, 21 (February, 1956), 13–18.

Anderson, Robert T., and Gallatin Anderson, "Voluntary Associations and Urbanization," *American Journal of Sociology*, 55 (November, 1959), 263–73.

Babchuk, Nicholas, and Ralph V. Thompson, "The Voluntary Associations of Negroes," *American Sociological Review*, 27 (October, 1962), 647–55.

Dotson, Floyd, "Participation in Voluntary Associations in a Mexican City," *American Sociological Review*, 18 (August, 1953), 380–86.

Gallagher, Orvoell R., "Voluntary Associations in France," *Social Forces*, 36 (December, 1957), 153–60.

Komarovsky, Mirra, "The Voluntary Associations of Urban Dwellers," *American Sociological Review*, 11 (December, 1946), 686–98.

Little, Kenneth, "The Role of Voluntary Associations in West African Urbanization," *American Anthropologist*, 59 (August, 1957), 579–96.

Smith, Joel, *et al.*, "Local Intimacy in a Middle-Sized City," *American Journal of Sociology*, 60 (November, 1954), 279–89.

Leisure and City Life

—

EIGHTEEN

All peoples devote part of their time to activities or interests that are not directly associated with work, although the amount of time given to such activities, and the character of the activities themselves, may vary from one group, community, or society to another. These activities and interests undergo change, responding to changes that occur in other parts of the social order. In the course of urbanization and industrialization, wherever it takes place, many changes occur in the nature of leisure. It is the purpose of this chapter to describe and interpret the nature of urban leisure and the changes that are occurring in leisure activities in urban society.

THE NATURE OF LEISURE

Leisure is here defined as the time which an individual has free from work or other duties and which may be utilized for purposes of relaxation, diversion, social achievement, or personal development. Like many other definitions, this one does not clearly demarcate leisure from non-leisure, or leisure activity from activity that is obligatory; indeed, what is often considered leisure-time behavior may be, in part, a response to social pressures or powerful inner drives, and may not, therefore, be a preferred form of behavior.

An individual's behavior as a wage earner, for example, is clearly not a leisure-time activity, even though it may afford relaxation and other satisfactions. But these satisfactions are merely by-products, not ends in themselves. If an individual returns from his place of employment at the end of the day to "work" in his garden or shop, this could be defined as leisure activity in terms of the motives involved. If the purpose is primarily to augment one's income by producing vegetables or making some product to sell, such activity could hardly be considered leisure; but if it is undertaken primarily for enjoyment, by one's self or family, then it would be a leisure activity. Yet a clear-cut distinction is hardly possible since different motives may be involved in the same activity.

Some activities outside the sphere of work may be mandatory and are therefore somewhat marginal to leisure. Church attendance, or participation in other organizational activities, may be obligatory; hence the time so devoted is not, strictly speaking, a leisure activity, although the personal responses may be the same as in voluntary participation. If such participation carries no reward other than personal gratification, and if such participation is voluntary, then it may be considered a leisure-time "pursuit."

Leisure-time activities take a multiplicity of forms. Some are home-centered, others are community-centered. Some are activities of individuals, others are group-oriented. Some are undertaken under the auspices of governmental organization, others are strictly private, either commercial or noncommercial. Some are "built into" existing institutions, such as schools or churches, others are completely detached from any institutional moorings. Some are designed mainly for spectators, others are participant-centered. Many of them are age-graded, or structured for males or females, or characteristic of a particular social stratum. Viewed in perspective, leisure-time activities in an urbanized society represent a vast complex of organizations, behavior patterns, and material equipment. Only in an affluent society can such a proliferation occur.

THE DYNAMICS OF LEISURE

In a dynamic urban society in which leisure is made available to the masses by a surplus of time and money, the mercurial character of leisure activity has some of the attributes of faddish or fashionable behavior. Indeed, fashions in leisure and in personal adornment have in common the attribute of dynamic change—here today but different next month or year.

Such are the dance crazes that suddenly, as if out of nowhere, become popular only to disappear about as suddenly, giving way to other crazes; or the song and tune hits, popular overnight, that provide mass entertainment until they shortly outlive their appeal; or the games that suddenly are widely accepted, but about as quickly are abandoned; or the new books and films that create a sensation, but are virtually forgotten at the end of the year; or the fashions in sports, such as boating, which are likely, in short time, to be replaced by other ephemeral activities having a new appeal. Though the dynamics of leisure is, in good part, a reflection of the dynamics of the entire social order of an urbanized society, it is also in part the creation of advertisers and promoters whose profit-taking depends on the changes in leisure behavior, especially as such behavior may involve consumption of merchantable goods or services.

Numerous writers on urbanism have commented on the tendency of urban residents to pursue their leisure outside the home. While this trend toward community-centered leisure is readily apparent, judging from the increasing variety of leisure activities available in the larger community setting, it should not obscure the fact that home-centered leisure looms large in the use of free time. This varies, of course, with such factors as age, education, and social class. The very young and the elderly are predominantly home-centered in their activities, whereas young and middle-aged adults are more disposed to find their activities in the community, or even outside it.

Recently in the United States there has been a veritable cult of "do-it-yourself" activities, usually undertaken in the home setting. To meet the needs of "do-it-yourself" faddists, a sizable industry has developed, having for its function the production and distribution of tools and other appropriate equipment for the home gardener, carpenter, cook-out addict, woodworker, amateur artist, and the like. There has indeed developed a considerable literature in the metropolitan press, especially in popular magazines, concerned with this aspect of leisure. Doubtless this trend in leisure reflects the interests of an increasing number of suburbanites whose home and community environs are especially favorable for such activities, more so than the environs of the apartment-house dweller in the city.

LEISURE AND CONFLICTING VALUES

In a famous book, Max Weber, the German sociologist, argued that the remarkable rise of industrialism in Europe and America was to be explained in considerable measure by what he called the "Protestant Ethic," which made a religious virtue of hard work, frugality, and industriousness.[1] Whatever may be the merit of Weber's thesis, it is an established fact that the philosophy of hard work was embraced by millions who sought spiritual redemption as well as material success through toil. Work was both an end in itself as well as a means to an

[1] Max Weber, *The Protestant Ethic and the Spirit of Capitalism* (1958). See the discussion in Chapter 2, p. 32, of this volume.

end; and blessed were those who toiled, including those whose toil lead to prosperity or even affluence, for this was added evidence that Providence had smiled beneficently upon them.

Although urbanization and industrialization, at least for the West, have created an era of abundance, both of wealth and leisure, the commitment of the masses to a philosophy of work has left many relatively unprepared for the judicious use of either the New Wealth or the New Leisure.[2] Some have clung tenaciously to the "ethic" of toil, viewing nonwork activity, and certainly idleness, as a machination of the devil.

Individual unpreparedness for abundant leisure in modern urban society may stem from two sources. One is the inability of many individuals to detach themselves effectively from the "ethic of work" to enjoy leisure without being haunted by guilt feelings that the time so spent is not sinful, or at least not wasteful. Such persons have not developed a style of life and set of values that include leisure as a major element. For them, time weighs heavily on their hands. Theirs may be an enforced idleness to be dreaded, not an achieved leisure to be enjoyed.

A second source is the confused situation resulting from the virtually unlimited number of possible choices to be made in the use of leisure time. In this respect the modern city is like a gigantic cafeteria with innumerable leisure "dishes" to be selected, but usually without much substantial information concerning the "nutritional" qualities of each dish or its personal or social implications. As the individual faces this cafeteria counter, he is often the object of constant and systematic efforts, by advertiser, promoter, or propagandist, to influence his choices, commonly at a price, or at least at a profit, pecuniary or otherwise. Commonly he has neither the knowledge nor intellectual sophistication to make a critical evaluation of these leisure offerings, but relies, perhaps unconsciously, on the "taste makers" and the "motivators." That he often becomes an avid but undiscriminating consumer is not surprising.

With the unprecedented amount of leisure time available for many middle class and working-class employees, there has come about a considerable change in the philosophy of work and leisure. Whereas the Protestant Ethic viewed leisure time as an opportunity for rest and relaxation which would enable the individual to work harder and more productively, with lasting benefits to himself and society, many now perceive work as a necessary and often unpleasant activity whose main function is to afford the individual more time to pursue his pleasures. For those with this outlook, leisure becomes an important end, and work the means to that end, rather than the reverse. No doubt these attitudes derive in part from the monotonous character of many work-tasks in urban society. The man on the assembly line, the girl in the typist pool, the file clerk in the big office, or the elevator operator—for them, and others like them, the job can hardly furnish an abundant life, even if it

[2] See especially John Galbraith, *The Affluent Society* (1958).

affords economic security. It is not surprising, then, that many of them seek exotic and thrill-packed activities away from the place of work.

Whereas man in folk communities furnished his own recreation, man in modern urban communities has generally had it furnished, either by commercial enterprises or by the community or society. Although it is not possible to make a precise distinction between "public" and "commercial" leisure, since the two often overlap at one point or another, the twentieth century has witnessed a phenomenal expansion of both types.

The commercialization of leisure has occurred wherever private economic enterprise has been an important feature of urban growth. This has been notably true of the West, and especially of the United States. In communist societies, however, leisure-time activities have been predominantly a function of government, which has not only provided the organization for such activities but also determined the form and content of the activities themselves.

Commercial enterprise has provided a large share of the leisure-time activities of the America people. Perhaps most important of all, in terms of time and money involved, is the entertainment provided by the mass media—television, radio, movies, newspapers, magazines, and so on. In the United States these media operate almost exclusively within the framework of private enterprise, being supported in the main by advertising or subscriptions. But in most countries the electronic media are "public," being maintained and operated by government agencies; and in communist societies, even the press is an agency of government.

"Professional" sports—baseball, football, basketball, horse racing—are commercial activities, carried on for profit. This is true of gambling in its varied forms, though in some countries lotteries are conducted by government agencies. Tourism is extensively commercialized, since tourist accommodations and facilities are generally maintained by private enterprises, although government is also involved in providing parks, highways, and other facilities for the use of tourists. Social centers such as dance halls, cocktail lounges, and bars are usually commercial undertakings, as are bowling alleys and pool rooms.

REDUCTION OF WORK TIME

Urbanization and industrialization have not always reduced the time the masses of workers must spend in earning a living. In the early stages of the Industrial Revolution it was fairly common for workers, in the United States and western Europe, to spend 12 or 14 hours a day on the

Mass recreation, a feature of city life, is often commercialized as well. Bathers swarm on the beach at Coney Island with the amusement park in the background. (Courtesy New York Convention and Visitors Bureau.)

job. Women and children were also employed for long hours at a stretch.[3] Under such working conditions there was neither much time nor energy left for the pursuit of pleasure, nor ample funds to spend on such pursuits. Nonwork time for adults was spent mainly in sleeping, eating, lovemaking, attending to household duties, visiting, and perhaps participating in church or other social functions. Leisure time in such societies was primarily for the elite, not the working masses.

Since around the turn of the century, however, the length of the working day or week has gradually declined in the urbanized countries of the world, allowing an increasing amount of time free from the responsibilities of earning a livelihood. In the middle decades of the present century the average work week for urban employees has been around 40 hours, compared with 50 to 70 hours a few decades earlier. The standard eight-hour day and five-day week have meant increased freedom from work during both the work week and the long weekends. With the rapid development of automation there is reason to believe that the work week will continue to be reduced, especially for certain classes of employees.

[3] See, for example, Charles Booth, *Life and Labor of the People of London* (9 vols., 1902), or Paul U. Kellogg (ed.), *The Pittsburgh Survey* (1914).

In Chicago a great audience listens to an open-air concert. (Courtesy Chicago Park District.)

Other changes have also provided additional time free from work. The span of working life of urban people has been greatly reduced, mainly as a result of two changes: the postponement of employment of those about to enter the world of work, and the compulsory retirement of workers at designated ages. The prolongation of work for young persons has been achieved mainly through the continuation of their education, at least through high school and often beyond. With increased longevity, most employed workers who attain the prescribed age of retirement can anticipate several more years during which time they are "free" to choose from an indefinite number of nonwork activities.

Vacations with full pay have afforded both the time and money necessary for various kinds of activities, including travel. Child labor laws have prohibited the employment of children below a stipulated age, usually 16, and social security legislation has made it financially possible for many low-income mothers to stay out of gainful employment while rearing their children. Recurrent periods of unemployment (seasonal lay-offs, strikes, or workless days occasioned by depressions) and the increased number of holidays during the year have also added to leisure time. Even the "coffee break" has become widely accepted in many urban establishments. Perhaps just as important as the increase in time for nonwork has been a rising income level for the masses, who now usually have funds to spend for purposes other than survival or mere comfort.

UNEVEN DISTRIBUTION OF LEISURE

Wilensky is of the opinion that the amount of leisure time in modern society has been greatly exaggerated.[4] The urban skilled worker, he says, may have gained the leisure time of his thirteenth-century counterpart, but the upper occupational classes have experienced an increase in the length of work-day, even though they may have longer vacations and be retired at an earlier age. One should therefore view cautiously the notion of a "leisure class."

There are, however, "leisure" categories which cut across occupational, economic, and age-sex boundaries. On the top economic levels there are those whose financial position is such that they can choose both their work and their leisure. Some of them choose not to work, at least very arduously; they are the playboys and playgirls of the metropolis or the fashionable resort. Others may have leisure forced upon them, whether they seek it or not; among them are workers who have been forcibly retired and for whom time may hang heavy on their hands since they are often unprepared, psychologically and otherwise, for a life of non-work.

Many are, as Wilensky puts it, leisure-stricken as well as poverty-stricken. It is the low-income, low status worker who has gained increased leisure time but who needs more work, in contrast to professionals and executives, who probably need more leisure time but who have an increasingly heavy work load.

For the masses of urban workers on the lower socioeconomic levels— excepting the unemployed, the retired, the underaged, and the incapacitated—there is a never-ending cycle of work and leisure, and for many of them work becomes the means to certain ends, one being the acquisition of the time and money necessary for leisure-time pursuits. As Mills graphically phrases it, "Each day men sell little pieces of their lives in order to buy them back each night and each week-end with the coin of 'fun.' With amusement, with love, with movies, with vicarious intimacy, they pull themselves into a sort of whole again, so that they are different men."[5] For these persons leisure-time activities are a form of escape from the routine and the tedium of the work-a-day world. It is their aim to keep work and leisure as far apart as possible, to isolate themselves from the world of work until they have to return to it at the beginning of the next day or week or month.

---

[4] Harold L. Wilensky, "The Uneven Distribution of Leisure," *Social Problems*, 9 (Summer, 1961), 55–56.

[5] C. Wright Mills, *White Collar* (1951), p. 237.

People without leisure

If the manual of clerical worker in the city closes his mind as well as the door on the job at the end of the day, the professional or executive is likely to work longer hours and even "take his work home" in a brief-case when he leaves his office or place of business. "It seems likely," writes Wilensky, "that we are headed toward an organization of work in which a small group of executives, merchants, professional experts, and politicians labor hard and long to control and service the masses, who in turn are going to 'take it easy' on a progressively shorter work week, in jobs that de-emphasize brawn and native shrewdness and play up discipline, reliability, and training." [6] It is the first category of workers for whom work and play will be more or less integrated and interdependent.

An additional category of persons for whom the era of affluence has not meant an abundance of leisure time are gainfully employed married women who have the dual responsibilities of holding a job and maintaining a household, the latter often without benefit of domestic assistance. Around one-third of the married women in the United States are gainfully employed; most of them live in cities, and they represent all strata of the social structure. Many workers, both male and female, engage in the practice of "moonlighting" (holding a secondary job, often in the evening after regular work hours). Generally, these are workers on the lower income levels who need to supplement their income. By its very nature, moonlighting means a reduction of leisure time.

Nonwork duties and leisure

Freedom from work does not necessarily mean a corresponding increase in leisure time. This seems to be particularly true of the urban middle and upper classes, who often have so many commitments that there is little time left when these obligations are met. The demands on the individual's time by kin-group or family, by civic, political, or occupational associations, by the church and related organizations, and by varied social clubs in whom participation may be virtually mandatory— all these weigh heavily on many persons. Only the strong-minded isolationist can resist their pressures.

In his vivid description of the "style of life" characterizing the "exurbanites," residents of an upper middle class commuting community near New York, Spectorsky notes that the long weekends, free from work obligations, are a continuing round of parties and other enervating activi-

---

[6] Harold L. Wilensky, "Work, Careers, and Social Integration," *International Social Science Journal*, 12 (1960), 558 (special issue on "Sociological Aspects of Leisure").

ties which are virtually mandatory for social acceptance in the prevailing status system.[7] If travel-to-work time is counted as a phase of work activity, the free time for employed "exurbanites" is strictly limited during the week. And although their wives have ample money to afford servants and modern household appliances, as well as large homes, most of their time is taken up with a variety of demanding tasks such as managing a household in a manner appropriate to status-striving families, driving the husband to the commuting train in the morning and meeting him in the evening, transporting small children to and from school or social gatherings, attending meetings of the PTA and other organizations, taking part in various financial drives or in local political activities, and so on. For them, leisure time is something of a mirage.

Similar patterns of leisure-time usage prevail in Crestwood Heights, an upper middle class suburb of Toronto.[8] Here both leisure and work tend to be geared to a fairly fixed time schedule. Unscheduled "loafing" is not an appropriate way to spend leisure.

Most leisure is spent in scheduled events: watching the fights on TV, regular bridge club tournaments, curling on Saturday, and the like. In many "play" activities there is a high degree of diligence, as the doctor knows who attempts to prescribe relaxed activity for a patient suffering from hypertension! Golf or gardening can be taken quite as seriously as business, and for many they *are* business.

Crestwooders nevertheless agree that the man works to have "time off," and that when he leaves his male environment of harsh exacting deadlines to return to his home and family, he expects and is expected to relax. Family life, however, is not entirely oriented around the father's work and leisure. His wife has her own activities outside the home which are carefully scheduled; and both have, as well, joint social engagements which bear on his career. The children have their school—which demands punctuality—scheduled appointments with dentist and dancing teacher, and numerous social activities. Home life is indeed often hectic, although there is for many a measure of quiet and relaxation in performing simple family duties and acts of mutual aid.[9]

ECONOMICS OF LEISURE

The financial outlay in materials and activities associated with leisure in the United States provides impressive evidence of the economic importance of this segment of American life. If the amount is less in other countries it is only because the people have less money or time to spend in this way. But in urbanized Europe, as in the United States, the expenditures for leisure activities are very great.

The editors of *Fortune* magazine estimated, in 1955, that the American

[7] A. C. Spectorsky, *The Exurbanites* (1955).
[8] John R. Seeley, R. Alexander Sim, and E. W. Loosely, *Crestwood Heights* (1956).
[9] *Ibid.*, pp. 64–65. Reprinted by permission of Basic Books, Inc., Publishers.

people were spending about 30.6 billion dollars annually for leisure activities, or about one and a half times the amount spent on clothing and shelter.[10] Leisure expenditures were presented in two categories: first, expenditures (about 18 billion dollars) on such things as amusements, athletics, hunting and fishing, domestic and foreign travel, boating, games and toys, and certain books and periodicals; second, consumer expenditures (about 12.6 billion dollars) for such things as alcohol, television, radio, records, musical instruments, and casual "eating out" for pleasure. Over 50 million decks of playing cards are sold annually.

In modern urban societies, therefore, leisure-time activities are so closely geared to the economy that no clear-cut separation of work and leisure is possible. This is clearly indicated by the vast amounts of work and wealth that go into the production of sundry objects, instruments, or equipment designed for leisure usage, and by the large numbers of persons who are employed in the production, distribution, or operation of these things. In addition, there are the multitudes who *work* to provide leisure-time necessities for countless other persons—professional athletes and their coaches, producers of mass-media content for mass consumption, directors of organized social activities such as play groups and clubs, professional performers in musical or dramatic organizations, librarians, instructors in various techniques or skills which may be used for diversion or relaxation or personal development. The number is legion, the variety almost endless. Perhaps no less than 10 per cent of the gainfully employed persons in the United States function to meet the needs of those with leisure on their hands.

If in modern urbanized societies the emphasis is greater on consumption than on production, this trend is especially true of activities and objects associated with leisure-time. In such a society almost everyone becomes a consumer of things that are processed, packaged, and presented to him ready for consumption—for a price.[11] In few other sectors of an economy, perhaps, is there so much persuasion and cajolery from the promoters and advertisers to purchase the offerings of the amusement-makers. Even the do-it-yourself devotees usually purchase their materials half-processed, with printed instructions. And those who prefer to spend their leisure more energetically must pay in taxes, donations, or rentals for the privilege of using parks, beaches, resorts, or other public facilities.

[10] Editors of *Fortune, The Changing American Market* (1955).
[11] See Vance Packard, *The Hidden Persuaders* (1957), for a popular presentation of the extent and techniques of organized persuasion in American society.

THE ORGANIZATION OF LEISURE

Most of the basic social institutions—government, religion, family, military, economic—define fairly clearly their central functions and the roles of persons associated with carrying out these functions. But, as Ennis has observed, there is no comparable institution of leisure, although in a sense leisure has become increasingly organized.[12] All of the basic institutions have tended to become multifunctional through the addition of functions bearing no necessary relationship to the central functions. Such a secondary function has been leisure. These ancillary functions usually involve no binding commitment on the part of the participants, as do the activities relating to the central functions: in an economic institution, for example, an employee *must* work, but the recreational provisions of the organization are usually optional. Although the organization has limited control over leisure-time usage, participation of its members in activities associated with the secondary function of leisure does give it a considerable measure of control over the workers, however indirect it may be. With the growth of bureaucracy there is increasing need for devices to enhance the loyalty of members to the organization, promote esprit de corps, and increase work efficiency. Leisure-time activity under organizational sponsorship is one device.

In modern urban society new forms of organization have emerged or institutional adaptations have been made to provide time and facilities for leisure-time usage. Most places of employment afford at least an annual fortnight of "vacation" time with full pay, and for many professionals, executives, and even government personnel the "time off from work" is usually longer, with additional "sick leave" allowed.

GOVERNMENT AND LEISURE

The expansion of governmental functions to include recreation has been a notable development in almost every country, but more particularly in countries which have been extensively urbanized and in which bureaucratic organization has undergone considerable expansion. Recreational facilities so provided are used, of course, by rural as well as city people, but the needs for these facilities have increased as more and more people become city dwellers. Such organizations as the National Park Service, the United States Forest Service, and the Fish and Wildlife Service are concerned with recreational facilities for both rural and urban residents. On the state level, government is similarly con-

[12] Philip Ennis, "Leisure in the Suburbs," in William Dobriner (ed.), *The Suburban Community* (1958), p. 260.

cerned with recreation. But it is perhaps in the sphere of municipal government that the most elaborate provisions are made to provide facilities for various leisure-time activities. Parks and other public recreation areas amounting to a total of 748,000 acres are maintained by some 3,000 cities in the United States.[13] In addition, most of the cities have recreational programs, under leadership, for persons of all ages. Included are such programs as music, art, drama, outdoor camping and craftsmanship, sports, public forums, and dancing. A specific function of local government is the regulation, in the public interest, of certain kinds of recreational activities.

OTHER ORGANIZATIONS PROVIDING LEISURE ACTIVITY

Some 25,000 industrial and commercial establishments likewise provide recreational facilities and programs for their employees.[14] Many companies own golf courses, bowling alleys, swimming pools, gymnasia, and summer resorts for their employees and families; others make use of public recreational facilities for intramural sports and other social and cultural activities.

Schools have also expanded their functions to include provisions for varied leisure activities, following the precept that "all work and no play makes Jack a dull boy." The extraordinary proliferation of extracurricular activities on all levels of education has been integrated in varying degrees with the educational process. In some instances, indeed, the extracurricular has virtually overshadowed the curricular! Many urban churches have included, in addition to regular worship, such activities as dancing, sports, outings, forum discussions, church dinners, dramatic performances, card playing, and so on.

Such organizations as the Y.M.C.A., Y.M.H.A., neighborhood centers, country clubs, and fraternal societies sponsor a multitude of leisure-time activities and programs. Organizations like the National Recreation Association, the National Industrial Recreation Association, the National Catholic Welfare Society, and others provide professional advisory and informational services to local communities and private organizations concerned with leisure.

VOLUNTARY ASSOCIATIONS AND LEISURE

The proliferation of voluntary associations in urban communities has been considered in another chapter. It would perhaps be correct to say

[13] George D. Butler, "The Structure of Public Leisure Agencies," *The Annals*, 313 (September, 1957), 122.

[14] Don L. Neer, "Industry," *The Annals*, 313 (September, 1957), 80.

that the majority of these organizations are concerned with some aspect of leisure time. Some are independent of other associations, but many are "built into" the structure of existing organizations such as churches, economic establishments, or political institutions. Wherever urbanism has strongly developed in any society, the growth of voluntary associations attests to the increase in leisure time. As Ennis has observed, "the more a community becomes fragmented into competing groups, the greater will be the proliferation of leisure organizations." [15]

Many of these associations tend to coalesce into larger organizations that have an integrative function. Local bowling teams, for example, may become associated with other teams in the Bowling Congress of America; or local groups of Boy Scouts and Girl Scouts are integrated with a network of state, regional, and national organizations. The Society for the Preservation of Barber Shop Quartet Singing in America (SPBSQSA) has 630 local "chapters" which are associated together in a national organization.[16] Some 12,000 local garden clubs maintain state organizations which support a national organization, the National Council of State Garden Clubs.[17]

Along with increasing organization of leisure has developed certain specialized occupational roles; indeed, there has been a tendency toward the professionalization of these roles. Although many persons engaged in organizing and directing leisure-time activities are amateurs, or at least volunteer part-time workers, an increasing number are trained specialists. In almost every American city there are numbers of specialized personnel, some public employees, others private, who are responsible in one way or another for organized leisure programs. This trend toward professionalization and specialization in a relatively new occupation has been closely associated with urbanization.

SPECIAL COMMUNITIES OF LEISURE

The era of abundant leisure time has produced the resort, a community more or less specialized in providing recreation for persons with leisure to spare and money to spend. Early resorts such as Tuxedo Park, New York, and Newport, Rhode Island, were exclusively for the elite. But as leisure time and surplus funds became more abundant for the masses, the resorts became less exclusive, catering to the tastes and interests of cosmopolitans in all stations of life and levels of cultural sophistication. Entertainment and accommodations became plentiful and reasonably cheap for those with limited funds, and also available for the financial aristocracy at a higher price. The roster of these communities of leisure

[15] *Ibid.*, p. 264.

[16] William Astor and Charlotte Astor, "Private Associations and Commercial Activities," *The Annals*, 313 (September, 1957), 94.

[17] *Ibid.*, p. 96.

is a long one; among them are Atlantic City, Palm Beach, and Las Vegas in the United States; Brighton and Blackpool in Britain; Scheveningen in Holland; Nice and Cannes on the French Riviera; Capri in Italy. Here plutocrat and proletarian can enjoy, each in his own way, the diverse entertainment of an affluent society. In addition to these well-known places are literally hundreds of other resorts, small and large, in many parts of the world.

Very different from the resort is the special community providing residential and recreational facilities for aged persons. Often these are subcommunities in or near a larger city. Commonly they are trailer parks occupied by elderly persons who have sought warmer climates. Many such parks cluster around the cities of Florida, southern California, and Arizona, but they are also found in other sections. The Bradenton (Florida) Trailer Park, for example, has more than a thousand living units.[18] Other Florida cities like St. Petersburg, Orlando, and West Palm Beach have become the mecca for thousands of elderly persons whose retirement has afforded them an abundance of leisure.[19] Trailer park residences are occupied, in the main, by working class and lower middle class persons; those of greater affluence generally live in hotels and apartments. Hoyt's study of the Bradenton Park indicated that more than half were retired workers or farmers, but only two per cent were teachers and other professionals.[20]

SPECIAL STUDIES OF LEISURE

The interests and values of urban people find expression in the ways they use their leisure time. These values are differentially expressed according to such factors as social class, age, sex, education, ethnicity, and personality. It is fairly well known that persons on different class, age, and educational levels tend to have somewhat different leisure tastes and interests, and that their activities in pursuit of these interests set them apart, to some degree, from those on other levels. It is also known that males and females, except small children, have rather different interests, and that ethnic groups are commonly distinguishable by their patterns of leisure-usage. These distinctions arise from different experiences in the processes of socialization and acculturation for particular human categories. In considerable measure the "tastemakers"—advertisers, movies, television, and so on—have produced these differentials, but they have also had a leveling effect in creating a "leisure culture" for the masses.

[18] G. C. Hoyt, "The Life of the Retired in a Trailer Park," *American Journal of Sociology,* 59 (January, 1954), 361–70.

[19] Irving L. Webber, "The Organized Social Life of the Retired: Two Florida Communities," *American Journal of Sociology,* 59 (January, 1954), 340–46.

[20] Hoyt, *op. cit.,* p. 363.

THE KANSAS CITY STUDY

In a research on leisure in Kansas City, Missouri, Havighurst recorded the differences in leisure-usage by classes of people—age, sex, economic status, and the like.[21] On the middle-aged level, for example, women were inclined to concentrate on reading and on formal and informal association, while men were more interested in gardening. Both groups tended to slacken off in their associational and sports interests with advancing years. Havighurst comments as follows:

> For example, an upper-middle-class man is his forties spends his leisure as follows: he attends a luncheon club once a week; he plays golf in season and perhaps handball; he spends a good deal of time on weekends looking after his lawn and caring for his flowers. The upper-lower-class man of the same age goes fishing on weekends, and on vacation; he works around the house a good deal, redecorating it and adding a new room at the back; he watches television several hours each evening and on weekends when he is not doing something else.[22]

Havighurst is of the opinion, however, that the variables of age, sex, and social class are perhaps less important than personality factors—the way individuals respond to leisure-time activities and the satisfactions they derive from such activities. Individuals whose leisure activities are quite different may nevertheless be similar in their responses and in the ways they view such activities. These similarities, or differences, cut across the usual boundaries of age, sex, social class, education. An urban upper middle class man, middle-aged, with a college education, may have in common with a working class man, also middle-aged, but with scant education, the capacity to participate enthusiastically in leisure-time activity, deriving much enjoyment from it, because such activity meets their personality needs. They may, indeed, prefer similar activities such as fishing. For others of similar or different class or age, leisure time may bring only ennui. From a social-psychological standpoint, in Havighurst's view, it is not so much the differences in form and content of leisure-time activity that count, although these may be important from certain points of view, but the subjective experiences of the individuals, either as active participants or inactive spectators.

THE CUYAHOGA COUNTY STUDY

In a study of social-class differences in use of leisure time in Cuyahoga County (Cleveland), Ohio, White found that the upper middle class

---

[21] Robert J. Havighurst, "The Leisure Activities of the Middle-Aged," *American Journal of Sociology*, 63 (September, 1957), 100–61.

[22] *Ibid.*, p. 161.

engaged in more activities during a designated week than did those on the lower socioeconomic levels.[23] But perhaps even more striking were the differences in the kinds of activities. Calculating the rates of use of leisure per 100 persons of all ages for several classes of activities, White found that the "use-rates" for certain types of activities increased from the higher to lower social-class levels, but for others there was an increase. In the use of parks and playgrounds, for example, the use-rate per 100 upper middle class persons was 1.6, for lower middle class 7.0, for upper lower class 12.2, and for the lower lower class 23. Somewhat similar differentials were observed in activities relating to community chest services, church activities, and the use of museums. In the case of commercial amusements the upper middle group had the lowest use-rate (68.9), but the rates for the other three classes were about the same (82 to 82.9). This use-rate pattern was reversed for home activities, use of libraries, participation in ethnic-racial organizations, and attendance at lecture-study groups.

White also found that the average number of hours spent in activities related to television, radio, movies, and sports was almost twice as great for the upper lower class as for the upper middle category when comparisons were made of males and females. Upper middle class males spent an average of 12 hours per week, compared with 21.7 hours spent by the upper lower males. But the time spent by the females in these activities was significantly lower, although the class differentials were about the same: upper middle females spent 7.7 hours, on the average, in these activities, while upper lower females spent 14.1 hours.

THE COLUMBUS STUDY

In a similar study of another metropolitan sample (Columbus, Ohio), Clarke found observable class differentials in leisure-time activities.[24] In a sample of 574 persons placed in occupational categories ranked according to five prestige levels, Clarke found that those in Occupational Class I (highest) participated most frequently in such activities as attending plays, concerts, and lectures, visiting museums or art galleries, reading for pleasure, attending movies, entertaining at home, and playing bridge. At the other extreme, those in the lowest occupational class, leisure time was spent most frequently in watching television, fishing, playing card games other than bridge, attending outdoor movies and baseball games, driving or riding in a car for pleasure, spending time at a tavern, and visiting a zoo.

[23] R. Clyde White, "Social Class Differences in the Use of Leisure," *American Journal of Sociology*, 61 (September, 1955), 145–50.

[24] Alfred C. Clarke, "Leisure and Occupational Prestige," *American Sociological Review*, 21 (June, 1956), 301–7.

Although some leisure-time activities such as polo and yachting are more or less exclusively upper class because of the cost involved, certain kinds of activities, originally followed only by the elite, have been taken up by many persons on the "common man" level. Among these is golf, initially an upper class sport but now followed by middle class and even some working-class people. In the social structure it has been downgraded. If the middle class person cannot afford a string of polo ponies or a stable of race horses or a yacht, at least he can rent a saddle horse for a few hours or even own or rent a boat with an outboard motor.

CARD PLAYING

Though not exclusively a class-oriented activity, card playing has nevertheless grown in popularity with increasing urbanization. A national survey conducted by the American Institute of Public Opinion in 1947 indicated that about 56 per cent of adult Americans played cards either regularly or occasionally.[25] More recently, a local study of card playing in Endicott, New York, a medium-sized city, revealed almost the same proportion of adults (57 per cent) as in the national sample played cards.[26] Very few of the persons reporting were professional card players or gamblers, or even card-playing addicts. Mostly they participated for reasons having little to do with card playing *per se*. Many of them found cards a pleasant and relaxing group activity which they could share intimately with friends or families. Some joined card clubs for status reasons; others played at public card parties held for such purposes as raising funds or bringing together the members of an organization; still others played to demonstrate their skill and their superiority over others. But, in general, the game was a substitute for conversation.

In their famous studies of Middletown, the Lynds noted a considerable increase in card-playing activities during the decade between the two researches, one in the 1920's, the other in the 1930's.[27] This trend has apparently continued unabated since then. The Lynds, like Crespi, attributed the popularity of cards to the need of a substitute for conversation. They say:

Most people have but a spotty fund of knowledge with which to carry on a prolonged conversation without becoming "heavy" or disputatious. All of this tends to make the effort to carry on an evening of talk over-strenuous and likely to be judged in the end as "not having got anywhere." Into this problematic situation has come bridge, the hostess' best friend and the universal social solvent: safe, orthodox, and fun. . . . What bridge has done is to institution-

[25] AIPO poll, *Public Opinion Quarterly*, 12 (Spring, 1948), 48.
[26] Irving Crespi, "The Social Significance of Card Playing as a Leisure-Time Activity," *American Sociological Review*, 21 (December, 1956), 717–22.
[27] Robert S. Lynd and Helen M. Lynd, *Middletown in Transition* (1937).

alize fun-in-small-groups, at the same time it is tending to drain serious talk from Middletown's leisure. It is an unparalleled device for an urban world that wants to avoid issues, to keep things impersonal, to enjoy people without laying oneself open or committing oneself to them, and to have fun in the process.[28]

NEIGHBORHOOD TAVERN AND COCKTAIL LOUNGE

Class differences in leisure-usage are clearly indicated in a study of the neighborhood tavern and cocktail lounge in Chicago.[29] The tavern, in general, is a workingman's recreational center. The Chicago taverns included in this study drew their patrons mainly from local neighborhoods; hence they tended to be social centers for informal contacts. Some of them attracted customers from particular ethnic or racial groups. There they regularly met their friends or neighbors and drank with them in an atmosphere of congeniality. They became, in a sense, a primary group having a continuity of informal social contacts.

The cocktail lounges, on the other hand, were located in or near a commercial district. Most of the patrons were middle or upper class persons, anonymously drawn from various sections of the city or from out of town. Whereas the habitues of the tavern were usually regular patrons, those of the lounges were more likely to be transients, city visitors for a day or week.

The upper middle class patrons interviewed spent from four to seven hours a week in drinking emporia, those in the lower middle class from seven to 12 hours; while the upper lower persons spent from 14 to 23 hours in such places. Clearly, the tavern is an important social center for the lower social classes, providing informal contacts which are not readily available in other situations. For the middle classes the cocktail lounge is only one of numerous available establishments providing an outlet for leisure time.

RECREATION AND METROPOLITAN DEVELOPMENT

A new dimension has been added to leisure by the concentration of an ever-larger proportion of the American population in metropolitan areas. About two-thirds of the United States population lived in such areas in 1960.[30] Although the United States has much open land suitable for outdoor recreation, the bulk of such land is distant from the expanding me-

---

[28] *Ibid.,* pp. 269–71. Reprinted by permission of Harcourt, Brace and World, Inc., publisher.

[29] David Gottlieb, "The Neighborhood Tavern and Cocktail Lounge," *American Journal of Sociology,* 62 (May, 1957), 559–62.

[30] See Chapters 3 and 4 for further discussion of metropolitan development in the United States.

tropolises: National parks and "wilderness areas" offer little relief to sweltering millions in the "asphalt jungle." A special survey conducted in the summer of 1960 by the Bureau of the Census revealed that three out of four Americans traveled less than 50 miles from home in order to enjoy a day's outdoor recreation.[31] Urban population, most of it in metropolitan areas, is expected to be 40 to 50 per cent greater in 1980 than in 1960. A review of the findings of a recent government-sponsored survey of needs in outdoor recreation stated: "The metropolitan transformation of American civilization is the commanding problem of outdoor recreation. This is the seat of demand which powers the whole system, and all public recreation programs must look to it for their specification."[32]

FACTORS INCREASING THE DEMAND FOR OUTDOOR RECREATION

In addition to the redistribution of population into metropolitan areas, several other factors contribute importantly to the demand for outdoor recreation facilities.[33] (1) *More people.* The over-all increase in population, due to high marriage and birth rates, means that even if all other factors remained constant, demand for recreation facilities would rise. (2) *More income.* Incomes have been rising in the United States and, as they have risen, expenditures for recreation have mounted more rapidly than other expenditures. Doubtless this reflects the fact that the incomes of most Americans are now high enough to allow considerable discretionary spending on other than necessities. (3) *More leisure.* Reduction of the work week has contributed to increased leisure of the working population, while early retirement and mechanization of household chores have contributed increased leisure to the nonworking population. (4) *More physical mobility.* Around 1900 the average American traveled about 500 miles annually. By 1955, largely because of the automobile, this figure rose to 5,000 miles per year. By 1985 the figure is expected to reach 7,700.

These factors are expected to produce a tripling of outdoor recreational pursuits between 1960 and 2000. This was a major finding of the Outdoor Recreation Resources Review Commission, established by Congress in 1958.[34] To meet the demand, the Commission recommended a five-point program, including development of a national outdoor recreation policy and a federal grants-in-aid program to the states.

[31] Cited in Gilbert Cross, "The Costly Crush to Get Outdoors," *Fortune* (July, 1962), 157.

[32] Harvey Perloff, quoted in *ibid.*, p. 158.

[33] This discussion is based on Regional Plan Association of New York City, *The Race for Open Space* (1960), pp. 21–22.

[34] Outdoor Recreation Resources Review Commission, *Outdoor Recreation for America* (January, 1962), p. 32.

OUTDOOR RECREATION IN THE NEW YORK REGION

A study in the New York metropolitan region highlights the problems of outdoor recreation in the nation's largest metropolis.[35] The study defined the New York metropolitan region as a 22-county unit including parts of New Jersey and lower Connecticut. Demand for outdoor recreation in this area will increase for the following reasons: (1) the 1955 population of 15 million is expected to increase to 24 million by 1985; (2) per capita real income in the region is expected to rise from $2,470 in 1955 to $4,350 in 1985; (3) increased leisure time is expected to rise in the region as in the nation generally; (4) it is estimated that the 3.9 million passenger cars in the New York region will increase to 8.6 million by 1985.

Despite a rising demand for recreational space, both the amount of land available for outdoor recreation and the rate of acquisition of land for public recreational uses have declined in the New York region. Shopping centers, airports, highways, and single-family homes on large lots consume vast amounts of open land. Projecting these land-use trends indicates that in the decades between 1955 and 1985 the New York region will add as much developed land as was added in the previous 300 years. In contrast, the public acquisition of land for recreation has declined. Prior to World War II, 15.7 acres of state and county parks were acquired in the region for every 1,000 population increase; since World War II, only seven acres have been acquired per 1,000 additional population. It has been suggested that the solution to the problem of metropolitan recreation lies not only in acquisition of land, but above all in the recognition that a new policy needs to be developed for the age of "mass leisure." [36]

SELECTED BIBLIOGRAPHY

BOOKS

Anderson, Nels, *Work and Leisure*. London: Routledge & Kegan Paul, 1961.
DeGrazia, Sebastian, *Of Time, Work, and Leisure*. New York: Twentieth Century Fund, 1962.
Denney, Reuel, and David Riesman, "Leisure in Industrial America," in Eugene Stanley (ed.), *Creating an Industrial Civilization*. New York: Harper, 1952.
Ennis, Philip, "Leisure in the Suburbs," in William Dobriner (ed.), *The Suburban Community*. New York: Putnam's, 1958.

[35] Regional Plan Association of New York City, *op. cit.*   [36] Cross, *op. cit.*

Graham, S., "Social Correlates of Adult Leisure-Time Behavior," in M. Sussman (ed.), *Community Structure and Analysis.* New York: Thomas Y. Crowell Company, 1959.

Jacobs, Norman (ed.), *Culture for the Masses.* Princeton: D. Van Nostrand, 1961.

Larrabee, Eric, and Meyersohn, Rolf (eds.), *Mass Leisure.* Glencoe, Ill.: The Free Press, 1959.

Riesman, David, *et al., The Lonely Crowd.* New Haven, Conn.: Yale University Press, 1950.

Rosenberg, Bernard, and David M. White (eds.), *Mass Culture.* Glencoe, Ill.: The Free Press, 1957.

Spectorsky, A. C., *The Exurbanites.* Philadelphia: Lippincott, 1955.

ARTICLES

Bendiner, Robert, "Could You Stand a Four-Day Week?" *The Reporter,* 17 (August, 1957), 12–15.

Clarke, Alfred C., "Leisure and Occupational Prestige," *American Sociological Review,* 21 (June, 1956), 301–7.

Crespi, Irving, "The Social Significance of Card Playing as a Leisure-Time Activity," *American Sociological Review,* 21 (December, 1956), 717–22.

Gottlieb, David, "The Neighborhood Tavern and the Cocktail Lounge," *American Journal of Sociology,* 62 (May, 1957), 559–62.

Havighurst, Robert J., "The Leisure Activities of the Middle-Aged," *American Journal of Sociology,* 63 (September, 1957), 152–63.

Hoyt, G. C., "The Life of the Retired in a Trailer Park," *American Journal of Sociology,* 59 (January, 1954), 361–70.

White, R. Clyde, "Social Class Differences in Use of Leisure," *American Journal of Sociology,* 61 (September, 1955), 145–50.

Wilensky, Harold L., "Work, Careers, and Social Integration," *International Social Science Journal,* 12 (1960), 555–60.

———— "The Uneven Distribution of Leisure," *Social Problems,* 9 (Summer, 1961), 32–56.

The Social Psychology
of Urban Life

PART FOUR

Personal Organization
and Disorganization in the City

NINETEEN

In Part Three of this book, we described the social aspects of urban society, the special features of urban social organization; now we shall turn our attention to an equally important, equally complex aspect of urbanism, namely, the urban personality, which is formed in part by the kinds of groups and institutions in which the individual participates. Thus, the two sides of urban society, the social and personal, are complementary, inseparable, and interdependent; together they add up to an extraordinarily complex whole.

Many of the generalizations about urban personality are not based on empirical studies, but are the result of logical deductions from a set of postulates about urban social life. For example, it has been postulated by some writers that because urbanites are subjected to a continuous barrage of emotional stimuli, their personalities will display symptoms of nervous ennui, cynicism, and superficiality. The well-known analyses of Wirth and Simmel illustrate this deductive, rather than empirical, approach.[1] Many analyses of urban personality also suffer from an anti-urban bias, stemming from the author's application of his rural values or from his observation of transitional problems. Consequently, the in-

[1] Georg Simmel, "The Metropolis and Mental Life," in *The Sociology of Georg Simmel,* translated, edited, and with an introduction by Kurt H. Wolff, (1950), pp. 409–24. Louis Wirth, "Urbanism as a Way of Life," *American Journal of Sociology,* 44 (July, 1938), 1–24. Wirth, an American sociologist, was a professor at the University of Chicago during the period when its Department of Sociology, under Robert Park and Ernest Burgess, was the most important center of urban studies in the United States. Wirth died in 1952 at the age of 55. The work of Simmel (1858–1918), a brilliant German theoretician, influenced Park and Burgess.

tegrative factors in urban personality have often been overlooked, while the disorganizing factors have been unduly emphasized. Despite these *caveats,* it is worthwhile to examine the general propositions about urban personality, for they sensitize us to the significant elements in urban experience with which city personalities must cope. Later in the chapter we shall present the findings of empirical studies, which, by indicating the intricacy of personality analysis, suggest that stereotyped notions of urban personality may apply to only a small proportion of the urban population.

IMPRESSIONS OF URBAN PERSONALITY

What features of urban social life affect human personality? What direction do these changes take? The analyses have stressed the complexity and impersonality of city life with the consequent expectation that city people would be more "nervous" and insensitive, although, as the compensating advantages of anonymity and variety, urbanites are also supposed to have increased freedom of thought and action. The four psychological traits most often pointed out as characteristic of city people are *anxiety* stemming from instabilities of status and the highly differentiated set of social roles to be performed; *emotional deprivation* resulting from personal isolation and from the impersonal contacts of city life; the process of *externalization* and superficiality imposed by large-scale organizations and mass society; *nervous enervation,* that is, blase attitudes and other protective psychological devices developed against the multiplicity of urban stimuli.

ANXIETY

All analyses of urban personality have hinged on the fact that the urbanite is involved in a specialized division of labor. He is necessarily involved, therefore, in a ramifying set of roles whose total structure he usually perceives dimly, if at all. It has been said that because the urbanite is just "a cog in a machine," he feels helpless and inadequate. Specialized roles are most obvious in the field of work, but specialization permeates virtually all aspects of urban life. Even one's recreational activities are likely to be commercialized and thus become another aspect of someone else's work role. Thus, for example, major league baseball, the urban spectator's pastime, is serious business for the players and the rest of the baseball industry.[2]

Specialization, in the city, is accentuated by rapid change; new roles are constantly being added and current roles become outmoded or their content changed. Witness the job categories added by the advent of tele-

[2] See Chapter 18, p. 421, for further discussion of the economic aspects of leisure.

vision and space flight. Meanwhile, the blacksmith has become a rarity, while the coal-miner and the railroad fireman promise to become so as machines take over many of their functions. Most recent management-labor disputes have arisen over the loss of jobs through automation. In the nonoccupational field, "teenager" illustrates a newly-developed role. The term "teenager" itself was rarely used before World War II, but the role has now expanded so rapidly that many commercial markets cater to this new subculture (for example, special magazines, much popular music), while learned volumes dissect it.[3] In an earlier day, "career girl" and "working wife" were new roles. Role specialization and change are not confined to cities, but they are more characteristic of the city and tend to originate there. In rural areas, the orientation to farming provides a central core of common occupational interest and sets limits to other role specialization.

The diversity and change which are built into the urbanite's roles may result in a weakening of the individual's psychological roots. Insecurity may result from the world of work—will one have a job or can one meet its demands? Even more importantly, the urban individual is cut off from a stable chain of cultural transmission and support. For example, while the farmer or the villager is usually able to pass on his work skills to his son, the urban father seldom has the opportunity for such transmission. Urban occupations remove the individual from his family not only for training and for work activity itself but often in social interests as well, thereby loosening the bonds of tradition and conformity. The father engaged in professional work, for example, often finds that his occupation leaves little time for his family or kin, and that even when they are together his work is too technical for mutual interest and discussion.

In addition, the fluidity of urban role structure has been conducive to the expectation and, often, the realization of vertical social mobility, a factor that increases the isolation of many urbanites. Communication and understanding between the generations of a family or between relatives who have moved into different levels of the class structure may be difficult. The individual finds he is not committed to the past way of life, and he may not have a clear idea of the future standards he will follow.

For all these reasons, stability and a sense of the meaning of life may be difficult for the urbanite to achieve. Anxiety is a likely product of the shifting sands of urban role structure.

EMOTIONAL DEPRIVATION

The specialized activities of the city are, of course, linked with the fact that city populations are large. Wirth's classic essay on the socially rele-

---

[3] For example, see James S. Coleman, *The Adolescent Society* (1961), and Jessie Bernard (ed.), "Teen-Age Culture," *Annals of the American Academy of Political and Social Science*, 338 (November, 1961), entire issue.

vant factors in city life identifies size, density, and heterogeneity, of
which size is the most important. Large size makes it impossible for all
the people of the city to have intimate personal knowledge of or interest
in one another. Contacts of such total involvement that they give the individual a sense of emotional fulfillment are called primary; secondary
contacts involve the individual only partially and yield much less emotional satisfaction; indeed, the individual may respond to these contacts
with complete indifference. The impersonality of such relationships, as
between clerk and customer and employer and employee, is illustrated
by the fact that sometimes their functions can be performed by machines,
the self-service counter and the vending machine replacing the clerk or
the dictating machine replacing the stenographer.

Sometimes secondary relationships require the person to conceal his
emotions. In many aspects of city life, the wearing of psychological masks
is virtually mandatory. The salesman, the floor manager, the receptionist,
the public relations man, the entertainer—these are occupational types
for whom masking is a *modus vivendi*. There are many others. They are
poseurs. Their behavior often belies their real feelings. Their synthetic
smile may be merely "window dressing," a device for manipulating or
pleasing customers and clients and smoothing the way to pecuniary or
other objectives.

The prevalence of secondary relationships in the city may yield a psy-
chic dividend, however. The urbanite may be less bound by the heavy
hand of custom, less influenced by gossip from his neighbors' tongues.
Although many of his relationships are contractual, and therefore are
binding by the force of law, they are also limited. Beyond the responsibilities which they impose, he has freedom of choice and action—freedom
to choose his friends, to use his leisure as he pleases, to live in a style be-
fitting his purse, to spend his money according to his own demands—or
those of his wife! There is not only freedom to choose, but also a wide
range of possible choices.

EXTERNALIZATION

The outer shell of form and appearance is very important in the city.
The multiple and transient contacts of the city place a premium on
visible cues for social placement. Hence the emphasis on consumption
patterns, fashion, and fads. One cannot take it for granted that others
will know what one is; one must show it. Status in the city is to some extent a matter of "putting up a front."

By force of circumstance, social control in the city must also employ
external measures, of which the clock and the calendar are among the
most important. Mumford has pointed out the vital role of the clock in
the development of industrial society.[4] The analysis of motion and the per-

---

[4] Lewis Mumford, *Technics and Civilization* (1934), pp. 13–18.

fection of various types of gears, escapements, and motive power provided immensely valuable technical experience for the invention and perfection of other precision machines. Development of the clock helped to create belief in "an independent world of mathematically measurable sequences: the special world of science." [5] Clocks employing gears and wheels were made in the fourteenth century, prior to the beginning of the Industrial Revolution. "The clock, not the steam engine, is the key machine of the modern industrial age," Mumford concludes.[6]

With the subsequent elaboration of a complex urban social structure, the clock has become an essential device for coordinating interdependent activities. In the city the machine or the boss sets the pace, and the individual is expected to keep in step. Many facets of metropolitan life are reduced to clocklike precision. Virtually all organized activities of the city, whether of work or play, are geared to time.

Other formal impersonal means of social control abound—policemen, hotel detectives, bank guards, highway troopers, and mechanized devices such as subway turnstiles, speed-timing by radar, and photographs automatically taken as a check is cashed.

Externalization is invariably associated with standardization, which is evident in status and social control, as already noted, and in many other areas of life. In its extreme form, standardization becomes the use of money as the measure of all things—and people. "How much is he worth?" Standardization involves viewing the externals of men and things with a calculating rational eye. As Simmel observed, ". . . in this attitude, a formal justice is often coupled with an inconsiderate hardness." [7]

Objective treatment of men and things leads to man's being treated as a thing, a highly efficient process well suited to the exigencies of the large scale of urban life, but one giving short shrift to his uniqueness and sensibilities. To this process of dehumanization, it may be tentatively suggested that urban man's reactions are of two types. First, he may attempt to assert his individuality by various attention-getting devices. If these devices are themselves of an external sort, such as extreme hairstyles or clothing, they only feed into the circle of superficiality and standardization. Or the individual may also assert his individuality by "playing along" with bureaucratic routine but saving the important parts of himself for leisure or the family.[8]

Second, the individual may not react at all to standardization, simply accepting the depersonalized view of himself. This lack of assertion of individuality can be very demoralizing, particularly if it is widespread in an urban population, and coupled with a lack of common goals and shared values. Individuals, lacking a sense of their own inner worth, are reduced to the "mass," shifting their loyalties, enthusiasms, and buying

[5] *Ibid.*, p. 15.   [6] *Ibid.*, p. 14.   [7] Simmel, *op. cit.*, p. 411.
[8] An adjustment similar to this is suggested by the section on "Autonomy" in David Riesman, Nathan Glazer, and Reuel Denney, *The Lonely Crowd* (1950), pp. 275–350, and there are echoes in William H. Whyte's advice to cheat on psychological tests given by employers in his *The Organization Man* (1957), pp. 449–56.

habits with the winds of impulse, the mass media, advertising, and the search for a "thrill."

In summary, the process of externalization is valuable and even necessary to urban society, because it provides visible guide lines for action in complex situations. But externalization may have paradoxical effects on the individual. It may exalt individuality, whether as an attention-getting device or on a more meaningful level; or it may reduce the individual to the "lowest common denominator."

NERVOUS ENERVATION

Nervous enervation more than physical exhaustion is a characteristic reaction to city life and labor. The jostling of crowds, the incessant clang of machines, the tenseness induced by trying to satisfy strangers, pleasant and unpleasant, whom one may never see again; the strains of communication (talking, listening, comprehending); the anxieties arising from the demands for punctuality and precision—these are the things that cause frayed nerves and a sickening sense of emotional depletion.

To protect one's own personality against the inexorable demands of city life is a problem that every urban person faces to a greater or less degree; more particularly it is a problem for those who are caught in the whirlpool of the market place. Escapism, either physical or psychological, is one device, or rather a series of devices. One may run away from it all —take a vacation in the country, repair after work to a quiet suburban home among the trees and flowers, or bar the outside world from one's city apartment. Or one may escape psychologically by building around himself a protective shell of callous indifference, even of cynicism. Except for his friends or relatives, he may avoid close identification with those about him, though perhaps observing the fictional rituals of politeness. A detached view of life and people in the city may be an effective means of maintaining one's personal balance. Theorists such as Wirth and Simmel have commented on the development of the blasé attitude and its other face, tolerance, as a protective reaction to the multiple stimuli of urban life.

EVALUATION OF IMPRESSIONS OF URBAN PERSONALITY

We have indicated that on the basis of inference from the specialized, impersonal nature of urban institutions, we should expect the urban dweller's personality to show anxiety, emotional deprivation, symptoms of externalization, and nervous enervation. Implicit in this formulation is the idea that urbanites have poor mental health. In the past decade or so the basis for these impressions of urban personality has been seriously challenged. Our knowledge of the social forces affecting urbanites has become more sophisticated than such pioneering analyses as those by Wirth and Simmel.

Studies have shown that the isolated anonymous urbanite is a gross oversimplification.[9] Instead it has been found that participation in the family and with kin occupies much of the time and interest of most urbanites and that ties to the neighborhood and local area are often strong; while, on the other hand, that only a minority of urban dwellers belong to any formal organization other than the church and that work interests seldom affect other areas of life, such as the formation of friendships and the family. Furthermore, it has been shown that other factors, particularly socioeconomic level, age, and marital status, are more highly related to how an individual behaves than city residence *per se*.

These new formulations of the nature of urban life lead us to expect that few, if any, clear-cut distinctions will exist between urban personality traits and those of people in other kinds of communities. We have already noted, however, the shortcomings of attempting to infer the psychological traits of city dwellers from a description of the social characteristics of urban life. Therefore, in the following section we will examine the empirical studies of urban personality traits. We shall focus on the question: Do urban personalities show the tensions which early urban theory had assumed? We shall find that the empirical studies leave many questions unanswered. On the whole, however, urban dwellers show fewer personality contrasts with those living in other communities than had been expected on the basis of the impressionistic analyses. Also, there is no definite evidence of their having more mental health problems, or other evidence of personal disorganization.[10]

STUDIES OF FOLK-URBAN PERSONALITY DIFFERENCES

The communities most different from cities are folk societies—small, isolated, nonliterate, and self-sufficient—for example, tribal and village societies. In such societies, technology is simple, there is little specialization, almost all contacts are primary, and the family is paramount. These social conditions, so very different from the city and seemingly more integrated, were supposed to be especially suited to the adjustment of

---

[9] See, for example, Albert Reiss, "An Analysis of Urban Phenomena," in Robert M. Fisher (ed.), *The Metropolis in Modern Life* (1955), pp. 41–51; Scott Greer, "Individual Participation in Mass Society," in K. Young and R. Mack (eds.), *Principles of Sociology: A Reader in Theory and Research* (1960), pp. 223–29; and Herbert J. Gans, "Urbanism and Suburbanism as Ways of Life: A Re-evaluation of Definitions," in Arnold Rose (ed.), *Human Behavior and Social Processes* (1962), pp. 625–48.

[10] If the city exerts any disorganizing effects they are probably temporary effects, resulting from the need for adjustment to the requirements of urban life. But reorganization is not disorganization. See pp. 461–63 in Chapter 20, for a fuller treatment of this point.

personality. The findings, however, suggest that personality adjustment in folk societies has been overrated.

REDFIELD'S AND LEWIS' FIELD REPORTS

We have an opportunity to examine personal adjustment in folk society by comparing the reports of two anthropologists who studied the same community. Redfield, who developed the concept of folk society, studied a number of Maya Indian communities on the Yucatan peninsula of southeastern Mexico. And, in 1926, Redfield studied Tepoztlan, a small Mexican agricultural village about 50 miles south of Mexico City. Oscar Lewis did field work in the same community, Tepoztlan, 17 years later, in 1943.[11] Redfield described the village as harmonious and the people as well-adjusted and content, but Lewis found considerable evidence of violence, cruelty, and suffering, and of strife both within the village and in its relations with other villages.

The reasons for such divergent reports on personality in folk society as Lewis' and Redfield's appear to lie in methodology and in attitudes.[12] The methodology of the social sciences is inadequate to deal with measures of disorganization and personal adjustment; our antiurban bias unconsciously predisposes us toward finding "sweetness and light" among folk populations. Other recent studies have indicated that Lewis' view of folk personal relationships is more accurate than Redfield's.[13] We have failed to realize that a precarious living off the land and an inescapable closeness to others may be as productive of anxiety and personal problems as urban specialization and impersonality.

MENTAL ILLNESS IN FOLK SOCIETY

The incidence of serious mental disorder in folk societies provides another way of comparing folk-urban personalities. Precise studies are few but indications are that simplicity of social structure has not "immunized" people against psychoses. A review of data on the extent of schizophrenia among primitive people, including some living in preliterate and tribal societies, suggests that the illness is neither absent nor rare. Similarly,

[11] Robert Redfield, *Tepoztlan—A Mexican Village* (1930); Oscar Lewis, *Life in a Mexican Village: Tepoztlan Re-Studied* (1951).

[12] A review of this general topic is given in Melvin Seeman, "An Evaluation of Current Approaches to Personality Differences in Folk and Urban Societies," *Social Forces,* 25 (December, 1946), 160–65.

[13] George Foster, "Interpersonal Relations in Peasant Society," *Human Organization,* 19 (Winter, 1960–61), 174–84; Joseph Lopreato, "Interpersonal Relations in Peasant Society: The Peasant's Point of View," *Human Organization,* 21 (Spring, 1962), 21–24. It should be noted that Tepoztlan is an example of peasant-folk society rather than the simpler tribal-folk society.

a survey of a wide variety of non-Western cultures, many of the folk type, shows the various psychoses are prevalent in such societies.[14]

One of the most thorough studies of the incidence of mental illness in a closely-knit nonindustrial community is Eaton and Weil's study of the Hutterites.[15] The Hutterites are an Anabaptist religious sect located in the Middle West, particularly in eastern South Dakota. They are farmers and have a very cohesive social structure based on their religious principles. Because their communities provide the individual Hutterite with such a high degree of support, it might be expected that mental illness would be rare. Eaton and Weil's study uncovered 199 cases (including 53 diagnosed as psychotic) of past or present mental illness among the 8,542 Hutterites. Thus, one in every 43 Hutterites either had active symptoms of mental disorder or had recovered from such a disorder. One clear finding emerges from the Hutterite study: it demolishes the stereotyped notion that people living in stable, self-contained communities necessarily have a negligible amount of mental illness.

STUDIES OF RURAL-URBAN PERSONALITY DIFFERENCES

Empirical studies of rural-urban personality differences are much more numerous than folk-urban comparisons. We shall compare the findings of empirical studies for ruralites on attitudes, personality adjustment, and mental illness. We shall find there is no clear indication of rural superiority, or even that ruralites differ very much personally from urbanites.

RURAL-URBAN COMPARISONS IN ATTITUDES

Tolerance has often been thought of as an attitude more characteristic of urban than rural dwellers. Since the city is culturally and racially more heterogeneous than the country, it is reasonable to assume that the urban dweller has a greater awareness than rural persons of divergent cultural norms. He may not accept the values of others, but at least he is aware of them, and often he must live and work with people who are different.

Does this mean, then, that city people, by and large, are less prejudiced, less bigoted, less intolerant of those who differ in race, religion, culture, nationality, moral qualities, or any other attributes? To answer the question adequately it would be necessary to state the problem in terms of a specific situation, employ an empirical measure of intolerance, and select representative samples of rural and urban persons matched for

---

[14] N. J. Demerath, "Schizophrenia among Primitives," in Arnold Rose (ed.), *Mental Health and Mental Disorder* (1955), pp. 215–22; Tsung-Yi Lin, "Effects of Urbanization on Mental Health," *International Social Science Journal*, 11 (1959), 24–33.

[15] J. Eaton and R. Weil, *Culture and Mental Disorders* (1955).

age, sex, and perhaps other attributes. The studies by Stouffer and Beers approximate these conditions.

Stouffer's Study of Political and Religious Tolerance.   One of the most significant studies of attitudes of the American people toward political and religious nonconformists was directed by Stouffer under the auspices of the Fund for the Republic.[16] A national sample of 4,933 persons was interviewed by staff members of the National Opinion Research Center and the American Institute of Opinion Research. A tolerance scale was constructed, and from this a three-level classification of the persons interviewed indicated roughly their degree of tolerance or intolerance.

In general, those living in cities of 100,000 or over and their suburbs (metropolitan areas) were the most tolerant, as shown by the percentage distribution of persons on the tolerance scale. Those living on farms were less tolerant than residents either of small towns or nonmetropolitan cities. Table 19 reveals these differences.

TABLE 19

**Percentage Distribution of Persons on Tolerance Scale,
by Type of Community**

Type of Community	Number	Less Tolerant	In-between	More Tolerant
Metropolitan areas	1,891	14	47	39
Other cities	1,362	19	51	30
Small towns	917	20	55	25
Farms	762	29	53	18

SOURCE: Samuel Stouffer, *Communism, Conformity, and Civil Liberties* (1955), p. 112.

Even when such important factors as education and regional location of the persons in the sample were held constant there still remained differences based upon type of community. These differences were by no means clearcut, but the same general pattern continued to exist, indicating that the differences cannot be explained solely in terms of education. The situation for the Middle West is presented in Table 20, adapted from the study.

These data suggest that the difference between metropolitan communities and smaller cities may not be very important, that the principal cleavage is between urban and rural communities. However, any such generalizations should be considered tentative.

More striking are the regional differences found in the study. The research revealed that when education and type of community were held constant regional differences continued to persist. For example, college

[16] Samuel Stouffer, *Communism, Conformity, and Civil Liberties* (1955).

TABLE 20

Percentage Distribution of Persons in the Middle West, Classified as "More Tolerant" on Scale of Tolerance, by Education and Type of Community

Educational Level	Farm	Small Town	Other Cities	Metropolitan Areas
College graduates	a	69	62	65
Some college	a	30	67	59
High school graduates	45	32	43	40
Some high school	13	10	22	37
Grade school	9	10	23	21

a No percentage calculations made when the number was less than 20. In the other regions the small number of cases in some of the categories makes the tables incomplete, but the general pattern is much the same as for the Middle West.
SOURCE: Samuel Stouffer, *Communism, Conformity, and Civil Liberties* (1955), p. 123.

graduates in the metropolitan South were less tolerant than college graduates in the metropolitan centers of the West, East, or Middle West. Similarly, persons on the grade school level were less tolerant in large southern cities than in communities of comparable size in other regions. For the urban population (metropolitan areas and smaller cities) the West showed the highest degree of tolerance of the major regions, with the South consistently the least tolerant.

Beers' Survey of Opinion Polls. Beers' survey of national opinion polls taken in the United States between 1946–50 compares farmers' opinions with those of various urban groups.[17] One important finding was that there were no cases of unanimity or near-unanimity among either the rural or the urban groups. Instead there was a wide variety of opinion within each group, particularly on the basis of occupation. Farm owners differed from other farm groups and urban executives differed from white collar workers or labor union members.

In general, however, farmers were more opposed than the urban groups to the expanding economic function of government, and to the unrestrained power of labor unions. Farmers were also slightly more isolationist in international affairs. These findings suggest that farmers are indeed more conservative; but the most important finding is that farmers did not differ from the urban public in being conservative. Thus, although only 14 per cent of the farmers favored more government regulation of business, the proportion of the general public in favor was also low—21 per cent. On the whole, farmers differed only in degree from the attitudes expressed by most of the population.

[17] Howard W. Beers, "Rural-Urban Differences; Some Evidence from Public Opinion Polls," *Rural Sociology,* 18 (March. 1953), 1–11.

The Stouffer and Beers studies indicate that there probably are differences in degree of tolerance between rural and urban populations. Their studies also suggest the major contrasts are between farmers and urban groups. Even then, the contrasts are not large, and other factors such as education and occupation prove equally important. We may expect differences based on residence to decline still further as modern transportation and communication continue to minimize rural isolation from the city.

RURAL-URBAN COMPARISONS IN PERSONALITY ADJUSTMENT

Few questions in urban sociology have generated more interest among both professionals and laymen as that of whether—and what kind of—personality differences exist between rural and urban dwellers.

A review of over 35 studies which compared rural and urban groups in the United States on a wide variety of personal attributes leads to the conclusion that there are no hard-and-fast rural-urban differences.[18] And a study of Finnish rural and urban groups suggests that these findings are not limited to the United States.[19]

The lack of sharp contrasts may lie in declining rural-urban differences as country folk, too, are geared to specialized production for distant markets and are effected by the mass media. Another reason may be that the usual "paper-and-pencil" personality tests lack sufficient depth to find existing differences.[20] Place of residence may affect personality, but other influential factors such as age and social class may be more important.

One of the most thorough surveys of personal adjustment was carried out in the United States as part of the Mental Health Study Act of 1955.[21] Researchers from the University of Michigan Survey Research Center interviewed 2,460 Americans over 21 years of age who were representative of the total population in terms of age, sex, education, income, occupation, and place of residence. Individuals in prisons, hospitals, and other institutions were excluded. This sample of the presumably normal adult population of the United States was questioned at length about its satisfaction in various areas of life. Nearly one in four of these adults said that at some time in life he had felt sufficiently troubled to need help,

[18] C. A. McMahan, "Personality in the Urban Environment," in T. Lynn Smith and C. A. McMahan (eds.), *The Sociology of Urban Life* (1951), pp. 748–60; Harald Swedner, *Ecological Differentiation of Habits and Attitudes* (1960), pp. 29–45.

[19] Kai Von Fieandt, "Psychological Effects of Urban and Rural Domiciles," *Acta Psychologica*, 14 (1958), 81–91.

[20] A recent study, using instruments alleged to measure subtle personality differences among normal people, found widespread differences among rural and urban boys in Michigan. See A. O. Haller and Carole Ellis Wolff, "Personality Orientations of Farm, Village, and Urban Boys," *Rural Sociology*, 27 (September, 1962), 275–93.

[21] Gerald Gurin, Joseph Veroff, and Sheila Feld, *Americans View Their Mental Health* (1960), pp. xxv, 228–30.

mainly in the areas of marriage, parenthood, the job, and psychological problems. One in seven actually sought help from religious, private, or public sources.

Dissatisfaction was apparently fairly widespread among Americans. Differences in feelings of satisfaction showed no consistent relationship to place of residence. Thus, people in metropolitan areas expressed more worrying and less happiness than other residential groups, but in marital adjustment, metropolitanites reported greater happiness and fewer feelings of inadequacy.

Most important was the fact that differences in level of gratification by place of residence were overshadowed by differences based on sex, age, education, and income. A young educated male farmer is perhaps more like a young educated male New Yorker than either of them is like his own father. Differences in place of residence are not crucial in feelings of personal satisfaction.

RURAL-URBAN COMPARISONS IN MENTAL ILLNESS

The pace of urban life has often been assumed to lead to higher rates of mental illness than in rural areas. Admission rates to mental hospitals in urban areas have consistently been higher than those in rural areas.[22] But we do not know where the patients come from originally. Also, it may be more inconvenient to keep a mentally ill person at home in the city than in the country. These factors may account for the relatively low rural rate of hospitalization for mental illness. It has been demonstrated that there are many unhospitalized psychotics in both city and country areas.

Surveys of total communities are a more reliable way of determining the extent of mental illness. The results of several of these surveys are presented in Table 21, showing only the rates of schizophrenic and manic-depressive psychoses. The communities include several predominantly rural ones: Thuringian (German) villages; the Danish island of Bornholm; and Williamson County, Tennessee. The comparisons with Baltimore rates of mental illness should be considered tentative since the various surveys differed widely in the ways they obtained their data. Nevertheless, the table shows that the Baltimore rate of schizophrenic and manic-depressive psychoses was higher than that of three rural areas, but was exceeded by that for the Danish farming and fishing community, Bornholm.

A more recent attempt to evaluate the prevalence of mental disorders in various types of communities was made in 1960 by Plunkett and

[22] Arnold Rose and Holger Stub, "Summary of Studies on the Incidence of Mental Disorders," in Arnold Rose (ed.), *Mental Health and Mental Disorder* (1955), pp. 99–101.

TABLE 21

Rates of Active and Recovered Cases of Schizophrenia and
Manic-Depressive Psychoses in Five Surveys
(per 100,000 population)

Thuringia	2.5
Tennessee	3.4
Bavaria	3.9
Baltimore	4.6
Bornholm	5.9

SOURCE: Paul Lemkau, C. Tietze, and M. Cooper, "A Survey of Statistical Studies in the Prevalence and Incidence of Mental Disorder in Sample Populations," *U. S. Public Health Reports*, 58 (December 31, 1943), 1920.

Gordon,[23] who reviewed 11 representative studies of urban and rural communities in the United States, published between 1916 and 1958. These studies included neuroses as well as psychoses. However, the studies differed so greatly in their orientation, personnel, populations considered, criteria of mental illness, case-finding techniques, and diagnostic categories that Plunkett and Gordon concluded that no direct comparisons of observed rates could be made. The prevalence rates per 1,000 for total mental disorder, for example, varied from 16.7 to 333.0. Accordingly, Plunkett and Gordon concluded that "the inconsistency of results is largely because each study has itself introduced an extrinsic variable between its findings and true prevalence." [24] They warn that "The most striking lesson from the prevalence survey is the stern and endlessly repeated admonition that true progress toward a grasp of mental illness in the population . . . will not begin until the validation and universal acceptance of a precise diagnostic system." [25]

Goldhamer and Marshall's Study of Historic Trends. The use of historic series of mental illness rates has been advocated as another way of determining whether urban populations are more prone to mental illness. If this is so then the rates should rise as more and more of the population live in cities. The outstanding historic study is that by Goldhamer and Marshall,[26] who established that accurate statistics were available for Massachusetts for several periods going back to the early nineteenth century. Goldhamer and Marshall also established the fact that mental hospitals were as available to the Massachusetts population then as they are now and that the diagnoses of doctors then were similar to those today, although the terminology differed.

[23] Richard Plunkett and John Gordon, *Epidemiology and Mental Illness* (1960), pp. 49–50, 90–93.
[24] *Ibid.*, p. 49.   [25] *Ibid.*, p. 93.
[26] Herbert Goldhamer and A. Marshall, *Psychosis and Civilization* (1953).

Goldhamer and Marshall computed that the rates for admission for psychosis in Massachusetts were 41 per 100,000 in 1840–45; 58 in 1880–84; and 85 in 1941, assuming in each case that the age structure of the population was that of 1840. This suggests that as urbanization proceeded so did mental illness. But Goldhamer and Marshall turned up a surprising and significant fact: When the over-all rates of admission were broken down by age groups, it was found that for those between ages 20 and 50 the admission rates were the same in the nineteenth as in the twentieth century! It was the age group over 50 which showed much higher admission rates in 1940. In other words, the fact that there are indeed proportionately more people in mental hospitals today than in the nineteenth century may result from an increasing tendency to hospitalize older people for mental disorders. This does not necessarily mean that old people have higher rates of mental illness today. Farm chores and country living make it easier to care for senile oldsters than do city apartments and jobs that keep the family away all day.

Goldhamer and Marshall's findings have raised much speculation. The fact remains that adults, aged 20 to 50, were hospitalized as often for mental illness in the nineteenth century as in the twentieth. This fact does not support the notion that mental illness has increased as our civilization has become more urban.

SUMMARY

Recent rural-urban comparisons based on empirical studies have not brought out any striking differences. Residents of rural areas, particularly farmers, appear to be somewhat less tolerant and more conservative, but there is a wide range of opinion among both ruralites and urbanites. In personality adjustment, studies have shown no consistent differences between rural and urban residents. Finally, rates of hospitalization for mental illness are clearly higher in urban areas, but available studies suggest the actual rates of mental illness are similar in rural and urban areas. Higher urban hospitalization rates are partly explained by a greater tendency in the city to hospitalize older patients.

The absence of clear-cut contrasts may be explained in various ways. (1) Major differences may have existed but have declined as specialization broke down the self-sufficiency of rural areas, and modern transportation and communication reduced their isolation. (2) The sampling methods and definitions of rural and urban vary from one study to another so the units cannot really be compared. (3) The instruments used to measure attitudes and personality are inadequate. (4) Age, sex, education, income, occupation, and other factors also affect values and psychological outlook and, on the whole, are more important than differences based on place of residence. (5) Rural-urban comparisons are often obscured by the fact that many people live in one kind of area but grew up in another. All of these factors undoubtedly have some influence as is evident in the various studies described, but which factors are most important has not yet been established.

We may conclude, after examining the empirical data on attitudes, personality adjustment, and mental illness, that easy generalizations about the disorganizing effects of city life on the individual are unwarranted. The following examination of studies of crime, suicide, and sexual deviation will also suggest a similar conclusion.

STUDIES OF RURAL-URBAN SOCIAL DEVIATION

CRIME AND DELINQUENCY

On the basis of the incidence of crimes known to the police it may be inferred that crime is more prevalent in urban than in rural communities. Yet these differences may be partly a matter of definition; they may also

TABLE 22

Offenses Known to Police, and the Rate per 100,000 by Class of City, 1961

Offense	Class of City		
	METROPOLITAN AREAS	OTHER CITIES	RURAL
Murder and non-negligent manslaughter	4.5	3.6	5.9
Forcible rape	10.4	4.1	6.8
Robbery	71.2	14.2	11.5
Aggravated assault	88.6	47.1	42.7
Burglary	570.6	357.0	234.8
Larceny	345.3	187.7	115.7
Auto theft	241.7	105.5	42.1

SOURCE: Federal Bureau of Investigation, *Uniform Crime Reports* (1961), p. 33.

reflect differences in the efficiency and honesty of law enforcement personnel, differences in the accuracy and completeness of records, or differences in social and economic conditions.[27] These differences are accentuated by the fact that submitting reports to the FBI for preparation of the Uniform Crime Reports is voluntary. Coverage is much more com-

---

[27] Strong criticism of crime statistics is given in Ronald Beattie, "Criminal Statistics in the United States, 1960," *Journal of Criminal Law, Criminology, and Police Science,* 51 (May–June, 1960), 49–65.

plete for urban areas than for rural areas; and the rural communities that do not contribute reports may be those with higher crime rates.

From the data in Table 22, it appears that for offenses as a whole there is a lower incidence in small and middle-sized cities and in rural areas than in large metropolitan centers. Even when generous allowance is made for inaccurate or incomplete data, the differences are impressive.

Interestingly, crimes of violence in rural areas (village and farm) are at a high level. Murder is proportionately more frequent in rural areas than in metropolitan areas and in other cities. Forcible rape is higher in rural areas than in cities, although the rate for metropolitan areas is highest of all. Assault rates are almost the same in rural areas and in nonmetropolitan cities; only in metropolitan areas are they appreciably higher. The reverse trend is true of offenses against property, such as burglary, larceny, and auto theft. It is only in these types of offenses that metropolitan areas and other cities consistently have much higher rates than rural areas. Possibly this is because there is more property to steal in the city and more opportunities for stealing it.

Table 23 indicates that high rates of physical aggression (homicides

TABLE 23

Fifteen Leading Countries in Rates per 100,000 Population of Homicide and Attempted Homicide, in Order of Frequency of Occurrence (1955–56)

Burma	60.17
Cuba	28.75 [a]
Thailand	20.10
Netherlands West Indies	15.00
Lebanon	12.53
Egypt	11.50
Ceylon	8.57
Israel	8.23
Guam	7.69
Alaska	7.62 [b]
Kenya	7.55
Pakistan	6.39
Yugoslavia	5.36 [c]
Turkey	5.11
Syria	4.90 [a]

[a] Data available only for 1954.
[b] Prior to Alaskan admission to statehood.
[c] Data available only for 1955.
SOURCE: Herbert Bloch, *Research Report on Homicide, Attempted Homicide, and Crimes of Violence* (Colombo: United States Operations Mission to Ceylon, August, 1960), p. 545. Professor Bloch compiled the data from statistics published by the International Criminal Police Organization.

and attempted homicides) can be found in many countries with large rural populations as well as in highly urbanized countries. It should be noted that the figures include attempted homicide as well as homicide itself, and hence are not comparable with those for murder in the United States.

Clinard's Studies of Rural and Urban Criminals. A comparative study of criminals with rural and urban backgrounds may cast more light on the problem of crime in rural and urban areas than a comparison of crime rates. Three related studies have examined the characteristics of rural and urban criminals. Clinard studied 200 property offenders in Iowa who were classified by farm, village, or urban residence before imprisonment.[28] A similar study was repeated in Iowa about 10 years later by Eastman.[29] Recently, Clinard repeated his original study with criminals of rural and urban background in Sweden.[30] The conclusions of the three studies with respect to the influence of rural and urban background on criminals convicted of offenses against property differ somewhat, but they agree on the importance of the community factor.

According to the original Clinard study, offenders with urban backgrounds tended to conform to criminal social patterns; that is, they conceived of themselves as criminals, made use of established techniques, spoke a criminal argot, frequently looked upon crime as a way of life or vocation, considered themselves enemies of the police and the courts, and associated with prostitutes, pimps, and racketeers. Village offenders manifested in a slight way some of the characteristic features of the criminal social pattern, but the prisoners with farm backgrounds showed few of these criminal traits. The same progression was evident in the Eastman and Swedish studies, but they did not disclose as clear-cut a criminal social type in cities as had the original study.

The significant findings of the three studies may be summarized as follows: (1) The urban environment is more conducive to crimes against property than are rural or village environments. These differences reflect differences in values and organization of rural and urban community life. The relative compactness of the rural community and the effective operation of such primary controls as gossip make it virtually impossible for a criminal culture to exist. In the metropolis, however, high mobility, anonymous relationships, and the prevalence of pecuniary values are conducive to crime and the development of criminal personalities. (2) However, differences between urban and rural environments are declining as rural and village areas become less isolated and urban values and behavior patterns are transmitted to them. Thus, the two later studies show

[28] Marshall B. Clinard, "The Process of Urbanization and Criminal Behavior," *American Journal of Sociology,* 48 (September, 1942), 202–13.

[29] Harold D. Eastman, "The Process of Urbanization and Criminal Behavior: A Restudy of Culture Conflict," unpublished Ph.D. dissertation, University of Iowa, 1954.

[30] Marshall B. Clinard, "A Cross-Cultural Replication of the Relation of Urbanism to Criminal Behavior," *American Sociological Review,* 25 (April, 1960), 253–57.

gang behavior among rural and village youth has increased. (3) Perhaps of most importance is the finding in the two later studies that the degree to which the urban environment produces a definite criminal social type may have been overstated.

SUICIDE

Like crime, suicide bears some relationship to urbanization. In general, there is a higher rate of suicide in urban than in rural areas, and a higher incidence in large cities than in small ones. Yet the size of the city is probably less important than social, economic, cultural, and other factors. American cities with a high percentage of adults, old people, and particularly elderly males usually have a higher suicide rate than communities with a different demographic structure. Pacific Coast cities—Seattle, Los Angeles, Oakland, and others—usually have a higher rate than cities elsewhere in the United States. American Negroes have a low suicide rate. Suicide is not generally the result of poverty—groups of middle or upper socioeconomic status have higher rates than the lower socioeconomic levels. Cities with a large Catholic population tend to have comparatively low rates. Most New England cities, for example, have rates below those of the urban population as a whole.

The incidence of suicide in a community is indicative of what Durkheim has called a state of *anomie*—the opposite of social cohesiveness. Undoubtedly this is the reason that suicide is usually prevalent in those sections of the city which manifest various forms of social disorganization, areas in which the incidence of divorce, desertion, homelessness, and crime is also high. This pattern has been shown in British as well as American cities.[31] It should be noted that these areas of the city also show a high rate of transiency. Many people drift to the city after they have become maladjusted elsewhere. It cannot be said that city life "caused" their suicides.

SEX DEVIATION

Kinsey's analysis of the sexual behavior of the American male reveals important rural-urban differences.[32] The proportions of males having premarital sex relations, intercourse with prostitutes, and homosexual intercourse were considerably higher for a sample of city men than for a rural sample. On the grade school level, 91 per cent of the city males between 21 and 25 had engaged in premarital intercourse, compared with 80 per cent of the farm males. Of those on the college level, in the same age

[31] Peter Sainsbury, *Suicide in London* (1955).
[32] Alfred C. Kinsey, *et al.*, *Sexual Behavior in the Human Male* (1948), pp. 455–58.

group, the percentages were 55 and 47, respectively. About one-third of the city males with a grade school education had been involved in homosexual activities between the ages of 16 and 20, compared with one-fifth of the farm males. These percentages rose to 46 and 26, respectively, for males on the high school level, but among college men they were 15 for urban males and 16 for rural men. About the same rural-urban differences were found for sexual relations with prostitutes. Kinsey believes the distinctive thing about homosexuality in the city is its organized character.

Analysis of the sexual behavior of females found fewer differences between those from rural and urban backgrounds.[33] One reason for this is that our mores for women are more uniform than those for men. Social ostracism is more frequent and more severe for women than for men who deviate sexually.

It should be noted that educational and social-class differences in sexual behavior may be as important as rural-urban differences. At least this is indicated by Kinsey's findings for both men and women. The cultural and socioeconomic differences have been extensively analyzed.[34] Apparently there are many sexual "worlds" among the American population, each largely ignorant of the attitudes and practices of others. The rural and urban "worlds" are not those most markedly different.

STUDIES OF PERSONALITY VARIATION
WITHIN THE CITY

The variations in personality adjustment within the city are in most cases greater than any variations revealed in rural-urban comparisons. The city is not one environment but many. There is evidence, for example, that some parts of the city have a higher incidence of mental and nervous disorders than other parts. The classic study of the ecology of mental disorders in Chicago, by Faris and Dunham, revealed that the incidence of schizophrenia, alcoholic psychoses, drug addiction, and general paresis was much higher in the slum area, and that the rates tended to decline from the Loop district in the center of the city to the peripheral areas.[35] There was one exception: manic-depressive psychoses showed no such pattern but were about as frequent in one section as another, although there was some tendency for manic-depressives to be on a higher socioeconomic level than the other psychotics. Suicide and crime rates also show variations from one section of the city to another. Illegitimacy, prostitution, and other forms of sexual deviation tend to be concentrated in particular areas of the city, though no section is entirely free of them.

[33] A. Kinsey, *et al.*, *Sexual Behavior in the Human Female* (1953), p. 686 and *passim*.

[34] See, for example, J. Himelhoch and S. F. Fava (eds.), *Sexual Behavior in American Society: An Appraisal of the First Two Kinsey Reports* (1955), pp. 175–211.

[35] R. E. L. Faris and H. Warren Dunham, *Mental Disorder in Urban Areas* (1939).

Social class appears to be one of the most important factors related to variations in personal adjustment. Since people of a given social class tend to live in the same neighborhood, this helps account for the variations in personality adjustment found among different sections of the city.

The Midtown Manhattan Study. A recent study in a densely settled section of Manhattan, at the heart of metropolitan New York City, demonstrates the relationship of social class to personality adjustment.[36] Semi-structured interviews were conducted at home with a representative sample of white adults, aged 20–59. The responses were rated independently by two psychiatrists in terms of the number and severity of psychological symptoms. The "well" group had no significant symptoms. The "mild" and "moderate" groups carried on their adult activities successfully despite psychological difficulties. The "impaired" group had symptoms of a neurotic or psychotic nature severe enough to handicap them considerably, sometimes completely, in everyday life. The table below contrasts the mental health ratings for the topmost and bottom-most socioeconomic levels. Table 24 shows that more than six times as many of the

TABLE 24

Mental Health Levels of Highest and Lowest Socioeconomic Strata in Midtown Manhattan Study

	Highest Socioeconomic Stratum	*Lowest Socioeconomic Stratum*
Well	30.0%	4.6%
Mild symptom formation	37.5	25.0
Moderate symptom formation	20.0	23.1
Impaired	12.5	47.3

SOURCE: Leo Srole, *et al., Mental Health in the Metropolis: The Midtown Manhattan Study* (1962), I, 230. Copyright 1962, McGraw-Hill Book Company, Blakiston Division. Used by permission.

members of the highest ranking socioeconomic group were classified as "well" (30.0 per cent), compared with the lowest ranking socioeconomic group (4.6 per cent).[37] The percentages are much closer for "mild" and

[36] Leo Srole, *et al., Mental Health in the Metropolis: The Midtown Manhattan Study* (1962), vol. I.

[37] It should be noted that the psychiatrists made their first mental health ratings "blind," that is, without knowledge of information which might identify the socioeconomic class of the individual. Thus, knowledge of the individual's class could not influence the psychiatrist's mental health rating. *Ibid.,* p. 413.

"moderate" symptom formation, with the highest socioeconomic stratum even having a larger percentage classified as showing "mild" symptom formation (37.5 per cent) than the lowest socioeconomic stratum (25.0 per cent). The highest stratum had only about one-eighth—12.5 per cent —of its members classified as "impaired," that is, having serious symptoms, while almost half—47.3 per cent—of the lowest ranking stratum were so classified. Table 24 clearly demonstrates that the highest socioeconomic stratum has proportionately few individuals with poor personal adjustment and proportionately many with good personal adjustment. The picture is just the reverse for the lowest socioeconomic stratum.

TABLE 25

Social Class and Rate of Treated Mental Illnesses, New Haven Study

Social Class	Rate per 100,000
I-II (highest)	556
III	538
IV	642
V (lowest)	1,659

SOURCE: A. B. Hollingshead and F. Redlich, *Social Class and Mental Illness* (1958), p. 210.

The New Haven Study. Serious mental illness, that is, psychosis, shows the same kind of relationship to social class as does general personality adjustment. The relationship is inverse, that is, the higher one variable the lower the associated variable. In this case, the higher the social class the lower the prevalence of mental illness. Hollingshead and Redlich's survey of treated psychiatric patients in New Haven gave the results shown in Table 25. The lowest social class, V, had a rate of treated mental illness, 1659 per 100,000 population, more than three times as great as that of the two top classes, 556.

URBANISM AS WAYS OF LIFE

The most fruitful approach to studying the psychological impact of the city lies in viewing the city as providing many different ways of life, rather than in thinking of urbanism as a single way of life. A recent analysis by Gans suggests there are at least five urban ways of life, based chiefly on social class and on stages of the family-cycle.[38]

[38] The following discussion is based on Gans, "Urbanism and Suburbanism as Ways of Life . . ." *op. cit.*, pp. 629–33. See also H. Gans, *The Urban Villagers* (1962), for a participant-observation study of one urban way of life.

(1) The "cosmopolites" are of varying socioeconomic levels and may be at any stage of the life-cycle, but are alike in the high value they place on the "cultural" facilities of the inner city. (2) The unmarried and childless vary by the permanency or transiency of these traits, but while they are unmarried, or married and childless, they participate actively in the varied activities of the city. (3) The "ethnic villagers" are immigrant groups such as the Italians, or migrant groups such as the Puerto Ricans, who carry on in urban enclaves the peasant life of their home communities. (4) The "deprived" are those whose handicaps of extreme poverty, emotional problems, and, especially, race prevent them from acquiring any but slum housing in the worst areas of the central city. (5) The "trapped" and the downwardly mobile are those for whom ownership of real estate, loss of social status, or other happenstance, has meant inability to move from crowded, deteriorated areas.

The first three types are protected from the disorganizing effects of urban life, even though they often live in densely populated, heterogeneous sections of the city where these effects would be expected to be at their height. The "cosmopolites" are protected by the organizing effects of the wide subculture to which they belong. The unmarried and the childless are detached from their local areas because they are not "tied down" by family obligations. The "ethnic villagers" are insulated because they have created their own effective local social structure which isolates them even from groups physically close to them.

It is only the last two groups—the "deprived," and the "trapped" and the downwardly mobile—upon whom the full impact of transient, anonymous urban neighborhoods fall. We have already noted that groups of these kinds do, in fact, have the highest mental illness rates in the city.

Although Gans' analysis was based on American cities, its findings are provocative and reinforce impressionistic observations made in cities in underdeveloped countries. Cosmopolites probably make up an even smaller percentage of the urban population in these cities than in cities in the United States. Their interests and outlook are often international. As professionals and white collar folk, even if they do not have much income, their intellectual and social life may be fairly broad and effectively detached from the traditional native life around them. The "villagers-in-the-city"—people who carry on their rural customs as they always have done—make up a large part of the population of cities in underdeveloped areas. Among the urban villagers there may also be distinctive ways of life reflecting religious or tribal affiliations. In India, Muslims and Hindus, at least on the lower social levels, lead quite different styles of life.

For cities both in developed and underdeveloped areas, there is no single urban pattern. Social status, family ties, ethnic affiliation, age, and other factors which modify urban environmental influences have to be studied in order to understand personality in the urban setting.

SELECTED BIBLIOGRAPHY

Books

De Ridder, J. C., *The Personality of the Urban African in South Africa.* London: Routledge & Kegan Paul, 1961.

Eaton, J., and R. Weil, *Culture and Mental Disorders.* Glencoe, Ill.: The Free Press, 1954.

Gans, Herbert, "Urbanism and Suburbanism as Ways of Life: A Re-evaluation of Definitions," in Arnold Rose (ed.), *Human Behavior and Social Processes.* Boston: Houghton Mifflin, 1962.

Goldhamer, Herbert, and A. Marshall, *Psychosis and Civilization.* Glencoe Ill.: The Free Press, 1953.

Hollingshead, A. B., and R. Redlich, *Social Class and Mental Illness.* New York: Wiley, 1958.

Longmore, Laura. *The Dispossessed: A Study of the Sex Life of Bantu Women in Urban Areas in and around Johannesburg.* London: Jonathan Cape, 1959.

Plant, J., *Personality and the Cultural Pattern.* New York: Commonwealth Fund, 1939.

Redfield, Robert, *Human Nature and the Study of Society.* Vol. 1, *The Papers of Robert Redfield.* Chicago: University of Chicago Press, 1962.

Rose, Arnold (ed.), *Mental Health and Mental Disorder.* Sections 2 and 3. New York: W. W. Norton and Co., 1955.

Rotondo, H., "Psychological and Mental Health Problems of Urbanization based on Case Studies in Peru," in P. Hauser (ed.). *Urbanization in Latin America.* Unesco Technology and Society series, 1961.

Sainsbury, Peter, *Suicide in London.* New York: Basic Books, 1955.

Simmel, Georg, "The Metropolis and Mental Life," in *The Sociology of Georg Simmel,* translated, edited, and with an introduction by Kurt Wolff. Glencoe, Ill.: The Free Press, 1950.

Srole, Leo, *et al.*, *Mental Health in the Metropolis: The Midtown Manhattan Study.* New York: McGraw Hill, 1962.

Swedner, Harald, *Ecological Differentiation of Habits and Attitudes.* Lund, Sweden: C. W. K. Gleerup, 1960.

Whyte, William H., *The Organization Man.* Garden City, N.Y.: Doubleday Anchor Books, 1957.

Wirth, Louis, *Community Life and Social Policy.* Chicago: University of Chicago Press, 1956.

Articles

Angell, R., "Moral Integration and Interpersonal Integration in American Cities," *American Sociological Review,* 14 (April, 1949), 245–51.

Beers, Howard, "Rural-Urban Differences: Some Evidence from Public Opinion Polls," *Rural Sociology,* 18 (March, 1953), 1–11.

Clinard, M., "Cross-Cultural Replication of the Relation of Urbanism to Criminal Behavior," *American Sociological Review,* 25 (April, 1960), 253–57.

Haller, A. O., and Carole Wolff, "Personality Orientation of Farm, Village, and Urban Boys," *Rural Sociology,* 27 (September, 1962), 275–93.

Killian, Lewis, and C. Grigg, "Urbanism, Race, and Anomia," *American Journal of Sociology,* LXVII (May, 1962), 661–65.

Reiss, Albert, "Rural-Urban and Status Differences in Interpersonal Contact," *American Journal of Sociology,* LXV (September, 1959), 162–95.

Wood, Arthur L., "Murder, Suicide, and Economic Crime in Ceylon," *American Sociological Review,* 26 (October, 1961), 744–53.

Adjustments of
Migrants to Cities

TWENTY

Historically, all cities have depended for their development on migrants from other types of communities, for, as noted in Chapter 1, cities are a relatively recent innovation. As cities grew they continued to "import" population, although urban communities also grow by natural increase, that is, the excess of urban births over urban deaths. The large-scale movement of people into urban areas has been accelerated in modern times as a result of complex social and economic forces, not only in the industrialized nations, but in nonindustrial countries as well.

The pouring of population into urban areas provides us with an opportunity for a unique insight into the nature of urban life. Some of the migrants are moving from one city to another, but most are moving from rural areas, and sometimes from peasant and even tribal settings, into cities. The impact of cities should be greatest on migrants, especially on those coming from nonurban areas. Study of urbanward migrants should, therefore, help us to understand the effects of the city. What changes does the city bring about in the ways of living and points of view of people? Does the city contribute to social and personal disorganization?

This chapter will examine the adjustment patterns of migrants to cities. Two kinds of migrants will be discussed—those moving across national boundaries (immigrants), and those moving from one community to another within the same country (internal migrants or in-migrants).

Migration represents a transition. On the whole, the difficulties of transition and adjustment are greater when the communities are very different. The greatest contrasts are found in the underdeveloped areas of the world, and the greatest problems of adjustment for migrants occur there, as peasants and tribesmen from traditional cultures and subsistence economies migrate to twentieth-century metropolitan capitals.

Problems arise mainly when migrants have to become accustomed to a new way of living. Since most migrants have come from nonurban communities, the problems of adjustment have been many and acute. It is important to note, however, that these problems are not an inherent part of city life. Once the migrants, or their children, have adjusted to city life the problems recede; and the city often ultimately brings a more satisfying way of life, physically and socially, than was available in the community of origin. For this reason, it is appropriate to call the effects of the city on migrants reorganizing rather than disorganizing. This should not blind us to the fact that the problems of migrants in cities are real, costly in human and material terms, and not easily solved.

The first major topic to be discussed will be the adjustment of immigrants and internal migrants to cities in the United States. Second, race as a factor in the adjustive process of migrants to American cities will be examined. Third, the special factors affecting the adjustment of migrants to cities in the underdeveloped regions of the world will be analyzed. Fourth, the selective factors in migration will be described.

IMMIGRANTS AND IN-MIGRANTS IN UNITED STATES CITIES

IMMIGRANTS AND THE PROBLEMS OF TRANSITION

Immigration has been such an important factor in providing labor and skill for the development of the United States that this country has been called "a nation of immigrants." Thus, the United States is an excellent testing-ground for study of the adjustment both of immigrants and internal migrants.

Immigrants' problems of adjustment have been most difficult for those who came from the impoverished villages of Europe. These people had to overcome not only the obstacles of language and custom, but had to acquire urban work skills as well. With such deficiencies, they were compelled to enter the urban labor force at the bottom level—usually as unskilled laborers—with low wages and poor housing as their lot. Often, too, they faced religious or ethnic discrimination, as, for example, did the Irish Catholic immigrants to Boston in the nineteenth century.[1]

Problems of acculturation, as well as physical problems of sanitation, health, housing, and education, were great. Many social services geared to helping immigrants came into existence at the end of the nineteenth and the beginning of the twentieth century when the greatest numbers came to the United States—almost nine million in the decade 1901–10.

[1] See Oscar Handlin, *Boston's Immigrants* (1959).

Settlement houses, such as Hull House in Chicago and the Henry Street settlement in New York City, were established in the slum neighborhoods where many immigrants lived. The settlement houses included a resident staff which conducted recreational programs as well as classes in English, citizenship, cooking, and other subjects. In another way, the "ward-heeler" politician, of the kind thinly fictionalized in Edwin O'Connor's *The Last Hurrah,* also provided services to bridge the gap between the immigrants and the larger American society. The "muckrakers" also flourished in this period and drew attention to urban problems, many of them relating to the immigrants. Jacob Riis' *How the Other Half Lives* exposed city slums, and Upton Sinclair's *The Jungle* described the working conditions of the meat-packing industry.

It was not so much the fact of immigration itself which created problems for the immigrants, as it was the vast social contrast between life in a small peasant village and in the industrial cities of the United States. This point is supported by a recent survey of mental health in one area of New York City. Mental health ratings for two kinds of immigrants living in the area were compared. Those who had come from European farms, villages, or small urban places and occupied a low socioeconomic status in Europe had poorer mental health than those who came from large or medium-sized European cities and had a higher socioeconomic position. The age distributions of the two groups were equalized. Table 26 shows

TABLE 26

Percentage Distribution of Mental Health Classification, by Types of European Immigrants, Standardized by Age

	Rural, Low Socioeconomic Status	Urban, Higher Socioeconomic Status
Well	10.2	17.9
Mild Symptom Formation	30.8	40.5
Moderate Symptom Formation	24.7	23.1
Impaired	34.3	18.5

SOURCE: Leo Srole, *et al., Mental Health in the Metropolis: The Midtown Manhattan Study* (1962), I, 262. Copyright 1962, McGraw-Hill Book Company, Blakiston Division. Used by permission.

that many more of the urban, higher status immigrants were classified as "well" or having only "mild symptoms," and many fewer were classified as emotionally "impaired," as compared with immigrants from rural, low status backgrounds.[2] Thus, slightly more than a third (34.3 per cent) of

[2] See Chapter 19, pp. 455–56, for a description of the ratings and other aspects of the study.

the rural, low status immigrants from Europe were classified as "impaired," that is, having many emotional handicaps in carrying out everyday activities, while less than a fifth (18.5 per cent) of the immigrants from urban, higher status European backgrounds were so classified. The transition to American cities was apparently less stressful psychologically for those who already had experience with living in cities and who had the necessary educational and occupational skills. Heavy burdens of adjustment fall on those immigrants without such experience or skills—and the vast majority of United States immigrants were in this category.[3]

THE SECOND GENERATION

Some authorities have contended that the burden of adjustment falls more heavily on the "second generation"—the native-born sons and daughters of foreign-born immigrants. The argument holds that the immigrants themselves are protected from the worst effects of disorganization by having grown up in a traditional culture whose values still guide their behavior as adults, even though they have moved to another community setting. Their children, however, are said to be caught between the conflicting demands of their parents' standards and those of American society transmitted to them by education and the mass media. Herberg argues, for example, that the second generation tends to reject religious participation because the religious customs which the parents attempt to pass on are often labeled as "inferior" or "odd" by American society.[4] Others have noted that culture conflict may lead to high crime rates in the second generation, because the conflict of values may result in no binding set of norms.[5] It has been established that delinquency rates are highest in the low-rent areas of the city where immigrants first settle, the rates remaining high no matter what particular immigrant group lives there.[6]

The validity of the second generation hypothesis has not been established. Research has only partially supported the contention that the second generation has low religious participation.[7] Many of the first generation, but particularly the second generation, advance socially and economically and move from the slum neighborhoods of first settlement, thereby also removing themselves from the delinquent patterns of such

[3] These adjustments are vividly described by the letters of the immigrants themselves in the classic study of W. I. Thomas and F. Znaniecki, *The Polish Peasant in Europe and America* (1918–20).

[4] Will Herberg, *Protestant–Catholic–Jew* (1955).

[5] An excellent summary of the argument, pro and con, is presented in J. T. Sellin, *Culture Conflict and Crime* (1938).

[6] Clifford Shaw, *Delinquency Areas* (1929).

[7] Bernard Lazerwitz, "The 'Three-Generation' Hypothesis: An Investigation of Findings by Herberg and Lenski," paper read at American Sociological Association meetings, Washington, D. C., August, 1962.

neighborhoods. Conflicts in values and standards may also express themselves psychologically among the second generation. But comparisons of
the mental health of the first and second generations show that the second
generation has better mental health than the parental generation.[8]

THE DECLINE OF IMMIGRATION

The last two or three decades have witnessed great changes in the
ethnic composition of the population, both urban and rural. Gates which
had been entered by millions of immigrants were all but closed in the
1920's, to be opened only slightly in the 1950's. The result was a steady
decline in the proportion of foreign-born persons from about one-seventh
of the population in 1910 to about one in twenty persons in 1960.

As Table 27 indicates, the foreign-born represent a much larger pro-

TABLE 27

**Percentage Distribution of U.S. Population by Race and Nativity,
for Urban and Rural Residents, 1950 and 1960**

	Urban		Rural	
	1950	1960	1950	1960
Native-born white	81.1	81.7	85.8	87.4
Foreign-born white	8.8	6.5	3.1	2.2
Negro	9.7	11.0	10.4	9.4
Other nonwhite	.3	.8	.7	1.1

SOURCE: Computed from *Statistical Abstract of the United States, 1962*, p. 29.

portion of America's city people than of her rural folk. True, there are
many ethnic pockets in rural areas, but with the exception of certain sections such as parts of Minnesota and Wisconsin, the rural ethnics represent a very small minority. In both urban and rural areas the proportions
of foreign-born are declining and will probably continue to decrease. The
simple fact is that foreign-born persons who die are not replaced by other
foreigners.

The immigrants' place in the social and economic life of United States
cities is being taken by migrants from rural areas within the United
States. Many of these in-migrants are nonwhite. The proportion of the
United States urban population which is Negro has increased steadily
over the years. As shown in the table above, Negroes made up 9.7 per cent
of the United States city population in 1950 and 11.0 per cent in 1960. It

[8] Leo Srole, *et al.*, *Mental Health in the Metropolis: The Midtown Manhattan
Study* (1962), I, 253–65.

is also most significant to note that by 1960 Negroes made up a larger percentage of the urban than of the rural population, in contrast to 1950 and previous census years.

Negroes, Puerto Ricans, Mexican-Americans (Americans of Mexican ancestry), and white southern "hillbillies" are the major rural groups migrating to American cities. Which particular group of migrants is most prevalent in a given city depends upon geographical accessibility. Thus, the Mexican Americans are moving most rapidly to the cities of Texas and the Southwest; the southern "hillbillies" are migrating to the industrial centers of Ohio, Indiana, Michigan, Missouri, and Illinois; the Negroes are generally moving North and West from the southern States; and the Puerto Ricans, whose migration is mainly by air, are settling most heavily in the large cities of the Northeast.

PROBLEMS OF LOW STATUS MIGRANTS FROM RURAL AREAS

These four groups migrating from rural areas within the United States to cities—Negroes, white southerners, Puerto Ricans, and Mexican-Americans—differ from the immigrants in that they are American citizens and, except for some Puerto Ricans and Mexican-Americans, English is their native language. But, like the bulk of our earlier immigrants, they must make the transition from the comparative simplicity of rural life to the complexities of the urban world. The in-migrants have taken over the unskilled, low-paying, low status jobs vacated by the immigrants who are declining in numbers and also ascending the socioeconomic ladder. The International Ladies Garment Workers Union, whose members formerly tended to be East European and Italian immigrants, is now made up increasingly of Negroes and Puerto Ricans. The in-migrants have also "inherited" the diseases associated with poor living conditions. In San Antonio, Texas, for example, the tuberculosis rate per 100,000 population in 1948–50 was 37 for Anglo-Americans, 70 for Negroes, and 125 for Mexican-Americans.[9] The discriminatory treatment and connotations of social inferiority formerly meted out to immigrant groups are now directed at the in-migrants. "No Irish Need Apply" has long since vanished from housing and job advertisements, but many restaurants in the Southwest refuse to serve "greasers" (Mexican-Americans), no matter how well-dressed; and much hostility has been voiced in New York City against the supposed increase in crime, welfare payments, and housing deterioration due to the Puerto Ricans.[10]

The in-migrants from rural areas now occupy the social and economic position in our cities that the immigrants occupied in a previous generation—and they suffer, as did the bulk of the immigrants, from the

[9] Clarence Senior, *Strangers—Then Neighbors* (1961), p. 18.
[10] *Ibid.*, pp. 17, 20–32.

dual burdens of poverty and urban inexperience. This is well-illustrated by comparing the rural in-migrants with other in-migrants. A study of migrants to Chicago reported that only those from rural-farm areas, especially the South, showed the low occupational status, high unemployment rate, and low educational status of "problem" migrants.[11] In contrast, migrants from rural nonfarm areas, and those migrating from another city to Chicago, had equal or higher socioeconomic status than the resident Chicago population.

Data from New York City also suggest that migrants with higher status and urban experience have few adjustment problems in cities.[12] The mental health ratings of those migrants of middle and upper class background who had moved to New York City from other urban places were, in fact, superior to those of similar status who had lived in New York City all their lives. The researchers suggested that the in-migrants might not be representative of the population of similar social status in their hometowns, but were perhaps the better adjusted and more able portion, who were attracted by the more abundant opportunities in New York City. The fact remains that these in-migrants, who were accustomed to living in cities and had easily marketable skills, had few problems in the city, at least as reflected in their mental health.

THE "HILLBILLIES"

The so-called "hillbillies" are a good case study of the inappropriate attitudes, values, and habits which lower class rural groups bring to the urban environment. They are Protestant, native white descendants of early Americans, of Anglo-Saxon stock from the Southern Appalachian and Ozark regions. Chicago's hillbilly population has been described as follows.

Settling in deteriorating neighborhoods where they can stick with their own kind, they live as much as they can the way they lived back home. Often removing window screens, they sit half-dressed where it is cooler, and dispose of garbage the quickest way. Their own dress is casual and their children's worse. Their housekeeping is easy to the point of disorder, and they congregate on front porches for the sort of motionless relaxation that infuriates bustling city people.

Their children play freely anywhere, without supervision. Fences and hedges break down; lawns go back to dirt. On the crowded city streets, children are unsafe, and their parents seem oblivious. Even more, when it comes to sex training, their habits—with respect to such matters as incest and statutory rape —are clearly at variance with urban legal requirements, and parents fail to appreciate the interest authorities take in their sex life.[13]

[11] Ronald Freedman, *Recent Migration to Chicago* (1950), p. 30ff.
[12] Srole, *op. cit.*, pp. 266–68.
[13] Albert N. Votaw, "The Hillbillies Invade Chicago," *Harper's Magazine* (February, 1958), p. 65. Reprinted by permission.

A study of the hillbillies as workers in a factory near Chicago showed their background had not prepared them for the highly formal, circumscribed behavior required by the extensive division of labor of industrial society.[14] The specialized jobs must be coordinated; hence the behavior of each worker must be dependable and predictable. The hillbillies, used to individual work on farms or in hunting and fishing, carried over into the factory the habit of working at their own pace and, as a consequence, disrupted productivity. Even such a minor item as punching a time card was novel to the hillbillies.

The industrial work adjustment of southern whites, as with other migrants from rural areas, is complicated by the fact that many are "sojourners"; that is, they are not yet fully committed to the city in terms of allegiance or financial dependence. Often having family farms and rural kin to depend on, the hillbillies frequently quit their jobs or take long weekends to go "home" for family occasions, because urban jobs or life are not to their liking. Some even limit their city "sojourn" to the winter when chores on their farms are less demanding. While in the city the migrants, many of whom are young adults, are freed from the traditional moral codes; sexual transgressions and general demoralization are a typical result.

Because absenteeism and unreliability lead to low seniority and little advancement, the hillbilly worker may develop no "stake" in his industrial job. This is also reflected in his lack of interest in unions or social security; thus he develops few ties or common interests with fellow-workers apart from those of his own background. In sum, his lack of ties to urban occupations is likely to make the hillbilly marginal from the point of view of his employer and fellow-workers.

Evidence suggests that the hillbillies' lack of integration into the urban world of work may be temporary. As they become convinced that industrialism offers a better living than their traditional productive system, they will be willing to put more into it—to seek approval from their supervisors and to make common cause with coworkers of other backgrounds. Paradoxically, the hillbillies attain a new identity of their own when they become aware that others regard them as one group. This new identity forms the basis for incipient voluntary associations and organizations for mutual aid. Another important consideration is that with further urban commitment whole families characteristically settle in the city, thus providing psychological support and motivation for the individual while also strengthening social control. The whole process of gradual restructuring of hillbilly attitudes and values which is suggested here echoes the re-organization which earlier immigrants experienced in the urban setting.

As with the immigrants, the transition is a painful one, and, as noted earlier, often appears to be *dis*organization rather than the *re*-organization it actually may be. The relatively small numbers of hillbillies in such

[14] This description is based on James S. Slotkin, *From Field to Factory* (1960).

cities as Chicago and Cincinnati are creating noticeable problems in education, housing, and welfare services.

The problems of the hillbillies are the more distinctive because this group has no "strikes" against it in terms of race, religion, or national origin. They are, in fact, the descendants of the early Americans so often pointed to with admiration. Their difficulties in adjusting to city life demonstrate the importance of low socioeconomic position and nonurban background as deterrents to satisfactory adjustment. It may be stated as a general principle that in-migrants with these background characteristics will have similar difficulties, despite the cultural setting. Thus, residents of Helsinki (Finland) who had been born in rural areas with no industry and had migrated to the capital less than two years before a study was conducted showed more signs of maladjustment and neuroticism on personality tests than either the native-born inhabitants of Helsinki or the stationary rural population.[15] In Poland, "sojourners" from peasant areas who worked temporarily in Warsaw showed slackening social control and poor work morale.[16]

INTERNAL MIGRATION AND PROBLEMS OF RACE AND ETHNICITY

The adjustment of many migrants to American cities is complicated by factors of color and race, problems which the European immigrants did not face. The question has been raised whether the visibility of color and the depth of racial prejudice will prevent these migrant groups from assimilating into the larger American society and moving up the socioeconomic ladder as the immigrant groups have done. Since each of the migrant groups from rural areas, except for the hillbillies, has a nonwhite component, this is an important question to answer.[17]

THE MEXICAN-AMERICANS

Although discrimination against Mexican-Americans is not embodied in state laws, as is discrimination against Negroes in the southern states, nevertheless, it is generally practiced and deeply entrenched. The situation was not widely recognized until the period following World War II, when a number of studies appeared.[18] These studies brought to light cases

[15] Kai Von Fieandt, "Psychological Effects of Urban and Rural Domiciles," *Acta Psychologica*, 14 (1958), 81–91.

[16] As abstracted in *Sociological Abstracts*, 7 (April, 1959), p. 107, from Stefan Nowakowski, "Hotel Robothiczy Na Tle Procesow Urbanizacji i Industrializacji," *Prezeglad Socjolognicny*, 12 (1958), 32–69.

[17] In recent United States censuses, Mexican-Americans have been classified as white; the Puerto Rican group is divided into white and nonwhite categories.

[18] This point is made and the studies cited in Charles C. Cumberland, "The United States-Mexican Border: A Selected Guide to the Literature of the Region," *Rural Sociology*, 25 (June, 1960), supplement, p. 71ff.

of lower wages for Mexican-Americans performing the same jobs as "Anglos," segregated schools, and, as the material result of discrimination, a much lower level of health, housing, and standard of living. Hostility and feelings of great social distance between the Anglos and the Mexican-Americans were found in measures of ethnic prejudice. It is revealing that a historical study of the Mexican-Americans in New Mexico concluded that they had achieved accommodation to the Anglo-Americans through separatism.[19]

THE PUERTO RICANS

The Puerto Ricans migrating to cities of the continental United States face racial discrimination as a new problem. In Puerto Rico, being of nonwhite race places only a minor handicap on the individual in competing for housing, jobs, education, and status. Census figures show that the migration from Puerto Rico is selective—a smaller percentage of nonwhite Puerto Ricans migrate to the continental United States than would be expected in terms of their proportion in the Puerto Rican population. The reverse migration is also selective—a larger percentage of the nonwhites return to Puerto Rico after spending some time in the continental United States.[20] The selectivity is in itself revealing of the pattern of discrimination.

The dilemma of race is compounded for the Puerto Ricans because the group includes both whites and nonwhites. In the 1960 census, about 10 per cent of the persons of Puerto Rican birth living in the continental United States were classified as nonwhite. Identification with the Puerto Rican group has been strengthened for those who are nonwhite and weakened for those who are white.[21] The nonwhite Puerto Rican found he could only avoid being stigmatized as a Negro by emphasizing his Spanish-speaking background, while the white Puerto Rican, especially in the second generation, found that by loosening his ethnic ties he could move into the general population.

The effect of race on the future adjustment of Puerto Ricans in the continental United States is unclear, but two alternative directions have been suggested.[22] If color consciousness in American society becomes more pronounced, then the Puerto Ricans may divide into three groups: recent arrivals, both white and nonwhite, will maintain Puerto Rican identity; among the Puerto Ricans settled for a longer period, and especially among the second and third generations, those of colored ancestry are likely to merge with the more numerous American Negro population while those of white ancestry are likely to become identified with the white Amer-

[19] Carolyn Zeleny, "Relations between the Spanish-Americans and Anglo-Americans in New Mexico: A Study of Conflict and Accommodation in a Dual-Ethnic Situation," Ph.D. dissertation, Yale University, 1944; cited in Cumberland, *op. cit.*, p. 76.

[20] Senior, *op. cit.*, p. 28.

[21] Oscar Handlin, *The Newcomers* (1959), p. 59.   [22] *Ibid.*, pp. 59–60.

icans. On the other hand, if the importance of color in American society declines, then all those of Puerto Rican ancestry, white and colored, are more likely to maintain their Puerto Rican identity.

NEGROES IN UNITED STATES CITIES

The integration of Negroes into United States cities is part of many major social problems. Not only are Negroes by far the most numerous of the nonwhite rural groups entering the cities, but their status is more dependent on what happens in the larger American society.

Except for the Negro, all of the immigrant and migrant groups have had a proud ethnic identity apart from their American identity, which filled the double function of sustaining them in the early period of discrimination and prejudice in the United States and in later marking them as a respectable American subgroup. None of this was possible for the American Negroes, since slavery abruptly cut them off from their African traditions. Their only meaningful identity was as Americans, but the position given them was so low as to constitute almost a nonidentity. The high rates of crime, delinquency, illegitimacy and other indexes of social disorganization among American Negro migrants in cities are a product of the marginal participation they have been allowed in American society. An example is the unstable Negro family life resulting from the inability of many Negro men to get steady, adequately paid employment. Thus, the family comes to depend on the women's earnings with unfortunate effects on children's supervision and on the marital relationship.

Residential and Educational Segregation.   There are several aspects of American cities which have changed since the time of heavy immigration from abroad, and these changes are important in evaluating the present and future adjustment of Negroes and other nonwhites. The most important change is that many of our cities are now metropolises,[23] and as such are larger and cover more territory than cities because they depend on fast automobile, bus, and truck transportation rather than on trolley, train, or subway. As metropolitan areas have grown there has been a pronounced tendency for the groups that are better established socioeconomically, especially those with children, to move to the more spacious, newer one-family homes on the outer sections of the metropolis. Low status migrants from rural areas, especially nonwhites, have settled in the deteriorating low-rent areas of the central core of the metropolis, with the result that residential segregation by race has been increased.[24]

Racial segregation in housing has profound consequences in many

[23] See Chapters 3, 4, 9, and 10 for a fuller description of metropolitan development.
[24] See Chapter 7, pp. 127–31, and Chapter 8, p. 164ff., for description of changes in racial segregation in American cities.

aspects of life, one of the most crucial of which is education. James B. Conant's study of the American high school includes a report on the educational facilities and problems of the large metropolitan areas, especially New York, Philadelphia, Detroit, Chicago, and St. Louis.[25] He contrasts the generally inferior central city schools with the general excellence of those in the suburban areas of the metropolis. Conant warns that the accumulation in our central cities of large numbers of young people, many of them Negro, who have little prospect of further education and few employment opportunities, is "social dynamite."[26]

Effects of the Metropolitan Economy and Government. Metropolitan development has brought changes not only in residential, and related educational, segregation, but also is based on a different economic system than previous urbanization was. The occupational structure of the metropolis is not advantageous to the new city residents from rural areas. Previous urban development, especially in the period of heavy immigration, had expanding opportunities for blue collar workers. The immigrants came at a time when the need for factory hands was at its peak. Now, technological advances, especially automation, have decreased the need for unskilled workers in cities. The poorly educated, unskilled migrant, whether white or nonwhite, thus finds he enters a metropolitan job market with shrinking requirements for untrained muscle power. He also finds there are increased hazards in self-employment of the neighborhood store type.

The metropolis the migrant enters differs also from the city entered by the immigrant in that government plays an increased role in its operation. Government has expanded various social welfare functions, such as unemployment insurance, social security, aid to dependent children, and subsidized low-cost housing; it has also moved strongly into economic regulation by enacting minimum wage laws, rent controls, and income taxes. Government has also become big business in the sense that it hires tens of thousands of employees, purchases tremendous quantities of goods and services, and places numerous contracts. The effect has been to make the new migrant groups more dependent on government for help in the climb up the socioeconomic ladder than the earlier immigrants had been.[27]

Negro and Puerto Rican in-migrants have not developed their own numerous philanthropic institutions—orphanages, homes for the aged, hospitals—which enabled the immigrants to find strong support within their own group. The future of migrants, especially nonwhite migrants, rests on effective public policy in a way that was not true for the immigrant groups. Governmental action against school segregation laws and bans on discrimination in housing and employment are important examples. It is significant that many of the gains of urban Negroes in

---

[25] James B. Conant, *Slums and Suburbs: A Commentary on Schools in Metropolitan Areas* (1961).

[26] *Ibid.*, p. 2. [27] Handlin, *The Newcomers, op. cit.*, pp. 104ff., 119.

white collar and professional employment have been under civil service or in public schools, colleges, and other institutions.

A final metropolitan change affects Negroes—the growth of their political power. This change stems largely from the concentration of Negroes in the metropolitan areas of the North and West where they are able to exercise their franchise. The seeking of political office and use of the ballot were an important method by which the immigrants secured their rights, and doubtless Negroes will also use the vote to good purpose. One authority notes, however, that some problems in Negro-white relations may ensue if continuing metropolitan residential segregation results in the domination of city legislatures by Negroes.[28]

Summary. Our discussion of race as a factor affecting nonwhite migrants' adjustments to cities may be summarized as follows:

1. Race is not the only factor affecting the adjustment of nonwhite migrants. The vast majority also have problems associated with low status and rural background. Race is an added handicap to the nonwhite groups in finding suitable urban housing and employment, but it is not their only handicap. Therefore, to some extent the adjustment problems of nonwhite migrants can be explained by the same processes as those which affected the adjustment of low status immigrants from rural areas.

2. Racial and color prejudice affect the integration of nonwhite groups into the city because they increase the reluctance of the dominant groups to accept these newcomers. There was prejudice against the immigrant groups, too, but it was much weaker, as shown by the fact that the immigrant groups were usually integrated into American society within three generations. Furthermore, color is highly visible as a mark of group identity, as the dilemma of identification for the nonwhite Puerto Rican illustrates. Also, the past effects of the color barrier have produced wide differences between white and nonwhite Americans, especially in the severe social deprivation and marginality among Negroes.

3. The communities to which the nonwhite migrants come are not the same as those to which the immigrants came. The new communities are metropolitan, which fact has important consequences for residential segregation, and for opportunities in education and employment. These aspects of metropolitan development do not appear to favor easy adjustment for nonwhite newcomers. However, the increased political leverage of Negroes in metropolitan areas may be an important compensation. The increased role of government in providing services of various kinds to low income groups also has important benefits for nonwhite migrants, as does direct government action against discrimination.

INTERNAL MIGRATION IN THE UNDERDEVELOPED REGIONS

Internal migration from rural areas is a major source of urban growth in other parts of the world, as well as in the United States. For migrants

[28] Morton Grodzins, "Metropolitan Segregation," *Scientific American*, 197 (July, 1957); cf. Grodzins, *The Metropolitan Area as a Racial Problem* (1958), pp. 13–15.

in the "underdeveloped" regions—Latin America, Africa, and Asia—the transition to an urban world is far more difficult, and the resulting problems much greater, than for internal migrants in the United States.

The differences center around the fact that in the underdeveloped countries the migrants to the city often become marginal urbanites in both a physical and a social sense. That they are *in* the city but not *of* the city is evident in the following ways. (1) Urban growth often stems from problems in rural areas rather than from opportunities in the cities. (2) The magnitude of urban growth has reached "flood" proportions, presenting almost unmanageable physical problems. (3) The dual physical structure of the cities—a small modern core ringed by shantytowns—mirrors the cultural clash between the wealthy westernized elite and the traditional ways and subsistence economy of peasants or tribesmen. (4) The ultimate social effects of migration to cities in the underdeveloped regions are not yet clear, although it seems safe to predict that the effects will not parallel those in the Western industrial nations. There is much disorganization, social and personal, but there are signs of readjustment in the development of stable "urban villages," in the continued vitality of family and kin relationships, and in the expansion of voluntary formal organizations.

FACTORS "PUSHING" MIGRANTS TO CITIES

The major forces behind cityward migration in the underdeveloped areas of the world lie in pressures in the rural areas which "push" a large part of the rural population to cities. Unable to earn a livelihood on the farms and in the villages, the migrants are not so much attracted by urban opportunity as they are expelled by rural poverty and insecurity that have resulted from overpopulation, fragmentation of land holdings into exceedingly small units, inefficient land use, and political realignments. The motive for such movement is in contrast to the history of cities in the industrialized parts of the world where migrants are drawn to cities by the "pull" of an expanding commercial and manufacturing economy.

Many underdeveloped nations are characterized by "overurbanization" —that is, there are more people living in cities than is justified by the productive capacity of the economy. The result is that in-migrants "pile up" without being immediately absorbed into the economy, accounting for the large numbers of unemployed. For example, in 1957 the per capita production of goods and services in Latin America was valued at $290, in contrast to $2,500 in the United States. Yet many countries of Latin America are highly urbanized.[29]

The rate of population growth is generally high throughout the world

[29] See Chapters 2 and 4 for comparative data on urbanization in the United States and other parts of the world.

Living conditions of migrants to cities. The flood of urban migration has severely strained urban facilities. This refugee family in Hong Kong eats, sleeps, and lives on the sidewalk. The father, a tailor, works here and also sells shoes here, some of which are visible in the case. (Courtesy American Friends Service Committee.)

—higher than it has ever been in the history of mankind—and it is highest of all in the underdeveloped areas. In almost all countries of Asia, Africa, and Latin America, population is growing at rates that will double the population in 35 years; in many the population will double in 25 years or less. In contrast, the growth rate of the United States population is such as to double the population in about 50 years, and most European populations are growing at considerably slower rates.[30]

Population expansion, coupled with the various land problems—shortage of agricultural land, wasteful methods of cultivation and feudal systems of land tenure—compel flight to the city. Rapidly growing populations cannot be supported in the rural areas of the underdeveloped nations because nonmechanized systems of agriculture have a limited carrying power. Lack of crop rotation and fertilizers, fragmentation of land into tiny holdings, and soil erosion are some aspects of nonscientific farming that plague these parts of the world. The lack of cultivable land for agri-

[30] Philip Hauser, "Demographic Dimensions of World Politics," *Science*, 131 (June 3, 1960).

View of a *favela*, or shantytown, in Rio de Janeiro. These squalid slums house at least a fifth of Rio's population, many of them migrants. Similar communities in Chile are called *callampas;* in Peru, *barriados;* in Venezuela, *ranchos.* (Courtesy Nancy Palmer Photo Agency [photograph by Nancy Flowers].)

cultural expansion is often an additional complication, as in India and other parts of Asia where rural densities are already very high.

Surveys of migrants to cities document the importance of economic "push." A study of a district in Tokyo found that younger sons were proportionately more numerous among the migrants. Younger sons made up 45 per cent of the men who were born in Tokyo or Yokohama, but 72 per cent of those who were not native residents of the city.[31] Younger sons migrate to the city because Japanese farms are usually only large enough for one heir to subsist on. A survey of 3,282 recent migrants to Lucknow, India, classified twice as many peasant migrants as having been "pushed" to the city by such factors as unemployment or insufficient land to cultivate, as had been "pulled" to the city by such reasons as prospects of better employment.[32] Similarly, in Peru, where peasants practice an ancient system of agriculture that ruins the soil, a survey of 17,000 heads of families now living in Lima but born in the provinces found that 61 per cent gave pressing economic reasons as the cause of their move to the city.[33]

Some migrants to the city are "pushed" by political events. About 5 per cent of the migrants in the Lucknow survey had come because of the partition of India and Pakistan in 1947. More recently, Tibetan refugees have fled to India. The creation of new national states and revolutionary uprisings have produced similar dislocations in Africa, Latin America, and the Far East. A little known group are the 12,500 Ambonese, former native residents of the Indonesian archipelago, who moved to the Netherlands in 1951 after Indonesia became a sovereign state. In supporting the Dutch against the Indonesian army they had put their money on the wrong horse, so to speak, and were under considerable pressure to move. Adjustment to a highly urbanized society was not easy for them.[34]

It must not be assumed that the city in underdeveloped areas has no "pulling" power in attracting rural migrants. It has. The point is that the "pull" is not usually economic opportunity. A small but significant minority come to cities for secondary or higher education or for technical training—6 per cent in the Lucknow survey and 9 per cent in the Lima survey. For most migrants, however, the "pull" of the city lies in the "bright lights." Knowledge of urban consumer goods and of urban diversity and excitement have penetrated even the most remote places by means of former migrants returning to visit and through the movies and radio. A random sample in five rural Egyptian villages disclosed that 50 per cent of the population listened to the radio.[35] Frustration and dissatisfaction

[31] R. P. Dore, *City Life in Japan* (1958), p. 123.

[32] R. Mukerjee and B. Singh, *Social Profiles of a Metropolis* (1961), p. 67.

[33] Jose Matos Mar, "The 'Barriadas' of Lima: An Example of Integration into Urban Life," in Philip Hauser, (ed.), *Urbanization in Latin America*, Unesco Tensions and Technology Series, No. 8 (1961), pp. 182–83.

[34] Tamme Wittermans and Noel P. Gist, "Urbanization and Integration of the Ambonese in the Netherlands," *Sociological Quarterly*, 2 (April, 1961), 119–34.

[35] Morroe Berger, *The Arab World Today* (1962), p. 86.

with rural poverty may be increased by contrast with the image of urban life usually displayed in the mass media.

The urban world has a social "pull," but it is usually an empty one. For the majority of migrants—illiterate or little educated, untrained, and unused to city ways—the move results merely in the transfer of rural problems and poverty to the city.

THE MAGNITUDE OF MIGRATION

The adjustment of the rural migrants in cities in underdeveloped countries is seriously hampered by the rapidity and volume of migration. The flood is continuous; before adequate housing, training, and services for one "wave" of migrants are provided another enters. Since migration is not usually prompted by economic opportunity in the city, it is not expected to slacken in times of economic slump.

In Latin America, seven of the 15 countries for which data are available will double their urban populations in less than 18 years; in Venezuela urban population will double in about 10 years.[36] In Asia and the Far East the scale of migration is not only very large but appears to be increasing since most countries in this region are in the initial stages of urbanization. City growth proceeded about three times as fast in India and the Federation of Malaya in the 1950's as in the 1920's.[37] Africa may have the highest rate of urbanization of all the underdeveloped regions. Estimates are that in the period 1955–61 there were 60 African cities with over 100,000 population.[38] Many of these cities were not even established until the twentieth century. Elisabethville, in the Republic of the Congo, was not founded until 1910, had over 100,000 inhabitants by 1948, and 183,000 in 1959. This growth rate is equalled by other African cities, some of which have quadrupled in population since World War II.[39]

The physical problems resulting from the magnitude of the urbanward migration are enormous. The living conditions of city areas where migrants settle cannot really be compared with the slums of cities in industrialized countries, for the standards are much lower. Houses are often shacks built on land obtained by squatters' rights. Some people have no houses, but make their homes on the sidewalk or rooftops. Water may be provided by a nearby river or by public taps in the streets. Interior electrification is rare, and paved streets and street lighting are usually conspicuous by their absence.

[36] Hauser, *Urbanization in Latin America, op. cit.,* p. 76.

[37] Population Branch of the Bureau of Social Affairs of the United Nations, "Demographic Aspects of Urbanization in the ECAFE Region," in Philip Hauser (ed.), *Urbanization in Asia and the Far East,* Unesco Tensions and Technology Series, No. 7 (1957), p. 106.

[38] United Nations, *Demographic Yearbook* (1960), Table 8.

[39] Kingsley Davis and Hilda H. Golden, "Urbanization and the Development of Pre-industrial Areas," *Economic Development and Industrial Change,* 3 (October, 1954), pp. 20–22; and *Demographic Yearbook* (United Nations, 1960), Table 7.

About one-half of the population of Calcutta, India, lives in *bustees*, that is, slums, and many more live in slums that are not so classified. The incomes of these families are so low that they cannot begin to afford decent housing for themselves. The Calcutta Metropolitan Planning Board estimated in 1963 that a subsidy of at least 70 per cent is necessary for them to have even the minimum of decent housing, a decent house being defined as a structure with a room and a half to be occupied by one family. A house of this type costs roughly 5,000 rupees, about a thousand dollars; but a large proportion of the families earn less than 100 rupees a month.

Most of the 65,000 Xhosa living in East London, a city of 100,000 in the Union of South Africa, have only one toilet per 100 inhabitants.[40] Less than half the 516 subdivisions in the city of Lucknow, India, have latrines.[41] These are not isolated instances.

We noted earlier how the provision of physical and social services for the immigrants and migrants to United States cities strained the resources of these prosperous and well-developed cities. The migrants to cities in the underdeveloped areas come in greater volume to cities much less equipped to handle them. The difficulties are accordingly magnified.

CULTURE CONFLICT IN THE CITY

The rapidly growing cities of the underdeveloped regions are typically characterized by a fundamental cultural conflict occasioned by the contacts, through population movement, between individuals with different social backgrounds. Because most of the cities were established as the administrative or trading outposts of Western colonial empires, a small westernized native elite developed. With the granting of political independence, this westernized group has customarily succeeded to governmental and business control, while the vast majority of native peasants or tribesmen retained many aspects of their religious, family, and economic organization. Therefore, the migrants now coming to the cities in such large numbers bring with them a way of life far removed from the demands of an industrial economy and from the standards of the westernized elite. The contrast is particularly sharp because there is only a small native middle class, its development having been stunted because the full range of urban occupations was not needed under colonialism.

The culture clash is reflected in the physical structure of many cities in the underdeveloped regions. In some cities, though not all, the "core" is in Western style and very modern, many buildings having been constructed fairly recently. Sometimes these businesses and residences are surrounded by a "ring" of transplanted rural villages or "shantytowns."

[40] Philip Mayer, *Townsmen or Tribesmen* (1961), p. 47.
[41] Mukerjee and Singh, *op. cit.*, p. 13.

The dual structure of such cities symbolizes the social, economic and occupational duality of their inhabitants.

The social distance between these groups is incomparably greater than that between urban residents in the United States and the stream of rural migrants to the cities. In the United States, all parts of the popu-

Two sisters in East London, South Africa—a study in contrasts. These sisters, members of the Xhosa tribe, typify the culture contrast within many African tribes. Although the sister at left is a domestic in town and has adopted a European way of life, the other sister follows traditional tribal practices. (Reproduced by permission of the Institute of Social and Economic Research, Rhodes University, from Philip Mayer, *Townsmen or Tribesmen*, Oxford University Press, 1961.)

lation, both rural and urban, are involved in the money economy and the specialized division of labor; thus, the rural migrants to cities move from a less to a more industrialized situation. In the underdeveloped regions, however, they move from a subsistence economy, organized around traditional values, directly to urban centers which must compete with the rest of the world on the basis of efficiency and maximum output.

Culture clashes in the mushrooming cities also occur among the various migrant groups themselves. The peasant typically owes his primary loyalty to his family and village, not to a national, an occupational, or any other nonlocal group. In tribal areas, the tribes constitute the main focus of life organization and loyalty. The provincialism of peasant villages and tribes generate hostility, suspicion, or avoidance when the migratory streams meet in the city. Caste differences and race are also important divisive factors in some cities.

THE SOCIAL EFFECTS OF MIGRATION

What happens to the social organization of migrant groups in the cities of underdeveloped areas? Does it follow the course of disorganization, restructuring, and reorganization that characterized immigrant experience in United States cities? These questions can as yet be only partially answered. However, we would be misguided in assuming that the ultimate effects of urbanization will produce a social organization similar to that of Western societies. It is highly probable that urban-industrial life is compatible with various forms of social organization. Certain economic and occupational changes must take place, but changes in the family, religious, and political systems do not necessarily follow.

The Urban Peasantry. From various urban communities in the underdeveloped areas come reports of the "urban peasantry"—villagers who have transplanted their peasant life to the city with minimum change or dislocation. Studies in Mexico City show that family structure, diet, dress, and religious and other belief systems were the same among those living in the city for 30 years or more as among recent arrivals.[42] This stability is associated with organizing one's life in the city, except for work contacts, around neighborhood units (*colonia*) and within them in still smaller, more cohesive units of dwellings facing on a common courtyard (*vecinidades*). Some cities in Asia and the Far East also show integrated folk cultures maintained by groups of fellow villagers and relatives living in a small section.[43]

Social Problems among Migrants. City life sometimes affects migrants

[42] Oscar Lewis, "The Culture of the *Vecinidad* in Mexico City: Two Case Studies," *Actas del XXXIII Congreso Internacional de Americanistas, San Jose* (July 20–27, 1958), pp. 387–402.

[43] "Summary Report of the General Rapporteur," in Hauser, *Urbanization in Asia and the Far East, op. cit.,* pp. 15–16, 19.

in ways that are not necessarily disorganizing. The position of women often becomes less subservient, partly because of their earning power in the city and partly because of the new role models available in the city.[44] The nuclear family appears to be increasingly prevalent among migrants, although the surprising fact is the general strength of the extended family and kinship ties.

There is, however, abundant evidence of social and personal disorganization among migrants in cities. In all of the underdeveloped regions, cities tend to show high rates of alcoholism, prostitution, immorality, and crime and delinquency. These conditions appear to be associated with the removal from the social control of the village and tribe, with cultural clash and conflicting standards, with the extreme poverty of many migrants, and with cities in which there is a high proportion of single males or other unattached individuals. Temporary migration, in which migrants, usually men, go to cities only seasonally or for several years, also contributes to disorganization among the migrants, and sometimes also in the peasant or tribal areas. This pattern is especially prevalent in the copper, diamond, and gold mining areas of Africa. In the Union of South Africa it has produced severe disorganization among the natives.[45]

The sex ratio in Calcutta, India, is about 60–40, the majority being males. The Calcutta Metropolitan Planning Board estimated in 1963 that some 50 per cent of the households of the city are either single-member or "messing families," the latter referring to groups of males who live together in a household, preserving some semblance of family life, but without females or children.

Personality Disorganization among Migrants. Insofar as data are available, the social disorganization of many migrants is reflected in personal disorganization. A representative sample comparing residents of a rural Peruvian village with those of an urban slum in Lima inhabited by migrants showed that the slum dwellers had more feelings of depression and inadequacy.[46] They also tended to perform less well under stress and to be more distrustful in their personal relationships than the villagers. It is important to note that the villagers, too, had a high degree of anxiety, although not as high as the migrants.

A revision of the Thematic Apperception Test was used to study the personalities of African Bantu men living in Johannesburg.[47] The TAT attempts to examine the deeper levels of personality. There are no comparative data for Africans not living in the city, but the urban group

[44] See, for example, Tanya Baker and Mary Bird, "Urbanisation and the Position of Women," *Sociological Review* (Keele, England), 7 (July, 1959), 99–122.

[45] Vivid portrayals are given in Mayer, *op. cit.*, and in Laura Longmore, *The Dispossessed* (1959).

[46] H. Rotondo, "Psychological and Mental Health Problems of Urbanization Based on Case Studies in Peru," in Hauser, *Urbanization in Latin America, op. cit.*, pp. 249–57.

[47] J. C. De Ridder, *The Personality of the Urban African in South Africa* (1961).

show many personal effects of their deprived racial position and the three-way culture clash of tribal, European, and urban ways. Analysis of the TAT responses indicated that the Africans had strong feelings of anxiety and insecurity. Such feelings are not unrealistic for, in addition to chronic poverty and racial discrimination, the Africans are plagued by gangs of "tsotsi" (detribalized delinquents modeling themselves on American gangsters) who roam the native sections of the city. The desire for money and material security also figures importantly as a personality trait, as does latent aggression. Tribal and Western (European and American) beliefs about family relationship and religion are mingled.

The prevalence of social and personal disorganization prompts the question whether it is likely to be permanent or just a stage on the road to reorganization. As noted earlier, no definite prediction can be made. A hopeful sign, however, is the tendency for some migrants to join voluntary associations in the city. Such organizations appear to be quite prevalent in West Africa, for example.[48]

Voluntary associations facilitate adjustment by providing the feeling of identity and purpose formerly supplied by the village or tribe, and are sometimes of direct economic benefit, as in labor unions. Many voluntary organizations have religious, political, or recreational aims. In joining voluntary associations the migrant is substituting organization on the basis of common interest for the organization on the basis of common locality and kinship which prevail in his village or tribe. Banding together with others of like purpose may enable migrants to transcend the narrow self-interest which their rural background and initial urban experience often foster. Participation in voluntary organizations may reduce culture clash and enable the migrants to take their place in the wider urban world.

EVALUATION OF MIGRANTS' ADJUSTMENTS

The adjustment of in-migrants to cities in underdeveloped areas lends itself to various interpretations. Many persons with rural backgrounds settle in cities and live their lives almost entirely in settlements of their own kind, without ever coming into contact with others of a different cultural background—except in the work or shopping situation. These are villagers within the city, and to a considerable extent they have transferred village culture to the city. For the most part, they don't identify with the city as a community, but only with their own restricted community. There is little or no civic consciousness among them, such as migrant groups experience in Western cities. They continue to be oriented psychologically and culturally toward their home village and their own kinship or tribal

---

[48] Kenneth Little, "The Role of Voluntary Associations in West African Urbanization," *American Anthropologist*, 59 (August, 1957), 579–96.

or caste group, rather than toward the urban community in which they live.

Are these people adjusted well or badly to city life? It depends on the perspective or on the criteria used. In some respects they are like the old-time immigrants in our own society. They certainly are not assimilated or acculturated into city culture, at least not very extensively or intensively. After leaving the work situation they may spend their time, quite satisfactorily, in the warm social climate of their fellow-villagers, who are also city residents. Perhaps the people who have the greatest difficulty in making an adjustment—at least from the point of view of prevailing norms of conduct—are the many detached or unattached men and women who do not reside in these cultural islands in the city.

SELECTIVE FACTORS IN MIGRATION

The heavy migration from rural areas has implications for the rural areas as well as the cities. This is particularly true if, as seems to be the case, the migrants to cities tend to be a superior portion of the rural population. It is not clear whether the selectivity is of those individuals who are innately superior. It is, however, quite clear that migration from rural areas is selective in terms of some degree of social and economic advantage.

We find this continues to be true among the most recent migrant groups. The hillbillies who migrate to cities do not come from the lowest strata of their home communities, as measured by their relative education and degree of skill.[49] Similarly, the West Indians migrating to Great Britain do not represent the "riffraff" of the Caribbean; many are in fact shocked at being considered working class in Great Britain.[50] Myths and rumors often circulate to the effect that migrants are the dregs of rural society, but the reverse is actually the case. Investigation of seven derogatory beliefs about the characteristics of Puerto Ricans in New York City were shown, for example, to have no factual basis.[51]

Little is known about whether migration to cities in the underdeveloped areas of the world is selective. The importance of overpopulation and rural poverty in "pushing" people to cities would suggest that selective factors play little part. Yet some studies in India indicate that the migrants are not the poorest villagers, as measured by financial and social status.[52]

[49] James S. Brown and George Hillery, "The Great Migration: 1940–60," in Thomas Ford (ed.), *The Southern Appalachian Region* (1962).
[50] Ruth Glass, *London's Newcomers* (1960), pp. 23ff., 106ff.
[51] Clarence Senior, *Strangers—and Neighbors* (1952 edition), pp. 15–21.
[52] Noel P. Gist, "Selective Migration in Urban South India," paper presented at World Population Conference, 1954, United Nations Document E/CONF.13/357; E. Eames, "Some Aspects of Urban Migration from a Village in North Central India," *The Eastern Anthropologist*, 8 (September–November, 1954), 13.

Over four decades ago, Ross called attention to "folk depletion" as a result of migrations from rural communities.[53] It was his view that the movement of rural people to cities was draining the countryside of its best brains, leaving, as he put it, "only fished-out ponds populated chiefly by bull-heads and suckers." Although these generalizations were provocative, they were based on subjective impressions rather than scientific analysis of actual migrations. Since that time a number of studies have been made, with various techniques of research employed and certain conflicting conclusions deduced.

Klineberg's Study of Negro Migrations.   The problem as formulated by Klineberg did not involve migrations from country to city, but rather interregional migrations from southern cities to communities in the North. He secured the academic grades of 562 Negro children who had attended the elementary schools of Nashville, Birmingham, and Charleston, and who had later migrated to a different area. When the grades of all the migrant children from the three cities were averaged together, the result was 49.3, about the same as the average (50) for the whole population.[54]

A second phase of the study was designed to ascertain if any changes in intelligence occurred after the migrants had lived in a northern community for varying lengths of time. Accordingly, nine series of intelligence tests were given to Negro children in the Harlem (New York) schools, the tests being so designed as to make possible a comparison between a northern-born control group and southern children who had been in New York City for lengths of time ranging from 1 to 11 years. The results of tests indicated the rise in intelligence was "roughly proportionate to length of residence in the more favorable environment." [55] Klineberg's conclusion was, then, that if northern Negroes rank higher than southern Negroes, the differences are not to be explained in terms of selective migrations but rather in terms of environmental influences. It is his view that the Negro who leaves the South is probably not superior in capacity to those who remain behind.

Klineberg's approach was refined in a Philadelphia study which compared successive IQ tests scores of the same Negro children at varying intervals, after they had migrated to Philadelphia from southern communities; Klineberg had used different groups of Negro migrant children who had lived in New York City for specified lengths of time. The Philadelphia study found that "there is a significant and continuous upward

[53] E. A. Ross, "Folk Depletion as a Cause of Rural Decline," *Publications American Sociological Society,* 11 (1917), 21–30.
[54] Otto Klineberg, *Negro Intelligence and Selective Migrations* (1935). Cf. his "The Intelligence of Migrants," *American Sociological Review,* 3 (April, 1938), 218–24.
[55] Klineberg, *Negro Intelligence and Selective Migrations, op. cit.,* p. 59.

trend in the intelligence test ratings of Southern-born Negro children as their length of residence in Philadelphia increased." [56] This supports Klineberg's findings in New York City.

Kansas and Missouri Studies. A different approach to the problem of intelligence and migration was made by Gist and Clark in a study of the selective character of rural-urban migrations in Kansas.[57] It was the assumption of the investigators that a more "satisfactory control of the cultural factor would be achieved if the traits of the groups to be compared had been measured when both were living in the same rural communities, before migration had occurred." Accordingly, intelligence test scores were secured for 2,544 students who had been enrolled in rural high schools in 1922–23, thirteen years before the study was made. Steps were then taken to ascertain the residential locations of the former students by securing the specific address of each individual in 1935.

Of the total number of individuals for whom data had been secured, approximately two-fifths had moved to cities. The mean I.Q. of the rural group was found to be 95, whereas the mean I.Q. of the group migrating to cities was 98. Although the differences were small, they were nevertheless statistically reliable.

So far as this study is concerned, the evidence seems to point to a selection of intelligence in rural-to-urban migrations. Yet there is no basis for assuming that the urban-bound migrants are genetically superior to those who remain in rural areas. "What the tests apparently measure, however inadequately, is a composite of the social experiences and backgrounds of the individuals, the richness or drabness of their home environments, their intellectual interests, their attitudes and values, the character of their emotional life, their ambitions, energy, and zeal, or lack of these qualities." [58]

Tests of hypotheses related to selective migrations in Missouri were made by Pihlblad and Gregory in 1952.[59] The Ohio Psychological Test given to 3,648 high school students in 1939–40 was used as a basis for determining selectivity in migration during a wartime decade. Most of the students were living on farms or in villages or small towns when the test was taken. Information on their place of residence in 1951–52 was subsequently secured. The investigators found that there was a "consistent tendency for mean test scores to increase with the size of community in which the subjects resided in 1952." Although the females ranked consistently higher than the males on this particular test, the

---

[56] Everett S. Lee, "Negro Intelligence and Selective Migration: A Philadelphia Test of the Klineberg Hypothesis," *American Sociological Review*, 16 (April, 1951), 227–33.

[57] Noel P. Gist and Carroll D. Clark, "Intelligence as a Selective Factor in Rural-Urban Migration," *American Journal of Sociology*, 44 (July, 1938).

[58] *Ibid.*, p. 56.

[59] C. T. Pihlblad and C. L. Gregory, "Selective Aspects of Migration Among Missouri High School Graduates," *American Sociological Review*, 19 (June, 1954), 314–24.

selective pattern for both groups was much the same. That is, migrants to cities tended to have a higher test intelligence than migrants to rural communities, and large cities tended to attract a somewhat higher level of tested intelligence than small cities.

SIGNIFICANCE OF SELECTIVE MIGRATION

One is hardly justified in stating dogmatically that cities are skimming off the intellectual cream of rural society, but enough research has been conducted to indicate, at least tentatively, that some selection of intelligence is involved in rural-urban migrations in the United States. Whether such selection occurs in other countries we do not know. To the extent that cities are attracting persons who are superior in education or native endowment, to this extent rural communities are deprived of their potential leadership or other contributions to social life. Unfortunately, there is no empirical evidence to indicate the actual losses or gains, but our general impression is that rural communities have sacrificed much of their effective leadership through out-migrations. Such a generalization is based on the assumption that some correlation exists between educational achievement and the effective exercise of civic leadership.

A Dutch sociologist, Hofstee, in reviewing the scientific literature on selective migration in Europe and the United States, holds that "migration as such is not necessarily selective with respect to intelligence and education." [60] One migrates, he believes, not just because of a desire to move, but because there may be better opportunities elseswhere. If there are opportunities in particular localities for persons of especially high intelligence or superior education, the tendency is for them to go to those localities. Since cities usually offer more occupational opportunities than the country for well-educated or otherwise intellectually competent persons, the attraction is primarily occupational rather than merely urban as such. Hofstee agrees that the literature shows a selection of the intellectually superior in rural-urban migrations, but the movement is to localities where the personal assets of intelligence can be rewarded with a suitable occupation. Change the nature of occupational opportunities in cities and the selective character of migration will likely change.

SELECTED BIBLIOGRAPHY

BOOKS

Beijer, G., *Rural Migrants in Urban Setting: An Analysis of the Literature on the Problem Consequent on the Internal Migration from Rural to Urban*

[60] E. W. Hofstee, *Some Remarks on Selective Migration*, Research Group for Europe Migration Problems, The Hague (1952), p. 7.

Areas in 12 European Countries, 1945–61. The Hague: Martinus Nijhoff, 1963.

Commager, Henry (ed.), *Immigration and American History.* Minneapolis: University of Minnesota Press, 1961.

Dore, R. P., *City Life in Japan: A Study of a Tokyo Ward.* Berkeley and Los Angeles: University of California Press, 1958.

Giffin, Roscoe, "Appalachian Newcomers in Cincinnati," in Thomas Ford (ed.), *The Southern Appalachian Region: A Survey.* Lexington, Ky.: University of Kentucky Press, 1962.

Glass, Ruth, *London's Newcomers: The West Indian Migrants.* Cambridge: Harvard University Press, 1961.

Handlin, Oscar, *The Newcomers: Negroes and Puerto Ricans in a Changing Metropolis.* Cambridge: Harvard University Press, 1959.

Hutchinson, E. P., *Immigrants and Their Children, 1850–1950.* New York: Wiley, 1956.

Mayer, Philip, *Townsmen or Tribesmen: Urbanization in a Divided Society.* Capetown, South Africa: Oxford University Press, 1961.

Senior, Clarence, *Strangers—Then Neighbors: From Pilgrims to Puerto Ricans.* New York City: Freedom Books (Anti-Defamation League of B'nai B'rith), 1961.

Slotkin, James, *From Field to Factory: New Industrial Employees.* Glencoe, Ill.: The Free Press, 1960.

Smythe, Hugh, and Mabel Smythe, *The New Nigerian Elite.* Stanford, Calif.: Stanford University Press, 1960.

United Nations, *Report on the World Social Situation Including Studies of Urbanization in Under-Developed Areas.* New York: Bureau of Social Affairs, United Nations Secretariat, 1957.

ARTICLES

Abu-Lughod, Janet, "Migrant Adjustment to City Life: The Egyptian Case," *American Journal of Sociology,* 67 (July, 1961), 22–33.

Brown, James, H. K. Schwarzweller, and J. J. Mangalam, "Kentucky Mountain Migration and the Stem-Family," *Rural Sociology,* 28 (March, 1963), 48–69.

Bruner, Edward, "Urbanization and Ethnic Identity in North Sumatra," *American Anthropologist,* 63 (June, 1961), 508–13.

Glazer, Nathan, "The Puerto Ricans," *Commentary,* 36 (July, 1963), 1–9.

Lee, Everett S., "Negro Intelligence and Selective Migration: A Philadelphia Test of the Klineberg Hypothesis," *American Sociological Review,* 16 (April, 1951), 227–33.

Yinger, J. Milton, and George Eaton Simpson, "The Integration of Americans of Mexican, Puerto Rican, and Oriental Descent," *Annals of the American Academy of Political and Social Science,* 304 (March, 1956), 124–31.

Zimmer, Basil. "Participation of Migrants in Urban Structures," *American Sociological Review,* 20 (April, 1955), 218–24.

Intergroup Relations
in the City

TWENTY-ONE

A look at some of the world's great cities attests to their cosmopolitanism. Possibly every race and nationality is represented in New York City. In this great metropolis there are as many Jews as in Israel, as many persons of German descent as there are residents of Bremen, as many Negroes as there are people in New Orleans, as many Italians as there are citizens of Florence. There are languages and art and customs from the four corners of the earth. Perhaps equally heterogeneous is Chicago, the great crossroads of the Middle West, which for decades was a mecca for Old World immigrants and dispossessed Negroes from the American South. San Francisco is a meeting place of peoples and cultures from the East and the West.

Looking across the seas, one finds the same phenomenon, varying only in degree of heterogeneity and in the character of social patterns. Bombay is populated by Hindus, Muslims, Sikhs, Parsees, Europeans, and Anglo-Indians; Singapore has Chinese, Malays, Eurasians, East Indians, and Indonesians; in Manila there are, in addition to the Filipinos, Americans, Chinese, and Japanese. Cities like Johannesburg are made up of Afrikaners, English, Africans, Chinese, and East Indians. Algiers and Casablanca are meeting places of Christian-French and Muslim-Arab cultures. Paris as one of the world's international crossroads attracts people from almost everywhere, as do London and Rome.

As people of different races and cultures jostle each other in the metropolis, all the social and psychological processes of human interplay are brought into focus and magnified. Stresses and strains occur, and traditional forms of interaction are often weakened as old racial and cultural

488

boundaries are crossed. New forms of social organization may arise, some reflecting cleavages along racial and cultural lines, others reflecting cooperative arrangements between individuals and groups that are different in these respects. Cultural interests and loyalties may fade as members of certain groups are rapidly integrated into the larger society while other groups, especially those of high racial visibility, remain in comparative isolation. If the city is a melting pot, as the playwright Israel Zangwill once said, it often boils over and sometimes explodes when human passions run high. And if it "melts," as no doubt it does, the blending process, whether biological or social, by no means occurs evenly for people of different color or culture.

PATTERNS OF RACIAL AND CULTURAL RELATIONS

Social systems differ greatly with reference to positions of racial or ethnic groups and to forms of interaction between people who are different in these respects. In Atlanta there is more discrimination against a Negro than there is in Amsterdam, and undoubtedly more in Memphis than in Montreal. A Muslim in Cairo or Casablanca may not discriminate against others on the basis of color, but he may draw a line between Christians or Jews and those of Islamic faith. A Bombay Brahmin resents racial discrimination, since he may himself have experienced it, but at the same time he may shun low-caste persons who are considered unclean. Johannesburg has one law for the black man, quite a different law for the white man.

Even within the same country there are marked variations in racial or ethnic relationships. Within a single city there are also differences in patterns of intercultural or interracial relations, just as there are variations in acceptance or rejection patterns of a particular ethnic or racial group like the Negro minority.

The same person may accept a Negro in one kind of situation and reject him in another. A white member of a labor union, for instance, may actually welcome a Negro to membership in his organization, and as fellow-members they may mingle and participate freely in the activities of the group. But he may reject the Negro as a neighbor, accept him with reluctance as a member of his church, and violently oppose the admission of Negro boys and girls to the school attended by his own children.

Such inconsistency may be interpreted as the differential influence exerted by the individual's own reference groups, which often supply him with racial or ethnic ideologies, specify the nature of his relations with Negroes (or others), and even bring pressure to obtain behavior appropriate to the prevailing ideology.[1] When the individual belongs to

[1] Joseph D. Lohman and Dietrich C. Reitzes, "Note on Race Relations in a Mass Society," *American Journal of Sociology*, 58 (November, 1952), 240–46.

several reference groups, as often happens in a city, this type of inconsistency is quite common.

THE RACE RELATIONS CYCLE THEORY

From early studies, mainly in Chicago, came the so-called "race relations cycle" theory, formulated initially by Park.[2] Park saw race relations
as a process, an unfolding and irreversible pattern, that occurs whenever
racial or ethnic groups, differing in culture and way of life, reside in the
same community. First there is *contact* between the groups, which leads
to *competition* for status and space. Sometimes competition is manifest
as *conflict*. Eventually there is some kind of intergroup adjustment or
accommodation which is then followed by *acculturation* and *assimilation*,
in which the groups come to share a common culture, together with its
values and beliefs and sentiments. Finally, there may be *amalgamation*,
the biological blending of the groups, though Park did not specify this
process as inevitable. The processes involved in the cycle theory were
invariably related to such ecological phenomena as segregation, invasion,
succession, and dispersion.

The life histories of many ethnic groups settling as immigrants in such
cities as Chicago and New York bear out the cycle theory, at least in part.
Among these groups were Czechs, Poles, Italians, Greeks, Swedes, Germans, Jews from various countries, and many other peoples. Most of them
entered the social structure at or near the bottom, as unskilled workers,
but as they gained an economic foothold their contacts widened and they
began to compete for jobs and space. All the while they began to acquire
many of the cultural and behavioral traits of the larger society, such as
language, manners, and style of life; ultimately they assimilated the
predominant values of the community, with the result that many tended
less and less to identify with their traditional ethnic group. Intermarriage
often occurred at some stage in the cycle. The logical denouement of this
process was the ultimate dissolution of particular ethnic groups as they
became merged, or submerged, in the larger community.[3]

While these processes have been somewhat applicable to numerous
ethnic groups in American cities, it is empirically unjustifiable to assume
that they are inevitable, or that they have cross-cultural relevance.[4] Even
Louis Wirth, one of Park's disciples, observed a tendency in the 1920's
for some Jews to return to the Ghetto after a period of disillusionment
resulting from their unsuccessful efforts to find acceptance in the larger

[2] Robert E. Park, *Race and Culture* (1949); a collection of papers by the distinguished sociologist.
[3] See Chapter 8 for discussion of the ecological aspects of accommodation, acculturation, and assimilation of ethnic groups.
[4] Amitai Etzioni, "The Ghetto: A Re-evaluation," *Social Forces*, 37 (1959), 260–65.

society.[5] In a recent study of Jews in Chicago, Rosenthal notes that the acculturative process has gone far—Jews are not distinguishable from non-Jews so far as their behavior, dress, style of life, or occupation is concerned—but that the assimilative process has not proceeded as Park had predicted.[6] In fact, many Jews, for one reason or another, voluntarily become segregated in order to preserve and perpetuate the basic values and beliefs of the group. Jewish self-consciousness has increased, and alienation of individual Jews from the group has declined. Possibly this increase in Jewish solidarity results in part from the Nazi efforts to destroy European Jews, partly from the establishment of a Jewish state, Israel.

If one views the processes of acculturation and assimilation cross-culturally, there is little to support the theory as a universal phenomenon. Arab-Muslims and French-Christians have lived alongside one another in Algerian cities for a long time, interacting in one way or another. Sometimes there has been harmony, sometimes conflict; doubtless a degree of acculturation and assimilation has occurred. But for the most part each of these ethnic segments has retained its own unique way of life, its own religious beliefs and practices, its own value systems. There is little evidence that the distinguishing identity of each group will disappear, at least in the foreseeable future; nor is there reason to believe that individuals will cease to identify with their own particular groups. What is true of North African cities is true also of Indian cities, where Hindus, Muslims, Christians, and other groups live alongside each other, often in tightly segregated districts, but without evidence of much acculturation or assimilation occurring.

NEGRO-WHITE RELATIONSHIPS AND THE URBAN IMPACT

In the urban milieu it is often difficult or even impossible to observe certain ceremonial or deferential forms of behavior that originated and became established in a rural social system. Masuoka writes of the changing patterns of racial contacts in American cities, but some of his observations would no doubt apply to the whole field of minority-majority group relations in the United States and elsewhere.

In a moving cultural environment of the urban community, personal relations based on ceremonial observance give way to the form of relations based on functional usefulness. Broadly speaking, it is to the moving hands of time and not to ceremonial observance that human beings in the city adjust their daily activities. Thus in the urban milieu the traditional Negro-white relationship is

[5] Louis Wirth, *The Ghetto* (1928).
[6] Erich Rosenthal, "Acculturation without Assimilation? The Jewish Community of Chicago," *American Journal of Sociology*, 64 (November, 1960), 274–88.

inevitably modified. . . . On the whole, the urban Negro is increasingly making it evident that the archaic racial etiquette is altogether unnecessary. Moreover, in the freedom of the city an infringement upon racial etiquette does not
call out in white persons the same degree of emotional disgust and anger as it
does in the isolated rural area. . . . As relations become more formal, as they
inevitably do in the city, adjustment is achieved more through formal channels
and less through the media of personal sentiment, attitude, and loyalty.[7]

When old relationships break down and new ones are not firmly established, personal and social disorganization among Negroes and other
minorities may be manifested in such behavior as crime, juvenile delinquency, immorality, domestic conflict, and even interracial combat. In
the United States many of the traditional relationships characterized by
deferential behavior of Negroes toward whites have given way in the city
to new institutional arrangements, but without the Negro's being permitted to share equitably in the benefits of a competitive society. This
in itself has been a source of frustration and tension.

If racial etiquette based upon sentiment and tradition has changed in
the Western metropolis, etiquette defining the relationships of caste and
religious groups in countries like India has commonly been modified under
the impact of metropolitan conditions. Undoubtedly the caste system in
India is giving way to a modified class system in which income, education,
power, and occupation become increasingly important as criteria of status.
This shift from caste to class is hastened by the conditions of living and
working in great metropolitan centers.

Work situations and social relationships

The modifying effect of a work situation on interracial or intercultural
relationships is well illustrated in the case of American industry in which
southern whites and Negroes work alongside each other, performing
similar tasks and drawing the same wages.[8] Such equality in the work
situation is usually not condoned by southern rural mores, but economic
need (by industrial managers for workers, by workers for jobs) softens
racial ideology concerning the status of Negroes. Equality, or at least
near-equality, in the job situation may not banish prejudice or hostility;
indeed, frictions may increase as a consequence of competition, and there
have been cases of violent outbursts of hostility, verbal and otherwise. But
under modern urban conditions of production and mass employment in
large-scale industry, the division of labor based upon race or caste distinctions is disappearing. This trend is not solely the result of economic

[7] J. Masuoka, "The City and Racial Adjustment," *Social Forces,* 27 (October,
1948), 39.
[8] Lewis M. Killian, "The Effect of Southern White Workers on Race Relations in
Northern Plants," *American Sociological Review,* 17 (June, 1952), 327–31.

changes in the systems of production; legal restrictions against work discrimination and the spread of a democratic ideology have also been contributing factors. The fact that mass industry in South Africa has not yet resulted in equalitarian work relationships suggests that the effect of industrialism on racial contacts varies greatly from one cultural situation to another.

URBAN MINORITY MOVEMENTS

It is in the city, more than in rural communities, that minority peoples are demanding, and often obtaining, the various freedoms denied them in a custom-dominated social order. Among these are the right to work, the right to a living wage, the right to adequate housing, the right to have a voice in political decisions, the right to organize for self-interest, and the right to an education. It is likewise in the city more than in rural areas that minority persons, as well as those in the majority, express the right to choose their friends or their spouses, even when racial or cultural barriers are crossed.

The city has logically become the locus for organized social movements: protest movements reflecting the aspirations of minority peoples for freedom and equality, or movements by the majority to maintain a superior position in a system of inequality. The ill-fated Garvey movement among American Negroes, for example, was centered in New York; the Black Muslims also have major centers in New York and Chicago. Indeed, organized efforts of Negroes throughout the United States to break the shackles of discrimination generally originate in a metropolis. In South Africa, Negroes and Asians in such cities as Durban and Johannesburg have organized to protect themselves against the increasing discrimination of whites and to gain at least a measure of the freedom which has been denied them.

The sharing of interests, convictions, and anxieties by members of racial or ethnic groups is commonly manifest in formal organizations through which some form of collective action may be carried out. If ethnic or racial groups represent a minority against which there is discrimination, it is all the more likely that organizations will be established for defensive or offensive purposes.

Such organizations have become an important feature of American urban society. Sometimes these organizations are local; more often, however, they are links in a larger chain of national or international scope. Frequently they include members from other racial or cultural groups. Among Negroes, The National Urban League, the National Association for the Advancement of Colored People, the Congress of Racial Equality (CORE), the Student Nonviolent Coordinating Committee, and the Southern Christian Leadership Crusade are groups that pursue a militant policy of defending the rights of Negroes in American life. Such organizations as the Anti-Defamation League of B'nai B'rith function not only to combat antisemitism and discrimination against Jews but to defend by legal means the rights of other minority people as well.

Accommodation in intergroup relations may occur on a formal or informal level, either within or outside the framework of organizational structures. Even the bare minimum of participation in the community involves accommodative and cooperative action, whether in the market place, the work situation, the voting booth, the school, or the church. Often individuals representing different racial or cultural groups cooperate in the main concerns of life without ever becoming intimate in their personal contacts, and without entering into each other's personal lives. The psychological, cultural, and ecological barriers separating them may be too high, but cooperate they do, nevertheless. In countless instances, however, the city is the scene of interpersonal contacts which cut across racial and cultural boundaries but which are warm, intimate, and informal. The occurrence of intergroup marriages is an illustration.

In the course of time, whether the intergroup relationships are formal or informal, there are reciprocal influences, sometimes manifest in the transmission, through borrowing or imitation, of cultural forms of objects that have some symbolic or utilitarian value. But if the intergroup contacts are both intimate and prolonged, if individuals representing different cultural backgrounds enter intimately into each other's lives and experiences, if there is a sharing of meanings and sentiments and beliefs, as well as behavioral patterns, this assimilative process results in a fusion of cultures and a blending of the heritages of the peoples involved. Whether the contacts are formal or informal, intermittent or prolonged, biological blending—the amalgamative process—may also occur, and commonly does.

These accommodative processes have occurred in varying degrees wherever peoples of differing race and culture have been thrown together to live and work in cities. With innumerable variations on the main themes, their occurrence is attested by the sagas of Old World immigrants who, by the tens of thousands, entered the gates of New World cities in both Americas. It is also the story of the American Negro, of the refugee, of countless others who have taken up residence in cities, sometimes by choice, sometimes not.

Ladino-Indian Relations. It would be erroneous to conclude that the accommodative processes always involve extensive blending of cultures or genes. If intergroup reciprocity and cooperation occur, it may be on the basis of inequality, and without much assimilation or acculturation on either side. Gillin [9] and Redfield [10] both cite the case of San Luis Jilotepeque, a small city in Guatemala, where the *Ladinos* (Europeans) and Indians reside and work together harmoniously in the same community, even though they differ greatly in race and culture. Furthermore, this successful accommodative relationship has not resulted in extensive acculturation or assimilation on either side. Although the Indians are subordinate in status to the *Ladinos*, and are sometimes exploited by the dominant group, no overt conflict of significance has occurred.

Parsee-Hindu Relations. A somewhat similar relationship exists between the Parsees and the Hindu majority in Bombay. Adherents of Zoroasterism, the Parsees migrated from Persia several centuries ago, settling in Bombay and adjacent communities. Although acculturation in certain respects has occurred, the Parsees have clung tenaciously to their religion and cultural traditions; and although they have been strong competitors of Hindu or Muslim businessmen, relationships between the Parsees and other groups have in general been characterized by harmony and good will. This may have been due in considerable measure to the magnanimous civic spirit of the Parsees, but perhaps also to their sustained effort to cooperate constructively with all groups in the city. Even though they are "people apart," both racially and culturally, they have a strong sense of identification both with the community of residence and with Indian society in general.

INTERGROUP COMPETITION IN CITIES

"City air," says the proverb, "makes men free." Taken symbolically, the proverb may mean freedom of competition, both for individuals and for groups. When individuals in a community do not differ appreciably in appearance or behavior, competition tends to be viewed mainly as an individual relationship. Even if a racial or ethnic minority is represented in a community by a very few persons, competition between them and others is highly individualized, and if conflicts arise from competitive situations they are largely personal in nature.

But if a minority group becomes so large or powerful that it appears to threaten the status of other groups, competition tends to assume more the character of intergroup than of interpersonal relations. Hostilities, if they arise, are generally directed primarily toward the collectivity rather than its individual members. When immigrants from abroad were relatively few in American cities, their presence was hardly noticed and their competition, if felt at all, was mainly an individual matter. But when

[9] John Gillin, "Race Relations without Conflict: A Guatemalan Town," *American Journal of Sociology,* 53 (March, 1948), 337–43.

[10] Robert Redfield, "Culture Contact without Conflict," *American Anthropologist,* 41 (July–September, 1939), 514–17.

their numbers increased to the point that they were considered a threat to the social or economic positions of numbers of the people, whether long-time residents or other newcomers, competitive consciousness shifted to a group basis: they were judged opprobriously and categorically as Jews, Polacks, Wops, Hunkies, Japs, and so on. Such has been the case for Negroes. As long as Negroes in northern cities represented a small and unobtrusive minority the reactions to them tended to be individualized; but when their numbers increased as a result of heavy in-migrations, competition shifted to a group basis. It was out of such a competitive situation that bitter conflicts sometimes emerged.

Wherever peoples of differing race, religion, nationality, or culture live and work together competitively in the same community, there is always a possibility that intergroup tensions will occur and will result in some form of discrimination. Whether the tensions so generated will culminate in overt conflict depends on the circumstances. In American cities almost every minority or majority group—racial, religious, or ethnic—has at one time or another been the object of hostility and sometimes of discrimination. For example, through a quasi-legal device known as a "protective covenant," property owners and realtors in many American cities agree not to rent or sell property to persons of a designated race or religion.[11] In some cities certain minorities are denied the use of public facilities or the right to reside wherever they choose in the community. The total effect is to isolate and segregate people from each other.

POWER AND INTERGROUP RELATIONS

Relationships between peoples who differ in culture or race, and particularly in social status, almost invariably involve the question of political and economic power and the exercise thereof.[12] Sometimes it is the numerical majority that sits in the seats of power, sometimes the minority. In the United States, political and economic power is concentrated mainly in the hands of the white majority, while in South Africa, it is wielded by a white minority. The possession of power is often an invitation to exploitation and discrimination, as has been the case in both the United States and South Africa. It has been especially true of colonialism, which almost always meant minority domination and very often the abuse of minority power. The French in Algeria, the Portuguese in Mozambique, the British in India, and the Belgians in the Congo are a few of the many possible examples.

[11] See Chapter 7, pp. 122–23, for a discussion of the legal status of protective covenants.

[12] R. A. Schermerhorn, "Power as a Primary Concept in the Study of Minorities," *Social Forces,* 35 (1956), 53–56.

Just as the "independence" movements against colonial domination have been basically a struggle for power, so has much of the racial conflict in the United States and South Africa. In both instances the struggle has been mainly between groups that differ in color and culture. The efforts of the dominant groups to disfranchise politically the subordinate people, or to prevent their enfranchisement, and the corresponding attempts by the subordinates to have access to the instruments of political power through the right to vote, are evidence of the element of power in racial and cultural conflict.

INTERGROUP CONFLICT

Conflict between racial or cultural groups may assume a variety of forms, depending upon historical and situational circumstances and other specific factors. In an analysis of urban racial violence in the United States, Grimshaw distinguishes four patterns of violence:

1. The "urban pogrom," characterized by a mass assault of one racial group, usually whites, upon a minority community: the race riot.
2. Mob action by groups directed against isolated members of another racial or cultural community: the lynching.
3. Spontaneous brawls, without direction or planning, which arise out of immediate situations.
4. Stray attacks by individuals or small groups on individuals of another race.[13]

Each of these types of conflict may vary according to specific situations, but they appear to be fairly applicable to conflict as it is manifest in different countries and between different kinds of racial or cultural groups. In some major conflicts all four patterns may occur more or less simultaneously. In some instances there may be concentrated aggression against property as well as against persons, including bombing, arson, and looting. Sometimes the conflict is highly organized, even directed by institutional functionaries; in other instances it is self-generating and lacking in institutional direction. Usually the governing body, through its police powers, attempts to maintain at least a semblance of order, although possibly to the advantage of one side or another.

For the most part, racial conflict in America has occurred between Negroes and whites, mainly in cities. Following World War I, a single year (1919) witnessed outbreaks of violence in 26 cities. Among the most violent of conflicts in the United States were those in Chicago,

[13] Allen D. Grimshaw, "Urban Racial Violence in the United States: Changing Ecological Considerations," *American Journal of Sociology,* 66 (September, 1960), 109–19. Cf. Richard D. Lambert, *Hindu-Muslim Riots.* Unpublished Ph.D. dissertation, University of Pennsylvania, 1951, pp. 217–21.

Washington, East St. Louis, Detroit, and Harlem in New York City. In most of these the losses in life and property, on both sides, were considerable. Generally these conflicts were sporadic, in the nature of violent action expressing pent-up hostilities and frustrations on the part of both Negroes and whites.

RACIAL CONFLICT IN WORLD CITIES

Often intense feelings of nationalism and the struggle for status equality and independence, or against status inequality and domination, have culminated in conflict in various cities of the world. These conflicts, of course, have not always been confined to cities, but have, in a sense, been national in scope. Tensions between the British and Egyptians produced a mass riot in Cairo in 1952, in which a vast amount of property was destroyed by mobs. For many years the cities of North Africa, especially Algiers and Oran, seethed with unrest as tensions between the French colonial overlords and the indigenous peoples assumed much of the character of a civil war, or at least a war for national independence—until independence was actually achieved in 1962. But it was also a struggle between peoples who differed in religion and way of life.

In the 1950's, Turkish nationalists attacked the Greek minority in Istanbul, burning, looting, and otherwise destroying large numbers of homes and shops belonging to the Greeks. The Istanbul riot was a reflection of intense feelings of nationalistic rivalry between the two countries, mainly over the dispute concerning the island of Cyprus. For several decades, Indian cities witnessed bloody riots between Hindus and Muslims, a conflict that was eventually resolved by the partition of India and the creation of Pakistan. Here, the conflict reflected not only nationalistic sentiments but also religious and other differences. There was a strong sense of status deprivation among the Muslim minority that reflected concern about real or alleged domination of the Hindu majority.

In 1958 colored residents of London were subjected to a series of violent attacks by British citizens who resented the presence and competition of "foreigners." For many years, and especially after World War II, people from the commonwealth countries had migrated to British cities, many of whom came from Africa and the West Indies, and were racially distinct from the Europeans. But with jobs, housing, and the necessary amenities of life in short supply, these outsiders were viewed by many as competitors who represented a serious threat to their own economic and social status. Competition in interpersonal relationships was exemplified in the associations of colored men and white girls, a situation which was resented by many white men. Having high racial visibility and distinctive habits, the colored persons were easily identified and thus became easy targets for many Britishers who resented their presence, or at least their competition, and who directed their hostilities against the colored men, either by economic or social discrimination or by physical assault. Swift action on the part of London officialdom, however, avoided the destructiveness that so often results from unbridled rioting.[14]

Racial and cultural conflict in South African cities has at times resulted in mass violence in which losses in life and property have been heavy. In 1949 mass rioting in Durban, a major city, occurred between Africans and Asians in which many lives were lost and much property pillaged. Here the violence erupted as pent-up feelings against discrimination and exploitation reached the boiling point, but instead of being directed against the dominant whites whose extreme racial policies antagonized all the nonwhite peoples, it was turned on the residents of Indian origin who were resented because they allegedly exploited the Africans. In 1961 destructive rioting broke out again, this time in Natal, another South African city, but it took the form of a violent reaction to the repressive measures of the Europeans against the colored peoples of the city. In both Durban and Natal, as in other communities of South Africa, the relations between the white Europeans on the one hand, and the Africans and Asians on the other, are so fraught with resentment that violent conflict becomes an ever-present likelihood.

THE MASS MOVEMENT FOR RACIAL EQUALITY IN THE UNITED STATES

When the United States Supreme Court announced its epoch-making decision in 1954 concerning racial integration in the public schools, the stage was set for a human drama whose unfolding was revolutionary in its implications for race relations and the position of the Negro minority in American society. In city after city, public schools were integrated racially; for the first time thousands of Negro and white children interacted as classmates and playmates in the same school.

But the weight of old habits and customs and traditions slowed down the integrative process and in some communities brought it to a dead stop. Massive opposition to integration developed in the South and in some border states. In numerous instances there was conflict as the forces of tradition, spearheaded by such organizations as the White Citizens Councils and the Ku Klux Klan, attempted to block the efforts of the integrationists to carry out the Supreme Court mandate.[15]

[14] For detailed discussions of race relations in Britain, see the following: Michael Banton, *White and Colored: The Behavior of British People toward Colored Immigrants* (1959); Ruth Glass, *London's Newcomers* (1961); J. S. G. Griffith, *et al.*, *Colored Immigrants in Britain* (1960). A section of the novel by Colin Macinnes, *Absolute Beginners* (1960), pp. 183–223, describes the British race riots in realistic detail.

[15] James W. Vander Zanden, "Seven Years of Southern Resistance," *The Midwest Quarterly*, 2 (1961), 273–84.

As the conflict deepened the scope of the struggle broadened. Under the leadership of the National Association for the Advancement of Colored People and other Negro organizations, and with support from many white individuals and organizations, Negroes demanded and vigorously sought the end of discrimination and segregation in all spheres of life. The battle was joined. For the first time in American history Negroes organized and directed a mass movement with no less a goal than the rights and privileges of full citizenship. In many respects this movement resembled the nationalist independence movements in countries until recently dominated by colonial powers.[16]

Backed by the force of federal court decisions, the movement employed a wide range of nonviolent techniques, including mass demonstrations, sit-in pressures, and boycotts. A resistant countermovement, often supported by the local judiciary and the police, as well as public opinion, attempted to block the mass efforts at integration. In many cities, large and small, violence erupted, but in community after community racial barriers were modified or eliminated altogether. It was the beginning of a new era in race relations. If there was not racial harmony at least there was a greater degree of racial equality.

INTERGROUP RELATIONS IN PARTICULAR CITIES

To provide concrete materials to reinforce and substantiate the discussion so far, we shall present in brief form an account of racial or cultural groups in several cities. These accounts may, at least, illustrate the great variability of interracial and intercultural relationships when viewed from a world perspective.

NEGROES IN CHICAGO

Over 800,000 Negroes reside in Chicago, most of them in a broad rectangular area extending for several miles south of the Loop. Until the second decade of the present century, the Negro community was comparatively small, but with the impetus to urbanward migration from two world wars the Negro population has grown more rapidly in recent decades than the population as a whole.

This influx of Negroes into Chicago has created situations in which Negro-white relationships have run the full gamut from violent conflict to harmonious cooperation. The golden age of race relations in Chicago was terminated when vast numbers of Negroes, mainly from the South, swarmed into a city with inadequate preparations for housing and employing such a large racial minority. Tensions increased as Negroes in-

[16] See E. Franklin Frazier, *Race and Cultural Contacts in the Modern World* (1957).

vaded, or threatened to invade, white residential districts, competed with whites for jobs, and intensified certain problems of moral behavior. In 1919 a five-day riot occurred in which many lives were lost and much property destroyed. Over the years numerous conflicts have taken place in sections where Negro-white competition for housing or jobs is most intense.

Aside from residential segregation, voluntary and involuntary, Negroes in Chicago encounter many forms of discrimination which function to restrict social and economic competition. Most of them are employed in low-income and low-status occupations—"Negro jobs" that are symbolic of inferior status in the social structure. There is a fairly definite job ceiling which is often lower for Negroes than for whites of comparable qualifications.[17]

Although Negroes and whites in Chicago interact at many points, they live a racially bifurcated existence for the most part. In their religious, recreational, and social life they participate mainly in separate institutional worlds. The imposition of restrictions on Negro participation has helped to create a race-consciousness that often asserts itself in protests against discrimination and in efforts by Negro leaders to improve the general position of the group. Yet social and economic stratification within the Negro community has created a wide gulf between the elite minority and the great majority of impoverished and dispossessed fellow-citizens.

Perhaps more than most American cities, Chicago's Negro population is residentially segregated in a large area extending southward from the inner Loop for a distance of several miles and accommodating upwards of a half-million persons.[18] So vast and complex is the Negro community of Chicago that the lives of many residents are almost completely encompassed by it. Among the changes that have altered the race relations situation somewhat are upgrading in occupations and improvement in housing through programs of urban renewal.

JEWS IN MINNEAPOLIS

Some 20,000 Jews live in Minneapolis.[19] Coming from various countries of Europe, they represent diverse cultural heritages. The bulk of the German Jews came in the latter part of the nineteenth century, along with thousands of other north European immigrants to settle in the Middle West. Eastern European Jews arrived later, many of them around 1900 or in the first two decades of the present century. Except for recent

[17] St. Clair Drake and Horace R. Clayton, *Black Metropolis* (1945). Cf. Otis Duncan and Beverly Duncan, *The Negro Population of Chicago* (1960).

[18] Davis McEntire, *Residence and Race* (1960).

[19] Albert I. Gordon, *Jews in Transition* (1949). For a further description of the acculturation of Jews, see Judith Kramer and Seymour Leventman, *Children of the Gilded Ghetto* (1961), which is discussed in Chapter 8, pp. 154–55.

refugees from totalitarian oppression, most of the Minneapolis Jews are lifelong citizens. Occupationally they are oriented toward proprietorial, clerical, and sales occupations, although a fairly high proportion are factory operatives. About three-fifths of them reside on the city's north side, and a third live in the area of original settlement a short distance from the central business district. Ecologically, the German Jews are separated from the Jews who came from eastern Europe.

Jews in Minneapolis have often been the objects of antisemitic feeling expressed in various forms of discrimination, exclusion, or avoidance. There are sections of "Christian" districts, mainly upper middle class, in which homes are unavailable to members of the Jewish community. Certain religious fundamentalist groups have from time to time spearheaded antisemitic campaigns. Jewish physicians have been denied membership on private hospital staffs, and Jewish internes have also encountered difficulties in securing internships. There are reports of job discrimination, and opposition to labor unions has at times been rationalized on the ground that they were dominated by Jews intent on causing trouble for the employers. Jews are seldom invited to membership in fashionable upper class clubs.

But there is another side, an important side, of Jewish-Gentile relations. Countering the antisemitic discriminators are individuals who have vigorously opposed discrimination and who have shared with Jews many social, civic, and economic activities. Jews and Gentiles have worked together on various community councils in fostering friendly relations between racial and cultural minorities in the city, including Negroes. The Jews are highly organized; one study showed 94 Jewish organizations, not counting the large number which had a mixed membership of Jews and non-Jews. Each adult was a member, on the average, of two Jewish organizations.

Some Jews in Minneapolis have rejected their Jewish heritage, preferring to be completely assimilated into non-Jewish society. These are the extreme assimilationists. But the great majority—the pluralists—wish to retain features of their heritage and have organized toward this end. They observe Jewish feast days and fast days, impart religious instruction to their children, maintain Jewish cultural and educational organizations, and support a newspaper published primarily in the interests of Jews. Solicitous of the welfare of their own group, Minneapolis Jews support a number of charitable organizations, both local and national. The Minneapolis Jewish community has a fairly strong sense of solidarity even though its members live and participate in a bicultural world.

THE CHINESE IN CITIES OF SOUTHEAST ASIA

Of the world's peoples the Chinese are among the most migratory, millions of them having pushed beyond the borders of China to settle in other countries of the region, mainly in the larger cities. In Bangkok, Jakarta, Singapore, Rangoon, and other metropolises they constitute a large segment of the local community, often dominating the economic life of the locality. As merchants and artisans they have prospered economically, many of them having risen to positions of power and affluence.

In Bangkok, for example, of the million people in the metropolis nearly one-fourth are Chinese.[20] Primarily because of their dominant position in the economy of the city, certain problems of intergroups relationships have arisen. Because many of the people of Thailand consider the Chinese a serious threat to the independence and welfare of the country, there is, consequently, considerable hostility against them, and steps have been taken to curtail their economic power by legislation barring them from certain occupations and land ownership. The Thai, however, are dependent upon the Chinese for important economic services, and the economy of the city and country could hardly function without them. Thus there is an accommodation of the two ethnic elements on the basis of economic interdependency but without cordiality, at least on the part of the Thai.

One factor that has greatly affected the relationships between the two peoples is the cultural self-sufficiency of the Chinese. Racially they are akin to the Thai, but culturally they are vastly different. In family organization, music, literature, language, and education a wide cultural chasm separates the two peoples. The Chinese are tightly organized into a network of voluntary associations, in contrast to the Thai, who maintain a loosely structured type of social organization. Because of their strong sense of group solidarity, the Chinese have apparently felt little need to identify with Thailand as a political society; their loyalties are mainly to their own group. These and other conditions have tended to set the two peoples apart, to increase the social distances between them, and to foster suspicions and hostilities on the part of the Thai. Coughlin says, "the Chinese community, particularly the one in Bangkok, is so self-sufficient that by becoming a part of its life, the individual is relieved of making more than a superficial compromise with the demands of Thai society. All social needs can be satisfied through community agencies— work, proper education, social status and recognition, protection, and security." [21] To this might be added the fact that the two peoples are ecologically segregated by residence in the community.

It would, however, be incorrect to say that no assimilation or acculturation of the Chinese has occurred. In numerous instances there are evidences of acculturative change, either to Western or to Thai culture. Some Chinese have Thai-ized their names, and an increasing number

[20] Richard J. Coughlin, "The Chinese in Bangkok: A Commercial-Oriented Minority," *American Sociological Review*, 20 (June, 1955), 311–16. Cf. Coughlin, *Double Identity: The Chinese in Modern Thailand* (1960).
[21] Coughlin, *Double Identity* . . . , *op. cit.*, p. 195.

of the younger Chinese have learned the Thai language. At the same
time the Chinese have become increasingly Westernized in one way or
another. "In so far as dress is concerned, and interest in popular music,
dancing, films, fads, and fashions, the typical Chinese youth is not greatly
different from his Western counterpart." [22]

INTERRACIAL RELATIONS IN BRAZILIAN CITIES

The major cities of Brazil—Rio de Janeiro, São Paulo, Salvador, Recife
—have large populations whose racial ancestry range from "full-blooded"
Caucasian, Negroes, or Indians to hybrids of varying racial combinations.
Unlike the United States, where all persons having *any* Negro ancestry
are defined as Negroes, and are generally assigned to low social status
on that basis, Negroes in Brazilian cities are generally assigned a social
status according to such qualities as education, occupation, and income.
Although color is a status symbol, it is only one of a number of symbols
of social class. In the social structure the Caucasians are mainly on the
higher social levels, and the *pretos*, or blacks, are predominantly at the
bottom, with most of the mulattoes occupying positions somewhere between the two. A black man or a mulatto who has acquired an education,
achieved economic success, and who displays other upper class symbols,
is socially acceptable on the higher levels.[23] As in other countries, the
actual nature of interpersonal and intergroup relations does vary somewhat from city to city.

Pierson cites a number of investigations concerning intergroup relations in various Brazilian cities. In Recife, intermarriage is extensive,
although the man usually chooses a lighter mate. There is visiting between
families who differ in color, but it is commonly confined to persons on
the same class level. Regardless of color, individuals are free to make use
of all public facilities such as parks, hospitals, cinemas, and transportation,
and to live in any section of the city they choose; but there is some discrimination against blacks in fashionable restaurants, barber shops, and
beauty parlors. Prejudice does exist, but it is mainly class rather than
race prejudice.

INTERGROUP RELATIONS IN HONOLULU

Intergroup relations in Honolulu have given that city a sociological
stamp probably unmatched by any other major community in the United
States, and perhaps by few in other parts of the world.[24] Here is a popu-

[22] *Ibid.*, p. 191.
[23] Donald Pierson, *Negroes in Brazil* (1942). Cf. Pierson's article, "Race Relations
in Portuguese America," in Andrew Lind (ed.), *Race Relations in World Perspective*
(1955), ch. 19; and Charles Wagley and Marvin Harris, *Minorities in the New
World* (1958), ch. 1.
[24] Andrew Lind, *People of Hawaii* (1958).

lation of differing races and cultures which has been extraordinarily successful in achieving not only "peaceful coexistence" but harmonious cooperation toward the objective of effective community life. Within the confines of this metropolis are persons whose ethnic origins include Hawaiian, Japanese, Chinese, Negroes, Filipinos, Koreans, Portuguese, Puerto Ricans, and Anglo-Saxons. In a very real sense Honolulu (and the remainder of Hawaii as well) is a unique racial and cultural "melting pot." Although each of the ethnic groups has maintained and preserved various elements of its own cultural heritage, assimilation to a common European culture has been both deep and extensive. Indeed, the assimilative process has gone so far that many of the younger "ethnics" have limited familiarity with the cultural heritage of their parents or other progenitors.[25]

The integration of the various ethnic elements into a common cultural "community" has been faciliated through intermarriage. Approximately one-third of the marriages are "mixed," but this varies considerably from one ethnic group to another. Intermarriage has occurred most extensively between the indigenous Hawaiians and other groups. Only about 10 per cent of the Japanese marry outside their own ethnic group, but this small proportion does not necessarily imply any hostility of the Japanese toward "outsiders"; rather, it represents a kind of ethnocentrism manifest in intragroup marriage preference.

Intergroup relations in general in Honolulu have been deeply influenced by changes in the relative socioeconomic positions of various ethnic groups. Many coolie laborers who were imported to work on the plantations tended, after a time, to gravitate to Honolulu, where they, or their descendants, became educated and commonly entered occupations that were both lucrative and prestigious.[26] Thus the Japanese and Chinese, and to some extent the Koreans, became highly successful in their efforts at upward mobility; less successful were the Portuguese, Puerto Ricans, and Filipinos; and perhaps least successful of all were the native Hawaiians who were uprooted from their own indigenous culture and unable, for one reason or another, to accommodate satisfactorily to the prevailing culture.

If intergroup relations in Honolulu are generally amicable, competition between groups that differ in race, culture, and class position is not entirely without prejudice, hostility, and even discrimination. Social distances may be considerable, especially between groups that are separated by social-class positions as well as by differences of race or culture. The Chinese and the Filipinos, or the Caucasians and the native Hawaiians, occupy quite different social worlds.

[25] C. K. Cheng, "A Study of Chinese Assimilation in Hawaii," *Social Forces*, 32 (1953), 163–67.

[26] See Edward Norbeck, *Pineapple Town* (1959), for a vivid account of intergroup relations in a company plantation town, and the changes that have occurred in the present century.

ANGLO-INDIANS OF INDIA

Another highly urbanized minority group, the Anglo-Indians of India, has a very different background, and its relationships with various groups have not always been mutually satisfactory. Most of the Anglo-Indians live in large cities such as Bombay, Calcutta, Madras, and Delhi. As racial hybrids, they are both European and Indian, but for the two centuries that India was governed by Britian they identified with the British, thought of England as their spiritual home, and in general considered themselves socially superior to other Indians. The British refused to accept them as social equals, and they were resented for their arrogance by many Indians. But if the British did not accept them as kith and kin, at least they favored them occupationally, reserving posts for them in transportation and communication.

With the departure of the British in 1947, the Anglo-Indians were forced to attempt a cultural and social reorientation, that is, to identify with India, not England, and to accept their status as Indians, not Europeans. The vast majority of them tend to cluster residentially in certain urban areas, which have come to exhibit the characteristics of an Anglo-Indian community.

Their acculturation is definitely Western. All of them are Christians; they have traditionally dressed in Western clothes; they eat Western food, speak English as their mother tongue, and in general accept the Western style of life. Few of them bothered to learn an Indian language. It is not surprising, therefore, that their self-isolation set them apart from the majority of Indian people. Although there was considerable hostility toward them, and doubtless some discrimination, at no time, so far as we are aware, was any aggressive overt action directed against them. As relationships between the Anglo-Indians and other groups are redefined, their status will probably change from marginality to full integration into the larger society.

SELECTED BIBLIOGRAPHY

BOOKS

Banton, Michael, *White and Colored: The Behavior of the British People toward Colored Immigrants*. New Brunswick, N.J.: Rutgers University Press, 1959.

Coughlin, Richard J., *Double Identity: The Chinese in Modern Thailand*. New Haven: Yale University Press, 1960.

Frazier, E. Franklin, *Race and Culture Contacts in the Modern World*. New York: Knopf, 1957.

———, *Black Bourgeoisie*. Glencoe, Ill.: The Free Press, 1957.

Handlin, Oscar, *The Newcomers: Negroes and Puerto Ricans in a Changing Metropolis*. Cambridge: Harvard University Press, 1959.

Kramer, Judith R., and Seymour Levantman, *Children of the Gilded Ghetto*. New Haven: Yale University Press, 1961.

Massarik, Fred, "The Jewish Community," in Marvin B. Sussman (ed.), *Community Structure and Analysis*. New York: Thomas Y. Crowell Company, 1959.

McEntire, Davis, *Residence and Race*. Berkeley: University of California Press, 1960.

Padilla, Elena, *Up from Puerto Rico*. New York: Columbia University Press, 1958.

ARTICLES

Blalock, H. M., "Urbanization and Discrimination in the South," *Social Problems*, 7 (Fall, 1958), 146–52.

Cheng, C. K., and Yamamura, Douglas S., "Interracial Marriage and Divorce in Hawaii," *Social Forces*, 36 (October, 1957), 77–85.

Cheng, C. K., "A Study of Chinese Assimilation in Hawaii," *Social Forces*, 32 (December, 1953), 163–67.

Etzioni, Amatai, "The Ghetto—A Re-evaluation," *Social Forces*, 37 (March, 1959), 248–54.

Gillin, John, "Race Relations without Conflict," *American Journal of Sociology*, 53 (November, 1948), 337–43.

Killian, Lewis M., and Charles M. Grigg, "Urbanism, Race, and Anomia," *American Journal of Sociology*, 67 (May, 1962), 661–66.

Nam, Charles B., "National Groups and Social Stratification in America," *Social Forces*, 37 (May, 1959), 328–33.

Rosenthal, Erich, "Acculturation without Assimilation? The Jewish Community of Chicago," *American Journal of Sociology*, 64 (November, 1960), 274–78.

Wittermans, Tamme, and Noel P. Gist, "The Urbanization and Integration of the Ambonese in The Netherlands," *Sociological Quarterly*, 2 (April, 1961), 119–33.

Communication, Public
Opinion, and the Community

———

TWENTY-TWO

Through communication a social system is held together. Communication makes possible the symbolic sharing of human experiences, providing common understandings and a common basis for collective action. The very word *community* implies common meanings and experiences that are *communicated*. Without communication there could be no consensus, no community consciousness, no community action. The emergence of mass societies in the modern world occurred *pari passu* with the development of instruments of communication capable of transmitting intelligence swiftly and over great distances, supplementing communication of a direct and interpersonal character.

URBAN SOCIETY AND THE MASS MEDIA

The spectacular growth of the mass media in modern urban society has been well-nigh revolutionary in shaping the form and content of social communication and indirectly the whole pattern of life. Never before in human history have so many people relied on mechanized media of communication to satisfy their basic needs and desires.

Modern urban society is made up of an infinite variety of groups whose members represent an equally infinite variety of social interests. The members of different groups commonly live apart from each other, represent different ethnic, economic, religious, and social backgrounds, and share different sets of experiences. Most of them never communicate with each other in an intimate, face-to-face relationship. To function as a collective unity the various parts of such a society or community must be held together by the thread of communication. In a mass society exemplified by the modern urbanized social order the very magnitude of the community, the heterogeneity of its culture, and the social and spatial apartness of its people limit the scope and effectiveness of interpersonal communication. It is in this kind of societal or community setting that mechanized mass media extend the lines of communication to thousands or millions of persons, providing the basis for some kind of consensus and collective social action.

GENERAL MASS MEDIA IN WESTERN SOCIETIES

The general mass media depend upon a mass appeal. They are unspecialized except, as in the case of the general daily press, they may be departmentalized, with separate sections devoted to special interests. Although such media may be owned and controlled by entrepreneurial groups primarily to enhance their own financial interests or political power, they are ostensibly maintained and operated in the interest of "the people." In their appeal to a wide range of actual or potential interests they tend to be nonselective of their audiences. This is especially true of the daily press, the radio, screen, and television, except for the comparatively few instances in which such media are operated for a select audience.

At any rate it may be said that such media cross the boundaries of racial, ethnic, religious, economic, class, sex, age, or educational groupings. Precisely because these media furnish information, propaganda, and entertainment to a nonselective audience they provide certain essentials for a common understanding or even collective action of a rather broad character. Urban dwellers obtain much of their knowledge of events from the news columns of the daily press, the radio, or television. It is only when similar informational news is made available to the masses that anything like consensus on broad public issues is possible.

The vastness of the audiences may provide a suggestion of the importance of the mass media in an urbanized society. In the United States the average weekday circulation of daily newspapers exceeds 59 million, and 48 million are sold on Sundays. The *New York Daily News*, for example, has a daily sale of around 2 million, which is perhaps exceeded in this country only by a few mass-circulation magazines. Berelson estimates that in the United States between 85 and 90 per cent of the adult population reads one or more newspapers more or less regularly, and from 60 to 70 per cent are regular readers of one or more magazines.[1] Mass circulation newspapers are also found in the large cities of Europe. In England, the *London Times* and the *Daily Express* each exceeds a

[1] Bernard Berelson, *The Library's Public* (1948).

a million copies sold daily. Countries in the early stages of urbanization, however, usually have a much smaller newspaper circulation.

The size of spectator audiences of the motion picture is equally impressive, according to Berelson. The weekly world audience of this medium is estimated at some 235 million persons; in the United States it is around 100 million. From 40 to 50 per cent of the adults in this country see a movie once every two weeks or oftener. In some respects the most important media of all, at least in terms of the size of the mass audience, are radio and television. Before television became widely adopted, it was estimated by Berelson that 90 to 95 per cent of the adult population listened to the radio 15 minutes or more a day. Television has even wider appeal, and it seems certain that its effect on the individual is greater.

Although the mass media are by no means restricted to cities, there is considerable evidence that city people are greater consumers of media content than rural dwellers. This would be particularly true of newspapers, books, and magazines, judging from the circulation of such literature. City dwellers more frequently own radio and television sets than do rural residents.

MASS MEDIA IN DEVELOPING COUNTRIES

The mass media have also been a feature of the growth of cities in underdeveloped countries, but the numbers of consumers are proportionally fewer than in the United States or Europe. In all of India, with a total population of about 450 million, including more than a hundred cities of over 100,000, there are only 491 daily newspapers having a total daily circulation of about 3.5 million, or an average of about 7,000 per newspaper. Even major metropolitan dailies have a daily circulation of less than 100,000. Whereas in the United States there are about 350 copies of newspapers for each 1,000 inhabitants, and in the United Kingdom about 590, in India and Egypt there are less than 25.

Similarly, the number of radio sets per 1,000 population is about 620 in the United States and 250 in Britain, but only two in India and 10 in Egypt.[2] The latter figures, however, are no reliable criteria of the size of the radio audience in India or Egypt, since "group listening" is widely practiced. The situation is much the same in the case of movies. In both the United States and Britain the number of cinema seats per 1,000 population is upwards of a hundred, compared with less than 10 in India and seven in Syria. Seventy per cent of all seats in movie houses and 85 per cent of all radio receiving sets are in Europe and North America.

There is reason to believe, however, that as cities expand in underdeveloped countries literacy will increase, perhaps even more rapidly

[2] Data from Wilbur Schramm (ed.), *The Process and Effects of Mass Communication* (1954), p. 74.

than the growth of cities. The number of consumers of mass media will increase correspondingly. Such mass media as radio, television, and the cinema are less directly associated with literacy of consumers than are newspapers and other printed media.

THE SPECIALIZED MEDIA

Because the persons who are identified with various social worlds are commonly widely separated, there must be dependence upon specialized media for the dissemination of pertinent information or opinion. The organization of interests on a regional, national, or international basis has been made possible by specialized media, and groups so organized are able to maintain esprit de corps and morale among their members through communication channels that make possible some sort of interaction between individuals most of whom are denied interpersonal contacts, except at conclaves or conventions. These media not only disseminate specialized information, but they are commonly also purveyors of propaganda in the interest of a particular group.

For some groups specialized media make possible a "sense of belonging" that probably could not otherwise exist. Through such media consensus develops with reference to issues of concern to the members. Under these circumstances the groups become a "public," and the consensus made possible by the mass media represents a public opinion on matters of concern to the members, who appraise a situation or problem from the same or similar vantage point. There is considerable evidence that persons in this special relationship tend to be influenced by the specialized media more than by general mass media. The labor press, for example, is an important instrumentality for the crystallization of "labor opinion" on matters of concern to organized workers.

Many organized groups in the United States have one or more specialized media whose contents are directed primarily to members of the organization, or possibly to nonmembers whose attitudes are to be influenced. These are the so-called house organs. There are thousands of such publications in American cities. Labor unions, fraternal societies, religious groups, educational associations, employers' organizations, professional groups—these are representative of organized groups maintaining specialized media essentially in the interest of their own members. In addition there are specialized media that represent certain interests of individuals who are not necessarily organized as a group—periodicals devoted to hunting or fishing, model airplanes, the movies, fashions, sports, backyard gardening, and the like. Numerous publications also serve the interests of large ethnic, racial, religious, or other minorities— the foreign-language press, the Negro press, the Catholic press, and so on. Even the general press is departmentalized for the benefit of readers with special interests.

THE "COMMUNITY PRESS" IN THE METROPOLIS

A unique medium of communication in the larger American cities is the "community press," published for distribution within a restricted urban locality or district. Some of these are "throw-away" papers that depend exclusively on advertising for financial support. Unlike city dailies that serve an entire area, community papers are concerned almost exclusively with events and personalities of a strictly local character. As such they are purveyors of neighborhood news, much of it about people whose names seldom if ever get into the columns of the mass circulation dailies. In this respect the community press resembles the small-town newspaper. It is a communication mechanism whereby neighborhood contacts can be reinforced and extended beyond the face-to-face level. Its success is apparently due mainly to the pleasure that people derive from reading about themselves, or other local residents whose identity is known to them, or about local happenings.

There were 81 such newspapers in Chicago in 1951. After interviewing 600 readers of three of the papers, Janowitz concluded that the community press is an important auxiliary of interpersonal communication in a local setting.[3] Readership ranged from 51 per cent to 61 per cent, and women read the papers more than did the men.

In purveying news of personalities and events, the Chicago community newspapers functioned both to reinforce direct social interaction and to provide what Janowitz calls "substitute gratification."[4] There was a positive relationship between the extent of direct neighborhood participation and reader interest about local affairs: those who participated most actively generally were interested in reading the social news. "We are interested in the neighborhood—that's what it gives you. . . . names of people we know," said one respondent. "We're going to put in a notice of the birthday of our little daughter. . . ."

But many persons who were relatively inactive in neighborhood activities also found satisfaction in reading the community newspaper. "It's very neighborly even if you don't know the people; you know the streets and you can just about figure out which house they live in," said a respondent. And another: "I always look for names. Maybe you do not know them, but you know they're neighbors."

MASS MEDIA AND BUREAUCRACY

The growth of bureaucracy in modern urban society is especially manifest in the mass media. Daily newspapers in large cities in the United

---

[3] Morris Janowitz, *The Community Press in an Urban Setting* (1952).
[4] *Ibid.*, pp. 162–63.

States and Europe have become fewer in number but have generally increased in size of circulation, though in some instances not as rapidly as population growth or the growth of cities. The number of daily newspapers in the United States declined from 2,086 in 1929 to 1,763 in 1961.[5] With increasing costs of operation, plus competition from radio and television, newspapers have often been able to survive only through mergers and other methods that have reduced the numbers and increased the size of the remaining papers. Numerous papers in the postwar period actually "went under," unable to make a profit even with large and increasing circulations.

This trend has had the effect of creating many one-newspaper cities. Such a monopoly may or may not affect the quality of journalistic output, but it does restrict the range and character of newspaper content to which the readers may be exposed. The development of newspaper chains, under central control and usually having a uniform editorial policy, still further extends this monopolistic trend. More than half the daily circulation of newspapers in the United States is under the control of chains. Thus all the newspapers in a chain may have the same, or similar, political philosophy expressed through their editorials, the same treatment of news, the same cartoons, the same columnists. And since bureaucracies are conservative in policy and practice, it is not surprising most metropolitan dailies in the United States have been conservative in their political orientation.

Even more pronounced has been the bureaucratization of television and motion pictures, and a corollary trend toward monopoly. A half-dozen major networks are responsible for most of the television programs in America. These gigantic broadcasting organizations are themselves parts of a far-flung corporate empire which includes the manufacturing of communications equipment and the actual transmission of programs. The National Broadcasting Corporation, for example, with its radio and television network, is a subsidiary of the Radio Corporation of America, which produces, among other things, all kinds of radio and television equipment. Similarly, a few large firms produce most of the motion pictures distributed in this country and abroad. These firms also own theaters, and as owners are able to select the films which are displayed.

Bureaucratic trends in the mass media have had the effect of concentrating many functions in a few major cities of each country, often in a single city. New York is the communications capital of the United States, with Washington perhaps second in this respect. In New York are located the "headquarters" of the major radio and television networks. Aside from being the center of control, New York is also the center of production for many national radio and television programs. Most of the books published in the United States, as well as magazines having a national

---

[5] *World Almanac* (1962), p. 542; and Alfred McClung Lee, *The Daily Newspaper in America* (1947), p. 717.

circulation, are edited and printed in New York and distributed from
that metropolis. Similarly, London is the communications center of the
United Kingdom, Paris of France, Rio de Janeiro of Brazil, and so on.

FUNCTIONS OF THE MASS MEDIA

THE ESCAPE FUNCTION

Perhaps the most obvious function of the mass media is to provide
amusement and relaxation for their audiences. In this respect they provide an escape from the problems and anxieties of everyday living. As
Klapper points out, however, there are many forms of escape.[6] Some
find in the mass media a respite from the routine and monotonous. Others
apparently escape from feelings of inferiority or insecurity by identifying
with mass-media personalities. Still others find release from emotional
tensions by losing themselves in the contents of the mass media and
thereby forgetting their troubles. The urban way of life in its total configuration appears to create a need for escape. The mass media serve such
a need. How well they serve it is a matter of opinion.

THE PROPAGANDA FUNCTION

That the mass media also serve as vehicles of propaganda there can
be no doubt, although little is known about the precise nature of these
influences. Where one or more media have a monopoly on the propaganda, so that the audience hears or sees only one side of an issue or
question, it is likely that the effects are greater than where there is no
monopoly of propaganda. But the effects are also dependent upon the
methods of dissemination and the content of the materials disseminated.
When Kate Smith, the popular radio star, broadcast from New York an
18-hour bond-selling propaganda campaign during World War II, she
used many types of appeals, mainly of an emotional character. The
response in terms of bond-buying was remarkable. This was monopolistic
propaganda in the sense that there was no systematic opposition to it. It
probably tended to reinforce existing attitudes by activating existing
predispositions toward bond buying, rather than to create new attitudes
toward the purchase of bonds.[7]

A study of the role of communication in the decisions of voters in a
presidential campaign was made in Erie County, Ohio (between Cleveland and Toledo) in the 1940's.[8] Obviously, the political propaganda was

[6] Joseph T. Klapper, *The Effects of Mass Communication* (1961), ch. 7.
[7] Robert K. Merton, *Mass Persuasion* (1946).
[8] Paul F. Lazarsfeld, Bernard Berelson, and Hazel Gaudet, *The People's Choice*
(1948).

nonmonopolistic since the mass media conveyed different political viewpoints and techniques of persuasion. In this particular situation there was evidence that the radio was more influential than the press, and specialized journalistic media were more influential than the general press. The *Farm Journal,* for example, was mentioned by persons interviewed as often as *Colliers,* despite great differences in circulation, and the Townsend publications were mentioned as frequently as *Life* or the *Saturday Evening Post.* On the basis of interviews with some 3,000 persons, the investigators concluded that only one-sixth were converted or reconverted by political propaganda, that about the same proportion was not affected one way or another, and that two-thirds had existing attitudes and predispositions reinforced.

THE STATUS-CONFERRAL FUNCTION

A major function of the mass media, the conferral of status, has been particularly true of the mass media in the United States, as evidenced by the considerable amount of space and time devoted to personal activities, achievements, and appearance. These personalized reports are thought, by some, to enhance the prestige of the individual, or of the group to which he belongs. The "social page" and "human interest" features in the press are avidly read by many persons, and if their own names or faces appear in a favorable light their self-esteem is enhanced, especially if it involves identification with prestigious situations, personalities, or activities.

THE INFORMATION-DISPENSING FUNCTION

Central to all functions of the mass media is the diffusion of information, whether in the form of facts or opinions. Indeed, all the other functions, latent or manifest, are subsidiary to the function of imparting intelligence to readers, listeners, or viewers. In a modern world of swiftly-moving events, grave crises, and changes that affect the lives of countless persons, the mass media do furnish much of the information—though not all— needed by the people who live in such a world. It is doubtful if an urban society could exist without the mass media, at least in its existing form.

WHAT MISSING THE NEWSPAPER MEANS

Most urban Americans are so addicted to newspaper reading that "missing the paper" is a genuine psychological deprivation. Two newspaper strikes in New York City, one in 1945 and another extending from

December 8, 1962 to March 31, 1963, provided opportunities for studying the effects of this deprivation. In 1945, deliverymen of eight newspapers in New York City went on strike for two weeks during which time most of the residents were unable to obtain their favorite papers. A study by Berelson of the public's reactions to the situation was revealing of the role of the daily newspaper in the lives of New Yorkers—and probably of other metropolitan dwellers as well.[9]

First of all, there was a sizable core of readers who found the daily newspaper indispensable as a source of information about, and interpretation of, public affairs. Secondly, many readers depended upon the newspaper as a tool for daily living. Among them were those who followed radio programs, motion picture announcements, financial and stock exchange information, department store advertising, and daily weather reports. Two women even followed obituary notices to make sure none of their friends died without their knowing it. Thirdly, newspaper reading had a respite function for many persons. Said one respondent: "I didn't know what to do with myself. I was depressed. There was nothing to read and pass the time. I got a paper on Wednesday and felt a whole lot better."

The study also revealed that newspaper reading had certain prestige value because the readers could appear informed in the presence of others and be better equipped to participate in conversation. "You have to read in order to keep up a conversation with other people," said one respondent. "It is embarrassing not to know if you are in company who discuss the news."

Finally, the study showed that many persons vicariously experienced social contacts through human interest stories, gossip columns, and society pages. Some of the readers enjoyed having vicarious contacts with distinguished personalities in the news, others missed seeing the names and pictures of their friends and acquaintances.

The 1962–63 strike, affecting all major newspapers in New York City, lasted 114 days. While the strike was in progress, six interim newspapers sprang into existence, but at best provided only partial substitutes for the regulars. A study conducted while the strike was in progress evaluated the effects of the news blackout on the conduct of public business.[10] It showed that during the strike, the dissemination of information on public matters was severely curtailed. Many local government statements and reports were shortened or withheld for later release, and law enforcement for protection of consumers and tenants was inhibited because offenders were not subject to the deterrence of vigorous publicity. Debate on a

[9] Bernard Berelson, "What 'Missing the Newspaper' Means," in Lazarsfeld and Stanton (eds.), *Communications Research, 1948–49* (1949), pp. 111–29.

[10] Clayton Knowles and Richard Hunt, "Public Policy in a Newspaper Strike," *Columbia Journalism Review*, 2 (Spring, 1963), 28–33.

number of important local questions was stifled. The process of governmental decision-making was hampered by the inability of officials and
politicians to send up trial balloons, and civic and minority groups experienced difficulty in making their opinions heard. The public was
deprived of the newspapers' watchdog services in connection with several
episodes involving questionable actions by public officials, which might
have led to prominent newspaper exposés in normal circumstances. The
strike clearly interfered with the normal processes of settling public
questions, but the study concluded that the full cost to the public welfare
could never be known.

COMMUNITY AND OPINION FORMATION

COMMUNITY SIZE AND PUBLIC OPINION

From opinion surveys comes evidence that the size and type of a
community are variables in the formation of opinion on certain public
issues. City people often differ from rural persons in their views on particular questions, and metropolites may differ from residents of smaller
communities. But there are other variables, such as race, social class,
religion, and occupation. Residents of one section of a city may also
differ in their opinions on public issues from those who live in a different
part of the community: suburbanites versus slum dwellers, for example.

In an analysis of the results obtained in researches conducted by the
American Institute of Public Opinion, Key concluded that farmers and
villagers were more disposed toward prohibition than were city dwellers,
but on the issue of daylight saving the reverse was true. Those expressing
a *favorable* opinion toward these two issues were apportioned percentage-
wise by type of community: [11]

	Daylight Saving	*Prohibition*
Farmers	24	50
Towns under 10,000	54	43
Cities 10,000 to 100,000	54	31
Cities over 100,000	73	23

Concerning issues of a highly complex character about which technical
knowledge may be limited to relatively few persons, differences between
various categories of people and types of communities may be small.
From data supplied by the Survey Research Center at the University
of Michigan, Key observed that on such issues as America's involvement
in international politics, the distribution of opinion was strikingly differ-

[11] V. O. Key, Jr., *Public Opinion and American Democracy* (1961), p. 115.

ent from that concerned with domestic matters. On a scale measuring the willingness for United States participation in international affairs there were only 10 percentage points difference between metropolitan residents (61) and rural persons (51); and except for the metropolitan fringe (53), the residents of other classes of cities were very similar in this respect. But even on this issue farmers tended to be more conservative than residents of cities or towns.

PERSONAL COMMUNICATION AND PUBLIC OPINION

It is an important fact, though an obvious one, that the mass media have supplemented rather than supplanted interpersonal communication. There is hardly a situation in which verbal intercourse does not play a role, whether it be communication of a formal or informal character. The whole social structure of society is reinforced by means of face-to-face communication in which the duties, responsibilities, privileges, and roles of individuals or groups are made explicit. It is probably a fact, even in the metropolis, that the behavior and ideas of people are influenced more by direct, personal communication than by impersonal communication through the various mass media.

How people make up their minds in voting

A study of voting behavior in Erie County, Ohio, revealed that personal influences were apparently more important than communication through the mass media in shaping the political decisions of voters.[12] On an average day during the presidential campaign, at least 10 per cent more people participated in discussions about the elections than listened to a campaign speech or read political news in a newspaper. Voters who had changed their minds in the course of the campaign mentioned the personal influence of friends or relatives more frequently than did individuals who had undergone no change of attitude. The investigators found that opinion leaders tended to rely on the mass media more than on personal contacts, but that they in turn influenced the voters mainly through direct political conversation.

It is almost axiomatic that people tend to be highly selective of things they read, see, or hear through the mass media—to avoid things they dislike or with which they disagree. It is an easy matter to flip the page of a newspaper or turn the radio off if the content is disliked or unappealing. Personal influence is more pervasive and often more persuasive: one cannot always easily escape being involved in a conversation, and often one is most effectively influenced when his psychological "guards" are down, which often is the case in personal relationship.

[12] Lazarsfeld, Berelson, and Gaudet, *op. cit.*

THE ELMIRA STUDY

Another study of voting behavior, conducted by Lazarsfeld and McPhee in Elmira, New York, likewise revealed the importance of personal influence in determining political decisions, although the evidence appeared to be somewhat indirect.[13] People tended to vote with their friends. If their friends were Republican, they tended to vote Republican; if Democratic, their vote was likely to be Democratic. For example, of 311 persons whose three closest friends were Republicans, 93 per cent indicated they intended to vote the Republican ticket. Contrariwise, of 116 persons whose three closest friends were Democrats, 81 per cent expected to vote Democratic.

Somewhat more direct evidence of personal influences was brought to light in the Elmira study, which revealed that those who shifted in their voting intentions were apparently influenced by their friends. Of those with three Republican friends, 56 per cent shifted toward the Republicans and 44 per cent toward the Democrats. But of those with three Democratic friends, 61 per cent shifted toward the Democrats and 38 per cent toward the Republicans.

It is clear, of course, that decisions to vote in a particular manner were not entirely the result of personal influence by friends; doubtless the selection of friends in the first place was based partly upon shared political convictions. The highly personalized communication between friends undoubtedly tended to reinforce existing political beliefs.

THE DECATUR STUDY

In a similar study conducted in the medium-sized city of Decatur, Illinois, Katz and Lazarsfeld interviewed some 800 women to ascertain how they arrived at decisions in four major spheres of social life: marketing, fashions, public affairs, and movie-going.[14] Starting with the assumption that urban society in the United States (and elsewhere) is characterized by innumerable associations and cliques which, as reference groups, influence the attitudes and behavior of members and nonmembers, the investigators attempted to ascertain just how this influence was exerted and who were the principal "influentials." They also assumed that the mass media are among the most influential forces in modern society, but that the influence exerted by the media in decision-making and opinion formation is often mediated through communication channels charac-

---

[13] Paul F. Lazarsfeld, and W. N. McPhee, *Voting: A Study of Opinion Formation in a Presidential Campaign* (1954).
[14] Elihu Katz and Paul F. Lazarsfeld, *Personal Influence* (1955).

terized by direct interpersonal contacts out of which opinions emerge. This they called the "two-step flow" of information or opinion.

In all four of these "areas," personal contacts were relatively more important in decision-making, according to the persons interviewed, than were the mass media, although magazines, newspapers, and radio did figure in the decisions. Some of these contacts were within the family group, others were outside. On matters relating to public affairs, married women were influenced a great deal by their husbands; in questions concerning marketing, women tended to influence other women; and in fashions, young women of similar status tended to influence each other.

OPINION LEADERS

In the three studies—Erie County, Elmira, and Decatur—the "opinion leader" played an important role in the formation of public opinion on social issues or consumer matters, supplementing and reinforcing the mass media. In these researches an opinion leader was defined operationally as a person whose opinions or judgments on public issues or consumer problems were sought more or less regularly by others. These leaders likewise sought the judgments of others. In any community there are many whose opinions are sought by no one, and whatever opinions they have on public questions may be borrowed rather than self-generated.

The opinion leaders in these researches differed from the nonleaders in certain respects. Generally they were more active in community associations, had a higher exposure to the content of the mass media, were better informed on public issues, and held definite opinions concerning certain issues. Actually, they were fairly evenly distributed throughout the social structure, with a balanced distribution between white collar and blue collar residents; but within each social stratum there was a tendency for the leaders to be better-educated than the nonleaders. Except for members of the same family, they were generally higher in social status than those who sought their opinions, but this social distance was not so great as to constitute a barrier to interpersonal communication. Manual workers, or their wives, tended to seek the judgments of opinion leaders who were also in the manual-working class; and professionals turned to other professionals for guidance in making up their minds. Thus, in unstructured situations in which decisions are not automatically made on the basis of tradition, opinion leaders play an important role in the formation of consensus and in decisions relating to such matters as consumer preferences.

PUBLIC OPINION AND COMMUNITY CONFLICT

Conflicts of one kind or another are virtually inherent in the nature of human relationships. When conflict centers around issues or problems of concern to numbers of persons, a "public opinion" may develop. Sometimes the issues stem from competition for status, power, or economic gain; in other instances, they derive from ideological and cultural differences of groups within a community. Certain conflicts originate in, and are confined to, a single community, such as a conflict centering around a local school-tax assessment issue. Others originate outside the community in which the conflict actually occurs. A strike in an industrial city, for example, may be initiated by union officials meeting in the national capital or elsewhere. In some instances conflicts may involve only one segment of a community, say a conflict between labor and management. But often the conflicts are communitywide, involving more or less directly all the inhabitants. Contests over the type of local government would be a case in point.

Viewing community conflict in the United States from a time perspective there is evidence that the nature of issues has changed during the past half-century. Religious conflicts have apparently declined in numbers and perhaps even in intensity as relationships between the major religious groups have become more harmonious. Issues arising from political, economic, or social reform, however, seem to have increased. Labor-management conflict fluctuates with changes in the economic barometer. The frequency and intensity of race conflict have fluctuated in recent years, and the nature of conflict itself has changed. In many southern communities the issue of segregation in its many aspects has become the center of mass demonstrations, legal action, and even physical violence.

The mass media, as one would expect, function as transmitters of information and even as manipulators of opinion on many issues. But if the conflict is widespread the mass media—newspapers, television, radio—cannot, or at least do not, furnish all the information that the partisans would like to know. Hence there is a tendency to rely increasingly on direct word-of-mouth communication, which offers fewer restraints on either the content or form of communication concerning the issues.[15] It is in this highly personalized communication, concentrated mainly among those whose ideas are similar, and often having the character of rumor and speculation, that public opinion becomes crystallized, policies formulated, and the proponents of one side or the other actively involved.

TYPES OF COMMUNITY CONFLICT

Coleman cites numerous instances of conflicts representing different issues.[16] In Athens, Tennessee, a group of World War II veterans attempted to wrest control of the local government from the entrenched regime. A conflict occurred in Scarsdale, New York, when it was charged that certain books in the public library were subversive. A bitter fight

[15] James S. Coleman, *Community Conflict* (1957), p. 13.   [16] *Ibid.*, pp. 4–5.

developed in Pasadena, California, over a proposed budget and school-tax assessment for the coming year. Numbers of communities have witnessed conflicts over the issue of fluoridation of the water supply, and in many others the issue of city-manager versus mayor-council type of government has resulted in a bitter contest. Nor are such conflicts limited to American cities. Bitter rioting occurred in London, England, in 1959 over an issue relating to certain racial minorities in the city. Brussels was the scene of rioting in 1962 between the Flemish and the Walloons, the major ethnic groups in Belgium.

When issues arise, controversy almost always ensues, leadership emerges, efforts are made to manipulate or influence opinion favorable to one side or another, and even physical violence may result. Eventually the issue is resolved, even if only temporarily. This may be achieved through the familiar technique of voting, but there are also other methods. Labor-management conflicts have been resolved by the technique of arbitration, by strikes, or by economic pressures. Sometimes an issue may diminish in importance as the climate of opinion changes, or other, more important, issues emerge. Often the issue is resolved in such a way as to permit the contesting groups to continue their functions, but only in a kind of unstable equilibrium, subject to a revival of the issue and the resumption of conflict between the interested groups.

Coleman observes that the character of economic and political structures of a community have an important bearing on the incidence and nature of conflicts.[17] Labor-management conflict is certainly more likely to occur in industrial than in nonindustrial cities. Economically self-sufficient communities more often have internal economic conflicts than suburbs; in the latter, occupational activities and interests of the residents commonly lie in other localities. Furthermore, the social-class composition of suburban populations tends to be more homogeneous than the population of central cities. Conflicts within suburban communities do occur, however, but they are more likely to center around such issues as educational values, ideological and moral questions, relations between "old timers" and recent arrivals, or community relationships to the central city.

Community conflicts centering initially around a single issue may spread to include a number of issues involving economic, religious, moral, racial, educational, or political beliefs. The Pasadena conflict which started over school-tax assessments eventually spread to include other issues pertaining to educational methods and philosophy. As conflicts widen and deepen entire groups may be involved—Catholics versus Protestants, Negroes versus whites, unionists versus management, and so on. In conflict situations individuals tend to identify with their appropriate reference groups, and on the basis of this identification the groups as entities often become involved.

[17] *Ibid.*, pp. 6–7.

SELECTED BIBLIOGRAPHY

BOOKS

Berelson, Bernard, "What 'Missing the Newspaper' Means," in Paul Lazarsfeld and Frank Stanton (eds.), *Communications Research 1948–49*. New York: Harper, 1949.

————, *et al.*, *Voting: A Study of Opinion Formation in a Presidential Campaign*. Chicago: University of Chicago Press, 1954.

Coleman, James S., *Community Conflict*. Glencoe, Ill.: The Free Press, 1957.

Janowitz, Morris, *The Community Press in an Urban Setting*. Glencoe, Ill.: The Free Press, 1952.

Klapper, Joseph T., *The Effects of Mass Communication*. Glencoe, Ill.: The Free Press, 1960.

Lang, Kurt, and Gladys Engel Lang, *Collective Dynamics*. Part 4. New York: Thomas Y. Crowell Company, 1961.

Lazarsfeld, Paul F., and Elihu Katz, *Personal Influence*. Glencoe, Ill.: The Free Press, 1955.

Merton, Robert K., "Patterns of Influence: A Study of a Local Community," in Paul Lazarsfeld and Frank Stanton (eds.), *Communications Research 1948–49*. New York: Harper, 1949.

Stouffer, Samuel A., *Communism, Conformity, and Civil Liberties*. New York: Doubleday, 1955.

ARTICLES

Jones, Robert W., "A Technique for Describing Community Structure through Newspaper Analysis," *Social Forces*, 37 (December, 1958), 102–8.

Kaufman, Walter C., and Scott Greer, "Voting in a Metropolitan Community," *Social Forces*, 38 (March, 1960), 196–205.

"New York: What Happened in the Newspaper Strike" (series of three articles), *Columbia Journalism Review*, 2 (Spring, 1963), 4–33.

Peterson, Warren A., and Noel P. Gist, "Rumor and Public Opinion," *American Journal of Sociology*, 57 (September, 1951), 159–67.

Riemer, S., and J. McNamara, "Contact Patterns in the City," *Social Forces*, 36 (December, 1957), 137–41.

Wirth, Louis, "Consensus and Mass Communication," *American Sociological Review*, 13 (February, 1948), 3–15.

The Image of the City

After the city has been detailed by censuses, chronicled by historians, measured by economists, described by architects, and surveyed by sociologists, something still remains to be considered; the city is also a source of emotion and nonrational opinions and biases. Few people regard cities dispassionately. Cities serve as dwelling places, but they are also places to sing about, to be lonesome for, to eulogize or condemn. Obviously, it is difficult to measure urbanism as a state of mind, and certainly it is impossible to apply any precise yardstick. Nevertheless, it is important to describe what we know of the sentiments and symbols attached to cities, if only to avoid possible attitudinal biases that may color research on urban life.

In this chapter various forms of urban symbolism are considered, together with the cultural and historical background of some of the ideas given expression by the symbols. Particular attention is given to the development of urban and anti-urban attitudes in the United States.

THE CITY AS A SYMBOL

The emotional and moral qualities assigned to urban life are an illustration of the symbolic meaning of the city. The city has been viewed as the embodiment of good or evil; as representing progress or decline; as being the arena of human alienation or human salvation. There can be no factually correct answers to the normative questions posed by such opposed views of urban life. The significance of such questions lies in their being asked at all, for this signifies that man is not neutral to cities, but surrounds them with values and beliefs. Hence cities become symbols, as well as things.

Types of Urban Symbolism

Symbols of the city are of many types, but they include spatial images, images of social and cultural characteristics, and temporal images.[1] The physical attributes of cities are so diverse that it is difficult for people to form an over-all description, even of a given city, except by short-hand symbolic representation. Thus, the Golden Gate Bridge "stands" for San Francisco, the French Quarter for New Orleans, and the downtown sky-line for New York City.[2] Preliminary investigation of the visual form in which urban residents perceive their cities suggests that they do indeed seek condensation and focus.[3] Lengthy interviews with long-time residents of Boston, Jersey City, and Los Angeles disclosed that in each city almost all of the sample had vivid images and associated sentiments composed of space and breadth of view, historic landmarks, vegetation and water, and so on. In fact, the residents of Los Angeles expressed dissatisfaction at the scarcity of easily identifiable focal points in their city. The spatial image of the city is related to the physical characteristics of the city, but the image is not an accurate map. Thus, none of the Bostonians, even the one who was born and raised in the district, included in their image of the city the large triangular area between the Back Bay and the South End, while they all included the Boston Common and certain other features.[4]

The social and cultural diversity of the city also require drastic symbolic condensation if the city is to be described as a whole. Verbal images may be used, as in analogy, personification, or adjectival lists of attributes. Thus, Milwaukee "sits in complacent shabbiness on the west shore of Lake Michigan," Chicago is "hog butcher for the world," Charleston is "feminine," or a city is labeled brawny, lusty, or smug, or the citizens are characterized as "proud Baltimoreans," or "proper Bostonians." [5]

Cities may be placed on a symbolic gradient of time as "dynamic," "adolescent," "progressive," or "conservative." "Whether the dominant set of images about change is one that pictures change as growth, development, discontinuity, or no change at all, anyone who makes temporal statements about a city necessarily is ordering a tremendous mass of events into a complex symbolic system." [6] The temporal symbolization of the city may be as simple as the adjectival designations noted by Strauss or as complex as the typology developed by Mumford, which is discussed below.

---

[1] This typology, and examples, are developed in Anselm Strauss, *Images of the American City* (1961).
[2] *Ibid.*, p. 9.   [3] Kevin Lynch, *The Image of the City* (1960).
[4] *Ibid.*, ch. 2.   [5] Strauss, *op. cit.*, pp. 12–13, 16, 22.   [6] *Ibid.*, p. 24.

The Golden Gate Bridge in San Francisco

The Acropolis in Athens

The Eiffel Tower in Paris

London's Big Ben

All photographs courtesy Trans World Airlines, Inc.

"Hell is a city much like London—a populous and smoky city," said the poet Shelley,[7] while others, with Samuel Johnson, have felt that "When a man is tired of London, he is tired of life; for there is in London all that life can afford." [8]

The theme that the country is better than the city—or vice versa—is probably as old as recorded history, and frequently has had religious overtones.[9] Thus, the Biblical statement that "the Lord God planted a garden eastward in Eden" [10] has sometimes been interpreted as indicating the divinely-designated superiority of the country: "God the first garden made, and the first city Cain," [11] or "God made the country, and man made the town." [12] In contrast, there is Oliver Wendell Holmes' rephrasing of Cowper's line into "God made the *cavern,* and man made the *house,*" [13] or William Cullen Bryant's poem, "Hymn of the City" (1830):

> Not in solitude
> Alone may man commune with heaven, or see
> Only in savage wood
> And sunny vale, the present Deity;
> Or only hear his voice
> Where the winds whisper and the waves rejoice.
>
> Even here do I behold
> Thy steps, Almighty!—here, amidst the crowd,
> Through the great city rolled,
> With everlasting murmur deep and loud—
> Choking the ways that wind
> 'Mongst the proud piles, the work of human kind. . . .

Agrarianism versus Urbanism. Rural-urban partisanship, at least in recent times, has more often had economic rather than religious overtones. The rise of industrial cities was especially important in initiating a long and continuing dialogue between proponents of the virtues of either

---

[7] "Peter Bell the Third," Part 3, stanza 1.

[8] James Boswell, *The Life of Samuel Johnson,* entry for September 20, 1777.

[9] Hughes has pointed out that ruralites and urbanites may each regard themselves as the pure followers of religion and notes that few, if any, of the great religions have avoided some conflict between these divergent rural-urban images of the "ideal man." Everett Hughes, "The Cultural Aspect of Urban Research," in L. D. White (ed.), *The State of the Social Sciences* (1956), p. 262.

[10] *Genesis,* 2:8.   [11] Abraham Cowley, "The Garden" Essay V (1664).

[12] William Cowper, "The Task," Book I (1785). The Cowley, Cowper, and similar quotations are traced back to the Genesis passage in John Bartlett, *Familiar Quotations,* 11th ed., p. 111.

[13] Cited in Arthur M. Schlesinger, *Paths to the Present* (1949), p. 224.

rural or urban life. A recent historical survey of opinions about community life in the United States notes that agrarianism—the belief that "a rural life, particularly one rooted in agriculture, is also the most humanly valuable" [14]—has remained strong despite the marked decline of rural farm population. Thus, Frank Lloyd Wright attributes to the urbanite "A vicarious life virtually sterilized by machinery." [15] Similarly, Baker Brownell states:

> In this age of wonders and defeat it is conceivable at least that men might dissolve entirely their alliance with living nature . . . and live entirely by artifice and material technology. . . .
>
> To abstract human beings by some technological procedure from this functional relationship with the life and creative persistence of the natural world around them would be literally to abstract them from life itself. They would no longer be men in a complete or formal sense. Their communities would disintegrate; their values disappear; that indeed is already happening in part as their relations with Nature become more indirect. The decline of the human community as we see it today corresponds to the decline of rural culture and economy.[16]

Mumford's Typology and the Industrial City. Probably the most comprehensive attempt to assess the impact of technology on the ultimate value of urban life has been made by Mumford who, following the scheme of Patrick Geddes, posited four major recent technological eras: *eotechnic,* based on the use of wind, water, and wood as power, which dominated western Europe from the tenth to eighteenth centuries; *paleotechnic,* based on the use of coal and iron, which became important in the eighteenth century and dominant by the end of the nineteenth, and is equivalent to the early Industrial Revolution; *neotechnic,* based on the use of electricity and the lighter metals, such as aluminum, which began in the 1880's and is now dominant; and *biotechnic,* which

> refers to an emergent economy already separating out more clearly from the neotechnic (purely mechanical) complex, and pointing to a civilization in which the biological sciences will be freely applied to technology, and in which technology itself will be oriented toward the culture of life. . . . In the biotechnic order the biological and social arts become dominant: agriculture, medicine, and education take precedence over engineering. Improvements, instead of depending solely upon mechanical manipulations of matter and energy will rest upon a more organic utilization of the entire environment, in response to the needs of organisms and groups considered in their manifold relations: physical, social, esthetic, psychological.[17]

[14] David R. Weimer (ed.), *City and Country in America* (1962), p. viii.
[15] Frank Lloyd Wright, "When Democracy Builds," in Weimer, *op. cit.,* p. 314.
[16] Baker Brownell, "The Human Community," in Weimer, *op. cit.,* pp. 324–25.
[17] Lewis Mumford, *The Culture of Cities* (1938), pp. 495–96.

Mumford also posits a typology of urban growth and decline: *eopolis,* the village community; *polis,* the city formed from adjacent villages; *metropolis,* a large city dominating the other communities in its region; *megalopolis,* the ever-larger and more powerful metropolis; *tyrannopolis,* the metropolis becoming socially and economically parasitic on the rest of the society; and *nekropolis,* the "death" of the city.[18] Significantly, Mumford regards the last three, the most urban stages, as destructive of human welfare and civilization. He does not believe, however, that the destructive urban cycle is initiated only by modern industrial technology, that is, with *paleotechnic* developments, for Mumford devotes much attention to ancient Rome and other urban centers which declined into *nekropolis.* However, he stresses that the industrial advances of the *paleotechnic* and *neotechnic* periods have enormously expanded the number and influence of very large cities; hence, the threat to fundamental human values has been greatly increased. According to Mumford, our cities are now at the *megalopolis* stage, and, unless brakes and widespread planning are applied to urban growth, dehumanization will result.

A brief discussion cannot do justice to the richness and complexity of Mumford's work. Certainly he assigns many positive functions to cities, but his main line of thought makes it clear that he regards the city, especially the contemporary large-scale city, as antithetical to man's happiness and fullest development. For Mumford, the ultimate values include (1) relatively small sized communities so that "human scale" can be preserved in social and economic activities, and (2) "organic" relationships between man and the environment. Hence, he has advocated planning "regional cities" which will necessarily be limited in size and scope, and the reorientation of technology from mechanical productivity to the service of man, that is, biotechnic technology. One may agree with Mumford, but one must also recognize that the equation of urban-industrial development with materialism and decline is a value-judgement.

THE CITY IN LITERATURE

Literature, which allows sentiments and values to be freely projected, is a rich source of urban symbolism. The city may, of course, be simply a locale for a novel or poem, but often it is an integral part of the action.

Analysis of twentieth-century novels about American life indicates that the city is a central theme.[19] Many modern novelists perceive the city as the distinctively contemporary way of life and try to distill its essential meaning by "revealing how it [the city] creates and definitely marks the

[18] *Ibid.,* pp. 284–92.
[19] This discussion is based on Blanche Gelfant, *The American City Novel* (1954), ch. 1.

people living in it." [20] This intention distinguishes "city novels" from those in which the place is relatively unimportant or irrelevant to the unfolding of character or plot.

There are at least three contemporary types of "city novel." (1) The "portrait" study reveals the city through a single character, usually a country boy who is discovering the city as a way of life, as in many of the novels of Theodore Dreiser and Thomas Wolfe. The change in character of the young person as he submits to city life or rebels against it reflects the author's evaluation of the personal impact of urbanism. (2) The "synoptic" novel, in which the city itself is the hero, attempts to present the totality of urban life and describes varied social worlds, many social relationships, and the tempo of change. John Dos Passos' *Manhattan Transfer* is a well-known example of this type. (3) The "ecological" city novel limits itself to a particular section of the city and focuses on the impact of urban life on a particular group. Thus, James Farrell's novels deal with Irish-Americans on the South Side of Chicago and Edith Wharton's with the upper class in fashionable areas of New York. In all instances the city novel is symbolic, for "in creating a unified impression [the author] uses particularized incidents as a means of arriving at underlying truths about city life. He offers an interpretation and judgment of the city—a way of seeing and evaluating it as an ordered pattern of experiences consistent with the inner principles of its being." [21]

Urban experience has produced not only conscious, formal literary symbolism, as in novels, but also the less structured expression of urban folklore; at least that is the conclusion of Botkin, the distinguished folklorist, who maintains that his colleagues have been going to remote rural areas to gather folk songs and stories while neglecting the urban folklore at their doorsteps.[22] Defining folklore as "a body of traditions, collective symbols and myths, folkways and folk-say, rooted in a place and in ways of living and looking at life," [23] Botkin collected a large amount of such material from newspapers, memoirs, travel writings, interviews, and recordings. He found that American cities possess folklore which has grown up around landmarks, streets, neighborhoods, place names, nicknames, local speech, foods, festivals, and the like.

He regards urban folklore as particularly interesting because it illustrates more fully than rural folklore the interchange between "folk" and "popular" art. As a pure form, folk art is oral, has limited acceptance, and is diffused by noncommercial and nonacademic media, while "popular" art is written, has wide acceptance, and is diffused by commercial mass media. Botkin's anthology includes the song "St. Louis Blues," which we may cite as an excellent example of the fusion of "folk" and "popular" elements.

[20] *Ibid.*, p. 4.   [21] *Ibid.*, p. 6.
[22] B. A. Botkin (ed.), *Sidewalks of America* (1954), pp. vii–x.   [23] *Ibid.*, p. vii.

ARE CITIES UN-AMERICAN?

In a provocative article, William H. Whyte asked, "Are Cities Un-American?" [24] He observed that although the United States is more urban than ever in a statistical sense, there appears to be a growing alienation between the city and what most people think of as the American way of life. Whyte pointed to metropolitan settlement patterns in which the middle classes live in bucolic, socially isolated suburbs, while the city core is populated largely by social and economic extremes and the "slightly odd"—ethnic and racial minorities, the very poor and the very rich, the old, and the unattached.

A major cause of the physical and social decline of American cities, according to Whyte, is poor city planning which reduces urban amenities so that those who have a choice move to a more attractive environment. However, Whyte also suggests that unimaginative city planning may be a symptom of a general lack of interest in and care about cities.

It is the contention of this book that most of the rebuilding under way and in prospect is being designed by people who don't like cities. They do not merely dislike the noise and the dirt and the congestion. They dislike the city's variety and concentration, its tension, its hustle and bustle. The new redevelopment projects will be physically in the city, but in spirit they deny it—and the values that since the beginning of civilization have always been at the heart of great cities.[25]

This line of thought suggests some of the questions we shall examine in this section. For example, is there an anti-urban bias in the United States? Is suburbia a reaffirmation of rural values?

RURALISM AS THE STANDARD

There is considerable evidence that ruralism is the yardstick by which Americans judge what is desirable and undesirable. There are, for example, numerous "rural survivals" in American urban life.[26] Thus, Americans regard living in single-family homes as more prestigious than living in apartment houses, and home ownership is preferred to rental. The high status assigned to living-room fireplaces—even those that are "false fronts"—and the acceptance of casual farm clothing—including

[24] William H. Whyte, "Are Cities Un-American?" *Fortune* (September, 1957), pp. 123–33. Reprinted in The Editors of Fortune, *The Exploding Metropolis* (1958).
[25] William H. Whyte, "Introduction," in *The Exploding Metropolis, op. cit.,* p. vii.
[26] Adolph Tomars, "Rural Survivals in American Urban Life," *Rural Sociology,* (December, 1943), 378–86.

blue jeans—by urbanites, are other instances exemplifying rural standards.[27]

Our stereotype of the personality and behavior of the "ideal man" also emphasizes rural characteristics. Tomars suggests that presidential candidates seek to identify themselves with farm origins or rural occupations to establish that they are "real" Americans.[28] In a more precise and comprehensive manner, William E. Henry concluded, after surveying concepts of the "normal" or "good" man, that even in the professional psychological literature, such concepts are built around notions of simplicity and stability associated with a quieter life than that of the city.[29]

In literature, too, there is a persistent anticity theme. In a recent review of the intellectual history of the United States, Herman Melville, Nathaniel Hawthorne, and Edgar Allen Poe are described as having "bad dreams of the city."[30] In their novels and stories of city life before the Civil War, ". . . the city scene was a backdrop for frightening experiences, personal defeat, icy intellectualism, heartless commercialism, miserable poverty, crime and sin, smoke and noise, dusk and loneliness."[31] The following dialogue, occurring on the arrival of rural newcomers to a large city, is illustrative:

> The ladies are first of all struck by the hardness of the pavements. "Are they so hard-hearted here?" asks Isabel. And Pierre replies: "Ask yonder pavements, Isabel. Milk dropped from the milkman's can in December, freezes not more quickly on those stones, than does the snow-white innocence, if in poverty it chance to fall in these streets." Isabel complains; " I like not the town" and asks "Thinks't thou, Pierre, the time will ever come when all the earth shall be paved?" And Pierre answers: "Thank God that never can be!"[32]

Wohl finds that the typical hero of the fiction of the middle and late nineteenth century is a virtuous country boy, such as Horatio Alger who succeeds in the city precisely because of his rural qualities.[33]

Analysis of American fiction dealing with New York City, 1846–1937, reveals that the city is consistently portrayed as evil either because it offers temptations and inducements to immoral behavior or because of the disintegrating effects of the desire for wealth and social prestige which characterize urban society.[34]

There is a certain ambivalence in the literary idealization of rural norms: after all, it is in the city that the Horatio Alger heroes make their mark—and they do not return to the country. Many of Melville's or Haw-

[27] *Ibid.*, and Botkin, *op. cit.*, p. ix. [28] Tomars, *op. cit.*
[29] Cited in Hughes, *op. cit.*, p. 266.
[30] Morton White and Lucia White, *The Intellectual versus the City* (1962), ch. 4.
[31] *Ibid.*, p. 37. [32] Herman Melville, *Pierre*, cited in White, *op. cit.*, p. 39.
[33] R. Richard Wohl, cited in Hughes, *op. cit.*, p. 266.
[34] Eugene Arden, "The Evil City in American Fiction," *New York History*, 35 (July, 1954), 59–79.

thorne's or Poe's "bad dreams" and "evils" of the city may have had a factual basis. Rapid urban growth brought manifold social problems, as well as a greater gap between rural and urban life styles, particularly in the latter part of the nineteenth century.[35]

History of American Viewpoints on the City

Another way of determining whether there is pro- or anti-urban bias in the United States is to examine the historic trend of opinion. Significantly, no studies have concluded that the weight of past and present opinion is pro-urban, although several studies have concluded that the underlying trend has been anti-urban, or at least ambivalent.

However, the studies also show that there have been important changes in the nature of anti-urbanism. Generally speaking, anti-urban sentiment was at a minimum in the colonial and early national period when cities were small and dominated by rural customs and interests. During the nineteenth century, as cities grew in size and power, and became increasingly differentiated from the countryside, distrust of the city mounted. The many difficulties attending rapid urban-industrial growth fostered the association of city life with social problems. But, cities also conferred many benefits and were clearly an ever more important part of the American scene. For these, and other reasons, although cities continued to be subjected to criticism, a new dialogue between ruralism and urbanism began, from which twentieth-century American attitudes toward the city are emerging.

Anti-urbanism among Intellectuals. The Whites' historical study of opinion among intellectuals in the United States concluded that

enthusiasm for the American city has not been typical or predominant in our intellectual history. Fear has been the more common reaction. For a variety of reasons our most celebrated thinkers have expressed different degrees of ambivalence and animosity toward the city. . . . We have no persistent or pervasive tradition of romantic attachment to the city in our literature or in our philosophy, nothing like the Greek attachment to the *polis* or the French writer's affection for Paris.[36]

Since the Whites' survey dealt with writers, philosophers, and members of the professions, it does not necessarily reflect popular opinion. Nevertheless, the prevalence of anti-urbanism among the most literate and thoughtful segment of society, many of whom were themselves city residents, is noteworthy.

The Whites' catalogue of anti-urban thought begins with Thomas Jefferson, who said in his *Notes on Virginia* (1784), "The mobs of great

[35] Arthur M. Schlesinger, *The Rise of the City, 1878–1898* (1933), p. 77.
[36] White and White, *op. cit.*, pp. 1–2.

cities add just so much to the support of pure government as sores do to the strength of the human body." [37] Jefferson advocated that all Americans should cultivate the land, except those workers—carpenters, masons, blacksmiths—whose products or skills were needed by farmers themselves. He suggested that, to curb urban growth, raw materials be sent to England for manufacturing. It was only after the War of 1812 made it clear that manufacturing centers were necessary for national survival that Jefferson abandoned his opposition to the encouragement of cities in the United States. Ultimately, then, he accepted cities as a necessary evil.

Other facets of anti-urbanism were displayed somewhat later in the nineteenth century. For the transcendentalist philosophers, Ralph Waldo Emerson and Henry David Thoreau, anti-urbanism was part of a metaphysical system in which Reason and Nature, supposedly rural characteristics, were exalted over Understanding and Artifice, the urban characteristics.[38] The transcendentalists flourished in the first half of the nineteenth century, but later philosophers representing such diverse systems as idealism and materialism also reacted negatively to the city.[39] Josiah Royce (1855–1916), an idealist, urged that large cities should be abandoned in favor of a "higher provincialism," for he believed that "Freedom . . . dwells now in the small social group, and has its securest home in the provincial life. . . . Apart from the influence of the province . . . the individual loses his right, his self-consciousness, and his dignity." [40] George Santayana, the Spanish-born materialist philosopher, who grew up in the United States and lived there until middle age, held that man's natural civilized state is agricultural and that men are reduced to proletarian status as "an unhappy effect of the monstrous growth of cities, made possible by the concentration of trade and the multiplication of industries." [41] For Santayana the ideal city was a rural center.

Among major authors, Hawthorne, Melville, and Poe before the Civil War, and Henry James, William Dean Howells, Frank Norris, and Theodore Dreiser after the Civil War all expressed distaste for the city. Although their presentations of the city ranged from the vivid mood interpretations of urban evil by Hawthorne, Melville, and Poe, to the literary realism of Howells and the naturalism of Norris and Dreiser, the evaluation of American urban life was ultimately negative. Thus, Howells, "one of our most eminent novelists of urban life ended his career living in New York but looking wistfully at the American village and the German city." [42] Some of Norris' and Dreiser's titles, *The Octopus, The Titan, The Pit,* are suggestive of the human alienation and degradation they saw as one consequence of the large-scale organization of the city.

Although the reform movement in American cities in the late nineteenth

[37] Cited in *ibid.,* p. 14.   [38] *Ibid.,* ch. 3.   [39] *Ibid.,* ch. 11.
[40] Josiah Royce, *Race Questions, Provincialism, and Other American Problems,* cited in *ibid.,* p. 183.
[41] George Santayana, *My Host the World,* cited in *ibid.,* p. 187.
[42] White and White, *op. cit.,* p. 116.

century and early twentieth century was founded on acceptance of the
city, the direction of reform also expressed a rural nostalgia. The Whites
credit William James, the pragmatist, as the inspiration of the movement
to study the city carefully as a basis for effectively improving it. Robert
Park, the influential urban sociologist at the University of Chicago, Jane
Addams, the social worker who founded Hull House settlement in
Chicago's slums, and John Dewey, the philosopher, are regarded as carrying out the pragmatic doctrine of James.[43] Significantly,

> . . . They wanted to decompose the city into spiritual units that would emulate
> village life. This is evident in Park's idealization of the primary group, in Jane
> Addams' hope that the settlement house would help fill the urban void, and in
> Dewey's plea for a revival of localism in his *Public and Its Problems*. All of
> these figures in the Age of Reform stressed the importance of community and
> communication in re-creating a livable urban life, but they sought to inject into
> the city the kind of face-to-face community they knew in their own small vil-
> lages and towns in the nineteenth century, before the radio, the automobile,
> the airplane, and television made less neighborly forms of communication
> possible.[44]

The Changing Focus of Anti-urbanism. The Whites found that significant changes in points of view toward the city occurred over time,
despite the persistence of the anti-urban theme. During the eighteenth
century, opinions of rural and urban life were relatively balanced and
nonpartisan. Thus, Benjamin Franklin, the leading Philadelphian, and
J. Hector St. John de Crèvecoeur, an agrarian writer, praised both the
city and the country.[45] This is perhaps explained by the absence of
marked contrasts between town and country in physical appearance or
way of life. Even by 1800, the largest city, Philadelphia, had reached only
70,000 is size. There were no city guidebooks and few "exposés" of urban
life.[46]

The most virulent anti-urbanism flourished in the nineteenth century, as
the transformation wrought by industrialization, heavy immigration, and
rapid growth became evident. The decades just before and just after
the Civil War witnessed the heaviest rates of urban growth in American
history. Between 1840 and 1850 the urban population grew by 92 per cent,
thereby almost doubling in ten years, while the following decades, 1850–
60 and 1860–70, had urban increases of 75 per cent and 59 per cent, respectively.

The intellectual grounds of anti-urbanism shifted after the Civil War.
Before the war, cities were attacked because they were *too civilized*, that
is, they did not measure up to the prevailing notions of romanticism

---

[43] *Ibid.*, chs. 9 and 10.   [44] *Ibid.*, p. 216.   [45] *Ibid.*, ch. 2.
[46] Bayrd Still, "The History of the City in American Life," *The American Review*
(Bologna, Italy), 2 (May, 1962), 20–37.

which valued unspoiled nature above all else. Unspoiled nature was a reality which was easily accessible to most Americans before the Civil War. "This does not mean that traditional romanticism can be expressed only in a period which is preponderantly non-urban, but it does suggest that it can flourish as the preponderant intellectual style only under such circumstances." [47] Only about one-twentieth of the American people lived in cities in 1800, but by 1870, a quarter of them lived in cities.

As a predominantly urban society emerged after the Civil War, intellectuals came to realize that any hopes for civilization would have to be realized in the city.

But they were not satisfied with mere possibilities. Urban intellectuals therefore turned upon the American city and criticized it for not living up to its possibilities and its promise; and as a result we find the growth of a city-based attack on the city itself, all in the name of the very things that a real romanticist would have scorned: science, sophistication, and order.

After the Civil War, cities were attacked because they were *not civilized enough.*

For the generation of post-Civil War intellectuals, for realists and pragmatists and naturalists, American city life was not deficient because it was artificial, rational, self-conscious, or effete. On the contrary, it was too wild, too vulgar, too ostentatious, too uncontrolled, too gaudy, too full of things that disturbed the sensibility of the fastidious . . . and too chaotic for scientifically ordered minds who sought a planned social order.[48]

Changes in rural-urban attitudes were also evident in the popular media. In the 1840's and 1850's cities had become large enough, numerous enough, and different enough to be the subject of intensive interest and attention in the popular press. In 1847, *Hunt's Merchant Magazine* began an extensive series of articles on cities and towns. Phelps' *Hundred Cities and Large Towns of America* appeared in 1852, while popular fiction described the mysteries and miseries of town life.[49] By the middle 1860's, curiosity was replaced by concern over urban problems, but toward the end of the nineteenth century such concern was tempered by a realization that the urban trend was irreversible and, in many ways, beneficial. Thus, although the evils of the city continued to be portrayed luridly in popular fiction, another side of the urban coin was shown, too. Clyde Fitch's play, *The City*, appearing in 1909, contains the lines: "What the city does is bring out what's strongest in us. She gives the man his opportunity, and it's up to him what he makes of it." [50] In the latter part of the nineteenth century, the change in popular portrayal of the farmer from "the sturdy

[47] White and White, *op. cit.*, p. 226.
[49] Still, *op. cit.*, pp. 24–25.
[48] *Ibid.*, pp. 229, 227.
[50] Cited in *ibid.*, p. 25.

yeoman" to the "hayseed" is also noteworthy.[51] The increasing prosperity and political power of urbanites, coupled with economic problems on the farm as agricultural mechanization and specialization outmoded the traditional self-sufficient family farmstead, contributed to a sense of rural inferiority, frustration, and unrest which expressed itself in several political movements in the post-Civil War period.[52]

On the urban scene, muckraking and the resulting social legislation were evidence of the energetic attack on urban problems in the late nineteenth and early twentieth century. Housing, sanitation, recreation, and industrial working conditions were among the urban evils subjected to scrutiny and improvement. The movement for reform of municipal government, exemplified in Lincoln Steffens' *The Shame of the Cities*, gained ground in this period, too. Fact-finding and reform appear to keynote the reaction to the city at this time. One study suggested that before World War I most urban spokesmen were planners, such as Daniel Burnham, moving spirit of the famous "Plan of Chicago." [53] However, the study notes that the optimism and faith of the planners began to decline.

> Beginning in the 1920's, a note of apology sounded in their ranks, and a growing conviction that the city needed friends is evidenced by the increasing number of persons who took to print in its behalf. . . . It seems to have taken the urban-centered disillusionments of the Progressive era and those following World War I to forge the social conscience essential to a mature critique of the city.[54]

In the process of re-evaluation, agrarian and urban points of view were involved in "a dialectic of thrust and counter-thrust" from which several attempts at a rational synthesis emerged. Regionalism is one such attempt; the Goodmans' proposals in *Communitas* are another.[55] However, the ferment over urban and rural points of view has by no means disappeared, as witness the emotion-laden controversy over the proposed establishment of a national Department of Urbiculture. A new point of view regarding urban communities may be in the making, but it has not yet solidified.

Is suburbia anti-urban?

What then of suburbs, our most characteristic contemporary community form? Do suburbs represent a flight from urbanism and a search for idealized rural values? Are suburbs an attempt to retreat from urban reality to a green cocoon? There are no definitive answers to these ques-

---

[51] Schlesinger, *Paths to the Present, op. cit.*, p. 229.

[52] *Ibid.*; see also the brilliant study by Henry Nash Smith, *Virgin Land: The American West as Symbol and Myth* (1950), which examines the shattering of the image of the American West as a Garden of Paradise.

[53] Weimer, *op. cit.*, p. viii.   [54] *Ibid.*, pp. viii–ix.   [55] *Ibid.*, p. ix.

Figure 23.

tions, partly because suburbs are still in flux,[56] but since they are important questions, available evidence is worth examining.

Dobriner, in noting that "the rural ideal is clearly invoked by the very labels given to suburban development—'Country Village,' 'Woodbury Knolls,' 'The Ridge,' 'Pinewood,'" and so on[57]—suggests that these names seem to promise the city dweller uncorrupted nature and a sense of community.

> The names of suburbia say, "Come back!" Come back to the *real* things—the green mansions, the sylvan hollows, and sun-sprayed meadows, the private, small and uncorrupted little green places. Come back to the permanent, immutable, and trusted forms of nature. . . . Return to the "Country Village" and Colonial America. No great heaving city this, no paranoid bureaucracy, just a simple untroubled rural village where there is a family and "roots" and friends. Everything is in order, and a man can see all the forces which shape his life.[58]

If these promises pull people to suburbs the promise may often be unfulfilled. Over-building and lack of planning often negate the outdoor attractions of the suburbs, and, as Dobriner points out elsewhere in his book, cleavages of social class and ethnicity often prevent suburban community harmony and integration. The important issue, however, is not so much whether suburbanites find allegedly rural virtues in the suburbs, but whether they went there in search of them.

Most data on suburban beliefs are impressionistic, and there have been few attempts to measure the pro- or anti-urban bias of suburbanites. Among the existing studies is one which examined the degree of "ruralism-urbanism" as values among the residents of New York City and adjacent suburbs.[59] For purposes of this study, "ruralism" (or "urbanism") was defined as a mind-set, that is, a group of attitudes and beliefs, and is not necessarily related to rural or urban residence or experience. Therefore, a 23-item questionnaire was designed to measure the way the rural or urban environment differentially appeared to embody "the good life" to individuals, rather than to measure factual knowledge about rural or urban life. For example, people were asked their degree of agreement or disagreement on such questions as, "For me, life on a farm would be extremely dull," and "I feel that the deepest appreciation of the fundamental relationships of life is found in the city." Three samples of residents were drawn: two from urban areas in New York City, one in the heart of the city and another further out but still within the city limits; the suburban sample was drawn from a rapidly-growing county adjacent to New York City. The three samples were matched by age, sex, marital

---

[56] See Chapter 9 for a discussion of the nature of suburbs, as well as changes apparently underway.

[57] William Dobriner, *Class in Suburbia* (1963), p. 73.   [58] *Ibid.*

[59] Sylvia F. Fava, unpublished manuscript, 1956.

status, education, length of residence, and size of community of childhood residence. Comparison of the "ruralism-urbanism" scores of the
matched samples showed that almost 70 per cent of the suburban sample
scored above the average, that is, were prorural, while only 43 per cent
of the outer-city sample and 33 per cent of the central city sample had
such scores. Suburbanites were, in other words, significantly more inclined than urbanities to project a positive image of farming and the open
country and a negative image of the city.[60]

After studying the political structure of suburbs, Robert Wood, a political scientist, concluded that it represented a renaissance of the small-
town and village ideal.[61] Suburban governments, according to Wood,
are typically small, ineffective, and expensive, unsuitable for coping with
metropolitan area problems. Yet suburbanites stubbornly resist efforts
at consolidation into larger governmental jurisdictions, and small-scale
suburban governments are, in fact, proliferating. Wood points out that the
attachment to suburban government is ideological, stemming from a
belief that the small community produces the best life, and the best
government.

Suburbia, defined as an ideology, a faith in communities of limited size and a
belief in the conditions of intimacy, is quite real. The dominance of the old
values explains more about the people and politics of the suburbs than any
other interpretation. Fundamentally, it explains the nature of the American
metropolis. . . . If these values were not dominant it would be quite possible
to conceive of a single gigantic metropolitan region under one government and
socially conscious of itself as one community. The new social ethic, the rise of
the large organization, would lead us to expect this development as a natural
one. The automobile, the subway, the telephone, the power line certainly make
it technically possible; they even push us in this direction.

But the American metropolis is not constructed in such a way; it sets its face
directly against modernity. Those who wish to rebuild the American city, who
protest the shapeless urban sprawl, who find some value in the organizational
skills of modern society must recognize the potency of the ideology. Until these
beliefs have been accommodated reform will not come in the metropolitan areas
nor will men buckle down to the task of directing, in a manner consonant with
freedom, the great political and social organizations on which the nation's
strength depends.[62]

Wood regrets that suburbs cling to small governments which are no
longer functional. He believes that in turning their backs on big government, suburbs have lost an opportunity to help make bigness livable.

[60] These findings raise further questions which are not dealt with here. For example,
do individuals with a prorural bias selectively migrate to the suburbs in the hope that
they can more easily live up to such values there; or does suburban living itself engender a prorural bias?
[61] Robert C. Wood, *Suburbia—Its People and Their Politics* (1958), ch. 1.
[62] *Ibid.*, pp. 18–19.

In a broader sense, he suggests that suburbs also represent the symbolic rejection of large organization and the large society in general and an unwillingness to forge a new social order based on them.[63] Riesman [64] and Whyte [65] have also suggested that the creation of suburbs may only enhance urban problems; instead of coping with central city decay and the new scale of industry and bureaucracy, suburbia insulates itself in an imitation small-town life which is itself sterile and stultifying.

The Suburban Image.   In sum, then, are suburbs anti-urban? Perhaps. The solid evidence describing suburbs or contrasting suburbanites with urbanites is too limited to be conclusive, although it is suggestive of anti-urbanism.

However, as several observers have pointed out, suburbia itself is also a myth.[66] Just as there are images of the city that are value-judgements rather than statements of fact, so there are images of suburbia. The images are diverse.

To some people suburbia represents the fulfillment of the American middle-class dream; it is identified with the continued possibility of upward mobility, with expanding opportunities in middle-class occupations, with rising standards of living and real incomes, and the gadgeted good life as it is represented in the full-color ads in the mass-circulation magazines. To less sanguine senses, for example, those of some architects, city planners, estheticians, and designers, suburbia represents a dreary blight on the American landscape, the epitome of American standardization and vulgarization, with its row upon monotonous row of mass-produced cheerfulness masquerading as homes, whole agglomerations or "scatterations" of them masquerading as communities. To these eyes, the new tract suburbs of today are the urban slums of tomorrow. There is a third group to whom the myth of suburbia is also important; I mean sociologists and other students of contemporary social and cultural trends. . . . [They tend] to see in suburbia the convergence of some of the apparently major social and cultural trends of our time (other-direction, social mobility, neoconservatism, status anxiety, and the like), thus making of suburbia a microcosm in which the processes at work in the larger society can conveniently be studied. Finally, the vocabularies of some recent left-wing critics of American society seem to have substituted the terms "suburb" and "suburban" for the now embarassingly obsolete term "bourgeois" as a packaged rebuke to the whole tenor of American life. What used to be condemned as "bourgeois values," "bourgeois style," and "bourgeois hypocrisy" are now simply designated as "suburban." [67]

Most images of suburbia are critical. Berger suggests that the critique of suburbia is part of the criticism of "chrome idols" and mass culture.

[63] *Ibid.*, ch. 7, especially pp. 301–2.
[64] David Riesman, "The Suburban Dislocation," *Annals,* 314 (November, 1957), 123–46.
[65] Whyte, "Are Cities Un-American?", *op. cit.*
[66] Bennett M. Berger, *Working-Class Suburb* (1960), ch. 1; Dobriner, *op. cit.*, ch. 1.
[67] Berger, *op. cit.*, pp. 99–100.

In the modern age, when, through the sheer lack of farm experience on the part of the vast majority of the population, agrarianism has lost its force as a normative standard, the familiar dialogue between ruralism and urbanism may peter out. In place of the nineteenth-century discussions of whether the city or the country is more "civilized," we may have discussions of whether urban or suburban life is more "cultured." [68] In place of the city versus the country debate we may have the city versus the suburb. This does not necessarily mean that suburbs are replacing the country in the sense of being rural: it does mean that suburbs, like all community forms, have the power to arouse emotion and partisanship. As new community forms arise, they become invested with symbolic meaning and enter the arena of public opinion.

SELECTED BIBLIOGRAPHY

BOOKS

Beshers, James M., *Urban Social Structure*, ch. 1. New York: The Free Press of Glencoe, 1962.

Botkin, B. A. (ed.), *Sidewalks of America: Folklore, Legends, Sagas, Traditions, Customs, Songs, Stories, and Sayings of City Folk*. New York: Bobbs-Merrill, 1954.

Coser, Lewis (ed.), *Sociology through Literature*. Englewood Cliffs, N.J., Prentice-Hall, 1963.

Gelfant, Blanche, *The American City Novel*. Norman, Okla.: University of Oklahoma Press, 1954.

Goodman, Percival, and Paul Goodman, *Communitas*. Chicago: University of Chicago Press, 1947.

Hughes, Everett C., "The Cultural Aspect of Urban Research," in L. D. White (ed.), *The State of the Social Sciences*. Chicago: University of Chicago Press, 1956.

Lynch, Kevin. *The Image of the City*. Cambridge, Mass.: Harvard University Press, 1960.

Mumford, Lewis, *The Culture of Cities*. New York: Harcourt, Brace, 1938.
————, *The City in History*. New York: Harcourt, Brace and World, 1961.

Smith, Henry Nash, *Virgin Land: The American West as Symbol and Myth*. Cambridge, Mass.: Harvard University Press, 1950.

Strauss, Anselm, *Images of the American City*. New York: The Free Press of Glencoe, 1961.

Weimer, David R. (ed.), *City and Country in America*. New York: Appleton-Century-Crofts, 1962.

White, Morton, and Lucia White. *The Intellectual versus the City*. Cambridge, Mass.: Harvard University Press, 1962.

Wood, Robert. *Suburbia—Its People and Their Politics*. Boston: Houghton Mifflin, 1958.

[68] Berger's analysis implies that the modern intellectual would argue that urban culture is "high" and suburban "low."

ARTICLES

Arden, Eugene, "The Evil City in American Fiction," *New York History*, 35 (July, 1954), 259–79.

Fava, Sylvia F., "Suburbanism as a Way of Life," *American Sociological Review*, 21 (February, 1956), 34–38.

Firey, Walter, "Sentiment and Symbolism as Ecological Variables," *American Sociological Review*, 10 (April, 1945), 140–48.

Holland, Robert B., "The Agrarian Manifesto—A Generation Later," *The Mississippi Quarterly*, 10 (Spring, 1957), 73–79.

Kolb, William, "The Place of Values in Urban Social Theory," *Alpha Kappa Deltan* (now *Sociological Inquiry*), 28 (Winter, 1958), 37–42.

Mills, C. Wright, "The Professional Ideology of Social Pathologists," *American Journal of Sociology*, 49 (September, 1943), 165–80.

Riesman, David, "The Suburban Dislocation," *The Annals of the American Academy of Political and Social Science*, 314 (November, 1957), 123–46.

Schlesinger, Arthur M., "The City in American History," *Mississippi Valley Historical Review*, 27 (June, 1940), 43–66.

Still, Bayrd, "The History of the City in American Life," *The American Review* (Bologna, Italy), 2 (May, 1962), 20–37.

Stone, Gregory, "City Shoppers and Urban Identification; Observations on Social Psychology of City Life," *American Journal of Sociology*, 60 (July, 1954), 36–45.

Tomars, Alfred, "Rural Survivals in American Urban Life," *Rural Sociology* (December, 1943), 378–86.

Whyte, William H., "Are Cities Un-American?", *Fortune*, LVI (September, 1957), 123–30.

Social Aspects of Urban Housing and Redevelopment

PART FIVE

Urban Housing

—

TWENTY-FOUR

Housing in its social aspects has become of increasing interest to behavioral scientists, including economists, political scientists, sociologists, and cultural anthropologists. This is so because the houses that people live in touch upon almost every facet of their lives and of the society as a whole.

SOCIAL PERSPECTIVES ON HOUSING

Housing constitutes a physical matrix in which human interaction occurs. The nature of this interaction is shaped in some measure by the physical conditions and appearance of the dwelling, and by the amount, design, and utilization of space, both within and outside the house itself. The interaction within this setting is in turn related both to the configurations of behavior and of personality structure of those who reside in the homes. The housing matrix is an important element, for example, in the socialization of the child and in his physical development. It likewise bears upon the structuring of family and neighborhood relations. Within this physical matrix intimate friendships and close kinship ties develop; but within it there may also be personal isolation, severe interpersonal or intergroup conflicts, any or all of which may have repercussions in the individual's subjective life—in anxieties, hostilities, romances, the fulfillment or unfulfillment of cherished ambitions, and so on.[1]

Aside from the physical matrix that housing affords for social interaction, it is also an important status symbol. Not only does the physical structure and its design have symbolic relevance for the status of its occupants, but its location in the community (whether in a prestige area or

[1] For a discussion of some of the social aspects of housing, see Robert K. Merton, "The Social Psychology of Housing," in Wayne Dennis (ed.), *Current Trends in Social Psychology* (1948), pp. 163–218.

not) and its appointments (as they may reveal class-conditioned tastes) are likewise symbolically significant. One of the usual imperatives of the middle and upper levels of the social structure in American cities is that families display a house and furnishings appropriate to their social class; and if they are upwardly mobile, it is also expected that they exhibit residential symbols acceptable to the social stratum to which they aspire. The upward movement of "status-seekers" is commonly associated with spatial movement—to the suburbs, for example—which involves a house or apartment having symbolic relevance for the anticipated status. But the system works both ways: the house may also be symbolic of low status, although low-income occupants themselves may not be especially concerned about the status symbolism of their house.

There is another way of viewing modern housing—from an institutional or organizational perspective. Housing in modern urban society involves a complex organization which is interrelated with many facets of social life: economic, political, legal, sociological, medical, ideological. It represents a convergence of numerous bureaucratic practices and interests, and also an arena of conflict between those with divergent philosophies—between persons favoring and others opposing public housing for low-income groups, or between those favoring and opposing racial segregation, or those committed to home ownership as opposed to rentership, and so on. Within the housing organization complex, numerous vested interests function as pressure groups to influence the interplay of public opinion or, more particularly, political or legal decisions. There is, for example, a complex structure of housing law on all levels of government. If, as the cliche has it, a man's house is his castle, a great many special functionaries are available to design, locate, finance, build, and rent or sell it for him (or to him), or perhaps even evict him from the property.

THE HOUSING PROBLEM

Why has the housing problem become acute? There are several reasons, and not all of them are equally applicable to cities in different countries. We shall attempt to designate a few of the conditions that have contributed to the housing crisis.

1. Although movements of population to cities have always created housing problems, the great tidal waves of urbanward migrants that have engulfed many cities in recent years have created housing shortages probably without precedent. War, revolution, and drought have forced people by the millions into cities as a means of survival. These uprooted migrants are in addition to those representing a more normal flow of population to cities.

2. Mass destruction of homes in wartime was incredible. A survey of 16 European countries (excluding Russia and German) in 1948 revealed that some 4.5 million dwelling units had been damaged or destroyed in World

War II, including one-fifth of all the homes in Greece and Poland.[2] A half-million homes in Britain were totally destroyed or made permanently uninhabitable.[3] Rangoon lost one-third of its houses, and in Manila about a quarter of a million homes were destroyed, representing about two-thirds of the residential property values.[4] A large part of the buildings in Tokyo was leveled by bombing, and in Nagasaki and Hiroshima hardly a house was left standing as the atomic bomb was introduced to the world.

3. In some countries there is both a shortage of materials for housing construction and a shortage of negotiable wealth with which to obtain the necessary materials.

4. National and municipal governments are often so hard-pressed financially and so beset by other problems that they are unable to make adequate financial provisions for housing reform.

5. Discrimination on the basis of race, religion, caste, or class has often made it difficult for minority groups to obtain standard housing.

6. Shoddy construction of houses and subsequent neglect of physical properties has turned many a residential district into a slum or quasi-slum soon after the homes were built. It is the policy of many owners to squeeze the last ounce of profit out of their rental properties at the cost of physical deterioration of their holdings.

7. Opposition of vested interests such as real-estate organizations to effective programs of slum rehabilitations and housing construction for low-income families has helped to perpetuate urban slums.

8. Abuse of property by occupants who are too ignorant, irresponsible, or physically incapacitated to care for it is not uncommon. Many take the position that if the property is neglected by the owner, it is not their responsibility to keep the place in repair.

9. The invasion of industry into residential areas has commonly had a blighting effect on property.

10. There are countless families the world over whose incomes are not sufficient for them to rent or purchase adequate shelter, even if it were available, which often it is not. Even in the United States, the most affluent of all countries, about one white urban family in ten, and one non-white urban family in three, had incomes less than $2,000 in 1960, a prosperous year.[5] Clearly, families on this income level are in no financial position to purchase modern homes, nor are they able to rent private dwellings meeting reasonable housing standards.[6] Stating the economics of the situation somewhat differently, private enterprise usually cannot construct

[2] Ernest Weissman, "Grave Deficit of Dwellings in Postwar Europe," *Housing and Town and Country Planning,* Bulletin 7 (1953), p. 15.

[3] *Housing in Britain,* Central Office of Information, London (1951), p. 9.

[4] C. M. Lorenze, "Housing Problems in the War-Devastated Areas of Asia and the Far East," *Housing and Town and Country Planning,* Bulletin 7 (1953), p. 7.

[5] *Statistical Abstract of the United States* (1962), p. 334.

[6] Home economists in the United States generally agree that families on the lower income levels should not spend more than one-fourth of their income on rent if they are to have enough left over for such essentials as food, clothing, medical care, taxes, and so on.

Deteriorated houses and drab lives. Vast numbers of people in the world's cities live in slums. The picture above shows conditions in the extensive slum area between Lima and Callao, two of Peru's leading cities. The lower picture is of slum housing in San Antonio, Texas, before demolition made way for a housing project. (Courtesy United Nations and Federal Public Housing Authority.)

modern dwellings to rent or sell profitably at the prices such low-income families can afford to pay.

HOUSING IN UNDERDEVELOPED COUNTRIES

As in all regions, housing in the underdeveloped countries ranges from the luxurious to the squalid. The contrasts are striking. Generally speaking, the proportion of city dwellers living under extremely adverse physical conditions is considerably greater in underdeveloped countries than in most of the urbanized societies. Although modern Western cities have vast acres of slums, by any reasonable standards these districts are almost luxurious compared with some of the slums of preindustrial societies.

More than half of the working-class families in major Indian cities live under highly congested conditions; commonly an entire family, and in some instances more than one family, occupy a single room. The heavy flow of migrants to such cities as Calcutta, Bombay, Madras, and Old Delhi has taxed the available housing facilities far beyond their capacity; many of the migrants live in flimsy sidewalk huts, or in clusters of mud huts erected at the outskirts.

A sample survey of 3,111 families in Old Delhi slums in 1956 revealed that each family occupied, on the average, 1.2 rooms.[7] Some 82 per cent of these families were living in one room, and less than 3 per cent occupied three or more rooms. When these figures are seen in relation to the average size of family, namely five persons, the extent of crowding is impressive, to say the least. In Bombay, the slum population is estimated to account for about 18 per cent of the city's population, or about 400,000 persons.[8] And in Calcutta, over 300,000 persons live on the pavements and sidewalks of the city, without benefit of a home; and of those living in houses at least three-fourths live in overcrowded quarters with more than two persons per room.[9]

Thousands of families in Singapore live under squalid and unsanitary conditions, often in hovels constructed of boxes, rusty corrugated iron, and bamboo, with no sanitary facilities.[10] The same situation prevails in Manila, where poor families live in makeshift shanties of scrap iron, canvas, clapboard, or other cast-off materials. In Algiers and Casablanca there are "oil can cities" scattered over the vacant places and occupied by impoverished families who have thrown together shelters of tent cloth and

---

[7] B. S. S. Pradesh, *The Slums of Old Delhi* (1958), p. 179.

[8] S. G. Bhave, "Urbanization in Maharashtra State," in Roy Turner (ed.), *India's Urban Future* (1961), p. 350.

[9] Richard L. Park, "West Bengal, Especially Calcutta," in Turner, *op. cit.*, pp. 384–85.

[10] J. M. Fraser, "Housing and Planning in Singapore," *Town Planning Review*, 23 (April, 1952), 5–25.

odd pieces of lumber, with walls made of oil cans fitted end to end.[11] In Johannesburg and other cities of South Africa at least a quarter of the African families live in shantytowns in which are erected hovels of packing cases, sheets of galvanized iron, or other materials that can be salvaged.[12]

Although squatting on public or private land is by no means new, this form of occupancy has attained mass proportions in the twentieth century. In many of the world's cities squatters by the thousands have hastily constructed shacks on land owned by others. Many of these dispossessed and uprooted peoples do not have so much as a roof over their heads. Whole families live openly on the streets and alleys of Indian cities. In inclement weather they find shelter in public buildings or on verandahs. In Hong Kong there is a class of squatters known as "street sleepers." The squatter problem in many cities is not only a problem of housing and health but one of broader legal, economic, and political implications.

But cities in the underdeveloped areas have extensive middle class and upper class residential districts in which the dwellings or apartments are attractive, comfortable, or even luxurious. In many of these countries there is an expanding middle class whose housing standards are being met by construction of large numbers of modern dwellings. For sheer luxury and esthetic attractiveness few cities in any country can match the homes built for the upper classes in Mexico City or Caracas.

HOUSING PROBLEMS IN INDUSTRIAL COUNTRIES

If the housing problem is almost overwhelming in underdeveloped countries, it is also acute in the highly urbanized and industrialized areas of the world. London's East End, occupied by the city's industrial workers, has long been known as one of Europe's major blighted districts. A survey in Britain revealed that upwards of a million city dwellings, or 6.5 per cent of the national total, were judged unfit for human habitation.[13] Some two million dwellings, or about one in seven, had less than three rooms per unit, and about one house in three was without a fixed bath.

In the five-story tenement slums of Naples, families are crowded into dark and unsanitary quarters at an incredible density. Slums in Paris have long housed the underprivileged residents of that city. The picture is similar in many other major cities of Europe and Latin America, where the old quarters, deteriorated and congested relics of the past, or fragile hovels

[11] Roger LeTourneau, "Social Change in the Muslim Cities of North Africa," *American Journal of Sociology*, 60 (May, 1955), 530.

[12] Leo Marquard, *Peoples and Policies of South Africa* (1952), pp. 49–52.

[13] F. T. Burnett and Sheila F. Scott, "A Survey of Housing Conditions in the Urban Areas of England and Wales: 1960," *The Sociological Review*, 10 (March, 1962), 76–77.

hastily constructed in recent years, exist alongside newer residential areas that bear the stamp of modern planning.

Few American cities are without their acres of slums. Behind the glittering façade of Chicago's lake shore stretch mile after mile of shabby dwellings. In New York's East Side, families are crowded into multistoried tenements that accommodate the low-income residents of that city, and the area known as Harlem, in upper Manhattan, is equally deteriorated and congested. In such southern cities as New Orleans, Birmingham, and Memphis the extent of housing blight and congestion is perhaps even greater. Small cities have slums of lesser magnitude, but otherwise they often match the deteriorated districts of Megalopolis. Only in recent years have systematic attempts been made to alter these conditions through public and private programs of urban renewal.

Slum conditions as presented here could hardly be considered typical of Western cities; indeed, most urban families are reasonably well-housed by any acceptable criteria. Generally speaking, housing for the upper middle and upper classes is comfortable, or even luxurious; only on the lower levels of the social structure are the housing problems critical.

HOUSING AND MINORITY GROUPS IN THE UNITED STATES

Disadvantaged minorities in the United States and elsewhere live under housing conditions that fall considerably below the standards maintained by the privileged classes. This is true of American Negroes, but it also applies to other groups such as American Indians, Spanish-name peoples of the Southwest, and Puerto Ricans in New York.

The housing problem for these racial or cultural minorities has several facets. Quantitatively, the housing shortage in the United States, in terms of available residences, is more acute for them than for most American families. Throughout the present century, at least until the 1950's, the percentage increase of nonwhite population (mainly Negroes) was greater every decade than the increase in available housing facilities. Between 1940 and 1950, for example, the nonwhite population increased more rapidly than the number of housing units occupied by Negroes.[14] For whites during the same period, the increase in housing facilities was greater than the rate of population growth. By the 1960's, however, construction of houses for nonwhites (as well as whites) increased more rapidly than the population. Even though this trend continues, it will be several years before the housing shortage for nonwhites is met.

Qualitatively, housing facilities for nonwhites have been inferior to those of whites. Using the generally accepted definition of "substandard" as housing that is in a dilapidated condition and without toilet, bath, and

[14] *Statistical Abstract of the United States* (1962), p. 758.

running water, one finds that nearly three-fourths of the dwelling units occupied by nonwhites, and two-thirds by Spanish-name families, were below the acceptable standard in 1950. In view of the fact that about four-fifths of all urban dwellings were "standard," the nature of the housing shortage for minorities is quite apparent.[15]

This situation varies considerably from one region or city to another. Housing is poorest in the South, both for whites and nonwhites, but the problem is especially acute for the latter. In Birmingham, Alabama, 88 per cent of the nonwhite housing and 32 per cent of housing occupied by whites was substandard in 1950. On the other hand, only 19 per cent of the nonwhites and 8 per cent of the whites in Los Angeles lived in substandard homes. Taking the urban population as a whole, the percentage of families residing in substandard homes was about three times as great for nonwhites as for whites. This situation may well be a major source of discontent.

Similar comparisons may be made for density of occupance and home ownership. In 1960, the median number of persons per dwelling unit occupied by whites was 3.3, but for houses occupied by nonwhites it was 4.0.[16] About one-third of the homes occupied by nonwhites in 1950 contained fewer rooms than persons, an indicator of "crowding," but this was true of only one-eighth of the dwelling units of whites.[17] From the beginning of the present century to about 1940, the percentage of home owners remained fairly stable—around 45 per cent for whites and 24 per cent for nonwhites. Since 1940 this picture has changed radically. In 1960, two-thirds of the whites and nearly two-fifths of the nonwhites were home owners.[18]

WHY MINORITIES ARE POORLY HOUSED

Why, then, are minority peoples in the United States so inadequately housed? There are several reasons, but two stand out as especially important. One is the limited purchasing power of nonwhites. For full-year, full-time work, nonwhite males in 1960 averaged $3,789, compared to $5,662 for white males.[19] When family rather than individual incomes are compared, the Negro-white difference is somewhat less, as a higher proportion of Negro family members are in the labor force. The low-income level of the nonwhite is in turn due to a number of conditions, including job discrimination and inability to earn higher incomes because of lack of skill or education. Even families with relatively high buying abilities may not

[15] Davis McEntire, *Residence and Race* (1960), p. 123.
[16] *Statistical Abstract of the United States* (1962), p. 758.
[17] McEntire, *op. cit.,* p. 127.
[18] *Statistical Abstract of the United States* (1962), p. 758.
[19] *The Economic Situation of Negroes in the United States,* U. S. Department of Labor, Bulletin S-3, revised 1962, p. 9.

have stable incomes and are therefore on the margin of the housing market.

A second reason for inadequate housing is discriminatory segregation. In most American cities Negroes and certain other minorities are denied free choice of residential location, regardless of their incomes. Bottled up in "ghettos," they are often forced to live under conditions of housing blight and congestion, not necessarily because they prefer such areas but because they have no alternative.

The housing situation for disadvantaged minorities in the United States is changing, however, and rather rapidly at that. With expanded occupational and educational opportunities available to nonwhite families, there has been a significant rise in their incomes which places them more firmly in the housing market. The average yearly earnings for full-time workers, cited above, show that in 1960 Negro men earned only 67 per cent as much as white men. However, in 1939 Negro men earned on the average only 45 per cent as much as white men. Although the barrier of residential discrimination still exists, significant legislative and attitudinal changes are taking place. Also, through urban renewal programs slums have been demolished to some extent and new homes constructed in many of the cities of the country.

HOUSING THE AGED

The problem of providing housing for the aged has been intensified during the past few decades, partly because of a steady increase in the proportion of older persons, partly because many children avoid responsibility for the support of their parents. Since most older persons have limited means of support, much of this responsibility has of necessity been assumed by the larger society. How to provide satisfactory housing for aged persons who themselves do not have sufficient means is a problem for which society has formulated no very satisfactory solution. The problem is as acute in urbanized Europe as in America.

The traditional means of housing the indigent aged in the United States has been the "old folks' home" or the "county poor farm," except those cared for by their own families or by religious or other groups. Old-age benefits or pensions for the working population have commonly been insufficient for elderly citizens to be comfortably housed in their declining years.

The housing needs of older persons are varied. Some, physically and mentally vigorous, are able to care for themselves, even to work at a gainful occupation; others, incapacitated, need constant custodial or nursing care. Housing preferences of older persons may be equally varied. Surveys of housing interests of aged persons in the United States indicate a rather wide range of choice, but on two points there is substantial agreement:

they prefer to live independently of their children or relatives, and they are averse to living in institutions.[20] Some wish to live in apartments, hotels, or boarding houses, with recreational or other facilities near at hand; the majority, however, prefer separate cottages for at least a semi-independent existence.

ADJUSTMENTS TO HOUSING SITUATIONS

THE FAMILY CYCLE AND HOUSING

Housing needs are seldom constant throughout the various stages of the family cycle. In the early stages of the cycle, that is during the child-rearing period, family incomes are often low, expenses mount as the family expands, and living space becomes inadequate. This is notably true of families on the lower levels of the income structure. Here the increase in the number of children is commonly far greater than the increase in family incomes. Pressures for space becomes acute, but the income needed to provide that space may not be forthcoming. This situation is exacerbated in the United States by the trend toward early marriages of couples just entering the labor market who have limited earning capacity. Their housing needs are likely to increase more rapidly than their purchasing power.

As the family moves into later stages of the cycle the situation may change. Normally the incomes rise with increased age and experience of the married couples, but family living expenses and the need for space decline as the children reach maturity and leave home, creating an "empty nest" situation. Couples in the middle or upper ages may not only have more space than they need, but also have difficulty adjusting to a relatively empty house.

A study in Chicago, by Duncan and Hauser, indicated the importance of the family cycle in the housing situation in that city.[21] During the six-year period, 1950–56, the increase in the number of families in the later stages of the cycle was greater than in the early, expanding stages. Although home ownership generally increased during this period, the proportion of home owners was greater for the "older" families than for those in the expanding stage, though between 1950 and 1956 the *rate* of increase in home ownership was more rapid for the "younger" families. During the period of study there was generally improvement in the quality of housing for families in all stages of the cycle, although the younger families were not as adequately housed as the older families.

The Chicago study also revealed that the proportion of families residing in single-family residences was greater for those in the later stages of the

---

[20] Wilma Donahue (ed.), *Housing the Aging* (1954), ch. 3.
[21] Beverly Duncan and Philip M. Hauser, *Housing a Metropolis—Chicago* (1960), ch. 7.

cycle than for the younger ones. However, there was a tendency for the older families to lighten the burden of household duties in single-family residences by moving to apartments or other types of residence. The authors of the research summarize their findings as follows, with the caution that the generalizations apply only to Chicago:

> Given the selected characteristics available, it appears that home ownership, occupancy of single-family homes, occupancy of newly-built units, and occupancy of standard units become more frequent as the family expands, and then become slightly less frequent as the family contracts.[22]

Housing needs, then, are closely associated with the family cycle. For the young married couple they are one thing; when children arrive and grow from childhood to maturity the needs change; in the "contracting" stage, when older children begin to leave the family group, the needs vary; and in the "empty nest" stage of the cycle they are again quite different. But there are deviations from this "typical" cycle. Some families are incomplete, that is, childless; others are broken by marriage or death; many persons never marry at all. Hence there may be corresponding deviations in housing needs.

The prevailing cyclical pattern for the nuclear family does not necessarily apply, however, to the extended or joint family group so widespread in underdeveloped countries. Hence the housing needs do not vary in the same way. The nuclear family *as a group* has its rise, decline, and eventual disappearance, but the joint family usually has a continuous existence as new members replace those who die or leave. So long as a joint family group remains intact there are thus no cyclical variations, as in the nuclear family; hence the housing needs tend to remain fairly constant, although the relocation of the group, or its numerical expansion or contraction, may create special needs.

HOUSING AND RESIDENTIAL MOBILITY

There is a definite relationship between housing needs, family cycles, and residential mobility. As Rossi observes, "The changes in needs generated by the life cycle changes become translated into residential mobility when the family dwelling does not satisfy the new needs." [23] During the early stages of the cycle housing needs tend to change rather rapidly, and often become acute. Hence there is a corresponding tendency toward high residential mobility in this period.

A number of studies in American cities indicate that about three-fifths of the residential moves within communities primarily represent efforts to find more satisfactory housing.[24] The sources of dissatisfaction leading to

[22] *Ibid.*, p. 251.   [23] Peter H. Rossi, *Why Families Move* (1955), p. 179.
[24] Nelson N. Foote, *et al.*, *Housing Choices and Housing Constraints* (1960), ch. 6.

change of residence appear to be the following, in descending order of importance: (1) living space, either too little or, occasionally, too much; (2) undesirable neighborhood, its social composition or physical characteristics; (3) high costs of housing; and (4) such secondary causes as landlord trouble or unsuitable design of the building.[25] But not all dissatisfied persons actually move. Foote and his associates estimate that the number of families dissatisfied with their housing is twice the number that actually move.[26] Furthermore, many families voluntarily move for reasons not directly connected with their satisfaction or dissatisfaction.

The problem of adjustment to new housing situations is always involved in residential mobility, and is especially important when residential movement is involuntary, as is often the case when dwellings are in the path of industrial shifts or of urban renewal developments. Often these problems of adjustment are intensified when families are forced to move to quarters in which there is a shortage of space in terms of their housing needs.

In American cities, as in others, many families have been forced to abandon dwellings marked for demolition in urban renewal programs. This means "relocation," either in homes of their own selection, or in dwellings especially constructed for them. Such movements often shatter the sentimental attachments to the old residences, or necessitate a new set of personal and family behavior patterns and the abandonment of old ones. Quite a different "style of life" may be the result. Such changes may, and often do, generate emotional stresses and interpersonal tensions, especially when families resist relocation. Families whose style of life has been appropriate for the permissive social environment of a slum may find the formal regulations of public housing uncomfortably restrictive of behavior.

A study of the "human" aspects of relocation in a midwestern city revealed numerous points of friction and unadjustment of families which had been removed from detached slum residences to apartments in a public housing project.[27] Some objected to the housekeeping regulations laid down and enforced by the management; some felt that the rentals were too high or the rent collectors too high-handed; others resented the rules concerning entertainment of guests in homes. One person expressed considerable feeling about his dog, which he had been forced to leave behind when he moved. "I love my dog," he said, "and I would prefer to live in a slum shack and have my dog with me than to reside in a new apartment without it." For many there was a nostalgic yearning for the "good old days."

In the course of time most relocated families probably make a reasonable adjustment to the new situation, accepting, or at least observing, the norms of behavior that are imposed and the style of life necessitated by the changed environment. Little is known, however, about the lasting ef-

---

[25] *Ibid.*, p. 156. [26] *Ibid.*, p. 155.
[27] Report of a seminar in urbanism at the University of Missouri, June, 1962.

fects on the personalities and social relationships of those who have been relocated.

THREE HOUSING TYPES: FUNCTIONS AND SYMBOLS

Viewed functionally and symbolically, as well as physically, there are innumerable types of housing situations. To provide a concrete picture of the differences between them, which may be very great, a description of three housing situations in specific communities will be presented in this section.

CRESTWOOD HEIGHTS

Housing in its social and cultural aspects was included in a notable research conducted in Crestwood Heights, an upper middle class suburb of Toronto.[28] In this rather fashionable community there is on display a variety of artifacts having not only utilitarian and esthetic functions but also symbolic relevance for social status of the occupants.

Viewing the Crestwood house "as a stage," the authors observe that it provides the setting for many human dramas with the enactment of varied roles by members of the family and others. The protocol for the performance of these roles varies according to the situation and the actors, whether for the daily dramas enacted by the family, or special performances in the form of dinners, cocktail parties, or other occasions.

The Crestwood home, both its contents and occupants, is frequently on display, remindful of a department store window, "charmingly arranged, harmoniously matched in color. On more than one occasion an interviewer had the experience of waiting while his hostess whisked the plastic covering off the furniture," [29] indicating that the living-room and dining-room furnishings were primarily for impressing outsiders rather than daily use by the family. In many houses the actual "living" room was the small den or "rumpus" room for informal day-by-day usage. Since the furnishings in the "display" room were primarily for enhancement of status through keeping up appearances, the parents usually prohibited boisterous behavior by their own or neighbors' children. Such behavior was more likely to be tolerated in the "recreation" rooms. In some instances, however, the family living room existed in fact as well as in name, with observable evidence of its daily use.

Furnishings were both an indicator of economic position and of class-conditioned tastes. The families were sufficiently affluent to acquire all

---

[28] John R. Seeley, R. Alexander Sim, and E. W. Loosley, *Crestwood Heights* (1956).

[29] *Ibid.*, p. 51.

the modern mechanical appliances for comfortable and convenient living, but they were not sufficiently affluent to obtain the most expensive furnishings and *objets d'art* commonly found in homes of the rich. There were no original Van Goghs or Renoirs, only originals of lesser artists, or perhaps inexpensive reproductions of masterpieces. Many families were preoccupied with fashion in furnishings—whether their possessions were passé or in style; whether the color scheme was harmonious, or the objects appropriately arranged. Such matters had considerable prestige potential.

The Crestwood house, say the authors, is intended to provide and enforce the privacy so greatly cherished by the occupants, although mechanical devices—telephone, radio, television—are constantly invading that privacy. But the house as it is arranged, and as protocol specifies, is a means of separating the family from the outside world, except on special occasions, when it serves the opposite function. It also serves to separate the members from each other. Individuals in the household have separate sleeping and working quarters, and in these parts of the house their privacy is inviolate, not to be invaded.

WEST END BOSTON

The physical characteristics, social functions, and symbolism of housing in West End, a deteriorated district of Boston, as described by Gans, stood in rather sharp contrast to the situation in Crestwood Heights.[30] Occupied mainly by working-class families of Italian descent, the area in its external appearances had all the earmarks of a noisy, rat-infested, smelly, deteriorated slum of high population density. But appearances were deceptive; within the residential structures the apartments were clean and orderly, though subjected to continuous daily use by the families and their friends.

Aside from the physical contrasts with Crestwood Heights, the social and symbolic differences were also important. Although, as Gans says, individuals and families could achieve the privacy of anonymity—and some did—mostly they tended toward "total immersion in sociability." Among the majority of West End families, social life, warm and friendly, was centered mainly in the home or adjacent streets. "The kitchen was normally the main arena of social activity. The living room was used mainly to house the television set, and, when visitors came, to allow the men to separate themselves from the women and carry on their own conversation."[31] Almost every evening friends or kinsmen gathered in the homes for informal talkfests which would last well into the night. Seldom was there formal entertainment. Nor was there the kind of privacy which the Crestwooders reserved for themselves in their homes, either privacy from outsiders or from one's own family group. Since much of social life

[30] Herbert Gans, *The Urban Villagers* (1962).   [31] *Ibid.*, p. 20.

took place on the streets, in public view of everyone, life had something of the character of a "goldfish bowl."

Status symbolism of housing had a different meaning for the West Enders than for the Crestwooders. Their houses and furnishings were not on "display" to impress outsiders. Most of the families in the area lived in similar dwellings and were in no position to make invidious comparisons. Strangers and casual acquaintances were seldom entertained in the homes, this privilege being extended mainly to intimates. The status of any family depended more on such qualities as moral stability, friendliness, and congeniality as a host than upon the exhibition of artifacts for symbolic purposes. "Thus," says Gans, "West Enders, unlike the middle class, do not have to put on an impressive front for such people (outsiders), and there is no need to have 'an address' or a well-manicured yard in a carefully zoned neighborhood. Indeed, the people who had to satisfy such status needs through housing could not live in the West End, and had to move." [32]

MEXICO CITY

In his "studies in the culture of poverty," Oscar Lewis graphically describes the style of life of a number of impoverished slum families in Mexico City.[33] One of these, the Gomez family, occupied a single room in a large *vecindad*, or neighborhood, in this instance a one-story tenement housing over 700 persons in 157 one-room apartments, an average of over four persons per room. Within the tenement the patios were crowded during the daytime with people and animals: dogs, children, turkeys, chickens, and perhaps even pigs. But in spite of the physical surroundings and primitive living facilities, the occupants developed a strong sense of community, particularly the younger members who met in various situations and who often formed lasting friendships. Lewis provides a vivid description of the Gomez style of life within the small apartment:

Inside the dark, windowless room, crowded with furniture, the Gomez family slept huddled under thin covers on a cold January morning. The smells of unwashed feet, sweat, shoe leather, and fried food pervaded the room. Augustin Gomez and his wife Rosa slept on a narrow cot against the right wall; she at the head and he at the foot. Alberto, the eldest son, aged twenty, Ester, the daughter, aged fourteen, and Juanito, the youngest son, aged six, all slept in the big bed which jutted out from the left wall across half the small room. When Augustin and Rosa quarreled, he would leave the narrow cot and exchange places with little Juanito, so that sometimes Ester would awaken in the morning to find that she had been sleeping between her father and her older brother. Rosa was the only one who lamented the sleeping arrangements. . . . The crowding had been even worse when Hector, their second son, had been

[32] *Ibid.*, p. 21.　　　[33] Oscar Lewis, *Five Families* (1959).

at home. But Augustin had thrown him out of the house almost a year ago, and now Hector slept in a tiny room with an old couple in a poorer *vecindad* a few blocks away.

The kitchen, just inside the front door, formed a passageway to the bedroom. This area had not been roofed when the *vecindad* was built and each tenant had to provide his own roof. Augustin had solved the problem by attaching two sheets of corrugated tar paper to a stick laid across the center, forming a low peak. The front portion was left open to allow smoke from the stove to escape. But it also permitted rain to enter. . . . The short left wall of the kitchen was entirely taken up by a gray cement washtub and the toilet. The toilet enclosure, with its half-shutter swinging door, was barely large enough to contain the low, rust-stained stool. It was a flush toilet but the chain had been broken for more than a year and Rosa had not troubled to fix it because there was rarely water in the tank. A pail of water, kept under the washtub, was used to flush the stool a few times a day, and a pile of torn-up newspaper tucked behind the water pipe served as toilet paper. The space was crowded with a collection of rags, cans, brushes, boxes, and bottles piled into a corner. More articles of the same kind, as well as the garbage tin, were stored under the kitchen washtub. Recently, following the example of other tenants, Hector had hung a pink flowered nylon shower curtain to hide the toilet area.[34]

The contrasts between the styles of life, including housing, of families in the areas just described are indeed sharp. At numerous points the contrasts are apparent: in the privacy available; in the status symbolism of the houses; in the density of occupance; in the use made of the dwellings; in physical equipment and conditions. Between areas in any one of the cities in which the houses existed the contrasts are equally sharp. This is the nature of city life.

Substandard housing is often occupied by persons characterized by low incomes (or none), irregular employment, limited education, low-status occupations, high spatial mobility, unstable life, low levels of ambition, and deviant behavior. Such residents may also be subject to ostracism on racial, religious, or cultural grounds and therefore denied many of the advantages enjoyed by others in privileged positions. The dwellings they live in become a symbol of their disadvantaged status, which in itself may be generative of frustrations and anxieties. If, therefore, slum districts with substandard housing exhibit more than their proportionate share of aberrant behavior and personalities, the explanation would have to be in terms of the total situation, which would include such variables as those mentioned above.

But substandard housing is also occupied by persons whose behavior is quite as conventional and stable as that of the population as a whole— sometimes even more so. There are indeed blighted districts in cities that appear to have no more than their proportionate share of "problem" people. Such an area is the West End, in Boston, described earlier. From his study of the area, and residence in it, Gans observed that most of the

[34] *Ibid.*, pp. 64–65. Reprinted by permission of Basic Books, Publishers, New York.

residents were economically self-sufficient, reasonably well-adjusted, and conventional in behavior, although a number of social deviants had moved into the district, partly to take advantage of the low rents.[35] But the deviants were not created by the district.

THE "EFFECTS" OF SUBSTANDARD HOUSING

Thus far in this chapter considerable emphasis has been placed on certain "problem" aspects of housing, including shortages of dwellings, physical deterioration, and room congestion. These are the more obvious conditions. It is generally believed that deteriorated districts in cities produce more than their proportionate share of crime, delinquency, vice, family disorganization, mental and physical disorders, and so on. There is indeed an impressive volume of data which do indicate a relationship between substandard housing and various "pathologies." The conclusion is sometimes drawn, therefore, that substandard housing tends to produce "problem people." But there seems to be no substantial evidence that housing *per se* determines the problems of behavior and personality; it is only one of many interrelated factors or conditions—social, psychological, cultural, physical—which have to be taken into consideration. About all that can be said with finality is that substandard housing is often associated with behavioral and personality problems. The actual determinants are another matter.

Because housing is such an important aspect of the physical environment in its relation to health, such serious diseases as tuberculosis, infantile paralysis, rickets, typhus, and syphilis usually appear more frequently in areas of substandard housing than in other sections of a city. Tuberculosis, for example, is likely to occur with unusual frequency in crowded dwellings having poor ventilation and a limited amount of sunlight. Typhoid is more frequent where plumbing facilities do not permit the sanitary disposal of human excreta. Overcrowding may increase the likelihood of friction between individuals, and this may lead to emotional or behavioral problems.

GROSS COMPARISONS

In Newark, New Jersey, Rumney compared two population groups: one a low-income population, formerly slum residents, living in a public housing project; the other a low-income population residing in a deteriorated area of the city.[36] He found that the incidence of illness and accidents was

[35] Gans, *op. cit.,* pp. 313–15.
[36] Rumney, Jay, "The Social Costs of Slums," *Journal of Social Issues,* 7 (1951), 77–83.

lower among the public housing families than among the slum residents. The tuberculosis rate per 10,000 persons for example, was 29 for the public housing residents and 59 in certain areas of substandard dwellings. In reviewing other studies, Rumney found that in Pittsburgh the infant mortality rate in public housing projects was 42 compared with 71 for existing slum areas, while juvenile delinquency rates per 10,000 population were 383 and 570, respectively.[37] Crimes "against the person" in a large public housing project in St. Louis declined, in three years, from two and one-half times the rate for the city as a whole to 15 per cent below the citywide rate, although the occupants, all Negroes, were formerly residents of a slum district with high rates.[38]

The validity of the results of such studies may be open to question because gross comparisons of entire groups are sometimes made without allowing for differences between or within the groups. In the Newark study, for example, 69 per cent of the population in one of the housing projects was Negro, compared with 17 per cent Negro in the population of the control ward; in another of the comparisons, 55 per cent of the rehoused group was Negro, but only 6 per cent in the control ward. Certainly in such matters as health or behavior race is an important variable, and unless it is properly taken into account in the comparisons the results may be in doubt.

The baltimore study

Probably the most comprehensive and methodologically sophisticated study of this type was carried out in Baltimore over a three-year period between 1955 and 1958.[39] Comparisons were made between a "test" sample of 300 families (1,341 persons) living in a public housing project and a "control" sample of 300 families (1,349 persons) residing in an unrehabilitated section of the city. Both groups consisted of Negro families with low incomes. The families were matched by a number of relevant items, including size of dwelling unit, age of the female head of the household, age of the oldest child, presence of the husband, number of children, and so on. The hypotheses tested were concerned with (a) incidence of illness (morbidity), (b) family and neighborhood relations and psychological states of the adults, and (c) school performance of the children. Data were obtained from official records and interviews with the residents.

The findings of the research indicated divergent tendencies. In some respects the rehoused test group showed up more favorably than the control group; in other instances the reverse was true; and in a great many of the comparisons there were no statistically significant differences, though

[37] *Ibid.* [38] *St. Louis Post Dispatch,* March 12, 1963.
[39] Daniel M. Wilner, *et al., The Housing Environment and Family Life* (1962).

certain tendencies that supported the hypotheses of differences were observed.

Morbidity rates, as a whole, were lower in the test than in the control group. This was the case for persons under 35, and especially for children. The incidence of disabilities from communicable diseases of childhood was notably lower in the housing project than in the control group. And for adults 35–59, the incidence of illness, for males and females, was higher in the control than in the test group, as measured both by the number of illnesses and days of disability. Taking the two groups in their entirety, the percentage with *no* illnesses was about the same.

Judged by a number of criteria specified in the questionnaire, residents of the housing project were somewhat better adjusted than the control group, even though there were inconsistent trends. The rehoused families, more than the control group, experienced a marked increase in neighboring, especially in mutual assistance activities such as helping out in household tasks or in times of illness; and the test women, in contrast to those in the control group, made many new and close friendships with their new neighbors in public housing projects.

The test families reported fewer quarrels and arguments, and more mutually-shared activities in household tasks and in leisure pursuits, than was true of the controls. They also showed more pride in the neighborhood, reported more activities in improving the area, and expressed more satisfaction with their style of of life, and living conditions in general, in the neighborhood.

A larger proportion of the test families than of the controls indicated an improvement in their position in society. However, there was no change in their levels of aspiration that would distinguish them from the other group. Among the test women, there was confirmation of the hypothesis that they would manifest improved morale, have more favorable self-images, and experience reduced anxieties, as indicated by their responses on a number of psychological scales.

Among the school children there was no appreciable difference between the results of intelligence and achievement scores for the two groups, but in school promotions the children in the housing project made a better showing than the other group. The differences in promotions, however, may have been due in part to different policies of the various schools attended.

Viewing the over-all picture, if this is possible, one might hazard the generalization that the rehoused families had profited psychologically, socially, and physiologically in their movement from substandard to standard housing. A follow-up study, after the test families had lived in the project for a few more years, would provide more valuable data for further testing of the hypotheses. Some of the effects of changed environment might not be apparent for a considerable length of time.

HOUSING AND SOCIAL ORGANIZATION

LARGE-SCALE ORGANIZATION

In recent years, in almost every country, housing has become increasingly associated with big business and big government. In metropolitan areas especially, the trend is toward large-scale undertakings by mammoth organizations, although much of the planning and construction in small cities and towns is still done by small enterprises, or even by the owners themselves.

Numerous private corporations in the United States have financed or constructed various kinds of housing projects. Even public housing, financed in the main by government, is usually built by large construction firms, under contract. Mass produced suburbs, mainly for middle class families, are examples of large-scale developments. Among the largest are the two Levittowns, one on Long Island, the other in Pennsylvania. Built by the Levitt corporation, they are the products of mass production on an unprecedented scale. Park Forest, a commuting suburb near Chicago, was also mass-produced as a corporate enterprise. Most of the dwellings in these and similar suburbs are detached single-family residences.

Several insurance corporations have invested heavily in housing, mainly for families on the higher income levels. As an investment for its enormous assets the Metropolitan Life Insurance, for example, developed eight projects costing around 200 million dollars and accommodating more than 100,000 persons. The largest of these is Parkchester, in New York, which includes some 42,000 rooms; other major Metropolitan projects are Stuyvesant Town and Peter Cooper Village, both in New York.

HOUSING AND GOVERNMENT

By the middle of the twentieth century housing in most countries had come to involve questions of broad public policy. This followed the recognition that socially and economically disadvantaged families often cannot, on their own initiative, obtain housing that meets acceptable standards of health and comfort. It is for this reason particularly that governments on all levels have entered the housing field in one way or another. Most commonly this has been through governmental financing or construction of low-rent housing for low-income families, though other kinds of subsidy are often provided from which families on the middle-income levels may also be beneficiaries.

Although municipal governments in American cities have been forced to give some attention to housing problems, it was not until the 1930's

The new look in housing. The structures in the center foreground are Stuyvesant Town and Peter Cooper Village, apartment projects erected by the Metropolitan Life Insurance Company on a slum site. Such large-scale urban developments, under either private or public auspices, are characteristic of new urban housing. (Courtesy Metropolitan Life Insurance Company.)

that the federal government became actively involved in housing reform. The first major enterprise was an emergency program, undertaken in 1933 at the depth of the depression. Viewed primarily as a measure to ease the critical employment situation by providing work for the jobless, the Public Works Administration constructed some 22,000 homes for low-income urban families.

In 1937 the federal government charted a new course by enacting legislation for a permanent housing authority (bureau) empowered to make loans to municipal agencies for slum-clearance and low-rent housing projects. The United States Housing Authority, so created, functioned primarily as a financial agency, furnishing loans to local communities meeting certain specifications in their plans for housing reform. The initial authorization was for 800 million dollars to be made available for the construction of 200,000 dwelling units. The program was interrupted by World War II, during which time construction was mainly for war workers. But by the end of the war, in 1945, some 193,000 dwellings had been built, and these subsequently were to house low-income families.

At this time the country was faced with a critical housing shortage, partly because of the heavy migrations of families to cities during and immediately after the war. Almost every available dwelling was occupied, even those virtually unfit for human habitation. The situation was especially acute for low-income families, particularly minority peoples such as Negroes, many of whom were forced to double up and live under incredibly crowded conditions.

In the face of organized opposition by realtors and other groups, new housing legislation was passed, primarily for the benefit of disadvantaged families. The Housing Act of 1949, the most comprehensive housing legislation in the country's history, was essentially an extension, in principle, of the Housing Act of 1937, except that it was broader in scope, with provisions for rehabilitation of slums by both private and public enterprise.

This Act empowered local communities, through their housing and development "authorities" (committees), to acquire slum districts, demolish deteriorated buildings, and dispose of the area for one purpose or another. The area so acquired could be sold to private enterprise for residential, industrial, or other purposes; it could be turned over to the community for public developments such as parks or schools; or it could be used for low-rent public housing. Subsequently, numerous housing laws were enacted, mostly as modifications of the 1949 Act. The program involved both public and private enterprise. Planning, financing, and overall management were mainly a function of government; the actual demolition and construction were carried out by private companies. By 1963 some 700,000 public housing units for low-income families had been constructed and a vast acreage of slums had been prepared for redevelopment.

NONPROFIT HOUSING ORGANIZATIONS

An important organizational development in numerous countries, excepting the United States, is cooperative housing. Nonprofit associations or cooperative building societies have engaged in extensive building operations for middle- and low-income families. There are numerous types of cooperative associations, but they all involve the basic principle of individuals and families banding together voluntarily to meet their housing needs. Some of these are cooperative credit societies which provide financial assistance in housing to members; some are cooperative building societies which are concerned with the construction of dwellings and other structures for the members. Often these associations combine to form a larger national federation. One variation is cooperative housing developed under the auspices of labor unions on behalf of their own members. In the United States the Amalgamated Clothing Workers Union has a housing division concerned with the development of cooperative housing. Still another variation is cooperative housing sponsored by religious bodies such as the Catholic Church.

Cooperative housing has perhaps developed more extensively in Europe than in most regions of the world. By the 1950's, cooperative associations had produced about 35 per cent of all the postwar dwellings constructed in Denmark, 33 per cent in The Netherlands, 27 per cent in Sweden, and 24 per cent in Switzerland.[40] Similar developments have also taken place in Great Britian, Germany, Norway, and Austria. About a fourth of all housing construction in Israel is on a cooperative basis.

HOUSING ASSOCIATIONS

Public interest in, and concern about, housing problems has given rise to varied associations. In the United States, for example, there are such organizations as the National Association of Housing Officials, concerned mainly with public housing; the National Association of Home Builders, an organization of private contractors and builders; and the Better Housing League, made up mainly of citizens interested in housing reform. There are, in addition, various national associations of such professional or business groups as architects, city planners, and real estate dealers. Numerous periodicals are published by, and generally in the interest of, these organizations.

Nor have organizations concerned with housing been limited to national scenes. The midcentury has witnessed the rise of numerous international organizations which have been concerned, in one way or another, with housing, especially residential facilities for low-income families. Foremost are various organizations which constitute a part of the United Nations. These include the Economic and Social Council; the Economic Commission for Asia and the Far East (ECAFE) and its special divisions related to housing; the International Labor Organization; the World Health Organization; and the section on Housing and Town Planning in the UN Bureau of Social Affairs. Others are the International Federation of Housing and Town Planning and the Inter-American Housing Center. These organizations are variously concerned with such matters as research in housing, financial problems and policies, seminars and educational programs related to housing, and the relation of housing to government and to broader programs of planning and urban renewal.

HOUSING PROGRAMS IN OTHER COUNTRIES

Housing programs have been initiated in many countries. In some countries the programs are well developed, in others they represent only

[40] *Housing, Building, and Planning,* issue on "Housing Through Nonprofit Organizations," Department of Economic and Social Affairs, United Nations, No. 10 (1956), p. 75.

a beginning. Space will not permit of an extended treatment of housing developments elsewhere, but to provide a basis for comparisons we shall present a brief discussion of housing programs in a few selected regions of the world.

HOUSING IN BRITAIN

Both public and private enterprise play an important role in Britain's housing program. Immediately after World War I the Housing and Town Planning Act of 1919 made all municipalities responsible for providing houses for low-income families.[41] Thus there developed a working relationship between local agencies and the central government whereby the center set standards, approved plans, and provided grants, while the municipalities acquired land, designed and built houses, and served as landlord. Between the two wars about a million houses were built by public housing authorities, and about three times as many by private enterprise.

With the acute housing shortage occasioned by World War II the burden of providing homes for the masses fell mainly on the central government and municipal authorities. During the immediate postwar years at least 90 per cent of the new homes were constructed by municipal housing authorities supported financially by the national government. By the 1960's, after the acute housing shortage ended, private enterprise assumed a major role in planning and construction of dwellings. Nevertheless, about one-fifth of all families in Britain reside in rented dwellings built under government auspices.

Once the postwar housing crisis was passed, a comprehensive program was launched toward the objective of urban rehabilitation, including the eradication of all slums. This program involved construction of multiple-dwelling apartments on land cleared of slum dwellings, and the development of large housing projects or "estates" beyond the outer limits of the major cities. The London County Council, one of the numerous housing authorities, has planned and is carrying out the construction of some 200,000 homes in the London metropolitan area.

HOUSING IN NORTHWEST EUROPE

The small countries of northwest Europe are advanced in their programs to eliminate slums and provide suitable housing for families on all economic levels. Many years ago the governments of these countries took official recognition of the fact that continued urban growth would create housing problems. Numbers of cities in Sweden, Holland, Denmark, and elsewhere acquired title to land lying on the outskirts of municipalities,

[41] Gordon Stephenson and H. R. Parker, "Urban Land Policies: United Kingdom," *Housing and Town and Country Planning*, Bulletin 7 (1953).

Vallingby, a planned suburb in Stockholm, Sweden, showing apartment houses of different kinds surrounding a restaurant and shopping center. Vallingby is 30 minutes by subway from the center of Stockholm. (Courtesy Swedish National Travel Office.)

thereby eliminating speculative inflation of land values as a factor in housing costs.[42] The municipality of Stockholm, for example, acquired some 20,000 acres and made them available for suburban housing developments, many for working-class families. In all these cities municipal housing authorities cleared slums, erected low-cost buildings, financed private construction, and exercised general control over housing operations. Each country has had a more or less comprehensive program involving housing construction under both public and private auspices.

It is probably correct to say that the Scandinavian countries have achieved standards of housing for the urban masses not attained by any other country in the world, unless it is Holland or Switzerland. In these countries the most deteriorated slums have been eliminated; and although there are still blighted and congested areas in the cities, the population in general, including low-income families, is comfortably housed.

HOUSING IN LATIN AMERICA

Most of the Latin American countries have undertaken programs of housing reform, but in view of the magnitude of the problem their accom-

[42] U. R. Nielsen, "Urban Land Policies: Denmark," *Housing and Town and Country Planning*, Bulletin 7 (1953), p. 64.

plishments have not been impressive except in a few cities. Public authorities have assumed the major responsibilities through slum clearance, construction of new homes for low-income families, and the provision of credit for home construction. In Bogota, Lima, Mexico City, Rio de Janeiro, and Santiago extensive slum clearance operations have demolished conspicuous shacktowns, whose occupants have been moved to temporary or permanent quarters built especially for them. Housing banks established in some of the countries provide credit for private organizations or individuals. In Caracas, a large apartment housing a thousand families was constructed on the site of a former slum.

On the whole, little more than a beginning has been made in a mass housing program. With at least 10 million slum dwellings in the cities, and with the number increasing yearly, it is clear that present achievements are far short of the needs. Even the distant future will probably not see all the slums demolished and the population rehoused.

SELECTED BIBLIOGRAPHY

BOOKS

Duncan, Beverly, and Philip M. Hauser, *Housing a Metropolis—Chicago.* Glencoe, Ill.: The Free Press, New York, 1960.

Fisher, Robert M., *Twenty Years of Public Housing.* New York: Harper, 1959.

Foote, Nelson N., *et al., Housing Choices and Housing Constraints.* New York: McGraw-Hill, 1960.

Gans, Herbert J., *The Urban Villagers.* New York: The Free Press of Glencoe, 1962.

Jacobs, Jane, *The Death and Life of Great American Cities.* New York: Random House, 1961.

Keats, John, *The Crack in the Picture Window.* New York: Ballantine Books, 1957.

McEntire, Davis, *Residence and Race.* Berkeley: University of California Press, 1960.

Merton, Robert K., "The Social Psychology of Housing," in Wayne Dennis (ed.), *Current Trends in Social Psychology.* Pittsburgh: University of Pittsburgh Press, 1948.

Rapkin, Chester, and William G. Grigsby, *Residential Renewal in the Urban Core.* Philadelphia: University of Pennsylvania Press, 1960.

Wilner, Daniel M., *et al., The Housing Environment and Family Life.* Baltimore: John Hopkins Press, 1962.

ARTICLES

Feldman, A. S., and C. Tilly, "Interaction of Social and Physical Space," *American Sociological Review,* 25 (December, 1960), 877–84.

Gutkind, P. C. W., "Congestion and Overcrowding: An African Urban Problem," *Human Organization,* 19 (Fall, 1960), 129–31.

Horne, F. S., "Interracial Housing in the United States," *Phylon,* 19 (April, 1958), 13–20.

Klutznick, Philip M., "The Provision of Shelter," *The Annals,* 314 (November, 1957), 39–45.

Marris, Peter, "Slum Clearance and Family Life in Lagos," *Human Organization,* 19 (Fall, 1960), 123–28.

McKee, James B., "Changing Patterns of Race and Housing," *Social Forces,* 41 (March, 1963), 253–60.

Mogey, John M., "Changes in Family Life Experienced by English Workers Moving from Slums to Housing Estates," *Marriage and Family Living,* 17 (May, 1955), 123–28.

Riemer, Svend, "Historical Outline of Housing," *Sociology and Social Research,* 44 (July, 1960), 394–401.

Tilly, C., "Occupational Rank and Grade of Residence in a Metropolis," *American Journal of Sociology,* 67 (November, 1961), 323–30.

Planning

TWENTY-FIVE

Planning is a means of directing social change and social relationships toward the ultimate objective of orderly and harmonious community processes. There are many forms and levels of planning, and many specific planning techniques. Some planning is done by agencies of government, some by citizens' groups having no official status. Some planning is segmental, concerned with a narrow phase of community life, some is comprehensive and communitywide in its scope. Planning is sometimes corrective and rehabilitative, sometimes preventive, sometimes concerned with the construction of entirely new community structures. There is planning for land use and planning for the use of a community's human and institutional resources. Planning may be either short-range or long-range, public or private.

The purpose of this chapter is to provide an overview of certain forms of planned social change in urban communities. In no sense is it intended as a comprehensive treatment of the subject, about which there is a vast literature, much of it specialized, technical, and even philosophical. But since social change is of central importance to urban sociologists and other social scientists, the systematic direction of social change in the city is of concern to them, even though they are not specialists in planning.

PLANNING IN HISTORICAL PERSPECTIVE

In a very real sense all cities have been planned, if not in their entirety at least in their various parts. Unlike Topsy, cities did not "just grow." Those who built the world's cties proceeded according to plans, even though the plans may have been individualized, segmental, and uncoordinated. It is perhaps because of this piecemeal character of much

574

planning without central direction that the growth and development of many cities appear haphazard, a dense jungle of people and structures.

The systematic planning of cities is by no means a twentieth-century phenomenon. History furnishes many examples of planning and community reconstruction in various forms. Early Egyptian and Mesopotamian cities were laid out in rectangular design. In modern times, the *Ringstrasse* of Vienna represents an attempt at reconstruction to permit of orderly city growth and movement of people. The famous boulevard and park system of Paris was developed by bold planning and reconstruction in the nineteenth century. Philadelphia's checkerboard street system was planned in 1682. Washington was designed in 1791 by the famous French architect and planner, L'Enfant. It is the best-known city plan in America.

The city planning movement, if such it can be called, had its beginnings in the latter part of the nineteenth century. As early as 1874 Sweden enacted a comprehensive city planning law, probably the first of its type. City planning exhibits at the Chicago World's Fair in 1893 helped to popularize the idea in the United States. The first city planning conference in this country was held in Washington in 1909. Throughout the present century cities have become increasingly concerned with ways and means of planning toward the objective of making cities more suitable places in which to live.

THE ORGANIZATION OF PLANNING

In the twentieth century the planning of cities has become "big business," conducted under both private and public auspices. The multiplicity of organizations concerned with community planning and development is a feature of modern urban society, at least of the democratic societies. In authoritarian countries most of the planning seems to be a virtual monopoly of government.

Most cities have official or semi-official planning commissions, often composed of lay citizens who possess no expertise in such matters as planning. In the United States there are some 2,500 such bodies. In larger cities the commission is commonly a department of municipal government with a technical staff that carries on a continuing program of research and planning. There are also private companies that provide, for a fee, specialized planning services to municipalities.

In the United States numerous multipurpose organizations include social planning as one of their functions. The National Urban League, concerned primarily with problems of Negroes, is an example; and similarly, in the case of councils of social agencies, which coordinate the work of various organizations in the general field of social welfare. The

The old and the new in planning. The upper picture shows the pattern of streets and buildings around the Arch of Triumph in Paris. This plan was completed in the nineteenth century. Below is a model of Harlow, one of Britain's "new towns" near London. These towns are designed to attract industry and industrial workers from the congested sections of the nearby metropolis. (Courtesy French Government Tourist Office and British Information Services.)

ubiquitous chambers of commerce are concerned with planning in one form or another, mainly from the point of view of local businessmen.

In addition there are many citizens' unofficial planning groups that function in such areas as health, housing, recreation, education, welfare, and so on. The Hyde-Park Community Conference on the south side of Chicago, for example, is an organization of local citizens interested in civic improvement, and committed to a program of social action to bring about needed changes.[1] Another such organization is the Perth-Royce Community Council, which serves a district of Toronto and which is concerned primarily with such matters as community recreation.[2]

The proliferation of organizations concerned with planning has as its counterpart the emergence of such specialized occupations as the professional city planner or the expert real estate appraiser. The establishment of university curricula in city and regional planning for the training of experts is evidence of a trend toward the rationalization of the planning process and the widespread recognition of its importance.

Planning in urban communities has also become an important function of government, on all levels, though the functions may vary from country to country. In general, there has been a trend toward centralization of government planning functions, though in the United States, at least, these functions have also expanded on the state and local levels. Numerous federal agencies such as the Housing and Home Finance Agency and the Department of Health, Education, and Welfare have been particularly active in planning having direct relevance to cities. Much of the directing and financing of programs in urban renewal and public housing has been carried on under the auspices of federal agencies.

FORMS OF PLANNING

ELEMENTS OF A PLAN

A comprehensive plan for a city or metropolitan area includes many elements. A major concern is the circulation of people and commodities. Hence a plan must give consideration to such aspects of transportation as street systems, airports, bus and railway routes and terminals, waterways and docks, parking facilities, and the control and regulation of traffic.

Another major concern is with orderly land use, which includes (1) a system of zoning to segregate business, industrial, and residential uses of land and (2) the control of design, placement, and construction of public and private buildings.

A third area of interest to planners is the cultural, educational, and

[1] Peter H. Rossi and Robert A. Dentler, *The Politics of Urban Renewal* (1961), ch. 5.
[2] Arthur Hillman, *Community Organization and Planning* (1950), pp. 169–71.

social life of the community. Hence a plan usually includes provisions for civic or community centers, public libraries, schools, and parks and playgrounds.

A fourth concern is with the health and physical needs of the community, including amenities that may be available to the modern city. Included here are plans dealing with civil defense, the disposal of waste products, hospitals, smoke abatement programs, and provisions for such utilities as gas, water, and electricity.

Fifth, a comprehensive plan includes provisions for urban rehabilitation, such as slum clearance, preventive measures against blight, and both public and private housing.

Finally, provision for local neighborhood facilities is commonly a feature of comprehensive plans, particularly those involving large-scale housing projects or new communities.

NEIGHBORHOOD PLANNING

The place of the neighborhood in community planning has been widely discussed but with little agreement, except that neighborliness, like all virtues, should be encouraged. Precisely how to integrate neighborhood and community plans is a matter on which authorities and others sometimes disagree. Neighborhoods in most built-up areas in American cities have not been systematically planned at all; even the concept of neighborhood planning seems to have emerged only after large-scale planning of sizable areas or entire communities became a reality.

Most of the large housing projects in American and European cities have included plans for local neighborhood services and participation. The new housing projects in England have given special attention to neighborhood facilities, including day nurseries for children, health centers, infant welfare clinics, playgrounds for children, branch libraries, swimming pools, communal laundries, and social centers for various group activities.[3] A notable application of neighborhood planning is in Stevenage, one of the new towns recently developed in Britain.[4] Six neighborhoods were planned for the town, each with provisions for a variety of facilities and activities. It was the idea of the planners that functional neighborhoods could integrate the activities of individuals and families into an organic whole.

Planning operations may, however, have the effect of disrupting or destroying rather than revitalizing neighborhood life. If these operations involve wholesale demolition of residential structures, almost invariably

[3] Charles Madge, "Survey of Community Facilities in the United Kingdom," *Housing and Town and Country Planning*, Bulletin 5 (1951), pp. 31–41.

[4] Harold Orlans, *Stevenage: A Sociological Study of a New Town* (1952), pp. 97–101.

the existing system of neighborhood relationships is seriously disrupted or even terminated since the neighbors may be separated when they are moved into new locations. According to Gans, this is what happened in Boston's West End when that blighted area was demolished to make way for an urban renewal program.[5] Marris observed the same thing in Lagos, Nigeria, when a rehousing program disrupted the pattern of neighborhood life in that city.[6] Progress by bulldozer thus may have the effect of pulverizing the intricate web of human relationships as well as the physical setting in which these relationships exist. For many, in the path of the bulldozer, this may be a traumatic experience.

ZONING

That aspect of planning in which community control is exercised over the use of private and public land is called zoning. For many cities in the United States zoning is the only form of planning, and even in these cities zoning regulations may be drawn up and enforced in a casual manner. Zoning regulations usually carry legal sanctions and are enforceable through the police power of a community.

Zoning ordinances represent the legal recognition that the community as a whole has a right to protect land against encroachments that would depreciate property values or be inimical to the health, morals, safety, or esthetic standards of the residents. They are a form of public control designed to minimize the social and economic waste that would accrue from unregulated competition for space.

Cities are zoned according to the functions assigned to various areas: districts devoted to heavy manufacturing, others to light manufacturing; commercial districts, either retail or wholesale, or districts available for offices; residential districts characterized by specific types or sizes of residences, including those having detached houses and others in which multifamily structures are permitted.

Zoning in a modern city is indispensable if an orderly change is to be achieved and if the wastefulness of unregulated competition is to be minimized. It was not until the latter part of the nineteenth century that certain European cities inaugurated such regulatory measures, while in the United States the first comprehensive law was inaugurated as late as 1916. The legacy of waste and inefficiency in the modern metropolis of today may be traced in part to the absence of effective regulations during the early periods of urban expansion in this country and Europe. Even to this date many cities in the underdeveloped regions have no effective zoning regulations, or if such are in existence they are freely ignored. Under these conditions land use is not specialized; cheek by jowl, one

---

[5] Herbert Gans, *The Urban Villagers* (1962).
[6] Peter Marris, *Family and Social Change in an African City* (1961).

may find residential, industrial, and commercial structures on the same site, or mansions located in the midst of mud huts.

PLANNING AND TRANSPORTATION

The modern city is geared to the movement of peoples and materials. This is pre-eminently true of cities in industrialized societies, somewhat less true of cities in preindustrial countries. But the trend everywhere is toward mechanization of transportation and the movement of increasing numbers of people and goods by machines, which are rapidly replacing "beasts of burden" and pedestrians as carriers.

In American cities people have turned increasingly to the passenger automobile and transport truck with the result that traffic congestion has become a major problem taxing the ingenuity of planners and administrators. The social and economic costs due to "friction of movement" are very high indeed. In European cities the traffic problem is less serious than in the United States or Canada, but even there the number of automobiles in use is increasing rapidly, often in cities whose streets were laid out centuries ago. Such traffic problems scarcely exist in most cities of the underdeveloped areas since there are comparatively few private automobiles or trucks.

The increased use of cars and trucks in the United States has been accompanied by a decline in the use of public transportation facilities, particularly buses, street cars, and subway trains. Three or four decades ago most city people rode public vehicles in their day-by-day movements in the city; today only about 16 per cent of urban workers use public transit facilities.[7] Between 1950 and 1958, use of public transit facilities fell from 17.2 billion to 9.7 billion rides per year, a decrease of 43 per cent.[8] Generally speaking, the larger the city the greater is the reliance on public facilities—Los Angeles being an apparent exception. The 1960 census reports indicate that, among the Standard Metropolitan Statistical Areas, in small SMSA's such as Eugene, Oregon, or Bay City, Michigan, the percentage of workers using public facilities was less than 2, whereas for Boston, New Orleans, Chicago, Philadelphia, Jersey City, and Newark the percentage ranged from 25 to 44. The New York SMSA was the only metropolitan region in which more than half (55 per cent) of the workers used public transportation in the journey to work.[9]

Public transportation has continued to play an important role in the movements of people in most cities of the world. In most of these cities

[7] *U. S. Census of Population: 1960. General Social and Economic Characteristics, United States Summary.* Final Report PC(1)-1C (1961), Table 94.
[8] *Guiding Metropolitan Growth,* Report of Committee for Economic Development (1960), p. 19.
[9] *U. S. Census of Population: 1960. Place of Work and Means of Transportation to Work, 1960.* Supplementary Report PC(S1)–41 (January 30, 1963).

Planned downtown shopping centers. Above: Automobiles are not permitted in the shopping center included in Rotterdam's rebuilt downtown area. Below: The mall of the Midtown Plaza in Rochester, New York. The Plaza, a business-shopping complex in the downtown area, covers 12 acres under one roof and has sublevel parking for 2,000 cars. (Courtesy Netherlands Information Service and Midtown Plaza, Rochester.)

public vehicles are heavily burdened. In many great cities surface facilities have been inadequate to transport the vast number of people "on the move." To relieve these pressures subway systems have been constructed, or are underway, in New York, London, Paris, Berlin, Philadelphia, Stockholm, Chicago, Madrid, Boston, Moscow, Budapest, and Tokyo, among others.

THE MASTER PLAN

One of the major features of city or metropolitan planning is a master plan, a comprehensive set of specifications and guidelines for the future community. Because no man can see with true prophetic vision all the events and changes that lie ahead, any comprehensive plan must of necessity have a tentative and dynamic character, subject to continuing revision in the light of additional data and the unfolding of community events.

The master plan for a community is a kind of blueprint, a prospectus for the future. "The elements of a master plan should be thought of as (a) a general pattern of land use and population distribution, (b) major channels of movement, and (c) systems of physical facilities." [10] Some of the features of a master plan can be presented visually on a map, but many essential elements such as policies, objectives, and evaluations of local situations can hardly be given such visual treatment. Nor can many of the plans of specific organizations in such areas as health or recreation be included in the master design; such plans are, in a sense, ancillary to the central prospectus.

The scope of a master plan depends in major part on the magnitude of the community and on the geographical and political boundaries within which the planners must function. Some master plans are concerned solely with the area within a particular municipality—city plans; others are developed within a much broader context to include all communities clustered around a central metropolis—metropolitan or regional plans. Because of the interdependency of communities within a metropolitan region, there has been a marked trend in recent years to plan for the region as a whole as well as for its constituent parts.

URBAN RENEWAL

Most of the world's cities bear witness to far-reaching changes that have disrupted community and institutional functions, hastened physical deterioration of many districts, and created living and working conditions

[10] Hugh R. Pomeroy, "The Planning Process and Public Participation," in Gerald Breeze and Dorothy E. Whiteman (eds.), *An Approach to Urban Planning* (1953), p. 18.

below standards generally considered favorable to social and physical well-being. A growing awareness of the problems created by these changes and of the urgent need to alleviate the conditions created by them has led to the formulation of many plans and programs for rehabilitation of the cities. Efforts at urban rehabilitation are by no means new, but it is perhaps only in the middle of the twentieth century that they have been undertaken on a large scale in many countries.

RENEWAL IN THE UNITED STATES

Urban renewal in American cities may be said to have its beginning in the slum clearance and public housing programs of the 1930's. Initially, the programs were designed primarily as economic pump-priming undertakings and to provide modern housing for underprivileged slum dwellers. After World War II a series of comprehensive legislative enactments specified a broad program of rehabilitation which included major slum clearance undertakings in cities willing to cooperate with the federal government. The legislative program provided for the purchase, by local authorities, of slum districts, the demolition of deteriorated structures, and further preparation of the area for different land use. Such districts could then be used for a variety of purposes: as sites for public housing projects; as locations for community parks, playgrounds, or public buildings; or as places for industrial development or the construction of private residences.

By the 1960's, most of the major American cities, and many smaller ones as well, had demolished large acreages of slum structures and had prepared the areas for various uses. In the three boroughs of New York City—Brooklyn, Manhattan, and the Bronx—about two square miles, or about 1.4 per cent of the total area, have been earmarked for urban renewal.[11] A slum district of over 400 acres in St. Louis was demolished in preparation for redevelopment.

In Pittsburgh, one of the cities undertaking a major renewal program, the central section of the city had shown clear evidence of decay. The so-called Golden Triangle had become drab and gray from decades of exposure to grimy smoke. A street plan designed over a century ago was inadequate for modern traffic. Surrounding the business district was a residential section that had become a sooty slum. The Monongahela and Allegheny rivers which joined at the point of the Triangle had become open sewers and a serious threat because of floods. Pittsburgh had the reputation of being the most smoke-ridden city in America.

To cope with this situation, an Urban Redevelopment Authority, supported by municipal, state, federal, and private funds, planned and

[11] Edgar M. Hoover, and Raymond Vernon, *Anatomy of a Metropolis* (1959), p. 204.

The Golden Triangle is refurbished. Pittsburgh's extensive rehabilitation of the central business district has altered the external appearance of the city. Above: 1947, before the clean-up and smoke abatement program was undertaken. Below: The Triangle as it appeared in the 1960's. (Courtesy Pittsburgh Chamber of Commerce.)

carried out a major rehabilitation program in the 400-acre district constituting the Triangle. Parking facilities were provided. Thoroughfares were redesigned and built to carry traffic around the Triangle. Slum and blighted buildings were demolished to make way for new office buildings. A smoke-abatement program was put into operation. On a tributary of the Allegheny a large dam was constructed to hold back flood waters. By the 1950's the entire downtown district had taken on a "new look."

URBAN RENEWAL ABROAD

Urban renewal projects are varied and numerous. In France, a new commercial section of the Greater Paris complex has been developed on a 150-acre blighted site, about 10 miles from the center of the city.[12] A new office center is rising in Rome on the grounds of an exposition planned for 1942, and in Madrid a new center of ministries has been located on a site previously occupied by small houses and a race track, about five miles from downtown. Milan has developed a new business center on a site damaged by war-time bombing. A bombed area in London has been developed for multipurpose uses—apartments, offices, shops—and planned in such a way as to separate pedestrian from vehicular traffic. Many if not all cities have been forced to construct new transportation routes, as the mass use of automobiles becomes more widespread.

PLANNING AND COMMUNITY SERVICES

The excessive demands made on existing institutions in the broad sphere of health, education, and welfare have necessitated some rational form of direction and planning if they are to function as needed. To some degree these demands rise from the flood-tide of population moving into the cities, and the shifting of population within metropolitan areas. There is an urgency for more and better schools, health facilities, and agencies to facilitate the adjustment of individuals and groups and the integration of diverse peoples into the social fabric of the community. In a few instances rather comprehensive programs of "community development" have been instituted, but the results, if any, are not yet certain.

Many of the problems are not new, but they have become increasingly acute as a result of the massive population shifts in recent years. Traditional institutions have often been unable to deal effectively with these problems. The influx of migrants of diverse racial, cultural, and economic

[12] Leo Grebler, "Urban Renewal in European Countries," *Journal of the American Institute of Planners,* 28 (November, 1962), 229–38.

backgrounds has intensified the problems of interracial and intercultural relationships, thus necessitating new forms of organization, or a revision of the functions of existing organizations, to meet the needs. Official and nonofficial agencies, such as interracial councils or bureaus of human relations, have been included as part of the community plans in many American cities.

RECREATION

There has been a growing acceptance of community responsibility in providing and regulating recreational facilities. Provisions for recreation often become incorporated into community planning programs. Some are features of master plans, others are provided by various organizations, public and private, within the community; still others are provided by state or national governments.

Many cities maintain official departments of recreation which are responsible for a wide range of leisure-time activities within the locality. Most of the large metropolitan communities have municipal park boards. And every American city, large and small, undertakes to regulate recreational facilities, public or private, in the interests of the community as a whole and the people who live in it.

The development of public parks and playgrounds has become an important aspect of community planning. Probably all the great cities of the world, and countless smaller ones, maintain a system of parks for free public use. The adequacy or inadequacy of the park acreages in particular cities reflects the planning undertaken in earlier days and the kinds of community leadership which existed. The extensive park system of Kansas City was established more than a half-century ago when the "city beautiful" movement was a source of inspiration of civic leaders and planners. Similarly, the large parks of Bangalore, India, were designed and laid out by the British in the nineteenth century.

With recognition by city planners and other leaders that total acreage in park land, or the existence of large parks, is no reliable criterion of the functional value of such areas, increasing emphasis has been placed on small parks and playgrounds that are strategically located for maximum use. Although not adding greatly to the park acreage of a city, neighborhood parks serve a useful purpose, especially for low-income families with small children. Urban renewal programs, as well as most programs for the planning of new cities, have usually included small parks and playgrounds as a part of the larger plan. Generally, the public housing projects in American and European cities have made provisions for such recreational areas.

But planning for recreation has gone far beyond provisions for parks and playgrounds. Aside from the recreational facilities provided by private organizations, community facilities for a wide range of activities have commonly been maintained for such activities as dramatics, musical programs, folk dances, athletics, handicraft work, and so on. The long summer vacations in American communities have created recreational needs for children and youth that can only be met by some kind of community planning. Community interest in planning and maintaining museums, art galleries, public libraries, zoos, and community social centers is indicative of the increasing importance of leisure in modern urban society.

PLANNING THE METROPOLITAN REGION

The growth of great multinucleated communities consisting of a major center and a cluster of satellites has created problems of regulation that can be dealt with only on a fairly large scale. These problems transcend political boundaries and cannot be met successfully by any single division of the larger community. There is, for example, need for an articulated system of transportation which cannot easily be achieved when various communities in the metropolitan complex act independently and without reference to the needs of the larger area or of neighboring municipalities. Since disease germs are not politically conscious and do not confine their activities to any particular district, the problem of safeguarding public health can be met successfully only on a metropolitan scale. One community may dump garbage or sewage into nearby streams, jeopardizing health over a wide area. Criminals, like disease germs, do not always confine their predatory activities to a single community; after committing an offense in one city they may escape to another to avoid arrest. Often a metropolitan district is a veritable maze of tax-levying, tax-collecting, and law-enforcing agencies.

Decentralization of population and industry and the rapid growth of suburban communities have necessitated planning within a larger metropolitan framework. But such planning is not easy to achieve because of conflicting interests of communities and the reluctance of some localities to subordinate their interests to the larger municipality. One fairly successful method has been the establishment of authorities to handle special problems on a metropolitan rather than a narrow community basis. Still another method has been through multilateral and bilateral agreements between different governing units within a metropolitan area.

THE NEW YORK METROPOLITAN REGION

In the late 1920's a regional plan of the New York area was drawn up and put into operation.[13] This plan applied to an area of some 5,500

[13] *Regional Survey of New York and Its Environs* (1927–31).

square miles lying in the states of New York, New Jersey, and Connecticut. It was addressed especially to such matters as trunk line railroads, suburban transit lines, waterway projects, major regional highways, parkways and boulevards, industrial sites, extensions of residential areas, public parks, and airports. The agency responsible for metropolitan planning is the Regional Plan Association, a nonprofit organization devoted to research on metropolitan problems, planning for orderly development of the region, and coordination of plans by municipal and country agencies. The Association is not an official government agency but is privately financed.

There are various other regional authorities and commissions in the New York area. These include the Triboro Bridge and Tunnel Authority which builds vehicular facilities; the Port of New York Authority which is concerned with the improvement of transportation within a designated area; the Tri-State Sanitation Commission concerned with waterway pollution; and an agency which deals with the water supply in four states. One of the functions of the Regional Plan Association is to assist in coordinating the work of specialized agencies which themselves are metropolitan in scope.

Some three decades after the initial survey of New York and its environs was made, another study was undertaken, also under the auspices of the Regional Plan Association and known as the New York Metropolitan Region Study.[14] This survey took into account the great changes that occurred after the first study, and of the problems created by these changes. The second study, more than the first survey, emphasized the economic and social features of the area, rather than its physical aspects. Both studies focused on the entire region, which includes 22 counties centering on Manhattan. Another recent survey, by Gottmann, deals with the vast urbanized region extending from New England to Washington, D. C., and including several hundred towns and cities.[15]

OTHER METROPOLITAN REGIONAL PLANS

The extensive demolition and redevelopment program carried out in Paris in the nineteenth century, while making that metropolis one of the most attractive cities in the world, did not allow for the rapid expansion of the city in recent decades. In 1934–35 a master regional plan was drawn for metropolitan Paris and is environs, which, among other things, provided for transportation routes and a permanent greenbelt around

[14] See Raymond Vernon, *Anatomy of a Metropolis* (1960), the generalized summary of the study. The complete series consists of nine specialized volumes, each dealing with particular aspects of the region. The initial survey also consisted of nine special reports, with a generalized summary, *Mastering a Metropolis*, by R. L. Duffus.

[15] Jean Gottmann, *Megalopolis* (1962). Published under the auspices of the Twentieth Century Fund. See Chapter 4, pp. 74–75, for further description of the study.

the city. All communities in the region are required to submit plans conforming to the master plan of the metropolitan area.[16]

About a fourth of the population of The Netherlands is concentrated in a metropolitanized region which includes Amsterdam, Rotterdam, The Hague, Leiden, and many smaller places in the western section. This region in its entirety is known as the *Rundstad,* or "rim city." Although each of the cities has its own plan, a regional plan for the area, part of a national plan, has been developed to provide an orderly expansion of the communities within the region. One of the features of the plan is the provision for permanent greenbelts between the cities.

The Greater London Plan covers an area of some 2,600 miles and extends to a distance of about 30 miles from the downtown area. The plan calls for the decentralization of about a million persons, thus relieving congestion within the densely settled sections. It also provides for decentralization of industry, the building of several new towns, electrification of the railway system, redesigning and improvement of highways, development of outlying parks, playing fields, and parkways, rehabilitation of congested areas, and the construction of peripheral shopping and amusement centers. Several organizations are responsible for carrying out the plans, among the most important being the London County Council. The Council has numerous functions, including housing and planning. Some of the major housing projects in the London area are planned, developed, and managed by the Council.[17]

METROPOLITAN PLANNING AND GOVERNMENT

Any planning program of a public character must be integrated with the structure of municipal government. In the case of regional or metropolitan planning this is difficult because of the proliferation of separate governmental bodies within the area. Many years ago Merriam called attention to the existence of some 1,600 governmental units in the metropolitan area of Chicago.[18] More recently, Wood found 1,467 distinct political units in the New York Metropolitan Region, each having power to raise and spend public monies.[19]

Various arrangements or proposals have been made in different cities to provide a framework through which metropolitan planning can be carried out. Sometimes this is complicated by state boundary lines. One such arrangement is a bistate agency which can be empowered by state

[16] Brian Chapman, "Paris," in William A. Robson (ed.), *Great Cities of the World* (1955), pp. 481–85.

[17] William A. Robson, "London," in *Robson, op. cit.,* pp. 272–76, 292–94.

[18] Charles E. Merriam, *et al., The Government of the Metropolitan Region of Chicago* (1933).

[19] Robert C. Wood, *1,400 Governments* (1961). This is a part of the New York Metropolitan Region Study discussed earlier.

legislatures to function for a metropolitan area divided by state boundaries. Often such agencies are little more than paper organizations because they may have only advisory functions or may have no clear role in the regular channels of government.

Another arrangement is the consolidation of city and county governments. In Boston, New York, Philadelphia, and New Orleans consolidations were worked out in the nineteenth century, but there is not much evidence that they have been successful, except possibly in the case of Philadelphia, which plan was completed in 1952, a century after it was initiated. Two recent developments are of note: the Miami, Florida, experiment in metropolitan government,[20] and the city-county merger of Nashville and surrounding Davidson County.[21]

Certain other compromise arrangements have been undertaken by various American cities for dealing with problems that are metropolitan in scope. Atlanta, for example, in 1951 annexed 82 square miles of fringe territory having a population of about 100,000. Other cities that have greatly increased their area by annexation since World War II are Dallas, Milwaukee, Fort Worth, and Kansas City. Another common arrangement is a city-county functional plan whereby a city and county, or a central city and specific suburbs, share certain facilities. Dallas, for example, has a city-county hospital system. Los Angeles County has contractual relations with various cities in the county to provide certain services pertaining to health, recreation, and fire protection.

METROPOLITAN TORONTO

Toronto has followed a different organizational principle in planning for the metropolitan area.[22] Within the district there are 13 separate municipalities having an aggregate population of about 1,250,000. One of the suburbs, York, has a population in excess of 100,000. Although some of the suburbs were unable to provide necessary services and facilities through independent action, they nevertheless resisted annexation. Yet there was no metropolitan authority empowered to deal with these problems. In 1953, however, the Metropolitan Toronto Act created a public corporation which would be responsible for an adequate water supply, sewage disposal, housing, education, arterial highways, metropolitan parks, certain welfare services, and the over-all planning of the area. The corporation was not only empowered to make plans but also to put them into operation, with all the powers of a municipality. It has jurisdiction over an area of some 250 square miles. The Metropolitan

[20] Edward Sofen, *The Miami Metropolitan Experiment* (1963).

[21] *Proposed Metropolitan Government Charter for Nashville and Davidson County* (1962).

[22] Frederick G. Gardiner, "Metropolitan Toronto: A New Answer to Metropolitan Area Problems," *Planning* (1953), 39–47.

Council consists of members selected both from the city of Toronto and from suburban municipalities.

COMMUNITY DEVELOPMENT

With the increase in pressing problems of cities, in part the result of the accumulation of population in urban centers during the past two or three decades, varied approaches have been undertaken to alleviate some of the conditions created by this growth of urban centers. One of these approaches is known as "community development." Although community development programs of one kind or another have existed for some time, the present emphasis tends to be in "self-help" undertakings in which citizens of an urban district or neighborhood are stimulated to participate in various collective undertakings for community betterment. Programs of community development are being emphasized especially in the underdeveloped regions, in cities as well as in villages.

The concentration of vast numbers of impoverished persons in the great cities of the underdeveloped regions has created slums the magnitude and sordidness of which are perhaps unsurpassed. The piling up of population in the cities has been so great that local, state, and national governments, with their limited financial resources, have been unable to alleviate the conditions of squalor and destitution. The problem seems almost insoluble—but not entirely so.

THE DELHI PILOT PROJECT

A notable experiment in urban community development was undertaken in Delhi, India, in 1958, to achieve civic improvement through the stimulation of self-help and citizen participation in community affairs.[23] The Delhi Pilot Project includes several procedures: (1) organization of small local development councils called Vikas Mandals; (2) formation of larger neighborhood councils made up of groups of Vikas Mandals; (3) establishment of volunteer organizations to plan self-help projects to improve conditions in the area; (4) improvement of the bazaars or market places; (5) citywide civic campaigns to improve the appearance of the city and rectify certain existing conditions; and (6) development of a health and welfare council and a community chest to coordinate the various welfare services with the citizens development councils.

Selected for the project were six areas ranging from 1,000 to 2,000 residents. Each project area was fairly distinctive in population compo-

[23] Marshall B. Clinard and B. Chatterjee, "Urban Community Development in India: The Delhi Pilot Project," in Roy Turner (ed.), *India's Urban Future* (1962), ch. 4. The Project received financial support from the Ford Foundation.

sition, physical conditions, and such social characteristics as caste, religion, occupation, and length of residence, but mostly the people were poor, uneducated, and without constructive civic interests. The central problem was to stimulate civic consciousness and local leadership so that the citizens would organize and work collectively toward the improvement of their respective local areas. Many specific projects were undertaken, including those concerned with physical improvement, sanitation, health and nutrition, recreation, handicrafts, education, and welfare work. By the 1960's the project was well advanced, with evidence of numerous achievements and an increase in civic interests. A similar project, on a larger scale, was later undertaken in Ahmedabad, India, an industrial city of a million population.

KARACHI AND DACCA PROJECTS

Similar community development programs in Karachi and Dacca, Pakistan, were undertaken in the 1950's. As a part of Pakistan's Second Five-Year Plan (1960–65) some 125 community development projects were planned to involve about a quarter of the urban population of the country. In Dacca, for instance, neighborhood councils were organized as a mechanism through which local citizens could participate in projects concerned with health, recreation, adult education, vocational training centers, organization of clubs for women and youth, and so on. The neighborhood councils were integrated into larger units for administrative purposes.[24]

PLANNING NEW CITIES

Most planning involves the modification of a community as it already exists, or the projection of change into the future. But the twentieth century has witnessed the planning of completely new cities or the extensive reconstruction of old cities, some of which were destroyed by military action. In this section some examples of such planning will be considered.

PLANNED CITIES IN THE UNITED STATES

Many new cities have been planned and developed since the turn of the twentieth century, but all of these have been comparatively small and mainly located near a metropolis. Some have been built by industrial firms, some by private real estate and housing corporations, and

[24] *Community Development in Urban Areas;* Report of the Secretary-General, United Nations (1961).

others by government agencies. Several new communities were built during or after World War II.

The atomic age has produced several new cities, the best known being Oak Ridge, Tennessee, Los Alamos, New Mexico, and Hanford, Washington, each of which was initially designed for the specialized function of conducting research into nuclear energy and of producing atomic bombs.

Some of the planned communities have been satellite cities within commuting distance of larger metropolitan centers. One of these is Park Forest, some 30 miles south of Chicago's downtown district. Opened for occupance in 1948, the community was developed under private auspices, and is designed for about 25,000 residents, most of whom represent middle-income, white collar families.

Industrial communities have been developed primarily as adjuncts to a factory, with the objectives of stabilizing the labor supply and increasing the efficiency and morale of workers. The city of Alcoa, near Knoxville, for example, was established in 1916 to accommodate workers employed by the Aluminum Company of America. Such cities usually have a liberal amount of space and modern facilities for both residential and recreational uses.

The first garden city in the United States was Radburn, New Jersey, built in the 1920's on a site near New York City. Although originally planned as a self-sufficient community, Radburn has become a commuter's suburb like many others in the area. The significance of Radburn is in its departure from conventual concepts in the planning of streets, residential neighborhoooods, and recreational areas.

During the depression of the 1930's, the Resettlement Administration of the national government planned and built three "greenbelt" cities. These communities were Greenhills, near Cincinnati; Greendale, in the vicinity of Milwaukee; and Greenbelt, between Washington and Baltimore. All of them were designed as commuters' suburbia, but were developed with the objective of providing most of the facilities for community life except employment. Conceived initially as model communities for demonstration purposes, the projects became the subject of a bitter ideological conflict. In the 1940's they were sold to private developers, thus terminating the role of the federal government in such planning projects.

BRITAIN'S "NEW TOWNS"

The New Towns Act of 1946 authorized the development of 15 new towns in the vicinity of Britain's large cities.[25] Eight are near London

[25] John Madge, "The New Towns Program in Britain," *Journal of the American Institute of Planners,* 28 (November, 1962), 208–19.

and the others in the vicinity of Newcastle, Glasgow, Edinburgh, Cardiff, and Leicester. All of them have been built around existing, relatively small communities. By 1963 the total population of these towns was on the order of a half-million, with none of them being larger than 60,000.

The inception of the New Towns came largely from Ebenezer Howard's garden city idea. A principal objective was to help relieve the great cities of population pressures by attracting families and industries from these metropolitan centers. A second objective was the revitalization of some of the smaller towns or cities which were selected as "cores" for new communities. Although the New Towns are located within a radius of 20 or 30 miles of a large city, they are not designed as commuters' suburbs. In order to make them economically self-sufficient, industries have been attracted from the metropolitan areas to provide a major basis for employment, and shopping centers have developed for the convenience of the residents of the new towns or adjacent communities.

Crawley, south of London, may be cited as an example. Built around the original town of 10,000, Crawley had a population of 54,000 in 1961, with 76 new industrial firms attracted to the community. Land use has been carefully planned for industry, recreation, shopping, and residence. All of the dwellings are within walking or cycling distance of places of employment, shopping centers, churches, or recreational establishments. The residential area consists of several planned neighborhoods, each containing houses for people with different incomes and styles of living. Surrounding the town is a permanent greenbelt.

During the period of development of the New Towns program there was considerable uncertainty about their future, that is, whether the experiment would be reasonably successful in terms of the objectives. By the time the projects were nearing completion in the 1960's, the program as a whole had received general approval, with considerable sentiment for an extension of the program to include the construction of additional New Towns to take care of the overflow from the great cities.[26]

CHANDIGARH, NEW CITY IN THE DESERT

When the partition of India occurred in the 1940's, the state of The Punjab was divided and the established capital, Lahore, went to Pakistan, thus leaving the Indian portion of the state without a capital.[27] Shortly after partition, several architects and planners, among them the distinguished French architect Le Corbusier, were commissioned to draw up plans for a new state capital, Chandigarh, to rise from the plains of The Punjab, in northwestern India. The situation was rather

[26] Madge, *ibid.*, p. 217.
[27] R. M. Panjabi, "Chandigarh: India's Newest City," *The Geographic Magazine,* 31 (1958), 401–14.

unique, one of the few instances in history in which planners were given a relatively free hand, unencumbered by traditional ideas, to plan an entirely new city. By the 1960's the plans were virtually complete and considerable progress had been made on construction. When completed, Chandigarh will cover an area of about 15 square miles, and will accommodate a maximum of a half-million inhabitants.

The residential portions of the city are divided into sectors, each of which is about three-fourths of a mile long and a half-mile wide. Each sector is a complete unit, and will include shops, a health center, swimming pool, banks, nurseries, schools, playgrounds, and a neighborhood center. A large part of the sectors is given over to parks and playgrounds for neighborhood use. The houses, built in rows, are situated around a large open space. In the middle of each sector is a band of park land.

A central sector will include a civic center, library, cinemas, and large shops. To the west of the center is an area reserved for colleges and a university, a museum, and a stadium, while to the north, in a large area, are the government buildings, including the Capitol and the High Courts.

A feature of the Chandigarh plan is the varied types of roads, each designed to be functional in its own way. Included are the highways that connect Chandigarh with other cities, straight grid roads that define the sectors, the main streets of each sector, local roads branching out from main streets and extending to the houses, and footpaths the length of the city and extending through the central parks. Dwellings on the outer periphery face inward and can be entered only from inside the sectors.

BRASILIA, A NEW NATIONAL CAPITAL

Some 600 miles north of Rio de Janeiro, in the sparsely settled interior of Brazil, a new national capital, Brasilia, has been constructed. Carved out of a tropical jungle, the new metropolis represents advanced, and certainly unconventional, ideas in planning and architecture. When completed, it will have all the major features of a modern metropolis, with accommodations for a half-million residents.

The overall plan, a prize-winning design in an international competition, provides a unique spatial arrangement of all institutional facilities and dwellings of various types.[28] In perspective, the design assumes the shape of an airplane with a long fuselage and sweptback wings. The "fuselage" is the civic and commercial center. At one end are government buildings, including the presidential palace and a university campus; in or near the middle are shops, a cultural area, an amusement section, a cathedral, and sites for embassies, hotels, and hospitals; at the opposite end are warehouses and terminal railway facilities for passen-

[28] Douglas Haskell, "Brasilia: A New Type of National City," *Architectural Forum,* 113 (November, 1960), 126–33.

gers and freight. Beyond the built-up area are an airport, playing fields, and a cemetery.

The "wings" are mainly blocks and superblocks of dwellings. Each of the superblocks has residential accommodations for some 3,000 persons, and each is a neighborhood unit with its own primary school and retail shops. About 100 superblocks are planned. A fairly large proportion of the dwellings are high-rise apartments, from 10 to 16 for each super-block. However, there are also sections for detached houses for workers, white collar employees, and retired persons, and an area reserved for spacious private homes for the well-to-do.

Brasilia represents an heroic effort to build, within a few years, a major metropolis complete in every detail. Boldly conceived as a metropolis functionally and esthetically appropriate for the modern age, Brasilia is destined to become one of the world's showplaces. Built at an estimated final cost to the Brazilian government of 450 million dollars, the success of the undertaking is still uncertain. There have been criticisms to the effect that the economy of the area is inadequate to maintain a function-ing metropolis of this magnitude and that it will be an economic liability to the country. There have also been criticisms that insufficient open spaces, in the form of parks and playgrounds, have been provided in the residential sectors.[29]

ROTTERDAM REBUILT

Some cities were so devastated by bombing during the war that exten-sive programs of reconstruction were necessary. Such a city is Rotterdam. In 1940, the German *Luftwaffe* virtually destroyed the inner portions of the great Dutch seaport. After the war the government undertook the difficult task of reconstruction, which resulted in an impressive restora-tion of a city that was largely ashes and rubble at the end of the conflict.

Included in the reconstructed central zone are various public and pri-vate structures designed to be functionally and esthetically harmonious. In one respect the planners departed from conventional conceptions by locating high-rise apartments in the central area close to shops, public buildings, banks, and other establishments. Since most of the occupants of these apartments would be within easy walking distance of their places of employment, it was anticipated that the problem of traffic congestion would be eased somewhat. Another distinctive feature of the inner zone is a shopping center known as the *Lijnbaan*, considered by many as a model. Some three blocks square, the shopping center consists mainly of small retail shops and restaurants on streets restricted to pedestrian traf-fic. At or near the edge of this center are the large department stores,

---

[29] Gilberto Freyre, "A Brazilian's Critique of Brasilia," *The Reporter*, 22 (March 31, 1960), 31–32.

The center of Rotterdam was almost entirely destroyed by disastrous air raids in World War II, but has been almost entirely rebuilt. All of the buildings of the downtown area shown are new except for the Stock Exchange at center-right. (Courtesy Netherlands Information Service.)

hotels, banks, and several public buildings such as the post office, city hall, and railway station.

SOCIOLOGICAL ASPECTS OF PLANNING

Urban community planning is always difficult because of the complexities of city life. The infinite variety and number of competing groups that often work at cross-purposes to each other, the conflicting interests of individuals who represent different cultural, racial, religious, economic, or political alignments, the sheer inertia that often adds up to actual resistance to proposed social change, the inability of individuals to agree either upon objectives or procedures—these are some of the conditions that make it difficult, sometimes even impossible, to translate plans into orderly social change. It is in such situations that the interplay of public opinion and community leadership becomes a force in the planning process, at least in democratic societies. The final outcome of some planning proposals may depend, in the final analysis, on the verdict of public opinion. Consequently, the effective communication to the public of relevant information may spell either the success or failure of any planning proposal.

Any sophisticated assessment of planning, in general or particular, must examine the character of the objectives, the methods employed to attain those objectives, and the prevalent values of the community, and particularly of the people who are supposed to be benefited by planning operations. Clearly this is no easy task. A good deal of planning has been undertaken with little or no reference to these considerations. Considerable criticism has therefore been directed against some of the plans which have been carried out. Lewis Mumford, one of America's foremost critics, has repeatedly warned against planning operations which ignore the functional and esthetic aspects of community life.[30] Apparently some planners have been almost entirely concerned with the physical changes in planning programs without much reference to the social effects of such planning. To remove or modify conditions of blight without reference to the values and mode of life of the people who live in such areas may have limited value. Such writers as Gans, for example, have strongly emphasized the values of cultural and social homogeneity, and particularly the sentimental relationships that may flourish in such areas, believing that much damage can be done by planning which does not take fully into account these sociological elements of neighborhood and community life.[31] Writers like Jane Jacobs have emphasized, as planning objectives, diversity in communities, self-help, and citizen participation,[32] in contrast to traditional procedures based on the notion of "doing something for the people."

SELECTED BIBLIOGRAPHY

BOOKS

Bollens, John (ed.), *Exploring the Metropolitan Community*. Berkeley: University of California Press, 1961.

Chapin, F. Stuart, Jr., *Urban Land Use Planning*. New York: Harper, 1957.

Gans, Herbert J., *The Urban Villagers*. New York: The Free Press of Glencoe, 1962.

Lubove, Roy, *The Progressives and the Slums*. Pittsburgh: University of Pittsburgh Press, 1963.

Meyerson, Martin, and Edward Banfield, *Politics, Planning and the Public Interest*. Glencoe, Ill.: The Free Press, 1955.

Mumford, Lewis, *The City in History*. New York: Harcourt, Brace and World, 1961.

Orlans, Harold, *Stevenage: A Sociological Study of a New Town*. London: Routledge & Kegan Paul, 1952.

[30] Lewis Mumford, *The City in History* (1961) and *The Culture of Cities* (1938).
[31] Herbert J. Gans, "Planning and Social Life: Friendship and Neighbor Relations in Suburban Communities," *Journal of the American Institute of Planners*, 27 (May and August, 1961), 134–84.
[32] Jane Jacobs, *The Death and Life of Great American Cities* (1961).

Perloff, Harvey (ed.), *Planning and the Urban Community*. Pittsburgh: University of Pittsburgh Press, 1961.

Rossi, Peter H., and Robert Dentler, *The Politics of Urban Renewal*. Glencoe, Ill.: The Free Press, 1961.

Webster, Donald, *Urban Planning and Municipal Public Policy*. New York: Harper, 1958.

Willhelm, Sidney, *Urban Zoning and Land-Use Theory*. New York: The Free Press of Glencoe, 1962.

Willmott, Peter, *The Evolution of a Community*. London: Routledge, 1963.

ARTICLES

Clinard, Marshall B., "The Delhi Pilot Project in Urban Community Development," *International Review of Community Development*, No. 7 (1961), pp. 161–71. Cf. Clinard, "Urban Community Development in India: The Delhi Pilot Project," in Roy Turner (ed.), *India's Urban Future*. Berkeley: University of California Press, 1962.

Foley, Donald L., "British Town Planning: One Ideology or Three," *British Journal of Sociology* (September, 1960).

Gans, Herbert J., "Planning and Social Life: Friendship and Neighbor Relations in Suburban Communities," *Journal of the American Institute of Planners*, 27 (May and August, 1961), 134–84.

Grebler, Leo, "Urban Renewal in European Countries," *Journal of the American Institute of Planners*, 28 (November, 1962), 229–38.

Haworth, Lawrence L., "An Institutional Theory of the City and Planning," *Journal of the American Institute of Planners*, 23 (1958), 135–43.

Holford, William, "Plans and Programs," *The Annals*, 314 (November, 1957), 94–100.

Madge, John, "The New Towns Program in Great Britain," *Journal of the American Institute of Planners*, 28 (November, 1962), 208–19.

Meyerson, Martin, and Barbara Terrett, "Metropolis Lost, Metropolis Regained," *The Annals*, 314 (November, 1957), 1–9.

Schnore, Leo, "A Planner's Guide to the 1960 Census of Population," *Journal of the American Institute of Planners*, 29 (February, 1963).

Index

Index